best-ever
slow cooking

best-ever
slow cooking

Catherine Atkinson and Jenni Fleetwood

BARNES & NOBLE

NEW YORK

This 2007 edition published by Barnes & Noble Publishing, Inc. by arrangement with Anness Publishing Ltd

Publisher: Joanna Lorenz
Editorial Director: Helen Sudell
Editorial Readers: Richard McGinlay, Joy Wotton and Jay Thundercliffe
Designer: Nigel Partridge
Photography: Karl Adamson, Edward Allwright, Steve Baxter, Nicki Dowey, James Duncan, Ian Garlick, Michelle Garrett, Amanda Heywood, Janine Hosegood, David Jordan, David King, Don Last, William Adams-Lingwood, Patrick McLeavey, Thomas Odulate, Craig Robertson, Bridget Sargeson, Sam Stowell
Recipes: Catherine Atkinson, Jane Bamforth, Alex Barker, Valerie Barrett, Michelle Berriedale-Johnson, Judy Bastyra, Kit Chan, Jacqueline Clarke, Carole Clements, Matthew Drennan, Sarah Edmonds, Joanna Farrow, Brian Glover, Nicola Graimes, Juliet Harbutt, Christine Ingram, Becky Johnson, Lucy Knox, Lesley Mackley, Sally Mansfield, Sallie Morris, Jennie Shapter, Anne Sheasby, Marlena Spieler, Steven Wheeler, Kate Whiteman, Rosemary Wilkinson, Elizabeth Wolf-Cohen, Jeni Wright
Production Controller: Lee Sargent

ISBN-13: 978 0 7607 8711 3
ISBN-10: 0 7607 8711 5

Printed and bound in China

10 9 8 7 6 5 4 3 2 1

Previously published as *Best-Ever Slow Cooker, One-Pot and Casserole Cookbook*

NOTES

Standard spoon and cup measures are level.

Large eggs are used unless otherwise stated.

Electric oven temperatures in this book are for conventional ovens. When using a fan oven, the temperature will probably need to be reduced by about 20–40°F. Since ovens vary, you should check with your manufacturer's instruction book for guidance.

Nutritional Analysis of recipes: The nutritional analyses on recipe pages are calculated per portion (i.e. serving or item), unless otherwise stated. If the recipe gives a range, such as Serves 4–6, then the nutritional analysis will be for the smaller portion size, i.e. serves 6.

Measurements for sodium do not include salt added to taste.

CONTENTS

INTRODUCTION

Long, slow cooking techniques have been used for centuries. From the earliest times, cooks discovered that meat roasted in the dying embers of the fire, or in a pot of gently bubbling stock suspended well above the flames, produced the tenderest results with rich, well-balanced flavors.

Cooking methods have developed and improved over the years, but no drastic changes were seen until the reduction of staff employed in richer households meant that very few people still had a cook who would spend the entire day preparing food.

Along with the gradual introduction of controllable range stoves and, eventually, the introduction of modern gas and electric ovens came an increased demand for dishes requiring less cooking time. In the latter half of the 20th century, more women went out to work, and time-saving became all-important.

Food manufacturers thrived on the sale of prepared ingredients that could reduce the number of hours spent in

Below: The gentle heat of the slow cooker allows delicate fish to cook beautifully.

the kitchen. Canned and dried soups, dehydrated prepared vegetables, main meals and "instant" desserts became very popular at the end of the 1960s and continued to be so throughout the 1970s.

The story of slow cooking

In the mid-1970s, the slow cooker was invented. It was originally designed for making baked beans and was marketed to the public as an appliance that would cook a wholesome meal unattended, ready to be served after a hard day's work. As such, it caught the attention of those with busy working lives. It lived up to its promise, and busy working mothers, families and students soon discovered its delights. The slow cooker's popularity continued for a decade.

However, with the booming economy years in the late 1980s and 1990s, the demand for economical cuts of meat fell. They were replaced by lean prime cuts, such as chicken breast portions and beef steak, which were more suited to fast cooking methods, such as grilling, broiling, and stir-frying. Time-saving appliances appeared on the scene,

Above: Impressive terrines can be made using the slow cooker as a bain-marie.

including the microwave—and with their arrival, many slow cookers were left to gather dust.

Changing attitudes

Toward the end of the 20th century and in the new millennium, there has been a change in attitudes toward food and a reverse in eating trends. Many people now demand natural food, with fewer artificial chemicals and more nutrients and flavor, rather than instant, quick-fix food. Genetically modified produce has not been welcomed everywhere, and sales of organic food have rocketed, along with requests for less tender, tastier cuts of meat. Slow-simmered casseroles, homemade soups, and traditional desserts are back in fashion, and so are slow cookers.

From tasty, wholesome family food to sophisticated entertaining, a slow cooker is a superb way to create wonderfully tender and flavor-packed meals. Its reputation for making delicious soups and succulent stews is well known, and the slow cooker is far more versatile than many people realize.

Because the slow cooker cooks gently, without the vigorous bubbling or fierce heat of some other cooking methods, delicate food, such as fish, fruit and vegetables, won't break up, even after

long cooking. Used as a bain-marie the slow cooker can produce divine creamy "baked" custards, the lightest sponge desserts, and tasty terrines and pâtés. The constant temperature makes it perfect for keeping party punches steaming hot and simmering preserves, so that the flavors mingle and the preserves are ready to eat without being left to mature.

There are many advantages to using a slow cooker. Not only does it produce delicious dishes with well-developed flavors, but once the food is in the slow cooker you can usually turn it on and forget about it. Because the slow cooker uses less electricity than a light bulb, it can be left unattended, which means you can be away from the kitchen all day and return when ready to serve.

Some slow cookers have timers that automatically switch to the warm setting when the food is cooked, and this is ideal for households who eat at different times. The remaining portions will still be deliciously moist for latecomers, and won't be overcooked or dry. As an added bonus, little steam or smell escapes from slow cookers.

You will be pleasantly surprised at the range of uses of the slow cooker. Although traditionally associated with cold weather foods, such as warming

Below: Pastry toppings for traditional pies are oven-cooked to retain their crispness.

casseroles, soups, and stews, you can also make delicious hot-weather dishes, such as chilled pâtés and terrines, light fish dishes, and summery Mediterranean-style pasta meals. The slow cooker really is invaluable when it is warm outside and you don't want to be confined to a steamy kitchen, with the oven pumping out heat. Simply switch on the slow cooker, and leave it while you get on with more important things.

Below: Individual servings can be cooked in single-portion ramekins in the slow cooker.

Above: The slow cooker makes excellent steamed chocolate and fruit puddings.

One-pot and clay-pot cooking

You can still take advantage of the benefits that a slow cooker brings by making meals cooked in just one pot, whether it be a large casserole dish, a clay baking dish, or a wok. Nourishing soups, delectable stews, spicy stir-fries, robust roasts, creamy risottos, and citrus custards all can be cooked in one-pot dishes. They are easy to prepare, a pleasure to serve, and the perfect choice for family and friends.

As with the slow cooker, cooking in a single pot is wonderfully liberating. All that is needed is a bit of leisurely preparation, and then the cook can relax, secure in the knowledge that there will be no last-minute sauces to make, and no tricky toppings to produce. Serving a selection of side dishes would defeat the object of one-pot cooking (and is largely unnecessary when vegetables are included anyway), so you have the perfect excuse for offering only the simplest accompaniments, sparing yourself the anxiety that comes with trying to get everything ready at precisely the same time.

One-pot dishes will seldom spoil if not eaten the moment they are ready. Some, like curries and casseroles, actually improve if made the day before, so that all the flavors can bed down together and blend. Stir-fries, pasta, and rice dishes need last-minute cooking, but if the preparation is done in advance, the effort is minimal.

This style of cooking is perfect for everyone, from students with a single hot plate to families who eat in shifts. The meal can be cooked in the oven, on top of the stove, or even in a free-standing appliance, such as a microwave oven, electric frying pan, or slow cooker. There are very few dishes to wash, and if there are any leftovers, you may well be able to transform them into tasty pie fillings, simply by sandwiching them inside ready-rolled puff pastry or phyllo.

The benefits of one-pot and clay-pot cooking

One-pot cooking can also be extremely healthy, especially if you use a clay pot, which ensures that vitamins and minerals are retained. This ancient form of cooking seals in all the food's natural juices by enclosing it in a porous clay container that has been soaked in water. As the container heats up, the water turns to steam, keeping the contents beautifully moist and tender. The only other liquid is that which comes from the food itself, so the full flavor of the food can be appreciated.

There's nothing new about cooking in clay. Thousands of years ago, hunters discovered that coating small birds and animals in clay before baking them in an open fire kept the meat juicy and

Above: Paella, a classic one-pot seafood and rice dish from Spain, is traditionally cooked in a shallow, two-handled pan.

Left: A whole chicken cooked with forty cloves of garlic makes the perfect pot-roast, and it, like other one-pot dishes, needs little attention once it is in the oven.

Below: Clay pots come in a whole host of sizes and shapes. These tiny shallow cazuelas can be used to bake individual portions of both savory and sweet tarts, roasted vegetables, and custards.

Left: The tall, conical tagine from north Africa is one of the many ancient clay-pot designs that are still widely used today.

cooker recipes, followed by a chapter for one-pot and clay-pot recipes, so that you can easily find dishes to suit your chosen method of cooking.

Most recipes are based on a family of four people, but if you have a small or large slow cooker or pan, the quantities can easily be halved to serve two, or doubled for eight. All recipes have been thoroughly tested, but it is important to get to know your slow cooker, as times can vary from one model to another. After trying a few recipes, you will know whether your slow cooker is faster or slower, and you will be able to adjust the recipe cooking times accordingly.

prevented it from burning. Chipping off the clay and throwing it away was wasteful and time-consuming, however. Clay pots were a huge improvement, and this material was used by many ancient civilizations. Today, clay pots based on ancient designs are still widely used all over the world. In North Africa, it is the conical tagine; in China, the sand pot; in Spain, the cazuela; and in France, the daubière and tian.

Chicken bricks, bean pots, and clay pots come in all shapes and sizes. They need to be treated kindly, but are surprisingly durable. If you've never used one—or have forgotten just how good they make food taste—this book will give you plenty of inspiration, along with ideas for other delicious one-pot dishes of every kind.

Using this book

Ideal for the first-time slow cooker user, as well as the more experienced slow cooker fan, this book offers practical advice and plenty of recipes that can be cooked just on the hob in any large pan or slowly in the oven in a clay pot. It contains a wonderfully detailed reference section with everything you need to know about ingredients, equipment, and techniques, so that you can feel completely confident.

Once you have mastered the basics, turn to the recipe chapters for a

selection of all-time classics, as well as unusual recipes that are sure to become household favorites. Step-by-step photographs show the key preparation stages of each recipe, to give successful results every time. For each type of dish, there is a chapter devoted to slow

Below: A glazed clay pot ensures that the flavors don't soak into the pot, which means that it can be used for both sweet and savory dishes.

SLOW COOKER BASICS

The basic principle behind the slow cooker is that it cooks food very slowly at a low temperature. The heat gradually builds up and is then maintained at an even temperature throughout cooking, to give perfect, tender results. Slow cookers are very simple and economical to use. They have a low wattage that consumes about the same amount of electricity as a light bulb, which makes them environmentally friendly as well.

Choosing a slow cooker
There is a very wide selection of slow cookers available. They come in a range of sizes, shapes, colors and prices, and it is these factors that you will need to think about before you decide which type of slow cooker is right for you.

When slow cookers were first manufactured, the earthenware or ceramic pots were permanently fixed into the heat-resistant plastic or aluminum outer casing. While it is still possible to buy models made this way, most modern versions have a removable cooking pot that fits snugly into an inner metal casing. The heating elements are safely situated between the inner and outer casings. This newer style not only simplifies cleaning up, but allows the cooking pot to be lifted out and taken to the table as a serving dish. In addition, food can be browned in the oven or under the broiler without causing damage to the outer casing.

The heat-resistant lid may be made of toughened glass or ceramic. The former has the advantage of allowing you to monitor the food's cooking progress without lifting off the lid and losing heat and moisture, although this may be hindered to some extent by steam and condensation gathering on the inside of the lid.

The range of designs and colors of slow cookers has increased in recent years. The original round-shaped rustic

cream and brown design with ceramic lid is still available, but alongside it you will now find much more contemporary-looking white, stainless-steel, and brightly colored models that will fit well in a bright, modern kitchen.

Slow cookers may be round or oval in shape. Round ones are superb for cooking casseroles, steaming desserts, and cooking cakes in round pans, while the oval version is better for pot-roasted meats and for use with loaf pans and terrines.

The size of different slow cookers can vary enormously—from a small $2\frac{1}{2}$-cup cooking pot to a huge $26\frac{1}{4}$-cup one. Of all the sizes, the most popular one is probably $14\frac{1}{4}$ cups, which will enable you to cook a wide range of dishes and easily cater for four people. However, the smaller versions, intended for cooking just one or two portions at a time, are a great asset for single people and couples and take up less space in the kitchen. They are also perfect for making hot dips and fondues.

Below: Oval-shaped slow cookers are perfect for cooking certain types of food, such as pot-roasted joints of meat, loaf-shaped terrines, and small whole fish.

Temperature settings
The cooking temperatures and settings on slow cookers vary slightly from model to model. The most basic (but perfectly adequate) models have three settings: off, low, and high. When the slow cooker is switched to low, the food will barely simmer; at the highest setting, it will simmer or even boil.

Other models have an additional medium setting, and some also have an auto setting. The auto setting is thermostatically controlled, so that the cooking temperature builds up to high, maintains it for a short time, then automatically switches to low to maintain the heat. It normally takes about an hour for the slow cooker to reach the "high" temperature, but this depends on the quantity of food being cooked and its initial temperature.

Most slow cooker models also have a power indicator light that remains on constantly during cooking—although in a few models it may switch off to indicate that the optimum temperature has been reached, so check the instructions.

Using a new slow cooker
Every model of slow cooker varies slightly, so it is important to read the manufacturer's instructions carefully before using. Even when using the same settings, some cookers will cook slower or faster than others.

To cover all models of slow cooker, the recipes in this book offer a range of cooking times. Depending on whether your own model cooks more slowly or quickly, you will either need to use the longer or shorter timing, or somewhere in between. Once you have used your new cooker a few times, it will be easy to know at a glance which cooking time you need to use.

Preheating

Some slow cookers need to be preheated on high for 15–20 minutes before cooking. However, always check the instructions first, because some models heat up quickly, making this step unnecessary, and the manufacturer may advise against heating the slow cooker when empty.

To preheat the slow cooker, place the empty cooking pot and lid in the slow cooker base, and switch the temperature onto the high setting. While the slow cooker heats up, prepare the ingredients for the recipe.

Slow cooker care

Always remove any labels and tags from a new slow cooker, then wash the ceramic cooking pot well in hot soapy water, rinse, and dry thoroughly.

After use, the slow cooker should be switched off before removing the ceramic cooking pot. If you don't want to wash the pot immediately after serving the food, it can be filled with warm water and left to soak for as long as necessary. However, do not immerse the entire pot in water for long periods of time, because the base is usually porous, and soaking may damage the pot. Very few cooking pots are dishwasher-proof, but it is worth checking the manufacturer's instructions; these should also inform you whether the cooking pot can be used on the stovetop or in the oven, microwave or freezer.

Never plunge the hot cooking pot into cold water immediately after use, or pour boiling water into an empty cold cooking pot. Subjecting it to a sudden change in temperature could cause it to crack. As with all electrical appliances, never immerse the outer casing in water or fill it with water. Nor should you use the metal inner casing without the ceramic cooking pot.

Scouring pads and abrasive cleaners will damage the outside of the cooker, so use a damp soapy cloth to clean it.

Above: Smaller slow cookers intended for cooking just one or two portions at a time are an asset for single people and couples.

During cooking, the cooking pot and lid will become very hot, so always use oven mitts when handling. The outer casing may also become hot after long cooking, so care should be taken when touching this, too.

The first few times you use a slow cooker, you may notice a slight odor. This is caused by the burning off of manufacturing residues, which is normal, and will lessen and disappear after time. After several months, the glaze on the cooking pot may become crackled; this is common with glazed stoneware and will not affect the slow cooker's efficiency.

Adapting your own recipes

Conventional recipes can be adapted for a slow cooker. The easiest way to adapt a recipe is to find a similar one in this book and use it as a guide to adapt the original recipe. As a general rule, the liquid content of a dish cooked conventionally can be reduced by as much as half in a slow cooker. Check toward the end of the cooking time, and add more hot liquid if necessary.

Tips for success

During cooking, steam will condense on the lid of the slow cooker, then slowly trickle back into the pot. This helps to form a seal around the lid, retaining heat, flavor, and cooking smells.

If possible, avoid lifting the lid during cooking, because this will cause heat loss and lengthen the cooking time. Unless a recipe states otherwise, the slow cooker should be left undisturbed. There is no need to stir food frequently, because the even cooking and low temperature help to prevent food from sticking or bubbling over. Should you need to lift the lid though, add an extra 15–20 minutes to the cooking time to make up for the heat lost.

If at the end of the cooking time the food is not quite ready, replace the lid and switch the slow cooker to high to speed up the cooking process. Once ready, many dishes can be kept hot for an hour or so without risk of spoiling, by switching the slow cooker to low.

Guide to cooking times

You can often introduce some flexibility to the total cooking time by adjusting the temperature setting. Certain foods, however, are only successful if cooked at the specified setting. Cakes, for example, should always be cooked on high for the entire cooking time, and pot-roasted meats and egg-based recipes should usually be started on high (or auto) for the first hour of cooking, then reduced. For dishes such as soups and casseroles, the cooking time may be shortened or extended to suit your needs by cooking on a higher or lower setting. As a rough guide, the cooking time on high is just over half that on low.

Low	Medium	High
6–8 hours	4–6 hours	3–4 hours
8–10 hours	6–8 hours	5–6 hours
10–12 hours	8–10 hours	7–8 hours

SLOW COOKER EQUIPMENT

To make most slow cooker recipes, you will only need a slow cooker. Stocks, soups, stews, casseroles, compotes, and pot roasts can all simply be cooked in the ceramic cooking pot. However, to make other dishes, such as cakes and pâtés that are cooked in a bain-marie, you will need suitable cookware that is watertight and which will fit inside the ceramic cooking pot.

Cake pans

When cooking cakes in the slow cooker, always use cake pans that have a fixed, non-removable base, rather than loose-based or springform pans. Before use, check that the pan is completely watertight by filling it with water and leaving it to stand for an hour; if it leaks, it is not suitable. You should also check that the pan will fit inside the ceramic cooking pot before you prepare it and fill it with mixture.

While it is important that the pan has a strong rigid shape, heat will penetrate more quickly if lighter, thinner pans are used. When using heavy-gauge metal pans, you will need to allow an extra 15–20 minutes cooking time.

Generally, round slow cookers can accommodate larger round and square cake pans than oval cookers. An 8-inch round pan or a 6½-inch square pan should fit comfortably in a 20-cup round cooker, providing the sides of the pans are straight and there is no protruding

lip or side handle. Oval cookers can also be used for round and square pans, if necessary, but the size will obviously be more limited.

The recipes in this book state which size and shape of pan to use, Try to stick to these as closely as possible—if the pan is too large, you will end up with a shallow cake; if it is too small, the mixture may overflow. Bear in mind, too, that the length of cooking time and the texture of the cake may be affected if the wrong pan is used.

Loaf pans

Perfect for making terrines, pâtés, and loaf-shaped cakes, these sturdy long, narrow metal pans are better suited to cooking in an oval-shaped slow cooker, which will accommodate their shape conveniently. A 14-cup oval slow cooker will hold a straight-sided 2-pound loaf pan or a 2-pound barrel-shaped ridged pan.

Ring pans

Kugelhopf pans and deep, ring-shaped pans that are not too wide are excellent for using in a slow cooker. The hollow tube in the center conducts heat into the middle of the cake, helping it to cook quickly and evenly. Ideally, choose

Below: Classic rectangular loaf pans are very useful for making terrines and chunky, country-style cooked pâtés.

Above: Rectangular, round, and heart-shaped pans can be used in the slow cooker as long as they fit comfortably inside the pot.

a pan with a central tube that is just a little higher than the outer rim of the pan. However, you should also check that the pan fits inside the slow cooker, and that the cooker lid can still fit tightly on top of the ceramic cooking pot when the pan is inside.

Other shaped pans

There are many other shapes of pan that may also be used in the slow cooker. These include small heart-, petal-, oval-, and hexagon-shaped pans. Before buying a pan to use in a slow cooker, it may be worth taking the internal measurement of the ceramic cooking pot first, to be sure the pan will fit inside.

Dariole molds

These little sandcastle-shaped pans are usually made of matt aluminum and come in various sizes, although molds with a 2½-inch diameter are the most popular. Dariole molds are useful for making single-portion-size cakes, desserts, and timbales, and are particularly good for making individual baked custards.

Soufflé and ramekin dishes

These pretty round dishes can be used as an alternative to metal cake pans, as well as for cooking pâtés and mousses. They are always straight-sided and may be made of glass, heatproof porcelain, or stoneware. Glass or porcelain are preferable because they conduct heat more quickly to the food inside. When using these dishes for cake-making, it is better to choose one with a perfectly flat base; occasionally they are slightly domed. Individual soufflé and ramekin dishes are miniature versions and can be used to make small, individual cakes, pâtés, and desserts such as baked custards.

Terrines

Usually rectangular in shape, these dishes may be made of porcelain, cast iron, or earthenware. When used to make pâté, they may double up as a serving dish. Some earthenware terrines aren't glazed, so are unsuitable for use in a bain-marie in a slow cooker. A loaf pan makes a good substitute.

Left: Thermometers can be used to check that meat is cooked properly.

Pudding bowls

Traditionally made of white earthenware, but also made of toughened glass, aluminum or polypropylene, pudding bowls have sloping sides, which make the top much wider than the base. They are ideal for making sweet and savory steamed puddings and can also be used to melt chocolate, butter, and similar ingredients in a bain-marie in the slow cooker. Bowls made from aluminum may have a clip-on lid with a handle attached. They are very good for making steamed meat and plain sponge puddings, because heat is conducted quickly. They are unsuitable for making acidic fruit desserts or similarly acidic recipes, because the acid will react with the metal.

Below: Soufflé dishes and ramekins can be used inside the slow cooker to make steamed desserts, custards, and pâtés.

Above: Metal pudding bowls with a clip-on lid and handle for easy lifting are great for making steamed meat puddings.

Meat thermometers

These useful instruments are the most reliable way of checking that meat is thoroughly cooked—this is particularly important for poultry, which can pass on salmonella bacteria when raw or partially cooked. Most thermometers have a stainless-steel body and a glass dial. By piercing the meat near the center toward the end of the cooking time, you can check the temperature inside the meat. The meat is ready to eat when the pointer on the dial reaches the appropriate wording; there are indications for types of meat including chicken, beef, lamb, and pork, as well as readings within some of those categories for rare, medium, and well-cooked meat. Choose a thermometer with a thin probe, so that it doesn't make large holes in the meat, causing juices to be lost. Do not leave the thermometer inside the meat during cooking, because exposure to steam in the slow cooker could damage the dial. Immediately after use, rinse the probe in hot soapy water, and wipe it clean; don't immerse the thermometer in water.

ONE-POT EQUIPMENT

If you are going to do a lot of cooking in just one pot, make it a good one. There's no point in planning a pot-roast for the whole family, only to find you haven't got a big enough pan, or that the one you have has a wobbly base. It is equally irritating to discover that your only decent casserole has a crack in it, or can only be used in the oven and not on top of the stove. Choose your cookware with care; it is worth investing in good quality equipment that will last.

Right:
Stainless-steel pans with a heavy base are a good choice for one-pot cooking.

Above: Frying pans with metal handles can be used under the broiler and in the oven.

For one-pot cooking, you need a large pan with a heavy base, which will conduct the heat evenly and help to prevent the food from scorching should you inadvertently allow the amount of liquid to get too low. A good quality stainless-steel pan would be an excellent choice, but it is important to choose one with an aluminum or copper base, since stainless steel does not conduct heat well. For long, slow cooking, cast-iron pans coated in vitreous enamel, are ideal, as they can also be used in the oven. When buying a frying pan, choose one with a heavy base. When cooking a frittata or a dessert such as tarte Tatin, it is essential to use a frying pan with a handle that can withstand the heat of the broiler or oven; a point worth considering when you are buying a new frying pan.

Woks

One of the most useful items in the kitchen, the wok need not be reserved solely for stir-frying. It is the ideal pan for quick-cooked creamy dishes such as beef Stroganoff. The wok can also be used for making a risotto. Woks that

Pots and Pans

When you are buying cooking equipment, it is very tempting to opt for a set of shiny pans, rather than individual items that might suit your purposes—and your personal circumstances—better.

Below left: A large pot with metal handles can be used on top of the stove and in the oven.

Left: Woks have either one or two handles.

Right: When buying casseroles, it is a good idea to choose different shapes and sizes.

Casseroles

For one-pot cooking, choose a casserole that is big enough to serve six, even if you usually cook for four. This will give you plenty of room for stirring the contents without risking splashes and scalds. The ideal pot will be one that can be used on top of the stove as well as inside it, so that if you do need to do any precooking, or if cooking juices need to be reduced by boiling, you will not require a second container. If you buy several casseroles, vary the shapes as well as the sizes. For cooking a whole chicken, for instance, an oval is more useful than a round dish. Look at the handles, too. It is important that they are easy to grasp, and that they do not become so hot that they are liable to burn you, even when you are using an oven glove. Appearance will obviously be a consideration, since you will be serving straight from the casserole, but consider practical aspects too.

have a flat base can be used on all types of stove. They can have either one or two handles. Those with two handles are good for deep-frying and general cooking, while the wok with one handle is designed especially for stir-frying. The single handle makes the wok easy to pick up so that the ingredients can be stirred and tossed in the wok at the same time.

FLAMEPROOF CASSEROLES

The most versatile casseroles are also flameproof and so can be used on top of the stove and under the broiler as well as in the oven.

FREESTANDING ELECTRIC COOKING POTS

It isn't vital to have a stove in order to cook a one-pot meal. Electric frying pans; slow-cookers (and combinations of the two); multipurpose appliances, in which you can shallow fry, deep fry or even cook a casserole, all have the advantage that they have easy temperature control, use very little electricity and are easy to clean.

Baking Dishes

There are plenty of one-pot recipes that benefit from being cooked in large, shallow dishes, from oven-roasted vegetables to layered potato bakes. Buy several different shapes, bearing in mind the size of your oven. Having two rectangular dishes that will fit side by side can be a real boon if you want to cook one meal for serving immediately and another for the freezer.

Ramekins

You will also find it useful to have six or eight ovenproof ramekin dishes, for baking single portions, such as individual soufflés and oven-baked desserts.

Below: Choose two ovenproof baking dishes that will fit next to each other in your oven.

CLAY-POT EQUIPMENT

Visit any market in any town the world over, and you will find clay cooking pots for sale. Some will be rough, rustic items, only suitable for display, but others—such as the Spanish cazuela or the North African tagine—will be intended not for the tourist trade, but for everyday cooking. Before buying, always seek local advice as to the durability and safety of the items, especially as regards any glazes that might be used. Buying a boxed item from a reputable store may not be as romantic, but it is probably more sensible. Clay cooking pots need special treatment, and it makes sense to follow the instructions that come with your particular utensil.

Left: *The classic, high, domed Romertopf dish (top) and a large oval clay pot that is especially designed for cooking whole fish.*

Romertopfs

Perhaps the most familiar unglazed clay pots are those produced by Romertopf. Their wide range includes items suitable for cooking meat, fish, fruit, vegetables, bread, and cakes. The classic Romertopf is a rectangular pot with a deep, wide base and a domed lid. These come in several sizes. Other shapes include a long oval, ideal for cooking a whole fish. This has a glazed base to prevent liquid from penetrating the clay and leaving behind a lingering fishy smell.

Lids are designed to fit snugly, so that they cannot accidentally slip off, but there is a narrow gap between the lid and the base that allows any excess steam to escape from the clay pot.

Right: *This deep, pan-shaped clay pot is designed for cooking bean dishes, but would also be good for baking potatoes, and for cooking soups and stews that have lots of liquid.*

Bean Pot/Potato Brick

There are several shapes of these deep, round pots. Some have a handle for easy lifting. Made entirely from clay, the pots have a domed lid. Although these pots are especially suitable for slowly cooking beans and pulses, they can also be used for soups and stews, and the shape is ideal for cooking both large and small potatoes. The potatoes are bathed in a layer of steam, which keeps them moist during cooking.

Whatever you are cooking, the pot and lid should first be soaked in water, then placed in a cold oven after the ingredients have been added.

Above: *The shape of these deep-based clay pots makes them ideal for baking potatoes and cooking beans and pulses.*

If you are cooking beans, check the recipe or the manufacturer's handbook. Before being added to the pot, some varieties, such as as kidney, cannellini, and soybeans, need to be brought to a boil in a pan of water, then boiled vigorously for about 10 minutes to eliminate toxins from the beans. Drain the beans, and leave them to cool before adding them to the bean pot. Any liquid added to the pot should be cold. This will prevent the pot from cracking or breaking.

Garlic Baker

This small terracotta dish with a domed lid is used for baking garlic. Like all clay pots, it must be placed in a cold oven and heated gradually. There is no need

Above: This large chicken brick is designed to hold a whole bird.

to soak the pot in water first. The inside of the dish is glazed, so the garlic juices will not permeate it. The baker will accommodate four to six garlic bulbs. A small cross must be cut in the top of each garlic bulb, or the tops can be sliced off, to prevent them from bursting during cooking. The steam they release will be trapped under the domed lid of the garlic baker and will keep the garlic cloves beautifully moist and tender. The garlic baker can also be used in a microwave oven.

Onion Baker

This clay pot looks like a larger version of the garlic baker. It consists of a shallow terracotta dish with a high, domed lid; it will accommodate four medium-size onions, and can also be used for cooking onion wedges, shallots, or pearl onions. The lid can be soaked in water first, so that it releases steam during cooking. The steam helps to tenderize the onions. Toward the end of cooking, the lid should be removed so that the onions turn brown and become caramelized.

Chicken Brick

This is a large, unglazed fire clay cooking dish with a high lid. The largest ones are designed to hold a whole chicken, guinea fowl or duck, but can also be used to cook any large piece of meat or poultry. Smaller chicken bricks are ideal for small birds and portions. There is no need to add fat or liquid to the pot unless the recipe specifically requires this.

Roasting onions in a clay pot gives them a wonderful, sweet taste, but the flavor can be enhanced even further by adding sprigs of fresh herbs. Pungent fresh herbs, such as rosemary, thyme, and oregano, work well; tuck small sprigs in among the vegetables for the best result.

Above:
The onion baker (left) and the garlic baker both have high, domed lids that are designed to trap steam during cooking.

Chinese Sand Pot

This covered earthenware pot, which is sometimes called a Chinese casserole, is usually glazed on the inside only and reinforced on the outside with wire. It comes from China, where it was originally used to cook stews over a slow charcoal fire. Several shapes and sizes are available. They are not expensive and can be bought in Asian and Chinese food and cooking equipment stores. The sand pot is ideal for slow-cooked dishes, such as soups and stews that are baked in the oven. Do not use sand pots on top of the stove unless the manufacturer recommends this. Sand pots are fairly fragile and are prone to crack easily. They do not need to be soaked before baking, but like other clay pots, are best placed in a cold oven.

Tagine

This North African cooking pot consists of a large, shallow base and a tall, conical lid. The dish that is cooked in it is also known as a tagine.

Left: The Chinese sand pot was designed for cooking over a slow charcoal fire, but it is equally at home in a modern oven.

The food is placed in the base. As it cooks, steam rises and is trapped in the lid, keeping the food moist. Tagines are traditionally made from glazed, brown earthenware, sometimes with a slightly rounded base. They come in a range of sizes, from small individual tagines to family-size ones that measure at least 8 inches across. There is also a modern version, with a heavy, cast-iron base and a glazed earthenware lid. Unlike the traditional tagine, which can be used only in the oven, or on a barbecue whose coals have been dowsed with sand, this design can also be used on top of the stove. This is very convenient,

since it means that onions, vegetables, and other ingredients, such as meat and poultry, can be browned in the base before the lid is fitted and the tagine is placed in the oven. Some glazed earthenware tagines can be used on top of the stove on a low heat, but it is best to use a heat diffuser; always check the manufacturer's instructions.

Above: The traditional tagine (above left) has a shallow base and a tall, conical lid, while the contemporary version (right) has a deeper, larger base.

WHAT'S IN A NAME?

Clay, earthenware, terracotta, stoneware—we use the terms interchangeably, but are they all the same thing? Clay is essentially the raw material; it is a fine-grained mix of mineral origin that occurs in sedimentary rocks and soils. It is malleable when moist, but hardens when it is heated. When pots that are made from clay are baked, they become earthenware.

Terracotta is an Italian word that means "baked earth." It has come to refer to a type of hard, brownish-red earthenware that is traditionally left unglazed.

Stoneware is stronger than earthenware, having been fired at a higher temperature. It is usually perfectly safe to put stoneware in a hot oven, but always check the manufacturer's instructions.

Cazuelas

These shallow, lidless earthenware dishes originated in Spain. They are made in a variety of sizes. The smallest, suitable for Catalan-style sweet custards, measure 4–5 inches across, while the largest—used for cooking savory dishes in the oven—measure 15 inches or even more. They vary in depth from about 1 inch to 3 inches. Cazuelas are either partially glazed on the outside, and fully glazed inside, or glazed inside and out. Neither type is soaked in water before use. After a while, the glaze on the cazuela may develop a slightly "crazed" appearance, but this is completely natural and will not affect the performance of the dish.

Individual cazuelas can be used for cooking single portions of a wide range of one-pot dishes, but they are absolutely ideal for making individual upside-down tarts. The lightly cooked vegetables are spread out on the base of the cazuelas, topped with rounds of puff pastry, then baked in the oven. The tarts can then be inverted onto serving plates.

Left: Spanish cazuelas come in a range of sizes and depths. The smallest are perfect for individual oven-baked custards, while the largest are good for slow-cooked stews and vegetable bakes, but will also accommodate whole fish and poultry as well as large joints of meat.

Tian

This traditional French baking dish originated in Provence. It is a shallow, usually oval, earthenware dish, and is used for baking vegetables, sometimes with rice and eggs. The dish that is cooked in it is also called a tian.

Right: Oval-shaped tians originated in Provence and are traditionally used for baking vegetables, but the shape is ideal for other oven-baked, one-pot dishes.

Glazed Earthenware Bakeware

A wide selection of glazed ovenproof earthenware is available. These dishes can often be put straight into a hot oven, or used under a hot broiler for browning. They are also suitable for use in the freezer. Unlike clay pots and porous earthenware, they do not need to be soaked in water before use and will not absorb the flavors of foods and so become tainted.

Right: A wide range of glazed earthenware bakeware is available – these dishes can often be used in the oven and under the broiler.

INGREDIENTS: BEEF

Enjoyed all over the world, there are dozens of classic beef dishes, from pot-roast brisket, to French boeuf bourguignonne, German sauerbraten, and Russian stroganoff. Beef's popularity is partly due to its versatility. There are many different cuts of beef, and many of these are suitable for a range of cooking methods. Beef tenderloin, for example, is perfect for cutting into steaks for broiling, strips for stir-frying, or baked whole, wrapped in pastry. Other cuts, such as the less expensive shin of beef, are unsuitable for roasting or broiling but are wonderful in stews and braised dishes—and are perfect for slow cooking.

Buying and storing

As with all meat, the flavor and texture of beef is determined by the breed of the animal, its feed, the environment in which it is reared and, ultimately, by the process of slaughtering and the treatment of the meat before it is cooked. While pork and lamb tend to come from very young animals, beef usually comes from those aged between 18 months and 2 years.

Beef should be hung to allow the flavor to develop and the texture to improve, preferably for at least two weeks. Well-matured beef has a deep, rich burgundy color, not a bright red hue, and the fat is a creamy color, or yellow, if the animal was grass-fed. Maturing is an expensive process because some water content will be lost through evaporation, so expect to pay a little more for well-hung meat. The leanest looking joint isn't always the best: for pot-roasting, casseroling,

Above: *Pot roast, also known as "eye of round," is a fairly lean cut of beef that is best slowly braised or pot-roasted.*

and braising, a marbling of fat running through the meat will provide flavor and basting to keep the meat moist.

Beef should be kept on a low shelf in the refrigerator, below any cooked foods and ingredients that will be eaten raw. When buying prepacked meat, check and observe the use-by date. Whether prepacked or loose, ground and cubed beef should be used within 1–2 days of buying; chops and small joints should be used within 3 days, and larger joints within 4–5 days.

Cuts of beef

Butchering techniques differ according to regional and cultural traditions, and also from country to country. Good butchers and larger supermarkets offer a range of cuts, and it is worth asking for their advice when buying.

Generally, cuts from the top of the animal, along the middle of the back, are tender because the muscles in this area do relatively little work. These are prime cuts that are good for quick cooking techniques, such as broiling and pan-frying, and tend to be the most expensive. Cuts from the neck, shoulders, and lower legs are full of flavor, but the texture is coarser and tougher because these are the parts of the animal that work the hardest. They require longer cooking by moist methods to ensure tender results—it is these cuts that are perfectly suited to cooking in the slow cooker. Slow, gentle stewing results in meltingly tender meat and a further developed flavor.

Left (from top): Thick flank makes good braising steak; thin flank produces rich-flavored steaks and is best suited to slow, moist methods of cooking. Flank steak is a lean cut with a coarse texture that becomes moist and tender when slowly braised.

Below: Neck is one of the less tender beef cuts but is delicious braised or stewed.

Blade or chuck These cuts come from the top forequarter and are relatively lean, marbled with just a little fat that keeps the meat moist. They are usually boned and sold together as braising steak. The long, gentle cooking of a slow cooker helps to tenderize the meat and intensifies its flavor. These cuts suit pot-roasting, casseroling, and braising.

Brisket This may be bought on the bone or boned and rolled, and comes from the lower part of the shoulder. It can be a fatty and somewhat tough cut of meat, but is excellent pot-roasted, braised or stewed in the slow cooker. It may also be salted or spiced before cooking, and served cold in thin slices.

Clod and neck Sometimes referred to as "sticking," these cuts come from the neck area and are fairly lean. They are often sold cut up as "stewing" steak. Slightly leaner than blade or chuck, they may also be sold ground.

Tenderloin, round, sirloin steak These lean, tender cuts from the back are usually cut into steaks for broiling or frying, or into strips for stir-frying, and occasionally they are used for roasting. They may be included in braised slow cooker recipes, particularly those cooked on a high setting, but there is little point in using such cuts in casseroles and similar long-cooked dishes, where less expensive cuts produce more flavorful results.

Flank Lean, thick flank, or top rump, comes from the hindquarter. In a whole piece, it is ideal for pot-roasting in the slow cooker. It is also sold thickly sliced as braising steak. Thin flank can be fatty and gristly. It can be stewed but is often sold ground.

Leg and foreshank The leg cut comes from the hind legs of the animal and foreshank from the forelegs. The latter is a tough cut that responds well to slow cooking. It is usually sold in slices with the bone in the center, and sinews and connective tissue running through; these and the marrow from the bones give the cooked meat a rich, gelatinous quality.

Ground beef This is made from meat from any part of the animal, which has been passed through a meat grinder. It can be used to make meat sauces and meatballs in the slow cooker. As a general rule, the paler the meat the higher the fat content, so look for dark meat with less fat.

Rib Forerib and forewing, or prime rib, are expensive joints, best served roasted. For the slow cooker, choose middle rib. It is a fairly lean joint, and best boned before braising or pot-roasting.

Round pot roast This is lean, but tough, and is excellent for pot-roasts and braised dishes. It is often salted and gently cooked, then pressed, and served cold.

Flank steak This braising cut can also be pot-roasted. It has a lean but somewhat coarse texture, and can be fast-fried or cooked very slowly, making it an ideal cut for the slow cooker.

VEAL

This meat comes from young calves so is very tender and lean. Most cuts are not well suited to cooking in the slow cooker. Exceptions are shoulder of veal, also known as the "oyster," which is sometimes cut into chunks for casseroles; and the knuckle, the bonier end of the hind leg, which can be cut into slices and used to make the Italian stew osso bucco.

Above: Chuck steak (top) and brisket (bottom) are tough cuts, but both have an excellent flavor. They are perfectly suited to long, slow stewing, which gives deliciously moist results.

Below: Knuckle (top) and shoulder (bottom) are two of the few cuts of veal suitable for the slow cooker.

BRING OUT THE TASTE

Beef is a well-flavored meat that is delicious cooked with robust ingredients and served with spicy accompaniments. Peppery mustards and spicy horseradish are classic accompaniments, while wasabi, a sharp-tasting Japanese horseradish gives a more unusual twist.

Other Asian flavorings, such as soy sauce and ginger, also work well. Perfect vegetable partners include potatoes, leeks, onions, parsnips, celery and celeriac.

LAMB

Though lamb cuts do not usually need tenderizing, the fragrant flavor of the meat is intensified by slow cooking. It is enjoyed around the world in a wealth of pot-roasts, casseroles, stews, tagines, curries, and braised dishes.

Buying and storing

Lamb comes from animals that are less than a year old; spring lamb comes from animals that are between three and five months old. Meat from older sheep is known as mutton and has a darker color and stronger flavor; it is rarely available. Look for firm, slightly pink lamb with a fine-grained texture. The younger the animal, the paler the meat. The fat should be creamy white, firm, and waxy. Avoid any meat that looks dark, dry or grainy.

Lamb should be kept covered on a low shelf in the refrigerator. Prepacked meat can be left in its packaging and used by the date given on the package. When buying loose meat, steaks and chops will keep for 2–3 days, while larger joints will keep for up to 5 days.

Above: Tender chump chops are good pan-fried, broiled, or braised.

Below: A small leg of lamb can be pot-roasted in the slow cooker; steaks cut from the leg are good for braises and casseroles.

Cuts of lamb

The lean, tender prime cuts are taken from the top of the lamb along the middle of the back and are often broiled, fried, or roasted. However, they may also be cooked using slow, moist methods. Tougher cuts from the neck and lower legs respond well to slow cooker methods.

Breast This inexpensive cut is fairly fatty and is often served boned and rolled, sometimes with stuffing. It can be braised in the slow cooker, but trim off the visible fat.

Chops and cutlets Loin chops and leg chops are thick and tender. Best-end chops or cutlets and middle-neck cutlets are thinner and should be trimmed of fat before slow cooking.

Leg This is the prime roasting joint and is often divided into two pieces: the shank end and the sirloin section. The shank is a flavorful cut and is good pot-roasted or gently braised. A small leg of lamb may be pot-roasted on the bone in a large or oval slow cooker, or it can be boned and stuffed. It may also be cut into leg steaks or cubed.

Middle neck and cross rib Relatively cheap and made tender by long, slow cooking, these are used in dishes such as Lancashire hot-pot and Irish stew.

Saddle of lamb Also called a double loin of lamb, this tender roasting joint is too big to cook in a slow cooker.

Shoulder This roasting joint from the forequarter is fattier than the leg, so should be trimmed before pot-roasting on or off the bone. Boneless shoulder can be cubed for casseroles.

Above: Tender noisettes cut from the rolled, boned loin (top) are better suited to quick cooking techniques, while lamb cutlets (bottom) are great for braised dishes.

PERFECT PARTNERS

Fragrant herbs and fruity flavors go well with lamb. Dried fruit is a common addition to lamb dishes all over the world; rosemary, thyme, and mint are popular herbs; and garlic and salty additions, such as anchovies and olives, are widely used in Mediterranean dishes. Vegetables that go well with lamb include new potatoes, peas, carrots, and beans such as navy and small cannellini.

Below: Dried prunes make a tasty addition to a Moroccan lamb tagine.

PORK

This light meat is rich-tasting and very versatile. It is also particularly good for slow cooking: whole joints can be pot-roasted, bacon and cured ham can be poached, chops can be braised, and cubes of meat stewed. Pork products, such as sausages and ground pork, are also fabulous prepared in the slow cooker, in dishes such as hearty stews and chunky pâtés and terrines.

Buying and storing

Traditionally, fresh pork was a food for late autumn. Pigs were fattened throughout summertime to provide fresh and cured meats during the colder months. However, with modern storage techniques, pork is no longer a seasonal meat and is available all year round.

Pork should be a pale brownish-pink in color with a smooth, moist, fine-grained texture. The fat should look white and firm. In older animals, the meat darkens to a deeper color, and the flesh is coarser and less tender.

Hygiene is very important when handling pork, and great care should be taken not to contaminate other foods with the meat juices. Store pork on a low shelf in the refrigerator, below any food that will be eaten raw. Keep prepacked meat in its packaging, and observe the use-by dates. Ground pork can be kept for up to 2 days, while pork chops and joints can be kept for 3 days.

CLASSIC FLAVORINGS

Pork is widely eaten in the U.S.A., and in South and Central America, Europe, and Asia. Because of its rich taste and texture, it goes well with fruity and acidic accompaniments. In New England, cranberries are favored, while in England, Germany, and France, apples are a popular choice. In other cuisines, peaches, apricots, and pineapple are all used. Pungent herbs and spices, such as sage, rosemary, thyme, and juniper, are often added to pork dishes, and throughout Europe cabbage is a popular vegetable accompaniment.

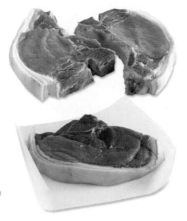

Above: Loin chops (top) and chump chops (bottom) are very good for braising.

Cuts of pork

Side This cut can be rolled and tied to make a neat joint and pot-roasted, or used for grinding and making sausages or terrines. Once a very fatty cut, today's belly pork tends to be leaner.

Chops Large and bony chump chops come from the hind loin, and leaner loin chops from the forelon. Both are good for braising. (A loin joint is better suited to oven-roasting than slow cooking.)

Leg or ham Often weighing more than 10 pounds, this cut is too big to be cooked in the slow cooker. However, it can be cut into two joints: the shank and the fillet. The shank can be pot-roasted, but is better oven-roasted. Leg fillet is cut across the top of the leg and is very tender. Leg steaks, cut from the top of the leg, are good for braising.

Neck end Cuts from this area include the sparerib, which is often cut into sparerib chops (different from Chinese-style spareribs, which are cut from the belly). They are good for braising.

Shoulder or blade Taken from the fore-end and sold on or off the bone, this can be pot-roasted, but is usually trimmed, cubed, and casseroled.

Tenderloin This lean, boneless, fine-textured piece of meat can be sliced into medallions or split lengthwise, stuffed, and tied. It may be cooked on a high setting in the slow cooker.

VARIETY MEATS

Known as "offal" in Europe, variety meats are all the offcuts from the carcass, including the organs, tail, feet, and head. Most variety meats are rich and highly flavored; they may be eaten on their own but are often used together with other meats—for example, in terrines and pâtés, and in steak and kidney pie. Many types of variety meat are good prepared in a slow cooker, particularly heart, tongue, and pig's feet, which become deliciously tender with slow, moist, gentle cooking. Unlike meat, which is often hung and matured for several weeks before using, variety meats do not keep well and should be bought very fresh and used quickly.

Bacon and ham

These are cured cuts of pork. Bacon is usually cured meat taken from the back and sides of the pig. Ham is the hind leg of a pig cut from the whole side, then cured separately. These cuts respond well to poaching in the slow cooker, as long cooking makes them very tender. Bacon chops are also good braised. Strips of bacon are often fried in a pan before adding to slow cooker stews.

Above: Rolled belly of pork is perfect for pot-roasting in the slow cooker.

POULTRY and GAME

The term poultry covers domesticated birds, including chicken, turkey, duck, goose, and guinea fowl, while game refers to wild birds and animals hunted for food, including pheasant, quail, wild rabbit, and venison. However, many game birds and animals are now farmed.

SMALL POULTRY

Chicken is probably the most popular of all small poultry, but there are many other types that are just as good.

Buying and storing

When buying fresh or chilled poultry, choose birds with soft blemish-free skin. Because poultry is highly susceptible to bacterial growth, keep it well chilled. Place loose poultry in a deep dish, and cover loosely. Check prepacked poultry to make sure that the package is sealed, and place on a plate, then store in the coldest part of the refrigerator. Check inside whole birds, and remove any giblets. Always wash hands, utensils, and surfaces after handling poultry.

When using frozen poultry, the safest way to thaw it is in the refrigerator. Place in a suitable container, and leave to defrost: for a 2–3 pound bird, allow about 30 hours in the refrigerator, or 8 hours at room temperature; for a 5-pound chicken, allow about 48 hours in the refrigerator, or 10 hours at room temperature. Once thawed or partially thawed, it should not be refrozen.

Below (from left to right): Corn-fed, free-range and organic chickens are widely available.

Types of small poultry

Poussin This is the French name for a young chicken that is only four to six weeks old and weighs 12 ounces –1½ pounds. These are very tender, with little fat, and will serve one or two people. They are ideal for pot-roasting, which gives moist, tender results.

Spring chicken These are sometimes called double poussins and will easily serve two. They are slightly larger birds, between six and ten weeks old, and weigh about 2 pounds.

Roasting chicken Sometimes known as a roaster, these prime birds are about 12 weeks old. They usually weigh about 3 pounds, but they may be as big as 6–7 pounds. The larger the bird, the better its value, because the proportion of meat to bone will be higher. They can be pot-roasted whole or in portions, poached, braised, or stewed.

Stewing or boiling chicken Rarely available from supermarkets, these birds are over one year old and tend to be large. Too tough for roasting, they are full of flavor and perfect for the slow cooker, as they need slow simmering. Either poach or use for soups and stews.

Guinea fowl These domestic fowl originated from the coast of Guinea in West Africa, hence their name. These birds are about the same size as a spring chicken. The flesh is delicate with a slightly gamey flavor. They can be cooked in the same way as chicken, but because they are quite dry, they respond best to moist cooking such as pot-roasting, braising, and stewing.

Cuts of chicken

A wide range of chicken portions are available fresh and frozen and are sold either individually, or in large, more economical packs. They may be sold on or off the bone.

Chicken quarters may be either leg joints or wing joints that have a portion of breast meat attached. The leg joint may be divided into thighs, small well-flavored dark meat joints, and drumsticks. Both need relatively long cooking in the slow cooker because the meat is compact.

Tender breast portions are entirely white meat; they are sold on or off the bone and may be skinned or unskinned. Portions on the bone have the most flavor when stewed or braised. Boneless chicken breast portions are sometimes referred to as fillets. The very small strips of chicken that can be found under the chicken breast are often sold separately. Supremes are chicken breast portions that include the wingbone, while part-boned breasts still have the short piece of bone leading into the wing and the fine strip of breastbone.

Jointing small poultry

This method of jointing can also be used for game birds, such as pheasant.

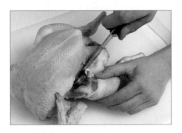

1 With the breast uppermost, use a sharp knife to remove the leg between the thigh and carcass. Cut, angling the knife inward, through the ball and socket joint. Repeat with the other leg.

2 Using poultry shears, cut along the breastbone, between the breast sections. Turn the bird over, and cut out the backbone. Using poultry shears, cut off the wing tips at the first joint.

3 Cut each breast section in half, leaving a portion of the breast attached to the wing. Next, cut each leg through the knee joint to separate the thigh and drumstick, making eight portions in all.

TURKEY

These substantial birds have dense meat that is lean and succulent. Fully grown, a turkey can weigh over 20 pounds and feed over 20 people. Whole birds won't fit in a slow cooker, but prepared joints and cuts are perfect for slow cooking.

Skinless, boneless breast fillets can be used in many different dishes. Turkey drumsticks can be large enough to provide a meal for three to four people. They can be pot-roasted, but are better braised or stewed until tender. Diced turkey is usually darker meat from the thigh or leg, and is ideal for casseroles and pâtés. Ground turkey can be used as an alternative to ground beef.

DUCK

Flavorful, juicy, and rich, duck is much fattier than chicken or turkey, with a higher proportion of bone to meat. Birds under 2 months old are called ducklings and are slightly leaner and more tender, but with less flavor. Wild duck has a stronger, more gamey taste than farmed duck but can be cooked in the same way. The slow cooker is unsuitable for cooking whole birds because of their awkward shape and fat content. However, duck breast portions can be used, providing the thick layer of fat is removed. Breast portions weigh about 8 ounces, making a generous serving for one. Skinned duck portions are ideal for braising, especially in citrus or fruit sauces, which tenderize and flavor.

Jointing a duck

Because ducks have a high proportion of bone to meat, it is better to cut the bird into four portions, dividing an equal amount of meat between them.

1 Place the duck, breast side up, on a board. Using poultry shears, trim off the wing tips at the first joint. Pull back the skin at the neck end, and cut out the wishbone. Cut the breast in half from the tail end to the neck.

Above: *Turkey is a versatile as well as economical meat.*

2 Separate the bird into two halves by cutting along each side of the backbone. Remove the backbone, and discard.

3 Cut each portion in half, sharing the meat as evenly as possible between the four portions.

GOOSE

These large, fatty birds are difficult to rear intensively, so fresh birds are usually only available from the late autumn until Christmas. Goose is much better suited to oven-roasting than cooking gently in the slow cooker.

GAME

Once hard to come by, game is now readily available from the supermarket. Fresh wild game remains seasonal and is only available during the months when hunting is allowed. Many types of game are now farmed and available all year round, while wild game is available frozen. Game can be divided into two types: game birds and furred game, which includes rabbit, hare, wild boar, and venison.

Buying and storing

Larger supermarkets and specialist butchers offer a good choice of game when in season and should be able to offer you advice on preparation and cooking. Game birds will not look as perfect as poultry, but check that they are not too damaged. Pheasant should be even in shape with a pleasant gamey aroma. Partridge will have a slightly stronger game smell and soft pale flesh. When buying grouse and quail, look for a moist fresh skin and choose birds with a high proportion of meat to bone.

Right: A brace of pheasant.

Below: Tiny quail are often farmed.

Below: Mallard is the most commonly available wild duck.

Birds that are sold in sealed packaging should be left in their packing and used by the date indicated. If you buy a bird "loose" from the butcher, remove the packaging when you get home, rinse the bird under cold running water, and pat dry with paper towels. Put the bird in a deep dish to catch any drips, and cover it tightly with plastic wrap. Store game birds in the coldest part of the refrigerator, and use within two days of purchase, or freeze right away. Before cooking wild game birds, rub your fingertips over the surface to try to locate any tiny balls of lead shot that may be left in them, then carefully cut them out with kitchen scissors or a filleting knife, and discard.

Types of game bird

Very young and tender birds are often roasted or spatchcocked and broiled, but most older game birds benefit from moist cooking techniques, such as pot-roasting, stewing, or braising. When pot-roasting dry game birds, such as cock pheasant, wrap slices of fatty bacon around the bird, then tie in place with string. This will help to baste and flavor the meat.

Pheasant One of the most plentiful of game birds, these are usually raised on managed estates in a similar manner to free-range farming. Traditionally they were sold in pairs, known as a brace (one male and one female). The tender hen pheasant would be roasted and the cock pheasant hung and stewed. In practice, supermarket pheasants are always young and tender. For the best results, pot-roast or stew pheasants. One bird should serve three or four people.

Grouse Native to Scotland, these birds feed on highland heather, which gives them a rich gamey flavor. They are quite small and

Below: Pigeon.

will serve one or two people. Ptarmigan and capercaillie are members of the grouse family, but are considered to have an inferior flavor compared to grouse. Young birds may be pot-roasted, but need to be kept moist with a layer of fat or fatty bacon over the breast. They are good stewed.

Partridge There are two main types: French or red-legged partridge, and the smaller English or gray-legged partridge, which has a better flavor. At their prime (around three months old), they weigh about 1 pound and it is usual to serve one per person. Older birds should always be casseroled or braised.

Wild duck These are less fatty than farmed ducks, so smaller ones may be cooked whole in a large slow cooker. Choose inland ducks because those from saltwater areas may have a fishy flavor.

Pigeon Wild and wood pigeon has a strong flavor and can be stewed slowly to tenderize the meat. Another traditional way of cooking an older bird is in a steamed pudding, often with beef steak inside a suet crust. Young pigeon is known as squab. They are reared commercially, although they are usually only available in the spring.

Quail This is now a protected species, so any quail for sale will have been farmed. They are tiny, so you will need two per person for a main course. They may be pot-roasted whole.

FURRED GAME

Most game needs to be hung before cooking to tenderize the flesh and develop the flavor. However, this is usually done by the butcher, so the meat is ready for cooking when you buy it.

Game is cooked in the same way as other meats, and recipes for similar types of meat are usually interchangeable. For example, wild boar can often be used instead of pork, farmed rabbit instead of chicken, and venison in place of beef in many recipes. Mature game should always be cooked using gentle, moist heat, as in braising and stewing, making it ideal for the slow cooker.

Deer

The word venison was once used to describe the meat of any animal killed for food by hunting. Today, in Britain and Australia, the term venison only refers to the meat from deer, although in North America it also includes meat from the reindeer, moose, caribou, elk, and antelope. Venison from deer is a lean, dark, close-textured meat. Much of it is now farmed and is more tender, with a slightly milder flavor, than venison from wild deer. Prime cuts, such as loin and fillet, are best roasted and served rare. Other cuts, such as shin, neck, and shoulder, benefit from marinating (red wine and juniper is traditional); they then need long and gentle cooking to tenderize and bring out the flavor of the meat.

Wild boar

Although hunted to extinction in Britain in the 17th century, wild boar is still found in Europe, Central Asia, and North Africa. The meat is dark-colored with a strong flavor and little fat, so it benefits from marinades with a little added oil. It can be cooked in exactly the same way as pork, but care must be taken, because the meat is dry and can easily become tough. Moist cooking methods work best.

Rabbit and hare

Although these animals belong to the same family, the meat is very different. Rabbit, especially if it has been farmed, is a paler, milder meat, similar to chicken. Hare, or jack rabbit as it is known in the United States, has a very strong, dark gamey flesh. The saddle of both can be roasted, but other cuts are best slowly stewed. Boneless rabbit and hare meat can be used in steamed puddings, terrines, and pâtés. Older hares are traditionally jugged (cooked in a casserole set over a pan of simmering water to temper the heat) to give deliciously tender results. Cooking gently in the slow cooker gives similar results.

Jointing a rabbit

A whole rabbit can be jointed into five pieces or more, depending on its size.

1 To joint a skinned and cleaned rabbit, use a large filleting knife to cut between the ball and socket joint at the top of each thigh to remove the hind legs.

2 Cut the body into three pieces. This will give you five pieces—two forelegs, two hind legs, and the saddle.

Above and left: Venison cuts that benefit from long, slow cooking include shin, shoulder, and neck (above, left to right) and haunch (left).

Above and right: Rabbit saddle is best roasted. Other rabbit cuts should be stewed.

Above and left: Cultivated hare has lean, dark meat and is available whole or in pieces.

FISH and SHELLFISH

The slow cooker is great for cooking fish, allowing the subtle flavor to develop slowly and also helping to retain the fish's shape as it cooks. Fish dishes that can be made in the slow cooker include terrines, soups, risottos, and pasta dishes, as well as simple steamed and poached fish. The slow cooker is also good for cooking many dishes containing raw and cooked shellfish. However, it is not suitable for cooking live shellfish, such as mussels and lobsters, because these require brief, fast boiling.

Most shellfish benefit from short cooking and should be added toward the end of cooking time, particularly when using precooked shellfish. One exception is squid, which requires either very brief or very long, slow cooking; anything in between gives tough results.

Buying and cooking

Always buy the freshest fish and shellfish available, from a supplier with a high turnover, and prepare and cook it within 24 hours. Fish and shellfish should smell fresh; if it has an unpleasant fishy or ammoniac odor, it is past its best. Most fish and shellfish from the supermarket has already been frozen, so shouldn't be refrozen; check this when you buy.

PREPARING FISH

Fish can be divided into two types: white and oily. These, in turn, can be divided into round and flat fish, which require slightly different preparation and cooking.

Round fish

This group includes white-fleshed fish such as cod, coley, and haddock, and oily fish such as salmon and mackerel. They have rounded bodies and eyes on either side of the head. The flesh is usually firm with largish flakes when cooked. Many are too big to be cooked whole in the slow cooker, so need to be sliced into steaks or filleted. A good fish dealer will often do this for you.

I To remove the scales, place the fish on a large sheet of newspaper. Scrape a fish scaler or knife against the skin, working from the tail to the head.

2 Using a filleting knife or thin, sharp knife, slit the fish open along the belly from the gills to the tail vent. Carefully scrape out the innards with a spoon, then rinse well under running water, inside and out. Cut off the head using a sharp knife.

3 To fillet the fish, lay it on its side, tail away from you. Make an incision along the backbone from head to tail, cutting through behind the gills. Starting at the head end, slide the knife between the fillet and bones to release the fillet.

4 To skin the fillet, lay it skin side down. Make a cut at the tail end, cutting through the flesh, but not the skin, so that the fillet can be lifted away slightly. Hold the tail firmly and "saw" the knife between the skin and flesh.

Flat fish

This group includes sole and plaice. Both eyes lie on their upper side and, because they lead an inactive life on the seabed, the flesh tends to be very delicate.

I Place the fish, light side down, on a board. Make a cut down the center using a sharp filleting knife, following the backbone, then make a second cut around the head.

2 Slide the knife under one fish fillet, inserting the blade between the flesh and bones. Holding the loosened corner, cut the flesh from the bones. Remove the second fillet in the same way, then turn the fish over and repeat.

3 The skins may be removed in the same manner as for round fish.

PREPARING SHELLFISH

You can often ask the fish dealer to prepare shellfish for you, but it is also easy to prepare at home.

Shrimp

Raw shrimp may be cooked in their shells or peeled first. The dark intestinal vein is usually removed.

I To peel, grip the head between your forefinger and thumb. Holding the body with your other hand, gently pull until the head comes off. Remove the legs, and peel the shell from the body. The tail may be pulled away or left on.

2 To remove the dark intestinal vein, make a shallow cut down the center of the back, and pull out the vein using a knife blade or a toothpick.

Preparing squid

Unlike other shellfish, which have their protective shell on the outside, the shell of the squid is found inside its body.

I Hold the body of the squid in one hand and the tentacles in the other, and gently pull apart. Cut the tentacles away from the head just below the eyes, and discard the head.

2 Remove the "quill" and soft innards from the body, and discard. Peel off the thin membrane, then rinse the body and tentacles under cold running water.

3 Using a sharp knife, slice the body into rings, or cut it into large pieces and lightly score in a criss-cross pattern.

COOKING FISH

Fish is well suited to simple cooking methods that retain its natural juices. Unlike meat, fish should be removed from the slow cooker as soon as it is done, otherwise it will become dry. It is ready when the flesh is still slightly translucent when eased away from the bone, and flakes easily.

Poaching

This is a good method for cooking large, fairly firm pieces of fish, such as steaks or chunky fillets. It can also be used for small whole fish. Fish stock, wine, water, and milk can all be used for poaching.

I Lightly grease the base of the ceramic cooking pot. Place four 6–8-ounce salmon fillets or similar in the base, leaving space between each one.

2 Pour over ⅔ cup dry white wine and 1¼ cups of boiling fish stock or water. Add a pinch of salt, 2 black peppercorns, a few slices of onion, 1 bay leaf, and a sprig of fresh parsley.

3 Cover the pot with the lid, and switch the slow cooker to high. Cook for 45 minutes–1½ hours, or until cooked. Serve with melted butter or a sauce, or leave to cool and serve with salad.

Braising

This method cooks the fish in a small amount of liquid, so that it is partly poached and partly steamed. It is a good technique for delicate flat fish fillets. Rolling the fish fillets helps to protect them during cooking and allows you to add a filling for extra flavor.

I Pour slightly less than ¼ inch white wine, cider, or fish stock into the ceramic cooking pot, and switch the slow cooker to high. Cover with the lid.

2 Blend 1 ounce butter with lemon or orange rind, salt, and pepper. Place four large, skinned lemon sole fillets on a board, and spread each with the butter.

3 Roll up the fillet to enclose the filling, and carefully place in the base of the ceramic cooking pot, with the loose end tucked underneath.

4 Sprinkle the fish with 1 tablespoon lemon juice. Cover with the lid, and cook for 45 minutes–1½ hours, or until the fish is opaque and cooked. Transfer to serving plates. Stir a little sour cream and chopped fresh parsley, dill, or cilantro into the cooking juices, and spoon over the fish.

VEGETABLES

Cooking vegetables in the slow cooker is a good way to ensure they are tender without being overcooked, which can spoil their texture and subtle flavors.

Onions

An essential ingredient in many slow cooker recipes, they take a long time to cook, so are often fried in oil before adding to the slow cooker.

Different types of onion have varying degrees of pungency. Large, yellow onions (often called Bermuda onions) are mild. Smaller, white onions, the most common type, have a stronger flavor; red onions are mild and sweet. Leeks are part of the onion family and have a milder flavor than onions; they cook more quickly. Garlic adds flavor;

Above: *The onion family includes scallions, red and white onions, and brown and banana shallots.*

CLEANING LEEKS

Leeks usually need careful cleaning to remove grit and dirt in the leaves.

1 Trim the root and coarse green tops, and discard. Remove any damaged or tough outer leaves.

2 Slit the top green part lengthwise about a third of the way down. Rinse well under cold running water, separating the layers as you do so.

---

the taste it imparts is milder when whole or sliced, and stronger when crushed or chopped. Slow cooking tames the pungency, so you may need to increase the amount in dishes cooked for more than 4 hours. Scallions are usually used raw, but have a delicate flavor when cooked.

Roots and tubers

These vegetables, which include carrots, rutabagas, turnips, parsnips, and potatoes, have a dense, sometimes starchy flesh. They take the longest time to cook in the slow cooker.

Cut roots and tubers into small pieces, no larger than 1 inch thick, and place in the base of the ceramic cooking pot, which is the hottest part during cooking. The vegetables should be immersed in the cooking liquid to ensure they soften, and to protect those roots and tubers, such as potatoes, that will discolor if exposed to air.

In braised dishes that use only a little liquid, it may be necessary to layer the ingredients. It does not matter if some of the meat on the surface is not covered with cooking liquid, as it will cook in the steam. If the dish contains ingredients that do not require long cooking, such as fish, sauté the root vegetables first.

Mushrooms

These add a deep color and rich taste to many dishes. They give off a lot of liquid, so if you add extra mushrooms to a recipe, adjust the liquid content.

White, cremini, and flat mushrooms are the most common cultivated types. White mushrooms have a mild taste; small whole ones are good in casseroles. Flat mushrooms have a stronger flavor and are usually sliced or left whole and stuffed. Cremini mushrooms have a darker brown skin, firmer texture, and a stronger, nuttier taste than white. Large ones are known as portabello mushrooms and have a meaty taste.

Portabello mushrooms, field blewitts, ceps, morels, and shiitake mushrooms are wild varieties with intense flavors. Delicate mushrooms, such as oyster and enoki, should be added to the slow cooker near the end of cooking. Dried mushrooms are used to thicken dishes by absorbing liquid. They should be pre-soaked in boiling water for a few minutes before adding, to remove any grit or dirt.

Above: Mushrooms have a distinctive taste and meaty texture.

Pumpkins and squashes

These come in many shapes, sizes, and colors. Cooking in the slow cooker helps to develop their flavor and retain their firm texture. They tend to produce a lot of liquid during cooking, so don't add too much extra liquid to braised dishes containing pumpkins or squashes.

Squashes can be divided into two varieties: summer and winter. Winter squashes have a dense, fibrous flesh and include pumpkins and butternut and acorn squashes. They all have sweet-tasting, deep-orange flesh. Summer squashes include patty pans and zucchini. They are picked young and have a high water content and delicate flesh that cooks quickly, so be careful not to overcook.

Shoot vegetables

This category covers a large number of vegetables, which vary widely in appearance and characteristics. Some, such as fennel, chicory, and celery, respond well to slow cooking, while others, such as asparagus and artichokes, are better cooked using conventional methods.

VEGETABLE FRUITS

Although tomatoes, bell peppers, and eggplants are all used as vegetables, botanically they are fruits.

Tomatoes

Great for slow cooking, these add a rich color and flavor to many dishes. They are juicy, so can be used as part of the cooking liquid. Long cooking can make the skins tough and seeds bitter, so these are best removed before cooking.

Bell peppers

Known as "sweet peppers" in Great Britain, these come in many colors, including red, orange, yellow, green, and purple. Green peppers are the unripe stage of peppers of other colors, such as red. Green peppers tend to lose their color and become bitter in slow cooked dishes, unless they are cut into very small pieces and added toward the end of cooking.

Below (from left): Butternut, acorn, and patty pan squashes make a great addition to slow cooked dishes.

Eggplant

Also known as "aubergines," eggplants range from large, glossy, dark-purple ones to the small, creamy-white egg-shaped ones. Very large eggplants may be slightly bitter, so should be salted after slicing or cubing and left for half an hour, then rinsed well. This process is also useful for drawing out liquid that would dilute the sauce of the dish.

Brassicas and green leafy vegetables

Brassicas, such as broccoli and cauliflower, should be broken or cut into small sprigs to ensure they cook evenly in the slow cooker. When using leafy vegetables, such as cabbage and spinach, shred them very finely and always add to hot liquid so they cook in the shortest possible time to retain their taste and texture.

CANNED AND FROZEN VEGETABLES

These make a useful last-minute addition to many dishes. They are particularly good time-savers because they require no further preparation. Cooked, canned vegetables should be well drained, then simply added 15 minutes before the end of cooking time.

Frozen vegetables, such as peas and corn, should be defrosted first and need a little more cooking. (For speedy defrosting, they can be placed in a strainer under cool running water.) Once added to the slow cooker, they should be cooked for 15–20 minutes.

GRAINS, PASTA, and BEANS

Cereal grains, pasta, and beans are all very versatile and can be used as a main ingredient or an accompaniment. Classic slow cooker dishes that use grains, pasta, and beans as the main ingredient include risottos, pilafs, lasagne, pasta bakes, and bean stews and curries.

RICE

Ordinary long grain rice doesn't cook well in the slow cooker, but converted rice gives excellent results. Also known as parboiled rice, it is soaked in water and then steamed under pressure, making it difficult to overcook. The grains remain separate during cooking, so it is particularly good for slow cooking, where the water bubbles very gently, if at all. The dry grains may appear more yellow than normal rice, but this coloration disappears during cooking; when fully cooked, the rice becomes bright white.

TYPES OF CONVERTED RICE

As well as white, long grain converted rice, there are several other varieties, all with their own unique cooking properties.

Converted brown rice Also known as "converted wholegrain rice," this is the whole rice grain complete with bran. It has a chewier texture and nuttier flavor than white long grain rice, and stands up best of all to long, slow cooking, still holding its shape after several hours on high.

Converted basmati rice Basmati rice is grown in northern India, the Punjab, parts of Pakistan, and in the foothills of the Himalayas. It has a unique taste and texture, and the word *basmati* means "fragrant one" in Hindi. Basmati is particularly good in pilafs and for serving with spicy Indian-style dishes.

Converted Italian rice Sometimes labeled "easy-cook risotto rice," this rice has short plump grains and a high proportion of starch, which gives a rich, creamy texture to dishes such as risotto.

Making slow cooker rice

A simple savory rice dish can be made easily in the slow cooker, and makes a good accompaniment for four people.

1 Grease the bottom of the ceramic cooking pot with 1 tablespoon butter, or 1 tablespoon sunflower-seed oil. Sprinkle 4–6 very finely chopped scallions over the butter or oil. Switch the slow cooker to high, and leave to cook for 20 minutes.

2 Add ¼ teaspoon ground turmeric or a pinch of saffron strands and 3 cups boiling vegetable stock to the pot. If the stock is unseasoned, add a pinch of salt as well.

3 Sprinkle generous 1½ cups converted rice over the stock, and stir well. Cover, and cook for about 1 hour, or until the rice is tender and the stock has been absorbed. Serve hot, or put into a shallow dish, stir in 2 tablespoons vinaigrette, and serve warm or cold.

Making risotto

A good risotto should be creamy and moist. Cooked conventionally, this is achieved by adding the cooking liquid gradually and stirring constantly. The gentle heat of the slow cooker and the use of converted Italian rice means that the liquid can be added all at once to produce a creamy risotto. This recipe for Risotto alla Milanese serves 3–4 people.

1 Gently fry 1 finely chopped onion in 1 tablespoon butter and 1 tablespoon olive oil in a frying pan until soft. Pour in ½ cup dry white wine, and heat until steaming but not boiling.

2 Transfer the mixture to the ceramic cooking pot, and switch the slow cooker to high. Cover with the lid, and cook for about 30 minutes, until boiling.

3 Sprinkle 1¼ cups converted Italian rice and a pinch of saffron strands into the pot. Pour in 3 cups boiling stock. Stir well, re-cover, and cook for about 45 minutes, stirring once halfway through cooking. The rice should be almost tender and most of the stock absorbed.

4 Turn off the slow cooker. Sprinkle ¾ cup freshly grated Parmesan cheese into the risotto and stir, then season with freshly ground black pepper.

5 Cover the pot, and leave to stand for about 5 minutes to allow the risotto to finish cooking. Taste, and adjust the seasoning if necessary, then serve with fine shavings of Parmesan.

COOK'S TIP

This recipe is for the classic Risotto alla Milanese, but the ingredients can be varied to create other risotto dishes. Try stirring pan-fried mushrooms or chopped cooked chicken into the risotto 15 minutes before the end of cooking.

OTHER GRAINS

As well as rice, there are many other grains that can be cooked successfully in a slow cooker. Whole grains, such as barley, quinoa, and whole wheat, can be served as an accompaniment instead of rice or potatoes, or as part of a main course. Whole rye grains need to be soaked in cold water overnight before cooking. This is not necessary for most grains, although presoaking will shorten the cooking time.

Cooking grains

The cooking times vary from grain to grain; quinoa and millet take the least time, while grains such as barley and rye take much longer. To speed up cooking and enhance the flavor, fry grains in a little oil for 2–3 minutes, before transferring to the slow cooker.

I Allow about 3 ounces per person for part of a main course. If the quantity of cooking liquid is not indicated on the package, place the grains in a measuring cup to check their volume, then measure three parts boiling water or stock to one part grain (millet is the exception, and needs four parts water).

2 Rinse the grains in a strainer under cold running water, then place in the ceramic cooking pot, and pour over the water or stock. Cover, and cook on high for 40 minutes–2 hours, or until tender.

PASTA

Both ordinary and easy-cook pastas can be used in the slow cooker. The latter gives the best results, but is not suitable for "all-day cooking"; the final result will be soft and soggy. As a general rule, pasta made from 100 percent durum wheat holds its shape better than the varieties made with eggs (all'uova). Fresh pasta is not suitable for slow cookers because it requires fast boiling in a large quantity of water. There is a huge range of pasta shapes, and the shape and size will affect cooking times.

"Precooked" lasagne sheets layered with meat or vegetables and white or cheese sauces, and stuffed cannelloni

tubes, covered with white or cheese sauce, will take about 2 hours on high, or 1 hour on high followed by 2 hours on low. The time taken will also be affected by the initial temperature of the sauces; the hotter they are to start with, the quicker the pasta will cook.

Large and medium shapes added to almost-cooked casseroles or near-boiling sauces will take 30–45 minutes on high. They will take less time if there is plenty of free cooking liquid, and if the sauce is thin. Whole-wheat pasta will take 10 minutes longer than white.

Small shapes, such as soup pasta, will take about 20 minutes on high. These can also be used to thicken casseroles or soups toward the end of cooking; the pasta absorbs some of the liquid.

BEANS

The slow cooker was invented for the commercial cooking of baked beans, cooking navy beans until perfectly tender, while still keeping their shape. The slow cooker is therefore great for cooking all dried beans, peas, and lentils.

Cooking beans

Most beans, peas, and lentils need to be soaked before cooking, but soaking times depend on the variety and also the age of the beans. Red lentils and split peas need no soaking; most beans should be soaked for at least 6 hours, and some, such as chickpeas, for 8–12 hours. Beans should not be left to soak for more than 24 hours. When they are fully soaked, the skin should look plump and smooth.

I Put the beans in a large bowl, cover with at least twice their volume of cold water, and leave to soak.

2 Drain the beans, then rinse under cold running water. Place the pulses in a large pan, and cover with cold water. Pour over enough cold water to come about 1½ inches above the beans. Bring to the boil, and boil rapidly, uncovered, for 10–15 minutes. (All beans, except for lentils and gunga peas, should be boiled fast before being transferred to the slow cooker, to destroy toxins.)

3 Remove the pan from the heat, and skim off any froth on the surface. Leave to cool for 5 minutes, then transfer the beans and cooking liquid to the ceramic cooking pot. The liquid should cover the pulses by at least ¾ inch; if necessary, top up with a little boiling water.

4 Add flavoring ingredients, such as bay leaves or sprigs of thyme, but do not add salt or acidic ingredients, such as tomato juice—these will toughen the beans and prevent them from cooking properly. Cover with the lid, and cook on high for 1¼–5 hours. (Cooking times vary according to the type of bean: kidney beans take about 1½ hours, and soya beans take 4½–5 hours. Canned beans or peas only need to be added to a dish about 30 minutes before the end of cooking time to warm through.)

FRUITS

The gentle simmering of the slow cooker makes it ideal for cooking all kinds of fruit to perfection. It is particularly good for poaching delicate fruits that have a tendency to break up during cooking, including soft fruits, such as currants and rhubarb. It can also be used to make desserts, such as cobblers and crumbles.

PREPARING FRUIT

Many fruits need only simple preparation, such as washing, while others need to be peeled, cored, seeded, or pitted before they are cooked.

Peeling

Fruits such as apples, pears, and peaches should be peeled before cooking.

To peel fruits such as apples and pears, use a vegetable peeler or a small paring knife to pare off the skin in thin strips. Apples can also be peeled in one single, spiral strip.

To peel fruits such as peaches and apricots, loosen the skins first. Make a tiny nick in the skin, then place in a bowl. Pour over boiling water to cover, and leave for 20–30 seconds. Lift out using a slotted spoon, rinse under cold water, and the skin should peel off easily.

Coring

Tough cores, seeds, and stems should be removed from fruit before cooking so that they do not spoil the dish.

When cooking chunks of fruit, first cut the fruit lengthwise into quarters. Remove the central core and seeds using a small knife, then peel and chop into smaller pieces as required.

When cooking whole fruits (for example, baked apples) you will need a special corer. Place the sharp "blade" of the corer over the stem end of the fruit, press down firmly, and twist. The core will come out with the corer.

Removing pits

Hard pits should always be removed from fruit before cooking, since they will become loose as the fruit cooks.

To pit larger fruits such as plums and apricots, cut around the crease in the fruit. Twist the halves apart, then carefully lever out the pit using the point of a small knife.

To pit cherries, it is easiest to use a special cherry pitter. Put the fruit in the pitter, with the end where the stalk was facing upward. Push the bar into the fruit to eject the pit.

COOKING FRUIT

Fruit can be cooked in all kinds of ways in a slow cooker, which is good for stewing and poaching, and can be used for "baking" as well.

Poaching and stewing

These techniques are slightly different. Poaching cooks fruit in a hot syrup, and is good for pears, fruits with pits, and figs. Stewing is used for fruit such as apples, berries, and rhubarb.

1 To stew rhubarb, cut 2 pounds rhubarb into 1-inch pieces. Put into the ceramic cooking pot with ¾–1 cup superfine sugar, sprinkling it between the layers. Pour over the juice of 1 large orange and ½ cup water.

2 Switch the slow cooker to high, and cook for 1½ hours, or until the rhubarb is tender but still holds its shape. Stir gently halfway through cooking.

Baking

Fruits such as whole apples, halved peaches, and figs can be "baked" in the slow cooker, with just a tiny amount of liquid to start the cooking process.

1 To make baked apples, you can use any type of apple. Keeping the fruits whole, remove the cores, then score the skin around the circumference.

2 Blend together ½ cup soft light brown sugar and ¼ cup finely chopped dried fruit, and use to fill the apples. Top each with a piece of butter and place in the ceramic pot on a square of foil shaped to form a saucer.

3 Pour ⅔ cup very hot water around the foil squares. Cover, and cook on high for 2–3 hours. If using cooking apples, check frequently, and remove as soon as they are tender; if overcooked, they may collapse.

To bake nectarines, figs, and oranges, place the halved or sliced fruits in the buttered ceramic cooking pot. Sprinkle a little lemon juice and sugar over each one and dot with butter. Pour 5 tablespoons water around the fruit, cover, and cook on high for 1½–2 hours, or until tender.

Making compotes

Compotes can be made with a single fruit, or several different types, cooked in a flavored syrup. They may be served hot or cold, as a dessert or for breakfast. The fruits should be ripe but still firm.

When using a slow cooker, all the fruits can be added at the same time, rather than in order of their cooking time. When using dried fruit, less extra sugar is needed because the fruit is already very sweet.

I Put 1 cup sugar in the ceramic cooking pot with 1¼ cups cold water. Add flavoring ingredients such as lemon rind.

2 Switch the slow cooker to high, and heat for about 30 minutes, then stir until the sugar dissolves completely. Cover the cooking pot with the lid, and heat for a further 30–45 minutes.

3 Add the fruit to the syrup. This could be 1 pound each prepared peaches, apricots, and cherries, or 1 pound each halved pears, plums, and apple slices. Cover, and cook for 1–3 hours, or until the fruit is tender. Serve hot, or allow to cool and transfer to a bowl before chilling. The compote will keep for several days in the refrigerator.

Making cobblers

Stewed and canned fruit are perfect for making these traditional baked desserts. Adding a little of the juice or syrup with the fruit produces steam and helps the cobbler to rise.

I Lightly grease the ceramic cooking pot with sweet butter. Add the fruit, cover the cooking pot with the lid, and switch the slow cooker to high. Canned fruit, such as peaches and berries, should be cooked for about 1 hour until hot and steaming; uncooked fruit, such as apple slices, should be cooked for 2–3 hours until tender.

2 When the fruit is nearly ready, make the cobbler topping. Sift ½ cup all-purpose flour, 1 teaspoon baking powder, and a pinch of salt into a bowl. Rub in 3 tablespoons butter, then add the finely grated rind of ½ lemon. Stir in ⅓ cup milk to make a thick batter, and spoon over the fruit. Cover, and cook on high for 45 minutes–1 hour, or until a skewer inserted into the topping comes out clean.

Making crumbles

Crumbles made in a slow cooker do not brown in the same way as conventional crumbles, but using brown flour, oats, butter, and crunchy sugar and a fairly dry fruit mixture gives similar results.

I Combine prepared fruit such as apple and peach slices with a little sugar and 1 teaspoon cornstarch. Add 2 tablespoons fruit juice or water, and switch the slow cooker to high.

2 Place ¾ cup whole-wheat flour and ½ cup jumbo oats in a mixing bowl. Rub in 6 tablespoons butter. Stir in ¼ cup raw sugar, then sprinkle over the fruit. Cover, and cook for 3–4 hours, or until the fruit and topping are cooked.

HERBS, SPICES, and FLAVORINGS

The judicious use of flavorings is the key to successful cooking. Some dishes require just a subtle hint, while others need more robust flavorings.

HERBS

While fresh herbs are usually considered superior, for slow cooker dishes dried herbs are often better. Delicate fresh leaves lose their pungency and color with long cooking, whereas dried herbs release their flavor slowly. As a general rule, fresh herbs should be added about 30 minutes before the end of cooking, or just before serving.

Some herbs dry more successfully than others. Thyme, marjoram, oregano, and sage dry very well, while parsley and chives lose their potency and color; it is better to use these herbs fresh at the end of cooking. Dried herb mixtures are often well flavored and worth using.

Buy dried herbs from a reliable source with a quick turnover, and look for small packages. "Freeze dried" herbs have a good fresh flavor. Store dried herbs in a cool, dark place for 6–9 months. Try to buy fresh herbs on the day you need them. They will keep for several days stored in the refrigerator.

Below: Robustly flavored rosemary and sage should be used sparingly.

Tender herbs

These herbs have soft, fragile leaves and need careful handling. They should be added in the last few minutes of cooking time, or to the finished dish. Popular tender herbs include pungent basil, which goes well with tomatoes and Mediterranean-style dishes; anise-scented chervil, dill, and tarragon, which go well with fish, eggs, and cream sauces; strong, refreshing mint; aromatic cilantro; lovage with its mild taste of celery; and the great all-rounder, parsley.

Robust herbs

These usually have tough, woody stems and pungent leaves and can withstand long cooking. They should be added at the start of slow cooking to extract and mellow their flavor, then removed just before serving. Popular robust herbs include richly flavored bay leaves, which are used in stocks, casseroles, marinades, and some sweet dishes; fragrant, aromatic oregano, marjoram, and thyme, which are very good in Mediterranean-style dishes; robust rosemary, which goes well with lamb; pungent sage, which complements pork; and aromatic kaffir lime leaves, which are used in Thai and Malaysian dishes.

SPICES

Warm, fragrant spices are usually added at the beginning of cooking time. However, some may become bitter if cooked for many hours, and should be added partway through cooking. Most spices are better used whole, rather than ground, in slow cooker dishes. Store spices in a cool, dark place, and check the sell-by date before using; they lose their taste and aroma with age. Whole spices will keep for up to 1 year; ground spices start to lose their pungency after about 6 months.

Left: Delicate dill has a mild aniseed flavor that goes well with fish.

BOUQUET GARNI

This simple bunch of herbs is a classic flavoring and is used in soups, casseroles and sauces.

Using a long piece of string, tie together a bay leaf with sprigs of parsley and thyme. Add to the slow cooker, and tie the string to the handle for easy removal.

Alternatively, place the herbs in a square of cheesecloth and tie into a loose bag. Flavorings such as peppercorns can also be added.

Hot spices

Many spices add heat to dishes—some give just a hint of warmth, others a fierce heat. The main hot spices are chili, ginger, pepper, and mustard.

There are more than 200 types of chile, of varying shapes, sizes, colors, and potencies. They can be bought fresh, dried, flaked, or ground. Chili powder may be hot or mild—from red hot cayenne pepper to mild, sweet paprika. There are also chili sauces, such as Tabasco or Thai chili sauce. All chiles and chili products can become bitter with long cooking and should be added partway through cooking.

Sweet, peppery ginger is used in both sweet and savory dishes and is available fresh, dried, ground, and preserved in syrup. Its close relative, galangal, is used in many Southeast Asian dishes. Warm, spicy fresh turmeric looks similar to fresh ginger root and is used in curries.

Black, white, and green peppercorns add a peppery bite to dishes. Black are the most aromatic. Black, brown, and white mustard seeds have a much more pungent aroma and kick, with the black seeds being the hottest. The heat diminishes with cooking, so add toward the end of cooking time.

Fragrant spices
Some plants are grown for their fragrant, aromatic seeds. These are sold whole and ground. Long, slow cooking softens the whole seeds and releases their taste. Popular seed spices include warm, aromatic cumin and coriander, which are used in Indian, North African and Middle Eastern dishes; pungent caraway seeds, which feature in many European dishes, especially pork- and cabbage-based ones, as well as baked recipes such as rye bread and sweet seed cake; and poppy seeds, which are often used in desserts in eastern Europe, and are also a popular topping for crusty bread. Other fragrant spices include warming allspice, cinnamon, cassia, and nutmeg; aromatic cardamom pods; pungent cloves; scented star anise; vanilla, which is mainly used in sweet dishes; gin-scented juniper berries, which go well with pork, game, and cabbage; delicate, bitter-sweet saffron, which is often used in rice and fish dishes; and sour tamarind, which is widely used in Indian and Southeast Asian cooking.

Above: There are many different varieties of chile.

Spice mixtures
As well as individual spices, there are a number of ground spice mixes that are widely used in both sweet and savory dishes. Popular mixes include apple pie spice, which is used in cakes and desserts; Chinese five-spice powder, which is used in many savory Chinese and Asian dishes; garam masala, a popular Indian spice mix that is added toward the end of cooking; and a wide variety of curry powders that vary in strength from mild to very hot. Jars of curry paste are also available.

OTHER FLAVORINGS
As well as herbs and spices, there are many other flavorings that can be used to enliven dishes—ranging from pungent sauces to delicate flower waters.

Savory sauces
There are many savory sauces that can be used to boost the flavor of dishes. They are strongly flavored and often salty, so usually only a splash or two is required. Mushroom ketchup and Worcestershire sauce can add a rich, rounded flavor to stews and casseroles. Dark and light soy sauce and other soy-based sauces, such as hoisin, are good in Asian-style braised dishes and soups. Fermented fish sauces are common in many cuisines and include anchovy sauce, oyster sauce, and nam pla (Thai fish sauce). They should be added at the beginning of cooking.

Sweet extracts
These have a rich, fragrant aroma and are usually used to flavor sweet dishes. You only need a little, sometimes just a few drops, to flavor a whole dish. Look for the real thing, and avoid artificial flavorings. Almond and vanilla extract are used to flavor cakes and desserts. Orange flower water and rose water have a delicate fragrance and should be added toward the end of cooking for the best flavor.

Alcohol
Because of the gentle heat, alcohol evaporates more slowly in a slow cooker, resulting in a stronger flavor. When adapting conventional recipes, the amount of alcohol should be reduced slightly. Beer, cider, and wine can be used in marinades and casseroles. Fortified wines, such as sherry, port, Marsala, and Madeira, can be used to enrich both sweet and savory dishes; a few spoonfuls should be added toward the end of cooking. Colorless fruit spirits, such as kirsch, and sweet liqueurs, such as amaretto, can be used to flavor desserts and sweet dishes.

GRINDING SPICES
Where ground spices are called for in a recipe, it is better to use whole spices and grind them yourself.

I Dry-fry whole spices in a heavy frying pan, shaking the pan over a medium-high heat for 1–2 minutes until the aroma is released.

2 Place the spices in a mortar and grind to a powder. To grind a larger quantity of spices, it is easier to use an electric spice grinder or a coffee grinder used solely for the purpose.

MAKING STOCK

A good stock forms the foundation of many dishes, from simple soups and classic sauces to warming casseroles and pot-roasts. Although ready-made stocks are available from supermarkets, making your own is easy and inexpensive. Most butchers and fish dealers will supply meat and fish bones and trimmings.

Making stock in a large pan on the stovetop is a simple process, but using a slow cooker is even easier because it can be left to bubble unattended for hours. A good stock must be simmered gently (rapid boiling will make it go cloudy), so the slow cooker comes into its own, keeping the stock at a bare simmer.

There are two types of stock: brown stock, where the bones and vegetables are roasted in the oven first, and white stock, where ingredients are only boiled. Clean vegetable peelings, celery leaves, and the stalks from fresh herbs are useful additions, providing extra flavor.

Always start making a stock with cold water; ideally this and any vegetables should be at room temperature. Use whole peppercorns because long cooking makes ground pepper taste bitter. If you make stock without salt, it can be used in dishes that include salty ingredients, such as smoked meats and fish, and as a base for reduced sauces.

Below: The ingredients used for stock can be varied according to what is available.

A good stock should be beautifully clear. Fat and other impurities will make it cloudy, so it is important to skim these off as the stock comes to simmering point, and at least once during cooking. Pour the stock through a strainer placed over a bowl, and leave to drip slowly, rather than squeezing the vegetables, which will spoil the clarity.

For the following recipes, you will need a slow cooker with a capacity of at least 10¼ cups. If your slow cooker is too small, the recipes can be halved, but the cooking times remain the same.

Basic meat stock

Used for meat dishes, such as casseroles, and as a base for light soups, basic meat stock is traditionally made from veal bones. Beef bones will also make a good stock but with a stronger flavor. Lamb bones may also be used, but this stock can only be used for lamb dishes. Some recipes include lean stewing meat, such as shin of beef, which gives a much meatier flavor. For this option, you will need 1 pound each bones and meat.

MAKES ABOUT 5 CUPS

1½ pounds beef or veal bones
1 onion, unpeeled and quartered
1 carrot, sliced
1 stick celery, sliced
6 black peppercorns
1 fresh bouquet garni
about 5 cups cold water

1 Using a meat cleaver, chop any large bones, so that they will fit into the slow cooker. (Cutting the bones into pieces will increase the flavor of the stock.)

2 Place the vegetables in the ceramic cooking pot. Add the peppercorns and bouquet garni, then place the bones on top, packing them tightly so that they fit in a single layer. Pour over the water, adding a little more, if necessary, to cover the bones, but leaving a space of at least 1½ inch between the water and the top of the pot. Cover, and cook on high or auto for 2 hours.

3 Using a slotted spoon, skim off any scum, and turn the temperature to low, or leave on auto and cook for 5 hours.

4 Strain the stock through a fine strainer, and leave to cool. This should be done quickly, ideally over a bowl of iced water.

5 Chill the stock for at least 4 hours, then remove the fat from the surface.

Brown meat stock

This stock is used as the base for classic beef consommé and other clear soups such as French onion soup. It also adds depth to the color and flavor of casseroles and braised meat dishes. The secret to the stock's rich color and flavor lies in the way the onion and bones are caramelized before simmering. However, take care not to let them burn, or the final stock will taste bitter.

MAKES ABOUT 5 CUPS

1½ pounds beef or veal bones
1 onion, unpeeled and quartered
1 carrot, sliced
1 stick celery, sliced
6 black peppercorns
1 fresh bouquet garni
about 5 cups cold water

1 Preheat the oven to 425°F. Using a meat cleaver, chop up the large bones, then place in a large, heavy roasting pan. Roast for 15 minutes, turning several times during cooking.

2 Add the vegetables to the pan, and cook for 15 minutes more, until the bones are well browned and the vegetables lightly tinged with color.

3 Transfer the bones and vegetables to the slow cooker, adding the peppercorns and bouquet garni. Pour in enough water to just cover, allowing a space of at least 1½ inches between the water and the top of the cooking pot. Cover with the lid, and cook on high or auto for 2 hours.

4 Using a slotted spoon, skim off any scum, then reduce the temperature to low or leave on auto. Cook for 4 hours.

5 Pour the stock through a fine strainer into a bowl, and cool quickly. Cover, and chill or freeze. Remove the fat from the surface of the stock before using.

STORING STOCK

Fresh stock should be covered and stored in the refrigerator as soon as it is cool, then used within 3 days. If it will not be needed in this time, freeze it in small quantities—1¼ cups is ideal. Line square-sided containers with freezer bags, leaving plenty overhanging the sides. Pour the measured stock into the bags, then freeze until solid. Remove the bags of stock, seal, label, and stack the blocks in the freezer.

White poultry stock

Raw poultry bones, chicken wings, or a cooked poultry carcass can be used to make this stock. It makes an excellent base for soups, white sauces, and for braising or stewing white meats. Including the onion skins does not add a great deal of extra flavor, but gives the stock a lovely, rich golden color.

MAKES ABOUT 4 CUPS

1 fresh or cooked poultry carcass
1 onion, unpeeled and roughly chopped
1 leek, roughly chopped
1 celery stick, sliced
1 carrot, sliced
6 white peppercorns
2 sprigs fresh thyme
2 bay leaves
about 4 cups cold water

1 Using poultry shears, cut the carcass into pieces, so that they will fit into the slow cooker. (This will also help to extract the flavor from the bones.)

2 Place the chopped onion, leek, celery, and carrot in the base of the ceramic cooking pot. Sprinkle over the peppercorns, then add the herbs, and top with the chopped poultry carcass.

3 Pour over the water, adding a little more to cover the chicken carcass, if necessary, but leaving a space of at least 1½ inches between the water and the top of the ceramic cooking pot. Cover the pot with the lid, then cook on high or auto for 2 hours.

4 Using a slotted spoon, skim off any scum that has risen to the surface of the stock. Reduce the temperature to low or leave on auto, re-cover, and cook for a further 3–4 hours.

5 Pour the stock through a fine strainer into a bowl, and cool quickly, ideally over a bowl of iced water.

6 Cover the stock, and store in the refrigerator, or freeze. Before using, remove the fat that has risen to the surface of the stock.

TURKEY GIBLET STOCK

This stock can be made in exactly the same way as white poultry stock. Use the giblets (including the liver) and neck of the turkey in place of the poultry carcass, and pour over 3¾ cups water.

Fish Stock

This light broth can be used as the base for delicate fish soups and hearty stews, as well as for poaching. It is the quickest and most easily made of all stocks.

Unlike other stocks, fish stock should not be simmered for very long, otherwise it will become bitter. Once the stock has come to simmering point (which will take about 1 hour), it should be kept at a bare simmer for no more than 1 hour.

Use only the bones of white fish such as sole and plaice. (The bones of oily fish such as mackerel are unsuitable.) Heads may be added, but the eyes and gills should be removed because these will spoil the final flavor. You can also use shrimp shells. The vegetables should be sliced finely to extract as much flavor as possible during cooking. To make a stock with a richer flavor, you can replace about ⅔ cup of the water with dry white wine.

MAKES ABOUT 3¾ CUPS

2 pounds fish bones and trimmings
2 carrots, finely sliced
1 onion, peeled and sliced
6 white peppercorns
1 bouquet garni
3¾ cups water

1 Rinse the fish bones and trimmings well under cold water, and cut any larger bones or pieces into several chunks so that they will easily fit inside the ceramic cooking pot.

2 Arrange the vegetables in the base of the cooking pot. Sprinkle over the peppercorns, add the bouquet garni, and place the fish bones on top.

3 Pour the cold water into the pot, adding a little more to cover the bones, if necessary, but leaving a space of at least 1½ inches between the water and the top of the cooking pot. Cover with the lid, then cook on high or auto for 1 hour until simmering.

4 Using a slotted spoon, skim off any scum that has risen to the surface. Reduce the temperature to low or leave on auto, re-cover, and cook for 1 hour. (Do not cook for longer than this.)

5 Using a fine strainer—or a course strainer lined with cheesecloth that has been briefly held under running water – pour the stock into a bowl, then cool quickly, ideally in a bowl of iced water. Cover with plastic wrap, and store in the refrigerator, or freeze.

Vegetable stock

You can vary the vegetables used in this recipe, but be sure to wash them well, and chop fairly small. Strong-tasting vegetables, such as turnips and parsnips, should be used in small quantities; their flavor will dominate otherwise. Starchy vegetables, such as potatoes, should be avoided; they will make the stock cloudy.

MAKES ABOUT 6¼ CUPS

1 large onion, left unpeeled
   and chopped
1 leek, roughly chopped
2 carrots, thinly sliced
1 celery stick, thinly sliced
2 bay leaves
1 sprig fresh thyme
a few fresh parsley stalks
6 white peppercorns
about 6¼ cups water

1 Put the vegetables, herbs, and peppercorns in the ceramic cooking pot, and pour over the water. Cover, and cook on high or auto for 2 hours.

2 Using a slotted spoon, skim off any scum. Reduce the temperature to low, or leave on auto, and cook for 2 hours.

3 Pour the stock through a fine strainer into a bowl, and leave to cool. Cover, and store in the refrigerator, or freeze.

Removing fat

Before using stock, the fat should be removed. The easiest way to do this is by cooling, then chilling the stock.

Pour the stock into a bowl, cover, and leave undisturbed in the refrigerator for at least 4 hours, or overnight. The fat will rise to the surface, setting in visible globules or a single layer if there is a lot of fat in the stock. Simply lift the fat from the top, or scoop off with a spoon.

1 If you don't have time to let the stock cool, let it settle for a few minutes, then skim off as much fat as possible, using a slotted spoon.

2 Next, draw an absorbent paper towel across the top to soak up any remaining surface fat. You may need to use two or three pieces of paper to remove the fat completely.

Another way to remove the fat is to leave the stock to cool, then lower several ice cubes into it. Gently move the ice cubes around for a few seconds, then remove. The fat will solidify and cling to the ice cubes, making it easy to remove. (This method will only work if the stock is cool.)

Reducing stocks

After straining and removing the fat from stock, it can be concentrated by returning it to the slow cooker and cooking uncovered on high for several hours to allow some of the water to evaporate. However, if you need a very concentrated stock, for a reduced sauce for example, the slow cooker is not suitable. To make very concentrated stocks, pour the stock into a pan, and boil rapidly on the stovetop.

READY-MADE STOCKS
If you do not have time to make your own stock, cartons of fresh stock can be found in the refrigerated section of many supermarkets. These make a good substitute. Good quality bouillon powders and liquid stocks may also be used, but take care with bouillon cubes because they are often strongly flavored and high in salt. Make them only in the recommended strength, and use in robustly flavored dishes.

MAKING SOUPS

Although many slow cooker soup recipes have lengthy cooking times, the actual preparation time for most is minimal, and they can then be left simmering on a low setting all day or overnight. Most soups benefit from long, gentle cooking, so there is no need to worry if they are left for a little longer than intended.

A good homemade stock forms the base of many soups, so it is well worth making large batches of stock and freezing it in convenient quantities. Alternatively, use good quality ready-made stock from the supermarket.

There are two basic techniques for making slow cooker soups. The easiest is to place the prepared ingredients in the ceramic cooking pot with either cold or near-boiling stock. This produces a fresh-flavored soup with a low fat content and is a good method for vegetable soups. However, it is less suitable for recipes containing onions, which take a long time to soften. The second, more usual method is to sauté or fry onions, other vegetables and/or meat in a frying pan before placing in the cooking pot. In some recipes, vegetables are simply softened, but in others they may be lightly browned, giving a richer flavor and deeper color.

Mixed vegetable soup

Almost any vegetable can be made into soup, but for the best results, use the freshest seasonal ingredients.

SERVES 4–6

1½ pounds mixed vegetables, such as
    carrots, celery, parsnips, potatoes
2 tablespoons butter
1 onion, finely chopped
1 teaspoon dried mixed herbs
3¾ cups near-boiling vegetable stock
⅔ cup milk or light cream (optional)
salt and ground black pepper

1 Prepare the mixed vegetables, then cut them into ¼-inch slices, sticks, or dice to ensure that they cook evenly and within the recommended time.

2 Melt the butter in a frying pan, add the onion, and fry gently, stirring frequently, for 10 minutes, until softened, but not colored.

3 Add the chopped vegetables to the pan, and fry for 2–3 minutes. Transfer the vegetables to the ceramic cooking pot, and switch the slow cooker to low.

4 Sprinkle over the dried mixed herbs, then pour in the stock. If you are using vegetables with a high water content, such as zucchini or squash, reduce the quantity of liquid. Others, such as potatoes and dried vegetables, soak up cooking juices, so add a little more liquid to compensate. (Bear in mind that it is easier to dilute the soup at the end of cooking, than to try to thicken a watery soup.)

5 Make sure that there is a gap of at least ¾ inch between the liquid and the top of the slow cooker, then cover with the lid and cook for 7–12 hours or until the vegetables are tender.

6 If using milk or cream, stir this in, and cook for a further 30 minutes to bring the soup back to boiling point. (Do not heat for longer than this because long heating may cause the soup to separate.) Season to taste, then serve.

ADAPTING SOUP RECIPES

Use this simple mixed vegetable soup recipe as a guide for making other soups. If you want to add meat or poultry to the soup, add it to the ceramic cooking pot at the start of cooking, and cook on high for at least 1 hour before reducing the heat to low. If you want to use fresh rather than dried herbs, stir in twice the quantity at the end of cooking time. Rather than using plain stock, use a mixture of stock and tomato juice, or a moderate amount of white wine or cider. Instead of stirring in cream, try adding crème fraîche instead.

Above: Using a hand blender is one of the easiest ways to make smooth soups, but be sure to keep the blade submerged in the soup to avoid spattering.

Pureeing soups

A few ladlefuls of soup can be pureed, then stirred back into the remaining liquid to thicken it, or the entire soup can be pureed to make it wonderfully smooth and velvety. When making chilled pureed soup, it is best to adjust the consistency after chilling because the soup will thicken considerably as it cools.

The simplest way to make pureed soup is using a handheld blender. It can be pureed while still in the slow cooker, and will not need reheating. You can also use a food processor or blender, but do not overfill it, because it may flood over the top. Most soups will need to be processed in two or more batches and, unless being served cold, will need to be reheated in the slow cooker or in a pan on the stovetop.

Soft vegetable soups can be pureed by hand. Press the mixture through a fine stainless-steel or plastic strainer, using a wooden "mushroom" or a large spoon. Alternatively, press the vegetables through a mouli-légumes, then stir in the cooking liquid. The soup will need to be reheated if serving hot.

Thickening soups

There are several ways to thicken soups. Cornstarch or arrowroot are probably the simplest. They can be blended with a little cold water to make a smooth paste, then stirred or whisked into the hot soup. Cornstarch will thicken boiling liquid instantly, but takes about 10 minutes to lose its raw flavor. Arrowroot thickens as soon as it reaches boiling point, but will become slightly thinner with prolonged cooking, so add in the last few minutes of cooking.

All-purpose flour can be sprinkled over fried onions before stirring in the stock, or blended with an equal quantity of softened butter or heavy cream and whisked into the finished soup a little at a time, cooking for a few minutes to thicken. Allow the soup to cook for at least 5 minutes to avoid a raw flour flavor.

Beaten eggs, egg yolks, or a mixture of eggs and cream can be used to thicken and enrich smooth soups. Always turn off the heat, and allow the soup to cool slightly before whisking in the egg mixture, otherwise it may curdle.

Breadcrumbs are sometimes used to thicken rustic and chilled soups. The breadcrumbs are stirred into the finished soup to soak up and thicken the liquid.

Garnishing soups

Adding a pretty garnish gives the final flourish as you serve soup, and can be as simple or complex as you like. A swirl of cream, crème fraîche, or yogurt, followed by a sprinkling of paprika or ground black pepper, can look great with smooth soups. Fresh chopped herbs make another simple but stylish garnish, adding color, flavor, and texture. Use strong herbs, such as sage and rosemary, in moderation.

For a richly flavored garnish, try adding a spoonful or swirl of pesto. It works especially well with Italian and Mediterranean soups. Grated, shaved, or crumbled cheeses also work well and are particularly good with vegetable and bean soups. Strongly flavored cheeses, such as Parmesan and Cheddar, or a crumbly cheese, such as Stilton, are ideal.

To add more substance, flavor, and texture to soups, try sprinkling over croutons or fried breadcrumbs. These are a classic soup garnish, and they add a crunchy texture that works with both smooth and chunky soups. To make croutons, cut thick slices of day-old bread (any type will do) into cubes. Shallow-fry in hot olive oil, turning them continuously, so that the cubes brown evenly, then drain on paper towels. Fried breadcrumbs can be made in the same way, but need less cooking time. To oven-bake croutons, toss them in a little oil, then bake in a shallow roasting pan at 400°F for 12–15 minutes.

Grilled cheesy croutes are the classic topping for French onion soup and can make a dramatic impact floating on top of a bowl of steaming hot soup. Simply rub thin slices of day-old baguette with peeled garlic cloves, then lightly toast both sides under a hot broiler. Sprinkle one side with grated Cheddar or Parmesan cheese, or sliced goat cheese, and put under a hot boiler until melted. Float one or two croutes on top of the soup just before serving.

Below: Crispy croutes coated in melted, bubbling cheese make an impressive garnish for a simple blended soup.

MAKING MARINADES

Marinating tenderizes and flavors meat, poultry, game, fish, and even vegetables and cheese. Although tenderizing may not be necessary when using a slow cooker, it is worth doing for the flavor. There are three basic types of marinade: moist, dry, and paste. Always use a nonmetallic dish for marinating.

Basic moist marinade

Moist marinades are usually made with oil and vinegar, or other acidic ingredients, such as wine, fruit juice, or yogurt. They add moisture as well as flavor.

Red meat, poultry, and game can be marinated for up to 2 hours at room temperature, or up to 24 hours in the refrigerator; small pieces of meat, such as steaks, chops, and cutlets, should be marinated for no more than 2 hours at room temperature, or 12 hours in the refrigerator; whole fish, fish fillets, and steaks should be marinated for up to 30 minutes at room temperature, or 2 hours in the refrigerator; vegetables need 30 minutes at room temperature, or 2 hours in the refrigerator; cheeses and tofu can be marinated for 1 hour at room temperature, or about 8 hours in the refrigerator.

SUFFICIENT FOR 2 POUNDS MEAT OR FISH OR 1½ POUNDS VEGETABLES

6 tablespoons olive oil
1–2 tablespoons cider vinegar
1 garlic clove, crushed
1 teaspoon dried thyme
½ teaspoon crushed peppercorns

1 Combine all the ingredients, using 1 tablespoon vinegar for fish and 2 tablespoons vinegar for meat or vegetables.

2 If you are marinating meat or fish with skin, make several shallow slashes in each piece, then place in a shallow dish.

3 Drizzle or brush the marinade over the food, making sure the pieces are completely covered, then leave to marinate, turning the pieces regularly.

Other moist marinades

You can make several other marinades, using the same techniques and timings as for the basic moist marinade.

Spicy yogurt marinade: Combine 1 cup plain yogurt, 2 crushed garlic cloves, ½ teaspoon each ground cumin and cinnamon and crushed black peppercorns, a pinch each of ground ginger, ground cloves, cayenne pepper, and salt. Use for chicken, lamb, and fish.

Hoisin marinade: Combine 1 cup hoisin sauce; 2 tablespoons each sesame oil, dry sherry, and rice vinegar; 4 finely chopped garlic cloves; ½ teaspoon soft light brown sugar; ¼ teaspon five-spice powder. Use this Chinese marinade for chops and chicken pieces.

Coconut and pineapple: Blend ¼ peeled, chopped pineapple, juice of ½ lime, and ⅔ cup coconut milk in a food processor. Use for chicken and pork.

Thai: Soak 2 tablespoons tamarind pulp in 3 tablespoons boiling water until softened, then press through a fine strainer into a pan. Finely chop 1 lemongrass stalk, 1-inch piece fresh galangal or ginger root, 2 shallots, 2 garlic cloves, 2 seeded green chiles, and 2 kaffir lime leaves, and place in a blender with 2 tablespoons each peanut oil and dark soy sauce. Blend to a paste and add to the pan. Bring to the boil, then leave to cool. Use for beef, pork, or chicken.

Wine: Combine 5 tablespoons wine, 2 tablespoons olive oil, 2 finely chopped shallots, a pinch of dried herbs or 2 teaspoons chopped fresh herbs, such as rosemary. Use red wine for red meat and duck, and white wine for chicken and fish.

Basic dry marinade

Also known as dry rubs, these herb and spice mixtures are rubbed into food shortly before cooking. They are used purely for flavoring and so are best used on fattier pieces of meat, oily fish, or for braised dishes. You can vary the flavor by using different spices, such as cardamom, dry-roasted cumin seeds, or a little chili powder, or try a dried herb mixture with some grated citrus rind.

SUFFICIENT FOR 2 POUNDS MEAT OR FISH

1 tablespoon dried thyme
1 tablespoon dried oregano
1 tablespoon garlic granules
1 tablespoon ground cumin
1 tablespoon ground paprika
½ teaspoon cayenne pepper
½ teaspoon ground black pepper

1 Combine the ingredients in a bowl, then transfer the mixture to a shallow dish, and spread out in an even layer.

2 Press each piece of meat or fish into the mixture to coat evenly, then gently shake off any excess. Arrange on a dish, cover with plastic wrap, and leave to marinate at room temperature for 30 minutes, or use immediately.

Paste marinades

Because these coat the food, it should be cooked above the level of the liquid —such as on a bed of vegetables.

Herb paste: Heat ¼ cup butter in a frying pan, and gently fry 4 ounces finely chopped shallots and ¼ teaspoon fennel seeds until the shallots are soft. Remove from the heat, and stir in 1-inch piece grated fresh ginger root, 2 tablespoons each chopped fresh dill and parsley, and 1 tablespoon finely chopped capers. Stir in 1–2 tablespoons sunflower-seed oil to make a paste. Spread over chicken pieces or tuck under the skin, or use to fill the cavity of a whole fish. Marinate for up to 1 hour at room temperature, or cook immediately. Use for food with a short cooking time.

Mexican chili paste: Combine the finely grated rind of 1 lime, 4 crushed garlic cloves, 2 tablespoons mild chili powder, 1 tablespoon ground paprika, 1 teaspoon ground cumin, ½ teaspoon dried oregano, and a pinch each of ground cinnamon and salt. Stir in 1 tablespoon olive oil and enough lime juice to make into a paste. Use for chicken and pork. Marinate for up to 1 hour at room temperature, or cook immediately.

Tandoori paste: Mix together 2 tablespoons each ground coriander, cumin, and garlic powder, 1 tablespoon each paprika and ground ginger, and 2 teaspoons each ground turmeric and chili powder with enough peanut oil to make a paste. Use for lamb, beef, chicken, and oily fish. Marinate for up to 2 hours at room temperature, or cover and leave overnight in the refrigerator. Scrape off the excess paste before cooking.

Fruit marinades

Certain fruits contain enzymes that soften the fibers of meat and tougher seafood, such as squid. Papaya, pineapple, and kiwi fruit all contain papain, which breaks down protein and is used in commercial tenderizers. Add a little of the juice to a marinade, or slice the fruit and place on top of the meat or fish, and leave for no longer than 15 minutes.

MARINATING TIPS

• The thicker a piece of food is, the longer it will need to marinate.
• When marinating meats such as game and white fish that can become dry during cooking, choose marinades containing less vinegar, wine, or fruit juice. These are suitable for fattier meats, such as lamb, and oily fish.
• During humid weather or in a warm kitchen, it is safer to marinate meat and fish in the refrigerator. In cooler weather, or for short marinating times, it is safe to leave the food at room temperature.
• As a general rule, dry herbs are better than fresh for marinades. When using fresh woody herbs, such as rosemary and thyme, crush the leaves to release their aroma.
• If you are frying or broiling marinated food before adding it to the slow cooker, pat it dry on paper towels first.
• Avoid adding salt to marinades; this will draw moisture from the food. If you want to season with salt, do so after marinating.

MAKING STEWS and CASSEROLES

The slow cooker's gentle, constant heat makes it perfect for making stews and casseroles. The lengthy cooking allows all cuts of meat to become tender and succulent, and even the toughest pieces can be turned into a flavorsome meal.

Stews, casseroles, carbonnades, hot-pots, and navarins are all names for what is, essentially, the same type of dish —meat and/or vegetables cooked in liquid in a cooking pot. Originally, the word stew described such dishes cooked on the stovetop, while casserole described dishes cooked in the oven, but now the names are largely interchangeable.

Choosing the right cut

Ideal meats for slow cooking are the cheaper cuts, such as brisket, chuck steak, blade-bone, shank, and knuckle. These cuts come from the part of the animal (usually the front) that has worked hardest, so have a looser texture and a good marbling of fat. During cooking, the connective tissues and fat dissolve to create a rich gravy, and the fibers open up and allow moisture to penetrate, making them juicy. These cuts also have far greater flavor than very lean ones.

More expensive cuts of meat, such as fine-grained and densely-textured sirloin steak and pork tenderloin, are delicious when cooked to rare or medium by quick-frying or broiling. However, they are less suitable for slow cooking because the tightness of the fibers prevents them from absorbing the liquid around them. This means that although they become tender when cooked in a slow cooker, the final stew will lack succulence and flavor.

Cutting meat into cubes

Tougher cuts of meat, such as stewing steak, cook more evenly and quickly if they are cut into small, even-size cubes: 1 inch is ideal. They should be slightly larger than the vegetables being cooked in the stew, because these will take a little longer to cook than the meat. Although excess fat should be removed, some marbling is useful for keeping the meat moist. Any excess fat can be skimmed off after cooking.

1 Trim the meat, cutting off the excess fat and any gristle, sinew, or membranes while it is in one piece.

2 Using a large sharp knife, cut the meat across the grain into 1-inch thick slices. These slices can be used for stews and casseroles. Cutting across the grain makes the fibers shorter, so that the meat is more tender.

3 To cut the meat into cubes, first cut the slices lengthwise into thick strips. Remove any fat or gristle as you go.

4 Cut each strip crosswise into 1-inch cubes. (When preparing meats such as shoulder of lamb, it may not be possible to cut into perfect cubes. Simply cut into even-size pieces, removing any fat or gristle as you go.)

Preparing chops

These are usually sold ready-prepared and fairly lean, but it is usually worth trimming a little before cooking. This will help them cook, look, and taste better.

1 Using sharp kitchen scissors or a sharp knife, remove the excess fat, cutting around the contours of the chop and leaving a little less than ¼ inch fat on the edge of each chop.

2 If you are going to prefry chops, such as bacon or gammon, before adding to the slow cooker, make shallow cuts with the knife all around the edge. The edge of the meat will then fan out during frying, preventing the meat from curling up, so that it stays in constant contact with the frying pan.

Preparing poultry

A variety of chicken and game portions can be used in stews and casseroles— from whole or diced breast portions, to drumsticks and thighs. Leaving the bones in the meat during cooking will enhance the flavor, or you may remove them (saving to use for stock) if you prefer. Generally, it is better to remove poultry skin before casseroling, because it won't crispen during the moist cooking.

To skin breast fillets, carefully pull the skin and thin membrane away from the meat. If you like, use a small, sharp knife to cut the meat off the rib bone and any remaining breastbone. Turn the breast portion over, and remove the thin, white central tendons from the meat.

To prepare scallops, cut the breast in half horizontally, holding your hand on top of the chicken breast as you cut. A chicken breast portion will yield two scallops, a duck breast portion three, and turkey four or more.

To skin and bone chicken thighs, use a sharp knife to loosen the skin, then pull it away from the meat. Carefully cut the flesh lengthwise along the main thigh bone, then cut the bone out, trimming the meat close to it.

Preparing vegetables

One of the unusual characteristics of slow cooking is that many types of vegetables take longer to cook than meat. To ensure that they cook within the recommended time, they should be cut into even-size pieces slightly smaller than the meat.

When preparing onions, slice them thinly or chop finely. If you want to have chunkier pieces, fry them until they are soft before adding to the slow cooker, because onion takes a long time to cook in a slow cooker.

Hard root vegetables such as carrots, potatoes, and turnips take the longest time to cook in the slow cooker. Cut them into ¼-inch dice, slices, or sticks. (Potatoes discolor when exposed to air, so make sure they are covered with liquid during cooking.)

COOK'S TIP

Some vegetables, such as bell peppers, become bitter if cooked too long; some types, especially green peppers, may discolor. They cook fairly quickly, so add these to the slow cooker 45 minutes— 1 hour before the end of cooking time.

LIQUIDS FOR CASSEROLES AND STEWS

The finished sauce is provided by a mixture of the juices from the meat and vegetables and the liquid that is added at the start of cooking. The long cooking time ensures plenty of flavor if you use water, although other liquids will give the dish a richer finish. You may need to adjust the quantity of liquid used, according to the main ingredients in the dish; vegetables such as mushrooms, for example, will give out a lot of moisture that will thin the sauce.

Stock Homemade stock is preferable, but you can use ready-made fresh stock, or good quality bouillon cubes or powder. Make these to the correct strength (you may only need a small portion of bouillon cube), because too much can produce an over-salty, artificial flavor. Try to use the flavor of stock that matches the dish. If you haven't got the appropriate meat stock, use vegetable stock instead.

Wine Red or white wine will add extra flavor, and its acidity will help to tenderize the meat. Choose a wine that you enjoy drinking, because a really cheap, acidic wine will spoil the finished dish. Generally, it is preferable to use a mixture of wine and stock, rather than wine alone.

Cider This flavors and tenderizes meat in the same way as wine, and is excellent in chicken and pork dishes, especially ones containing fruit. Unless you require a very sweet finish, use hard or medium cider.

Beer Pale or brown ale or stout makes a rich dark sauce and cooks without a hint of its original bitterness. Too much can be overpowering, though, so use a mixture of beer and stock.

Tomatoes These add flavor to the dish. You can use chopped fresh or canned tomatoes, bottled strained tomatoes, concentrated paste, or tomato juice.

BASIC TECHNIQUES

There are two basic ways of making slow cooker stews and casseroles: a simple one-step method, where cold raw ingredients are placed in the ceramic cooking pot, and a second method, in which the meat and some or all of the vegetables are fried beforehand.

Making a one-step stew

Irish stew is a classic one-step stew, and the recipe given here is a perfect guide to cooking any stew using this technique. All the ingredients are placed in the ceramic cooking pot without pre-frying. This reduces preparation time and is also suitable for those on a reduced-fat diet.

The stock or cooking liquid is usually cold, but may be hot to speed up the cooking process. For the tenderest results, casseroles should be cooked on a low setting. However, when the ingredients are cold to begin with, and especially if cooking larger pieces of meat, it is better to start the cooking on the high or auto setting for 1–2 hours.

SERVES 4

2 pounds boned shoulder of lamb
   or 8 neck of lamb chops
1 pound onions
2 pounds potatoes
1 carrot, sliced (optional)
sprig of thyme or bay leaf (optional)
2½ cups lamb
   or vegetable stock
salt and ground black pepper

1 Using a sharp knife, trim all excess fat from the lamb, then cut the meat into 1¼-inch pieces. (If using lamb chops, these may be left whole.)

2 Using a sharp knife, slice the onions and potatoes as thinly as possible.

3 Place the onions at the bottom of the ceramic cooking pot, then arrange the potatoes, carrot, and herbs, if using, on top and finally the meat. Lightly season each layer with salt and pepper.

4 Pour the stock over the meat. If necessary, add a little more stock to cover the meat. Cover the slow cooker with the lid, and cook on auto or high for 2 hours.

5 Using a large spoon, skim off any scum that has risen to the surface. Re-cover the pot and leave on auto, or switch to low and cook for a further 4–6 hours, or until the meat and vegetables are very tender and juicy.

Making a prefried stew

This method is used for the majority of stews and casseroles, because it adds color and an intense rich flavor. The natural sugars in the ingredients are broken down by pre-frying, and the sweet, complex flavors are released. While precooking meat improves the taste and appearance of the cooked casserole, it is also useful to give vegetables the same treatment, especially onions because they take much longer to tenderize than meat in a slow cooker.

SERVES 4–6

2 pounds lean stewing steak
3 tablespoons all-purpose flour
¼ cup butter
2 tablespoons oil
12 pearl onions, peeled
4 ounces white mushrooms
1 garlic clove, crushed
1¼ cups red wine
⅔ cup near-boiling beef stock
1 bay leaf
2 tablespoons chopped fresh parsley
salt and ground black pepper

1 Trim the meat and cut into 1-inch cubes. Season the flour with salt and black pepper, and either spread out on a plate or place in a plastic bag. Roll the meat in the flour, or add a few cubes at a time to the bag, shaking until coated, then remove, and coat the next batch. Shake off any excess and reserve.

2 Melt half the butter with half of the oil in a large frying pan. (If you prefer, you can reduce the fat slightly by using a non-stick frying pan.)

3 When the butter sizzles, fry the meat in two or three batches. (Do not try to cook too much meat at once, because it will start to stew, rather than brown.) Turn the meat frequently, so that it browns on all sides. Lift the meat out of the pan with a slotted spoon, and transfer to the ceramic cooking pot.

4 Heat the remaining butter and oil in the frying pan, then add the onions and cook until glazed and golden brown. Transfer to the ceramic cooking pot, using a slotted spoon. Add the mushrooms and garlic to the pan and cook for 2–3 minutes until browned, then transfer to the cooking pot.

5 Sprinkle any remaining flour into the pan juices, and stir to mix. Gradually mix in the red wine, followed by the stock.

6 Stir the sauce to loosen any sediment from the base of the pan, and heat to simmering point. Pour over the meat and vegetables, and add the bay leaf, pressing it down into the liquid.

7 Cover the slow cooker with the lid, and switch to high or auto. Cook for 1 hour, then leave on auto or switch to low, and cook for a further 6–8 hours, or until the meat and vegetables are tender. Alternatively, cook on high throughout for 4–5 hours. Sprinkle over the parsley just before serving.

Thickening stews

There are many different ways to thicken the sauces of stews and casseroles. **Flour** Meat is often fried before being put in the ceramic cooking pot, and can be first dusted in flour, which will act as a thickener for the juices as the meat cooks. Do not over-brown the flour, as this gives it a bitter flavor; only fry until light brown.

Alternatively, you can add flour toward the end of the cooking time by whisking in a paste made from equal quantities of flour and butter. Allow extra cooking time to allow the flour to cook and lose its "raw" flavor.

Cornstarch or arrowroot These very fine flours can both be used as thickeners. They should be blended with a little water or other cold liquid before being stirred into the stew.

Pasta and rice If it becomes obvious partway through cooking that the stew or casserole will be too thin, you can stir in a little pasta or converted rice, which will absorb some of the liquid. These should be added about 45 minutes before the end of the cooking time. (Lentils and grains, such as pearl barley, will also act as thickeners, but these must be added early in the cooking time to cook thoroughly.)

Reduction If the sauce is too thin when cooking is complete, lift out the meat and vegetables with a slotted spoon, and set aside. Pour the liquid into a wide pan or frying pan and boil fast to reduce the liquid. Add the meat and vegetables to the reduced sauce, and gently reheat. This is a useful technique with delicate fish and chicken, which may break up if overcooked.

Skimming off fat

If the dish has produced a lot of fat during cooking, you may wish to remove it before serving. Most will rise to the surface, so that you can simply skim it off the top, using a large kitchen spoon. Additional fat can be removed using absorbent paper towels. Simply rest the paper towel on the surface of the stew, and remove as soon as it has soaked up the fat. If you have made the dish in advance, chill it in the refrigerator, so that the fat solidifies on the top of the stew or casserole. It can then be lifted or scooped off.

BRAISING

This technique involves slow cooking in very little liquid in a dish with a tight-fitting lid; the trapped steam keeps the food moist during cooking. Instead of cutting meat into small chunks, it is sliced into larger, even-size pieces, or in some cases, such as chops or lamb shanks, left whole. Braising also works well for large pieces of firm, meaty fish, which can be placed on a bed of vegetables, with just enough liquid to cover them.
The slow cooker is perfect for braising, because the heat is so gentle, and the lid forms a tight seal, so that any steam condenses on the inside of the lid and trickles back into the pot.

Preparing meat for braising

Always trim excess fat from meat before braising, then skim any fat from the surface before serving. To ensure even cooking, all the pieces of meat should be of a similar thickness.

1 Cut the meat into slices about ¾ inch thick. At the narrower end cut slightly thicker slices.

2 Place the thicker slices on a chopping board, cover with a sheet of waxed paper, and gently beat with a rolling pin or meat hammer to flatten.

If you want to pound all the meat, to help tenderize it, you can start by cutting it all into thick slices, about 1 inch thick, then pounding it to flatten.

Braising lamb shanks

On the whole lamb joints are tender and quite fatty and do not benefit from being braised. Lamb shanks, however, are lean and tough, so benefit from long, slow, moist cooking. Thickly sliced meat, such as braising steak, and small joints, such as topside, can be cooked in the same way.

SERVES 4

4 lamb shanks
1 red onion, very finely chopped
1 garlic clove, crushed
sprig of fresh thyme
1 teaspoon chopped fresh rosemary
1 teaspoon ground paprika
1 tablespoon balsamic vinegar
4 tablespoons olive oil
¾ cup red wine
⅔ cup lamb or vegetable stock
chopped fresh parsley
salt and ground black pepper

1 Using the point of a sharp knife, gently prick the shanks at intervals all over.

2 Combine the onion, garlic, thyme, rosemary, paprika, vinegar, and 2 tablespoons of the oil. Brush over the shanks, place in a shallow, nonmetallic dish, cover, and leave to marinate for 2 hours at room temperature, or up to 24 hours in the refrigerator. (Marinating starts the tenderizing process, but is not essential.)

3 Brush the marinade off the lamb and set aside. Heat the remaining 2 tablespoons oil in a frying pan, and lightly brown the shanks all over. Transfer to the ceramic cooking pot, and season with salt and pepper.

4 Add the reserved marinade to the frying pan, and pour in the wine and stock. Bring almost to the boil, stirring, then pour over the shanks.

5 Cover with the lid and switch to high or auto. Cook for 1 hour, then leave on auto, or reduce to low and cook for a further 6–8 hours, or until very tender, turning the meat halfway through.

6 Using a slotted spoon, transfer the lamb shanks to a warmed serving plate. Skim off any fat from the cooking juices, then check the seasoning. Stir in the parsley, and spoon over the shanks.

Braising red cabbage

Many types of vegetable respond well to braising, becoming meltingly tender with an intense flavor. Red cabbage is used here, but fennel and celery are also very good braised. Fennel should be cut into thin, even slices from the top through the root end; sticks of celery can be left whole or cut into shorter pieces.

SERVES 4–6

1 red cabbage, about 2 pounds
1 pound stovecooking apples, peeled, cored, and chopped
2 tablespoons soft light or dark brown sugar
2 tablespoons red wine vinegar
¾ cup near-boiling water
salt and ground black pepper

1 Discard the tough outer leaves of the cabbage, cut it into quarters, and remove the hard stalk. Shred the cabbage finely.

2 Put the cabbage, apples, sugar, vinegar, salt, and pepper into the ceramic cooking pot, and toss together. Pack down firmly, then pour over the water.

3 Cover with the lid, and switch to high for 3–4 hours, or to low for 6–8 hours, stirring halfway through.

Reheating braised dishes, casseroles, and stews

Braised dishes, casseroles, and stews are often served the day after they are made because their flavor improves with keeping and reheating. The improvement in taste is less obvious in dishes made in the slow cooker, because the long gentle cooking has already allowed the flavors to develop and mingle. However, if you do plan to reheat a dish, it is important to cool it as quickly as possible—but you should never plunge the hot ceramic cooking pot into cold water, because this may cause it to crack.

1 When cooking is complete, remove the ceramic cooking pot from the slow cooker, and place on a pot stand for at least 10 minutes, taking off the lid to allow steam to escape. (Do not remove the lid for braised vegetables; you want to retain the moisture with these.)

2 Place the ceramic cooking pot in a washing-up bowl of cool but not very cold water. Leave for about 15 minutes, or until the surrounding water starts to feel warm. (Don't overfill the bowl or the water may overflow into the prepared dish; the water should come just over halfway up the cooking pot.)

3 Remove the ceramic cooking pot, and pour away the warmed water. Refill the bowl with very cold water, replace the ceramic cooking pot, and add a few ice cubes or frozen ice packs to speed up the cooling process. Leave until the food is completely cool.

4 Cover the ceramic cooking pot with the lid, and place in the refrigerator until needed, or transfer the contents to another container, if you prefer.

5 The slow cooker is not suitable for reheating the dish. It will take too long for the contents to reheat to ensure food safety. Check whether the ceramic cooking pot is suitable for use on the stovetop or in the oven. Remove the dish from the refrigerator at least 30 minutes before reheating.

6 If necessary, transfer the food to a suitable pan or casserole dish, then reheat gently over a low heat on the stovetop, or in the oven at 325°F, until simmering. For safety, meat dishes must come to a gentle simmer and be maintained at that temperature for at least 30 minutes. Any fresh herbs should be added at this stage, a few minutes before serving.

TOPPINGS

Adding a topping to casseroles and braised dishes can transform them into a special meal. It is also an easy way to create a one-pot meal with no need for extra accompaniments. Many toppings are arranged on top of the casserole or braise and cooked as an integral part of the dish. Others are cooked separately, then served with the dish.

Dumplings

These are ideal for casseroles and stews, but are unsuitable for braised dishes because they need plenty of simmering liquid to cook in. If the casserole is cooking on a low setting, increase the temperature to high about 30 minutes before adding the dumplings. This recipe makes enough to serve four.

I Sift I cup self-rising flour and a little salt and pepper into a mixing bowl. Stir in 2 ounces shredded beef or vegetable suet. Mix in about 5 tablespoons chilled water to make a soft but not sticky dough.

2 Using floured hands, shape the mixture into 8 medium or 12 small round dumplings. Alternatively, roll out into a "rope" with a diameter of about 1 inch, and cut off 1-inch pieces.

3 Remove the lid from the slow cooker. Working quickly so that heat isn't lost, lower the dumplings into the casserole, spacing them slightly apart. Cover and cook on high for 45 minutes–1 hour, or until well risen and firm. Do not lift the lid during cooking, or the dumplings won't rise properly. (Alternatively, the dumplings can be cooked separately in a covered shallow pan of simmering stock for 30 minutes. Lift out using a slotted spoon, and serve with the casserole.)

FLAVORING DUMPLINGS

Dumplings can be flavored in many ways. Good choices include herbs or flavored liquids, such as stock, white wine, or cider, instead of water.
Herb and mustard dumplings go well with rich beef casseroles. Sift I teaspoon mustard powder with the flour and stir in 2–3 tablespoons chopped fresh parsley.
Lemon and tarragon dumplings are good with chicken, turkey, and fish casseroles. Stir in the finely grated rind of ½ lemon and 3 tablespoons chopped fresh tarragon.
Caraway and sour cream dumplings work well with beef and veal goulash. Stir in I teaspoon caraway seeds, and mix the dry ingredients together with a mixture of half sour cream and half chilled water.
Mushroom dumplings go well with beef and pork casseroles. Stir 2 ounces very finely chopped mushrooms into the dumpling mixture.
Rosemary dumplings are good with lamb casseroles. Stir in ½–1 teaspoons chopped fresh rosemary.

Potato toppings

Sliced, grated, and mashed potatoes make a good topping for casseroles and some braised dishes. If you like, they can be browned in the oven or under a broiler before serving. Sliced and grated potatoes are usually added at the beginning of cooking; mashed potatoes are added toward the end. All these recipes make enough to serve four.

Sliced potato topping: Thinly slice 1½ pounds potatoes, and arrange over the top of the casserole at the beginning of cooking. Make sure there is just enough liquid to cover the potatoes. Cover with the lid, and cook on low for 8–10 hours, or on high for 4–5 hours, until tender. To brown the top before serving, brush the potatoes with a little melted butter, and place under a hot broiler for 3–4 minutes.

Grated potato topping: Grate 1½ pounds potatoes, then blanch in boiling salted water for 5 minutes. Drain well and squeeze out any excess liquid. Stir in 1 tablespoon melted butter or olive oil, then sprinkle evenly over the surface of the casserole. Cook on low for 4–6 hours, or on high for 2–3 hours. If you like, brown under the broiler.

Creamy mashed potato topping:
Boil 2 pounds peeled floury potatoes until tender. Drain well, return to the pan, and add ¼ cup butter, or 2 tablespoons olive oil. Mash with a potato masher until smooth, then beat in 5 tablespoons hot milk or cream, salt, pepper, and grated nutmeg. Spoon on top of the casserole or braised dish, spreading out evenly. Cover, and cook in the slow cooker for 1 hour. Alternatively, bake in an oven preheated to 375°F for 30 minutes, or brown the top under a medium broiler.

Polenta toppings
This golden-yellow cornmeal topping goes well with Mediterranean-style stews. Mixed with flour, milk, and egg, polenta makes a delicious cornbread topping.

Basic polenta topping: Bring 8 cups water with 1 teaspoon salt to the boil in a large, heavy pan. Remove the pan from the heat, and pour in 3 cups fine polenta, whisking continuously. Return the pan to the heat, and stir for 15 minutes, until thick. Season well with salt and pepper. This soft polenta can be used in the same way as mashed potato topping.

Polenta triangles: Spoon the basic polenta mixture onto a wet board and spread out to ½ inch thick. Leave to set for 1 hour, then cut into triangles. One hour before the end of cooking time, arrange the polenta on top of the casserole. To serve, brush with olive oil, sprinkle with grated Parmesan cheese, and broil.

Cornbread topping: Mix 1½ cups fine cornmeal with 1 tablespoon whole-wheat flour and 1 teaspoon baking powder. Make a well in the center, and add 1 beaten egg and ¾ cup milk. Mix, then quickly spoon over the top of the casserole. Cover, and cook for 1 hour until firm. If you like, brown under a broiler.

Crumble toppings
These can be cooked in the slow cooker, but are much better baked in the oven. They work well with braised dishes and chunky casseroles with only a little sauce or gravy. This recipe serves four.

1 Sift 1½ cups all-purpose white or whole-wheat flour and a pinch of salt into a bowl. Rub in 7 tablespoons butter or margarine, until the mixture resembles very fine breadcrumbs.

2 Stir in ½ cup chopped nuts, or 2–3 tablespoons rolled oats, 1 ounce grated sharp Cheddar cheese, or 1 ounce sunflower seeds.

3 Preheat the oven to 375°F. Sprinkle the topping over the casserole in an even layer, then bake uncovered for 30 minutes until golden.

Bread toppings
Sliced, cubed, or crumbled, many types of bread may be used, from sliced white to textured whole-grain.

Bread crumb topping: Preheat the oven to 300°F. Combine 1½ cups bread crumbs with 2 tablespoons chopped fresh parsley and 2 finely chopped garlic cloves. Sprinkle over the casserole, and bake for about 30–40 minutes until golden.

Cheesy French bread topping: Lightly toast 6–12 thick slices of day-old French bread on both sides. Rub one side of each slice with a halved garlic clove, then spread with a little French mustard. Sprinkle over 1 cup coarsely grated Gruyère cheese, and broil until the cheese bubbles. Arrange on top of the casserole, and serve immediately.

POT-ROASTING

This method of cooking small or large joints of meat and whole poultry in a small amount of liquid, usually with herbs and vegetables, is ideal for less tender cuts of meat, poultry, and game that are low in natural fat. It makes them wonderfully succulent and tender and minimizes shrinkage. The meat is nearly always browned before being placed in the slow cooker with a little liquid and other ingredients. Sometimes the meat is marinated before cooking, especially beef and game, which can be dry.

When choosing joints of meat for pot-roasting, small pieces weighing no more than 2½ pounds are ideal. If the meat is irregularly shaped, it will cook less uniformly and may be awkward to carve, so boned joints such as sirloin, silverside, and topside should be tied; shoulder of lamb should be both boned and tied before pot-roasting.

Tying a boneless joint

You will need fine string for tying joints of meat. Store it in a plastic bag or box, rather than leaving loose in a drawer, so that it does not get dirty.

I Roll or arrange the meat joint into a neat shape. Tie it lengthwise with a piece of string. This should be pulled tightly and double-knotted, because the meat will shrink a little during cooking. (You may need to ask someone to help you do this.)

2 Tie the joint widthwise at regular intervals about I inch apart, knotting and trimming the ends of string as you go. Apply even pressure when tying each length of string, to keep the shape of the joint as neat as possible.

Boning a shoulder of lamb

Lamb shoulder is made up of three bones: the flat blade bone, the thin arm bone, and the knuckle.

I Place the shoulder on a board, and trim off any excess fat. Insert a sharp knife into the larger end of the lamb joint, then slice it along the flat blade bone, working toward the center. Turn the meat over, and repeat on the other side. Twist out the blade bone.

2 Put the lamb, skin side down, on the board. Cut along the line of the arm and knuckle bones, scraping the meat off the bones, then remove them.

3 Cut through the flesh where the blade bone was, and open out the meat. It can now be stuffed, then rolled and tied.

Tying a shoulder *en ballon*

As an alternative to rolling and tying a shoulder of lamb, it can be tied *en ballon*; this is a round cushion shape that is served sliced into wedges.

I Lay the meat out flat, skin side down. If you like, spoon stuffing into the middle. Pull one corner of the joint into the center, and secure it with a skewer.

2 Do the same with the other four corners, tucking in the remains of the shank and securing them by tying a loop of string around the "ballon."

3 Turn the joint over, and continue tying loops of string at even spaces around the ballon, to make six or eight sections. Tie a knot at the crossover point on each side as you go.

Pot-roasting brisket of beef

Other cuts of beef, such as silverside and topside, can be cooked in this way. Stuffed breast or shoulder of lamb also work very well.

SERVES 4–6

2½ pounds rolled brisket
2 tablespoons beef dripping
    or vegetable shortening
2 onions, cut into 8 wedges
2 carrots, quartered
2 sticks celery, cut into 2-inch lengths
2 bay leaves
2 sprigs of fresh thyme
1¼ cups near-boiling beef stock
salt and ground black pepper

1 Season the meat well with salt and pepper. Heat the dripping or vegetable fat in a large, heavy pan until hot. Add the meat and turn frequently, using two spoons, until browned. If the fat gets too hot before the meat is browned, add a little cold butter to cool it. Lift out the meat, and transfer to a plate.

2 Pour away some of the fat, leaving about 1 tablespoon in the pan. Add the onions, carrots, and celery, and cook for a few minutes or until lightly browned and beginning to soften. Browning the vegetables will add flavor and color to the pot-roast, but take care not to darken them too much or the stock will become bitter. Arrange a single layer of vegetables in the base of the cooking pot, then place the meat on top, adding any juices from the plate. Put the remaining vegetables around the sides of the meat, and tuck in the fresh herbs.

3 Pour the stock into the pan, and bring to the boil, stirring in any sediment.

4 Pour the stock over the meat and vegetables; it should barely cover them, leaving most of the meat exposed.

5 Cover the slow cooker with the lid, and switch to high. Cook for 4 hours, then reduce the temperature to low, and cook for a further 2–3 hours, or until the meat is cooked through and very tender. Once or twice during cooking, turn the meat and baste. Avoid using any sharp utensils when doing so, because they may puncture the outer layer and allow juices to escape.

6 Lift out the meat, and place on a warmed serving dish. Cover with a piece of foil, and leave it to rest; 15 minutes will be sufficient to allow the fibers to relax and let the juices settle, making the meat easier to carve.

7 Meanwhile, skim any fat from the juices and stock in the cooking pot. Serve as a gravy with the meat. (If you like, thicken the juices with cornstarch or arrowroot first.) Normally the vegetables are discarded, but these may be served with the meat as well.

Pot-roasting chicken

A whole chicken can be pot-roasted in exactly the same way as a joint of beef or lamb, but this technique is unsuitable for large chickens weighing more than 3½ pounds. Avoid stuffing the cavity, although you may add a quartered onion or lemon for flavoring.

SERVES 4

⅔ cup dry white wine or hard cider
2 bay leaves
2½–3 pounds chicken
1 lemon, quartered
1 tablespoon sunflower-seed oil
2 tablespoons sweet butter
⅔ cup boiling chicken stock
1 tablespoon cornstarch blended with
    2 tablespoons water or wine
salt and ground black pepper

1 Pour the wine into the ceramic cooking pot. Add the bay leaves, and switch the slow cooker to high. Meanwhile, rinse or wipe the chicken, and pat dry using a paper towel. Season the cavity, then add the lemon quarters.

2 Heat the oil and butter in a heavy frying pan. Brown the chicken on all sides, then transfer it to the ceramic cooking pot. If the chicken has been trussed, untie it before placing in the cooking pot. This will allow the heat to penetrate more easily.

3 Pour the stock over the chicken, then cover with the lid and cook on high for 3½–4½ hours, or until the juices run clear when pierced with a thin knife or skewer, or a meat thermometer inserted into the thickest part of the thigh reads 170°F. (Chicken and other poultry must be cooked on high throughout.)

4 Lift the chicken out of the cooking pot, place on a warmed serving dish, cover with foil, and leave to rest for 10–15 minutes before serving. Meanwhile, skim the juices, stir in the cornstarch mixture, and cook on high for 10 minutes, then serve as a sauce.

POACHING

This gentle method of cooking keeps food wonderfully moist. It differs from boiling, because the heat is so low that only the occasional bubble breaks the surface of the liquid. It is ideal for delicate meats, such as poultry and fish, which can overcook and disintegrate if fiercely boiled. Poaching also allows you to skim off the scum and fat that faster boiling would bubble back into the liquid, making it cloudy and spoiling the flavor. The slow cooker is perfect for poaching, because it keeps the heat constant and steady and needs little attention.

Poaching chicken

Unlike pot-roasting, the slow cooker can be used for poaching large chickens and other poultry, although it is important to check that it will fit comfortably in the ceramic cooking pot. There should be enough space for it to be completely immersed in liquid and room for liquid to circulate around the sides. Because the cavity of the bird will be filled with poaching liquid, the bird will be cooked from the inside and the outside.

SERVES 4

3-pound oven-ready chicken
1 onion
2 carrots
2 leeks
2 celery sticks
a few fresh parsley stalks
2 bay leaves
6 black peppercorns
½ teaspoon salt

1 Remove any trussing string from the chicken. Remove any loose pieces of fat from inside the chicken, then rinse the cavity under cold water, and place the chicken in the ceramic cooking pot.

2 Trim the onion at the stem and root end, but do not peel (the skin will add a rich golden color to the stock). Cut the onion into six or eight wedges. Wash and trim the carrots, leeks, and celery, then roughly chop or slice them and add to the cooking pot, packing them in around the chicken.

3 Tie the herbs together, and add to the pot with the peppercorns and salt.

4 Pour in enough near-boiling water to just cover the chicken, pouring it over the vegetables and the chicken. Cover with the lid, switch the slow cooker to high, and cook for 1 hour.

5 Skim off any scum and fat using a slotted spoon. Re-cover the pot, and cook for 2–2½ hours, or until the chicken is cooked and tender. To check the chicken is cooked, insert a meat thermometer into the thickest part, where the thigh joins the body; it should read 170°F. (Alternatively, insert a skewer into the thickest part; the juices should show no traces of pink. If they are clear, lift the chicken out of the pot, and double-check on the other side.)

6 Remove the chicken from the pot, using a large fork inserted into the cavity to lift it up. Leave the chicken to rest for 10 minutes before carving. Alternatively, if you plan to eat the chicken cold, leave it to cool completely on a wire rack placed over a large plate to catch any drips. (The wire rack will allow air to circulate around the chicken, helping it to cool more quickly.)

7 Leave the cooking liquid to cool for a few minutes, then ladle into a colander set over a large bowl. Leave to drip; do not press the vegetables or the stock will become cloudy. Cool the stock quickly by placing the bowl in cold water.

8 If you plan to eat the chicken cold, as soon as it is cool, cover with plastic wrap, and store in the refrigerator. (Leave the skin on, because this will help to keep the meat moist.) Use within 2 days of cooking.

9 When the stock is cool, cover with plastic wrap, and place in the refrigerator. Any fat in the stock will rise to the surface and can be removed easily and discarded. The stock can be kept for up to 3 days, or it can be frozen in airtight containers for up to 6 months.

Poaching gammon

Gammon is the cured hind leg of the bacon pig. Once cooked, it is known as ham. When serving the meat in slices, poaching is the best cooking method, producing tender, juicy results. However, if you wish to serve it whole, it can be glazed after poaching and briefly baked.

SERVES 6–8

4-pound boned middle gammon joint
1 onion
6 whole cloves
2 carrots, halved
1 bouquet garni
10 black peppercorns
hard cider (optional)

1 Place the meat in the ceramic cooking pot, cover with cold water, and leave to soak for 2–24 hours to remove the salt. (Mild cured gammon shouldn't need long soaking, but it is preferable to soak smoked gammon for the longer time.)

2 Drain the gammon, then return it to the cooking pot. Peel the onion, stud with the cloves, and add to the pot with the carrots, herbs, and peppercorns. If you find it difficult to squeeze the onion down the side of the gammon, halve it.

3 Pour in enough cold water or cider, or a mixture of the two, to just cover the gammon. Switch the slow cooker to high, cover with the lid, and cook for 1 hour. Skim off any scum, using a slotted spoon, then re-cover, and cook for a further 4–5 hours. Check and skim the surface once or twice during cooking.

4 Lift the ham out of the pot, and place on a board. Slice, and serve hot, or allow to cool, then wrap in foil, and store in the refrigerator for up to 5 days.

5 Strain the cooking liquid into a bowl, and leave to cool. (Taste the stock when hot; if it is very salty, use sparingly in dishes, and do not add additional salt.) Chill the stock, and remove any fat from the surface. Store in the refrigerator, and use within 2 days. Alternatively, freeze for up to 6 months.

GLAZING HAMS

After poaching, lift the ham into a foil-lined baking dish, and leave to cool for 15 minutes. Snip the string off the ham, then slice off the rind, leaving a thin, even layer of fat. Score the fat in diagonal lines, then score in the opposite direction to make a diamond pattern. Brush the warm joint with about 3 tablespoons lime marmalade, and sprinkle with 3 tablespoons raw sugar. Push whole cloves into the corners of the diamond shapes after glazing, if you like. Bake at 425°F for about 20 minutes, until the fat is brown and crisp. Serve hot or cold.

Poaching fish

The delicate texture of fish benefits from simple cooking. Poaching brings out its flavor and keeps it moist. Both whole fish and fillets can be poached in the slow cooker, but first check that there is enough room for the fish, as well as space to maneuver a fish spatula.

Fish can be poached in cold liquid, but it will retain its shape and texture if added to hot liquid. Larger pieces of fish, such as steaks or cutlets, will take no more than 45 minutes on high, or 1½–2 hours on low, but take care not to overcook, and check frequently. Fish is ready when the flesh is only slightly translucent when eased away from the bone, or flakes easily when tested with the point of a sharp knife or skewer.

Poaching fruit

Apples, pears, fruits with pits, such as plums, and soft fruit, such as figs, can be poached whole, halved, or sliced. Even fragile fruit, such as rhubarb, will retain its shape when cooked in a slow cooker. Cooking times will depend on the size and ripeness of the fruit, but as a rough guide, tender fruit, such as figs and rhubarb, will take about 1½ hours on high; ripe or near-ripe fruit, such as plums or apples, will take about 2 hours on high; and harder, less ripe fruit, such as pears, will take 3–5 hours on high, or 6–8 hours on low.

The classic poaching liquid is syrup and usually consists of 1 part sugar to 2 parts water. Flavoring ingredients such as spices or a pared strip of lemon rind can be added to the liquid, as can red or white wine, cider, or fruit juice sweetened with sugar.

1 Put the sugar, poaching liquid, and any flavorings into the ceramic cooking pot, and switch the slow cooker to high. Cook for 1 hour, stirring occasionally to dissolve the sugar.

2 Add the fruit, cover, and cook until the fruit is barely tender. Leave the fruit to cool in the syrup, or remove and place in a serving dish. Strain the syrup over the fruit, or simmer gently to thicken.

USING the SLOW COOKER as a BAIN-MARIE

While many dishes are cooked directly in the ceramic cooking pot, others may be cooked in a bain-marie – in a pan or dish placed inside the cooking pot and surrounded by barely simmering water. This technique is good for making pâtés, terrines, cakes, steamed puddings, and custard-based desserts. To allow the water to move freely around the cooking container, an upturned saucer or metal pastry ring is often placed on the base of the cooking pot. This is important if the cooking pot has a slightly concave base.

MAKING PÂTÉS AND TERRINES

When raw meat and eggs are used, make sure that the depth of the mixture is no greater than 2¼ inches, otherwise the pâté may not cook thoroughly. This is especially important with pork and chicken. A 1-pound terrine or loaf pan measuring about 8 x 4 x 2¼ inches and holding a volume of 3¾ cups is an ideal size.

Making classic pork pâté

You can use this recipe as a guide for making other pâtés. You can vary the proportions of the main ingredients, and can use lean ground beef or pork in place of the veal.

SERVES 6

8 ounces rindless smoked fatty
   bacon strips
8 ounces boneless belly of pork
6 ounces veal
4 ounces chicken livers
3 tablespoons dry white wine
1 tablespoon brandy
½ teaspoon dried thyme
½ teaspoon dried rosemary
1 garlic clove, crushed
½ teaspoon salt
¼ teaspoon ground mace
ground black pepper

1 Place an upturned saucer or metal pastry cutter in the base of the ceramic cooking pot. Pour in about 1 inch of very hot water, then turn the slow cooker to high.

2 Taking 5 ounces of the bacon, stretch one strip at a time on a board, using the back of a large knife. Use to line a 1-pound loaf pan, or a 3¾-cup round dish, leaving the bacon overhanging the sides.

3 Finely chop the remaining bacon and place in a large bowl. Trim the belly of pork, veal, and chicken livers, then grind using the medium blade of a grinder, or place in a food processor, and chop roughly. Add to the bowl.

4 Spoon the white wine and brandy over the meat. Add the herbs, garlic, and seasonings, then mix well. Transfer the mixture to the pan or dish, pressing down lightly. Fold the overhanging bacon over the top of the filling, then cover with a piece of foil.

5 Place the pâté in the slow cooker, then pour enough very hot water around it to come nearly to the top. Cook on high for 4–6 hours. To test whether the pâté is cooked, push a thin skewer into the center, and press lightly around the edges of the hole; the liquid should be clear, not cloudy or pink.

6 Carefully remove the pâté from the slow cooker, and leave to cool on a wire rack. Cover, and chill for several hours, then unmold, and keep covered until ready to serve. (If you like, the pâté can be pressed before chilling.)

PRESSING PÂTÉS

After cooling the cooked pâté, you may "press" it to give it a slightly firmer texture and to make it easier to slice. Cover the pâté with waxed paper or plastic wrap. Top with a board that fits exactly inside the pan, and place several weights or cans on the board. (Alternatively, use bags of rice or lentils, which can be molded to fit into the top of the pan.) Leave until completely cool, then chill overnight (still weighted if you want a really firm texture).

Making mousseline pâté

A mousseline pâté has a light, smooth, creamy texture. Allow plenty of time to prepare it, because you will need to chill the mixture between each stage. Mousseline pâtés are extremely rich, so serve thinly sliced with bread or salad.

SERVES 8

1 tablespoon butter
1 shallot, finely chopped
1 tablespoon brandy or sherry
8-ounce skinless chicken breast portion
2 ounces chicken livers, trimmed
1 tablespoon fresh white bread crumbs
1 egg, separated
1¼ cups heavy cream
salt and ground white pepper

1 Lightly oil and line a 1-pound loaf or terrine pan, or a 3¾-cup baking dish, with parchment paper. Melt the butter in a small pan, add the shallot, and cook for about 5 minutes until soft. Turn off the heat, then stir in the brandy or sherry. Place the mixture in a bowl, and leave to cool.

2 Meanwhile, roughly chop the chicken breast portion and livers, then place in a food processor and puree for about 30 seconds. Add the shallot mixture and bread crumbs to the chicken, and process until very smooth. Return the mixture to the bowl, and chill for 30 minutes.

3 Meanwhile, place an upturned saucer or metal pastry cutter in the bottom of the ceramic cooking pot. Pour in about 1 inch of very hot water, then turn the slow cooker to high.

4 Set the bowl of chicken puree over a larger bowl filled with crushed ice and water. Lightly whisk the egg white with a fork until frothy, and beat into the puree, a little at a time. Beat in the egg yolk.

5 Gradually add the cream, mixing well between each addition. Season with salt and white pepper, then spoon the mixture into the prepared pan, and level the top. Cover with plastic wrap or foil.

6 Place the pan or terrine in the slow cooker, then pour enough hot water around to come nearly to the top. Cook on high for 3–4 hours, or until firm.

7 Carefully remove the pâté from the slow cooker, and leave to cool on a wire rack. Chill well before slicing and serving.

Making a studded terrine

Attractive terrines can be made using the mousseline mixture and studding it with vegetables or layering it with other meats, such as strips of chicken or ham.

SERVES 8

3 ounces fine asparagus stalks
3 ounces green beans, topped and tailed
4 ounces carrots, peeled and cut into matchstick strips
½ quantity mousseline pâté mixture

1 Lightly oil and line a 1-pound loaf pan or terrine, or a 3¾ cup baking dish, with parchment paper. Cook the vegetables, one type at a time, in boiling water for 1 minute. Drain, plunge into cold water, then drain again.

2 Spread a layer of the mixture in the bottom of the pan. Arrange the asparagus lengthwise, with gaps between each, then cover with a thin layer of the pâté.

3 Repeat the layers using the beans and carrots and finishing with the remaining pâté mixture. Smooth the top. Cover with plastic wrap or foil, and cook in the same way as the chicken mousseline for 2½–3½ hours.

MAKING STEAMED PUDDINGS and DESSERTS

The slow cooker is perfect for cooking sticky steamed sponges and custards. It keeps the water at a very gentle simmer, reducing the risk of the water bubbling up and spoiling the dish.

Making a steamed sponge

Sponge puddings cooked in steam have a surprisingly light, moist texture. They were traditionally made using shredded beef or vegetarian suet, but this modern version uses a creamed cake mixture. Make sure that all the ingredients are at room temperature before you start.

SERVES 4–6

½ cup butter, at room temperature
generous ½ cup superfine sugar
½ teaspoon vanilla extract
2 eggs, lightly beaten
1½ cups self-rising flour
about 3 tablespoons milk

1 Place an upturned saucer or metal pastry cutter in the bottom of the ceramic cooking pot. Pour in 1 inch very hot water, then preheat the slow cooker on high. Grease a 3¾-cup ovenproof bowl and line the base with a piece of waxed paper or parchment paper.

2 Cream the butter, sugar, and vanilla extract together in a large mixing bowl until pale and fluffy. Add the eggs, a little at a time, beating thoroughly. If the mixture begins to curdle, beat in a spoonful of the flour.

3 Sift half the flour over the creamed mixture, and fold in using a large metal spoon. Sift over the rest, and fold in with 2 tablespoons of the milk. If necessary, add the remaining milk to make a soft dropping consistency, then spoon into the heatproof bowl.

4 Cover the pudding with waxed paper and foil, and tie with string. Lower into the slow cooker, then pour enough water around the bowl to come halfway up the sides. Cover with the lid, and cook on high for 4–5 hours, or until well risen and springy to the touch. Lift out of the slow cooker, and remove the foil. Turn out onto a serving plate, peel off the paper, and serve.

HOW TO COVER A STEAMED PUDDING

1 Brush a sheet of waxed paper with softened butter, then place the unbuttered side on a sheet of foil. Make a pleat about ¾ inch wide in the middle to allow the pudding to rise. (If fresh fruit is included in the pudding, you must use waxed paper; otherwise, a double piece of foil may be used.)

2 Cover the bowl with the pleated waxed paper and foil, allowing it to overlap the rim by 1 inch. Tie the foil securely with fine string.

3 Make a loop with the string at the top of the bowl to make a secure handle. This will enable the bowl to be lifted in and out of the ceramic cooking pot easily.

Making baked egg custard

A lightly set, creamy-textured custard is ideal for serving hot or cold. It can be enjoyed on its own or with all manner of desserts, such as fruit pies, steamed sponges, and crumbles.

SERVES 4–6

butter or flavorless oil, for greasing
2 cups milk
3 eggs
3 tablespoons superfine sugar
pinch of freshly grated nutmeg

1 Place an upturned saucer or metal pastry cutter in the bottom of the ceramic cooking pot. Pour in about 1 inch of very hot water, then turn the slow cooker to high.

2 Lightly grease the base and sides of a 3¾-cup heatproof dish. Heat the milk in a pan until it is steaming hot, without letting it boil.

3 Whisk the eggs and sugar lightly in a bowl, then slowly pour over the hot milk, whisking all the time. Pour the mixture through a fine strainer into the prepared dish, and sprinkle the top with a little grated nutmeg.

4 Cover the dish with plastic wrap, and place in the slow cooker. Pour in enough near-boiling water to come just over halfway up the sides of the dish. Put the lid on the slow cooker, then switch to the low setting, and cook for 4 hours, or until the custard is lightly set. Serve hot or cold.

Making crème brûlée

You can use the basic baked egg custard mixture to make other custard-based desserts, such as crème brûlée, which is a rich, creamy baked custard topped with a crisp layer of caramelized sugar.

1 Make the custard, whisking 1 teaspoon vanilla extract into the egg and sugar mixture, then use ⅔ cup heavy cream and 1¼ cups light cream in place of the milk.

2 Strain the custard into a pitcher, then pour into four or six individual ramekins, first making sure that the ramekins will fit inside the cooking pot in a single layer.

3 Cover each dish with plastic wrap, then place in the ceramic cooking pot. Pour enough near-boiling water around the dishes to come three-quarters of the way up the sides. Cover with the lid, and cook on low for about 3 hours, or until set.

4 Remove the custards from the slow cooker, and leave to cool. Sprinkle the tops with ½ cup superfine sugar. Place under a hot broiler, and cook until the sugar melts and caramelizes. Cool, then chill.

Making bread and butter pudding

This favorite dessert can be made using the classic baked custard mixture.

1 Make the custard using 1¼ cups milk and ⅓ cup heavy cream.

2 Butter 8 medium slices of bread, then cut each in half diagonally. Arrange the slices in a 4 cup, buttered baking dish, first making sure that it will fit in the cooking pot.

3 Pour the custard over the bread, and sprinkle 2 tablespoons raw sugar and a little grated nutmeg over the top. Cover with plastic wrap, and put the dish in the cooking pot. Pour enough near-boiling water around the dish to come two-thirds up the sides. Cover with a lid, and cook on high for 3–4 hours, or until the custard has set. Serve the pudding warm.

Making cheese and vegetable strata

This savory bread and butter pudding can be made using the baked custard mixture. Simply leave out the sugar, and season well with salt and black pepper.

1 Cook 1 thinly sliced leek and 1 large finely chopped onion in 2 tablespoons butter until soft. Stir in 2 tablespoons chopped fresh chives or parsley.

2 Remove the crusts from 8 slices of bread, then cut into fingers. Arrange one-third of the bread fingers in a buttered 7½-cup soufflé dish. Top with half the vegetable mixture. Repeat the layers, ending with bread.

3 Pour the custard mixture over the strata, then sprinkle ¾ cup finely grated Cheddar cheese over the top. Cover with buttered foil, then put in the ceramic cooking pot, and pour enough near-boiling water around the dish to come halfway up the sides. Cover, and cook on high for 3–4 hours until lightly set. Cut into wedges, and serve warm.

Making rice pudding

Cooked in the slow cooker, rice pudding is wonderfully rich and creamy. Unlike baked versions, it doesn't form a thick skin on the top. Add flavorings such as grated nutmeg at the beginning, or partway through cooking.

SERVES 4–6

2 tablespoons softened butter
generous ⅓ cup pudding rice, rinsed
    and drained
4 tablespoons superfine sugar
3 cups milk
¾ cup unsweetened condensed milk

1 Thickly butter the ceramic cooking pot, taking it about halfway up the sides. Add the rice, sugar, milk, evaporated milk, and any flavorings, and stir to mix.

2 Cover with the lid, and cook on high for 3–4 hours, or on low for 5–6 hours, until the rice is cooked and most of the milk has been absorbed.

3 Stir the pudding at least twice during the last 2 hours of cooking. If the mixture gets too thick toward the end, stir in a little more milk.

MAKING CAKES

Many cakes can be made successfully in a slow cooker—in particular, moist cake mixtures, such as carrot cake and gingerbread, that normally require long cooking at low temperatures. These types of cake usually benefit from being left to mature before eating, but this is not necessary when they are cooked in the slow cooker. The slow cooker is also good for making lightly textured, rich-flavored sponge cakes. However, it is not suitable for whisked sponges and cakes, because these need fast cooking at a high temperature.

Cakes can be cooked either in a pan with a fixed base or in a straight-sided soufflé dish. Before you line a pan and fill it with cake mixture, make sure it will fit in the ceramic cooking pot. It is a good idea to test that the pan is watertight: fill it with water, and leave for a few minutes to check for leakages.

The baking pan should be lined with waxed paper that has been greased with a little flavorless oil, or parchment paper. This makes it easier to remove the cake from the pan

Base-lining

Some recipes only require the base of the pan to be lined. This technique can be used to line any shape of pan, whether round, square, or rectangular.

Place the pan on a sheet of waxed paper or parchment paper and, using a pencil, draw round the pan. Cut just inside the line so that the paper will fit neatly inside the pan. Using a paper towel drizzled with a flavorless oil, grease the inside of the pan, and place the lining paper in the base, pressing it right into the corners.

Lining round cookware

The sides, as well as the base, of a pan or soufflé dish, will often need to be lined.

1 Place the pan or soufflé dish on a sheet of waxed paper and draw round it. Cut inside the line. Cut strips of paper, about ½ inch wider than the depth of the pan or dish. Fold up the bottom edge by ½ inch, then make cuts about ½ inch apart from the edge of the paper to the fold.

2 Brush the inside of the pan or dish with oil, then position the paper strips around the side of the pan so that the snipped edge sits on the base. Place the paper circle in the base.

Lining a square pan

You can line a square pan with a single piece of waxed paper.

Put the pan on a square of waxed paper, which allows the depth of the pan on all four sides. Draw around the base of the pan. Cut in from the edge to each corner of the square. Fold in each side along its pencil line, making a firm crease. Lightly brush the inside of the pan with oil, then fit the paper inside, making sure it fits well into the corners.

Lining a loaf pan

Unlike a square pan, it is easier to line a loaf pan with two strips of paper.

1 Cut a strip of waxed paper the length of the pan base and wide enough to cover the base and long sides. Cut another strip of paper, the same width as the pan base and long enough to cover the base and ends of the pan.

2 Lightly brush the inside of the pan with oil, then press the two pieces of paper into position, creasing it where it meets the edges of the base of the pan.

Making dark chocolate cake

Steaming in the slow cooker gives this cake a deliciously moist texture and rich flavor.

SERVES 8–10

¾ cup butter, at room temperature
½ cup soft light brown sugar
¼ cup clear honey
3 eggs, lightly beaten
1¼ cups self-rising flour
¼ cup unsweetened cocoa powder
2 teaspoons milk
1 teaspoon vanilla extract
whipped cream, for the filling (optional)

1 Place an upturned saucer or metal pastry cutter in the ceramic cooking pot. Pour in 1 inch of very hot water, then switch the slow cooker to high.

2 Grease and line a 7-inch fixed-base round cake pan or soufflé dish, at least 3 inches deep.

3 Put the butter, sugar, and honey in a bowl, and cream together until pale and fluffy. Beat the eggs into the creamed mixture a little at a time, beating well after each addition. If the mixture curdles, mix in a little of the measured flour.

4 Sift the flour and cocoa over the cake mixture. Using a large metal spoon, gently fold in with the milk and vanilla extract. Spoon the mixture into the prepared pan, and level the surface.

5 Loosely cover the cake pan with lightly oiled foil. Put the pan in the ceramic cooking pot, and then pour enough near-boiling water around the pan to come just over halfway up the sides.

6 Cover with the lid, and cook on high for 3 hours. To test if the cake is cooked, insert a skewer into the center of the cake. Leave for a few seconds, then remove; it should come away clean. If any mixture sticks to the skewer, re-cover, and cook for 30 minutes more.

7 Remove the cake from the ceramic cooking pot, and place on a wire rack for 10 minutes before turning out of the pan. Leave to cool, then cut in half, and fill with whipped cream, if you like.

DECORATING CAKES

Cakes cooked in a slow cooker darken in color, but they do not brown in the same way as an oven-baked cake. As a result, many will benefit from decorating.

Decorating uncooked cakes
Many cakes can be decorated before they are put in the slow cooker. Note that light sponges and wet cake mixtures cannot hold heavy decorations.

Glistening sugar is an easy and effective way of decorating cakes. Different types of sugar can be sprinkled over the top of an uncooked cake. Good choices include superfine sugar, larger crystals of granulated or raw sugar, and brown sugar crystals.

Chopped and sliced nuts can be sprinkled over cakes in the same way as sugar. Toast them first.

Halved nuts and candied fruits can be arranged in decorative patterns on fruit cakes and stiff cake batters. After cooking, brush over a little warmed honey or sugar syrup to glaze.

Decorating cooked cakes
After cooking, cakes can be decorated in a number of different ways.

Frosting can transform a simple cake into something special. To make fudge frosting, break 2 ounces semisweet chocolate into the cooking pot, and add 2 cups sifted confectioners' sugar, ¼ cup butter, 3 tablespoons milk, and 1 teaspoon vanilla extract. Switch the slow cooker to high for 15–25 minutes, or until the chocolate has melted. Remove the cooking pot, stir to mix, then beat until thick, and spread over the cake.

American frosting can be made by placing a bowl in the ceramic cooking pot, then pouring enough near-boiling water around the bowl to come just over halfway up the sides. Switch the slow cooker to high. Place 12 ounces superfine sugar in the bowl with ½ teaspoon tartaric acid and 2 egg whites. Whisk continuously until the mixture holds its shape. Spread over the cake in peaks.

MAKING SAVORY SAUCES

Sauces add flavor, color, texture, and moisture to food. Many can be made in the slow cooker, from classic simmered sauces to emulsions that are made by using the slow cooker as a bain-marie. Here are just a selection of classic sauces that can be used for cooking or for serving with other dishes.

Making fresh tomato sauce

This sauce can be used as the base for pasta dishes, or can be combined with meat or poultry to make a rich cooking sauce. You can use 2 × 14-ounce cans chopped plum tomatoes instead of fresh, if you prefer. This recipe will make about 2 cups.

1 Pour 1 tablespoon olive oil into the ceramic cooking pot. Add 2 crushed garlic cloves and the finely grated zest of ½ lemon. Stir, then cover with the lid, and switch the slow cooker to high. Cook for 15 minutes.

2 Peel and roughly chop 2 pounds ripe tomatoes, and add to the cooking pot with 4 tablespoons vegetable stock or red wine, 1 teaspoon dried oregano, and a pinch of superfine sugar. Stir to combine, then cover with the lid, and cook on low for 3 hours.

3 Stir in 3 tablespoons chopped fresh basil, and season to taste with salt and ground black pepper.

Making white sauce

To make white sauce in a slow cooker, heat the milk, then whisk in a mixture of butter and flour. This recipe will make about 2 cups.

1 Pour 1⅔ cups milk into the ceramic cooking pot. Add flavoring ingredients (such as a bay leaf, mace, a few parsley stalks, half a peeled onion, and 4 black peppercorns). Switch the slow cooker to high, and heat for 1 hour, or until simmering.

2 Blend 1½ tablespoons softened butter with scant ¼ cup all-purpose flour to make a paste.

3 Remove the flavoring ingredients from the milk, using a slotted spoon. Add the paste in small spoonfuls, and whisk into the hot milk until thickened.

4 Cover with the lid, and cook for about 30 minutes, stirring occasionally. Season with salt and extra pepper if needed.

HOT EMULSION SAUCES

These rich, creamy sauces can be made very successfully using the slow cooker as a bain-marie.

Making hollandaise sauce

The rich flavor of hollandaise sauce goes well with fish, shellfish, and many vegetables. Take your time making it, because it may curdle if the butter is added too quickly. This recipe will make about 1¼ cups.

1 About 30 minutes before making the sauce, remove ¾ cup sweet butter from the refrigerator. Cut into tiny cubes, and leave to come to room temperature.

2 Pour about 2 inches near-boiling water into the ceramic cooking pot. Cover the slow cooker with the lid to retain the heat, and switch to high.

3 Put 4 tablespoons white wine vinegar in a pan with 4 black peppercorns, I bay leaf, and some mace (optional). Bring to the boil, and simmer until reduced to I tablespoon. Remove from the heat and dip the base of the pan into cold water to prevent further evaporation.

4 Beat 3 egg yolks with I tablespoon of the butter and a pinch of salt in a heatproof bowl that will fit in the slow cooker. Strain in the reduced vinegar. Place the bowl in the ceramic cooking pot, and pour enough boiling water around the bowl to come just over halfway up the sides. Whisk for about 3 minutes until beginning to thicken.

5 Beat in the remaining butter a little at a time, making sure that each addition of butter is completely incorporated before adding the next. The mixture will slowly thicken and emulsify. Season with salt and ground black pepper. Switch the slow cooker to low, and keep the hollandaise warm for up to I hour. (If the sauce starts to curdle, add an ice cube, and whisk vigorously; the sauce should combine. If this doesn't work, whisk I egg yolk with I tablespoon lukewarm water, and slowly whisk into the separated sauce.)

Making beurre blanc

This simple butter sauce is served with poached or broiled fish and poultry. It can be varied by adding chopped fresh herbs, such as chives or chervil, to the finished sauce. It is extremely rich, and only a small amount is needed per serving. This recipe will make about I cup.

I Pour about 2 inches of near-boiling water into the ceramic cooking pot. Cover with the lid, and switch the slow cooker to high.

2 Pour 3 tablespoons each of white wine and white wine vinegar into a pan. Add 2 finely chopped shallots, and bring to the boil. Simmer until reduced to about I tablespoon liquid.

3 Strain the mixture into a heatproof bowl that will fit in the slow cooker, then pour enough boiling water around the bowl to come halfway up the sides.

4 Whisk in I cup chilled diced butter, adding it piece by piece, and making sure that each addition is completely incorporated before adding the next. Season with salt and ground black pepper before serving.

Making a sabayon sauce

Light and airy sabayon sauce is thickened with egg. It goes well with vegetable and pastry dishes. This recipe will make about 1¼ cups.

I Half-fill the ceramic cooking pot with near-boiling water, cover with the lid, and switch to high.

2 Place a heatproof bowl over the water in the slow cooker; the base should just touch the water, but the rest of the bowl should be above the water. Place 4 egg yolks with I tablespoon white wine vinegar in the bowl, and whisk until pale. Add 6 tablespoon red or white wine, or stock and whisk again.

3 When the sauce is thick and frothy, season to taste and serve immediately.

MAKING SWEET SAUCES

A sweet sauce adds the finishing touch to a dessert, and the slow cooker is excellent for making fruit purees, creamy custards, and rich chocolate sauces.

Making fresh fruit coulis
Cooking soft fruits, such as raspberries, blackberries, blueberries, blackcurrants, plums, cherries, and apricots, brings out their natural flavor. This recipe will make about 1½ cups.

1 Put 3 cups prepared fruit in the ceramic cooking pot with 3 tablespoons water. Stir in a little sugar, and add a dash of lemon juice. Cover with the lid, and cook on high for 1–1½ hours or until very soft.

2 Remove the cooking pot from the slow cooker, and leave to cool slightly. Pour the fruit into a food processor or blender, and process until smooth. Press the puree through a strainer to remove any seeds or skins.

3 Taste the sauce, and stir in a little more sugar or lemon juice, if needed. Cover and chill until required. If you like, stir in 3 tablespoons liqueur, such as Kirsch, before serving. The coulis can be stored in the refrigerator for up to 5 days.

Making dried fruit sauce
Dried fruits, such as apricots, can also be made into sauces. This recipe will make about scant 2½ cups.

1 Place 6 ounces dried apricots in the ceramic cooking pot, pour over 2 cups orange juice, cover, and leave to soak overnight.

2 Place the ceramic pot in the slow cooker, and cook on high for 1 hour, or until the apricots are tender. Puree in a food processor or blender, and serve warm or cold. If necessary, dilute the sauce with a little extra fruit juice.

Making custard
Custard is the classic dessert sauce and can also be used as the basis for many desserts. The slow cooker maintains a gentle, constant heat, so the custard can be made directly in the ceramic cooking pot, rather than in a bain-marie. It can be served hot or cold, and can also be flavored: try stirring 3 ounces chopped semisweet chocolate or 3 tablespoons rum or brandy into hot custard. For extra richness, replace some of the milk with light or heavy cream. This recipe will make about 2½ cups.

1 Pour 2 cups of milk into the ceramic cooking pot. Split a vanilla bean lengthwise, and add it to the milk. Heat on high for 1 hour, or until the milk reaches boiling point.

2 Meanwhile, whisk together 5 egg yolks and scant ½ cup superfine sugar in a bowl until the mixture is pale and thick.

3 Whisk 1 teaspoon cornstarch into the egg mixture. (This will help the custard to thicken and prevent curdling.)

4 Remove the vanilla bean, and pour the hot milk over the egg mixture, whisking all the time. Pour the mixture back into the ceramic cooking pot, and stir until slightly thickened. Bring the custard to simmering point; do not let it boil, or it may curdle. Cook until it is thick enough to coat the back of a wooden spoon.

Making sabayon sauce
This frothy sauce goes well with elegant desserts and dainty pastries. This recipe makes about scant 2 cups.

1 Pour about 2 inches near-boiling water into the ceramic cooking pot. Cover with the lid, and switch to high.

2 Put 4 eggs and ¼ cup superfine sugar in a heatproof bowl, first checking that it will fit comfortably in the slow cooker. Beat well until the mixture becomes a paler color, then whisk in generous ½ cup sweet white wine.

3 Place the bowl in the ceramic cooking pot, and pour enough boiling water around it to come just over halfway up the sides. Continue whisking the sauce for 10 minutes until it is very thick and frothy. Serve hot or cold.

Making creamy chocolate sauce
This dark, velvety smooth sauce should be served with desserts that can stand up to its deep, rich flavor.

1 Pour scant 1 cup heavy cream, 4 tablespoons milk, and ½ teaspoon vanilla extract into the ceramic cooking pot. Switch the slow cooker to high, and heat for about 45 minutes.

2 Turn off the slow cooker. Add 5 ounces chopped bittersweet chocolate, and stir continuously until it has melted. Serve warm.

Making glossy chocolate sauce
This sweet pouring sauce is ideal for serving with profiteroles and ice cream.

Put 8 ounces chopped semisweet chocolate, 4 tablespoons light corn syrup, 4 tablespoons water, and 2 tablespoons sweet butter into the ceramic cooking pot. Switch the slow cooker to high, and heat, stirring, for 30 minutes until melted. Serve warm.

Making white chocolate sauce
This sweet creamy sauce is good served warm with fresh summer fruits.

1 Pour about 2 inches very hot water into the cooking pot. Cover with the lid, and switch the slow cooker to high.

2 Put 7 ounces white chocolate and 2 tablespoons heavy cream into a heatproof bowl. Place in the cooking pot, and pour enough near-boiling water around the bowl to touch the base.

3 Stir the mixture until melted, then stir in 4 tablespoons heavy cream and 4 tablespoons milk. Heat for 5 minutes, then remove from the heat, and whisk.

Making caramel sauce
This rich, creamy sauce is delicious poured over sweet pastries and pastry desserts.

1 Put 2 tablespoons sweet butter and 6 tablespoons soft dark brown sugar in the ceramic cooking pot. Switch the slow cooker to high, and heat for about 20 minutes, stirring occasionally, until the butter has melted and the sugar has dissolved.

2 Stir ⅔ cup heavy cream into the sauce, and cook for 20 minutes, stirring occasionally, until smooth. Serve warm or cold.

Making butterscotch sauce
This buttery sauce is very sweet and rich, and should be served in small quantities.

1 Put ¼ cup sweet butter, 6 tablespoons soft light brown sugar, ¼ cup superfine sugar, and scant ½ cup light corn syrup into the ceramic cooking pot. Heat on high for 20 minutes, stirring, until the sugar has dissolved.

2 Gradually stir in ⅔ cup heavy cream and 1 teaspoon vanilla extract. Serve warm.

MAKING FONDUES

Fondues are tremendous fun for informal entertaining, and if you already own a slow cooker you won't need a special fondue set to keep the dip warm at the table. The smaller models of slow cooker are ideal for fondue-making, because they are deeper, and the mixture must be at least 2 inches deep for dipping. Cheese, chocolate, and butterscotch fondues can all be made in the slow cooker. Meat fondues cooked in hot oil are unsuitable because the slow cooker does not reach a high enough temperature.

Making cheese fondue

There are many versions and variations of this hot cheese dip. The classic Swiss cheese fondue, traditionally enjoyed after an exhausting day of Alpine skiing, usually uses hard cheeses, such as Emmenthal and Gruyère, and slightly softer ones, such as Appenzeller.

This basic recipe serves four to six people and can be used as a guide for creating your own variations. Try using beer, cider, ale, or milk in place of the white wine, or add brandy in place of Kirsch. Alternatively, you can vary the cheese, using sharp Cheddar, or Monterey Jack. You can buy packets of cheese mixtures for fondues, but check the label carefully; *fromage fondu* is a term for a blended cheese product and not a cheese for fondue-making.

1 Rub the inside of the ceramic cooking pot with the cut half of a clove of garlic. This will impart a subtle flavor to the fondue. Pour in ⅔ cup dry white wine. Cover with the lid, then switch the slow cooker to high, and heat for 45 minutes.

2 In a small bowl, blend 2 teaspoons cornstarch with 1 tablespoon Kirsch to make a smooth paste, then stir in a pinch of freshly grated nutmeg, and season well with ground black pepper.

3 Stir the cornstarch mixture into the hot wine until thickened and smooth. (The cornstarch will help to prevent the fondue separating once the cheese is added.)

4 Sprinkle 8 ounces grated Gruyère or Emmenthal cheese over the wine, and stir until completely melted. Switch the slow cooker to low, and continue stirring until the fondue is thoroughly blended and smooth. Add a little more wine if the mixture seems too thick. The fondue is now ready to serve, or can be kept warm on low for up to an hour.

SPECIALITY FONDUES
While the Swiss fondue is classic, other countries have their own versions. *Fonduta* is a creamy fondue made with Fontina cheese from the Piedmontese region of Italy. The Dutch *kaasdoop* is a similar hot cheese dip. The French make fondue using Comte and Beaufort cheese.

SAVORY DIPPERS
Savory fondues are usually served with cubes of crusty bread, which are speared onto long-handled forks for dipping: Swiss tradition has it that anyone who loses their piece of bread in the fondue has to pay a forfeit. There are lots of other foods that can be dipped into the fondue as an alternative to bread:

• Crispy bacon rolls: rinded fatty bacon strips cut in half widthwise, rolled, and skewered, then broiled or oven-baked.
• Cooked cocktail sausages.

• Small whole mushrooms, broiled or lightly fried.

• Vegetable crudités such as florets of raw cauliflower.

Making chocolate fondue

This smooth, not-too-sweet fondue makes a deliciously indulgent dessert. It is made using equal quantities of chocolate and cream, so you can easily increase the quantities to feed more people, if necessary. This recipe makes enough to serve four people.

If you prefer, you can use other types of chocolate, such as milk or white; be sure to choose a good quality chocolate that is intended for melting, because many brands of eating chocolate are difficult to melt.

This recipe can also be used as a guide for a fudge fondue. Simply omit the liqueur and add 2½ ounces chopped caramel chocolate bars in place of the bittersweet chocolate.

I Pour ⅔ cup heavy cream into the ceramic cooking pot, and switch the slow cooker to high. Stir in 1 tablespoon orange or coffee liqueur, then cover with the lid, and heat for about 30 minutes.

2 Finely chop 5 ounces bittersweet chocolate, and sprinkle over the hot cream mixture. Stir with a wooden spoon until melted and well blended, then switch the slow cooker to low.

3 Keep the chocolate fondue warm for up to 30 minutes, or serve immediately. For a thicker fondue, turn off the slow cooker, and leave to cool for 10 minutes.

Butterscotch fondue

This rich, creamy fondue is especially good served with sweet fruits, such as pineapples, pears, and bananas. This recipe will serve four to six people.

I Cut ½ cup sweet butter into small cubes, and place in the ceramic cooking pot. Add 1 cup molasses sugar, and heat on high for about 15 minutes, until the butter starts to melt.

2 Pour in scant 1 cup heavy cream, and stir until the sugar dissolves completely.

3 Stir in ½ teaspoon vanilla extract, then cover with the lid and cook on high for 30 minutes, stirring occasionally, until the sauce is smooth and creamy. Switch the slow cooker to low, and keep warm for up to 1 hour.

4 Before serving, turn off the slow cooker, and leave for 10 minutes to allow the sauce to cool and thicken slightly.

SWEET DIPPERS

As with savory fondues, there are all manner of sweet and fruity treats that you can dip into hot chocolate or butterscotch fondues.

• Pink and white marshmallows, bitesize strawberries, and marzipan cut into small shapes.

• Fresh fruits such as seedless grapes, tangerine segments, pineapple cubes, sliced figs and kiwis. (Toss any fruits that are likely to discolor, such as apples, in a little orange juice.)

• Plain cake, such as Madeira or fruit cake, cut into small cubes. Cut up the cake a few hours before serving to allow it to dry out and firm up.

MAKING PRESERVES

The slow cooker is excellent for making chutneys, curds, and syrups. Although it is unsuitable for making jams and jellies, because the temperatures reached are too low to achieve setting point, it can be used for softening fruits at the start of many of these recipes. It is particularly useful for the long simmering needed to soften citrus fruits for marmalades.

Making chutney

Long, gentle cooking in the slow cooker produces chutneys with a well-developed flavor. As a result, slow cooker chutneys can often be eaten immediately and do not need to be matured beforehand. Because the slow cooker allows little evaporation, only chutneys with a relatively low liquid content are suitable. Those whose main ingredients contain a lot of liquid, such as rhubarb, tomatoes, and large zucchini, should be avoided because the juices will not evaporate sufficiently to make a thick, spoonable preserve.

You can use the following fruity apple chutney recipe as a guide to making other chutneys. Vary the ingredients, depending on your preference, seasonal availability, and the dried fruits that you have at hand.

MAKES JUST OVER 3 POUNDS

8 ounces onions
1½ pounds stovecooking apples
1 ounce fresh ginger root
3 garlic cloves, crushed
2 cups soft light brown sugar
¾ cup cider vinegar
1 pound mixed dried fruit, such as
    apricots, peaches, figs, dates, prunes,
    or golden raisins
1 teaspoon salt

I Peel and finely chop the onions, and place in the ceramic cooking pot. Quarter, core, peel, and roughly chop the apples into even-size pieces, and add to the onions. Peel the ginger, then finely chop, and add to the pot. (If the ginger is tough and fibrous, grate it rather than chopping, squeeze the juices into the pot, then discard the fibers.)

2 Add the garlic, sugar, and cider vinegar to the ceramic cooking pot, and switch the slow cooker to high.

3 Heat, uncovered, for 30 minutes, then stir until the sugar has completely dissolved. Cover with the lid, and cook for 6 hours, stirring occasionally.

4 Toward the end of cooking time, chop the dried fruit into small, even-size pieces, and stir into the chutney with the salt. Cover and cook for 2–3 hours, or until the chutney is thick, stirring once or twice toward the end of cooking.

5 Spoon the chutney into hot sterilized jars, and seal with vinegar-proof tops. Label and store in a cool dark place. Use within 6 months of making, and once opened, store in the refrigerator.

Making fruit curd

Using the slow cooker as a bain-marie is a great way to make fruit curds, because the temperature of the water won't get too hot and spoil the preserve. You can use this basic citrus-fruit curd recipe as a base for other fruit curds. To make a passion fruit curd, use 2 tablespoons less citrus juice, and stir in the seeds and pulp of 2 passion fruits at the end of cooking. If you prefer a richer, firmer preserve, replace some of the beaten egg with 2 egg yolks.

MAKES ABOUT 1½ POUNDS

finely grated rind of 3 lemons,
    4 limes, or 2 oranges
    (preferably unwaxed or organic)
⅔ cup lemon, lime, or orange juice
1¾ cups superfine sugar
8 tablespoons sweet butter, diced
⅔ cup beaten eggs

I Pour 2 inches hot water into the ceramic cooking pot, and switch the slow cooker to high. Put the citrus rind and juice, sugar, and butter into a large heatproof bowl, first checking that it will fit in the slow cooker.

2 Put the bowl in the slow cooker, and pour enough near-boiling water around the bowl to come just over halfway up the sides. Leave for 15 minutes, stirring occasionally, until the sugar has dissolved and the butter has melted. Remove the bowl from the ceramic cooking pot, and leave to cool for a few minutes. Turn the slow cooker to low.

Making cordial

The slow cooker is the perfect vehicle for infusing flavors such as citrus rind and spices. It brings the liquid very slowly to the boil and maintains it at a constant, low temperature, ensuring that maximum flavor is extracted. It is therefore perfect for making cordials, as well as syrups for fruit compotes. This recipe is for lemon cordial, but you can use the same method to make other flavors. Try using the rind of 2 oranges and the juice of 1 lemon. Alternatively, omit the lemon rind, and use 10 scented rose petals, 1 split vanilla bean, and the juice of 1 lemon.

3 Pour the beaten eggs through a strainer into the fruit mixture, and whisk to combine. Cover the bowl with foil, then return it to the slow cooker.

4 Cook on low for 1–1½ hours, stirring every 15 minutes, until the curd thickens and lightly coats the back of the spoon.

5 Remove the bowl from the slow cooker, and pour the curd into small warmed sterilized jars. If you prefer a smooth curd, pour through a strainer before potting.

6 Cover each jar with a waxed disk and cellophane, then label. Store in a cool, dark place or the refrigerator, and use within 3 months. Once opened, store in the refrigerator, and use within 1 week.

2 Put the peel and cheesecloth bag in the ceramic cooking pot, then pour over the water and lemon juice. Cover the pot with the lid, and switch the slow cooker to high. Cook for 4–6 hours, or until the peel is tender. (The peel must be really soft before adding the sugar.)

MAKES ABOUT 5 CUPS

3 large juicy lemons, preferably
    unwaxed or organic
1¾ cups superfine sugar
sparkling mineral water and ice, to serve

Making marmalade

Although the slow cooker can't be used to bring marmalade to setting point, it is ideal for the long simmering of the peel. This recipe will fit in a 14¼-cup slow cooker, but you can double or halve the quantities as necessary.

MAKES ABOUT 6 POUNDS

2 pounds Temple oranges
6¼ cups near-boiling water
juice of 2 lemons
9 cups sugar

1 Wash and scrub the oranges. Cut them in half, squeeze out the juice, and reserve. Remove the pips and membrane from the peel, and tie them in a piece of cheesecloth. Slice the orange peel thinly or thickly, as preferred.

3 Remove the cheesecloth bag, and leave until cool enough to handle. Squeeze the liquid from it into a large, heavy pan. Transfer the rind and cooking liquid from the slow cooker to the pan. Add the orange juice and sugar, and heat gently, stirring until the sugar has dissolved.

4 Bring the mixture to the boil, and boil rapidly for about 15 minutes, until the marmalade reaches 220°F on a sugar thermometer. (Alternatively, place a spoonful of the marmalade on a chilled saucer, and leave to cool for 1 minute. Press gently with your finger, and it should wrinkle; if not, continue boiling.)

5 Remove the pan from the heat and skim off any scum, using a slotted spoon. Leave to stand for 15 minutes, then stir to distribute the peel evenly. Ladle the marmalade into hot sterilized jars, seal and label. Store in a cool, dark place, and use within one year of making.

1 Wash the lemons, then thinly pare off the rind, leaving the bitter white pith behind. Put the rind in the cooking pot with the sugar and 4 cups cold water. Cover, and switch the slow cooker to high.

2 Heat for 30 minutes, then stir until the sugar has dissolved. Cook for a further 1½ hours, then leave to cool.

3 Halve the lemons and squeeze out the juice. Stir into the syrup, then pour through a stainless-steel or plastic strainer. Pour into sterilized bottles, seal, and label. Store in the refrigerator for up to 10 days. Dilute to taste with mineral water, and serve over ice.

SLOW COOKER SAFETY

The slow cooker is an extremely efficient and safe way to cook food. It is, however, an electrical appliance, and some basic common-sense safety precautions should be followed. Because slow cooker models vary, always take the time to read the instruction manual supplied by the manufacturer before use.

Cooker care

Looking after your cooker is simple but very important. When you first unwrap and remove your slow cooker from its box, check that it isn't damaged in any way, that the plug (which has hopefully been provided) is attached properly, and if you bought your slow cooker in another country, that the voltage on the rating plate of the appliance corresponds with your house electricity supply. If you are in any doubt, consult a qualified electrician before using the slow cooker.

Before you use the slow cooker for the first time, wash the ceramic cooking pot in warm soapy water, and dry it thoroughly. Stand the slow cooker on a heat-resistant surface when in use, making sure that the mains lead is tucked away safely; the slow cooker should not touch anything hot or hang over the edge of the table or work-top, in case it falls off accidentally.

Take extra care if you have young children (or curious pets), and position the slow cooker out of reach. After an hour or so of cooking, the slow cooker can become very hot; not just the

Below: Do not submerge the slow cooker in water. If it needs cleaning, make sure it is unplugged, and use a damp, soapy sponge.

Above: Protect your hands from the hot cooker and escaping steam with a pair of padded oven gloves.

ceramic cooking pot, but the outer casing and the lid as well. Always use oven gloves when lifting the lid (do this away from you to prevent scalding from steam or drips), and when removing the cooking pot from inside the slow cooker.

Do not switch on the slow cooker if the ceramic cooking pot is empty (the only exception to this would be if the manufacturer recommends preheating). As soon as you have finished cooking, remove the plug from the socket to prevent the slow cooker from being switched on accidentally.

Never immerse the outer casing of the slow cooker in water—this would be extremely dangerous, risking electric shock and fatal injury, because the outer casing contains the electrical elements that heat the ceramic cooking pot.

You should never use the outer casing for cooking without the ceramic cooking pot in place. If you need to clean the casing, do so with warm soapy water and a damp cloth, and be absolutely sure that the appliance is unplugged before you put it in contact with water.

Ensuring food safety

Slow cookers cook food slowly using a gentle heat—the precise temperature will vary from model to model, but the average is from about 200°F on the low setting to about 300°F on the high setting. Bacteria in food is destroyed at a temperature of 165°F, so as long as the food is cooked for the appropriate length of time, as stated in the

recipe, this temperature will be reached quickly enough to ensure that the food is safe to eat. However, additional factors may affect the slow cooker's ability to reach the desired temperature, and you should be aware of the following to ensure food safety:

• Avoid placing the slow cooker near an open window or in a draught.

• Do not lift the lid during cooking time unless instructed to do so in the recipe.

• Do not add ingredients that are frozen or part-frozen to the ceramic cooking pot, because they will increase the length of time needed to reach the required cooking temperature, and the timings given in the recipe will not be sufficient.

• Increase the cooking time in extreme cold temperatures, where the kitchen temperature is considerably lower than normal, and check food is cooked before serving, particularly poultry and pork.

Checking meat is cooked

When it comes to food safety, one of the main things to look out for is that meat is properly cooked—in particular, poultry and pork. A meat thermometer is a worthwhile investment if you are planning to cook whole joints of meat and poultry in your slow cooker. It is the most reliable way to ensure that the inside of the meat has reached a high enough temperature to kill any potentially harmful bacteria, without losing its juices and becoming dry and overcooked.

Below: A meat thermometer is easy to use and gives an accurate temperature reading to let you know when meat is safe to eat.

Above: A skewer or the tip of a sharp knife can be inserted into a thick part of a meat joint to check that it is thoroughly cooked.

When using a meat thermometer, the tip of the stainless-steel probe should be inserted as near the center of the meat as possible, but not touching any bone. Meat thermometers have different markings for various meats, indicating rare and pinkish lamb and beef, through to medium and well cooked. Pork and poultry must always be cooked thoroughly to avoid the risk of food poisoning, as they can pass on harmful bacteria when raw or partially cooked; always err on the side of caution, and go for well cooked, rather than risk the meat being underdone and therefore unsafe.

To check that meat is cooked without a thermometer, insert the tip of a thin sharp knife or skewer into the thickest part of the meat joint, and hold it there for 20 seconds. For medium to well-cooked lamb or beef, the juices will be almost clear, and the knife will feel hot on the back of the hand. When cooking pork or poultry, it is essential that the meat juices should be completely clear. If there is any trace of pink, the meat is not ready to eat and should be cooked for a further 30 minutes; check again with the skewer or knife before serving.

With poultry, you can double check by giving the leg a tug—it should have some give in it and not be resistant. If you are still unsure, make a deep cut where the thigh joins the body; there should be no visible trace of pink meat. If there is, cook the meat for a further 30 minutes, then check again.

FOOD SAFETY TIPS

Basic food safety recommendations should be followed when preparing or using food in the slow cooker.

• Food should always be at room temperature when it is added to the slow cooker, otherwise it will take longer to reach the safe cooking temperature. However, ingredients such as meat and fish should not be left out of the refrigerator for longer than is necessary, so remove from the refrigerator just to take off the chill, and keep covered with plastic wrap.

• Marinating food in the ceramic cooking pot before cooking saves on dishwashing, but the cooking pot will become cold in the refrigerator, so remove it at least 1 hour before you plan to start cooking.

• Large joints of meat and whole poultry should be cooked at a high temperature for the first 1–2 hours to accelerate the cooking process. Switch the slow cooker to low for the remaining cooking time.

• Avoid lifting the lid of the ceramic cooker during the cooking time, especially in the early stages. It takes 15–20 minutes to recover the lost heat each time the lid is removed, so it will take much longer to reach a safe temperature.

• Don't be tempted to partially cook meat or poultry, then refrigerate for subsequent cooking. Also avoid reheating precooked dishes in the slow cooker.

• Frozen foods should always be thoroughly thawed before being placed in the slow cooker. If added when frozen, they will increase the time the food takes to reach a safe temperature. If adding frozen vegetables toward the end of cooking time, thaw them first under cold running water.

• Soak dried beans, in particular red kidney beans, overnight and then fast-boil them on the stovetop for 10 minutes in a pan of fresh cooking water to destroy toxins before adding to the slow cooker.

ONE-POT COOKING TECHNIQUES

Cooking a dish in a single pot doesn't demand any particular expertise, but mastering a few simple techniques will make for greater efficiency, especially when preparing the ingredients. Many one-pot dishes need very little attention while they are actually cooking, but it is important to follow the instructions in individual recipes as regards stirring.

Stewing, Braising, and Casseroling Meat

These are long, slow, and moist methods of cooking either in the oven or on top of the stove. The meat is browned first to seal in the natural juices and improve the flavor and color of the finished dish, then it is simmered slowly at low temperature in liquid—wine, water, beer, or stock.

1 Trim off any excess fat from the meat. For stewing and casseroling, cut the meat into 1-inch cubes. For braising, use thickly cut steaks or cut the meat into thick slices.

2 Toss the meat, a few pieces at a time, in seasoned flour, then shake off any excess. The flour coating browns to give the casserole a good flavor and also thickens the liquid.

3 Heat 2 tablespoons sunflower-seed oil in a flameproof casserole. Add the meat, in batches, and cook over high heat. When the meat is well browned on all sides, use a slotted spoon to remove it before adding the next batch.

4 Add the sliced or chopped onions and other vegetables to the remaining fat and juices in the casserole, and cook, stirring occasionally, for about 5 minutes.

5 Return the meat to the casserole, add herbs, and pour in the cooking liquid. Stir to loosen the residue from the base of the pan, then heat until simmering. Simmer gently on the stovetop or in the oven until the meat is tender. The casserole may be covered for the entire cooking time or uncovered toward the end to let excess liquid evaporate.

Pot-roasting Meat

This slow method of cooking is ideal for slightly tough cuts of meat, such as beef pot-roast, lamb shoulder and shanks, and the narrow end of a leg of pork.

1 Heat a little sunflower-seed oil in a large flameproof casserole until very hot. Add the meat, and cook over high heat, turning frequently, until browned on all sides. Remove the meat from the pan.

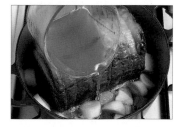

2 Add the onions, leeks, and any root vegetables to the pan, then cook, stirring constantly, for a few minutes. Replace the meat on top of the vegetables, and pour in a little liquid, such as stock, wine, or beer. Cover, and cook gently in the oven until the meat is tender.

Casseroling Chicken

Moist cooking methods not only bring out the flavor of poultry, but also offer the opportunity for herbs, spices, and aromatics to permeate the light meat thoroughly. Whole birds, cuts, and portions can be casseroled.

I Brown the poultry pieces or bird all over first. Remove from the pan before softening chopped onion, carrot, celery, and other flavoring ingredients in the fat remaining in the pan.

2 Replace the poultry before adding the chosen liquid—stock, wine, or canned tomatoes. Season the casserole well, then bring it just to simmering point. Cover it closely, and simmer very gently on top of the stove, or cook in the oven at 350°F.

COOKING TIMES FOR CASSEROLING CHICKEN
- For a whole bird allow 20 minutes per 1 pound, plus 20 minutes.
- Large portions 45–60 minutes.
- Boneless breast portions about 30 minutes.
- Chunks 20–40 minutes.

Pan-frying Meat

This is the traditional cooking method for beef steaks, such as sirloin, fillet, and rib; it is also good for veal scallops and chops, lamb loin, leg, and rib chops, as well as noisettes, and pork chops, steaks, and scallops.

I Cook steaks and chops in the minimum of fat, then add flavored butter when serving, if you like. Dab a little sunflower-seed oil on paper towels, and use to grease the pan lightly. Heat the pan until it is very hot (almost smoking). Add the steak or chops, and cook for 2–4 minutes on each side.

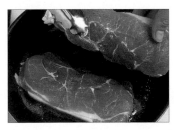

2 Pan-fry other lean cuts of meat in a mixture of butter and oil. Butter burns easily, so heat the oil in the pan first, and add the butter just before the meat to avoid this. Make sure that the butter and oil are sizzling before adding the meat. Cook on both sides until browned. Beef and thin cuts of meat, such as scallops, will be ready to serve. For some thicker cuts and meat such as pork that needs to be well cooked, reduce the heat to low once the meat is browned, and cook for 10–15 minutes, or until cooked through. Test by piercing the center of the meat with the point of a sharp knife.

Pan-frying Poultry

This quick cooking method is ideal for boneless chicken breast portions, Once the meat is cooked, the cooking juices can be made into a tasty sauce; simply stir in a little cream, add some chopped herbs, and season to taste.

When frying poultry, remember that it must be cooked through. Scallops and boneless breast portions cook quickly, so are ideal for pan-frying over high heat, but uneven thicker portions require careful cooking. With larger pieces, reduce the heat to low once the chicken is browned, and cook it slowly for up to 30 minutes so that the center is cooked.

Stir-frying

This is a fast method of cooking tender meat. The meat should be cut into thin slices across the grain, and then cut into fine, long strips. Use a wok or a large, heavy frying pan.

Heat a little oil in a wok or frying pan until it is smoking hot. Add the meat, in batches, and stir-fry over high heat. Remove the cooked meat before adding a fresh batch. When all the meat is cooked, add the other ingredients, and stir-fry over slightly lower heat.

CLAY-POT COOKING TECHNIQUES

Used with care, clay cooking pots last for years, but it is very important to follow the manufacturer's instructions closely. The advice that follows should be read in conjunction with your handbook.

Preparing a Clay Pot
All unglazed clay cooking pots must be soaked in cold water before every use. This is essential because it is the water retained in the clay that provides the moisture required during cooking. Ideally, the soaking time should be about 20 minutes. If it is the first time you have used the pot, leave it to soak for at least 30 minutes.

Place both the pot and its lid in a sink of cold water, inverting the lid on top of the base if necessary. The entire pot and the lid must be submerged. This thorough soaking is recommended before every use. If you are really short of time, you can just hold the pot under cold running water for about 1 minute, but this is not so satisfactory as soaking.

You can use your clay pot for lots of different recipes, but should avoid cooking fish or any highly flavored dish in it the first time you use it. If you have more than one clay pot, consider keeping separate pots for savory and sweet dishes.

Partially Glazed Clay Pots
Also available are clay pots that are glazed on the inside, but which have unglazed lids. With this type of pot, only the lid needs to be soaked, and this is done by holding it under cold running water for a few minutes. The ingredients are put into the pot, seasoned, and moistened with stock. The lid is fitted,

and the pot is placed in a cold oven, which is then heated to 425°F. Steam released from the soaked lid helps to keep the food moist as it bakes. The lid can be removed toward the end of the cooking time to let the food brown, if necessary.

Cooking with a Clay Pot
Most clay pots should be used only in the oven. Unglazed pots are sensitive to sudden changes of temperature, which can cause the pot to crack or break if it is placed directly over the heat.

Some clay pots can be used on top of the stove on very low heat, but it is recommended that a heat diffuser or flame-tamer is used. These are available from specialist cookware stores.

1 Some recipes suggest lightly cooking vegetables or meat in a frying pan to brown them before adding them to the clay pot. If you do this, let the browned foods cool slightly before putting them into the cold clay pot.

2 Once the browned foods have been added, it is okay to pour in warm or lukewarm cooking liquids. If what is in the pot is cold, any liquid added should be at room temperature.

USING A HEAT DIFFUSER

If your handbook states that your pot can safely be used on top of the stove, you can obviously do so, but always use a heat diffuser between the heat source and the pot.

Some cazuelas can be used on top of the stove with a heat diffuser.

Cooking in an Oven
An unglazed clay pot must always be heated gradually.

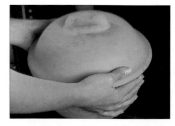

Place the clay pot in a cold oven and then heat to the required temperature. It might crack if subjected to a sudden change of temperature.

You will notice that the recipes in this book advise you to place the clay pot, which will be cold, in a cold oven, then set the oven temperature to let the oven and clay pot heat slowly.

An electric oven heats up quite gradually, giving the clay pot plenty of time to acclimatize. If, however, you are using a traditional gas oven, the flames may be too fierce for the cold clay pot. You should start by setting the oven temperature to 375°F. After 5 minutes, increase the temperature to 400°F. Continue to increase the temperature of the oven gradually, each time raising it to the next setting on your oven, until the temperature specified in the recipe has been reached.

The exact cooking times for recipes containing liquids may vary from oven to oven, as the time taken for the liquid to come to a boil will differ.

Cooking with a Cast-iron Tagine on a Stovetop

In addition to the classic all-earthenware tagines, which can't be used on a stovetop, there is a modern version that has an earthenware lid and cast-iron base. The base can be used on the top of any type of stove, be it gas, electric, or wood-burning, to brown ingredients, such as onions, vegetables, or meat before the other ingredients and liquid are added. The pot is then covered, and the tagine or stew is simmered gently on top of the stove or in the oven.

Place the cast-iron tagine base on the stovetop, add a little oil, and heat. Add the vegetables or other ingredients, and cook over medium-high heat, stirring occasionally, until browned.

Browning in a Clay Pot

A certain amount of browning will occur during cooking, depending on the cooking temperature, cooking time, and type of food. Some recipes suggest removing the lid for a short period toward the end of the cooking time to enhance the color of baked items and roasts, and also to develop a crisper finish. The oven temperature for clay-pot cooking is fairly high, so the browning process will take only a few minutes; keep a close check on the food.

To remove the lid, lift the clay pot out of the oven using pot holders, and place it on a pot stand, wooden board, or folded dish towel. Take care when lifting the lid to avoid any escaping steam.

Adding Liquids to a Clay Pot

Never add boiling liquids—or even very hot liquids—to a cold clay pot, or the sudden change in temperature may cause the claypot to crack.

If you need to add liquid to the clay pot during the cooking period, this liquid should be hot. This not only avoids a sudden temperature change, but also ensures that the food isn't cooled too much, which would slow the cooking.

Adding Flavorings

To get the best results, place herb sprigs and spices in among vegetables that are to be roasted or underneath cuts of meat. This will ensure that the flavor penetrates as deeply as possible.

Adding Ingredients during Cooking

In some recipes, ingredients that don't need to be cooked for long, such as shrimp or cooked ham, are added toward the end of the cooking time.

Remove the pot from the oven using pot holders, and remove the lid. Add the cold food, and stir well to ensure that it is distributed evenly, then re-cover the pot, and return it to the oven.

Cooking on a Barbecue

Moroccan tagines are sometimes placed on a barbecue, but they should not be too near the heat source. It is best to wait until the coals have all turned gray. Cover the coals with some sand, to make the heat less concentrated, and then let the tagine heat up slowly by initially placing it at the edge of the barbecue and gradually moving it to the hottest part.

Using a Clay Pot for Baking

Clay pots can be used for baking cakes, breads, and sponge-based desserts. It is, however, best to keep a separate clay pot for sweet foods or, alternatively, use earthenware that is glazed inside.

If you use a clay pot for baking, it is a good idea to line the base of the clay pot with a piece of baking parchment, so that the food doesn't stick to the base and is easy to remove after baking.

SAFETY FIRST

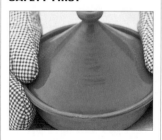

When you remove any type of clay pot from the oven, either to add extra ingredients or to serve, protect your hands with pot holders. Place the pot on a folded towel, wooden board, heatproof mat, or pot stand, as sudden contact with a cold surface could cause the pot to crack. Do the same with the lid, when you lift it off.

Clay pots should never be used under the broiler or in the freezer, as the sudden change in temperature could cause the clay pot to crack or break.

Microwave Cooking

Clay pots can be used to cook foods in the microwave oven, as well as in a conventional oven. One of the advantages with using a clay pot for microwave cooking is that, because it is moist from soaking, it will absorb some of the microwave energy. This slows down the cooking process, which is perfect for protecting delicate foods, cooking foods more evenly, and pot-roasting less tender cuts of meat, whole chickens, or game birds.

Select a clay pot that will fit inside your microwave oven. The smaller, rectangular, or round pots are ideal.

Prepare the pot as for oven cooking, by soaking it in water for 20 minutes. When setting the cooking time, refer to your microwave handbook for detailed instructions on using a clay pot, as each appliance is different. If you are adapting an existing microwave recipe, expect the food to take slightly longer to cook in a clay pot. The food is usually cooked on full (100%) power, but it may also be cooked on medium-high (70%), or medium (50%) settings so that the food simmers, rather than boils.

A safety note worth remembering is that because a clay pot is moist and absorbs microwave energy, it will become hot—hotter, in fact, than many other types of microwave cookware. Make sure you use pot holders to lift the clay pot out of the microwave, and always place the pot and lid on a pot stand, wooden board, mat, or folded dish towel when removing it from the oven, both for your own safety, and to avoid subjecting the pot to severe temperature changes.

ADAPTING RECIPES FOR CLAY-POT COOKING

A wide range of foods can be cooked in a clay pot, and you may wish to try using it for some of your favorite dishes. Find a clay-pot recipe in this book that is similar to the one you want to make, and use it as a blueprint. The main differences in cooking techniques that should be observed are these:

• When an unglazed or partially glazed clay pot is used, the oven must not be preheated.

• When the pot is put into the cold oven, it is heated gradually until it reaches the required cooking temperature. If the dish contains liquid, it must be heated until it boils. This is likely to be at a higher temperature than when cooking in another type of container, because the pot forms an insulating layer between the heat of the oven and the food. When the liquid boils, the oven temperature may then be reduced, so that the contents of the pot simmer.

• If you are using a gas stove, it is essential that you increase the temperature gradually or the transition from cold to blasting heat may cause the pot to crack.

• You will probably have to extend the cooking time to take into account the fact that the ingredients, including any liquids, are cold when put into the oven, which also starts off cold. When foods are roasted with little or no liquid, however, the cooking time stays about the same because the higher cooking temperature compensates for the insulation of the clay pot.

• Because of the moist environment, food cooked in a clay pot doesn't overcook quickly when the lid is on, however, it is important to check the food frequently if the lid is removed toward the end of cooking to promote browning, as the top of the food can easily scorch.

Cleaning and Storing Clay Pots

Before using a clay pot for the first time, brush it thoroughly inside and out to remove any loose clay particles left from the manufacturing process. Rinse the pot after brushing, then drain it. If you intend to cook in it right away, then soak it thoroughly in cold water first.

After using the pot a few times, you may notice a color change. This is completely natural and is part of the character of a clay pot. As with a well-seasoned frying pan or wok, this effect is owing to a protective layer that builds up with use and enhances the cooking qualities of the pot.

Washing the Pot

1 Wash a clay pot promptly after every use, using a brush and hot water. A soft-bristled brush is fine if the pot is not too dirty, otherwise use a firm-bristled brush. Add liquid detergent to the water if this is recommended in your handbook, as this helps to get rid of stubborn stains. Avoid using abrasive cleaning materials such as detergents, as these may affect the porous nature of the clay and may impair its cooking qualities.

2 Having washed the pot, rinse it under hot water, then stand it upside down on paper towels to drain thoroughly.

Using a Dishwasher

Most glazed earthenware dishes can be washed in the dishwasher, but some manufacturers do not recommend washing clay pots that way. Check your manufacturer's handbook.

Removing Food Residue

Sometimes food may bake onto the surface of a clay pot, especially if it has been used for cooking without the cover. Soaking the pot in hot water to which a little liquid detergent has been added is usually sufficient to release the residue. Leave the pot to soak overnight if the residue is particularly stubborn. Some earthenware dishes can be filled with hot water to remove baked-on food, but do not leave them immersed in hot soapy water.

1 If an unglazed clay pot becomes tainted with residual flavors, soak it overnight in cold water containing baking soda. If the problem is severe, or if smells still linger, fill the pot with cold water, add baking soda, and place it in a cold oven.

2 Set the oven to 350°F, and leave the clay pot to heat in the oven for about 20 minutes. Increase the temperature of the oven to 400°F, and continue to heat for 20 minutes more, then increase the oven temperature again to 450°F, and leave the pot at this temperature for 30 minutes to 1 hour.

3 Carefully lift the pot out of the oven using pot holders, and then discard the contents. Scrub the interior of the pot gently before rinsing it thoroughly with very hot water. Turn the pot and lid upside down on a rack, and leave to dry at room temperature. It is worth following this cleaning procedure after about a hundred uses, to clean the pores of your clay pot. This will let it take up water with the same efficiency as when it was brand new.

Storing the Pot

Before you put a clay pot away, make sure that it is not only completely clean, but also thoroughly dried.

Invert the lid into the base. This is not only for safety and so that it takes up less room in your kitchen, but also because placing the lid on the pot as for cooking could encourage molds and mildew to grow on the inside surfaces of the pot and lid.

It is for this reason that the pot must also be stored somewhere dry and airy. Do not leave it in a damp place. It is the nature of a clay pot to absorb moisture, so it is important to keep it completely dry during storage. Do not wrap the clay pot or seal it in a plastic bag during storage.

SLOW COOKER SOUPS

The slow cooker truly excels when it comes to soup-making—the long, gentle cooking allows the flavors to develop fully over time, giving rich, flavorsome results. This chapter draws on recipes from around the world, from North African Spiced Soup, Asian-style Duck Consommé, and Galician Broth, to French Onion Soup with Cheese Croutes, Chicken Soup with Knaidlach, and Genoese Minestrone. There are also soups for every occasion—from Spicy Pumpkin Soup for a hearty lunch and Chilled Tomato and Sweet Pepper Soup for a summer lunch party to delicate Greek Avgolemono for an elegant start to a meal.

FRENCH ONION SOUP with CHEESE CROUTES

Probably the most famous of all onion soups, this hearty, warming dish was traditionally
served as a sustaining early-morning meal to the porters and workers of Les Halles
market in Paris. Use large yellow Bermuda onions for the best result.

SERVES 4

3 tablespoons butter
2 teaspoons olive oil
2½ pounds onions, peeled and sliced
1 teaspoon superfine sugar
1 tablespoon all-purpose flour
1 tablespoon sherry vinegar
2 tablespoons brandy
½ cup dry white wine
4 cups boiling beef, chicken, or duck stock
1 teaspoon chopped fresh thyme
salt and ground black pepper

For the croutes
4 slices day-old French bread,
    about 1 inch thick
1 garlic clove, halved
1 teaspoon French mustard
½ cup grated Gruyère cheese

1 Put the butter and olive oil in the ceramic cooking pot, and heat on high for about 15 minutes until melted.

2 Add the onions to the pot, and stir to coat well in the melted butter and oil. Cover with the lid, then place a folded dish towel over the top to retain all the heat, and cook for 2 hours, stirring halfway through cooking time.

3 Add the sugar and stir well. Cover again with the lid and folded dish towel, and continue cooking on high for 4 hours, stirring two or three times, to ensure the onions are coloring evenly. At the end of this time, they should be a dark golden color.

4 Sprinkle the flour over the onions, and stir to mix. Next, stir in the vinegar followed by the brandy, then slowly blend in the wine. Stir in the stock and thyme, and season with salt and pepper. Cook on high for a further 2 hours, or until the onions are very tender.

5 For the croutes, place the bread slices under a low broiler, and cook until dry and lightly browned. Rub the bread with the cut surface of the garlic, and spread with mustard, then sprinkle the grated Gruyère cheese over the slices.

6 Turn the broiler to high, and cook the croutes for 2–3 minutes, until the cheese melts, bubbles, and browns. Ladle the soup into warmed bowls, and float a Gruyère croute on top of each. Serve immediately.

Energy 418Kcal/1747kJ; Protein 11.5g; Carbohydrate 51.8g, of which sugars 19.4g; Fat 15.9g, of which saturates 8.2g; Cholesterol 33mg; Calcium 209mg; Fiber 5.3g; Sodium 1195mg.

CARROT and CILANTRO SOUP

Root vegetables, such as carrots, are great for slow cooker soups. Their earthy flavor becomes rich and sweet when cooked slowly over a gentle heat and goes perfectly with robust herbs and spices, and their texture becomes beautifully smooth when pureed.

SERVES 4

1 pound carrots, preferably young
    and tender
1 tablespoon sunflower-seed oil
3 tablespoons butter
1 onion, chopped
1 stick celery, plus 2–3 pale leafy tops
2 small potatoes, peeled
3¾ cups boiling vegetable stock
2 teaspoons ground coriander
1 tablespoon chopped fresh cilantro
⅔ cup milk
salt and ground black pepper

3 Pour the boiling vegetable stock over the vegetables, then season with salt and ground black pepper. Cover the pot with the lid, and cook on low for 4–5 hours until the vegetables are tender.

4 Reserve 6–8 tiny celery leaves from the leafy tops for the garnish, then finely chop the remaining celery tops. Melt the remaining butter in a large pan, and add the ground coriander. Fry for about 1 minute, stirring constantly, until the aromas are released.

5 Reduce the heat under the pan, and add the chopped celery tops and fresh cilantro. Fry for about 30 seconds, then remove the pan from the heat.

6 Ladle the soup into a food processor or blender, and process until smooth, then pour into the pan with the celery tops and cilantro. Stir in the milk, and heat gently until piping hot. Check the seasoning, then serve garnished with the reserved celery leaves.

1 Trim and peel the carrots, and cut into chunks. Heat the oil and 2 tablespoons of the butter in a pan, and fry the onion over a gentle heat for 3–4 minutes until slightly softened. Do not let it brown.

2 Slice the celery, and chop the potatoes, and add them to the onion in the pan. Cook for 2 minutes, then add the carrots, and cook for a further 1 minute. Transfer the fried vegetables to the ceramic cooking pot.

Energy 168Kcal/697kJ; Protein 3g; Carbohydrate 11.9g, of which sugars 9.2g; Fat 12.4g, of which saturates 6g; Cholesterol 24mg; Calcium 94mg; Fiber 3.1g; Sodium 758mg.

TOMATO and FRESH BASIL SOUP

Peppery, aromatic basil is the perfect partner for sweet, ripe tomatoes—and it is easy to grow at home in a pot on a sunny kitchen windowsill. Make this soup in late summer when fresh tomatoes are at their best and most flavorsome.

SERVES 4

1 tablespoon olive oil
2 tablespoons butter
1 onion, finely chopped
2 pounds ripe tomatoes,
    roughly chopped
1 garlic clove, roughly chopped
2½ cups vegetable stock
½ cup dry white wine
2 tablespoons sun-dried tomato puree
2 tablespoons shredded fresh basil
⅔ cup heavy cream
salt and ground black pepper
whole basil leaves, to garnish

1 Heat the oil and butter in a large pan until foaming. Add the onion, and cook gently for about 5 minutes, stirring, until the onion is softened but not brown, then add the chopped tomatoes and garlic.

2 Add the stock, white wine and sun-dried tomato puree to the pan, and stir to combine. Heat until just below boiling point, then carefully pour the mixture into the ceramic cooking pot.

3 Switch the slow cooker to the high or auto setting, cover with the lid, and cook for 1 hour. Leave the slow cooker on auto, or switch to low and cook for a further 4–6 hours, until tender.

4 Leave the soup to cool for a few minutes, then ladle into a food processor or blender and process until smooth. Press the pureed soup through a strainer into a clean pan.

5 Add the shredded basil and the cream to the soup, and heat through, stirring. Do not allow the soup to reach boiling point. Check the consistency, and add a little more stock if necessary. Season, then pour into warmed bowls, and garnish with basil. Serve immediately.

Energy 335Kcal/1387kJ; Protein 3.1g; Carbohydrate 11.7g, of which sugars 10.8g; Fat 28.9g, of which saturates 16.4g; Cholesterol 65mg; Calcium 50mg; Fiber 3g; Sodium 168mg.

CHILLED TOMATO and BELL PEPPER SOUP

Inspired by the classic Spanish soup, gazpacho, which is made with raw salad vegetables,
this soup is cooked first and then chilled. Broiling the peppers gives a slightly smoky
flavor, but you can leave out this step to save on preparation time, if you like.

SERVES 4

2 red bell peppers
2 tablespoons olive oil
1 onion, finely chopped
2 garlic cloves, crushed
1½ pounds ripe, well-flavored tomatoes
½ cup red wine
scant 2 cups vegetable or chicken stock
½ teaspoon superfine sugar
salt and ground black pepper
chopped fresh chives, to garnish

For the croutons
2 slices white bread, crusts removed
3 tablespoons olive oil

1 Cut each pepper into quarters, and remove the core and seeds. Place each quarter, skin side up, on a broiler rack. Broil until the skins are blistered and charred, then transfer to a bowl, and cover with a plate.

2 Heat the oil in a frying pan. Add the onion and garlic, and cook gently for about 10 minutes until soft, stirring occasionally. Meanwhile, remove the skin from the peppers, and roughly chop the flesh. Cut the tomatoes into chunks.

3 Transfer the onions to the ceramic cooking pot, and add the peppers, tomatoes, wine, stock, and sugar. Cover, and cook on high for 3–4 hours, or until the vegetables are very tender. Leave the soup to stand for about 10 minutes to cool slightly.

4 Ladle the soup into a food processor or blender, and process until smooth. Press through a fine strainer into a bowl. Leave to cool before chilling in the refrigerator for at least 3 hours.

5 Meanwhile, make the croutons. Cut the bread into cubes. Heat the oil in a frying pan, add the bread, and fry until golden. Drain well on paper towels.

6 Season the soup to taste with salt and pepper, then ladle into chilled bowls. Serve topped with a few croutons and a sprinkling of chopped chives.

Energy 262Kcal/1090kJ; Protein 3.5g; Carbohydrate 17.6g, of which sugars 11.5g; Fat 18g, of which saturates 2.6g; Cholesterol 0mg; Calcium 4/mg; Fiber 3.4g; Sodium 499mg.

SPICY PUMPKIN SOUP

This stunning golden-orange soup has a smooth velvety texture, and a delicate taste, which is subtly spiced with cumin and garlic. Long, slow cooking really gives the flavors time to develop and come together to make a wonderful autumnal dish.

SERVES 4

2 pounds pumpkin, peeled
   and seeds removed
2 tablespoons olive oil
2 leeks, trimmed and sliced
1 garlic clove, crushed
1 teaspoon ground ginger
1 teaspoon ground cumin
3 cups near-boiling chicken stock
salt and ground black pepper
4 tablespoons plain yogurt, to serve
cilantro leaves, to garnish

COOK'S TIP
To save time, reheat the soup on the
stovetop rather than in the slow cooker.

1 Using a sharp knife, cut the pumpkin into large chunks. Place the chunks in the ceramic cooking pot.

2 Heat the oil in a large pan, and add the leeks and garlic. Cook gently until softened but not colored.

3 Add the ginger and cumin to the pan, and cook, stirring, for a further minute. Tip the mixture into the ceramic cooking pot, pour over the chicken stock, and season with salt and black pepper.

4 Cover the slow cooker with the lid, switch to low, and cook for 6–8 hours, or until the pumpkin is very tender.

5 Ladle the soup, in batches if necessary, into a food processor or blender, and process until smooth. Return the soup to the rinsed out cooking pot, cover, and cook on high for 1 hour, or until piping hot. Serve in warmed individual bowls, with a swirl of plain yogurt and a few cilantro leaves.

Energy 89Kcal/372kJ; Protein 2.3g; Carbohydrate 6.2g, of which sugars 4.7g; Fat 6.3g, of which saturates 1.1g; Cholesterol 0mg; Calcium 75mg; Fiber 3.1g; Sodium 127mg.

WILD MUSHROOM SOUP

This robust, creamy soup is ideal for a simple lunch or supper, served with chunks of nutty whole-grain bread spread with fresh butter. The rich flavor and color of the soup are further enhanced by the addition of dried wild mushrooms and a dash of Madeira.

SERVES 4

¼ cup dried wild mushrooms,
   such as morels, ceps, or porcini
2½ cups hot chicken or vegetable stock
2 tablespoons butter
1 onion, finely chopped
1 garlic clove, crushed
1 pound white or other cultivated
   mushrooms, trimmed and sliced
1 tablespoon all-purpose flour
fresh nutmeg
¼ teaspoon dried thyme
4 tablespoons Madeira or dry sherry
4 tablespoons crème fraîche or
   sour cream
salt and ground black pepper
chopped fresh chives, to garnish

4 Stir in the Madeira or sherry and the remaining stock, and season with salt and pepper. Bring to the boil, then transfer to the ceramic cooking pot. Cook for 1 hour, then switch to low, or leave on auto and cook for a further 3–4 hours, or until the mushrooms are very tender.

5 Ladle the soup into a food processor or blender, and process until smooth. Strain it back into the pan, pressing it with the back of a spoon to force the puree through the strainer.

6 Reheat the soup until piping hot, then stir in half the crème fraîche or sour cream. Ladle into warmed bowls, swirl a little of the remaining crème fraîche or sour cream on top of each, and sprinkle with chives.

COOK'S TIP
Dried mushrooms have a rich, intense flavor and are perfect for boosting the flavor of cultivated mushrooms, which can often be rather bland.

1 Put the dried mushrooms in a strainer, and rinse under cold running water to remove any grit, then place in the ceramic cooking pot. Pour over half of the hot chicken or vegetable stock, and cover with the lid. Switch the slow cooker to the auto or high setting.

2 Place the butter in a large pan, and melt over a medium heat. Add the chopped onion, and cook for 5–7 minutes until softened and just golden.

3 Add the garlic and fresh mushrooms to the pan, and cook for 5 minutes. Sprinkle over the flour, then grate some nutmeg into the mixture, and add the thyme. Cook for 3 minutes more, stirring all the time, until blended.

Energy 143Kcal/592kJ; Protein 3.7g; Carbohydrate 8.2g, of which sugars 3.7g; Fat 9g, of which saturates 5.3g; Cholesterol 22mg; Calcium 41mg; Fiber 2g; Sodium 174mg.

GENOESE MINESTRONE

In the Italian city of Genoa, pesto is stirred into minestrone to add extra flavor and color.
This tasty version is packed with vegetables and makes an excellent vegetarian supper
dish when served with bread. To save time, you can use ready-made bottled pesto.

SERVES 4

2 tablespoons olive oil
1 onion, finely chopped
2 celery sticks, finely chopped
1 large carrot, finely chopped
1 potato, weighing about 4 ounces,
   cut into ½-inch cubes
4 cups vegetable stock
3 ounces green beans, cut into
   2-inch pieces
1 zucchini, thinly sliced
2 Italian plum tomatoes, peeled
   and chopped
7-ounce can cannellini beans, drained
   and rinsed
¼ Savoy cabbage, shredded
1½ ounces dried "quick-cook" spaghetti
   or vermicelli, broken into short lengths

For the pesto
about 20 fresh basil leaves
1 garlic clove
2 teaspoons pine nuts
1 tablespoon freshly grated
   Parmesan cheese
1 tablespoon freshly grated
   Pecorino cheese
2 tablespoons olive oil

1 Heat the olive oil in a pan, then add the chopped onion, celery, and carrot and cook, stirring, for about 7 minutes, until the vegetables begin to soften.

2 Transfer the fried vegetables to the ceramic cooking pot. Add the potato cubes and vegetable stock, cover the cooking pot with the lid, and cook on high for 1½ hours.

3 Add the green beans, zucchini, tomatoes, and cannellini beans to the pot. Cover, and cook for 1 hour, then stir in the cabbage and pasta, and cook for a further 20 minutes.

4 Meanwhile, place all the pesto ingredients in a food processor. Blend to make a smooth sauce, adding 1–3 tablespoons water through the feeder tube to loosen the mixture if necessary.

5 Stir 2 tablespoons of the pesto sauce into the soup. Check the seasoning, adding more if necessary. Serve hot, in warmed bowls, with the remaining pesto spooned on top of each serving.

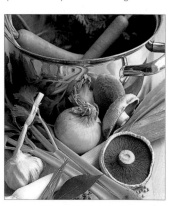

Energy 263Kcal/1098kJ; Protein 8.5g; Carbohydrate 25.1g, of which sugars 7g; Fat 14.9g, of which saturates 2.8g; Cholesterol 5mg; Calcium 103mg; Fiber 5.4g; Sodium 1034mg.

GALICIAN BROTH

This classic Galician soup from the north coast of Spain needs long, slow cooking to give the flavors time to develop fully. Traditionally, it would be made with young, green leafy turnip tops, but in this version tasty collards are used instead.

SERVES 6

1-pound gammon, in one piece, soaked
   overnight in cold water
2 bay leaves
2 onions, sliced
2 teaspoons paprika
1½ pounds baking potatoes, cut into
   1-inch chunks
8 ounces collards
15-ounce can navy or cannellini
   beans, drained
ground black pepper

COOK'S TIP
Bacon knuckles can be used instead of the gammon. The bones will give the stock a delicious flavor. If there is any broth left over, you can freeze it and use it as stock for another soup.

1 Drain the gammon, and put it in the ceramic cooking pot with the bay leaves and onions. Pour over just enough fresh cold water to cover the gammon. Switch to high, cover, and cook for 1 hour.

2 Skim off any scum, then re-cover and cook for 3 hours. Check, and skim the broth once or twice if necessary.

3 Using a slotted spoon and a large fork, carefully lift the gammon out of the slow cooker and onto a board. Add the paprika and potatoes to the broth, and cook for 1 hour.

4 Meanwhile, discard the skin and fat from the gammon, and cut the meat into small chunks. Add it to the slow cooker, and cook for a further 2 hours, or until the meat and potatoes are tender.

5 Remove the cores from the collards, then roll up the leaves, and cut into thin shreds. Add to the slow cooker with the beans and cook for 30 minutes.

6 Remove the bay leaves from the broth, season with black pepper to taste, and serve piping hot.

Energy 273Kcal/1147kJ; Protein 21.4g; Carbohydrate 33.7g, of which sugars 5.3g; Fat 6.7g, of which saturates 2g; Cholesterol 17mg; Calcium 113mg; Fiber 6.7g; Sodium 974mg.

NORTH AFRICAN SPICED SOUP

The great advantage of cooking soup in the slow cooker is that all the flavors have a chance to develop and mingle. This technique is particularly well suited to richer soups with complex spicing, such as this version of the Moroccan national soup harira.

3 Mix together the cinnamon, turmeric, ginger, cayenne pepper, and 2 tablespoons of stock to form a paste, then add to the pot with the carrots, celery, and remaining stock. Stir well, and season. Cover, and cook for 1 hour.

4 Add the chopped tomatoes, potatoes, chickpeas, and saffron to the pot. Cook for 4–5 hours until the vegetables are tender. Stir in the cilantro and the lemon juice, then check the seasoning, and adjust if necessary. Ladle into warmed bowls, and serve piping hot, with fried wedges of lemon, if you like.

SERVES 6

1 large onion, very finely chopped
4 cups near-boiling vegetable stock
1 teaspoon ground cinnamon
1 teaspoon ground turmeric
1 tablespoon grated fresh ginger root
pinch cayenne pepper
2 carrots, finely diced
2 celery sticks, finely diced
14-ounce can chopped tomatoes
1 pound potatoes, finely diced
14-ounce can chickpeas, drained
5 strands saffron
2 tablespoons chopped fresh cilantro
1 tablespoon lemon juice
salt and ground black pepper
fried wedges of lemon, to serve (optional)

1 Place the chopped onion in the ceramic cooking pot, and add 2½ cups of the nearly-boiling vegetable stock.

2 Switch the slow cooker to high or auto, cover with the lid, and cook for about 1 hour, until the onion is soft and translucent.

Energy 166Kcal/705kJ; Protein 7.5g; Carbohydrate 30.3g, of which sugars 7.4g; Fat 2.5g, of which saturates 0.3g; Cholesterol 0mg; Calcium 62mg; Fiber 5.3g; Sodium 335mg.

AVGOLEMONO

This light, delicate soup is a great favorite in Greece and is a fine example of a few carefully chosen ingredients combining to make a delicious dish. It is essential to use a stock that is well flavored, so use homemade if you can.

SERVES 4

3¾ cups near-boiling chicken stock
⅓ cup converted white rice
3 egg yolks
2–4 tablespoons lemon juice
2 tablespoons finely chopped fresh parsley
salt and ground black pepper
lemon slices and parsley sprigs, to garnish

4 Slowly add the egg mixture to the soup in the ceramic cooking pot, whisking all the time. The soup will thicken slightly and turn a pretty yellow.

5 Taste, and add more lemon juice and seasoning if necessary. Stir in the parsley, and serve immediately, garnished with lemon slices and parsley sprigs.

COOK'S TIP
When adding the egg mixture, you need to be careful not to let the soup curdle. You should avoid whisking the mixture into boiling liquid, so allow the soup to cool very slightly before whisking in the egg mixture in a slow, steady stream. Do not reheat the soup.

1 Pour the stock into the ceramic cooking pot. Cover with a lid, and cook on high for 30 minutes, or until it reaches boiling point.

2 Stir in the rice, cover, and cook for 45 minutes, or until the rice is tender. Season to taste with salt and pepper. Switch off the slow cooker, remove the lid, and leave to stand for 5 minutes.

3 Meanwhile, whisk the egg yolks in a bowl, then add about 2 tablespoons of the lemon juice, whisking constantly until the mixture is smooth and bubbly. Add a ladleful of the hot soup to the egg mixture, whisking continuously.

Energy 90Kcal/410kJ; Protein 3.3g; Carbohydrate 11.1g, of which sugars 0.3g; Fat 4.8g, of which saturates 1.3g; Cholesterol 151mg; Calcium 26mg; Fiber 0.1g; Sodium 211mg.

CABBAGE, BEET, and TOMATO BORSCHT

There are numerous versions of this classic soup, which originates in eastern Europe. Beets and sour cream are the traditional ingredients in every borscht, but other ingredients tend to be many and varied. This version has a deliciously sweet and sour taste and can be served piping hot or refreshingly chilled.

SERVES 6

1 onion, chopped
1 carrot, chopped
6 raw or vacuum-packed (cooked, not
    pickled) beets, 4 diced
    and 2 coarsely grated
14-ounce can chopped tomatoes
6 new potatoes, cut into bitesize pieces
1 small white cabbage, thinly sliced
2½ cups vegetable stock
3 tablespoons sugar
2–3 tablespoons white wine vinegar
    or cider vinegar
3 tablespoons chopped fresh dill
salt and ground black pepper
sour cream and dill, to garnish
buttered rye bread, to serve

1 Put the onion, carrot, diced beets, tomatoes, potatoes, and cabbage into the ceramic cooking pot, and pour over the vegetable stock. Cover the cooking pot with the lid, and cook on high for about 4 hours, or until the vegetables are just tender.

2 Add the grated beets, sugar, and vinegar to the pot, and stir to combine. Cook for a further hour until the beets are cooked.

3 Taste the soup, checking for a good sweet/sour balance, and add more sugar and/or vinegar if necessary. Season to taste with plenty of salt and freshly ground black pepper.

4 Just before serving, stir the chopped dill into the soup, and ladle into warmed soup bowls. Garnish each serving with a generous spoonful of sour cream and plenty more fresh dill, then serve with thick slices of buttered rye bread.

VARIATIONS
• Borscht is often served cold in summer. To serve chilled, leave it to cool at room temperature, then chill in the refrigerator for at least 4 hours. Ladle into bowls, each containing an ice cube, and top with a large spoonful of sour cream.
• For a different garnish, try scattering finely chopped hard-boiled egg or scallions over the top.

Energy 125Kcal/531kJ; Protein 3.5g; Carbohydrate 27.8g, of which sugars 7g; Fat 0.7g, of which saturates 0.1g; Cholesterol 0mg; Calcium 58mg; Fiber 3.2g; Sodium 357mg.

POTAGE of LENTILS

In this soup, red lentils and vegetables are cooked slowly until very soft, then pureed to give a rich and velvety consistency. On a hot day, serve chilled with extra lemon juice.

SERVES 4

3 tablespoons olive oil
1 onion, chopped
2 celery sticks, chopped
1 carrot, sliced
2 garlic cloves, peeled and chopped
1 potato, peeled and diced
generous 1 cup red lentils
3 cups near-boiling vegetable stock
2 bay leaves
1 small lemon
½ teaspoon ground cumin
cayenne pepper or Tabasco sauce, to taste
salt and ground black pepper
lemon slices and chopped fresh Italian
    parsley, to serve

1 Heat the oil in a frying pan. Add the onion, and cook, stirring frequently, for 5 minutes, or until beginning to soften. Stir in the celery, carrot, garlic, and potato. Cook for a further 3–4 minutes.

2 Tip the fried vegetables into the ceramic cooking pot, and switch to high. Add the lentils, vegetable stock, bay leaves, and a pared strip of lemon rind, and stir briefly to combine.

3 Cover the slow cooker with a lid, and cook on auto or high for 1 hour.

4 Leave the cooker on auto, or switch to low and cook for a further 5 hours, or until the vegetables and lentils are soft and tender.

5 Remove and discard the bay leaves and lemon rind. Process the soup in a food processor or blender until smooth. Tip the soup back into the cleaned cooking pot, stir in the cumin and cayenne pepper or Tabasco, and season.

6 Cook the soup on high for a further 45 minutes, or until piping hot. Squeeze in lemon juice to taste, and check the seasoning. Ladle into warmed bowls, and top each portion with lemon slices and a sprinkling of chopped fresh parsley.

Energy 300Kcal/1265kJ; Protein 15.0g; Carbohydrate 40.1g, of which sugars 3.6g; Fat 9.6g, of which saturates 1.3g; Cholesterol 0mg; Calcium 47mg; Fiber 3.9g; Sodium 456mg.

CHICKEN SOUP with KNAIDLACH

This famous Jewish soup is often made using a whole chicken cut into portions and slowly simmered in a huge stockpot. If you have a very large slow cooker, you can double the quantities given here, using a small whole chicken; the cooking times will remain the same. The knaidlach are cooked separately, so that the clarity of the soup is retained.

SERVES 4

2 chicken portions, about 10 ounces each
1 onion
5 cups boiling chicken stock
2 carrots, thickly sliced
2 celery sticks, thickly sliced
1 small parsnip, cut into large chunks
small pinch of ground turmeric
2 tablespoons roughly chopped fresh
    parsley, plus extra to garnish
1 tablespoon chopped fresh dill
salt and ground black pepper

For the knaidlach
¾ cup medium matzo meal
2 eggs, lightly beaten
3 tablespoons vegetable oil
2 tablespoons chopped fresh parsley
½ onion, finely grated
pinch of chicken bouillon cube (optional)
about 6 tablespoons water
salt and ground black pepper

1 Rinse the chicken pieces, and put them in the ceramic cooking pot. Peel the onion, keeping it whole. Cut a small cross in the stem end, and add to the pot with the stock, carrots, celery, parsnip, turmeric, salt, and pepper.

2 Cover with the lid, and cook on high for 1 hour. Skim off the scum that comes to the surface. (Scum will continue to form, but it is only the first scum that rises that will detract from the appearance and flavor of the soup.)

3 Cook for a further 3 hours, or until the chicken is tender. Remove the chicken, discard the skin and bones, and chop the flesh. Skim the fat off the soup, then return the pieces of chicken. Stir in the parsley and dill, and continue cooking while you make the knaidlach.

4 Put the matzo meal, eggs, oil, parsley, onion, chicken stock, if using, and water in a large bowl. Mix together well; it should be the consistency of a thick, soft paste. Cover and chill for 30 minutes, until the mixture has become firm.

5 Bring a pan of water to the boil, and have a bowl of cold water next to the stove. Dip two tablespoons into the cold water, then take a spoonful of the matzo batter. With wet hands, roll it into a ball, then slip it into the boiling water, and reduce the heat so that the water simmers. Continue with the remaining matzo batter, then cover the pan, and cook for 15–20 minutes.

6 Remove the knaidlach from the pan with a slotted spoon, and divide between individual serving bowls. Leave them to firm up for a few minutes. Ladle the hot soup over the knaidlach, and serve sprinkled with extra chopped parsley.

VARIATIONS
• Instead of knaidlach, the soup can be served over cooked rice or noodles.
• To make knaidlach with a lighter texture, separate the eggs, and add the yolks to the matzo mixture. Whisk the whites until stiff, then fold into the batter.

Energy 586Kcal/2451kJ; Protein 38.2g; Carbohydrate 42.6g, of which sugars 6.3g; Fat 30.3g, of which saturates 7.7g; Cholesterol 272mg; Calcium 131mg; Fiber 3.7g; Sodium 802mg.

SPINACH and ROOT VEGETABLE SOUP

This is a typical Russian soup, traditionally prepared when the first vegetables of spring appear. You will need to use a large slow cooker to accommodate the spinach.

SERVES 4

1 small turnip, cut into chunks
2 carrots, diced
1 small parsnip, cut into large dice
1 potato, peeled and diced
1 onion, chopped
1 garlic clove, finely chopped
¼ celeriac bulb, diced
3 cups boiling vegetable or chicken stock
6 ounces fresh spinach, roughly chopped
1 small bunch fresh dill, chopped
salt and ground black pepper

For the garnish
2 hard-boiled eggs, sliced lengthwise
1 lemon, sliced
2 tablespoons fresh parsley and dill

COOK'S TIP
For the best results, use the best quality vegetable or chicken stock.

1 Put the turnip, carrots, parsnip, potato, onion, garlic, celeriac, and stock into the ceramic cooking pot. Cook on high or auto for 1 hour, then either leave on auto or switch to low, and cook for a further 5–6 hours, until the vegetables are soft and tender.

2 Stir the spinach into the cooking pot, and cook on high for 45 minutes, or until the spinach is tender but still green and leafy. Season with salt and pepper.

3 Stir in the dill, then ladle the soup into warmed bowls, and serve garnished with egg, lemon, and a sprinkling of fresh parsley and dill.

Energy 67Kcal/280kJ; Protein 3g; Carbohydrate 11.5g, of which sugars 7g; Fat 1.3g, of which saturates 0.1g; Cholesterol 0mg; Calcium 121mg; Fiber 3.9g; Sodium 499mg.

ASIAN-STYLE DUCK CONSOMMÉ

The Vietnamese community in France has had a profound influence on French cooking.
As a result, you will find many classic French dishes brought together with Asian flavors.

SERVES 4

1 small carrot
1 small leek, halved lengthwise
4 shiitake mushrooms, thinly sliced
soy sauce
2 scallions, thinly sliced
finely shredded watercress or
   Chinese cabbage
ground black pepper

For the consommé
1 duck carcass (raw or cooked), plus
   2 legs or any giblets, trimmed of fat
1 large onion, unpeeled, with root
   end trimmed
2 carrots, cut into 1-inch pieces
1 parsnip, cut into 1-inch pieces
1 leek, cut into 1-inch pieces
2 garlic cloves, crushed
1 tablespoon black peppercorns
1-inch piece fresh ginger root,
   peeled and sliced
4 thyme sprigs or 1 teaspoon dried thyme
1 small bunch fresh cilantro

3 Line a strainer with cheesecloth, and strain the consommé into a bowl, discarding the bones and vegetables. Leave to cool, then chill for several hours or overnight. Skim off any congealed fat, and blot the surface with a paper towel to remove all traces of fat.

4 Cut the carrot and leek into 2-inch pieces. Cut each piece lengthwise into thin slices, then stack, and slice into thin julienne strips. Place the julienne strips in the clean ceramic cooking pot with the sliced shiitake mushrooms.

5 Pour over the consommé, and add a few dashes of soy sauce and some ground black pepper. Cover, and cook on high for about 45 minutes, or until piping hot, skimming off any foam that rises to the surface, with a slotted spoon.

6 Adjust the seasoning, and stir in the scallions and watercress or Chinese cabbage. Ladle into warmed bowls, and sprinkle with the fresh cilantro leaves.

1 To make the consommé, put the duck carcass, legs or giblets, onion, carrots, parsnip, leek, and garlic in the ceramic cooking pot. Add the peppercorns, ginger, thyme, and cilantro stalks (reserve the leaves), and enough cold water to cover the bones, leaving at least a 1½-inch space at the top of the pot.

2 Cover the pot with the lid, and cook on high or auto for 2 hours. Skim off any surface scum, then reduce the temperature to low or leave on auto. Cover, and cook for a further 4 hours, removing the lid for the last hour.

Energy 96Kcal/406kJ; Protein 7.1g; Carbohydrate 12.1g, of which sugars 7.9g; Fat 2.5g, of which saturates 0.6g; Cholesterol 28mg; Calcium 51mg; Fiber 4g; Sodium 47mg.

HOT and SOUR SHRIMP SOUP

This salty, sour, spicy hot Thai soup, known as Tom Yam Kung, *is a real classic. Cooking the stock in the slow cooker maximizes the flavor before the final ingredients are added.*

SERVES 4

1 pound raw jumbo shrimp,
   thawed if frozen
3¾ cups near-boiling light chicken stock
   or water
3 lemongrass stalks
6 kaffir lime leaves, torn in half
8 ounces straw mushrooms, drained
3 tablespoons Thai fish sauce
4 tablespoons fresh lime juice
2 tablespoons chopped scallion
1 tablespoon fresh cilantro leaves
4 fresh red chiles, seeded and
   thickly sliced
salt and ground black pepper

1 Peel the shrimp, reserving the shells. Using a sharp knife, make a shallow cut along the back of each shrimp, and use the point of the knife to remove the thin black vein. Place the shrimp in a bowl, cover, and place in the refrigerator until ready to use.

2 Rinse the reserved shrimp shells under cold running water, then put them in the ceramic cooking pot, and add the chicken stock or water. Cover with the lid, and switch the slow cooker to high.

3 Using a pestle, bruise the bulbous end of the lemongrass stalks. Lift the lid of the ceramic pot, and quickly add the lemongrass stalks and half the torn kaffir lime leaves to the stock. Stir well, then re-cover with the lid, and cook for about 2 hours until the stock is fragrant and aromatic.

4 Strain the stock into a large bowl, and rinse out the ceramic cooking pot. Pour the stock back into the cleaned pot. Add the drained mushrooms, and cook on high for 30 minutes.

5 Add the shrimp to the soup, and cook for a further 10 minutes, until the shrimp turn pink and are cooked.

6 Stir the fish sauce, lime juice, scallion, cilantro, chiles, and remaining lime leaves into the soup. Taste, and adjust the seasoning if necessary. The soup should be sour, salty, spicy, and hot.

Energy 127Kcal/536kJ; Protein 27g; Carbohydrate 1.4g, of which sugars 1.2g; Fat 1.4g, of which saturates 0.3g; Cholesterol 315mg; Calcium 133mg; Fiber 0.7g; Sodium 2715mg.

ONE-POT, CLAY-POT SOUPS

There's something supremely comforting about hot soup, and when you prepare it yourself, the aroma insures that the pleasure starts long before you lift the ladle. Nourishing, easy to digest, quick to cook, and convenient, soup provides the perfect meal-in-a-bowl at lunchtime or a warming after-school snack, and when served as a first course, it gives guests a real sense of welcome. Mediterranean Leek and Fish Soup with Tomatoes, Italian Farmhouse Soup, Seafood Chowder, and Bean and Pistou Soup are just some of the treats in store.

CATALAN POTATO and FAVA BEAN SOUP

While they are in season fresh fava beans are perfect, but canned or frozen are just as good in this creamy, richly flavored soup.

SERVES 6

2 tablespoons olive oil
2 onions, chopped
3 large mealy potatoes, diced
1 pound fresh shelled fava beans
7½ cups vegetable or chicken stock
1 bunch cilantro, finely chopped
⅔ cup light cream
salt and ground black pepper
fresh cilantro leaves,
    to garnish

COOK'S TIP
Fava beans sometimes have a tough outer skin, particularly if they are large. To remove this, first cook the beans briefly in boiling water, then peel off the skin, and add the tender, bright green center part to the soup.

1 Heat the olive oil in a large pan, add the chopped onions, and cook, stirring occasionally with a wooden spoon, for about 5 minutes, until they are just softened but not brown.

2 Add the diced potatoes, shelled fava beans (reserving a few for garnishing), and vegetable or chicken stock to the pan. Bring to a boil, then simmer gently for 5 minutes.

3 Stir in the finely chopped cilantro and simmer for 10 minutes more.

4 Process the soup, in batches, in a food processor or blender, then return the soup to the rinsed-out pan.

5 Stir in the cream (reserving a little for garnishing), season, and bring to a simmer. Serve garnished with more cilantro leaves, beans, and cream.

SPANISH POTATO and GARLIC SOUP

Traditionally served in shallow earthenware dishes, this delicious, classic Spanish soup is a great choice for vegetarians.

SERVES 6

2 tablespoons olive oil
1 large onion, thinly sliced
4 garlic cloves, crushed
1 large potato, halved and cut
    into thin slices
1 teaspoon paprika
14-ounce can chopped tomatoes, drained
1 teaspoon thyme leaves, plus extra
    chopped thyme leaves, to garnish
3¾ cups vegetable stock
1 teaspoon cornstarch
salt and ground black pepper

COOK'S TIP
Paprika is a popular spice in many Spanish dishes. It is made from red bell peppers that are dried and powdered into a coarse-grained spice. It has a slightly sweet, mild flavor and a rich red color.

1 Heat the oil in a large, heavy pan, add the onion, garlic, potato, and paprika and cook, stirring occasionally, for about 5 minutes, or until the onions have softened but not browned.

2 Add the chopped tomatoes, thyme leaves, and vegetable stock to the pan and simmer for 15–20 minutes, until the potatoes have cooked through.

3 In a small bowl, mix the cornstarch with a little water to form a smooth paste, then stir into the soup. Bring to a boil, stirring, then simmer for about 5 minutes, until the soup has thickened.

4 Using a wooden spoon, break up the potatoes slightly, then season to taste. Serve the soup garnished with the extra chopped thyme leaves.

Catalan Potato and Broad Bean Soup: Energy 236Kcal/990kJ; Protein 9.3g; Carbohydrate 30.3g, of which sugars 4.6g; Fat 9.4g, of which saturates 3.8g; Cholesterol 14mg; Calcium 94mg; Fiber 6.8g; Sodium 30mg.
Spanish Potato and Garlic Soup: Energy 86Kcal/359kJ; Protein 1.5g; Carbohydrate 11.5g, of which sugars 4.4g; Fat 4.1g, of which saturates 0.6g; Cholesterol 0mg; Calcium 15mg; Fiber 1.5g; Sodium 12mg.

LENTIL and PASTA SOUP

This rustic vegetarian soup makes a warming winter meal and goes especially well with multigrain or crusty Italian bread.

SERVES 4–6

¾ cup brown lentils
3 garlic cloves, unpeeled
4 cups water
3 tablespoons olive oil
2 tablespoons butter
1 onion, finely chopped
2 celery stalks, finely chopped
2 tablespoons sun-dried tomato paste
7½ cups vegetable stock
a few fresh marjoram leaves
a few fresh basil leaves
leaves from 1 fresh thyme sprig
½ cup dried small pasta shapes, such as
    macaroni or tubetti
salt and ground black pepper
tiny fresh herb leaves,
    to garnish

1 Put the lentils in a large pan. Smash one of the garlic cloves using the blade of a large knife (there's no need to peel it first), then add it to the lentils. Pour in the water, and bring to a boil. Simmer for about 20 minutes, or until the lentils are tender. Tip the lentils into a strainer, remove the garlic, and set it aside. Rinse the lentils under cold water, and leave to drain.

2 Heat 2 tablespoons of the oil with half the butter in the pan. Add the onion and celery, and cook gently for 5 minutes.

3 Crush the remaining garlic, then peel, and mash the reserved garlic. Add to the pan with the remaining oil, the tomato paste, and the lentils. Stir, then add the stock, herbs, and salt and pepper. Bring to a boil, stirring. Simmer for 30 minutes, stirring occasionally.

4 Add the pasta, and bring the soup back to a boil, stirring. Reduce the heat, and simmer until the pasta is just tender. Add the remaining butter to the pan, and stir until melted. Taste the soup for seasoning, then serve hot in warmed bowls, sprinkled with herb leaves.

Energy 206Kcal/865kJ; Protein 8.1g; Carbohydrate 23.5g, of which sugars 1.7g; Fat 9.5g, of which saturates 3g; Cholesterol 9mg; Calcium 24mg; Fiber 1.9g; Sodium 42mg.

ITALIAN FARMHOUSE SOUP

Root vegetables form the base of this chunky, minestrone-style main meal soup. You can vary the vegetables according to what you have at hand.

SERVES 4

2 tablespoons olive oil
1 onion, coarsely chopped
3 carrots, cut into large chunks
6–7 ounces turnips, cut into
    large chunks
6 ounces rutabaga, cut into
    large chunks
14-ounce can chopped Italian tomatoes
1 tablespoon tomato paste
1 teaspoon dried mixed herbs
1 teaspoon dried oregano
2 ounces dried bell peppers, washed and
    thinly sliced (optional)
6¼ cups vegetable stock or water
½ cup dried small macaroni
    or conchiglie
14-ounce can red kidney beans, rinsed
    and drained
2 tablespoons chopped fresh Italian parsley
salt and ground black pepper
freshly grated Parmesan cheese,
    to serve

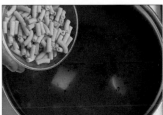

1 Heat the olive oil in a large pan, add the onion, and cook over low heat for about 5 minutes, until softened. Add the carrot, turnip, and rutabaga chunks, canned chopped tomatoes, tomato paste, dried mixed herbs, dried oregano, and dried peppers, if using. Stir in salt and pepper to taste.

2 Pour in the vegetable stock or water, and bring to a boil. Stir well, cover the pan, then lower the heat, and simmer for 30 minutes, stirring occasionally.

3 Add the pasta to the pan, and bring quickly to a boil, stirring. Lower the heat and simmer, uncovered, for about 5 minutes, until the pasta is only just tender, or according to the instructions on the packet. Stir frequently.

4 Stir in the kidney beans. Heat through for 2–3 minutes, then remove the pan from the heat, and stir in the parsley. Taste the soup for seasoning. Serve hot in warmed soup bowls, with grated Parmesan cheese handed separately.

Energy 248Kcal/1047kJ; Protein 10.2g; Carbohydrate 38.6g, of which sugars 14.9g; Fat 7g, of which saturates 1.1g; Cholesterol 0mg; Calcium 139mg; Fiber 10.6g; Sodium 422mg.

BROCCOLI, ANCHOVY, and PASTA SOUP

This wonderfully chunky and flavorful soup is from Puglia in the south of Italy, where anchovies and broccoli are often used together.

SERVES 4

2 tablespoons olive oil
1 garlic clove, finely chopped
¼–⅓ fresh red chile, seeded and
    finely chopped
2 drained canned anchovies
1 small onion, finely chopped
scant 1 cup bottled strained tomatoes
3 tablespoons dry white wine
5 cups vegetable or light
    chicken stock
11 ounces broccoli flowerets
1¾ cups dried orecchiette pasta or other
    medium-size pasta shapes
salt and ground black pepper
freshly grated Romano cheese,
    to serve

1 Heat the oil in a large pan. Add the garlic, chile, anchovies, and onion, and cook over low heat, stirring constantly, for 5–6 minutes.

2 Add the tomatoes and wine, with salt and pepper to taste. Bring to a boil, cover, then cook over low heat, stirring occasionally, for 12–15 minutes.

3 Pour in the stock. Bring to a boil, then add the broccoli, and simmer for about 5 minutes. Add the pasta and bring back to a boil, stirring. Simmer, stirring frequently, for 7–8 minutes, until the pasta is just tender, or according to the package instructions. Taste for seasoning. Serve hot, in warmed bowls. Hand around grated Romano separately.

PASTA SQUARES and PEAS in BROTH

This thick, filling Italian soup, flavored with pancetta or bacon and prosciutto, is traditionally made with homemade pasta and fresh peas. In this modern, more convenient version, ready-made fresh lasagne sheets are used with frozen peas, to save time.

SERVES 4–6

2 tablespoons butter
2 ounces pancetta or rindless smoked
    fatty bacon, coarsely chopped
1 small onion, finely chopped
1 celery stalk, finely chopped
3½ cups frozen peas
1 teaspoon tomato paste
1–2 teaspoon finely chopped fresh
    Italian parsley
4 cups chicken stock
11 ounces fresh lasagne sheets
about 2 ounces prosciutto, diced
salt and ground black pepper
freshly grated Parmesan cheese, to serve

1 Melt the butter in a large pan, and add the pancetta or rindless smoked bacon, with the chopped onion and chopped celery. Cook together over low heat, stirring constantly, for 5 minutes.

2 Add the frozen peas to the pan, and cook, stirring, for 3–4 minutes. Stir in the tomato paste and finely chopped parsley, then add the chicken stock, with salt and pepper to taste. Bring to a boil. Cover, lower the heat, and simmer the soup for 10 minutes.

3 Meanwhile, using a large, sharp knife and a rule, cut the lasagne sheets into ¾-inch squares.

4 Taste the soup for seasoning. Drop the pasta into the pan, then stir, and bring to a boil. Simmer for 2 minutes, or until the pasta is just tender, then stir in the prosciutto. Serve hot with grated Parmesan handed around separately.

COOK'S TIP
Take care when seasoning the soup with salt, because of the saltiness of the pancetta and the prosciutto.

Broccoli, Anchovy and Pasta Soup: Energy 268Kcal/1131kJ; Protein 10.3g; Carbohydrate 41.2g, of which sugars 5.2g; Fat 7.3g, of which saturates 1.1g; Cholesterol 1mg; Calcium 69mg; Fiber 3.9g; Sodium 182mg.
Pasta Squares and Peas in Broth: Energy 175Kcal/730kJ; Protein 9.5g; Carbohydrate 19.7g, of which sugars 2.6g; Fat 7.1g, of which saturates 3.2g; Cholesterol 19mg; Calcium 24mg; Fiber 4g; Sodium 236mg.

CORN and POTATO CHOWDER

This creamy yet chunky soup is rich with the sweet taste of corn. It's excellent served with thick, crusty bread and topped with some grated Cheddar cheese.

2 Heat until the oil and butter are sizzling, then reduce the heat to low. Cover the pan, and cook gently for about 10 minutes, until the vegetables are just softened, shaking the pan occasionally.

3 Pour in the stock, season with salt and pepper to taste, and bring to a boil. Reduce the heat, cover the pan again, and simmer gently, stirring occasionally, for about 15 minutes, or until the vegetables are tender.

SERVES 4

1 onion, chopped
1 garlic clove, crushed
1 medium baking potato, chopped
2 celery stalks, sliced
1 green bell pepper, seeded and sliced
2 tablespoons sunflower-seed oil
2 tablespoons butter
2½ cups vegetable stock
1¼ cups milk
7-ounce can cannellini or navy beans
11-ounce can corn
good pinch of dried sage
salt and ground black pepper
freshly grated Cheddar cheese,
    to serve

1 Put the onion, garlic, potato, celery, and green bell pepper into a large, heavy pan with the sunflower-seed oil and butter.

4 Add the milk, canned beans, and corn—including their liquids. Stir in the dried sage, and simmer, uncovered, for 5 minutes, then check the seasoning, and adjust to taste. Serve hot in bowls, sprinkled with the grated Cheddar cheese.

Energy 275Kcal/1161kJ; Protein 9.6g; Carbohydrate 43.3g, of which sugars 16.5g; Fat 8.3g, of which saturates 1.8g; Cholesterol 4mg; Calcium 141mg; Fiber 5.5g; Sodium 441mg.

BEAN and PISTOU SOUP

This hearty vegetarian soup is a typical Provencal-style soup, richly flavored with a homemade garlic and fresh basil pistou sauce.

SERVES 4–6

scant 1 cup dried navy beans, soaked
    overnight in cold water
scant 1 cup dried cannellini beans, soaked
    overnight in cold water
1 onion, chopped
5 cups hot vegetable stock
2 carrots, coarsely chopped
8 ounces Savoy cabbage, shredded
1 large potato, about 8 ounces,
    coarsely chopped
8 ounces green beans, chopped
salt and ground black pepper
fresh basil leaves, to garnish

For the pistou
4 garlic cloves
8 large, fresh sprigs basil leaves
6 tablespoons olive oil
4 tablespoons freshly grated
    Parmesan cheese

3 Add the chopped carrots, shredded cabbage, chopped potato, and green beans to the bean pot. Season with salt and pepper, cover, and return the pot to the oven. Reduce the oven temperature to 350°F, and cook for 1 hour, or until all the vegetables are cooked right through and the flavors have mingled.

4 Meanwhile, place the garlic and basil in a mortar and pound with a pestle, then gradually beat in the oil. Stir in the grated Parmesan. Stir half the pistou into the soup, and then ladle into warmed soup bowls. Top each bowl of soup with a spoonful of the remaining pistou, and serve garnished with basil.

1 Soak a bean pot in cold water for 20 minutes, then drain. Drain the soaked navy and cannellini beans, and place in the bean pot. Add the chopped onion, and pour over sufficient cold water to come 2 inches above the beans. Cover and place the pot in an unheated oven. Set the oven to 400°F and cook for about 1½ hours, or until the beans are cooked through and tender.

2 Drain the beans and onions. Place half the beans and onions in a food processor or blender, and process to a paste. Return the drained beans and the bean paste to the bean pot. Add the hot vegetable stock.

Energy 305Kcal/1281kJ; Protein 17.2g; Carbohydrate 34.6g, of which sugars 7.5g; Fat 11.8g, of which saturates 3.3g; Cholesterol 10mg; Calcium 215mg; Fiber 10.8g; Sodium 133mg.

MEDITERRANEAN SAUSAGE and PESTO SOUP

This hearty soup makes a satisfying one-pot meal that brings the summery flavor of basil to midwinter meals. Thick slices of warm crusty bread make the perfect accompaniment.

SERVES 4

oil, for deep-frying
1 pound smoked pork sausages
a handful of fresh basil leaves
1 tablespoon olive oil
1 red onion, chopped
1 cup red lentils
14-ounce can chopped tomatoes
   with herbs
4 cups chicken stock or water
salt and ground black pepper
4 tablespoons pesto,
   to serve

COOK'S TIP

The flavor of smoked sausages is very good in this soup, but you could use ordinary fresh sausages if you like. Choose coarse-textured sausages, such as Toulouse.

1 Heat the oil for deep-frying to 375°F, or until a cube of day-old bread browns in about 60 seconds. Slice one of the sausages diagonally, and deep-fry for 2–3 minutes, or until brown and crisp. Add the basil leaves, and deep-fry for a few seconds, until crisp. Lift out the sausage slices and basil leaves, using a slotted spoon, and drain them on paper towels. Strain the oil into a bowl.

2 Heat the olive oil in the pan, add the chopped red onion, and cook until softened. Coarsely chop the remaining sausages, and add them to the pan. Cook, stirring, for about 5 minutes, or until the sausages are cooked.

3 Stir in the lentils, tomatoes, and stock or water, and bring to a boil. Reduce the heat, cover, and simmer for about 20 minutes. Cool the soup slightly before processing it in a blender. Return the soup to the rinsed-out pan.

4 Reheat the soup, add seasoning to taste, then ladle into warmed individual soup bowls. Sprinkle the soup with the deep-fried sausage slices and basil, and swirl a little pesto through each portion just before serving. Serve with plenty of warm crusty bread.

Energy 738Kcal/3075kJ; Protein 26.2g; Carbohydrate 46.7g, of which sugars 6.9g; Fat 50.9g, of which saturates 15.8g; Cholesterol 53mg; Calcium 86mg; Fiber 4.5g; Sodium 885mg

MOROCCAN SPICED LAMB SOUP

Classic north African spices—ginger, turmeric, and cinnamon—are combined with garbanzo beans and lamb to make this hearty, warming soup.

SERVES 6

½ cup garbanzo beans, soaked overnight
1 tablespoon butter
8 ounces lamb, cut into cubes
1 onion, chopped
1 pound tomatoes, peeled and chopped
a few celery leaves, chopped
2 tablespoons chopped fresh parsley
1 tablespoon chopped fresh cilantro
½ teaspoon ground ginger
½ teaspoon ground turmeric
1 teaspoon ground cinnamon
7½ cups water
scant ⅓ cup green lentils
3 ounces vermicelli or
    ¾ cup soup pasta
2 egg yolks
juice of ½–1 lemon
salt and ground black pepper
fresh cilantro, to garnish
lemon wedges, to serve

1 Drain the garbanzos, rinse under cold water, and set aside. Melt the butter in a large, flameproof casserole or pan, and cook the lamb and onion, stirring, for 2–3 minutes, until the lamb is browned.

2 Add the chopped tomatoes, celery leaves, herbs, and spices and season well with ground black pepper. Cook for about 1 minute, then stir in the water, and add the green lentils and the soaked, drained and rinsed garbanzos.

3 Slowly bring to a boil and skim the surface to remove the froth. Boil rapidly for 10 minutes, then reduce the heat, and simmer very gently for 2 hours, or until the garbanzos are very tender.

4 Season with salt and pepper, then add the vermicelli or soup pasta to the pan, and cook for 5–6 minutes, until it is just tender. If the soup is very thick at this stage, add a little more water.

5 Beat the egg yolks with the lemon juice, and stir into the simmering soup. Immediately remove the soup from the heat, and stir until thickened. Pour into warmed serving bowls, and garnish with plenty of fresh cilantro. Serve the soup with lemon wedges.

COOK'S TIP

If you have forgotten to soak the garbanzos overnight, place them in a pan with about four times their volume of cold water. Bring very slowly to a boil, then cover the pan, remove it from the heat, and let stand for 45 minutes before using as described in the recipe.

Energy 248Kcal/1042kJ; Protein 16.3g; Carbohydrate 25.8g, of which sugars 4.1g; Fat 9.5g, of which saturates 4g; Cholesterol 101mg; Calcium 64mg; Fiber 3.6g; Sodium 70mg.

CHINESE CHICKEN and CHILE SOUP

Ginger and lemongrass add an aromatic note to this tasty, refreshing soup, which can be served as a light lunch or an appetizer.

2 Place the Chinese sand pot in an unheated oven. Set the temperature to 400°F, and cook the soup for 30–40 minutes, or until the stock is simmering and the chicken and vegetables are tender.

3 Add the scallions and mushrooms, cover, and return the pot to the oven for 10 minutes. Meanwhile, place the noodles in a large bowl, and cover with boiling water—soak for the required time, following the package instructions.

4 Drain the noodles, and divide among four warmed serving bowls. Stir the soy sauce into the soup, and season with salt and pepper. Divide the soup among the bowls, and serve immediately.

COOK'S TIP

Rice noodles are available in a variety of thicknesses and can be bought in straight lengths or in coils or loops. They are a creamy white color and very brittle in texture. Rice noodles are precooked, so they only require a very short soaking time—check the package for exact timings. Vermicelli rice noodles are very fine and will need to be soaked for only a few minutes.

SERVES 4

5 ounces boneless chicken breast portions, cut into thin strips
1-inch piece fresh ginger root, finely chopped
2-inch piece lemongrass stalk, finely chopped
1 red chile, seeded and thinly sliced
8 baby corn cobs, halved lengthwise
1 large carrot, cut into thin sticks
4 cups hot chicken stock
4 scallions, thinly sliced
12 small shiitake mushrooms, sliced
1 cup vermicelli rice noodles
2 tablespoons soy sauce
salt and ground black pepper

1 Place the chicken strips, chopped ginger, chopped lemongrass, and sliced chile in a Chinese sand pot. Add the halved baby corn and the carrot sticks. Pour over the hot chicken stock, and cover the pot.

Energy 168Kcal/707kJ; Protein 13.7g; Carbohydrate 26.1g, of which sugars 3.1g; Fat 1g, of which saturates 0.2g; Cholesterol 26mg; Calcium 25mg; Fiber 1.7g; Sodium 853mg.

CHICKEN and LEEK SOUP with PRUNES and BARLEY

This recipe is based on the traditional Scottish soup, Cock-a-leekie. The unusual combination of leeks and prunes is surprisingly delicious.

3 Bring the stock to a boil, then reduce the heat, and cover the pan. Simmer gently for 1 hour. Skim off any scum when the water first starts to boil and occasionally during simmering.

4 Add the chicken breast portions to the pan, and continue to cook for another 30 minutes, until they are just cooked. Leave until cool enough to handle, then strain the stock. Reserve the chicken breast portions and the meat from the carcass. Discard all the skin, bones, cooked vegetables, and herbs. Skim as much fat as you can from the stock, then return it to the pan.

5 Add the pearl barley to the stock. Bring to a boil over medium heat, then lower the heat, and cook very gently for 15–20 minutes, until the barley is just cooked and tender. Season the soup with 1 teaspoon each salt and ground black pepper.

6 Add the ready-to-eat prunes to the pan, then thinly slice the remaining leeks, and add them to the pan. Bring to a boil, then cover the pan, and simmer gently for about 10 minutes, or until the leeks are just cooked.

7 Slice the chicken breast portions and then add them to the soup with the remaining chicken meat from the carcass, sliced or cut into neat pieces. Reheat the soup, if necessary, then ladle it into warm, deep soup plates, and sprinkle with plenty of chopped parsley to serve.

SERVES 6

⅔ cup pearl barley
1 chicken, weighing about 4¼ pounds
2 pounds leeks
1 fresh bay leaf
a few fresh parsley stalks and
   thyme sprigs
1 large carrot, thickly sliced
10 cups chicken or
   beef stock
14 ounces ready-to-eat prunes
salt and ground black pepper
chopped fresh parsley, to garnish

1 Rinse the pearl barley thoroughly in a strainer under cold running water, then cook it in a large pan of boiling water for about 10 minutes. Drain the barley, rinse well again, and drain thoroughly. Set aside in a cool place.

2 Cut the breast portions off the chicken and set aside, then place the remaining chicken carcass in the pan. Cut half the leeks into 2-inch lengths, and add them to the pan. Tie the herbs together into a bouquet garni, and add to the pan with the carrot and stock.

Energy 273Kcal/1158kJ; Protein 21.7g; Carbohydrate 44.4g, of which sugars 27.2g; Fat 2.1g, of which saturates 0.4g; Cholesterol 47mg; Calcium 70mg; Fiber 7.5g; Sodium 55mg.

BOUILLABAISSE

Perhaps the most famous of all Mediterranean fish soups, this recipe, originating from Marseilles in the south of France, is a rich and colorful mixture of fish and shellfish, flavored with tomatoes, saffron, and orange.

SERVES 4–6

3–3½ pounds mixed fish and shellfish, such
    as red snapper, John Dory, monkfish,
    large shrimp, and clams
5 cups water
8 ounces tomatoes
pinch of saffron threads
6 tablespoons olive oil
1 onion, sliced
1 leek, sliced
1 celery stalk, sliced
2 garlic cloves, crushed
bouquet garni
1 strip pared orange rind
½ teaspoon fennel seeds
1 tablespoon tomato paste
2 teaspoons Pernod
4–6 thick slices French bread
3 tablespoons chopped fresh parsley
salt and ground black pepper

1 Remove the heads, tails, and fins from the fish, and put in a large pan, with the water. Bring to a boil, and simmer for 15 minutes. Strain, and reserve the liquid.

2 Cut the fish into large chunks. Leave the shellfish in their shells.

3 Scald the tomatoes, then drain, and refresh in cold water. Peel and chop them. Soak the saffron in 1–2 tablespoons hot water. Heat the oil in the cleaned pan, add the onion, leek, and celery, and cook until softened. Add the garlic, bouquet garni, orange rind, fennel seeds, and tomatoes, then stir in the saffron and liquid and the fish stock. Season with salt and pepper, then bring to a boil, and simmer for 30–40 minutes.

4 Add the shellfish, and boil for about 6 minutes. Discard any clams that remain closed. Add the fish, and cook for 6–8 minutes more, until it flakes easily. Using a slotted spoon, transfer the fish to a warmed serving platter. Keep the liquid boiling, and add the tomato paste and Pernod, then check the seasoning. Place a slice of bread in each soup bowl, pour the broth over it, and serve the fish separately, sprinkled with the parsley.

Energy 338Kcal/1418kJ; Protein 42.2g; Carbohydrate 12.8g, of which sugars 3.8g; Fat 13.2g, of which saturates 1.9g; Cholesterol 100mg; Calcium 55mg; Fiber 1.6g; Sodium 239mg.

MEDITERRANEAN LEEK and FISH SOUP with TOMATOES

This chunky soup, which is almost a stew, makes a robust and wonderfully aromatic meal in a bowl. Serve it with crisp-toasted croutes spread with a spicy garlic mayonnaise.

SERVES 4

2 tablespoons olive oil
2 large thick leeks, white and green
    parts separated
1 teaspoon crushed coriander seeds
good pinch of dried red chili flakes
11 ounces small salad potatoes,
    thickly sliced
7-ounce can chopped tomatoes
2½ cups fish stock
⅔ cup fruity white wine
1 fresh bay leaf
1 star anise
1 strip pared orange rind
good pinch of saffron threads
1 pound white fish fillets, such as sea bass,
    monkfish, cod, or haddock, skinned
1 pound small squid, cleaned
9 ounces uncooked peeled shrimp
2–3 tablespoons chopped
    fresh parsley
salt and ground black pepper

For the garlic croutes
1 short French loaf, sliced and toasted
spicy garlic mayonnaise

1 Gently heat the olive oil in a pan, then thinly slice the green part of the leeks. Add with the crushed coriander seeds and the dried red chili flakes, and cook for 5 minutes, stirring occasionally.

1 Gently heat the olive oil in a pan, then thinly slice the green part of the leeks. Add with the crushed coriander seeds and the dried red chili flakes, and cook for 5 minutes, stirring occasionally.

3 Bring to a boil, then reduce the heat, and partly cover the pan. Simmer for about 20 minutes, until the potatoes are tender. Taste and adjust the seasoning.

4 Cut the fish into chunks. Cut the squid sacs into rectangles, and score a criss-cross pattern into them without cutting right through.

5 Add the fish to the soup, cook gently for 4 minutes, then add the shrimp, and cook for 1 minute. Add the squid and the thinly sliced white part of the leek, and cook, stirring occasionally, for 2 minutes.

6 Stir in the chopped parsley, and serve with the toasted croutes topped with spicy garlic mayonnaise.

Energy 383Kcal/1615kJ; Protein 52g; Carbohydrate 17.8g, of which sugars 4.7g; Fat 9.4g, of which saturates 1.6g; Cholesterol 427mg; Calcium 107mg; Fiber 3.2g; Sodium 326mg.

COCONUT and SEAFOOD SOUP with GARLIC CHIVES

The long list of ingredients in this Thai-inspired recipe could mislead you into thinking that this soup is complicated. In fact, it is very easy to put together.

SERVES 4

2½ cups fish stock
5 thin slices fresh ginger root
2 lemongrass stalks, chopped
3 kaffir lime leaves, shredded
1 ounce garlic chives (1 bunch), chopped
½ ounce fresh cilantro
1 tablespoon vegetable oil
4 shallots, chopped
1¾ cups coconut milk
2–3 tablespoons Thai fish sauce
3–4 tablespoons Thai green curry paste
1 pound uncooked jumbo shrimp, peeled and deveined
1 pound prepared squid
a little lime juice (optional)
salt and ground black pepper
4 tablespoons fried shallot slices, to serve

1 Pour the stock into a pan, and add the slices of fresh ginger, the chopped lemongrass, and half the lime leaves.

2 Add half the chopped chives to the pan with the cilantro stalks. Bring to a boil, then reduce the heat. Cover the pan, then simmer gently for 20 minutes. Strain the stock.

3 Rinse the pan, then add the oil and shallots. Cook over medium heat for 5–10 minutes, stirring occasionally, until the shallots are just beginning to brown. Stir in the stock, coconut milk, the remaining lime leaves, and half the fish sauce. Heat gently until the soup is just simmering, then cook over low heat for 5–10 minutes.

4 Stir in the curry paste and the peeled shrimp, and cook for 3 minutes. Add the squid, cook for 2 minutes more. Add the lime juice, if using, and season.

5 Stir in the remaining fish sauce, chopped chives, and the chopped cilantro leaves. Serve the soup in warmed, shallow bowls sprinkled with fried shallots.

VARIATIONS

• Instead of squid, you could add 14 ounces firm white fish, such as monkfish, cut into small pieces.
• You could also replace the squid with fresh mussels. Steam 1½ pounds closed mussels in a tightly covered pan for about 3 minutes, or until the shells have opened. Discard any that remain shut, then remove the mussels from their shells.

Energy 282Kcal/1185kJ; Protein 37.9g; Carbohydrate 7.7g, of which sugars 6g; Fat 11.3g, of which saturates 1.9g; Cholesterol 473mg; Calcium 156mg; Fiber 0.7g; Sodium 451mg.

CLAM, MUSHROOM, and POTATO CHOWDER

The delicate, sweet taste of clams and the soft earthiness of wild mushrooms combine
with potatoes to make this a great meal on its own—fit for any occasion.

SERVES 4

48 clams, scrubbed
¼ cup sweet butter
1 large onion, chopped
1 celery stalk, sliced
1 carrot, sliced
8 ounces assorted wild and
    cultivated mushrooms
8 ounces mealy potatoes,
    thickly sliced
5 cups boiling light chicken or
    vegetable stock
1 thyme sprig
4 parsley stalks
salt and ground black pepper
fresh thyme sprigs,
    to garnish

1 Place the clams in a large, heavy pan, discarding any that are open. Add ½ inch of water to the pan, then cover, and bring to a boil. Cook over medium heat for 6–8 minutes, shaking the pan occasionally, until the clams open (discard any clams that do not open).

2 Drain the clams over a bowl, and remove most of the shells, leaving some in the shells as a garnish. Strain the cooking juices into the bowl, add all the clams, and set aside.

3 Add the butter, onion, celery, and carrot to the pan, and cook gently until softened but not colored. Add the mushrooms, and cook for 3–4 minutes, until their juices begin to appear. Add the potato slices, the clams and their juices, the stock, thyme, and parsley stalks.

4 Bring to a boil, then reduce the heat, cover, and simmer for 25 minutes. Season to taste, ladle into soup bowls, and garnish with thyme sprigs.

Energy 203Kcal/848kJ; Protein 10.8g; Carbohydrate 15.8g, of which sugars 5.2g; Fat 11.2g, of which saturates 6.8g; Cholesterol 60mg; Calcium 66mg; Fiber 2.4g; Sodium 696mg.

SEAFOOD CHOWDER

Chowder takes its name from the French word for cauldron—chaudière—the type of pot once traditionally used for soups and stews. Like most chowders, this is a substantial dish, which is good served with crusty bread for a lunch or supper.

SERVES 4–6

generous 1 cup drained,
   canned corn
2½ cups milk
1 tablespoon butter
1 small leek, sliced
1 small garlic clove, crushed
2 rindless smoked fatty bacon strips,
   finely chopped
1 small green or red bell pepper, seeded
   and diced
1 celery stalk, chopped
generous ½ cup white long
   grain rice
1 teaspoon all-purpose flour
scant 2 cups hot chicken or
   vegetable stock
4 large scallops
4 ounces white fish fillet, such as
   monkfish or flounder
1 tablespoon finely chopped fresh
   Italian parsley
good pinch of cayenne pepper
2–3 tablespoons light
   cream (optional)
salt and ground black pepper
crusty bread, to serve

1 Place half the drained corn in a food processor or blender. Add a little of the milk, and then process until the mixture is thick and creamy. Set aside.

COOK'S TIP

If you don't have a food processor, then simply chop the corn very finely, and transfer to a bowl. Beat in the milk, a little at time, until the mixture is thick and creamy.

2 Melt the butter in a large, heavy pan. Add the leek, garlic, and bacon, and gently fry for 4–5 minutes until the leek has softened but not browned.

3 Add the green or red bell pepper and the chopped celery, and cook over very gentle heat for 3–4 minutes more, stirring frequently, until the bell pepper and celery have softened slightly.

4 Stir in the rice, and cook for a few minutes, stirring occasionally, until the grains begin to swell, then sprinkle the flour evenly over the top of the rice and vegetables. Cook for about 1 minute, stirring constantly, then gradually stir in the remaining milk and the hot stock.

VARIATIONS

You can use other shellfish in place of the scallops if you prefer—try fresh or frozen shrimp, or mussels or clams, which are equally good in or out of their shells. Leave frozen shellfish to thaw at room temperature before adding to the chowder. Undyed, naturally smoked haddock or cod would make a delicious alternative fish.

5 Bring the mixture to a boil over medium heat, then lower the heat, and stir in the creamed corn mixture, with the whole corn. Season well.

6 Cover the pan, and simmer very gently for about 20 minutes, or until the rice is tender, stirring occasionally. Add a little more chicken or vegetable stock or water to the pan if the mixture thickens too quickly, or if the rice begins to stick to the base of the pan.

7 Cut the corals away from the scallops and set them aside, slice the white flesh into ¼in pieces. Cut the white fish fillet into bitesize chunks.

8 Add the scallops and chunks of fish to the chowder. Stir gently, then cook for 4 minutes.

9 Stir in the scallop corals, if you like, chopped parsley, and cayenne. Cook for a few minutes more until the scallops are just cooked and heated through, then stir in the cream, if using. Adjust the seasoning, and serve the chowder with thick slices of crusty bread.

Energy 263Kcal/1106kJ; Protein 19.2g; Carbohydrate 32.8g, of which sugars 10.4g; Fat 6.5g, of which saturates 3.2g; Cholesterol 40mg; Calcium 149mg; Fiber 1.6g; Sodium 353mg.

SLOW COOKER FIRST COURSES AND LIGHT MEALS

Whether you are planning a light lunch with friends, or a delicate first course for a special dinner party, the slow cooker is perfect for cooking a beautiful dish while giving you the time to concentrate on something else.

Among the tasty appetizers here are a pretty Haddock and Smoked Salmon Terrine, Cardamom Chicken Mousselines, and Red Lentil and Goat Cheese Pâté. For a delicious trouble-free lunch, there are mouthwatering Baked Eggs with Creamy Leeks, Mushroom and Zucchini Lasagne, and a Savory Nut Loaf that is sensational when served with a spicy fresh tomato sauce.

MUSHROOM and BEAN PÂTÉ

This light and tasty pâté is delicious served on whole-wheat toast or with crusty French bread and makes an excellent vegetarian appetizer or light lunch served with salad.

SERVES 8

6 cups mushrooms, sliced
1 onion, finely chopped
2 garlic cloves, crushed
1 red bell pepper, seeded and diced
2 tablespoons vegetable stock
2 tablespoons dry white wine
14-ounce can red kidney beans, rinsed and
    drained
1 egg, beaten
1 cup fresh whole-wheat breadcrumbs
2 teaspoons chopped fresh thyme
2 teaspoons chopped fresh rosemary
salt and ground black pepper
salad leaves, fresh herbs,
    and tomato wedges,
    to garnish

VARIATION

To make a lighter, milder-tasting pâté, use small or regular-size cannellini beans in place of the kidney beans.

1 Put the mushrooms, onion, garlic, red pepper, vegetable stock, and wine in the ceramic cooking pot. Cover, and cook on high for about 2 hours, or until the vegetables are almost tender, then set aside for about 10 minutes to cool.

2 Tip the vegetable mixture into a food processor or blender, and add the rinsed kidney beans. Process to make a smooth puree, stopping the machine once or twice to scrape down the sides.

3 Lightly grease and line a 2-pound loaf pan. Put an inverted saucer or metal pastry ring in the bottom of the ceramic cooking pot. Pour in about 1 inch of hot water, and switch the slow cooker on to high.

4 Transfer the mushroom mixture to a bowl. Add the egg, breadcrumbs, and herbs, and season with salt and pepper. Mix together thoroughly, then spoon the mixture into the prepared pan, and cover with plastic wrap or foil.

5 Put the pan in the slow cooker, and pour in enough boiling water to come just over halfway up the sides of the pan. Cover with the lid, and cook on high for 4 hours, or until lightly set.

6 Remove the pan from the ceramic cooking pot, and place on a wire rack until completely cool. Refrigerate for several hours, or overnight if preferred. Turn out of the pan, remove the lining paper, and serve in slices, garnished with salad leaves, herbs, and tomato wedges.

Energy 85Kcal/358kJ; Protein 5.5g; Carbohydrate 12.3g, of which sugars 3.8g; Fat 1.6g, of which saturates 0.4g; Cholesterol 28mg; Calcium 47mg; Fiber 3.7g; Sodium 187mg.

RED LENTIL and GOAT CHEESE PÂTÉ

The slightly smoky, earthy flavor of red lentils provides a perfect partner to tangy goat cheese, making a pâté that will be a hit with vegetarians and non-vegetarians alike.

SERVES 8

1 cup red lentils
1 shallot, very finely chopped
1 bay leaf
2 cups near-boiling
    vegetable stock
½ cup soft goat cheese
1 teaspoon ground cumin
3 eggs, lightly beaten
salt and ground black pepper
melba toast and arugula leaves,
    to serve

1 Place the lentils in a strainer, and rinse well under cold running water. Drain, then tip the lentils into the ceramic cooking pot, and add the shallot, bay leaf, and hot vegetable stock.

2 Switch the slow cooker to high, cover, and cook for 2 hours, or until all the liquid has been absorbed and the lentils are soft and pulpy. Stir once or twice toward the end of the cooking time to prevent the lentils sticking to the pot.

3 Turn off the slow cooker. Tip the lentil mixture into a bowl, remove the bay leaf, and leave to cool uncovered, so that the steam can evaporate. Meanwhile, wash and dry the ceramic cooking pot.

4 Lightly grease the base of a 3¾-cup loaf pan with oil, and line the base with waxed paper. Put an upturned saucer or metal pastry ring in the bottom of the ceramic cooking pot, and pour in about 1 inch of hot water. Turn the slow cooker to high.

5 Put the goat cheese in a bowl with the cumin, and beat together until soft and creamy. Gradually mix in the eggs until blended. Stir in the lentil mixture, and season well with salt and pepper.

6 Tip the mixture into the prepared pan. Cover with plastic wrap or foil. Put the pan in the slow cooker, and pour in enough boiling water to come just over halfway up the sides. Cover the slow cooker with the lid, and cook for 3–3½ hours, until the pâté is lightly set.

7 Carefully remove the pan from the slow cooker, and place on a wire rack to cool completely. Chill in the refrigerator for several hours, or overnight.

8 To serve, turn the pâté out of the pan, peel off the lining paper, and cut into slices. Serve with melba toast and arugula.

Energy 136Kcal/573kJ; Protein 9.8g; Carbohydrate 16g, of which sugars 0.9g; Fat 4.1g, of which saturates 2.6g; Cholesterol 13mg; Calcium 34mg; Fiber 1.4g; Sodium 97mg.

CHEESE-STUFFED PEARS

These pears, with their scrumptious creamy topping, make a sublime dish when served with a simple salad. If you don't have a very large slow cooker, choose short squat pears rather than long, tapering ones, so that they will fit in a single layer.

SERVES 4

¼ cup ricotta cheese
¼ cup dolcelatte cheese
1 tablespoon honey
½ celery stick, finely sliced
8 green olives, pitted and
  roughly chopped
4 dates, pitted and cut into
  thin strips
pinch of paprika
2 medium barely ripe pears
⅔ cup apple juice
salad leaves, to serve (optional)

4 Pour the apple juice around the pears, then cover with the lid. Cook on high for 1½–2 hours, or until the fruit is tender. (The cooking time will depend on the ripeness of the pears.)

5 Remove the pears from the slow cooker. If you like, brown them under a hot broiler for a few minutes. Serve with salad leaves, if you like.

COOK'S TIP
These pears go particularly well with slightly bitter and peppery leaves, such as chicory and arugula. Try them tossed in a walnut oil dressing.

1 Place the ricotta cheese in a bowl, and crumble in the dolcelatte. Add the honey, celery, olives, dates, and paprika, and mix together well until creamy and thoroughly blended.

2 Halve the pears lengthwise. Use a melon baller or teaspoon to remove the cores, and make a hollow for the filling.

3 Divide the ricotta filling equally between the pears, packing it into the hollow, then arrange the fruit in a single layer in the ceramic cooking pot.

Energy 236Kcal/992kJ; Protein 6.9g; Carbohydrate 35.6g, of which sugars 35.6g; Fat 8.2g, of which saturates 5.0g; Cholesterol 24mg; Calcium 141mg; Fiber 4.1g; Sodium 261mg.

COUNTRY-STYLE TERRINE with LEEKS

Traditionally, this sort of French pork terrine contains pork liver and egg to bind the mixture together. This version uses leeks instead to give a lighter result. In France, cornichons (small dill pickles or gherkins) and mustard are served as accompaniments.

3 Reserve two of the bacon strips for the garnish, then finely chop the remaining bacon. Add to the pork mixture along with the leeks, herbs, spices, salt, and pepper. Mix together, using a wooden spoon or your fingertips, until thoroughly combined.

4 Lightly grease the base and sides of a 5-cup heatproof dish or loaf pan with oil, and then line with waxed paper. Put an upturned saucer or metal pastry ring in the base of the ceramic cooking pot, and pour in 1 inch of hot water. Turn the slow cooker to high.

5 Spoon the meat mixture into the prepared dish or pan, pressing it into the corners. Tap firmly to settle the mixture, and smooth the top. Arrange the bay leaves and reserved bacon (trimmed to size) on top, then cover with foil.

6 Place the dish or pan in the slow cooker, and pour in enough boiling water to come just over halfway up the sides. Cover with the lid and cook for 4–5 hours or until cooked; the juices of the pâté should run clear when pierced with a skewer. Lift out of the ceramic cooking pot, and leave to cool in the dish or pan.

7 Put the dish or pan on a tray, then place a foil-covered plate or board (just smaller than the size of the dish or pan) on top of the pâté. Weight the plate or board with two or three large cans or other heavy objects, and chill for several hours, or preferably overnight.

SERVES 8

12 ounces trimmed leeks
2 tablespoons butter
2 garlic cloves, finely chopped
2 pounds lean pork leg or shoulder
4 ounces rinded smoked fatty bacon
1 teaspoon chopped fresh thyme
3 sage leaves, finely chopped
¼ teaspoon quatre épices (see Cook's Tip)
¼ teaspoon ground cumin
½ teaspoon salt
½ teaspoon ground black pepper
3 bay leaves

COOK'S TIP

Quatre épices is a classic French spice mix containing ground cloves, cinnamon, nutmeg, and pepper.

1 Cut the leeks lengthwise, wash well, and slice thinly. Melt the butter in a large heavy pan, add the leeks, then cover and cook over medium-low heat for about 10 minutes, stirring occasionally. Add the garlic, and continue cooking for a further 10 minutes, until the leeks are very soft. Set aside to cool.

2 Trim off any excess fat and gristle from the pork, then cut the meat into 1-inch cubes. Working in two or three batches, put the meat into a food processor fitted with a metal blade; the bowl should be about half full. Pulse to chop the meat to a coarse puree. Alternatively, pass the meat through the coarse blade of a meat grinder. Transfer the meat to a large mixing bowl, and remove any white stringy pieces.

Energy 211Kcal/884kJ; Protein 27.5g; Carbohydrate 1.3g, of which sugars 1g; Fat 10.7g, of which saturates 4.4g; Cholesterol 87mg; Calcium 20mg; Fiber 1.0g; Sodium 395mg.

BAKED EGGS with CREAMY LEEKS

Enjoy these deliciously creamy eggs for a light lunch or supper with toast and a salad.
You can use other vegetables in place of the leeks, such as pureed spinach or ratatouille.

3 Melt the butter in a small frying pan, and cook the leeks over a medium heat, stirring frequently, until softened.

4 Add 3 tablespoons of the cream and cook gently for about 5 minutes, or until the leeks are very soft and the cream has thickened a little. Season with salt, black pepper and nutmeg.

5 Spoon the leeks into the ramekins or soufflé dishes, dividing the mixture equally. Using the back of the spoon, make a hollow in the center of each pile of leeks, then break an egg into the hollow. Spoon 1–2 teaspoons of the remaining cream over each egg, and season lightly with salt and pepper.

6 Cover each dish with plastic wrap, and place in the slow cooker. If necessary, pour in a little more boiling water to come halfway up the sides of the dishes. Cover, and cook for 30 minutes, or until the egg whites are set and the yolks are still soft, or a little longer if you prefer the eggs firmer.

SERVES 4

1 tablespoon butter, plus extra
   for greasing
8 ounces small leeks, thinly sliced
4–6 tablespoons whipping or
   heavy cream
freshly grated nutmeg
4 eggs
salt and ground black pepper

VARIATION
To make herb and cheese eggs, put 1 tablespoon heavy cream in each dish with some chopped herbs. Break in the eggs, add 1 tablespoon heavy cream and a little grated cheese, then cook as before. This is the perfect recipe for a lazy weekend brunch.

1 Pour about 1 inch hot water into the ceramic cooking pot, and switch the slow cooker to high.

2 Using a pastry brush, lightly butter the base and insides of four ¾-cup ramekins or individual soufflé dishes.

Energy 239Kcal/990kJ; Protein 8.5g; Carbohydrate 2g, of which sugars 1.6g; Fat 21.9g, of which saturates 11.4g; Cholesterol 266mg; Calcium 58mg; Fiber 1.2g; Sodium 110mg.

SAVORY NUT LOAF

Ideal as an alternative to the traditional meat roast, this wholesome dish is perfect for special occasions. It is also particularly good served with a spicy fresh tomato sauce.

SERVES 4

2 tablespoons olive oil, plus extra
    for greasing
1 onion, finely chopped
1 leek, finely chopped
2 celery sticks, finely chopped
3 cups mushrooms, chopped
2 garlic cloves, crushed
15-ounce can lentils, rinsed and drained
1 cup mixed nuts, such as hazelnuts,
    cashew nuts, and almonds, finely
    chopped
½ cup all-purpose flour
½ cup grated sharp Cheddar cheese
1 egg, beaten
3–4 tablespoons chopped fresh
    mixed herbs
salt and ground black pepper
chives and sprigs of fresh Italian parsley, to
    garnish

1 Place an upturned saucer or metal pastry ring in the base of the ceramic cooking pot. Pour in about 1 inch of hot water and switch the slow cooker to high.

2 Lightly grease the base and sides of a 2-pound loaf pan or terrine—first making sure it will fit in the slow cooker —and line the base and sides of the pan with baking parchment.

3 Heat the oil in a large pan, add the onion, leek, celery, mushrooms, and garlic, then cook for 10 minutes, until the vegetables have softened. Do not let them brown.

4 Remove the pan from the heat, then stir in the lentils, mixed nuts and flour, grated cheese, beaten egg, and herbs. Season well with salt and black pepper, and mix thoroughly.

5 Spoon the nut mixture into the prepared loaf pan or terrine, pressing right into the corners. Level the surface with a fork, then cover the pan with a piece of foil. Place the loaf pan in the ceramic cooking pot, and pour in enough near-boiling water to come just over halfway up the side of the dish.

6 Cover the slow cooker with the lid, and cook for 3–4 hours, or until the loaf is firm to the touch.

7 Leave the loaf to cool in the pan for about 15 minutes, then turn out onto a serving plate. Serve the loaf hot or cold, cut into thick slices and garnished with fresh chives and sprigs of Italian parsley.

Energy 484Kcal/2019kJ; Protein 23.7g; Carbohydrate 34.1g, of which sugars 5.1g; Fat 29g, of which saturates 5.4g; Cholesterol 69mg; Calcium 238mg; Fiber 8.7g; Sodium 128mg.

PASTA with MUSHROOMS

Slow-cooking a mixture of mushrooms, garlic, and sun-dried tomatoes together with white wine and stock makes a rich and well-flavored pasta sauce. Served with warm ciabatta, this makes a truly excellent vegetarian lunch dish.

SERVES 4

½ ounce dried porcini mushrooms
½ cup hot water
2 cloves garlic, finely chopped
2 large pieces drained sun-dried tomato
   in olive oil, sliced into thin strips
½ cup dry white wine
½ cup vegetable stock
2 cups cremini mushrooms, thinly sliced
1 handful fresh Italian parsley,
   roughly chopped
4 cups dried short pasta shapes, such as
   ruote, penne, fusilli, or eliche
salt and ground black pepper
arugula and/or fresh Italian parsley,
   to garnish

1 Put the dried porcini mushrooms in a large bowl. Pour over the hot water, and leave to soak for 15 minutes.

2 While the mushrooms are soaking, put the garlic, tomatoes, wine, stock, and cremini mushrooms into the ceramic cooking pot, and switch the slow cooker to high.

3 Tip the porcini mushrooms into a strainer set over a bowl, then squeeze them with your hands to release as much liquid as possible. Reserve the soaking liquid. Chop the porcini finely. Add the liquid and the chopped porcini to the ceramic cooking pot, and cover the slow cooker with the lid. Cook on high for 1 hour, stirring halfway through cooking time to make sure that the mushrooms cook evenly.

4 Switch the slow cooker to the low setting, and cook for a further 1–2 hours, until the mushrooms are tender.

5 Cook the pasta in boiling salted water for 10 minutes, or according to the instructions on the package. Drain the pasta, and tip it into a warmed large bowl. Stir the chopped parsley into the sauce, and season to taste with salt and black pepper. Add the sauce to the pasta, and toss well. Serve immediately, garnished with arugula and/or parsley.

VARIATIONS

Fresh wild mushrooms can be used instead of cremini mushrooms, although they are seasonal and often expensive. A cheaper alternative is to use a box of mixed wild mushrooms, available from good supermarkets and delicatessens.

Energy 420Kcal/1787kJ; Protein 15.1g; Carbohydrate 84.9g, of which sugars 5.1g; Fat 2.6g, of which saturates 0.3g; Cholesterol 0 mg; Calcium 61mg; Fiber 4.8g; Sodium 14mg.

MUSHROOM AND ZUCCHINI LASAGNE

This is the perfect lasagne for vegetarians. Adding dried porcini to fresh cremini
mushrooms intensifies the flavor. The dish can be made and assembled in
the slow cooker early in the day, then left to cook. Serve with crusty Italian bread.

SERVES 6

For the tomato sauce
½ ounce dried porcini mushrooms
½ cup hot water
1 onion
1 carrot
1 celery stick
2 tablespoons olive oil
14-ounce cans chopped tomatoes
1 tablespoon sun-dried tomato paste
1 teaspoon granulated sugar
1 teaspoon dried basil
   or mixed herbs

For the lasagne
2 tablespoons olive oil
¼ cup butter
1 pound zucchini, thinly sliced
1 onion, finely chopped
6 cups cremini mushrooms, thinly sliced
2 garlic cloves, crushed
6–8 non-precook lasagne sheets
½ cup freshly grated Parmesan cheese
salt and ground black pepper
fresh oregano leaves, to garnish
Italian-style bread,
   to serve (optional)

For the white sauce
3 tablespoons butter
⅓ cup all-purpose flour
3¾ cups milk
freshly grated nutmeg

1 Put the dried porcini mushrooms in a bowl. Pour over the hot water, and leave to soak for 15 minutes. Tip the porcini and liquid into a strainer, set over a bowl, and squeeze the mushrooms with your hands to release as much liquid as possible. Chop the mushrooms finely, and set aside. Strain the soaking liquid through a fine strainer, and reserve.

2 Chop the onion, carrot, and celery finely. Heat the olive oil in a pan, and fry the vegetables until softened. Place in a food processor with the tomatoes, tomato paste, sugar, herbs, porcini and soaking liquid, and blend to a puree.

3 For the lasagne, heat the olive oil and half the butter in a large pan. Add half the zucchini slices, and season to taste. Cook over a medium heat, turning the zucchini frequently, for 5–8 minutes, until lightly colored on both sides. Remove from the pan with a slotted spoon, and transfer to a bowl. Repeat with the remaining zucchini.

4 Melt the remaining butter in the pan, and cook the onion for 3 minutes, stirring. Add the cremini mushrooms, chopped porcini, and garlic, and cook for 5 minutes. Add to the zucchini.

5 For the white sauce, melt the butter in a large pan, then add the flour and cook, stirring, for 1 minute. Turn off the heat, and gradually whisk in the milk. Bring to the boil, and cook, stirring, until the sauce is smooth and thick. Season with salt, black pepper, and nutmeg.

6 Ladle half of the tomato sauce into the ceramic cooking pot, and spread out to cover the base. Add half the vegetable mixture, spreading it evenly. Top with about one-third of the white sauce, then about half the lasagne sheets, breaking them to fit the cooking pot. Repeat these layers, then top with the remaining white sauce, and sprinkle with grated Parmesan cheese.

7 Cover the ceramic cooking pot with the lid, and cook on low for 2–2½ hours or until the lasagne is tender. If you like, brown the top under a medium broiler. Garnish with a sprinkling of fresh oregano leaves, and serve with fresh Italian-style bread.

Energy 421Kcal/1757kJ; Protein 15.5g; Carbohydrate 32.9g, of which sugars 15g; Fat 26.2g, of which saturates 12.4g; Cholesterol 49mg; Calcium 346mg; Fiber 3.8g; Sodium 310mg.

CHICKEN and PISTACHIO PÂTÉ

This easy version of a classic French charcuterie can be made with white chicken breast portions or a mixture of light and dark meat for a more robust flavor. Serve it as an elegant appetizer for a special dinner, or with salad for a light lunch.

SERVES 8

oil, for greasing
1¾ pounds boneless chicken meat
¾ cup fresh white breadcrumbs
½ cup heavy cream
1 egg white
4 scallions finely chopped
1 garlic clove, finely chopped
3 ounces cooked ham, cut into small cubes
½ cup shelled pistachio nuts
2 tablespoons green peppercorns
    in brine, drained
3 tablespoons chopped fresh tarragon
pinch of grated nutmeg
salt and ground black pepper
French bread and salad, to serve

1 Line the base of a 5-cup round or oval heatproof dish (such as a soufflé dish) with waxed paper, then lightly brush the base and sides with oil.

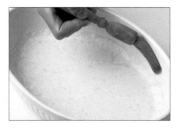

2 Put an upturned saucer or metal pastry ring in the base of the ceramic cooking pot, and pour in about 1 inch of hot water. Switch the slow cooker to high.

3 Cut the chicken meat into cubes, then put in a food processor, and blend until fairly smooth. (You may need to do this in batches depending on the capacity of your food processor.) Alternatively, pass the meat through the medium blade of a food mill. Remove any white stringy pieces from the ground meat.

4 Place the breadcrumbs in a large mixing bowl, pour over the cream, and leave to soak.

5 Meanwhile, lightly whisk the egg white with a fork, then add it to the soaked breadcrumbs. Add the minced chicken, scallions, garlic, ham, pistachio nuts, green peppercorns, tarragon, nutmeg, salt, and pepper. Using a wooden spoon or your fingers, mix thoroughly.

6 Spoon the mixture into the prepared dish, and cover with foil. Place the dish in the ceramic cooking pot, and pour a little more boiling water around the dish to come just over halfway up the sides. Cover the slow cooker with the lid, and cook for about 4 hours, until the pâté is cooked through.

7 To check whether the pâté is cooked, pierce with a skewer or fine knife—the juices should run clear. Carefully lift out of the slow cooker and leave the pâté to cool in the dish. Chill in the refrigerator, preferably overnight.

8 To serve, turn out the pâté onto a serving dish, and cut into slices. Serve with crusty French bread and salad.

VARIATIONS
• You can use turkey breast fillet in place of some or all of the chicken, and serve with a tangy cranberry sauce.
• Pale green pistachio nuts look very pretty in this pâté, but you can use hazelnuts instead; they are equally good.
• This pâté also makes a perfect dish for a special picnic or a cold buffet. Serve with a delicately flavored herb mayonnaise.

Energy 321Kcal/1344kJ; Protein 36.6g; Carbohydrate 3.7g, of which sugars 1.2g; Fat 17.9g, of which saturates 7.7g; Cholesterol 125mg; Calcium 37mg; Fiber 0.7g; Sodium 379mg.

CARDAMOM CHICKEN MOUSSELINES

These light chicken mousselines, served with a tangy tomato vinaigrette, make an elegant appetizer. They should be served warm rather than hot, so as soon as they are cooked, turn off the slow cooker, and leave to cool for half an hour before eating.

SERVES 6

12 ounces skinless, boneless
  chicken breast portions
1 shallot, finely chopped
1 cup full-fat soft cheese
1 egg, lightly beaten
2 egg whites
crushed seeds of 2 cardamom pods
4 tablespoons white wine
⅔ cup heavy cream
oregano sprigs, to serve

For the tomato vinaigrette
12 ounces ripe tomatoes
2 teaspoons balsamic vinegar
2 tablespoons olive oil
sea salt and ground black pepper

1 Roughly chop the chicken, and put in a food processor with the finely chopped shallot. Process until the mixture becomes fairly smooth.

2 Add the soft cheese, beaten egg, egg whites, crushed cardamom seeds, and white wine to the chicken mixture, and season with salt and ground black pepper. Process again until the ingredients are thoroughly blended.

3 Gradually add the cream, using the pulsing action, until the mixture has a smooth and creamy texture. Transfer the mixture to a bowl, cover with plastic wrap, and chill in the refrigerator for about 30 minutes.

4 Meanwhile, prepare six ⅔-cup ramekins or dariole molds, checking first that they will all fit in the slow cooker. Lightly grease the base of each one, then line. Pour about ¾ inch hot water into the ceramic cooking pot, and switch the cooker to high.

5 Divide the chicken mixture among the prepared dishes, and level the tops. Cover, each with foil, and place in the ceramic cooking pot. Pour in a little more near-boiling water to come half-way up the dishes. Cover and cook for 2½–3 hours, or until the mousselines are firm; a skewer or thin knife inserted into the middle should come out clean.

6 Meanwhile, peel, quarter, seed, and finely dice the tomatoes. Place them in a bowl, sprinkle with balsamic vinegar, and season with a little salt. Stir well.

7 To serve, unmold the mousselines onto warmed plates. Place small spoonfuls of the tomato vinaigrette around each plate, then drizzle over a little olive oil, and grind over a little black pepper. Garnish with sprigs of fresh oregano.

Energy 191Kcal/795kJ; Protein 18.1g; Carbohydrate 2g, of which sugars 2g; Fat 11.6g, of which saturates 5g; Cholesterol 96mg; Calcium 30mg; Fiber 0.7g; Sodium 130mg.

FISH TERRINE

This colorful layered terrine makes a spectacular appetizer or main course on a special occasion. It is particularly good for entertaining because it can be made in advance, chilled until ready to serve, then arranged on plates at the last minute.

SERVES 6

1 pound skinless white fish fillets
8 ounces thinly sliced smoked salmon
2 egg whites, chilled
¼ teaspoon each salt and ground
    white pepper
pinch of freshly grated nutmeg
1 cup heavy cream
2 ounces small tender fresh spinach leaves
lemon mayonnaise, to serve

1 Cut the white fish fillets into 1-inch pieces, removing any bones. Spread out the fish pieces on a plate, cover with plastic wrap, and chill in the freezer for 15 minutes until very cold.

2 Lightly oil a 5-cup terrine or loaf pan. Line the base and sides of the pan with the smoked salmon slices, making sure they overlap each other all the way around and letting them hang over the edges of the pan.

3 Remove the white fish from the freezer, then place in a food processor, and blend to make a very smooth puree. (You may need to stop the machine and scrape down the sides two or three times as you do this.)

4 Add the egg whites, one at a time, processing after each addition, then add the salt, pepper, and nutmeg. With the machine running, pour in the cream, and stop as soon as it is blended. (If over-processed, the cream will thicken.)

5 Transfer the fish mixture to a large glass bowl. Put the spinach leaves into the food processor, and process to make a smooth puree. Add one-third of the fish mixture to the spinach, and process briefly until just combined, scraping down the sides once or twice.

6 Pour about 1 inch of very hot water into the ceramic cooking pot. Place an upturned saucer or metal pastry ring in the base, then turn the slow cooker onto high.

7 Spread half the plain fish mixture in the base of the pan. Spoon the green fish mixture over the top, and smooth it level, then cover with the remaining plain mixture. Fold the overhanging pieces of smoked salmon over the top to enclose the mixture. Tap the pan to settle the mixture and remove any air pockets, then cover the pan with a double layer of lightly oiled foil.

8 Put the pan in the slow cooker, and pour in enough boiling water to come just over halfway up the sides. Cook for 3–3½ hours, or until a skewer inserted into the terrine comes out clean. Leave the terrine to cool in the pan, then chill in the refrigerator until firm.

9 To serve the terrine, turn out onto a board, remove the lining paper, and slice. Arrange the slices on individual plates, and serve with lemon mayonnaise.

Energy 340Kcal/1409kJ; Protein 23.2g; Carbohydrate 0.8g, of which sugars 0.8g; Fat 27.1g, of which saturates 14.7g; Cholesterol 110mg; Calcium 50mg; Fiber 0.2g; Sodium 201mg.

HADDOCK and SMOKED SALMON TERRINE

This substantial terrine makes a superb dish for a summer buffet. It is very good served with dill mayonnaise or a tangy mango salsa instead of the crème fraîche or sour cream.

SERVES 6

1 tablespoon sunflower-seed oil, for greasing
12 ounces smoked salmon
2 pounds haddock fillets, skinned
2 eggs, lightly beaten
7 tablespoons low-fat crème fraîche
   or sour cream
2 tablespoons drained bottled capers
2 tablespoons drained soft green or
   pink peppercorns
salt and ground white pepper
low-fat crème fraîche or sour cream,
   peppercorns, fresh dill and arugula, to
   serve

1 Pour about 1 inch of warm water into the ceramic cooking pot. Place an upturned saucer or metal pastry ring in the base, then turn the slow cooker on to high. Lightly grease a 4-cup loaf pan or terrine. Use some of the smoked salmon slices to line the pan or terrine, letting them hang over the edge. Reserve the remaining salmon.

2 Cut two long slices of the haddock the length of the pan or terrine, and cut the remaining haddock into small pieces. Season with salt and pepper.

3 Combine the eggs, crème fraîche or sour cream, capers, and soft peppercorns in a bowl. Season with salt and pepper, then stir in the small pieces of haddock. Spoon half the mixture into the mold, and smooth the surface with a spatula.

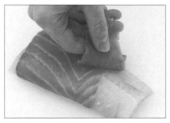

4 Wrap the long haddock fillets in the reserved smoked salmon. (Don't worry if there isn't enough salmon to cover them completely.) Lay the wrapped haddock fillets on top of the fish mixture in the pan or terrine.

5 Spoon the rest of the fish mixture into the pan or terrine, and smooth the surface. Fold the overhanging pieces of smoked salmon over the top, and cover tightly with a double thickness of foil.

6 Tap the terrine to settle the contents, then place in the slow cooker, and pour in enough boiling water to come just over halfway up the sides. Cook for 3–4 hours, or until a skewer inserted into the terrine comes out clean.

7 Remove the terrine from the slow cooker, but do not remove the foil cover. Place two or three large, heavy cans on the foil to weight it, and leave until cold. Chill in the refrigerator for 24 hours.

8 About 1 hour before serving, remove the terrine from the refrigerator, lift off the weights, and carefully remove the foil. Gently invert the terrine onto a serving plate, and lift off the mold.

9 Cut the terrine into thick slices, using a sharp knife. Serve with crème fraîche or sour cream, peppercorns, dill sprigs, and arugula leaves.

Energy 316Kcal/1326kJ; Protein 46.1g; Carbohydrate 0.4g, of which sugars 0.4g; Fat 14.5g, of which saturates 6.2g; Cholesterol 170mg; Calcium 653mg; Fiber 0g; Sodium 1228mg.

ONE-POT, CLAY-POT FIRST COURSES AND LIGHT MEALS

When you are cooking a first course, appetizer, or snack for family or friends, the most successful dishes are often the simplest, so anything that can be cooked in one pot is a sure winner. Whether you opt for a simple pasta dish, such as Linguine with Arugula, a hot and spicy clay-pot treat, such as Potato Wedges with Tomato and Chili Salsa, or Pork Ribs with Ginger and Chili, or use your wok to make a stir-fry, everyone will be glad you chose the easy option.

BRAISED BABY LEEKS in RED WINE with AROMATICS

Coriander seeds and oregano lend a Greek flavor to this dish of braised leeks. Serve it as part of a mixed hors d'oeuvre or as a partner for baked white fish.

SERVES 6

12 baby leeks or 6 thick leeks
1 tablespoon coriander seeds,
    lightly crushed
2-inch piece cinnamon stick
½ cup olive oil
3 fresh bay leaves
2 strips pared orange rind
5–6 fresh or dried oregano sprigs
1 teaspoon sugar
⅔ cup fruity red wine
2 teaspoons balsamic or
    sherry vinegar
2 tablespoons coarsely chopped fresh
    oregano or marjoram
salt and ground black pepper

1 If using baby leeks, simply trim the ends, but leave them whole. Cut thick leeks into 2–3-inch lengths.

2 Place the coriander seeds and cinnamon in a pan wide enough to take all the leeks in a single layer. Cook over medium heat for 2–3 minutes, until the spices give off a fragrant aroma, then stir in the olive oil, bay leaves, orange rind, fresh or dried oregano, sugar, wine, and balsamic or sherry vinegar. Bring to a boil, and simmer for 5 minutes.

3 Add the leeks to the pan. Bring back to a boil, reduce the heat, and cover the pan. Cook the leeks gently for 5 minutes. Uncover, and simmer gently for another 5–8 minutes, until the leeks are just tender when tested with the tip of a sharp knife.

4 Use a slotted spoon to transfer the leeks to a serving dish. Boil the pan juices rapidly until reduced to about 5–6 tablespoons. Add salt and pepper to taste, and pour the liquid over the leeks. Leave to cool.

5 The leeks can be left to stand for several hours. If you chill them, bring them back to room temperature again before serving. Sprinkle the chopped herbs over the leeks just before serving.

COOK'S TIP
Genuine balsamic vinegar from Modena in northern Italy has been produced for over 1,000 years. It has a high sugar content and wonderfully strong bouquet. It is a very dark brown color and has a deep, rich flavor with hints of herbs and port. Nowadays you can find quite good balsamic vinegar in supermarkets. It is expensive, but the flavor is so rich that you only need to use a little.

Energy 185Kcal/768kJ; Protein 2.9g; Carbohydrate 5.7g, of which sugars 4.5g; Fat 15.1g, of which saturates 2.2g; Cholesterol 0mg; Calcium 52mg; Fiber 3.9g; Sodium 7mg.

POTATO WEDGES with TOMATO and CHILE SALSA

This is a healthier version of traditionally baked potato skins; the clay pot keeps the potato flesh wonderfully moist and fluffy.

SERVES 4

6 potatoes, about 4 ounces each
3 tablespoons olive oil
salt and ground black pepper

For the tomato and chile salsa
4 juicy ripe tomatoes
1 sun-dried tomato in olive
    oil, drained
3 scallions
1–2 fresh red or green chiles, halved
    and seeded
1 tablespoon extra virgin
    olive oil
2 teaspoons lemon juice

COOK'S TIP
Varieties of potato that produce a fluffy texture when baked are best for these wedges. Good types to use include russet Burbank potatoes and long white potatoes.

1 Soak the clay pot or a potato pot in cold water for 20 minutes, then drain. Scrub the potatoes, and dry with paper towels. Cut each potato lengthwise into four wedges. Brush with a little of the oil, and sprinkle with salt and pepper.

2 Place the potatoes in the clay pot, and cover with the lid. Place in an unheated oven, set the temperature to 400°F, and cook for 55–60 minutes, or until the potatoes are tender.

3 Meanwhile, finely chop the tomatoes, sun-dried tomato, scallions, and chile, and combine with the olive oil and lemon juice. Cover and leave to stand to let the flavors mingle.

4 Uncover the potatoes, brush with the remaining olive oil, and bake, uncovered, for 15 minutes more, until slightly golden. Divide the potato wedges and salsa among four serving bowls and plates, and serve immediately.

Energy 238Kcal/1001kJ; Protein 4g; Carbohydrate 30.8g, of which sugars 4.9g; Fat 11.9g, of which saturates 1.8g; Cholesterol 0mg; Calcium 23mg; Fiber 2.6g; Sodium 28mg.

BRAISED GRAPE LEAVES

This popular eastern Mediterranean dish keeps moist when cooked slowly in a clay pot.

SERVES 4

12 fresh grape leaves
2 tablespoons olive oil
1 small onion, chopped
2 tablespoons pine nuts
1 garlic clove, crushed
⅔ cup cooked long grain rice
2 tomatoes, peeled, seeded, and
    finely chopped
1 tablespoon chopped fresh mint
1 lemon, sliced
⅔ cup dry white wine
scant 1 cup vegetable stock
salt and ground black pepper
lemon wedges, to serve

1 Soak the clay pot in cold water for 20 minutes, then drain. Blanch the grape leaves in a pan of boiling water for about 2 minutes, or until they darken and soften. Rinse the leaves under cold running water, and leave to drain.

2 Heat the oil in a frying pan, add the onion, and cook for 5–6 minutes, stirring frequently, until softened. Add the pine nuts and crushed garlic and cook, stirring constantly, until the onions and pine nuts are a golden brown color.

3 Stir the onion mixture into the rice, with the tomatoes, mint, and seasoning.

4 Place a spoonful of the rice mixture at the stalk end of each grape leaf. Fold the sides over the filling, and roll up tightly.

5 Place the stuffed grape leaves close together, seam side down, in the clay pot. Place the lemon slices on top. Pour over the wine and sufficient stock just to cover the lemon slices.

6 Cover with the lid, and place in an unheated oven. Set the oven to 400°F, and cook for 30 minutes. Reduce the temperature to 325°F, and cook for 30 minutes more. Serve hot or cold, with lemon wedges.

Energy 258Kcal/1072kJ; Protein 4.6g; Carbohydrate 28.8g, of which sugars 5.5g; Fat 11.1g, of which saturates 1.2g; Cholesterol 0mg; Calcium 49mg; Fiber 2.1g; Sodium 11mg.

PAN-FRIED HAM and VEGETABLES with EGGS

A perfect family supper dish, this is very easy to prepare. Serve with plenty of hot, crusty bread—Italian ciabatta is particularly good.

3 Add the zucchini and bell peppers to the onion and garlic, and cook over medium heat for 3–4 minutes.

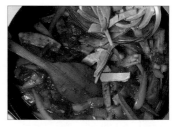

4 Stir in the paprika, tomatoes, tomato paste, ham, and seasoning. Bring to a boil, and simmer gently for 15 minutes.

5 Reduce the heat to low. Make four wells in the tomato mixture, break an egg into each, and season. Cook over gentle heat until the white begins to set.

SERVES 4

2 tablespoons olive oil
1 onion, coarsely chopped
2 garlic cloves, crushed
6 ounces cooked ham
8 ounces zucchini
1 red bell pepper, seeded and
    thinly sliced
1 yellow bell pepper, seeded and
    thinly sliced
2 teaspoons paprika
14-ounce can chopped tomatoes
1 tablespoon sun-dried tomato paste
4 eggs
1 cup coarsely grated
    Cheddar cheese
salt and ground black pepper
crusty bread, to serve

1 Heat the olive oil in a deep frying pan. Add the onion and garlic, and cook for 4 minutes, stirring frequently, or until just beginning to soften.

2 While the onions and garlic are cooking, cut the ham and zucchini into 2-inch long batons. Set the ham aside.

6 Preheat the broiler. Sprinkle the cheese over the vegetables, and broil for about 5 minutes, until the eggs are set. Serve immediately with bread.

Energy 350Kcal/1457kJ; Protein 24.4g; Carbohydrate 11.4g, of which sugars 10.7g; Fat 22.8g, of which saturates 9.3g; Cholesterol 244mg; Calcium 276mg; Fiber 3.1g; Sodium 817mg.

WILD MUSHROOM and SUN-DRIED TOMATO SOUFFLES

These impressive little soufflés are baked in individual earthenware pots. They are packed with rich, Italian flavors and are remarkably easy to prepare and cook.

SERVES 4

½ cup dried porcini mushrooms
3 tablespoons butter, plus extra
    for greasing
4 teaspoons grated Parmesan cheese
⅓ cup all-purpose flour
1 cup milk
½ cup grated sharp
    Cheddar cheese
4 eggs, separated
2 sun-dried tomatoes in oil, drained
    and chopped
1 tablespoon chopped fresh chives
salt and ground black pepper

1 Place the dried mushrooms in a bowl, pour over enough warm water to cover, and leave to soak for 15 minutes. Grease four individual earthenware soufflé dishes with a little butter. Sprinkle the grated Parmesan cheese into the soufflé dishes, and rotate each dish to coat the sides with cheese. Preheat the oven to 375°F.

2 Melt the 3 tablespoons of butter in a large pan, remove from the heat, and stir in the flour. Cook over low heat, stirring constantly, for 1 minute. Remove the pan from the heat, and gradually stir in the milk. Return to the heat, and bring to a boil, stirring constantly, until the sauce has thickened.

COOK'S TIP
A variety of different dried mushrooms are available—any can be used instead of the porcini.

3 Remove the sauce from the heat, then stir in the grated Cheddar cheese and plenty of seasoning. Beat in the egg yolks, one at a time, then stir in the chopped sun-dried tomatoes and the chives. Drain the soaked mushrooms, then coarsely chop them, and add them to the cheese sauce.

4 Whisk the egg whites until they stand in soft peaks. Mix one spoonful into the sauce, then carefully fold in the remainder. Divide the mixture among the soufflé dishes, and bake for 25 minutes, or until the soufflés are golden brown on top, well risen, and just firm to the touch. Serve immediately—before they sink.

Energy 290Kcal/1207kJ; Protein 14.7g; Carbohydrate 11.6g, of which sugars 3.9g; Fat 20.8g, of which saturates 11.2g; Cholesterol 232mg; Calcium 274mg; Fiber 0.6g; Sodium 305mg.

LINGUINE with ARUGULA

This is a first course that you will find in many a fashionable restaurant in Italy. It is very quick and easy to make at home and is worth trying for yourself.

SERVES 4

12 ounces fresh or dried linguine
½ cup extra virgin olive oil
1 large bunch arugula, about 5 ounces,
    stalks removed, shredded
    or torn
1 cup freshly grated
    Parmesan cheese
salt and ground black pepper

VARIATION
Oil-based pasta sauces, such as this one, are best served with fine, long pastas such as linguine. Spaghetti, capelli d'angelo, bucatini, or fettuccine would work just as well in this recipe.

1 Cook the pasta in a large pan of salted, boiling water for 8–10 minutes, until it is just tender, or according to the instructions on the package. As soon as the pasta is cooked, drain thoroughly.

2 Heat about 4 tablespoons of the olive oil in the pasta pan, then add the drained pasta, followed by the arugula. Toss over medium to high heat for 1–2 minutes, or until the arugula is just wilted, then remove the pan from the heat.

3 Tip the pasta and arugula into a warmed, large serving bowl. Add half the freshly grated Parmesan cheese and the remaining olive oil. Add a little salt and black pepper to taste.

4 Toss the mixture quickly to mix, and serve immediately. Hand around the remaining Parmesan cheese.

COOK'S TIP
Buy arugula by the bunch from a fruit and vegetable store. The type sold in small cellophane packages in supermarkets is usually very expensive. Always check when buying arugula that all the leaves are bright green. In hot weather, arugula leaves quickly turn yellow.

Energy 585Kcal/2451kJ; Protein 19g; Carbohydrate 65.4g, of which sugars 3.5g; Fat 29.2g, of which saturates 7.1g; Cholesterol 19mg; Calcium 311mg; Fiber 3.3g; Sodium 260mg.

SPAGHETTI with GARLIC and OIL

This simple pasta dish from Rome can be made in less than 15 minutes. Use fresh chiles if you like and, since the oil is so important, the very best extra virgin olive oil.

SERVES 4

14 ounces fresh or dried spaghetti
6 tablespoons extra virgin olive oil
2–4 garlic cloves, crushed
1 dried red chile
1 small handful fresh Italian parsley, coarsely chopped
salt

COOK'S TIP
Don't use salt when you are preparing the hot oil, garlic, and chile mixture, because the salt will not dissolve sufficiently. This is why plenty of salt is recommended for cooking the pasta.

1 Cook the pasta in a large pan of salted boiling water, according to the package instructions, until it is just tender, adding plenty of salt to the water (see Cook's Tip).

2 When the pasta is just tender, drain it by tipping it into a large colander, then transfer it to a warmed, large serving bowl. Rinse out the pasta pan and dry.

3 Heat the olive oil in the pan. Add the crushed garlic and the whole dried chile, and stir over low heat for 1–2 minutes, until the garlic is just beginning to brown. Remove the chile and discard.

4 Pour the hot olive oil and cooked garlic mixture over the pasta, add the coarsely chopped fresh Italian parsley, and toss vigorously until the pasta glistens, then serve immediately.

Energy 495Kcal/2084kJ; Protein 12.4g; Carbohydrate 74.5g, of which sugars 3.6g; Fat 18.5g, of which saturates 2.6g; Cholesterol 0mg; Calcium 50mg; Fiber 3.5g; Sodium 7mg.

SPAGHETTI with BUTTER and HERBS

This is a versatile recipe. You can use just one favorite herb or several—basil, Italian parsley, rosemary, thyme, marjoram, or sage would all work well.

SERVES 4

14 ounces fresh or dried spaghetti
   alla chitarra
2 good handfuls mixed fresh herbs,
   plus extra herb leaves and flowers
   to garnish
½ cup butter, diced
salt and ground black pepper
freshly grated Parmesan cheese, to serve

I Cook the pasta in a large pan of salted boiling water for 10–12 minutes, until just tender or according to the instructions on the package.

2 Using a large sharp knife, chop the fresh herbs coarsely or finely, whichever you like.

COOK'S TIP
Square-shaped chitarra spaghetti is the traditional type for this sauce, but you can use any type of long thin pasta, such as ordinary spaghetti or spaghettini, or even linguine.

VARIATION
If you like the flavor of garlic, add one or two crushed cloves to the pan when melting the butter.

3 Drain the pasta in a colander, and then return the pasta to the pan. Add the butter, and heat until it melts and sizzles, then add the chopped herbs and salt and pepper to taste.

4 Toss the pasta over medium heat until it is thoroughly coated in the butter and herbs.

5 Serve the pasta immediately in warmed shallow bowls, sprinkled with some extra herb leaves and flowers. Hand around a bowl of freshly grated Parmesan separately.

SPAGHETTI with CHEESE and BLACK PEPPER

This dish is very quick and easy to cook, perfect for a midweek supper. The flavors are very simple, so choose a strong-tasting cheese and a good extra virgin olive oil. Romano is traditional in this dish, but Parmesan could also be used.

SERVES 4

14 ounces fresh or
   dried spaghetti
1⅓ cups freshly grated
   Romano cheese
about 1 teaspoon coarsely ground
   black pepper
extra virgin olive oil, to taste
salt

I Cook the fresh or dried pasta in a large pan of salted boiling water until it is just tender, or according to the instructions on the package.

2 As soon as the spaghetti is cooked, drain it, leaving it a little moister than usual, then tip the spaghetti straight into a large warmed serving bowl.

3 Add the freshly grated cheese, lots of black pepper, and salt to taste. Toss the pasta well to mix, then moisten with as much olive oil as you like. Serve the pasta immediately.

DEVILED KIDNEYS on BRIOCHE CROUTES

The expression "deviled" dates from the 18th century. It was used to describe dishes or foods that were seasoned with hot spices giving a fiery flavor that was associated with the devil and the heat of hell—in this case, cayenne pepper and Worcestershire sauce provide the "fire."

SERVES 4

8 mini brioche slices
2 tablespoons butter
1 shallot, finely chopped
2 garlic cloves, finely chopped
1½ cups mushrooms, halved
¼ teaspoon cayenne pepper
1 tablespoon Worcestershire sauce
8 lamb's kidneys, halved and trimmed
⅔ cup heavy cream
2 tablespoons chopped fresh parsley,
    to garnish

1 Preheat the broiler to high and toast the brioche slices until they are a golden brown color on both sides. Set aside, and keep warm.

2 Melt the butter in a large, heavy frying pan until it is just foaming. Add the finely chopped shallot, finely chopped garlic, and halved mushrooms, then cook for about 5 minutes, or until the shallot is just beginning to soften. Stir in the cayenne pepper and the Worcestershire sauce, and simmer the mixture for about 1 minute, stirring constantly with a wooden spoon.

3 Add the kidneys to the pan and cook for 3–5 minutes on each side. Finally, stir in the cream, and simmer for about 2 minutes, or until the sauce is heated through and slightly thickened.

4 Transfer the brioche croutes to warmed plates. Top with the kidneys. Sprinkle with the chopped parsley, and serve immediately.

COOK'S TIPS
• If you can't find mini brioches, you can use a large brioche instead. Slice it thickly, and stamp out croutes using a 2-inch round cutter.
• If you like, the brioche croutes can be fried rather than toasted. Melt 2 tablespoons butter in the frying pan, and fry the croutes until crisp and golden on both sides. Remove from the pan, and drain on paper towels.

Energy 367Kcal/1526kJ; Protein 12.7g; Carbohydrate 18.6g, of which sugars 2.5g; Fat 27.4g, of which saturates 16.3g; Cholesterol 222mg; Calcium 66mg; Fiber 1g; Sodium 299mg.

PORK RIBS with GINGER and CHILI

Ginger, garlic, and chili are used to flavor the sweet-and-sour sauce that coats these ribs.
Cook the pork ribs in a covered clay pot first to tenderize the meat, then uncover the dish
so the ribs become deliciously sticky and brown.

SERVES 4

16–20 small meaty pork ribs, about
    2 pounds total weight
1 onion, finely chopped
2-inch piece fresh ginger root,
    peeled and grated
2 garlic cloves, crushed
½–1 teaspoon chili powder
4 tablespoons soy sauce
3 tablespoons tomato paste
3 tablespoons honey
2 tablespoons red wine vinegar
3 tablespoons dry sherry
4 tablespoons water
salt and ground black pepper

1 Soak the clay pot in cold water for
20 minutes, then drain. Place the ribs in
the clay pot, arranging them evenly.

2 Combine the onion, ginger, garlic, chili
powder, soy sauce, tomato paste, honey,
wine vinegar, sherry, and water.

3 Pour the sauce over the ribs, and toss
to coat them. Cover the clay pot, and
place in an unheated oven. Set the oven
to 425°F. Cook for 1 hour.

4 Remove the lid, baste the ribs and
season with salt and pepper. Cook
uncovered for 15–20 minutes, basting
the ribs two to three times during the
cooking. Serve with steamed rice or
baked potatoes.

COOK'S TIPS
• For a stronger flavor, place the ribs
in a shallow dish, coat them evenly with
the sauce, cover and marinate in a cool
place for 1–2 hours before cooking in
the clay pot.
• If you cannot get hold of fresh ginger
root, ginger in sunflower-seed oil (sold in
small jars) is available from major
supermarkets. It is in a paste form and
can simply be added when the flavor of
fresh ginger root is required. Use
2 teaspoons instead of the fresh ginger.

Energy 633Kcal/2637kJ; Protein 42.9g; Carbohydrate 11.5g, of which sugars 11.2g; Fat 45.2g, of which saturates 14.1g; Cholesterol 149mg; Calcium 43mg; Fiber 0.5g; Sodium 250mg.

LAMB'S LIVER and BACON CASSEROLE

The trick when cooking liver is to seal it quickly, then simmer it gently and briefly. Prolonged and/or fierce cooking makes liver hard and grainy. Boiled new potatoes tossed in lots of butter go well with this simple casserole.

SERVES 4

2 tablespoons extra virgin olive oil or
   sunflower-seed oil
8 ounces rindless unsmoked lean bacon
   strips, cut into pieces
2 onions, halved and sliced
2 cups cremini
   mushrooms, halved
1 pound lamb's liver, trimmed
   and sliced
2 tablespoons butter
1 tablespoon soy sauce
2 tablespoons all-purpose flour
⅔ cup hot, well-flavored
   chicken stock
salt and ground black pepper

1 Heat the oil in a frying pan, add the bacon, and cook until crisp. Add the sliced onions to the pan, and cook for about 10 minutes, stirring frequently, or until softened. Add the mushrooms to the pan, and cook for 1 minute more.

2 Use a slotted spoon to remove the bacon and vegetables from the frying pan, and keep warm. Add the liver to the fat remaining in the pan, and cook over high heat for 3–4 minutes, turning once to seal the slices on both sides. Remove the liver from the pan, and keep warm.

3 Melt the butter in the frying pan, add the soy sauce and flour, and blend together. Stir in the stock and bring to a boil, stirring until thickened. Return the liver, bacon, and vegetables to the pan, and heat through for 1 minute. Season with salt and pepper to taste, and serve immediately with new potatoes and lightly cooked green beans.

Energy 418Kcal/1739kJ; Protein 34.2g; Carbohydrate 9.3g, of which sugars 2.6g; Fat 27.3g, of which saturates 9.5g; Cholesterol 527mg; Calcium 34mg; Fiber 1.3g; Sodium 1257mg.

TENDERLOIN of BEEF STROGANOFF

Legend has it that this Russian recipe was devised by Count Paul Stroganov's cook to use beef frozen by the Siberian climate. The only way that it could be prepared was cut into very thin strips. The strips of lean beef were served in a brandy-flavored cream sauce.

3 Cook the onion and garlic over low heat, stirring occasionally, until the onion has softened. Add the mushrooms, and stir-fry over high heat for 1–2 minutes. Transfer the vegetables and their juices to a dish, and set aside.

4 Wipe the frying pan, add the remaining oil, and heat. Coat a batch of meat with flour, then cook over high heat until well browned. Remove from the pan, then coat, and cook another batch. When the last batch is cooked, replace all the meat and vegetables. Add the brandy, and simmer until it has almost evaporated.

SERVES 8

2½ pounds beef tenderloin
2 tablespoons all-purpose flour
large pinch each of cayenne pepper
    and paprika
5 tablespoons sunflower-seed oil
1 large onion, chopped
3 garlic cloves, finely chopped
6½ cups cremini mushrooms, sliced
5 tablespoons brandy
1¼ cups beef stock
    or consommé
1¼ cups sour cream
3 tablespoons chopped fresh
    Italian parsley
salt and ground black pepper

1 Thinly slice the beef across the grain, then cut it into fine strips. Season the flour with the cayenne and paprika.

2 Heat half the oil in a large frying pan, and add the chopped onion and garlic.

5 Stir in the beef stock or consommé and seasoning, and cook, stirring frequently, for 10–15 minutes, or until the meat is tender and the sauce is thick and glossy. Add the sour cream, stir well, and sprinkle with the chopped fresh Italian parsley. Serve immediately with plain boiled rice and a simple salad.

COOK'S TIP
If you do not have a very large frying pan, it may be easier to cook this dish in a large, flameproof casserole.

Energy 399Kcal/1659kJ; Protein 34.6g; Carbohydrate 6.5g, of which sugars 3g, Fat 23.9g, of which saturates 9.8g; Cholesterol 114mg; Calcium 56mg; Fiber 1.1g; Sodium 85mg.

SWEET-and-SOUR PORK STIR-FRY

This is a great idea for a quick family supper. Remember to cut the carrots into small, thin strips so that they cook in time.

SERVES 4

1 pound pork tenderloin
2 tablespoons all-purpose flour
3 tablespoons oil
1 onion, coarsely chopped
1 garlic clove, crushed
1 green bell pepper, seeded and sliced
12 ounces carrots, cut into thin strips
8-ounce can bamboo shoots, drained
1 tablespoon white wine vinegar
1 tablespoon soft brown sugar
2 teaspoons tomato paste
2 tablespoons light soy sauce
salt and ground black pepper

1 Thinly slice the pork. Season the flour, and toss the pork in it to coat.

2 Heat the oil in a wok or large frying pan, and cook the pork over medium heat for about 5 minutes, until golden and cooked through. Remove the pork with a slotted spoon, and drain on paper towels. You may need to do this in several batches.

3 Add the onion and garlic to the wok or frying pan, and cook for 3 minutes. Stir in the bell pepper and carrots, and stir-fry over high heat for 6–8 minutes, or until beginning to soften slightly.

4 Return the meat to the pan with the bamboo shoots. Add the remaining ingredients with ½ cup water, and bring to a boil. Simmer gently for 2–3 minutes, or until piping hot. Taste, and adjust the seasoning, if necessary, and serve the stir-fry immediately.

VARIATION
Finely sliced strips of skinless, boneless chicken breast portions can be used in this recipe instead of the pork.

Energy 324Kcal/1357kJ; Protein 27.9g; Carbohydrate 23.9g, of which sugars 16.2g; Fat 13.6g, of which saturates 3g; Cholesterol 71mg; Calcium 63mg; Fiber 4.2g; Sodium 646mg.

PORK CHOW MEIN

This is a very speedy dish to cook, but make sure that you prepare all the ingredients before you start to cook. If you don't have a wok, use a very large frying pan instead.

SERVES 4

6 ounces medium egg noodles
12 ounces pork tenderloin
2 tablespoons sunflower-seed oil
1 tablespoon sesame oil
2 garlic cloves, crushed
8 scallions, sliced
1 red bell pepper, seeded and chopped
1 green bell pepper, seeded
    and chopped
2 tablespoons dark soy sauce
3 tablespoons dry sherry
¾ cup bean sprouts
3 tablespoons chopped fresh
    Italian parsley
1 tablespoon toasted sesame seeds

1 Soak the noodles according to the package instructions, then drain well.

2 Thinly slice the pork. Heat the sunflower-seed oil in a wok or large frying pan, and cook the pork over high heat until golden brown and cooked through.

3 Add the sesame-seed oil to the wok or pan, with the garlic, scallions, and bell peppers. Cook over high heat for 3–4 minutes, or until beginning to soften.

4 Reduce the heat slightly, then stir in the soaked noodles, with the dark soy sauce and dry sherry. Stir-fry for about 2 minutes. Add the bean sprouts, and cook for 1–2 minutes more. If the noodles begin to stick to the pan, add a splash of water. Stir in the chopped parsley, and serve the chow mein sprinkled with the toasted sesame seeds.

Energy 404Kcal/1696kJ; Protein 26.9g; Carbohydrate 40.2g, of which sugars 8.5g; Fat 14.8g, of which saturates 3.3g; Cholesterol 68mg; Calcium 45mg; Fiber 3.7g; Sodium 683mg.

MINTED LAMB STIR-FRY

Lamb and mint have a long-established partnership that works particularly well in this full-flavored stir-fry. Serve with plenty of crusty bread.

SERVES 2

10 ounces boneless lamb shoulder or
    leg steaks
2 tablespoons sunflower-seed oil
2 teaspoons sesame oil
1 onion, coarsely chopped
2 garlic cloves, crushed
1 fresh red chile, seeded and
    finely chopped
3 ounces fine green beans, halved
8 ounces fresh spinach, shredded
2 tablespoons oyster sauce
2 tablespoons Thai fish sauce
1 tablespoon lemon juice
1 teaspoon sugar
3 tablespoons chopped
    fresh mint
salt and ground black pepper
fresh mint sprigs, to garnish
noodles or rice, to serve

1 Trim the lamb of any excess fat, and cut into thin slices. Heat the sunflower-seed and sesame oils in a wok or large frying pan, and cook the lamb over high heat until browned. Remove with a slotted spoon, and drain on paper towels.

2 Add the onion, garlic, and chile to the wok, cook for 2–3 minutes, then add the beans, and stir-fry for 3 minutes.

3 Stir in the shredded spinach with the browned meat, oyster sauce, Thai fish sauce, lemon juice, and sugar. Stir-fry for 3–4 minutes more, or until the lamb is cooked through.

4 Sprinkle in the chopped mint, and toss lightly, then adjust the seasoning. Serve piping hot, garnished with mint sprigs, and accompanied by noodles or rice.

Energy 438Kcal/1819kJ; Protein 31.9g; Carbohydrate 9.3g, of which sugars 8g; Fat 30.6g, of which saturates 9.1g; Cholesterol 105mg; Calcium 229mg; Fiber 3.6g; Sodium 1879mg.

STIR-FRIED CRISPY DUCK

This stir-fry would be delicious wrapped in flour tortillas or steamed Chinese pancakes, with a little extra warm plum sauce.

2 Heat the oil in a wok or large frying pan, and cook the duck over high heat until golden and crisp. Keep stirring to prevent the duck from sticking. Remove the duck with a slotted spoon, and drain on paper towels. You may need to cook the duck in several batches.

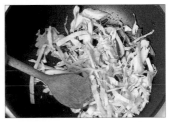

3 Add the scallions to the wok or frying pan, and cook for 2 minutes. Stir in the cabbage, and cook for 5 minutes, or until it is softened and golden.

SERVES 2

10–12 ounces boneless duck breast
2 tablespoons all-purpose flour
4 tablespoons oil
1 bunch scallions, halved lengthwise and
  cut into 2-inch strips, plus extra
  to garnish
2½ cups finely shredded
  green cabbage
8-ounce can water chestnuts, drained
  and sliced
½ cup unsalted cashew nuts
4 ounces cucumber, cut into strips
3 tablespoons plum sauce
1 tablespoon light soy sauce
salt and ground black pepper

1 Remove any skin from the duck breast, then trim off a little of the fat. Thinly slice the meat into even-size pieces. Season the flour with plenty of salt and pepper, and use it to coat each piece of duck completely.

4 Return the duck to the pan with the water chestnuts, cashews, and cucumber. Stir-fry for 2 minutes. Add the plum sauce and soy sauce, and season to taste, then heat for 2 minutes. Serve garnished with the sliced scallions.

Energy 682Kcal/2846kJ; Protein 36.9g; Carbohydrate 41.3g, of which sugars 26.3g; Fat 44.4g, of which saturates 7.5g; Cholesterol 151mg; Calcium 174mg; Fiber 5.8g; Sodium 844mg.

MUSSELS and CLAMS with LEMONGRASS and COCONUT CREAM

Lemongrass has an incomparable flavor and aroma and is widely used in Thai cooking, especially with seafood. If you have difficulty obtaining fresh baby clams for this recipe, then use a few extra mussels instead.

SERVES 6

4–4½ pounds mussels
1 pound baby clams
½ cup dry white wine
1 bunch scallions, chopped
2 lemongrass stalks, chopped
6 kaffir lime leaves, chopped
2 teaspoons Thai green curry paste
scant 1 cup coconut cream
2 tablespoons chopped
    fresh cilantro
salt and ground black pepper
garlic chives, to garnish

1 Clean the mussels by pulling off the beards, scrubbing the shells well, and removing any barnacles. Discard any broken mussels or any that do not close when tapped sharply. Wash the clams.

COOK'S TIP
The kaffir lime tree is native to Southeast Asia, and both the leaves and fruit rind are used in cooking. Dried kaffir lime leaves, available from supermarkets, can be used in place of fresh—add them at the beginning of the cooking time, and remove and discard just before serving.

2 Pour the white wine into a large, heavy pan, and add the scallions, chopped lemongrass stalks, kaffir lime leaves, and Thai green curry paste. Simmer over low heat until the wine has almost evaporated.

3 Add the mussels and clams to the pan, cover tightly, and steam the shellfish over high heat for 5–6 minutes, or until the shells open.

4 Using a slotted spoon, transfer the cooked mussels and clams to a heated serving bowl, and keep hot. At this stage, discard any shellfish that remain closed. Strain the cooking liquid into the clean pan, and gently simmer until it is reduced to about 1 cup.

5 Stir in the coconut cream and fresh cilantro, with plenty of salt and pepper to taste. Increase the heat, and simmer gently until the sauce is piping hot. Pour the sauce over the mussels and clams, and serve immediately, garnished with garlic chives.

Energy 132Kcal/563kJ; Protein 19.6g; Carbohydrate 3.1g, of which sugars 3g; Fat 3.4g, of which saturates 0.6g; Cholesterol 44mg; Calcium 239mg; Fiber 0.3g; Sodium 288mg.

SAFFRON MUSSELS with WHITE WINE and GARLIC

Mussels are easy to cook in a clay pot, and they stay deliciously moist. The saffron adds a lovely pungent flavor as well as its characteristic yellow color to the creamy sauce.

SERVES 4

few saffron threads
2¼ pounds mussels in their shells
2 tablespoons butter
2 shallots, finely chopped
2 garlic cloves, finely chopped
scant 1 cup dry white wine
4 tablespoons heavy cream or
   crème fraîche
2 tablespoons chopped fresh parsley
salt and ground black pepper
French bread, to serve

1 Soak a large clay pot in cold water for about 20 minutes, then drain. Put the saffron in a small bowl, add 1 tablespoon boiling water, and leave to soak.

2 Scrub the mussels, pull off the beards, and discard any open mussels that don't close when tapped. Place all the closed mussels in the soaked clay pot.

3 Melt the butter in a frying pan, add the shallots and garlic, and cook gently for 5 minutes, to soften. Stir in the wine and saffron water, and bring to a boil. Pour the liquid over the mussels.

4 Cover the clay pot, and place in an unheated oven. Set the oven to 425°F. Cook the mussels for 15 minutes, then remove the pot from the oven, and, firmly holding the lid on, shake the pot. Return the pot to the oven and cook for 10 minutes more, or until the mussels have opened.

COOK'S TIP
Saffron is the stigma of a type of crocus. It is an expensive spice and is sold as thin, wiry threads. It has a mild aroma and adds a slightly pungent flavor to both sweet and savory dishes, and also to buns, cakes, and breads. However, the main characteristic of saffron is the distinctive yellow color it imparts once diluted in a liquid.

5 Using a slotted spoon, transfer the mussels to four warmed serving bowls (discard any that have not opened). Mix the cream or crème fraîche and parsley into the cooking liquid, and season to taste. Pour the cooking liquid over the mussels, and serve immediately with French bread to soak up the sauce.

Energy 224Kcal/935kJ; Protein 13.5g; Carbohydrate 1.8g, of which sugars 1.4g; Fat 14.7g, of which saturates 8.5g; Cholesterol 64mg; Calcium 164mg; Fiber 0.2g; Sodium 201mg.

PENNE with CREAM and SMOKED SALMON

This modern way of serving pasta is popular all over Italy. The three essential ingredients combine together beautifully, and the dish is very quick and easy to make. Accompany with salad greens, ciabatta bread, and some sparkling wine for an easy but impressive meal.

SERVES 4

3 cups dried penne
4 ounces thinly sliced
    smoked salmon
2–3 fresh thyme sprigs
2 tablespoons sweet
    butter, diced
⅔ cup light cream
salt and ground black pepper

VARIATION

Although penne is the traditional pasta to serve with this sauce, it also goes very well with fresh ravioli stuffed with spinach and ricotta.

COOK'S TIP

This dish can be served as an appetizer or a main course.

1 Cook the dried pasta in a large pan of salted boiling water for 10 minutes, until it is just tender, or according to the instructions on the package.

2 Meanwhile, using sharp kitchen scissors, cut the smoked salmon slices into thin strips, about ¼ inch wide. Strip the leaves from the thyme sprigs, and rinse in cold water.

3 Drain the pasta, and return it to the pan. Add the butter and heat gently until melted, then stir in the cream with about a fourth of the smoked salmon and thyme leaves, and season with pepper. Heat gently for 3–4 minutes, stirring constantly. Check the seasoning. Divide among four warmed bowls, top with the remaining salmon and thyme leaves, and serve immediately.

Energy 459Kcal/1936kJ; Protein 19.1g; Carbohydrate 65.7g, of which sugars 3.8g; Fat 15.2g, of which saturates 8.2g; Cholesterol 44mg; Calcium 62mg; Fiber 2.6g; Sodium 592mg.

SHRIMP with BAKED GARLIC and ROASTED TOMATOES

Packed full of wonderful Mediterranean flavors, this simple, gutsy dish makes a marvelous first course for a dinner party.

SERVES 4

4 small garlic bulbs
4–5 tablespoons olive oil
1¼ pounds baby plum tomatoes on
    the vine
16 raw jumbo shrimp, in
    their shells
a few sprigs of fresh thyme
salt and ground black pepper
lemon wedges and warm crusty bread,
    to serve

COOK'S TIPS

• If you can't find small garlic bulbs, use
one large one, and bake it in the oven for
about 50 minutes, or until the cloves are
soft and creamy.
• Spread a little of the baked garlic on the
bread, and drizzle with olive oil.

1 Cut a small cross in the top of each
bulb of garlic. Place the bulbs in a garlic
baker, brush with half the olive oil, and
sprinkle with a little salt and ground
black pepper.

2 Place the garlic baker in an unheated
oven, set the temperature to 400°F, and
bake the garlic for about 40 minutes.
The garlic cloves should be soft and
creamy—if not, return them to the oven
and bake for 10 minutes more.

3 Place the tomatoes and shrimp in a
shallow earthenware baking dish. Drizzle
over the remaining olive oil, sprinkle with
thyme sprigs, and season. Place the dish
in the oven after the garlic has been
cooking for 30 minutes; turn the shrimp
after 7 minutes.

4 Arrange the garlic, tomatoes, and
shrimp on a warmed serving plate, and
serve with lemon wedges and plenty of
crusty bread.

Energy 183Kcal/761kJ; Protein 11.7g; Carbohydrate 8g, of which sugars 4.3g; Fat 11.8g, of which saturates 1.8g; Cholesterol 98mg; Calcium 53mg; Fiber 2.3g; Sodium 107mg.

COD and SHRIMP GREEN COCONUT CURRY

This quick curry takes just minutes to make. If you can't find green masala curry paste at your local supermarket, simply substitute another variety—the curry will be just as good.

SERVES 4

1½ pounds cod fillets, skinned
6 tablespoons green masala
    curry paste
¾ cup canned coconut
    milk or scant 1 cup coconut cream
6 ounces raw or cooked,
    peeled shrimp
fresh cilantro, to garnish
basmati rice, to serve

VARIATION

Any firm fish, such as monkfish, can be used instead of cod. Whole fish steaks can be cooked in the sauce, but allow an extra 5 minutes' cooking time, and baste them with the sauce from time to time.

1 Using a sharp knife, cut the skinned cod fillets into 1½-inch pieces.

2 Put the green masala curry paste and the coconut milk or cream into a frying pan. Heat to simmering, and simmer gently for 5 minutes, stirring occasionally.

3 Add the cod pieces and shrimp (if raw) to the cream mixture, and cook gently for 5 minutes. If using cooked shrimp, then add them after this time, and heat through. Garnish the curry with fresh cilantro, and serve immediately with basmati rice.

Energy 255Kcal/1066kJ; Protein 39g; Carbohydrate 2.4g, of which sugars 2.3g; Fat 9.9g, of which saturates 1.5g; Cholesterol 163mg; Calcium 78mg; Fiber 0.4g; Sodium 235mg.

FISH STEW with LEMONGRASS

Lemongrass and ginger give this delicate stew of fish, shrimp, new potatoes, and broccoli an appetizing aromatic flavor.

SERVES 4

2 tablespoons butter
6 ounces onions, chopped
4 teaspoons all-purpose flour
1⅔ cups light fish stock
⅔ cup white wine
1-inch piece fresh ginger root, peeled and
    finely chopped
2 lemongrass stalks, trimmed and
    finely chopped
1 pound new potatoes, scrubbed and
    halved if necessary
1 pound white fish fillets
6 ounces large, cooked, peeled shrimp
10 ounces small broccoli flowerets
⅔ cup heavy cream
4 tablespoons chopped fresh
    garlic chives
salt and ground black pepper
crusty bread, to serve

3 Remove the skin from the fish fillets, and cut the fillets into large chunks. Add the chunks of fish to the pan with the shrimp, broccoli, and cream. Stir gently.

4 Simmer gently for 5 minutes, taking care not to break up the fish. Adjust the seasoning, and sprinkle in the chives. Serve with plenty of crusty bread.

1 Melt the butter in a large pan. Add the onions, and cook for 3–4 minutes. Stir in the flour, and cook for 1 minute.

2 Stir in the fish stock, wine, ginger, lemongrass, and potatoes. Season and bring to a boil. Cover, and cook for 15 minutes.

Energy 515Kcal/2148kJ; Protein 34.9g; Carbohydrate 27.6g, of which sugars 5.9g; Fat 27.4g, of which saturates 16.2g; Cholesterol 202mg; Calcium 131mg; Fiber 3.7g; Sodium 218mg.

GINGERED SEAFOOD STIR-FRY

This would make a lovely summer supper. Serve with lots of bread to mop up the juices and some chilled dry white wine. It would also be good as a first course for four.

SERVES 2

1 tablespoon sunflower-seed oil
1 teaspoon sesame oil
1-inch piece fresh ginger root, peeled
    and finely chopped
1 bunch scallions, sliced
1 red bell pepper, seeded
    and finely chopped
4 ounces small "queen" scallops
8 large shrimp, peeled
4 ounces squid rings
1 tablespoon lime juice
1 tablespoon light soy sauce
4 tablespoons coconut milk
salt and ground black pepper
mixed salad greens and crusty bread,
    to serve

1 Heat the sunflower-seed and sesame oils in a wok or large frying pan, and cook the chopped ginger and sliced scallions for 2–3 minutes, stirring frequently, until golden brown. Add the chopped red bell pepper, and cook, stirring constantly, for 3 minutes more.

2 Add the scallops, shrimp, and squid rings to the wok or frying pan, and cook over medium heat, stirring occasionally with a wooden spoon, for about 3 minutes, until all the seafood is opaque and just cooked through. Add the lime juice and light soy sauce.

3 Pour in the coconut milk, and mix well, then simmer the sauce, uncovered, for 2 minutes, until it begins to thicken slightly.

4 Season the stir-fry well. Arrange the mixed salad greens on two individual serving plates, and spoon over the seafood mixture with the juices. Serve the seafood with plenty of crusty bread to mop up the juices.

Energy 284Kcal/1194kJ; Protein 37.6g; Carbohydrate 11.9g, of which sugars 8.8g; Fat 9.9g, of which saturates 1.6g; Cholesterol 303mg; Calcium 120mg; Fiber 2.2g; Sodium 884mg.

TUNA FRITTATA

This is the ultimate meal in a pan—easy to prepare and easy to serve. For a stronger cheese flavor, try a creamy goat cheese in place of the soft white cheese.

SERVES 2–3

2 tablespoons butter
1 tablespoon olive oil
1 onion, finely chopped
6 ounces zucchini, halved lengthwise
    and sliced
1¼ cups cremini mushrooms, sliced
2 ounces asparagus tips
4 eggs, beaten
scant ½ cup farmer's cheese
    or ricotta cheese
2 tablespoons chopped fresh thyme
7-ounce can tuna, in olive oil, drained and
    coarsely flaked
4 ounces cooked, peeled shrimp
salt and ground black pepper

1 Heat the butter and oil in a nonstick frying pan. Add the chopped onion, and cook for 3 minutes, then add the sliced zucchini, mushrooms, and asparagus tips, and cook for 10 minutes more, or until beginning to soften and brown.

2 Beat together the eggs, cheese, chopped thyme, and plenty of seasoning until they are well combined.

3 Stir the tuna into the pan, add the shrimp, and season well. Heat through gently. Pour over the egg mixture, and cook over gentle heat for 5 minutes.

4 Push the egg away from the sides to let the uncooked egg run onto the pan. Preheat the broiler to medium, and broil the omelet to set and brown the surface. Serve cut in wedges.

Energy 465Kcal/1935kJ; Protein 39.6g; Carbohydrate 3.9g, of which sugars 2.5g; Fat 32.6g, of which saturates 13g; Cholesterol 435mg; Calcium 174mg; Fiber 1.4g; Sodium 1033mg.

SLOW COOKER FISH AND SHELLFISH

Delicious, healthy, and perfectly suited to cooking in a slow cooker, fish and shellfish can be used in a fabulous range of dishes. The gentle heat of this method cooks the delicate flesh to perfection every time. Although large whole fish, such as salmon, are too big for the slow cooker, smaller fish, such as herring and red mullet, fillets, fish steaks, and shellfish are perfect. Unlike meat, fish cooks relatively quickly in the slow cooker, so is ideal for combining with rice or pasta. It is incredibly versatile and can be cooked in all manner of ways, to make both light and hearty dishes. Try Salmon Risotto with Cucumber for a light and sophisticated summer dish, or comforting Fish Pie as a winter warmer.

CREAMY ANCHOVY and POTATO BAKE

This classic Scandinavian dish of potatoes, onions, and anchovies cooked with cream makes a hearty winter lunch or simple supper, served with a refreshing salad. In Norway and Sweden, it is often served as a hot appetizer.

2 Use half of the butter to grease the base and sides of the ceramic cooking pot, and layer half the potatoes and onions in the base of the dish.

3 Drain the anchovies, reserving 1 tablespoon of the oil. Cut the anchovies into thin strips, and lay these over the potatoes and onions, then layer the remaining potatoes and onions on top.

4 Combine the light cream and anchovy oil in a small pitcher, and season with a little ground black pepper. Pour the mixture evenly over the potatoes, and dot the surface with butter.

5 Cover and cook on high for 3½ hours, or until the potatoes and onions are tender. Brown under a hot broiler, if you like, then drizzle over the double cream, and sprinkle with parsley and pepper. Serve with fresh crusty bread.

SERVES 4

2¼ pounds maincrop potatoes
2 onions
2 tablespoons butter
2 x 2-ounce cans anchovy fillets
⅔ cup light cream
⅔ cup heavy cream
1 tablespoon chopped fresh parsley
ground black pepper
fresh crusty bread, to serve

COOK'S TIP
This recipe can also be served as an appetizer for six, or as a side dish to accompany a main meal.

1 Peel the potatoes, and cut into slices slightly thicker than ½ inch. Cut the slices into strips slightly more than ½ inch wide. Peel the onions, and cut into very thin rings.

Energy 378Kcal/1580kJ; Protein 11.3g; Carbohydrate 37.9g, of which sugars 6.4g; Fat 21.2g, of which saturates 11.4g; Cholesterol 54mg; Calcium 1460mg; Fiber 11.5g; Sodium 133mg.

SALMON RISOTTO with CUCUMBER

A classic risotto is time-consuming to make because the stock must be added very gradually and requires constant attention from the cook. Here, the wine and stock are added all at once, making it far easier, yet still giving a delicious, creamy texture.

SERVES 4

2 tablespoons butter
small bunch of scallions,
    finely sliced
½ cucumber, peeled, seeded,
    and chopped
generous 1 cup converted Italian rice
3 cups boiling vegetable
    or fish stock
½ cup white wine
1 pound salmon fillet, skinned
    and diced
3 tablespoons chopped fresh tarragon
salt and ground black pepper

1 Put the butter in the ceramic cooking pot, and switch the slow cooker to high. Leave to melt for 15 minutes, then stir in the scallions and cucumber. Cover, and cook for 30 minutes.

2 Add the rice to the pot, and stir, then pour in the stock and wine. Cover with the lid, and cook for 45 minutes, stirring once halfway through cooking.

3 Stir the diced salmon into the risotto, and season with salt and pepper. Cook for a further 15 minutes, or until the rice is tender and the salmon just cooked. Switch off the slow cooker, and leave the risotto to stand for 5 minutes.

4 Remove the lid, add the chopped tarragon, and mix lightly. Spoon the risotto into individual warmed serving bowls or plates, and serve immediately.

COOK'S TIP
Frozen peas can be used instead of cucumber, if you like. These should be defrosted and stirred into the risotto at the same time as the salmon.

Energy 506Kcal/2122kJ; Protein 28.4g; Carbohydrate 51.3g, of which sugars 2.8g; Fat 20g, of which saturates 5.9g; Cholesterol 70mg; Calcium 91mg; Fiber 1.4g; Sodium 266mg.

SPECIAL FISH PIE

Fish pie topped with melting, cheesy bread crumbs is the ultimate comfort food and is always a firm family favorite. Serve with plenty of lightly steamed green vegetables such as asparagus spears, green beans, or sugar snap peas.

SERVES 4

12-ounce haddock fillet, skinned
2 tablespoons cornstarch
1 cup drained, canned corn
1 cup frozen peas, defrosted
4 ounces peeled cooked shrimp
½ cup cream cheese
⅔ cup milk
¼ cup whole-wheat bread crumbs
½ cup grated Cheddar cheese
salt and freshly ground black pepper

1 Cut the haddock into bitesize pieces, and place in a mixing bowl. Sprinkle with the cornstarch, and toss thoroughly to coat the pieces evenly.

2 Add the corn, peas, and shrimp to the coated haddock pieces, and mix together well. In a separate mixing bowl, blend together the cream cheese, and milk, season with salt and ground black pepper, and pour over the fish mixture. Stir well to combine.

3 Spoon the fish mixture into the ceramic cooking pot. Switch the slow cooker to high, cover with the lid, and cook for 2 hours.

4 Meanwhile, combine the bread crumbs and grated cheese. Spoon the mixture evenly over the top of the dish. Remove the ceramic cooking pot from the slow cooker, and brown the top under a moderate broiler for 5 minutes, until golden and crisp. Serve hot.

COOK'S TIP
To make a more economical dish, leave out the shrimp, and replace them with the same weight of haddock. Alternatively, to make a more extravagant dish, use more shellfish, replacing some of the haddock with the same weight of scallops and shelled mussels.

Energy 306Kcal/1283kJ; Protein 31.3g; Carbohydrate 12.2g, of which sugars 2.1g; Fat 15.1g, of which saturates 9.2g; Cholesterol 153mg; Calcium 224mg; Fiber 0.6g; Sodium 736mg.

SMOKED TROUT CANNELLONI

This delicious dish makes a great change to the classic meat or spinach and cheese cannelloni that are usually served. You can also buy smoked trout ready-filleted, which can save on preparation time. If you buy fillets you will need only about 8 ounces.

SERVES 4

2 tablespoons butter, plus extra
    for greasing
1 large onion, finely chopped
14-ounce can chopped tomatoes
½ teaspoon dried mixed herbs
1 smoked trout, weighing
    about 14 ounces
¾ cup frozen peas, thawed
1½ cups fresh white bread crumbs
16 cannelloni tubes
1½ tablespoons freshly grated
    Parmesan cheese
salt and ground black pepper
mixed salad,
    to serve (optional)

For the sauce
3 tablespoons butter
⅓ cup all-purpose flour
2½ cups milk
1 bay leaf
freshly grated nutmeg

VARIATION
To make a more economical dish, use a drained 7-ounce can of tuna in oil in place of the trout.

1 Melt the butter in a frying pan, add the onion, and cook gently for about 10 minutes, until soft, stirring frequently. Stir in the chopped tomatoes and dried herbs, and simmer uncovered for a further 10 minutes, or until the sauce is very thick.

2 Meanwhile, skin the smoked trout, using a sharp knife. Carefully flake the flesh, and discard all the bones. Add the fish to the tomato sauce, then stir in the peas and bread crumbs, and season with plenty of salt and black pepper.

3 Lightly grease the base and halfway up the sides of the ceramic cooking pot. Carefully spoon the trout filling into the cannelloni tubes, and arrange the filled tubes in the base of the slow cooker, placing them side by side.

4 To make the sauce, melt the butter in the pan, and add the flour. Cook for 1 minute, stirring, then gradually whisk in the milk, and add the bay leaf. Cook over a medium heat, whisking constantly until the sauce thickens, then simmer for 2–3 minutes, continuing to stir. Remove the bay leaf, and season to taste with salt, pepper, and nutmeg.

5 Pour the sauce over the cannelloni, and sprinkle with grated Parmesan. Cover, and cook on high or auto for 1 hour.

6 Switch the slow cooker to low, or leave on auto, and cook for 1–1½ hours, or until the cannelloni is tender. If you like, brown the top under a moderate broiler before serving. Serve with a mixed salad, if using.

Energy 669Kcal/2811kJ; Protein 41.5g; Carbohydrate 74.5g, of which sugars 15.1g; Fat 24.9g, of which saturates 11.9g; Cholesterol 116mg; Calcium 353mg; Fiber 3.1g; Sodium 390mg.

CANNELLONI SORRENTINA-STYLE

There is more than one way of making cannelloni. For this fresh-tasting dish, sheets of cooked lasagne are rolled around a tomato, ricotta, and anchovy filling. You can, of course, use traditional cannelloni tubes, if you prefer.

SERVES 4–6

1 tablespoon olive oil, plus extra for greasing
1 small onion, finely chopped
2 pounds ripe Italian tomatoes, peeled and finely chopped
2 garlic cloves, crushed
1 teaspoon dried mixed herbs
⅔ cup vegetable stock
⅔ cup dry white wine
2 tablespoons sun-dried tomato paste
½ teaspoon sugar
16 dried lasagne sheets
generous 1 cup ricotta cheese
4½-ounce package mozzarella cheese, drained and diced
2 tablespoons shredded fresh basil, plus extra basil leaves to garnish
8 bottled anchovy fillets in olive oil, drained and halved lengthwise
⅔ cup freshly grated Parmesan cheese
salt and ground black pepper

1 Heat the oil in a pan, add the onion, and cook gently, stirring, for 5 minutes until softened. Transfer to the ceramic cooking pot, and switch on to high. Stir in the tomatoes, garlic, and herbs. Season with salt and black pepper to taste, then cover the slow cooker with the lid, and cook for 1 hour.

2 Ladle about half of the tomato mixture out of the cooking pot, place in a bowl and set aside to cool.

3 Stir the vegetable stock, white wine, tomato paste, and sugar into the tomato mixture remaining in the slow cooker. Cover with the lid, and cook for a further hour. Turn off the slow cooker.

4 Meanwhile, cook the lasagne sheets in batches in a pan of salted boiling water for 3 minutes or according to the instructions on the packet. Drain the sheets of lasagne. Separate them, and lay them out on a clean dish towel until needed.

5 Add the ricotta and mozzarella to the tomato mixture in the bowl. Stir in the shredded fresh basil, and season to taste with salt and black pepper. Spread a little of the mixture over each lasagne sheet. Place one halved anchovy fillet across the width of each sheet, close to one of the short ends. Starting from the end with the anchovy, roll up each lasagne sheet to form a tube.

6 Transfer the tomato sauce in the slow cooker to a food processor or blender, and puree until smooth. Wash and dry the ceramic cooking pot, then lightly grease the base and halfway up the sides with a little oil.

7 Spoon about a third of the pureed sauce into the ceramic cooking pot, covering the base evenly. Arrange the filled cannelloni seam-side down on top of the sauce. Spoon the remaining sauce over the top.

8 Sprinkle with the Parmesan. Cover the slow cooker with the lid, and cook on high or auto for 1 hour, then switch to low or leave on auto, and cook for a further hour until the cannelloni is tender. Brown under the broiler, if you like, then serve garnished with basil.

Energy 546Kcal/2293kJ; Protein 25.5g; Carbohydrate 54.3g, of which sugars 9.7g; Fat 24.1g, of which saturates 13.4g; Cholesterol 58mg; Calcium 301mg; Fiber 3.5g; Sodium 282mg.

TUNA LASAGNE

This delicious, comforting dish is perfect for a family supper or casual entertaining, and is incredibly simple to make. Use precooked sheets of lasagne, breaking them into smaller pieces as necessary to fit the shape of your slow cooker.

SERVES 6

5 tablespoons butter, plus extra
    for greasing
1 small onion, finely chopped
1 garlic clove, finely chopped
4 ounces mushrooms, thinly sliced
⅓ cup all-purpose flour
¼ cup dry white wine
⅔ cup heavy cream
2½ cups milk
3 tablespoons chopped fresh parsley
2 × 7-ounce cans tuna in oil
2 canned pimientos, cut into strips
1 cup mozzarella cheese, grated
8–12 sheets precooked lasagne
3 tablespoons freshly grated
    Parmesan cheese
salt and ground black pepper
Italian-style bread, such as ciabatta,
    and green salad,
    to serve

1 Lightly grease the base and halfway up the sides of the ceramic cooking pot.

2 Melt 2 tablespoons of the butter in a large pan, add the onion, and fry gently for 5 minutes until almost soft but not colored. Add the garlic and mushrooms, and cook for a further 3 minutes, stirring occasionally. Tip the vegetables into a bowl, and set aside.

3 Melt the remaining 3 tablespoons of butter in the pan. Sprinkle over the flour, and stir in. Turn off the heat, then gradually blend in the wine, followed by the cream and milk. Gently heat, stirring constantly, until the mixture bubbles and thickens. Stir in the parsley and season well with salt and ground black pepper.

4 Reserve 1¼ cups of the sauce, then stir the mushroom mixture into the remaining sauce.

5 Drain the tuna well, and tip into a bowl. Flake the fish with a fork, then gently mix in the pimiento strips, grated mozzarella, and a little salt and pepper.

6 Spoon a thin layer of the mushroom sauce over the base of the ceramic cooking pot, and cover with 2–3 lasagne sheets, breaking them to fit. Sprinkle half of the tuna mixture over the pasta. Spoon half of the remaining sauce evenly over the top, and cover with another layer of lasagne sheets. Repeat, ending with a layer of lasagne. Pour over the reserved plain sauce, then sprinkle with the Parmesan cheese.

7 Cover the slow cooker with the lid, and cook on low for 2 hours, or until the lasagne is tender.

8 If you like, brown the top of the lasagne under a medium broiler, and serve with bread and a green salad.

Energy 554Kcal/2315kJ; Protein 32.2g; Carbohydrate 28.9g, of which sugars 7.4g; Fat 34.7g, of which saturates 18.5g; Cholesterol 110mg; Calcium 371mg; Fiber 0.6g; Sodium 616mg.

POACHED FISH in SPICY TOMATO SAUCE

This traditional Jewish dish is known as Samak. It is usually served with flatbreads, such as pitta or matzos, but you can serve it with plain boiled rice or noodles, if you prefer.

SERVES 4

1 tablespoon vegetable or olive oil
1 onion, finely chopped
⅔ cup bottled strained tomatoes
⅓ cup boiling fish or vegetable stock
2 garlic cloves, crushed
1 small red chile, seeded and
  finely chopped
pinch of ground ginger
pinch of curry powder
pinch of ground cumin
pinch of ground turmeric
seeds from 1 cardamom pod
juice of 1 lemon,
  plus extra if needed
2 pounds mixed firm white fish fillets
2 pounds chopped fresh cilantro
2 tablespoons chopped fresh parsley
salt and ground black pepper

1 Heat the oil in a frying pan, add the onion, and cook gently, stirring, for 10 minutes until soft but not colored.

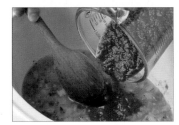

2 Transfer the onions to the ceramic cooking pot, then stir in the tomatoes, stock, garlic, chile, ginger, curry powder, cumin, turmeric, cardamom, lemon juice, salt, and pepper. Cover, and cook on high or auto for 1½ hours, until the mixture is just simmering.

3 Add the fish to the pot, cover, and continue cooking on auto or low for 45 minutes–1 hour, or until the fish is tender. (The flesh should flake easily.)

4 Lift the fish onto warmed serving plates. Stir the fresh herbs into the sauce, then taste, and adjust the seasoning, adding more lemon juice, if necessary. Spoon the sauce over the fish and serve immediately.

Energy 224Kcal/942kJ; Protein 42g; Carbohydrate 4.1g, of which sugars 3.1g; Fat 4.4g, of which saturates 0.6g; Cholesterol 104mg; Calcium 34mg; Fiber 0.8g; Sodium 151mg.

COCONUT SALMON

Salmon is quite a robust fish, and responds well to being cooked with this fragrant blend of spices, garlic, and chili. Coconut milk adds a mellow touch and a creamy taste.

SERVES 4

1 tablespoon oil
1 onion, finely chopped
2 fresh green chiles, seeded and chopped
2 garlic cloves, crushed
1-inch piece fresh ginger root, grated
¾ cup coconut milk
2 teaspoons ground cumin
1 teaspoon ground coriander
4 salmon steaks, each about 6 ounces
2 teaspoons chili powder
½ teaspoon ground turmeric
1 tablespoon white wine vinegar
¼ teaspoon salt
fresh cilantro sprigs, to garnish
rice tossed with scallions,
    to serve

VARIATION

Trout fillets go well with spices and can be used instead of salmon in this dish.

1 Heat the oil in a pan, add the onion, chiles, garlic, and ginger, and fry for 5–6 minutes, until fairly soft. Place in a food processor with ½ cup of the coconut milk, and blend until smooth.

2 Tip the paste into the ceramic cooking pot. Stir in 1 teaspoon of the cumin, the ground coriander, and the rest of the coconut milk. Cover, and cook on high for 1½ hours.

3 About 20 minutes before the end of cooking time, arrange the salmon steaks in a single layer in a shallow glass dish. Combine the remaining 1 teaspoon cumin, the chili powder, turmeric, vinegar, and salt in a bowl to make a paste. Rub the mixture over the salmon steaks, and leave to marinate at room temperature while the sauce finishes cooking.

4 Add the salmon steaks to the sauce, arranging them in a single layer, and spoon some of the coconut sauce over the top to keep the fish moist while it cooks. Cover with the lid, reduce the temperature to low, and cook for 45 minutes–1 hour, or until the salmon is opaque and tender.

5 Transfer the fish to a serving dish, spoon over the sauce, and garnish with fresh cilantro. Serve with the rice.

Energy 363Kcal/1512kJ; Protein 35.9g; Carbohydrate 5.1g, of which sugars 4.2g; Fat 22.2g, of which saturates 3.8g; Cholesterol 88mg; Calcium 59mg; Fiber 0.5g; Sodium 275mg.

MIXED FISH JAMBALAYA

As with the Spanish paella, the ingredients used to make this classic Creole dish can be varied according to what is available. The name jambalaya is thought to have come from the French word for ham—jambon—and the Creole word for rice—à la ya.

SERVES 4

2 tablespoons oil
6 strips rinded smoked fatty bacon, chopped
1 onion, chopped
2 sticks celery, sliced
2 garlic cloves, crushed
1 teaspoon cayenne pepper
2 bay leaves
1 teaspoon dried oregano
½ teaspoon dried thyme
4 tomatoes, skinned, seeded, and chopped
3 cups boiling vegetable or fish stock
1 tablespoon tomato paste
1½ cups converted rice
8 ounces firm white fish, such as haddock, skinned, boned, and cubed
4 ounces cooked shrimp
salt and ground black pepper
4 scallions and 4 cooked shrimp in their shells, to garnish

1 Heat the oil in a frying pan, and cook the bacon over a medium-high heat for 2 minutes. Reduce the heat, add the onion and celery, and cook for a further 5–10 minutes, or until soft and beginning to turn brown.

2 Transfer the mixture to the ceramic cooking pot, and switch the slow cooker to high. Add the garlic, cayenne pepper, bay leaves, oregano, thyme, tomatoes, boiling stock, and tomato puree. Stir well to mix, then cover with the lid, and cook for about 1 hour.

3 Sprinkle the rice over the tomato mixture, followed by the cubes of fish. Season with salt and pepper, and stir. Re-cover, and cook for 45 minutes.

4 Add the shrimp, and stir, then cook for 15 minutes, or until the fish and rice are tender and most of the liquid has been absorbed. Serve garnished with scallions and shrimp in their shells.

COOK'S TIP
If you like a really hot, spicy bite to your jambalaya, serve with a little hot chili sauce for sprinkling over at the table.

Energy 243Kcal/1015kJ; Protein 23.2g; Carbohydrate 6.5g, of which sugars 5.4g; Fat 14g, of which saturates 3.4g; Cholesterol 126mg; Calcium 64mg; Fiber 1.6g; Sodium 1303mg.

HOKI BALLS in TOMATO SAUCE

This simple fish dish is ideal for serving to young children because there is no risk of bones. For adults, it can be spiced up with a dash of chili sauce. It is low in fat and therefore ideal for anyone on a low-fat or low-cholesterol diet.

2 Meanwhile, cut the fish into large chunks, and place in a food processor. Add the bread crumbs and the chives or scallions, and season with salt and pepper. Process until the fish is finely chopped but still has some texture.

3 Divide the mixture into 16 even-size pieces, then roll them into balls with damp hands. Put the fish balls on a plate, and chill in the refrigerator until needed.

4 About 30 minutes before the end of the sauce's cooking time, take the fish balls out of the refrigerator, and leave them to stand at room temperature.

5 Add the fishballs to the sauce in a single layer. Cook for 1 hour on high, then reduce the temperature to low, and cook for a further hour, or until the fish balls are thoroughly cooked. Serve hot, garnished with chives and accompanied by steamed green vegetables.

SERVES 4

14-ounce can chopped tomatoes
2 ounces white mushrooms, sliced
1 pound hoki or other firm white fish
  fillets, skinned
¼ cup whole-wheat bread crumbs
2 tablespoons chopped fresh chives
  or scallions
salt and ground black pepper
chopped fresh chives, to garnish
steamed green vegetables,
  to serve

COOK'S TIP

If hoki is not available, you can use the same weight of cod, haddock, or whiting.

1 Pour the chopped tomatoes into the ceramic cooking pot, then add the sliced mushrooms and a little salt and ground black pepper. Cover with the lid, switch the slow cooker to high, and cook for about 2 hours.

Energy 116Kcal/490kJ; Protein 22.2g; Carbohydrate 4.6g, of which sugars 2.9g; Fat 1.0g, of which saturates 0.1g; Cholesterol 52mg; Calcium 27mg; Fiber 1.0g; Sodium 125mg.

RED MULLET BRAISED on a BED of FENNEL

These pretty pink fish have a wonderful firm flesh and sweet flavor. They are usually cooked whole, but you can remove the heads if there is not enough room in your slow cooker to fit them all in a single layer. Other small whole fish, such as sardines, or fish fillets, such as salmon, cod, and hake, can also be cooked in this way.

SERVES 4

2 teaspoons fennel seeds
1 teaspoon chopped fresh thyme
2 tablespoons chopped fresh parsley
1 clove garlic, crushed
2 teaspoons olive oil
4 red mullet, weighing about
    8 ounces each
lemon wedges, to serve

For the fennel
8 ripe tomatoes
2 fennel bulbs
2 tablespoons olive oil
½ cup boiling fish or
    vegetable stock
2 teaspoons balsamic vinegar
salt and ground black pepper

1 Crush the fennel seeds using a mortar and pestle, then work in the chopped thyme and parsley, garlic, and olive oil.

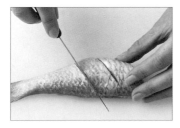

2 Clean and scale the fish, and trim off the fins. Use a sharp knife to make deep slashes on each side of the fish.

3 Push the herb paste into the cuts in the fish, and spread any excess inside the body cavities. Place the fish on a plate, loosely cover with plastic wrap, and leave to marinate. On a warm day, it is best to place the marinating fish in the refrigerator, and then bring to room temperature about 20 minutes before cooking.

4 Meanwhile, prepare the bed of fennel. Put the tomatoes in a heatproof bowl, add boiling water to cover, and leave to stand for 1 minute. Drain and cool under cold running water, and peel off the skins. Quarter the tomatoes, seed, and cut into small dice.

5 Trim the feathery fronds from the fennel (these can be kept for garnishing), then cut the bulbs into ½-inch slices from the top to the root end.

6 Heat the olive oil in a frying pan, and cook the fennel slices over a medium heat for about 10 minutes, or until just starting to color.

7 Transfer the fennel to the ceramic cooking pot. Add the diced tomatoes, hot stock, balsamic vinegar, salt, and pepper, cover with the lid, and cook on high for 2 hours.

8 Give the fennel sauce a stir, then place the red mullet on top in a single layer. Cover, and cook for 1 hour, or until the fish is cooked through and tender. Serve immediately, with lemon wedges for squeezing over.

COOK'S TIP
Red mullet is highly perishable, so be sure to buy very fresh fish. Look for specimens with bright eyes and skin, and that feel firm. The liver is considered a delicacy, so if your fish dealer will clean them for you, ask for the liver along with the fish.

Energy 194Kcal/816kJ; Protein 26.5g; Carbohydrate 4.2g, of which sugars 4.1g; Fat 8.1g, of which saturates 1.2g; Cholesterol 63mg; Calcium 95mg; Fiber 3.0g; Sodium 239mg.

HADDOCK with SPICY PUY LENTILS

Dark brown Puy lentils have a delicate taste and texture and hold their shape during cooking, which makes them particularly good for slow cooker dishes. Red chile pepper and ground cumin add a hint of heat and spice without overpowering the flavor of the fish.

SERVES 4

¾ cup Puy lentils
2½ cups near-boiling vegetable stock
2 tablespoons olive oil
I onion, finely chopped
2 celery sticks, finely chopped
I red chile, halved, seeded
    and finely chopped
½ teaspoon ground cumin
four thick 5-ounce pieces of
    haddock fillet or steak
2 teaspoons lemon juice
2 tablespoons butter, softened
I teaspoon finely grated lemon rind
salt and ground black pepper
lemon wedges, to garnish

I Put the lentils in a strainer, and rinse under cold running water. Drain well, then tip into the ceramic cooking pot. Pour over the hot vegetable stock, cover with the lid, and switch the slow cooker on to high.

2 Heat the oil in a frying pan, add the onion and cook gently for 8 minutes. Stir in the celery, chile, and cumin, and cook for a further 2 minutes, or until soft but not colored. Add the mixture to the lentils, stir, re-cover, and cook for about 2½ hours.

3 Meanwhile, rinse the haddock pieces, and pat dry on paper towels. Sprinkle them with the lemon juice. In a clean bowl, beat together the butter, lemon rind, salt, and a generous amount of ground black pepper.

4 Put the haddock on top of the lentils, then dot the lemon butter over the top. Cover, and cook for 45 minutes–I hour, or until the fish flakes easily, the lentils are tender, and most of the stock has been absorbed. Serve immediately, garnished with the lemon wedges.

COOK'S TIP
Any firm white fish can be cooked in this way. Both cod and swordfish give particularly good results.

Energy 366Kcal/1538kJ; Protein 38.9g; Carbohydrate 25.2g, of which sugars 3.2g; Fat 12.8g, of which saturates 4.3g; Cholesterol 82mg; Calcium 64mg; Fiber 4.7g; Sodium 353mg.

SKATE with TOMATO and OLIVE SAUCE

The classic way of serving skate is with a browned butter sauce, but here it is given a Mediterranean twist with tomatoes, olives, orange, and a dash of Pernod. If time allows, soak the skate in salted water for a few hours before cooking, to firm up the flesh.

SERVES 4

1 tablespoon olive oil
1 small onion, finely chopped
2 fresh thyme sprigs
grated rind of ½ orange
1 tablespoon Pernod
14-ounce can chopped tomatoes
1 cup stuffed green olives
¼ teaspoon superfine sugar
4 small skate wings
all-purpose flour, for coating
salt and ground black pepper
1 tablespoon basil leaves, to garnish
lime wedges, to serve

COOK'S TIP

Pernod gives this dish a deliciously distinctive taste of aniseed, but for those who don't like the flavor, use 1 tablespoon vermouth instead.

1 Heat the oil in a pan, add the onion, and fry gently for 10 minutes. Stir in the thyme and orange rind, and cook for 1 minute. Add the Pernod, tomatoes, olives, sugar, and a little salt and pepper, and heat until just below boiling point.

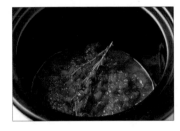

2 Tip the mixture into the ceramic pot, and switch on to high. Cover with the lid, and cook for 1½ hours.

3 Meanwhile, rinse the skate wings under cold water, and pat dry with paper towels. Sprinkle the flour on a large, flat dish, and season well with salt and ground black pepper. Coat each skate wing in the flour, shaking off any excess, then place on top of the tomato sauce.

4 Re-cover the ceramic cooking pot, and reduce the temperature to low. Cook for 1½–2 hours, or until the skate is cooked and flakes easily.

5 Place the fish onto warmed serving plates, and spoon over the sauce. Sprinkle over the basil leaves, and serve with a wedge of lime for squeezing over.

Energy 144Kcal/606kJ; Protein 15.5g; Carbohydrate 8.1g, of which sugars 3.7g; Fat 4.8g, of which saturates 0.7g; Cholesterol 35mg; Calcium 37mg; Fiber 1.4g; Sodium 366mg.

LEMON SOLE and PROSCIUTTO ROULADES

In this elegant dish, prosciutto and delicately textured lemon sole are rolled around a subtle herb and lemon stuffing. Serve this dish for a special dinner party with new potatoes tossed in butter, and lightly steamed asparagus.

2 Remove most of the fat from the prosciutto. Lay two overlapping slices on a board, and place a sole fillet on top, skinned side up.

3 Mix the walnuts, bread crumbs, parsley, eggs, lemon rind, and pepper together, and spread a quarter of the mixture over the fish fillet, then press down gently. Starting at the thicker end of the fillet, carefully roll up the fish and ham to enclose the filling.

4 Repeat with the remaining prosciutto, fish, and filling, then secure each roll with a toothpick.

5 Place the fish seam side down in the ceramic cooking pot. Cover with the lid, then turn the temperature down to low. Cook for 1½–2 hours, or until the fish flakes easily. Remove the cocktail sticks, and serve immediately with freshly cooked vegetables.

SERVES 4

2 teaspoons sweet butter,
  at room temperature
½ cup dry white wine
4 large lemon sole fillets, about
  5 ounces each
8 thin slices of prosciutto, about
  4½ ounces in total
½ cup chopped toasted walnuts
1½ cups fresh white bread crumbs
2 tablespoons finely chopped fresh parsley
2 eggs, lightly beaten
1 teaspoon finely grated lemon rind
ground black pepper
new potatoes and steamed green
  vegetables, to serve

1 Smear the inside of the ceramic cooking pot with the butter. Pour in the wine, and switch the slow cooker to high. Skin the fish fillets, and check that all the bones have been removed, then pat dry with paper towels.

Energy 363Kcal/1521kJ; Protein 38g; Carbohydrate 9.6g, of which sugars 1.5g; Fat 17.3g, of which saturates 3.6g; Cholesterol 201mg; Calcium 134mg; Fiber 0.8g; Sodium 714mg.

BASQUE-STYLE TUNA

In Spain, this traditional fisherman's stew is known as marmitako. *It was formerly cooked at sea on the fishing boats, and takes its name from the cooking pot, known in France as a* marmite. *The rich flavorings go perfectly with the robust taste of chunky tuna.*

SERVES 4

2 teaspoons olive oil
1 onion, finely chopped
1 clove garlic, finely chopped
⅓ cup white wine, preferably Spanish
⅔ cup boiling fish
    or vegetable stock
7-ounce can chopped tomatoes
1 teaspoon paprika
½ teaspoon dried crushed chiles
1 pound waxy new potatoes,
    cut into ½-inch chunks
1 red and 1 yellow bell pepper,
    seeded and chopped
1 small sprig of fresh rosemary
1 bay leaf
1 pound fresh tuna,
    cut into 1-inch chunks
salt and ground black pepper
crusty bread, to serve

3 Stir the chunks of tuna into the sauce. Cover, and cook for 15–20 minutes, or until the fish is firm and opaque.

4 Remove the rosemary and bay leaf, then ladle the stew into warmed dishes, grind over a little more black pepper, and serve with crusty bread.

1 Heat the oil in a large frying pan, add the onion, and fry gently for 10 minutes until soft and translucent. Stir in the garlic, followed by the wine, stock, tomatoes, paprika, and chiles. Bring to just below boiling point, then carefully pour the mixture into the ceramic cooking pot.

2 Add the chunks of potato, red and yellow bell peppers, rosemary, and bay leaf to the pot, and stir to combine. Cover the slow cooker with the lid, and cook on high for 2–2½ hours, or until the potatoes are just tender, then season the sauce to taste with salt and a little ground black pepper.

Energy 797Kcal/1256kJ; Protein 30.1g; Carbohydrate 27.5g, of which sugars 9.6g; Fat 6g, of which saturates 1.2g; Cholesterol 57mg; Calcium 39mg; Fiber 3.2g; Sodium 397mg.

COD with CARAMELIZED ONIONS

After very long slow cooking, sliced onions become caramelized and turn a deep golden color with a fabulously rich, sweet flavor, which is further enhanced here by the addition of balsamic vinegar. Tangy caper and cilantro butter adds a fresh, sharp contrast.

SERVES 4

3 tablespoons butter
2 teaspoons olive oil
2½ pounds yellow onions, peeled
    and finely sliced
1 teaspoon superfine sugar
2 tablespoons balsamic vinegar
2 tablespoons vegetable stock,
    white wine or water
4 x 5-ounce thick cod fillets

For the butter
½ cup butter, softened
2 tablespoons capers,
    drained and chopped
2 tablespoons chopped fresh cilantro
salt and ground black pepper

1 Put the butter and oil in the ceramic cooking pot, and heat on high for about 15 minutes, until melted.

2 Add the sliced onions, and stir to coat well in the butter and oil. Cover the pot with the lid, then place a folded dish towel over the top to retain all the heat. Cook for 2 hours, stirring halfway through cooking time.

3 Sprinkle the sugar over the onions, and stir well to mix. Replace the lid and folded dish towel, and cook on high for 4 hours, stirring two or three times, to ensure the onions color evenly. At the end of the cooking time, they should be a dark golden color.

4 Add the vinegar to the onions and stir in the stock, wine, or water. Cover again, and cook for 1 hour; the onions should now be fairly tender. Season with a little salt and pepper, and stir well. Arrange the cod fillets on top of the onions, and cook for a final 45 minutes–1 hour, or until the fish flakes easily.

5 Meanwhile, make the caper and cilantro butter. Cream the butter in a small bowl until soft, then beat in the capers, cilantro, salt, and pepper. Roll up the butter in foil, plastic wrap, or waxed paper to form a short log shape, twisting the ends to secure them. Chill in the refrigerator or freezer until firm.

6 To serve, spoon the onions and fish onto warmed serving plates. Slice off disks of the butter, and top each piece of fish with one or two slices. Serve immediately, with the butter melting over the hot fish.

Energy 534Kcal/2213kJ; Protein 31.3g; Carbohydrate 25g, of which sugars 18.1g; Fat 35g, of which saturates 20.6g; Cholesterol 152mg; Calcium 96mg; Fiber 4.2g; Sodium 334mg.

SWORDFISH in BARBECUE SAUCE

This is an ideal way to cook any firm fish steaks. The warmly spiced smoky sauce goes particularly well with meaty fish, such as swordfish, shark, and tuna. Choose smaller, thicker fish steaks rather than large, thinner ones, so that they will fit in the slow cooker.

SERVES 4

1 tablespoon sunflower-seed oil
1 small onion, very finely chopped
1 garlic clove, crushed
½ teaspoon chili powder
1 tablespoon Worcestershire sauce
1 tablespoon soft light brown sugar
1 tablespoon balsamic vinegar
1 tablespoon American mustard
⅔ cup tomato juice
4 swordfish steaks, about 4 ounces each
salt and ground black pepper
fresh Italian parsley, to garnish
boiled or steamed rice, to serve

1 Heat the oil in a frying pan, add the onion, and cook gently for 10 minutes, until soft. Stir in the garlic and chili powder, and cook for a few seconds, then add the Worcestershire sauce, sugar, vinegar, mustard, and tomato juice. Heat gently, stirring, until nearly boiling.

2 Pour half the sauce into the ceramic cooking pot. Rinse the swordfish steaks, pat dry on paper towels, and arrange in a single layer on top of the sauce. Top with the remaining sauce.

3 Cover the slow cooker with a lid, and switch on to high. Cook for 2–3 hours, or until the fish is tender and cooked.

4 Carefully transfer the fish to warmed serving plates, and spoon the barbecue sauce over the top. Garnish with sprigs of Italian parsley, and serve immediately with boiled or steamed rice.

COOK'S TIP
For a really smoky barbecue flavor, use a crushed dried chipotle chile instead of the chili powder.

Energy 158Kcal/670kJ; Protein 27.3g; Carbohydrate 4.9g, of which sugars 4.5g; Fat 3.5g, of which saturates 0.6g; Cholesterol 59mg; Calcium 21mg; Fiber 0.2g; Sodium 114mg.

SPINACH and NUT STUFFED HERRINGS

It is difficult to cook large whole fish in a slow cooker, but smaller fish, such as sardines and herrings, are ideal. Their slightly oily flesh is perfectly suited to slow cooking, too, because it helps to keep the fish wonderfully moist.

SERVES 4

3 tablespoons sweet butter
1 teaspoon sunflower-seed oil
¼ cup pine nuts
1 small onion, finely chopped
6 ounces frozen spinach, thawed
1 cup white bread crumbs
⅓ cup grated Parmesan cheese
pinch of freshly grated nutmeg
5 tablespoons fish or vegetable stock
    or white wine
4 small herrings, heads removed,
    and boned
salt and ground black pepper
lemon wedges, to serve

4 Put the onion and spinach in the mixing bowl with the pine nuts, and add the bread crumbs, cheese, nutmeg, salt, and pepper. Mix the ingredients with a fork until thoroughly combined.

7 Arrange the fish on the base of the ceramic cooking pot in a single layer. Cover the pot with the lid, and cook for 1½–2½ hours, or until the fish is cooked. (Test the flesh with a fork; it should flake easily when ready.)

8 Carefully lift the stuffed fish out of the slow cooker onto warmed serving plates, and serve with lemon wedges.

COOK'S TIP
This dish is perfect for a simple, tasty supper, but it is great for entertaining, too. Serve with a tasty couscous salad tossed with plenty of herbs and raisins. The sweetness of the dried fruit goes particularly well with the spinach and pine nut stuffing, and complements the rich flavor of the fish.

1 Heat 2 tablespoons of the butter and sunflower-seed oil in a frying pan until melted. Add the pine nuts and gently fry for 3–4 minutes, until golden. Lift them from the pan with a slotted spoon, leaving the fat behind, and place in a mixing bowl.

2 Add the finely chopped onion to the pan and cook gently for 10 minutes, stirring frequently, until soft.

3 Meanwhile, place the thawed spinach in a fine strainer, and press out as much liquid as possible. (Use your hands to squeeze out the liquid, or press firmly with the back of a spoon.)

VARIATIONS
• Other kinds of nuts can be used in place of pine nuts in the stuffing. Try chopped hazelnuts or walnuts instead.
• As an alternative to nuts, add 1 tablespoon chopped dried apricots to the stuffing.

5 Smear the remaining 1 tablespoon of butter over the base of the ceramic cooking pot, and pour in the stock or wine. Cover with the lid, and switch the slow cooker on to high.

6 Using a sharp knife, make three shallow cuts down each side of the fish, then spoon the stuffing into the cavities, packing it in quite firmly. Bring the edges of the fish together, and secure with wooden toothpicks.

Energy 351Kcal/1462kJ; Protein 24g; Carbohydrate 7.6g, of which sugars 1.9g; Fat 23.9g, of which saturates 6.9g; Cholesterol 78mg; Calcium 619mg; Fiber 1.5g; Sodium 624mg.

NORTHERN THAI FISH CURRY

Thin, soupy, strongly flavored curries are typical of the northern region of Thailand. Fragrant lemongrass, zesty galangal, and salty Thai fish sauce come together to give this dish its characteristic Thai flavor. Serve with lots of sticky rice to soak up the juices.

5 Add the shallots, garlic, galangal or ginger, lemongrass, chili flakes, fish sauce, and sugar to the pot, and stir to combine. Cover with the lid, and cook for 2 hours.

6 Add the cubes of salmon to the stock, and cook for 15 minutes. Turn off the slow cooker, and leave to stand for a further 10–15 minutes, or until the fish is cooked through. Serve immediately.

SERVES 4

1 pound salmon fillet
2 cups near-boiling vegetable stock
4 shallots, very finely chopped
1 garlic clove, crushed
1-inch piece fresh galangal or ginger, finely chopped
1 lemongrass stalk, finely chopped
½ teaspoon dried chili flakes
1 tablespoon Thai fish sauce
1 teaspoon palm sugar or light brown sugar

COOK'S TIP

Allow the fish to return to room temperature before adding to the stock, so that the temperature of the liquid doesn't fall below simmering point.

1 Wrap the salmon fillet in plastic wrap, and place in the freezer for 30–40 minutes to firm up slightly.

2 Unwrap the fish, and carefully remove and discard the skin. Using a sharp knife, cut the fish into 1-inch cubes and remove any stray bones with your fingers or a pair of tweezers.

3 Place the cubed fish in a bowl, cover with plastic wrap, and leave to stand at room temperature.

4 Meanwhile, pour the hot vegetable stock into the ceramic cooking pot, and switch the slow cooker to high.

Energy 216Kcal/902kJ; Protein 23.2g; Carbohydrate 2.7g, of which sugars 2.2g; Fat 12.6g, of which saturates 2.1g; Cholesterol 56mg; Calcium 30mg; Fiber 0.2g; Sodium 522mg.

GREEN FISH CURRY

Fresh-tasting, spicy curries made with coconut milk are a classic of Thai cuisine. This slow cooker version of green curry uses dry unsweetened shredded coconut and cream to give a really rich taste and texture, which is offset by the generous use of spices, chile, and fragrant herbs.

SERVES 4

1 onion, chopped
1 large fresh green chile, halved, seeded, and chopped, plus extra slices to garnish
1 garlic clove, crushed
½ cup cashew nuts
½ teaspoon fennel seeds
2 tablespoons dry unsweetened shredded coconut
⅔ cup water
2 tablespoons vegetable oil
¼ teaspoon cumin seeds
¼ teaspoon ground coriander
¼ teaspoon ground cumin
⅔ cup heavy cream
4 white fish fillets, such as cod or haddock, skinned
¼ teaspoon ground turmeric
2 tablespoons lime juice
salt
3 tablespoons chopped fresh cilantro, plus extra to garnish
boiled rice, to serve

1 Place the onion, chile, garlic, cashew nuts, fennel seeds, and coconut in a food processor with 3 tablespoons of the water, and blend to make a smooth paste. Alternatively, work the dry ingredients to a paste in a mortar with a pestle, then stir in the water.

2 Heat the oil in a frying pan, and fry the cumin seeds for 1 minute, until they give off their aroma. Add the coconut paste, and fry for 5 minutes, then stir in the ground coriander, cumin, and remaining water. Bring to the boil, then let the mixture bubble for 1 minute.

3 Transfer the mixture to the ceramic cooking pot. Stir in the cream, cover with the lid, and switch the slow cooker to high. Cook for 1½ hours.

COOK'S TIP
Do not leave the fish to marinate for longer than 15 minutes, because the texture will be spoiled.

4 Toward the end of cooking time, prepare and marinate the fish. Cut the fillets into 2-inch chunks, and put them in a glass bowl. Combine the turmeric, lime juice, and a pinch of salt in a separate bowl, and pour it over the fish. Use your hands to rub it into the fish. Cover with plastic wrap, and leave to marinate for 15 minutes.

5 Stir the fish into the sauce, re-cover, and cook for 30 minutes–1 hour, or until the fish flakes easily. Stir in the cilantro. Spoon the curry into a warmed bowls. Garnish with chopped cilantro and sliced green chile, and serve with rice.

Energy 511Kcal/2118kJ; Protein 36.1g; Carbohydrate 6.4g, of which sugars 3.9g; Fat 37.9g, of which saturates 18.8g; Cholesterol 132mg; Calcium 50mg; Fiber 2g; Sodium 153mg.

ONE-POT, CLAY-POT FISH AND SHELLFISH

For a healthy, speedy meal with superb flavor, fish and shellfish are the perfect choice. Cooking on top of the stove means that you can check the dish frequently, and serve it the moment it is ready. Italian Fish Stew would make a fine dish for a family meal, Seafood Risotto is a good choice for an impromptu supper with friends, while a more formal dinner would provide the perfect opportunity for trying Octopus and Red Wine Stew, Fish with Fregola, or a colorful Seafood Paella.

ITALIAN FISH STEW

Italians are renowned for enjoying good food, and this stew is a veritable feast of fish and shellfish in a delicious tomato broth—ideal for a family lunch.

SERVES 4

2 tablespoons olive oil
1 onion, thinly sliced
a few saffron threads
1 teaspoon dried thyme
large pinch of cayenne pepper
2 garlic cloves, finely chopped
2 × 14-ounce cans tomatoes, drained
    and chopped
¾ cup dry white wine
8 cups hot fish stock
12 ounces white, skinless fish fillets, such
    as haddock or cod, cut into pieces
1 pound monkfish, cut into pieces
1 pound mussels, scrubbed
8 ounces small squid, cleaned and cut
    into rings
2 tablespoons chopped fresh basil
    or parsley
salt and ground black pepper
thickly sliced bread, to serve

1 Heat the olive oil in a large, heavy pan. Add the onion, saffron threads, thyme, cayenne pepper, and salt to taste. Stir well, and cook over low heat for 10 minutes, until the onion is soft. Add the garlic and cook for 1 minute more.

2 Stir in the chopped tomatoes, dry white wine, and hot fish stock. Bring to a boil, and boil for 1 minute, then reduce the heat to low and simmer gently for 15 minutes.

COOK'S TIP
Cayenne pepper has quite a hot, spicy flavor and was originally made from a type of chile from the Cayenne region of French Guiana. It should be used sparingly.

3 Add the fish pieces to the tomato mixture in the pan, and stir gently. Gently simmer the stew over low heat for 3 minutes more.

4 Add the mussels and squid rings, and simmer for about 2 minutes, until the mussels open. Discard any that remain closed. Stir in the basil or parsley, and season to taste. Ladle into warmed soup bowls, and serve with bread.

Energy 337Kcal/1423kJ; Protein 49.8g; Carbohydrate 8.3g, of which sugars 7.3g; Fat 8.8g, of which saturates 1.5g; Cholesterol 196mg; Calcium 112mg; Fiber 2.2g; Sodium 226mg.

OCTOPUS and RED WINE STEW

Fresh octopus can be quite difficult to handle, so unless you're happy to clean and prepare it for this traditional Greek dish, buy one that's ready for cooking.

SERVES 4

2 pounds prepared octopus
1 pound onions, sliced
2 bay leaves
1 pound ripe tomatoes
4 tablespoons olive oil
4 garlic cloves, crushed
1 teaspoon sugar
1 tablespoon chopped fresh oregano
    or rosemary
2 tablespoons chopped fresh parsley
⅔ cup red wine
2 tablespoons red wine vinegar
chopped fresh herbs, to garnish
warm bread and pine nuts, to serve

COOK'S TIP

The octopus, along with cuttlefish and squid, is a member of the mollusk family—their main shared characteristic is that they have no shell. Octopus can be very tough, so it needs long, slow cooking to tenderize it.

1 Put the octopus in a large pan of gently simmering water with one-fourth of the onions and the bay leaves. Cover the pan, and cook gently for 1 hour.

2 While the octopus is cooking, plunge the tomatoes into boiling water for 30 seconds, then refresh in cold water. Peel off the skins, and chop coarsely.

3 Drain the octopus and, using a small sharp knife, cut it into bitesize pieces. Discard the head.

4 Heat the oil in the pan, and cook the octopus, the remaining onions, and the garlic for 3 minutes. Add the tomatoes, sugar, herbs, wine, and vinegar, and cook, stirring, for 5 minutes.

5 Cover the pan, and cook over the lowest possible heat for about 1½ hours, until the red wine and tomato sauce is thickened and the octopus is tender. To serve, garnish with fresh herbs, and serve with plenty of warm bread, and pine nuts to sprinkle on top.

Energy 371Kcal/1556kJ; Protein 42.5g; Carbohydrate 12.5g, of which sugars 9.9g; Fat 14.5g, of which saturates 2.4g; Cholesterol 108mg; Calcium 113mg; Fiber 2.7g; Sodium 16mg.

GOAN FISH CASSEROLE

The cooking of Goa is a mixture of Portuguese and Indian; the addition of tamarind gives a slightly sour note to the spicy coconut sauce.

SERVES 4

1½ teaspoons ground turmeric
1 teaspoon salt
1 pound monkfish fillet, cut into
    eight pieces
1 tablespoon lemon juice
1 teaspoon cumin seeds
1 teaspoon coriander seeds
1 teaspoon black peppercorns
1 garlic clove, chopped
2-inch piece fresh ginger root,
    finely chopped
1 ounce tamarind paste
⅔ cup hot water
2 tablespoons vegetable oil
2 onions, halved and sliced lengthwise
1⅓ cups coconut milk
4 mild fresh green chiles, seeded and cut
    into thin strips
16 large raw shrimp, peeled
2 tablespoons chopped fresh cilantro
    leaves, to garnish

1 Combine the ground turmeric and salt in a small bowl. Place the monkfish in a shallow dish, and sprinkle over the lemon juice, then rub the turmeric and salt mixture over the fish fillets to coat them completely. Cover, and chill until ready to cook.

COOK'S TIP

Tamarind, which is also known as Indian date, is a popular spice throughout India, Southeast Asia, and the Caribbean. It has little smell, but the distinctive sour, yet fruity taste makes up for this. It is often used in curries and spicy dishes and is available from Indian and Southeast Asian stores and some large supermarkets.

2 Put the cumin seeds, coriander seeds, and black peppercorns in a blender or small food processor, and process to a powder. Add the garlic and ginger, and process for a few seconds more.

3 Preheat the oven to 400°F. Combine the tamarind paste and the hot water, and set aside.

4 Heat the oil in a frying pan, add the onions, and cook for 5–6 minutes, until softened and golden. Transfer the onions to a shallow earthenware dish.

VARIATION

You may use any firm white fish fillets, such as cod, halibut, or hake, instead of the monkfish in this casserole.

5 Add the fish fillets to the oil remaining in the frying pan, and cook briefly over high heat, turning them to seal on all sides. Remove the fish from the pan, and place on top of the onions.

6 Add the ground spice mixture to the pan, and cook over medium heat, stirring constantly, for 1–2 minutes. Stir in the tamarind liquid, coconut milk, and chile strips, and bring to a boil. Pour the sauce into the earthenware dish to coat the fish completely.

7 Cover the earthenware dish, and cook the fish casserole in the oven for about 10 minutes. Add the shrimp, pushing them into the liquid, then cover the dish again, and return it to the oven for 5 minutes, or until the shrimp turn pink. Do not overcook them, or they will toughen. Check the seasoning, sprinkle with cilantro leaves, and serve.

Energy 220Kcal/926kJ; Protein 28g; Carbohydrate 12.8g, of which sugars 10.5g; Fat 6.8g, of which saturates 1g; Cholesterol 113mg; Calcium 103mg; Fiber 1.4g; Sodium 720mg.

MOROCCAN FISH TAGINE

This spicy, aromatic dish proves just how exciting an ingredient fish can be. Serve it with couscous, which you can steam in the traditional way in a colander on top of the tagine.

SERVES 8

3 pounds firm fish fillets, skinned
   and cut into 2-inch chunks
4 tablespoons olive oil
1 large eggplant, cut into
   ½-inch cubes
2 zucchini, cut into
   ½-inch cubes
4 onions, chopped
14-ounce can chopped tomatoes
1⅔ cups bottled
   strained tomatoes
scant 1 cup fish stock
1 preserved lemon, chopped
scant 1 cup olives
4 tablespoons chopped fresh cilantro,
   plus extra cilantro leaves
   to garnish
salt and ground black pepper

For the harissa

3 large fresh red chiles, seeded
   and chopped
3 garlic cloves, peeled
1 tablespoon ground coriander
2 tablespoons ground cumin
1 teaspoon ground cinnamon
grated rind of 1 lemon
2 tablespoons sunflower-seed oil

1 Make the harissa. Process everything in a food processor to a smooth paste.

2 Put the fish in a wide bowl, and add 2 tablespoons of the harissa. Toss to coat, cover, and chill for at least 1 hour.

COOK'S TIP
To make the fish go further, add 1¼ cups cooked garbanzo beans to the tagine.

3 Heat half the olive oil in a shallow, heavy pan. Add the eggplant cubes, and cook for about 10 minutes, or until they are golden brown. Add the zucchini, and cook for 2 minutes more. Remove the vegetables from the pan using a slotted spoon, and set aside.

4 Add the remaining olive oil to the pan, add the onions, and cook over low heat for about 10 minutes, until golden brown. Stir in the remaining harissa, and cook for 5 minutes, stirring occasionally.

5 Add the vegetables, and combine with the onions, then stir in the chopped tomatoes, bottled strained tomatoes, and fish stock. Bring to a boil, then lower the heat, and simmer for about 20 minutes.

6 Stir the fish chunks and preserved lemon into the pan. Add the olives, and stir gently. Cover, and simmer over low heat for about 15–20 minutes. Season to taste. Stir in the chopped cilantro. Serve with couscous, if you like, and garnish with cilantro leaves.

Energy 263Kcal/1099kJ; Protein 32.3g; Carbohydrate 8.3g, of which sugars 7g; Fat 11.3g, of which saturates 1.7g; Cholesterol 75mg; Calcium 57mg; Fiber 3.2g; Sodium 360mg.

FISH PLAKI

Greece has so much coastline, it's no wonder that fish is so popular there. Generally, it is treated simply, but in this recipe the fish is cooked with onions and tomatoes.

SERVES 6

1¼ cups olive oil
2 onions, thinly sliced
3 large, well-flavored tomatoes,
    coarsely chopped
3 garlic cloves, thinly sliced
1 teaspoon sugar
1 teaspoon chopped fresh dill
1 teaspoon chopped fresh mint
1 teaspoon chopped fresh celery leaves
1 tablespoon chopped fresh Italian parsley
1¼ cups water
6 hake or cod steaks
juice of 1 lemon
salt and ground black pepper
extra fresh dill, mint or parsley sprigs,
    to garnish

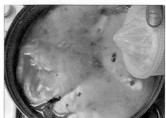

1 Heat the oil in large, heavy sauté pan or flameproof casserole. Add the onions, and cook, stirring, until pale golden, then add the tomatoes, garlic, sugar, dill, mint, celery leaves, and parsley with the water. Season with salt and pepper, then simmer, uncovered, for 25 minutes, until the liquid has reduced by one-third.

2 Add the fish steaks, and cook gently for 10–12 minutes, until the fish is just cooked. Remove the pan or casserole from the heat, and add the lemon juice. Cover, and leave to stand for 20 minutes before serving. Arrange the fish in a dish, and pour the sauce over. Garnish with herbs, and serve warm or cold.

Energy 455Kcal/1885kJ; Protein 79g; Carbohydrate 6.5g, of which sugars 5.3g; Fat 34.9g, of which saturates 5g; Cholesterol 69mg; Calcium 64mg; Fiber 2.2g; Sodium 103mg.

SEAFOOD PIE with RÖSTI TOPPING

In this variation of a classic fish pie, a mixture of white fish and shellfish are combined with a creamy herb-flavored sauce and finished with a grated potato topping.

SERVES 4

1 pound 10 ounces potatoes, unpeeled
   and scrubbed
¼ cup butter, melted
12 ounces cod or haddock fillets, skinned
   and cut into bitesize pieces
4 ounces cooked, peeled shrimp
4 ounces cooked, shelled mussels
8–12 shelled queen scallops
¼ cup butter
1 onion, finely chopped
½ cup all-purpose flour
scant 1 cup dry white wine
1¼ cups fish or vegetable stock
7 tablespoons heavy cream
2 tablespoons chopped fresh dill, plus
   extra sprigs to garnish
1 tablespoon chopped
   fresh parsley
4 tablespoons freshly grated
   Parmesan cheese
salt and ground black pepper

1 Place the potatoes in a large pan. Cover with cold water, and bring to a boil. Cook for 10–15 minutes, or until they are only just tender.

VARIATIONS

• For a speedy version of these individual pies, buy ready-prepared potato rösti and sprinkle it evenly over the fish and sauce as in step 6.

• To make an alternative topping, cook the potatoes until soft, drain, and mash with a little milk and butter. Spoon the mashed potato over the fish and sauce, and top with cheese as in step 6.

• Add 2 tablespoons chopped capers to the sauce at the end of step 5.

2 Drain the potatoes well, and set aside until they are cool enough to handle. Peel, and coarsely grate the parboiled potatoes into a large mixing bowl. Stir in the melted butter, and season well with salt and pepper.

3 Preheat the oven to 425°F. Divide the pieces of cod or haddock and the shrimp, mussels, and scallops among four individual 7½-inch rectangular earthenware dishes.

4 Melt the butter in a large pan, add the onion, and cook for 6–8 minutes, stirring occasionally with a wooden spoon, or until softened and light golden. Sprinkle in the flour, and stir thoroughly with a wooden spoon until well blended.

5 Remove the pan from the heat, and gradually pour in the wine and stock, stirring constantly until smooth. Bring to a boil, stirring constantly, then stir in the cream, dill, and parsley, and season. Pour the sauce over the fish.

6 Sprinkle the grated potato evenly over the fish and sauce in the dishes, and top with the grated Parmesan cheese. Bake for 25 minutes, or until the topping is crisp and golden and the fish is cooked. Serve hot, garnished with dill.

COOK'S TIP

Choose waxy potatoes for this dish and cook until barely tender. Mealy potatoes are too soft and will break up, so if you have only mealy potatoes, opt for the mashed potato option (see Variations).

Energy 770Kcal/3215kJ; Protein 47.3g; Carbohydrate 44.5g, of which sugars 4.5g; Fat 42.4g, of which saturates 25.5g; Cholesterol 236mg; Calcium 298mg; Fiber 2.7g; Sodium 626mg.

SHELLFISH TAGINE

The distinctive mixture of spices and chiles used in this tagine is known as charmoula—a classic Moroccan marinade for fish, meat, and vegetable dishes.

SERVES 4

4 tablespoons olive oil
4 garlic cloves, sliced
1–2 fresh green chiles, seeded
    and chopped
a large handful of Italian parsley,
    coarsely chopped
1 teaspoon coriander seeds
2½ teaspoons ground allspice
6 cardamom pods, split open
½ teaspoon ground turmeric
1 tablespoon lemon juice
12 ounces scorpion fish or red snapper
    fillets, cut into large chunks
8 ounces squid, cleaned and
    cut into rings
1 onion, chopped
4 tomatoes, seeded and chopped
1¼ cups warm fish or vegetable stock
8 ounces large, raw shrimp
1 tablespoon chopped fresh cilantro
salt and ground black pepper
lemon wedges, to garnish
couscous or rice and crusty bread,
    to serve

1 Place the olive oil, garlic, chiles, parsley, coriander seeds, allspice, and cardamom pods in a mortar, and pound to a smooth paste using a pestle. Stir in the ground turmeric, salt, pepper, and lemon juice.

VARIATIONS

Scorpion fish is the traditional choice for this dish, and red mullet or snapper makes a good, authentic alternative, but there's no reason why you shouldn't substitute other fish—try red bream, porgy, or even halved cod or hake steaks.

2 Place the chunks of fish in a large glass or china bowl with the squid rings, add the spice paste, and toss together. Cover and leave the fish to marinate in the refrigerator for about 2 hours, or longer, if there is sufficient time.

3 Place the chopped onion, seeded and chopped tomatoes, and fish or vegetable stock in a tagine (see Cook's Tip), and cover. Place the tagine in an unheated oven, and set the oven to 400°F. Cook the vegetables for 20 minutes.

4 Remove the fish from the marinade, then drain well. Set aside the squid and any excess marinade, then place the fish in the tagine with the vegetables. Cover, and cook in the oven for 5 minutes.

5 Add the shrimp, squid rings, and the remaining marinade to the tagine, and stir to combine. Cover the tagine, and return it to the oven for 5–10 minutes, or until all the fish, shrimp, and squid are cooked right through.

6 Taste the sauce, and season to taste with salt and pepper, if necessary, then stir in the chopped cilantro. Serve immediately, garnished with lemon wedges. Serve the tagine with couscous or rice and crusty bread to soak up the juices.

COOK'S TIPS

• A tagine is a traditional Moroccan stew, and it is also the name given to the shallow earthenware cooking dish with a tall, conical, earthenware lid in which the stew is traditionally cooked. A shallow, earthenware baking dish or a soaked, shallow clay pot can be used in place of a tagine.
• To ensure that the fish fillets have no tiny bones left in the flesh after filleting, lay the fillets on a board, skin side down, and run your hand gently over the surface of the flesh. Pull out any bones that you find, using a pair of tweezers.

Energy 301Kcal/1261kJ; Protein 37.2g; Carbohydrate 7.1g, of which sugars 5.5g; Fat 14g, of which saturates 2.2g; Cholesterol 269mg; Calcium 128mg; Fiber 2.2g; Sodium 251mg.

FISH with SPINACH and LIME

Fresh herbs and hot spices are combined to make the charmoula marinade that is used to flavor this delicious Moroccan-style dish. Crusty bread makes a good accompaniment.

SERVES 4

1½ pounds white fish,
    such as haddock, cod, sea bass,
    or monkfish
sunflower-seed oil, for frying
1¼ pounds potatoes, sliced
1 onion, chopped
1–2 garlic cloves, crushed
5 tomatoes, peeled and chopped
13 ounces fresh spinach, chopped
lime wedges, to garnish

For the charmoula
6 scallions, chopped
2 teaspoons fresh thyme
4 tablespoons chopped Italian parsley
2 tablespoons chopped fresh cilantro
2 teaspoons paprika
generous pinch of cayenne pepper
4 tablespoons olive oil
grated rind of 1 lime and 4 tablespoons
    lime juice
salt

1 Cut the white fish into large, even-size pieces, discarding any skin and bones. Place the fish in a large, shallow dish.

2 Blend together the ingredients for the charmoula. Season with salt. Pour over the fish, stir to mix, and leave in a cool place, covered with plastic wrap, to marinate for 2–4 hours.

3 Heat about ¼ inch oil in a large, heavy pan, add the potato slices, and cook, turning them occasionally, until they are cooked right through and golden brown. Drain the fried potatoes on paper towels.

4 Pour off all but 1 tablespoon of the oil from the pan, and add the onion, garlic, and tomatoes. Cook over gentle heat for 5–6 minutes, stirring occasionally, until the onion is soft. Place the potatoes on top, and then add the spinach.

5 Place the marinated fish pieces on top of the chopped spinach in the pan, and pour over all of the marinade. Cover the pan tightly, and cook for 15–18 minutes. After about 8 minutes of the cooking time, carefully stir the contents of the pan with a wooden spoon, so that the pieces of fish at the top are distributed throughout the dish.

6 Cover the pan again, and continue cooking, but check occasionally—the dish is cooked once the fish is just tender and opaque and the spinach has wilted. Serve the dish hot, with wedges of lime and plenty of warm crusty bread, if you like.

Energy 433Kcal/1810kJ; Protein 37.3g; Carbohydrate 28.9g, of which sugars 9.4g; Fat 19.3g, of which saturates 2.8g; Cholesterol 78mg; Calcium 206mg; Fiber 5.2g; Sodium 260mg.

FISH with FREGOLA

This Sardinian speciality is a cross between a soup and a stew. Serve it with crusty Italian country bread to mop up the juices.

SERVES 4–6

5 tablespoons olive oil
4 garlic cloves, finely chopped
½ small fresh red chile, seeded and
   finely chopped
1 large handful fresh Italian parsley,
   coarsely chopped
1 red snapper, about 1 pound, cleaned,
   with head and tail removed
1 porgy, about 1¼ pounds, cleaned, with
   head and tail removed
12 ounces–1 pound thick cod fillet
14-ounce can chopped plum tomatoes
1½ cups dried fregola
1 cup water
salt and ground black pepper

1 Heat 2 tablespoons of the olive oil in a large, flameproof casserole. Add the chopped garlic and chile, with about half the chopped fresh parsley. Cook over medium heat, stirring occasionally, for about 5 minutes.

2 Cut all of the fish into large chunks—including the skin and the bones in the case of the snapper and porgy—and add the pieces to the casserole. Sprinkle with 2 tablespoons more of the olive oil, and cook for a few minutes more.

3 Blend together the ingredients for the charmoula. Add salt. Pour over the fish, stir, and leave in a cool place, covered with plastic wrap, to marinate for 2–4 hours.

4 Add the fregola, and simmer for about 5 minutes, then add the water and the remaining oil. Simmer for 15 minutes, until the fregola is just tender.

5 If the sauce becomes too thick, add more water, then taste for seasoning. Serve hot, in warmed bowls, sprinkled with the remaining parsley.

VARIATION
Any white fish fillet can be used instead of cod in this dish. Monkfish, haddock, hake, or flounder could all be used.

COOK'S TIPS
• Fregola is a tiny pasta shape from Sardinia. If you can't get it, use a tiny soup pasta (*pastina*), such as *corallini* or *semi de melone*.
• You can make the basic fish sauce several hours in advance or even the day before, bringing it to a boil and adding the fregola just before serving.

Energy 300Kcal/1256kJ; Protein 29.6g; Carbohydrate 17.3g, of which sugars 2.3g; Fat 12.9g, of which saturates 1.7g; Cholesterol 44mg; Calcium 79mg; Fiber 1.1g; Sodium 126mg.

SEAFOOD PAELLA

There are as many versions of paella as there are regions of Spain. Those from near the coast contain a lot of seafood, while inland versions add chicken or pork. Here the only meat is the chorizo—essential for an authentic flavor.

SERVES 4

3 tablespoons olive oil
1 large onion, chopped
2 fat garlic cloves, chopped
5 ounces chorizo, sliced
11 ounces small squid, cleaned
1 red bell pepper, seeded
  and sliced
4 tomatoes, peeled, seeded, and diced,
  or 7-ounce can tomatoes
generous 2 cups chicken stock
7 tablespoons dry white wine
1 cup short grain Spanish rice
  or risotto rice
large pinch of saffron threads
1¼ cups fresh or frozen peas
12 large cooked shrimp, in the shell, or
  8 langoustines
1 pound mussels, scrubbed
1 pound clams, scrubbed
salt and ground black pepper

1 Heat the olive oil in a large sauté pan or a paella pan, add the onion and garlic, and cook until the onion is translucent. Add the chorizo, and cook until golden.

2 If the squid are very small, you can leave them whole; otherwise cut the bodies into rings and the tentacles into pieces. Add the squid to the pan, and sauté over high heat for 2 minutes, stirring occasionally.

3 Stir in the bell pepper slices and the diced tomatoes, and simmer gently for 5 minutes, until the bell pepper slices are tender. Pour in the stock and wine, stir well, and bring to a boil.

4 Stir in the rice and saffron, and season to taste with salt and pepper. Spread the contents of the pan in an even layer over the base. Bring the liquid back to a boil, then lower the heat, and simmer gently for 10 minutes.

5 Add the peas, shrimp or langoustines, mussels, and clams, stirring them gently into the rice. Cook gently for another 15–20 minutes, until the rice is tender and all the mussels and clams have opened. If any remain closed, discard them. If the paella seems dry, add a little more stock. Gently stir everything together, and serve piping hot.

Energy 613Kcal/2566kJ; Protein 43.1g; Carbohydrate 57.7g, of which sugars 10g; Fat 21.8g, of which saturates 5.4g; Cholesterol 313mg; Calcium 246mg; Fiber 4.4g; Sodium 639mg.

SEAFOOD RISOTTO

Creamy, saffron-flavored rice makes the perfect foil for shellfish. Ready-prepared, frozen seafood mixtures, which include shrimp, squid, and mussels, are ideal for making this quick and easy dish—remember to thaw them before cooking.

SERVES 4

4 cups hot fish or
    shellfish stock
¼ cup sweet butter
2 shallots, chopped
2 garlic cloves, chopped
1¾ cups risotto rice
⅔ cup dry white wine
½ teaspoon powdered saffron, or
    a pinch of saffron threads
14 ounces mixed prepared seafood,
    thawed if frozen
2 tablespoons freshly grated
    Parmesan cheese
2 tablespoons chopped fresh Italian
    parsley, to garnish
salt and ground black pepper

I Pour the fish or shellfish stock into a large, heavy pan. Bring it to a boil, then pour it into a large, heatproof pitcher or bowl, and keep warm.

2 Melt the butter in the rinsed-out pan, add the shallots and garlic, and cook over low heat for 3–5 minutes, stirring occasionally, until the shallots are soft but not colored. Add the rice, stir well to coat the grains completely with butter, then pour in the dry white wine. Cook over medium heat, stirring occasionally, until the wine has been absorbed by the rice.

COOK'S TIP
It is essential to use proper risotto rice, such as arborio or carnaroli, for this dish; it has a wonderfully creamy texture when cooked but still retains a "bite."

3 Add a ladleful of hot stock and the saffron, and cook, stirring constantly, until the liquid has been absorbed. Add the seafood, and stir well. Continue to add hot stock, a ladleful at a time, waiting until each quantity has been absorbed before adding more. Stir the mixture for about 20 minutes in all, until the rice is swollen and creamy, but still with a little bite in the middle.

VARIATION
Use peeled shrimp, or cubes of fish such as cod or salmon in place of the mixed prepared seafood.

4 Vigorously mix in the freshly grated Parmesan cheese, and season to taste, then sprinkle over the chopped parsley, and serve immediately.

Energy 547Kcal/2284kJ; Protein 27.3g; Carbohydrate 71.3g, of which sugars 17g; Fat 13.8g, of which saturates 8.2g; Cholesterol 229mg; Calcium 195mg; Fiber 0.2g; Sodium 350mg.

BAKED SEA BREAM with TOMATOES

John Dory, halibut, or sea bass can all be cooked this way. If you prefer to use filleted fish, choose a chunky fillet, such as cod, and roast it skin side up. Roasting the tomatoes brings out their sweetness, which contrasts beautifully with the flavor of the fish.

SERVES 4–6

8 ripe tomatoes
2 teaspoons sugar
scant 1 cup olive oil
1 pound new potatoes
1 lemon, sliced
1 bay leaf
1 fresh thyme sprig
8 fresh basil leaves
1 sea bream, about 2–2¼ pounds,
   cleaned and scaled
⅔ cup dry white wine
2 tablespoons fresh white breadcrumbs
2 garlic cloves, crushed
1 tablespoon finely chopped fresh parsley
salt and ground black pepper
chopped fresh Italian parsley or basil
   leaves, to garnish

1 Preheat the oven to 475°F. Cut the tomatoes in half lengthwise, and arrange them in a single layer in a baking dish, cut side up. Sprinkle with sugar, salt, and pepper, and drizzle over a little of the olive oil. Roast for 30–40 minutes, until lightly browned. Remove the tomatoes from the dish, and set aside.

2 Meanwhile, cut the potatoes into ½-inch slices. Place in a large pan of salted water, and parboil for 5 minutes. Drain, and set aside.

3 Grease the baking dish with a little more of the oil. Arrange the potatoes in a single layer with the lemon slices on top; sprinkle on the herbs. Season, and drizzle with half the remaining oil. Lay the fish on top, and season. Pour over the wine and the rest of the oil. Arrange the tomatoes around the fish.

4 Combine the bread crumbs, garlic, and parsley; sprinkle over the fish. Bake for 30 minutes. Garnish with chopped parsley or basil.

Energy 440Kcal/1840kJ; Protein 26g; Carbohydrate 21.5g, of which sugars 6.6g; Fat 26.7g, of which saturates 3.4g; Cholesterol 51mg; Calcium 76mg; Fiber 2g; Sodium 205mg.

FILLETS of SOLE in RED WINE SAUCE

Forget the old maxim that red wine and fish do not go well together. The robust sauce
adds color and richness to this excellent dish, which is more than elegant enough for a
dinner party. Halibut and John Dory are also good cooked this way.

SERVES 4

4 fillets of sole, about 6–7 ounces
    each, skinned
10 tablespoons chilled butter, diced, plus
    extra for greasing
4 ounces shallots, thinly sliced
scant 1 cup robust red wine
scant 1 cup fish stock
salt and ground black and white pepper
fresh Italian parsley leaves, or chervil,
    to garnish

1 Preheat the oven to 350°F. Season the
fish fillets on both sides with salt and
ground black pepper. Generously butter
a shallow flameproof dish that is large
enough to take all the sole fillets in a
single layer. Spread the shallots in an
even layer in the dish, and lay the fish
fillets on top. Season well with salt and
ground black pepper.

2 Pour in the red wine and fish stock,
cover the dish with a lid or foil, and then
bring the liquid to just below boiling
point. Transfer the dish to the oven, and
bake for 6–8 minutes, or until the sole is
just cooked.

3 Using a metal spatula, lift the fish and
shallots onto a serving dish, cover with
foil, and keep hot.

4 Transfer the dish to the stove, and
bring the cooking liquid to a boil over
high heat. Cook it until it has reduced by
half. Lower the heat, and whisk in the
chilled butter, one piece at a time, to
make a smooth, shiny sauce. Season with
salt and ground white pepper; set the
sauce aside, and keep hot.

5 Divide the shallots among four
warmed plates, and lay the sole fillets
on top. Pour the sauce over and around
the fish, and garnish with the fresh Italian
parsley, or chervil.

Energy 515Kcal/2142kJ; Protein 35.6g; Carbohydrate 2.6g, of which sugars 1.9g; Fat 36.7g, of which saturates 19.5g; Cholesterol 156mg; Calcium 98mg; Fiber 0.4g; Sodium 452mg.

MONKFISH with ARUGULA PESTO, BELL PEPPERS, and ONIONS

Colorful Mediterranean vegetables complement richly flavored monkfish layered with pesto sauce in this impressive-looking clay pot dish.

SERVES 4

2 pounds monkfish tail
2 ounces arugula
2 tablespoons pine nuts
1 garlic clove, chopped
⅓ cup freshly grated
　　Parmesan cheese
6 tablespoons olive oil
3 tablespoons lemon juice
2 red bell peppers, halved
2 yellow bell peppers, halved
1 red onion, cut into wedges
2 zucchini, cut into
　　1-inch slices
4 fresh rosemary sprigs
salt and ground black pepper

3 Place the arugula, pine nuts, chopped garlic, freshly grated Parmesan cheese, 3 tablespoons of the olive oil, and 1 tablespoon of the lemon juice in a food processor or blender, and process to form a smooth paste.

1 Remove any skin or membrane from the monkfish. Using a large, sharp knife, cut along one side of the central bone, as close to the bone as possible, and then remove the fish fillet. Repeat on the other side. Set aside.

2 Soak a fish clay pot in cold water for 20 minutes, then drain, and set aside.

VARIATIONS
• Salmon tail fillets or thick fillets of cod or haddock could be used in place of the monkfish. Remove the skin from the fish, and run your hand along the other side to check for any hidden bones, and, if necessary, remove these with tweezers.
• Arugula makes an interestingly peppery pesto, but other leafy herbs can be used to make this sauce. Basil is the classic choice, but Italian parsley is also good.

4 Lay one fish fillet out flat, cut side up, and spread with the pesto. Place the remaining fillet on top, cut side down, on top of the layer of pesto. Tie the fish with string at regular intervals to seal together. Sprinkle with plenty of salt and pepper to season, and set aside.

5 Cut each bell pepper half into three, lengthwise. Remove the core and seeds.

6 Place the pieces of bell pepper in the clay pot with the onion wedges and zucchini slices. In a small bowl, combine 1 tablespoon of the olive oil and the remaining lemon juice, and sprinkle over the vegetables. Mix well, and season with salt and plenty of black pepper.

7 Tuck the fresh rosemary sprigs in among the vegetables. Cover the clay pot, and place in an unheated oven. Set the temperature to 425°F, and cook the vegetables for 20 minutes.

8 Remove the clay pot from the oven, place the monkfish parcel in the center of the vegetables, and brush it with 1 tablespoon of the olive oil. Sprinkle the remaining oil over the vegetables. Cover the pot again, then return it to the oven, and cook for 20–25 minutes more, or until the monkfish is cooked through and turns opaque.

9 To serve, cut the fish into thick slices, removing the string, if you like, and serve with the cooked vegetables.

Energy 477Kcal/1991kJ; Protein 47g; Carbohydrate 14.7g, of which sugars 13.7g; Fat 25.8g, of which saturates 4.5g; Cholesterol 42mg; Calcium 160mg; Fiber 4.3g; Sodium 139mg.

BAKED MONKFISH with POTATOES and GARLIC

This simple supper dish can be made with other fish. Sauce tartare or a thick vinaigrette flavored with chopped gherkins and hard-cooked egg are delicious accompaniments.

3 Pour the main batch of stock over the potatoes, and bake, uncovered, stirring once or twice, for about 50 minutes, or until the potatoes are just tender.

4 Nestle the monkfish tail into the potatoes, and season to taste with salt and ground black pepper. Mix the 3 tablespoons of stock with the wine, and use to baste the monkfish two or three times during cooking. Bake the monkfish and potatoes for 10–15 minutes.

5 Finely chop the remaining garlic. Melt the remaining butter, and toss it with the fresh bread crumbs, chopped garlic, most of the chopped parsley, and seasoning. Spread the crumb mixture over the monkfish, pressing it down gently with the back of a spoon.

SERVES 4

¼ cup butter
2 onions, thickly sliced
2¼ pounds waxy potatoes, peeled and
   cut into small chunks
4 garlic cloves
a few fresh thyme sprigs
2–3 fresh bay leaves
scant 2 cups vegetable
   or fish stock, plus 3 tablespoons
2 pounds monkfish tail in one piece,
   membrane removed
2–3 tablespoons white wine
1 cup fresh white bread crumbs
½ cup fresh Italian parsley,
   finely chopped
1 tablespoon olive oil
salt and ground black pepper

1 Preheat the oven to 375°F. Melt half the butter in a shallow flameproof dish, and cook the onions for 5 minutes, until soft. Stir in the potatoes.

2 Slice two of the garlic cloves, and add them to the dish with the thyme and bay leaves, and season with salt and pepper.

6 Drizzle the olive oil over the crumb-covered fish, then return the dish to the oven, and bake for 10–15 minutes more, or until the bread crumbs are crisp and golden brown and all the liquid has been absorbed. Sprinkle the remaining chopped parsley onto the potatoes and fish, and serve immediately.

Energy 529Kcal/2230kJ; Protein 45.8g; Carbohydrate 54g, of which sugars 6.5g; Fat 15g, of which saturates 7.4g; Cholesterol 63mg; Calcium 67mg; Fiber 3.5g; Sodium 245mg.

JANSSON'S TEMPTATION

*A traditional Swedish favorite, this rich gratin is utterly moreish. As food writer Jane
Grigson pointed out, the name probably does not refer to a specific Jansson but means
"everyone's temptation" as Jansson is a common Swedish surname.*

SERVES 4–6

¼ cup butter
2 pounds potatoes
2 large, sweet onions, sliced
2 × 2-ounce cans anchovies in olive
   oil, drained
scant 2 cups whipping cream or
   half and half heavy and
   light cream
a little milk (optional)
salt and ground black pepper

1 Preheat the oven to 400°F. Use
1 tablespoon of the butter to grease the
base and sides of a shallow, 6¼-cup
earthenware baking dish.

4 Lay half of the onions on top of the
potatoes, season with black pepper,
and dot with butter. Lay the anchovies
on top of the onions, then add the
rest of the sliced onions, and top with
the remaining potatoes.

5 Mix the cream with 2 tablespoons
cold water, and pour this mixture over
the potatoes and onions in the dish.
Add a little milk, if necessary, to bring
the liquid to just below the top of the
final layer of potato batons.

6 Dot the potatoes with the remaining
butter, then cover the dish with foil, and
bake for 1 hour.

7 Reduce the oven temperature to
350°F, and remove the foil from the top
of the dish. Bake for 40–50 minutes
more, or until the potatoes are tender
when tested with a knife and golden
brown in color.

2 Using a small sharp knife, carefully cut
the potatoes into thin slices, then cut
the slices into fine batons.

3 Toss the potato batons with salt and
ground black pepper, and sprinkle half
of them in the base of the prepared
ovenproof dish.

COOK'S TIPS
• It is important to cover the gratin with
foil for the first half of the cooking time,
so that the potatoes don't brown or dry
out too much.
• If you are using whole, salted anchovies
or small whitebait or smelts, they will
need to be boned. If they are very salty,
soak in a little milk for about 30 minutes
before using.
• Serve with small glasses of chilled
schnapps and cold beer for an authentic
Swedish flavor.

Energy 509Kcal/2111kJ; Protein 9.1g; Carbohydrate 31.5g, of which sugars 7.8g; Fat 39.3g, of which saturates 23.7g; Cholesterol 107mg; Calcium 121mg; Fiber 2.1g; Sodium 743mg.

BAKED SARDINES with CAPER and TOMATO STUFFING

Sardines are often a popular choice for cooking on the barbecue, but you can enjoy these delicious Mediterranean-style baked sardines all year round.

SERVES 4

16 fresh sardines, cleaned
8–12 cherry tomatoes, on the vine, sliced
3 tablespoons capers, chopped
½ small red onion, very finely chopped
4 tablespoons olive oil
grated rind and juice 1 lemon
3 tablespoons chopped fresh parsley
1 tablespoon chopped fresh basil
fresh basil sprigs and lemon wedges,
    to garnish
crusty bread, to serve

COOK'S TIP
Removing the bones before cooking, as in step 1 of this recipe, makes the sardines easier to eat.

1 Remove the backbone from the sardines by placing slit side down on a cutting board. Using your fingers, push firmly along the length of the backbone to loosen it from the flesh. Turn the sardine over, and pull out the bone; cut the ends with a sharp knife to release it. Repeat with the remaining sardines.

2 Place the tomato slices inside each sardine; they may stick out slightly, depending on the size of the fish. Mix the capers and red onion together, and place on top of the tomatoes.

3 Preheat the oven to 400°F. Lay the sardines in a single layer in a large earthenware dish.

4 Combine the olive oil, lemon rind and juice, parsley, and basil, and drizzle over the sardines. Bake the sardines for about 10 minutes, or until the flesh flakes easily. Garnish with basil and lemon wedges, and serve with plenty of crusty bread to mop up the sauce.

Energy 214Kcal/887kJ; Protein 13.3g; Carbohydrate 3.4g, of which sugars 3g; Fat 16.4g, of which saturates 3.1g; Cholesterol 0mg; Calcium 89mg; Fiber 1.3g; Sodium 78mg.

SALMON BAKED with POTATOES and THYME

This is clay-pot cooking at its most sophisticated—a mouthwatering combination of potatoes and onions braised in thyme-flavored stock and topped with perfectly tender pepper-crusted salmon fillets.

SERVES 4

1½ pounds waxy potatoes,
    thinly sliced
1 onion, thinly sliced
2 teaspoons fresh thyme leaves
scant 2 cups vegetable or fish stock
3 tablespoons butter,
    finely diced
4 skinless salmon fillets, about
    5 ounces each
2 tablespoons olive oil
1 tablespoon black peppercorns,
    coarsely crushed
salt and ground black pepper
fresh thyme, to garnish
snow peas or sugar snap peas,
    to serve

1 Soak a fish clay pot in cold water for 20 minutes, then drain.

2 Layer the potato and onion slices in the clay pot, seasoning each layer and sprinkling with thyme. Pour over the stock, dot with butter, cover, and place in an unheated oven.

3 Set the oven to 375°F. Bake the potatoes for 40 minutes, then remove the lid, and bake for 20 minutes more, or until they are almost cooked.

4 Meanwhile, brush the salmon fillets with olive oil, and coat with crushed black peppercorns, pressing them in, if necessary, with the back of a spoon. Place the salmon on top of the potatoes, cover, and cook for 15 minutes, or until the salmon is opaque, removing the lid for the last 5 minutes. Serve garnished with fresh thyme sprigs and with snow peas or sugar snap peas to accompany.

Energy 517Kcal/2160kJ; Protein 33.4g; Carbohydrate 28.4g, of which sugars 3.1g; Fat 30.8g, of which saturates 9g; Cholesterol 96mg; Calcium 17mg; Fiber 1.9g; Sodium 14/mg.

BAKED SEA BASS with LEMONGRASS and RED ONIONS

Moist, tender sea bass is flavored with a combination of traditional Thai ingredients in this simple, but mouthwatering clay-pot dish.

SERVES 2–3

1 sea bass, about 1½ pounds, cleaned
   and scaled
2 tablespoons olive oil
2 lemongrass stalks, thinly sliced
1 red onion, finely shredded
1 fresh chile, seeded and
   finely chopped
2-inch piece fresh ginger root,
   finely shredded
3 tablespoons chopped fresh cilantro
rind and juice of 2 limes
2 tablespoons light soy sauce
salt and ground black pepper

COOK'S TIP
This recipe will taste delicious using a variety of fish, such as red snapper, salmon, or tilapia. Depending on the weight of the fish, you may need to use two smaller fish rather than one whole one.

1 Soak a fish clay pot in cold water for 20 minutes, then drain. Make four or five diagonal slashes on both sides of the fish. Repeat the slashes on one side in the opposite direction to give an attractive cross-hatched effect. Rub the sea bass inside and out with salt, pepper and 1 tablespoon of the olive oil.

2 Combine the Thai ingredients—the lemongrass, red onion, chile, ginger, cilantro, and lime rind.

3 Place a little of the lemongrass and red onion mixture in the base of the clay pot, then lay the fish on top. Sprinkle the remaining mixture over the fish, then sprinkle over the lime juice, soy sauce, and the remaining olive oil. Cover, and place in an unheated oven.

4 Set the oven to 425°F, and cook the fish for 30–40 minutes, or until the flesh flakes easily when tested with a knife. Serve immediately.

Energy 298Kcal/1248kJ; Protein 43.7g; Carbohydrate 1.6g, of which sugars 1.1g; Fat 13g, of which saturates 1.9g; Cholesterol 180mg; Calcium 298mg; Fiber 0.3g; Sodium 156mg.

SWORDFISH STEAKS with MANGO and AVOCADO SALSA

Meaty swordfish steaks, marinated in a tangy mix of lime juice, cilantro, and chile, served with a vibrant fruity salsa.

SERVES 4

4 swordfish steaks, about 5 ounces each
lime wedges and shredded scallions,
    to garnish

For the marinade
rind and juice of 2 limes
2 garlic cloves, crushed
1 fresh red chile, seeded and
    finely chopped
2 tablespoons olive oil
2 tablespoons chopped fresh cilantro
salt and ground black pepper

For the salsa
1 mango
4 scallions, thinly sliced
1 fresh red chile, seeded and
    finely chopped
2 tablespoons chopped fresh cilantro
2 tablespoons lime juice
2 tablespoons olive oil
1 ripe avocado

3 Place the swordfish steaks in the clay pot, and pour the marinade over them. Cover, and place in an unheated oven. Set the oven to 425°F, and bake for 15–20 minutes, or until the fish is cooked. The time will vary depending on the thickness of the steaks.

4 To complete the salsa, using a sharp knife, cut the avocado in half, remove the pit, then coarsely dice the flesh. Stir it into the prepared salsa ingredients, and mix well. Serve the swordfish steaks with a mound of salsa, garnished with lime wedges and shredded scallions.

1 Place the swordfish steaks in a shallow nonmetallic dish. Combine the marinade ingredients, and pour over the swordfish. Cover, and leave to marinate in the refrigerator for 2 hours, or longer if you have sufficient time.

2 Soak a fish clay pot in cold water for 20 minutes, then drain. To prepare the salsa, peel the mango and slice the flesh off the pit. Cut the flesh into coarse dice. Add the scallions, chile, cilantro, lime juice, and olive oil. Toss the ingredients together, cover, and set aside to let the flavors blend.

Energy 311Kcal/1297kJ; Protein 29g; Carbohydrate 5.5g, of which sugars 5.3g; Fat 19.4g, of which saturates 3.3g; Cholesterol 69mg; Calcium 30mg; Fiber 1.3g; Sodium 212mg.

SLOW COOKER POULTRY AND GAME

The slow cooker is perfect for making all manner of stews, casseroles, and curries, and this chapter is packed with fantastic, healthy recipe ideas using poultry and game as the basis. Chicken is always a firm favorite, and the versatility of the slow cooker means that there is something here for everyone. In addition, there are plenty of other poultry and game dishes to whet the appetite, using turkey, guinea fowl, and rabbit. All of these recipes draw their inspiration from favorite cuisines around the world, giving a wonderful choice of dishes for every occasion. Try Mexican Drunken Chicken, Indian Chicken Korma, Creole Jambalaya, or French Duck Stew.

TURKEY and TOMATO HOT-POT

Often reserved for festive meals, turkey makes a great choice for any occasion. Here the meat is shaped into balls and simmered with rice in a richly flavored tomato sauce.

SERVES 4

white bread loaf, unsliced
2 tablespoons milk
1 garlic clove, crushed
½ teaspoon caraway seeds
8 ounces ground turkey
1 egg white
1½ cups near-boiling chicken stock
14-ounce can chopped tomatoes
1 tablespoon tomato paste
½ cup converted rice
salt and ground black pepper
1 tablespoon chopped fresh basil,
    to garnish
zucchini ribbons,
    to serve

1 Using a serrated knife, remove the crusts and cut the bread into cubes.

2 Place the bread in a mixing bowl, and sprinkle with the milk, then leave to soak for about 5 minutes.

3 Add the garlic clove, caraway seeds, turkey, and salt and pepper to the bread, and mix together well.

4 Whisk the egg white until stiff, then fold, half at a time, into the turkey mixture. Chill in the refrigerator.

5 Pour the stock into the ceramic cooking pot. Add the tomatoes and tomato paste, then switch to high, cover with the lid, and cook for 1 hour.

6 Meanwhile, shape the turkey mixture into 16 small balls. Stir the rice into the tomato mixture, then add the turkey balls. Cook on high for a further hour, or until the turkey balls and rice are cooked. Serve with the zucchini.

Energy 187Kcal/797kJ; Protein 18.2g; Carbohydrate 26.6g, of which sugars 3.9g; Fat 1.7g, of which saturates 0.5g; Cholesterol 32mg; Calcium 44mg; Fiber 1g; Sodium 212mg.

LAYERED CHICKEN and MUSHROOM BAKE

*This rich, creamy dish makes a hearty winter supper. The thick sauce combines with
juices from the mushrooms and chicken during cooking to make a well-flavored gravy.*

2 Add 2 tablespoons of the butter to
the pan, and heat gently until melted.
Stir in the leek, and fry gently for about
minutes. Sprinkle the flour over the
leeks, then turn off the heat, and
gradually blend in the milk until smooth.
Slowly bring the mixture to the boil,
stirring all the time, until thickened.

3 Remove the pan from the heat, and
stir in the Worcestershire sauce, if using,
mustard, diced carrot, mushrooms, and
chicken. Season generously.

4 Arrange enough potato slices to
cover the base of the ceramic cooking
pot. Spoon one-third of the chicken
mixture over the top, then cover with
another layer of potatoes. Repeat
layering, finishing with a layer of potatoes.
Dot the remaining butter on top.

5 Cover and cook on high for 4 hours,
or until the potatoes are cooked and
tender when pierced with a skewer.
If you like, place the dish under a
moderate broiler for 5 minutes
to brown, then serve.

SERVES 4

1 tablespoon olive oil
4 large chicken breast portions,
  cut into chunks
3 tablespoons butter
1 leek, finely sliced into rings
¼ cup all-purpose flour
2½ cups milk
1 teaspoon Worcestershire sauce
  (optional)
1 teaspoon whole-grain mustard
1 carrot, finely diced
3 cups white mushrooms, thinly sliced
2 pounds potatoes, thinly sliced
salt and ground black pepper

1 Heat the olive oil in a large pan.
Add the chicken, and fry gently until
beginning to brown. Remove the chicken
from the pan, using a slotted spoon,
leaving any juices behind. Set aside.

Energy 461Kcal/1943kJ; Protein 42.4g; Carbohydrate 43.8g, of which sugars 5.2g; Fat 14.1g, of which saturates 6.4g; Cholesterol 126.3mg; Calcium 49mg; Fiber 4.3g; Sodium 351mg.

APRICOT and ALMOND STUFFED CHICKEN

Couscous makes a delicious and simple base for this sweet-and-sour stuffing flavored with dried apricots and crunchy toasted almonds. A couple of spoonfuls of orange jelly marmalade adds tanginess to the sauce, as well as thickening it slightly.

SERVES 4

¼ cup dried apricots
⅔ cup orange juice
4 skinned boneless chicken breast portions
⅓ cup instant couscous
⅔ cup boiling chicken stock
¼ cup chopped toasted almonds
¼ teaspoon dried tarragon
1 egg yolk
2 tablespoons orange jelly marmalade
salt and ground black pepper
boiled or steamed basmati and wild rice,
   to serve

1 Put the dried apricots in a small bowl, and pour over the orange juice. Leave to soak at room temperature while you prepare the remaining ingredients.

2 Using a sharp knife, cut a deep pocket horizontally in each chicken breast portion, taking care not to cut all the way through. Put the chicken portions between two sheets of oiled parchment paper or plastic wrap, then gently beat with a rolling pin or meat hammer until slightly thinner.

3 Put the couscous in a bowl, and spoon over ¼ cup of the stock. Leave to stand for 2–3 minutes, or until all the stock has been absorbed.

4 Drain the apricots, reserving the juice, then stir them into the couscous along with the chopped almonds and tarragon. Season with salt and black pepper, then stir in just enough egg yolk to bind the mixture together.

5 Divide the stuffing equally between the chicken portions, packing it firmly into the pockets, then securing with wooden toothpicks. Place the stuffed chicken portions in the base of the ceramic cooking pot.

6 Stir the orange marmalade into the remaining hot stock until dissolved, then stir in the orange juice. Season with salt and pepper, and pour over the chicken. Cover the pot, and cook on high for 3–5 hours, or until the chicken is cooked through and tender.

7 Remove the chicken from the sauce, and keep warm. Tip the sauce into a wide pan, and boil rapidly until reduced by half. Carve the chicken into slices on the diagonal, and arrange on serving plates. Spoon over the sauce, and serve immediately with basmati and wild rice.

COOK'S TIP

Sautéed spinach or steamed green vegetables make a great accompaniment to this dish. They go particularly well with the sweet, fruity stuffing.

Energy 379Kcal/1604kJ; Protein 40.2g; Carbohydrate 38g, of which sugars 27g; Fat 8.5g, of which saturates 1.3g; Cholesterol 155mg; Calcium 61mg; Fiber 1.6g; Sodium 117mg.

HEN in a POT with PARSLEY SAUCE

Although harder to find nowadays, a boiling fowl will feed a family well. A large chicken could replace the boiling fowl. Serve with potatoes boiled in their jackets and cabbage.

SERVES 6

3½–4 pound boiling fowl or
   whole chicken
½ lemon, sliced
small bunch of parsley and thyme
1½ pounds carrots, cut into large chunks
12 shallots or small onions, left whole

For the sauce
½ cup butter
½ cup all-purpose flour
1 tablespoon lemon juice
4 tablespoons chopped Italian parsley
⅔ cup milk
salt and ground black pepper
sprigs of Italian parsley, to garnish

VARIATION
A small joint of ham or bacon can also be added to the pot if available. Soak it overnight in cold water before cooking, and do not add any extra salt without tasting first. A boiling fowl with a small joint of bacon, weighing 2–2¼ pounds in total, should feed 8–10 people. Red cabbage makes a tasty accompaniment.

1 Remove any trussing string and loose pieces of fat from inside the boiling fowl or chicken, then rinse under cold water, and place in the ceramic cooking pot. Add the lemon, parsley and thyme, carrots, and onions, and season well.

2 Pour in near-boiling water to just cover the fowl and vegetables. Cover with the lid, switch the slow cooker to high, and cook for 1 hour.

3 Skim off any scum and fat, using a slotted spoon. Re-cover the pot, and cook for 2–2½ hours, or until the fowl is cooked and tender. Using a slotted spoon, lift the fowl onto a warmed serving dish, arrange the vegetables around it, and keep warm.

4 Strain the cooking liquid into a pan, and boil uncovered to reduce by a third. Strain, and leave to settle for 2 minutes, then skim the fat off the surface.

5 Melt the butter in a pan, add the flour, and cook, stirring, for 1 minute. Gradually stir in the stock (there should be about 2½ cups) and bring to the boil.

6 Add the lemon juice, parsley, and milk to the pan. Season with salt and ground black pepper, and simmer the sauce for another 1–2 minutes.

7 To serve, pour a little of the sauce over the fowl, and add the carrots and onions, then garnish with a few sprigs of fresh parsley, and take to the table for carving. Pour the rest of the sauce into a warmed sauceboat and serve separately.

Energy 509Kcal/2114kJ; Protein 36.2g; Carbohydrate 20.1g, of which sugars 12.2g; Fat 32g, of which saturates 11.4g; Cholesterol 195mg; Calcium 109mg; Fiber 4g; Sodium 214mg

CHICKEN FRICASSÉE

Traditionally made with chicken, rabbit, or veal, this fricassée dish has a wonderfully rich and flavorsome sauce that is further enhanced with cream and fresh herbs. The meat is first seared in fat, then braised in stock with vegetables until tender. It is a perfect dish for entertaining, because you can prepare it in advance and then simply leave it to simmer while you enjoy the company of your guests.

SERVES 4

20 small even-size pearl onions or shallots
2½–3 pounds chicken, cut into pieces
2 tablespoons butter
2 tablespoons sunflower-seed oil
3 tablespoons all-purpose flour
1 cup dry white wine
2½ cups boiling chicken stock
1 bouquet garni
1 teaspoon lemon juice
3 cups white mushrooms
⅓ cup heavy cream
3 tablespoons chopped fresh parsley
salt and ground black pepper
mashed potatoes and steamed seasonal
    vegetables, to serve

1 Put the onions or shallots in a bowl, add just enough boiling water to cover them, and leave to soak.

2 Meanwhile, rinse the chicken pieces well in cold water, and pat dry with paper towels.

3 Melt half the butter with the oil in a large frying pan. Add the chicken pieces and cook, turning occasionally, until lightly browned all over. Using a slotted spoon or tongs, transfer the chicken pieces to the ceramic cooking pot, leaving the juices behind.

4 Stir the flour into the pan juices, then blend in the wine. Stir in the stock, and add the bouquet garni and the lemon juice. Bring the mixture to the boil, stirring all the time, until the sauce has thickened. Season well, and pour over the chicken. Cover the pot with the lid, and switch the slow cooker to high.

5 Drain and peel the onions or shallots. (Soaking them in boiling water loosens the skins, making them easy to peel.) Trim the stalks from the mushrooms.

6 Clean the frying pan, then add the remaining butter, and heat gently until melted. Add the mushrooms and onions or shallots, and cook for 5 minutes, turning frequently until they are lightly browned. Tip into the ceramic cooking pot with the chicken.

7 Re-cover the slow cooker with the lid, and cook on high for 3–4 hours, or until the chicken is cooked and tender. (To test that the chicken is cooked through, pierce the thickest part of one of the portions with a skewer or thin knife; the juices should run clear.)

8 Using a slotted spoon, remove the chicken and vegetables to a warmed serving dish. Add the cream and 2 tablespoons of the parsley to the sauce, and whisk to combine. Check the seasoning, adjust if necessary, then pour the sauce over the chicken and vegetables.

9 Sprinkle the fricassée with the remaining parsley, and serve with mashed potatoes and seasonal vegetables.

COOK'S TIP
A classic bouquet garni is made up of parsley stalks, a sprig of thyme, and a bay leaf. You can tie these together with a piece of string, or tie the herbs in a small square of cheesecloth. Some people like to add rosemary as well.

Energy 613Kcal/2563kJ; Protein 53.1g; Carbohydrate 36.4g, of which sugars 17.9g; Fat 25g, of which saturates 11.1g; Cholesterol 196mg; Calcium 128mg; Fiber 5.3g; Sodium 396mg.

SPRING CHICKEN SLOW-BRAISED in SMOKY BACON SAUCE

Sweet, succulent, and tangy with the flavor of apples and aromatic thyme, this delicious stew makes a great alternative to the classic roast. Baby spring chickens are also known as poussin and can weigh 12oz–1¼pounds. Be sure to buy large ones, because the smaller birds are only big enough for a single serving.

SERVES 4

2 large spring chickens
2 tablespoons sweet butter
2 teaspoons sunflower-seed oil
4 ounces chopped bacon pieces
  or smoked fatty bacon
2 leeks, washed and sliced
2¼ cups small white mushrooms,
  trimmed
½ cup apple juice,
  plus a further 1 tablespoon
½ cup chicken stock
2 tablespoons clear honey
2 teaspoons chopped fresh thyme
  or ½ teaspoon dried
8 ounces crisp red apples
2 teaspoons cornstarch
salt and ground black pepper
creamy mashed potatoes and
  pan-fried or steamed baby leeks,
  to serve

3 Add the chopped bacon to the pan, and cook for about 5 minutes, stirring occasionally, until beginning to brown.

4 Using a slotted spoon, transfer the bacon to the ceramic cooking pot, leaving all the fat and juices behind.

5 Add the leeks and mushrooms to the pan, and cook for a few minutes until they begin to soften and the mushrooms begin to release their juices.

1 Using a sharp, heavy knife or a meat cleaver, carefully split the spring chickens in half to make four portions. Rinse the portions well under cold running water, then pat dry using paper towels.

2 Heat the butter and sunflower-seed oil in a large pan, and add the spring chicken portions. Fry, turning the pieces over, until lightly browned on all sides. Transfer the chicken portions to the ceramic cooking pot, leaving the cooking fat in the pan.

6 Pour ½ cup apple juice and the chicken stock into the pan, then stir in the honey and thyme. Season well with salt and ground black pepper.

7 Bring the mixture almost to boiling point, then pour over the chicken and bacon. Cover the ceramic cooking pot with the lid, switch the slow cooker to high, and cook for 2 hours.

8 Quarter, core, and thickly slice the apples. Add them to the cooking pot, submerging them in the liquid to prevent them from turning brown. Cook for a further 2 hours, or until the chicken and vegetables are cooked and tender.

9 Remove the chicken from the cooking pot, place on a plate, and keep warm.

10 Blend the cornstarch with the 1 tablespoon apple juice, and stir into the cooking liquid until thickened. Taste and adjust the seasoning, if necessary.

11 Serve the chicken on warmed plates with sauce poured over the top. Accompany with mashed potatoes and pan-fried or steamed baby leeks.

COOK'S TIP
Always check that chicken is thoroughly cooked before serving, to avoid any risk of salmonella. To test, pierce the thickest part of the meat with a skewer or thin knife; the juices should run clear.

Energy 465Kcal/1945kJ; Protein 32.8g; Carbohydrate 25.9g, of which sugars 20.7g; Fat 26.3g, of which saturates 9.5g; Cholesterol 172mg; Calcium 40mg; Fiber 3.3g; Sodium 632mg.

TARRAGON CHICKEN in CIDER

Aromatic tarragon has a distinctive flavor that goes wonderfully with both cream and chicken. This recipe is truly effortless, yet provides an elegant dish for entertaining or a special family meal. Serve with sautéed potatoes and a green vegetable.

SERVES 4

12 ounces small pearl onions
1 tablespoon sunflower-seed oil
4 garlic cloves, peeled
4 boneless chicken breast portions,
   skin on
1½ cups hard cider
1 bay leaf
scant 1 cup crème fraîche
   or sour cream
2 tablespoons chopped fresh tarragon
1 tablespoon chopped fresh parsley
salt and ground black pepper

1 Put the button onions in a heatproof bowl, and pour over enough boiling water to cover. Leave to stand for at least 10 minutes, then drain, and peel off the skins. (They should come off very easily after soaking.)

2 Heat the oil in a frying pan, add the onions, and cook gently for 10 minutes, or until lightly browned, turning them frequently. Add the garlic, and cook for a further 2–3 minutes. Using a slotted spoon, transfer the onions and garlic to the ceramic cooking pot.

3 Place the chicken breast portions in the frying pan, and cook for 3–4 minutes, turning once or twice until lightly browned on both sides. Transfer the chicken to the ceramic cooking pot.

4 Pour the cider into the pan, add the bay leaf and a little salt and pepper, and bring to the boil.

5 Pour the hot cider and bay leaf over the chicken. Cover the ceramic cooking pot with the lid, and cook on low for 4–5 hours, or until the chicken and onions are cooked and very tender. Lift out the chicken breasts. Set aside while you finish preparing the cider sauce.

COOK'S TIP
When preparing and cooking poultry, always be sure to wash utensils, surfaces, and hands afterwards to avoid risk of contamination or food poisoning. Use a plastic or glass chopping board when cutting all poultry, meat, or fish because they are easier to wash and much more hygienic. Wooden boards are absorbent and should therefore be avoided.

6 Stir the crème fraîche or sour cream and the herbs into the sauce. Return the chicken breasts to the pot, and cook for a further 30 minutes on high, or until piping hot. Serve the chicken immediately, with lightly sautéed potatoes and a green vegetable, such as cabbage.

VARIATIONS
• Guinea fowl and pheasant portions can also be cooked in this way. Try using white wine in place of the cider, and serve with creamy mashed potatoes and steamed baby carrots drizzled with a little melted butter.
• Try using 1 or 2 sprigs of fresh thyme in place of the tarragon. It gives a very different flavor but is equally good. Serve with rice and roasted tomatoes.

Energy 520Kcal/2167kJ; Protein 36.9g; Carbohydrate 12.1g, of which sugars 9.2g; Fat 33.9g, of which saturates 12.9g; Cholesterol 184mg; Calcium 90mg; Fiber 1.5g; Sodium 138mg.

CHICKEN with CHIPOTLE SAUCE

Spicy-hot and deliciously rich and smoky, this dish of chicken cooked in a rich chili sauce is great served with rice for a tasty, healthy supper. The puree can be prepared ahead of time, making this recipe ideal for casual entertaining.

SERVES 6

6 chipotle chiles
scant 1 cup boiling water
scant 1 cup chicken stock
3 tablespoons vegetable oil
3 onions
6 boneless chicken breast portions
salt and ground black pepper
fresh oregano, to garnish

COOK'S TIP

Spicy-hot, wrinkled, dark red chipotle chiles are smoke-dried jalepeños and have a really rich taste. To really bring out their flavor, they need long, slow cooking—making them perfect for slow cooker casseroles.

1 Put the dried chiles in a bowl, and cover with the boiling water. Leave to stand for about 30 minutes until very soft. Drain, reserving the soaking water in a measuring pitcher. Cut off the stalk from each chile, then slit the chile lengthwise, and scrape out the seeds with a small, sharp knife.

2 Chop the chiles roughly, and put in a food processor or blender. Add enough chicken stock to the soaking water to make it up to 1⅔ cups, then pour into the food processor or blender. Process until smooth.

3 Heat the oil in a frying pan. Halve and slice the onions, and add them to the pan. Cook, stirring, over a medium heat for 5 minutes, or until soft but not colored.

4 Transfer the onions to the ceramic cooking pot, and switch to high. Sprinkle the onion slices with a little salt and ground black pepper.

5 Remove the skin from the chicken breast portions, and trim off any pieces of fat. Arrange in a single layer on top of the onion slices. Sprinkle with a little salt and several grindings of black pepper.

6 Pour the chili sauce over the chicken, making sure that each piece is evenly coated. Cover with the lid, and cook for 3–4 hours, or until the chicken is cooked through but still moist and tender. Garnish with fresh oregano, and serve.

Energy 235Kcal/989kJ; Protein 36.9g; Carbohydrate 5.9g, of which sugars 4.2g; Fat 7.3g, of which saturates 1.1g; Cholesterol 105mg; Calcium 26mg; Fiber 1.1g; Sodium 92mg.

DRUNKEN CHICKEN

Flavored with a mixture of sherry and tequila, this rich, fruity casserole makes a great meal for any occasion. Serve with bowls of plain boiled rice to soak up the juices, or with warmed flour tortillas to scoop up the chicken and sauce.

SERVES 4

1 cup raisins
½ cup sherry
1 cup all-purpose flour
½ teaspoon salt
½ teaspoon ground black pepper
3 tablespoons vegetable oil
8 skinless chicken thighs
1 onion, halved and
    thinly sliced
2 garlic cloves, crushed
2 tart eating apples
1 cup sliced almonds
1 slightly under-ripe plantain, peeled
    and sliced
1¼ cups boiling chicken stock
½ cup tequila
chopped fresh herbs, to garnish

1 Put the raisins in a bowl, and add the sherry. Set aside to soak.

2 Meanwhile, combine the flour, salt, and pepper, and spread the mixture out on a large plate. Heat 2 tablespoons of the oil in a large frying pan. Coat each chicken thigh in the seasoned flour, then fry, turning, until browned all over. Drain well on kitchen paper.

3 Heat the remaining oil in the pan, add the onion, and fry for 5 minutes, or until soft and beginning to brown. Stir in the garlic, then remove the pan from the heat. Tip the onions and garlic into the ceramic cooking pot, and switch the slow cooker to high.

4 Peel, core, and dice the apples. Add them to the ceramic cooking pot, then sprinkle with the almonds, plantain slices, and raisins. Pour in the sherry, chicken stock, and tequila and stir to combine.

5 Add the chicken pieces to the fruit and vegetable mixture, pressing them down into the stock so that they are completely covered. Cover with the lid, and cook for 3 hours, or until the chicken thighs are very tender.

6 Check the chicken is cooked: pierce the thickest part with a sharp knife or skewer; the juices should run clear. Cook for a little longer, if necessary.

7 Taste the sauce, and add a little more salt and ground black pepper if necessary. Serve the chicken piping hot, sprinkled with chopped fresh herbs.

Energy 529Kcal/2227kJ; Protein 23.1g; Carbohydrate 63.7g, of which sugars 34.1g; Fat 11.5g, of which saturates 1.8g; Cholesterol 94.5mg; Calcium 76mg; Fiber 2.9g; Sodium 401mg.

CARIBBEAN PEANUT CHICKEN

Peanut butter adds a delicious richness and depth of flavor to this spicy rice dish.
It is a classic ingredient used in many slow-cooked Caribbean curries and stews.

3 Meanwhile, heat the remaining oil in a frying pan, add the onion, and fry for 10 minutes until soft. Transfer to the ceramic cooking pot, and switch the slow cooker to high. Add the chopped tomatoes and chile, and stir to combine.

4 Put the peanut butter into a bowl, then blend in the stock, adding a little at a time. Pour the mixture into the ceramic cooking pot, season, and stir. Cover with the lid, and cook for 1 hour.

5 About 30 minutes before the end of cooking time, remove the chicken from the refrigerator, and leave it to come to room temperature.

6 Add the chicken and the marinade to the ceramic cooking pot, and stir to mix. Re-cover, and cook for 1 hour.

7 Sprinkle the rice over the casserole, then stir to mix. Cover, and cook for a final 45 minutes–1 hour, or until the chicken and rice are cooked and tender. Serve immediately, garnished with lemon or lime wedges for squeezing over, and sprigs of fresh parsley.

SERVES 4

4 skinless, boneless chicken
 breast portions
3 tablespoons peanut or
 sunflower-seed oil
1 garlic clove, crushed
1 teaspoon chopped fresh thyme
1 tablespoon curry powder
juice of half a lemon
1 onion, finely chopped
2 tomatoes, peeled, seeded, and chopped
1 fresh green chile, seeded and sliced
4 tablespoons smooth peanut butter
3 cups boiling chicken stock
1½ cups converted white rice
salt and ground black pepper
lemon or lime wedges and
 sprigs of fresh Italian parsley,
 to garnish

1 Cut the chicken breast portions into thin strips. In a bowl, mix together 1 tablespoon of the oil with the garlic, thyme, curry powder, and lemon juice.

2 Add the chicken strips to the ingredients in the bowl, and stir well to combine. Cover with plastic wrap, and leave to marinate in the refrigerator for 1½–2 hours.

Energy 635Kcal/2677kJ; Protein 45.8g; Carbohydrate 70.7g, of which sugars 4.4g; Fat 20.8g, of which saturates 4.1g; Cholesterol 105mg; Calcium 65mg; Fiber 2.1g; Sodium 354mg.

JAMAICAN JERK CHICKEN

*The word "jerk" refers to the herb and spice seasoning traditionally used to marinate
meat in Jamaica. It was originally used only for pork, but jerked chicken is just as good.*

SERVES 4

8 chicken pieces, such as thighs and legs
1 tablespoon sunflower-seed oil
1 tablespoon sweet butter

For the sauce
1 bunch of scallions, trimmed and
    finely chopped
2 garlic cloves, crushed
1 hot red chile pepper, halved,
    seeded, and finely chopped
1 teaspoon ground allspice
½ teaspoon ground cinnamon
1 teaspoon dried thyme
¼ teaspoon freshly grated nutmeg
2 teaspoons raw sugar
1 tablespoon all-purpose flour
1¼ cups chicken stock
1 tablespoon red or white wine vinegar
1 tablespoon lime juice
2 teaspoons tomato paste
salt and ground black pepper
salad leaves or rice, to serve

VARIATION
For jerked pork, sauté 4 pork loin steaks
(each about 3½ ounces) in oil for 30 seconds
on each side. Make the jerk sauce as above,
using vegetable instead of chicken stock.
Cook in the same way as the chicken recipe
above, and serve with plain boiled rice and
chargrilled pineapple wedges.

1 Wipe the chicken pieces, then pat dry
on paper towels. Heat the oil and butter
in a frying pan until melted, then add the
chicken, in batches if necessary, and cook
until browned on all sides. Remove with
a slotted spoon, leaving the fat in the
pan, and transfer to the ceramic cooking
pot. Switch the slow cooker to high.

2 Add the scallions, garlic, and chile to
the frying pan, and cook gently for 4–5
minutes, or until softened, stirring
frequently. Stir in the allspice, cinnamon,
thyme, nutmeg, and sugar. Sprinkle in the
flour, and stir to mix, then gradually add
the chicken stock, stirring until the
mixture bubbles and thickens. Remove
the pan from the heat.

3 Stir the vinegar, lime juice, tomato
paste, and some salt and ground black
pepper into the sauce. Pour over the
chicken pieces, cover with a lid, and
cook on high for 3–4 hours, or until the
chicken is cooked and very tender.

4 Remove the chicken from the sauce,
and place on a serving dish. Taste the
sauce, and adjust the seasoning, then
serve separately, with salad leaves or
rice as an accompaniment.

COOK'S TIP
There are many recipes for jerk seasoning,
but all include chiles, allspice, and thyme.
The spicy sauce not only flavors the meat,
but also tenderizes it.

Energy 189Kcal/794kJ; Protein 21g; Carbohydrate 7g, of which sugars 3.1g; Fat 8.8g, of which saturates 3.1g; Cholesterol 10/mg; Calcium 24mg; Fiber 0.5g; Sodium 238mg.

SPICY CHICKEN JAMBALAYA

This classic Creole dish is great for a family supper, served with a simple salad.
Spicy red Spanish chorizo sausage gives the stew a real flavor boost. It is available from
most large supermarkets, or from specialist Mediterranean stores and delicatessens.

SERVES 6

8 ounces skinless, boneless chicken
   breast portions
6-ounce piece raw smoked gammon
   or bacon
2 tablespoons olive oil
1 large onion, peeled and chopped
2 garlic cloves, crushed
2 sticks celery, diced
1 teaspoon chopped fresh thyme or
   ½ teaspoon dried thyme
1 teaspoon mild chili powder
½ teaspoon ground ginger
2 teaspoons tomato paste
2 dashes of Tabasco sauce
3 cups boiling chicken stock
1½ cups converted rice
4 ounces chorizo sausage (cooked), sliced
2 tablespoons chopped fresh Italian
   parsley, plus extra,
   to garnish
salt and ground black pepper

1 Cut the chicken into 1-inch cubes, and season with salt and pepper. Trim any fat off the gammon or bacon, then cut the meat into ½-inch cubes.

2 Heat 1 tablespoon of the olive oil in a pan, add the onion, and fry gently for about 5 minutes, until beginning to color. Stir in the garlic, celery, thyme, chili powder and ginger, and cook for about 1 minute. Transfer the mixture to the ceramic cooking pot, and turn the slow cooker to high.

3 Heat the remaining 1 tablespoon olive oil in the pan, add the chicken pieces and fry briefly until lightly browned. Add the chicken to the ceramic cooking pot with the gammon or bacon cubes.

4 Add the tomato paste and Tabasco sauce to the stock, and whisk together. Pour into the slow cooker, cover with the lid, and cook on high for 1½ hours.

5 Sprinkle the rice into the pot, and stir to mix. Cover, and cook on high for 45 minutes–1 hour, or until the rice is almost tender and most of the stock has been absorbed. Check toward the end of cooking time, and add a little extra hot stock or water if the mixture is dry.

6 Stir in the chorizo, and cook on high for a further 15 minutes, or until heated through. Stir in the chopped parsley, then taste, and adjust the seasoning. Turn off the slow cooker, and leave to stand for 10 minutes. Stir with a fork to fluff up the rice, then serve garnished with chopped fresh parsley.

Energy 384Kcal/1617kJ; Protein 21.2g; Carbohydrate 48.6g, of which sugars 2.9g; Fat 13g, of which saturates 3.6g; Cholesterol 43mg; Calcium 57mg; Fiber 1.1g; Sodium 630mg.

DOROWAT

The long-simmered stews eaten in Ethiopia are known as wats and are traditionally served with a pancake-like flatbread called injera. Hard-boiled eggs are added to the sauce toward the end of cooking, so that they soak up the flavor of the spices.

SERVES 4

2 tablespoons vegetable oil
2 large onions, chopped
3 garlic cloves, chopped
1-inch piece peeled and finely
    chopped fresh ginger root
¾ cup chicken or vegetable stock
1 cup bottled strained tomatoes or
    14-ounce can chopped tomatoes
seeds from 5 cardamom pods
½ teaspoon ground turmeric
large pinch of ground cinnamon
large pinch of ground cloves
large pinch of grated nutmeg
3-pound chicken, cut into 8–12 portions
4 hard-boiled eggs
cayenne pepper or hot paprika,
    to taste
salt and ground black pepper
roughly chopped fresh cilantro and
    onion rings, to garnish
flatbread or rice, to serve

1 Heat the oil in a large pan, add the onions, and cook for 10 minutes, until softened. Add the garlic and ginger, and cook for 1–2 minutes.

2 Add the stock and the bottled strained tomatoes or chopped tomatoes to the pan. Bring to the boil and cook, stirring frequently, for about 10 minutes, or until the mixture has thickened, then season.

COOK'S TIP
Check the sauce just before you add the hard-boiled eggs. If it seems too thick, add a little more stock.

3 Transfer the mixture to the ceramic cooking pot, and stir in the cardamom, turmeric, cinnamon, cloves, and nutmeg. Add the chicken in a single layer, pushing the pieces down into the sauce.

4 Cover with the lid, and cook on high for 3 hours. Remove the shells from the eggs, then prick the eggs a few times with a fork or very fine skewer. Add to the sauce, and cook for 30–45 minutes, or until the chicken is cooked through and tender. Season to taste with cayenne pepper or hot paprika. Garnish with cilantro and onion rings, and serve with flatbread or rice.

Energy 388Kcal/1629kJ; Protein 54.6g; Carbohydrate 13g, of which sugars 9.6g; Fat 13.4g, of which saturates 2.8g; Cholesterol 13mg; Calcium 81mg; Fiber 2.5g; Sodium 311mg.

FRAGRANT CHICKEN CURRY

Lentils are used to thicken the sauce in this mild, fragrant curry, and fresh cilantro gives
the dish a really distinctive, fresh taste. The generous quantities of spinach mean that you
won't need an additional vegetable dish to balance the meal.

2 Add the chicken to the lentil mixture, pressing it down in a single layer. Cover, and cook on high for 3 hours, or until the chicken is just tender.

3 Add the spinach to the pot, pressing it down into the hot liquid. Cover, and cook for a further 30 minutes, until wilted. Stir in the chopped cilantro.

4 Season the curry with salt and pepper to taste, then serve garnished with fresh cilantro sprigs and accompanied with basmati rice and poppadums.

COOK'S TIP
You will need a large slow cooker to accommodate all the spinach in this recipe. It will shrink down during cooking, but the initial volume is large. If you have a small slow cooker, use thawed, well-drained frozen spinach instead.

SERVES 4

½ cup red lentils
2 tablespoons mild curry powder
2 teaspoons ground coriander
1 teaspoon cumin seeds
1½ cups boiling vegetable
   or chicken stock
8 chicken thighs, skinned
8 ounces fresh shredded spinach
1 tablespoon chopped fresh cilantro
salt and ground black pepper
sprigs of fresh cilantro,
   to garnish
white or brown basmati rice
   and poppadums, to serve

1 Place the lentils in a strainer, and rinse under cold running water. Drain well, then put in the ceramic cooking pot with the curry powder, ground coriander, cumin seeds, and stock. Cover, and cook on high for 2 hours.

Energy 591Kcal/2490kJ; Protein 75.5g; Carbohydrate 38.2g, of which sugars 3.9g; Fat 16.1g, of which saturates 3.9g; Cholesterol 171mg; Calcium 426mg; Fiber 9.4g; Sodium 880mg.

CHICKEN in a CASHEW NUT SAUCE

The Moguls had a profound impact on Indian cuisine, and the resulting style of cooking is known as Mughlai food. One of their legacies is the use of nut paste, which is used here to give the curry a rich yet delicately flavored sauce.

SERVES 4

1 large onion, roughly chopped
1 clove garlic, crushed
1 tablespoon tomato paste
½ cup cashew nuts
1½ teaspoons garam masala
1 teaspoon chili powder
¼ teaspoon ground turmeric
1 teaspoon salt
1 tablespoon lemon juice
1 tablespoon plain yogurt
2 tablespoons vegetable oil
1 pound chicken breast fillets,
    skinned and cubed
2¼ cups white mushrooms
1 tablespoon golden raisins
1¼ cups chicken or vegetable stock
2 tablespoons chopped fresh cilantro,
    plus extra to garnish
rice and fruit chutney,
    to serve

1 Put the onion, garlic, tomato paste, cashew nuts, garam masala, chili powder, turmeric, salt, lemon juice, and yogurt in a food processor and process to a paste.

2 Heat the oil in a large frying pan or wok, and fry the cubes of chicken for a few minutes, or until just beginning to brown. Using a slotted spoon, transfer the chicken to the ceramic cooking pot, leaving the oil in the pan.

3 Add the spice paste and mushrooms to the pan, lower the heat, and fry gently, stirring frequently, for 3–4 minutes. Tip the mixture into the ceramic pot.

4 Add the golden raisins to the pot, and stir in the chicken or vegetable stock. Cover with the lid, and switch the slow cooker to high. Cook for 3–4 hours, stirring halfway through the cooking time. The chicken should be cooked through and very tender, and the sauce fairly thick.

5 Stir the chopped cilantro into the sauce, then taste, and add a little more salt and pepper, if necessary. Serve the curry from the ceramic cooking pot, or transfer to a warmed serving dish, and garnish with a sprinkling of chopped fresh cilantro. Serve with rice and a fruit chutney, such as mango.

Energy 239Kcal/1006kJ; Protein 31.6g; Carbohydrate 10.7g, of which sugars 7.6g; Fat 8.1g, of which saturates 1.7g; Cholesterol 78.9mg; Calcium 39mg; Fiber 1.9g; Sodium 696mg.

CHICKEN KORMA

The use of ground almonds to thicken the sauce gives this mild, fragrant curry a beautifully creamy texture. Its mild taste makes it particularly popular with children.

SERVES 4

¾ cup sliced almonds
1 tablespoon ghee or butter
1½ pounds skinless, boneless chicken
    breast portions, cut into
    bitesize pieces
1 tablespoon sunflower-seed oil
1 onion, chopped
4 green cardamom pods
2 garlic cloves, crushed
2 teaspoons ground cumin
1 teaspoon ground coriander
pinch of ground turmeric
1 cinnamon stick
good pinch of chili powder
1 cup coconut milk
½ cup boiling chicken stock
1 teaspoon tomato paste (optional)
5 tablespoons light cream
1–2 tablespoons fresh lime
    or lemon juice
2 teaspoons grated lime or lemon rind
1 teaspoon garam masala
salt and ground black pepper
saffron rice and poppadums, to serve

1 Dry-fry the sliced almonds in a frying pan until pale golden. Transfer about two-thirds of the almonds to a plate, and continue to dry-fry the remainder until they are slightly deeper in color.
Put the darker almonds on a separate plate, and set them aside to use for the garnish. Leave the paler almonds to cool, then grind them until fine in a spice grinder or coffee mill used for the purpose.

2 Heat the ghee or butter in the frying pan, and gently fry the chicken pieces until evenly brown. Transfer to a plate.

3 Add a little sunflower-seed oil to the fat in the pan, if necessary, then fry the onion for 8 minutes. Stir in the cardamom pods and garlic, and fry for a further 2 minutes, until the onion is soft and just starting to color.

4 Add the ground almonds, cumin, coriander, turmeric, cinnamon stick, and chili powder to the frying pan, and cook for about 1 minute. Transfer the mixture to the ceramic cooking pot, and switch the slow cooker to high.

5 Add the coconut milk, stock, and tomato paste, if using, to the pot, and stir in. Add the chicken, and season with salt and pepper. Cover with the lid, and cook on high for 3 hours, or until the chicken is cooked and very tender.

6 Stir the cream, citrus juice and rind, and the garam masala into the curry, and cook on high for 30 minutes. Check the seasoning, garnish with the reserved almonds, and serve immediately with saffron rice and poppadums.

Energy 410Kcal/1714kJ; Protein 45.7g; Carbohydrate 7.8g, of which sugars 6.4g; Fat 22g, of which saturates 6g; Cholesterol 136mg; Calcium 98mg; Fiber 1.9g; Sodium 202mg.

CHICKEN and SPLIT PEA KORESH

A traditional Persian Koresh—a thick saucy stew served with rice—is usually made with lamb, but here chicken is used to create a lighter, lower-fat dish.

SERVES 4

¼ cup green split peas
3 tablespoons olive oil
1 large onion, finely chopped
1 pound boneless chicken thighs
1½ cups boiling chicken stock
1 teaspoon ground turmeric
½ teaspoon ground cinnamon
¼ teaspoon grated nutmeg
2 tablespoons dried mint
2 eggplants, diced
8 ripe tomatoes, diced
2 garlic cloves, crushed
salt and ground black pepper
fresh mint, to garnish
plain boiled rice, to serve

1 Put the split peas in a large bowl. Pour in cold water to cover, and leave to soak for at least 6 hours or overnight.

2 Tip the split peas into a strainer, and drain well. Place in a large pan, cover with fresh cold water, and bring to the boil. Boil rapidly for 10 minutes, then rinse, drain, and set aside.

3 Heat 1 tablespoon of the oil in a pan, add the onion, and cook for about 5 minutes. Add the chicken, and cook until golden on all sides, then transfer to the ceramic cooking pot. Add the split peas, hot chicken stock, turmeric, cinnamon, nutmeg, and mint, and season well with salt and black pepper.

4 Cover the pot with the lid, and cook on high or auto for 1 hour. Switch the slow cooker to low, or leave on auto, and cook for a further 3 hours, or until the chicken is just cooked and the split peas are nearly tender.

5 Heat the remaining 2 tablespoons of oil in a frying pan, add the diced eggplants, and cook for about 5 minutes, until lightly browned. Add the tomatoes and garlic, and cook for a further 2 minutes.

6 Transfer the eggplants to the ceramic cooking pot, stir to combine, then cook for about 1 hour. Sprinkle with fresh mint leaves to garnish, and serve with plain boiled rice.

Energy 298Kcal/1251kJ; Protein 29.1g; Carbohydrate 18.5g, of which sugars 10.2g; Fat 12.5g, of which saturates 2.3g; Cholesterol 118mg; Calcium 48mg; Fiber 4.5g; Sodium 206mg.

BRAISED GUINEA FOWL with RED CABBAGE

The slightly gamey flavor of guinea fowl is complemented perfectly by the sweet, fruity
flavor of red cabbage, braised in apple juice and scented with juniper berries.

SERVES 4

1 tablespoon sweet butter
½ red cabbage, weighing
   about 1 pound
3 pounds oven-ready guinea
   fowl, jointed
1 tablespoon sunflower-seed oil
3 shallots, very finely chopped
1 tablespoon all-purpose flour
½ cup chicken stock
⅔ cup apple juice
1 tablespoon soft light brown sugar
1 tablespoon red wine vinegar
4 juniper berries, lightly crushed
salt and ground black pepper

VARIATIONS
• Other mild-tasting poultry or game such
as chicken or pheasant can be used in
place of the guinea fowl, if preferred.
• Add to the fruity flavor of the cabbage
by adding 1 tablespoon golden raisins to
the pot before cooking.

1 Use half the butter to grease the
ceramic cooking pot. Cut the cabbage
into wedges, removing any tough outer
leaves and the central core. Shred the
cabbage finely, then place in the ceramic
cooking pot, packing it down tightly.

2 Rinse the guinea fowl portions, and
pat dry with paper towels. Heat the
remaining butter and the oil in a pan,
and brown the guinea fowl on all sides.
Lift from the pan, leaving the fat behind,
and place on top of the red cabbage.

3 Add the shallots to the frying pan, and
cook gently for 5 minutes. Sprinkle with
the flour, cook for a few seconds, then
gradually stir in the stock followed by
the apple juice. Bring to the boil, stirring
continuously, until thickened. Remove
from the heat, stir in the sugar, vinegar,
and juniper berries, and season.

4 Pour the sauce over the guinea fowl,
cover, and cook on high for 4 hours, or
until the meat and cabbage are tender.
Check the seasoning and serve.

Energy 456Kcal/1907kJ; Protein 44.5g; Carbohydrate 20g, of which sugars 15g; Fat 22.5g, of which saturates 6.7g; Cholesterol 225mg; Calcium 96mg; Fiber 3.1g; Sodium 15mg.

GUINEA FOWL and SPRING VEGETABLE STEW

*Resembling a well-flavored chicken stew, this tasty dish of guinea fowl cooked with
spring vegetables and flavored with mustard and herbs is a sure winner.*

SERVES 4

3½ pounds guinea fowl
3 tablespoons all-purpose flour
3 tablespoons olive oil
4 ounces pancetta, cut into tiny cubes
1 onion, chopped
3 cloves garlic, chopped
scant 1 cup white wine
8 ounces baby carrots
8 ounces baby turnips
6 baby leeks, cut into 3-inch lengths
sprig of fresh thyme
1 bay leaf
2 teaspoons Dijon mustard
⅔ cup boiling chicken
    or vegetable stock
8 ounces shelled peas
2 tablespoons chopped fresh parsley
1 tablespoon chopped fresh mint
salt and ground black pepper

1 Joint the guinea fowl into eight pieces.
Wipe or lightly rinse them, then pat dry
on paper towels. Season the flour with
salt and pepper, and toss the guinea fowl
portions in it. Set aside any leftover flour.

2 Heat 2 tablespoons of the oil in a
large frying pan, add the pancetta, and
fry over a medium heat until lightly
browned, stirring occasionally. Using a
slotted spoon, transfer the pancetta to
the ceramic cooking pot, leaving any fat
and juices in the frying pan.

3 Add the guinea fowl portions to the
pan, and fry, turning, until browned on
all sides. Arrange the guinea fowl
portions in a single layer in the cooking
pot on top of the pancetta.

4 Add the remaining 1 tablespoon oil to
the frying pan, add the onion, and cook
for 3–4 minutes, until just beginning to
soften. Add the garlic, and cook for
about 1 minute, then stir in the reserved
flour. Gradually stir in the wine, and bring
to the boil. Pour over the guinea fowl.

5 Add the carrots, turnips, and leeks to
the cooking pot with the thyme and bay
leaf. Blend the mustard with the stock,
season with salt and pepper, and pour
over. Cover with the lid, and cook on
high for 3–4 hours, or until the guinea
fowl and vegetables are tender.

6 Add the peas to the stew, and cook
for a further 45 minutes. Taste, and
adjust the seasoning, then stir in most of
the fresh herbs. Divide the stew among
four warmed serving plates, sprinkle the
remaining fresh herbs over the top, and
serve immediately.

COOK'S TIPS
• To save time on preparation, ask your
butcher to joint the guinea fowl for you.
• Rabbit has a delicate flavor that goes
well with the tender spring vegetables and
herbs used in this stew. Try using eight
rabbit joints in place of the guinea fowl.

Energy 581Kcal/2425kJ; Protein 50.5g; Carbohydrate 29.1g, of which sugars 11.2g; Fat 26.5g, of which saturates 7.4g; Cholesterol 224mg; Calcium 109mg; Fiber 6.9g; Sodium 668mg.

DUCK STEW with OLIVES

This method of cooking duck with olives, onions, and wine has its roots in Provence, in France. The sweetness brought out by slow-cooking the onions balances the saltiness of the olives beautifully. Simple, creamy mashed potatoes make a perfect accompaniment.

SERVES 4

4 duck quarters or breast portions
8 ounces pearl onions, peeled
½ teaspoon superfine sugar
2 tablespoons all-purpose flour
1 cup dry red wine
1 cup duck or chicken stock
1 bouquet garni
1 cup pitted green or black olives, or a
   combination
salt and ground black pepper

1 Put the duck skin side down in a large frying pan, and cook for 10–12 minutes, turning to color evenly, until browned on both sides. Lift out with a slotted spoon, and place skin side up in the ceramic cooking pot. Switch the slow cooker to high.

2 Pour off most of the fat from the pan, leaving about 1 tablespoon behind. Add the onions, and cook over a medium-low heat until beginning to color. Sprinkle over the sugar, and cook for 5 minutes, until golden, stirring frequently. Sprinkle with the flour, and cook, uncovered, for 2 minutes, stirring frequently.

3 Gradually stir the red wine into the onions, followed by the stock. Bring to the boil, then pour over the duck. Add the bouquet garni to the pot, cover with the lid, and cook on high for 1 hour.

4 Turn the slow cooker to low, and cook for a further 4–5 hours, or until the duck and onions are very tender.

5 Put the olives in a heatproof bowl, and pour over very hot water to cover. Leave to stand for about 1 minute, then drain thoroughly. Add the olives to the casserole, re-cover with the lid, and cook for a further 30 minutes.

6 Transfer the duck, onions, and olives to a warm serving dish or individual plates. Skim all the fat from the cooking liquid, and discard the bouquet garni. Season the sauce to taste with black pepper and a little salt, if needed, then spoon over the duck and serve

COOK'S TIPS
• Taste the stew before adding more salt; if the olives were salty, the stew will not need any more.
• The skin may be removed from the duck before cooking, if you prefer, and the duck pieces cooked in 1 tablespoon oil for a few minutes to brown them.

Energy 414Kcal/1736kJ; Protein 47.3g; Carbohydrate 8.2g, of which sugars 2.3g; Fat 18.5g, of which saturates 5.2g; Cholesterol 257mg; Calcium 67mg; Fiber 1.6g; Sodium 917mg.

PAPPARDELLE with RABBIT

This rich-tasting dish comes from northern Italy, where rabbit sauces are very popular.
It is ideal for entertaining, as the sauce can be kept warm in the slow cooker until needed.

SERVES 4

½ ounce dried porcini mushrooms
⅔ cup warm water
1 small onion
½ carrot
½ celery stick
2 bay leaves
2 tablespoons butter or 1 tablespoon
  olive oil
1½ ounces pancetta or rindless fatty
  bacon, chopped
1 tablespoon roughly chopped fresh Italian
  parsley, plus extra to garnish
9 ounces boneless rabbit meat
4 tablespoons dry white wine
7-ounce can chopped Italian plum
  tomatoes or scant 1 cup
  bottled strained tomatoes
11 ounces fresh or dried pappardelle
salt and ground black pepper

1 Put the dried mushrooms in a bowl,
pour over the warm water, and leave to
soak for 15 minutes. Finely chop the
vegetables, either in a food processor or
by hand. Make a tear in each bay leaf, so
that they will release their flavor when
added to the sauce.

2 Heat the butter or oil in a large frying
pan until just sizzling. Add the chopped
vegetables, pancetta or bacon, and the
parsley, and cook for about 5 minutes.

3 Add the rabbit pieces, and fry on
both sides for 3–4 minutes. Transfer the
mixture to the ceramic cooking pot, and
switch to the high or auto setting.
Add the wine and tomatoes.

4 While the mixture is starting to heat
through, drain the mushrooms, and pour
the soaking liquid into the slow cooker
through a fine strainer. Chop the
mushrooms, and add to the mixture,
with the bay leaves. Season to taste with
salt and black pepper. Stir well, cover
with the lid, and cook for 1 hour.
Reduce the setting to low or leave on
auto, and cook for a further 2 hours, or
until the meat is tender.

5 Lift out the rabbit pieces, cut them
into bitesize chunks, and stir them back
into the sauce. Remove and discard the
bay leaves. Taste the sauce, and season,
as necessary. The sauce is now ready to
serve, but can be kept hot in the slow
cooker for 1–2 hours.

6 About 10 minutes before serving,
cook the pasta according to the
instructions on the package. Drain the
pasta, add to the sauce, and toss well to
mix. Serve immediately, sprinkled with
fresh parsley.

VARIATION
If you prefer, or if rabbit is not available,
this dish can be made with chicken instead.

Energy 393Kcal/1653kJ; Protein 23g; Carbohydrate 46g, of which sugars 4.9g; Fat 13.3g, of which saturates 5g; Cholesterol 46mg; Calcium 80mg; Fiber 1.1g; Sodium 128mg.

RABBIT CASSEROLE with JUNIPER

Because rabbit is such a lean meat, casseroling is an ideal way to cook it, helping to keep it really moist and juicy. Using a well-flavored marinade improves both the taste and texture of the meat. Chicken leg portions make an excellent alternative to rabbit if you prefer. Serve with steamed new potatoes and whole baby carrots.

SERVES 4

2 pounds prepared rabbit pieces
1 onion, roughly chopped
2 garlic cloves, crushed
1 bay leaf
1½ cups fruity red wine
2 sprigs of fresh thyme
1 sprig of fresh rosemary
1 tablespoon juniper berries
2 tablespoons olive oil
½ ounce dried porcini mushrooms
2 tablespoons chopped fresh parsley
2 tablespoons chilled butter
salt and ground black pepper

4 Meanwhile, put the mushrooms in a heatproof bowl, and pour over ⅔ cup boiling water. Leave to soak for 1 hour, then drain, reserving the soaking liquid, and finely chop the mushrooms. Put the mushrooms in a small bowl, and cover with plastic wrap to keep them moist.

5 Pour the soaking liquid from the mushrooms into the ceramic cooking pot. Cook for a further 2 hours. Lift out the rabbit pieces with a slotted spoon, and strain the cooking liquid, discarding the vegetables, herbs, and juniper berries. Wipe the ceramic cooking pot clean, then return the rabbit and cooking liquid. Add the mushrooms, and season.

6 Cover, and cook for a further hour, or until the meat and mushrooms are cooked and tender. Stir in the chopped parsley, then lift out the rabbit pieces, and arrange on a warmed serving dish. Cut the chilled butter into small cubes, and whisk it into the sauce, one or two pieces at a time, to thicken. Spoon the sauce over the rabbit, and serve.

1 Put the rabbit pieces in a glass or ceramic dish with the onion, garlic, bay leaf, and wine. Bruise the thyme and rosemary to release their flavor, and lightly crush the juniper berries, and add them to the dish. Toss to combine. Cover, and marinate in the refrigerator for at least 4 hours or overnight, turning the pieces once or twice, if possible.

2 Remove the rabbit from the marinade, reserving the marinade, and pat dry with paper towels. Heat the oil in a frying pan, add the rabbit pieces, and fry for 3–5 minutes, turning to brown all over. Transfer the meat to the ceramic cooking pot.

3 Pour the marinade into the frying pan, and bring to boiling point. Pour over the rabbit, cover the ceramic cooking pot with the lid, and switch the slow cooker to high. Cook for about 1 hour.

Energy 356Kcal/1483kJ; Protein 32g; Carbohydrate 3.2g, of which sugars 2.3g; Fat 17.5g, of which saturates 6.3g; Cholesterol 163mg; Calcium 30mg; Fiber 0.6g; Sodium 66mg.

HARE POT PIES

The full, gamey flavor of hare is perfect for this dish, but boneless rabbit, venison, pheasant, or any other game meat can be used instead. The meat filling is cooked in the slow cooker until tender and succulent—this can be done the day before if you like—before being topped with pastry and finished in the oven.

3 Heat the remaining oil in the pan, and fry the hare in batches until well browned. When all the meat has been cooked, return it to the pan. Sprinkle over the flour, and cook, stirring, for a few seconds, then gradually stir in the Madeira and stock, and bring to the boil.

4 Transfer the hare mixture to the ceramic cooking pot, and cook for 1 hour. Switch the slow cooker to low or leave on auto, and cook for a further 5–6 hours, until the meat and vegetables are tender. Stir in the chopped parsley, then set aside to cool.

5 To make the pies, preheat the oven to 425°F. Spoon the hare mixture into four individual pie dishes. Cut the pastry into quarters, and roll out on a lightly floured work surface to make the pie covers. Make the pieces larger than the dishes. Trim off any excess pastry, and use the trimmings to line the rim of each dish.

6 Dampen the pastry rims with cold water, and cover with the pastry lids. Pinch the edges together to seal in the filling. Brush each pie with beaten egg yolk, and make a small hole in the top of each one to allow steam to escape.

7 Stand the pies on a baking tray, and bake for 25 minutes, or until the pastry is well risen and dark golden. If the pastry is browning too quickly, cover with foil after 15 minutes to prevent it from overbrowning.

SERVES 4

3 tablespoons olive oil
1 leek, sliced
8 ounces parsnips, sliced
8 ounces carrots, sliced
1 fennel bulb, sliced
1½ pounds boneless hare, diced
2 tablespoons all-purpose flour
4 tablespoons Madeira
1¼ cups game
    or chicken stock
3 tablespoons chopped fresh parsley
1 pound puff pastry, thawed
    if frozen
beaten egg yolk, to glaze

VARIATION

You can make one large single pie, instead of four individual ones, if you like.

1 Heat 2 tablespoons of the oil in a large pan. Add the leek, parsnips, carrots, and fennel, and cook for about 10 minutes, stirring frequently, until softened.

2 Using a slotted spoon, transfer the vegetables to the ceramic cooking pot. Cover with the lid, and switch the slow cooker to the high or auto setting.

Energy 906Kcal/3784kJ; Protein 45g; Carbohydrate 60.4g, of which sugars 10g; Fat 53.7g, of which saturates 15.9g; Cholesterol 107mg; Calcium 180mg; Fiber 7.6g; Sodium 553mg.

ONE-POT, CLAY-POT POULTRY AND GAME

This chapter lifts the lid on delicious main courses using chicken, duck, pheasant, grouse, guinea fowl, pigeon, venison, and rabbit. All are made effortlessly on top of the stove or in a freestanding electric cooker. You'll be reminded of old favorites such as Coq au Vin, Chicken Casserole with Winter Vegetables, and Hunter's Chicken and invited to try some exciting new flavors, such as Guinea Fowl with Beans and Curly Kale, Mediterranean Duck with Harissa and Saffron, or Grouse with Orchard Fruit Stuffing. For a great experience you'll be sure to repeat, try Spicy Venison Casserole.

CHICKEN with GARBANZOS and ALMONDS

The almonds in this tasty Moroccan-style recipe are precooked until soft, adding an interesting texture and flavor to the chicken.

SERVES 4

½ cup blanched almonds
½ cup garbanzo beans, soaked overnight
   and drained
4 part-boned chicken breast portions, skinned
4 tablespoons butter
½ teaspoon saffron threads
2 Bermuda onions, thinly sliced
3¾ cups chicken stock
I small cinnamon stick
4 tablespoons chopped fresh Italian
   parsley, plus extra to garnish
lemon juice, to taste
salt and ground black pepper

I Place the almonds and the soaked and drained garbanzos in a large, flameproof casserole of water, and bring to a boil. Boil for 10 minutes, then reduce the heat. Simmer for I–I½ hours, until the garbanzos are soft. Drain the garbanzos and almonds, and set aside.

2 Place the skinned chicken pieces in the casserole, together with the butter, half of the saffron, and salt and plenty of black pepper. Heat gently, stirring, until the butter has melted.

3 Add the onions and stock, bring to a boil, then add the reserved cooked almonds, garbanzos, and cinnamon stick. Cover with a tightly fitting lid, and cook very gently for 45–60 minutes, until the chicken is completely tender.

4 Transfer the cooked chicken to a serving plate, and keep warm. Bring the sauce to a boil, and cook over a high heat until it is well reduced, stirring frequently with a wooden spoon.

5 Add the chopped parsley and remaining saffron to the casserole, and cook for 2–3 minutes more. Sharpen the sauce with a little lemon juice, then pour the sauce over the chicken, and serve, garnished with extra fresh parsley.

CHICKEN with TOMATOES and HONEY

A thick tomato and honey sauce coats chicken pieces in this subtly spiced dish.

SERVES 4

2 tablespoons sunflower-seed oil
2 tablespoons butter
4 chicken portions
I onion, grated or very finely chopped
I garlic clove, crushed
I teaspoon ground cinnamon
good pinch of ground ginger
3–3½ pounds tomatoes, peeled, cored,
   and coarsely chopped
2 tablespoons honey
⅓ cup blanched almonds
I tablespoon sesame seeds
salt and ground black pepper
chopped fresh Italian parsley, to garnish

I Place the oil and butter in a large, flameproof casserole. Add the chicken, and cook over medium heat for about 3 minutes, until it is lightly browned.

2 Add the grated or chopped onion, garlic, cinnamon, ginger, tomatoes, and plenty of seasoning, and heat gently until the tomatoes begin to bubble.

3 Lower the heat, and then cover the casserole. Simmer very gently, stirring and turning the chicken occasionally, for about I hour, or until it is completely cooked through.

4 Lift out the chicken pieces, and transfer them to a plate. Increase the heat, and cook the tomato sauce until it is reduced to a thick purée, stirring frequently. Stir in the honey, cook for I minute, then return the chicken pieces to the casserole, and cook for 2–3 minutes more to heat through.

5 Transfer the chicken and sauce to a warmed serving dish, and sprinkle with the blanched almonds and sesame seeds. Serve hot, garnished with parsley.

COOK'S TIP
To blanch whole almonds, place them in a strainer and lower it into boiling water. Cook the almonds for 2–3 minutes, then remove the strainer from the water. Pinch the softened almond skin between your thumb and finger to squeeze it off.

Chicken with Chickpeas and Almonds: Energy 463Kcal/1935kJ; Protein 45.2g; Carbohydrate 18.6g, of which sugars 7g; Fat 23.6g, of which saturates 7.9g; Cholesterol 132mg; Calcium 110mg; Fiber 4.8g; Sodium 179mg.
Chicken with Tomatoes and Honey: Energy 579Kcal/2413kJ; Protein 33.7g; Carbohydrate 20.7g, of which sugars 19.2g; Fat 40.8g, of which saturates 10.5g; Cholesterol 178mg; Calcium 103mg; Fiber 5.2g; Sodium 192mg.

HUNTER'S CHICKEN

This traditional dish sometimes has strips of green pepper in the sauce instead of the mushrooms. Creamed potato or polenta makes a good accompaniment.

SERVES 4

¼ cup dried porcini mushrooms
2 tablespoons olive oil
1 tablespoon butter
4 chicken portions, on the bone, skinned
1 large onion, thinly sliced
14-ounce can chopped tomatoes
⅔ cup red wine
1 garlic clove, crushed
leaves of 1 fresh rosemary sprig,
    finely chopped
1¾ cups fresh portabello mushrooms,
    thinly sliced
salt and ground black pepper
fresh rosemary sprigs, to garnish

1 Put the porcini in a bowl, add 1 cup warm water, and soak for 20 minutes. Squeeze the porcini over the bowl, strain the liquid, and reserve. Finely chop the porcini.

2 Heat the oil and butter in a large, flameproof casserole until foaming. Add the chicken portions, and sauté over a medium heat for 5 minutes, or until golden brown. Remove the pieces, and drain on paper towels.

3 Add the sliced onion and chopped porcini mushrooms to the pan. Cook gently, stirring frequently, for about 3 minutes, until the onion has softened but not browned. Stir in the chopped tomatoes, red wine, and reserved mushroom soaking liquid, then add the crushed garlic and chopped rosemary, with salt and pepper to taste. Bring to the boil, stirring constantly.

4 Return the chicken to the casserole, and turn to coat with the sauce. Cover with a tightly fitting lid, and simmer gently for 30 minutes.

5 Add the fresh mushrooms to the casserole, and stir well to mix into the sauce. Continue simmering gently for 10 minutes, or until the chicken is tender. Taste for seasoning. Serve hot, with creamed potato or polenta, if you like. Garnish with the rosemary sprigs.

Energy 310Kcal/1299kJ; Protein 38.2g; Carbohydrate 9.2g, of which sugars 7.5g; Fat 10.8g, of which saturates 3.3g; Cholesterol 113mg; Calcium 38mg; Fiber 2.4g; Sodium 128mg.

SEVILLE CHICKEN

Oranges and almonds are a favorite ingredient in southern Spain, especially around Seville,
where the orange and almond trees are a familiar and wonderful sight.

SERVES 4

1 orange
8 chicken thighs
all-purpose flour, seasoned with
    salt and pepper
3 tablespoons olive oil
1 large Bermuda onion,
    roughly chopped
2 garlic cloves, crushed
1 red bell pepper, seeded and sliced
1 yellow bell pepper, seeded and sliced
4 ounces chorizo, sliced
½ cup sliced almonds
generous 1 cup brown basmati rice
2½ cups chicken
    or vegetable stock
14-ounce can chopped tomatoes
¾ cup white wine
generous pinch of dried thyme
salt and ground black pepper
fresh thyme sprigs, to garnish

3 Add the chorizo, stir-fry for a few minutes, then sprinkle over the almonds and rice. Cook, stirring, for 1–2 minutes.

4 Pour in the chicken or vegetable stock, chopped tomatoes, and white wine, then add the reserved orange peel and the dried thyme. Season well. Bring the sauce to simmering point, stirring, then return the chicken to the pan.

5 Cover tightly, and cook over a very low heat for 1–1¼ hours, until the rice and chicken are tender. Just before serving, add the orange segments and juice, and allow to cook briefly to heat through. Season to taste, garnish with sprigs of fresh thyme, and serve.

1 Pare a thin strip of peel from the orange, using a vegetable peeler, and set it aside. Peel the orange, then cut it into even segments, working over a bowl to catch any excess juice. Dust the chicken thighs with plenty of seasoned flour.

2 Heat the olive oil in a large frying pan, and fry the chicken pieces on both sides until nicely brown. Transfer the browned chicken to a plate. Add the chopped onion and crushed garlic to the pan, and fry for 4–5 minutes until the onion begins to brown. Add the sliced red and yellow peppers to the pan, and fry, stirring occasionally with a wooden spoon, until they are slightly softened.

Energy 861Kcal/3598kJ; Protein 65.3g; Carbohydrate 67.1g, of which sugars 17.1g; Fat 34g, of which saturates 5.6g; Cholesterol 155mg, Calcium 172mg, Fiber 6.3g, Sodium 453mg.

MUSTARD BAKED CHICKEN

In this recipe, a mild, aromatic whole-grain mustard makes a tasty way of cooking chicken. Speciality mustards are freely available in delicatessens and wholefood shops. Serve with new potatoes and peas or snow peas.

SERVES 4–6

8–12 chicken joints, or 1 medium chicken,
   about 2¼ pounds, jointed
juice of ½ lemon
2–3 tablespoons whiskey mustard
2 teaspoons chopped fresh tarragon
sea salt and ground black pepper

VARIATION
A whole chicken can also be baked
this way. Allow about 1½ hours in
an oven preset to 350°F. When cooked,
the juices will run clear without any
trace of blood.

1 Preheat the oven to 375°F. Put the chicken joints into a large shallow baking dish in a single layer, and sprinkle the lemon juice over the chicken to flavor the skin. Season well with sea salt and black pepper.

2 Spread the mustard over the joints, and sprinkle with the chopped tarragon. Bake in the preheated oven for 20–30 minutes, or until thoroughly cooked, depending on the size of the chicken pieces. Serve immediately.

Per portion Energy 426Kcal/1768kJ; Protein 40.3g; Carbohydrate 0g, of which sugars 0g; Fat 29.3g, of which saturates 8.1g; Cholesterol 215mg; Calcium 13mg; Fiber 0g; Sodium 146mg

ROAST FARMYARD DUCK with APPLES and CIDER

Sharp fruit flavors offset the richness of duck: orange is the classic, but stovecooking apples are used here with hard cider. Serve with a selection of vegetables, including roast potatoes and, perhaps, some red cabbage

SERVES 4

4½ pounds oven-ready duck or duckling
1¼ cups hard cider
4 tablespoons heavy cream
sea salt and ground black pepper

For the stuffing
6 tablespoons butter
2 cups fresh white bread crumbs
1 pound stovecooking apples,
   peeled, cored, and diced
1 tablespoon sugar,
   or to taste
freshly grated nutmeg

1 Preheat the oven to 400°F. To make the stuffing, melt the butter in a pan, and gently fry the bread crumbs until golden brown. Add the apples to the bread crumbs with salt, pepper, the sugar, and a pinch of nutmeg. Mix together well.

2 Wipe the duck out with a clean, damp cloth, and remove any obvious excess fat (including the flaps just inside the vent). Rub the skin with salt. Stuff the duck with the prepared mixture, then secure the vent with a small skewer.

COOK'S TIP
The giblets aren't required for this recipe, but you can remove the liver and set it aside to use in a warm salad. The remaining giblets can be used later, with the duck carcass, to make a delicious stock for soup.

3 Weigh the stuffed duck, and calculate the cooking time, allowing 20 minutes per 1 pound. Prick the skin all over with a fork to allow the fat to run out during the cooking time, then lay it on top of a wire rack in a roasting pan, sprinkle with freshly ground black pepper, and put it into the preheated oven to roast.

4 About 20 minutes before the end of the estimated cooking time, remove the duck from the oven, and pour off all the fat that has accumulated under the rack (reserve it for frying). Slide the duck off the rack into the roasting pan, and pour the cider over it. Return to the oven, and finish cooking, basting occasionally.

5 When the duck is cooked, remove it from the pan, and keep warm while you make the sauce. Set the roasting pan over a medium heat, and boil the cider to reduce it by half. Stir in the cream, heat through, and season. Meanwhile, remove the stuffing from the duck. Carve the duck into slices, or quarter it using poultry shears. Serve with a portion of stuffing and the cider sauce.

Energy 572Kcal/2397kJ; Protein 31.5g; Carbohydrate 34.6g, of which sugars 13.1g; Fat 33.1g, of which saturates 17.8g; Cholesterol 211mg, Calcium 74mg, Fiber 2.4g, Sodium 498mg

OVEN-ROASTED CHICKEN with MEDITERRANEAN VEGETABLES

This is a delicious—and trouble-free—alternative to a traditional roast chicken. The recipe also works very well with guinea fowl.

SERVES 4

4–5 pounds roasting chicken
⅔ cup extra virgin olive oil
½ lemon
a few fresh thyme sprigs
1 pound small new potatoes
1 eggplant, cut into 1-inch cubes
1 red or yellow bell pepper, seeded
   and cut into fourths
1 fennel bulb, trimmed and cut
   into fourths
8 large garlic cloves, unpeeled
coarse salt and ground black pepper

1 Preheat the oven to 400°F. Rub the chicken all over with olive oil, and season with pepper. Place the lemon half inside the bird, with a sprig or two of thyme. Put the chicken, breast side down, in a large roasting pan. Roast for about 30 minutes.

2 Remove the chicken from the oven, and season with salt. Turn the chicken right side up, and baste with the juices from the pan.

3 Arrange the potatoes around the chicken, and roll them in the cooking juices until they are thoroughly coated. Return the roasting pan to the oven, to continue roasting.

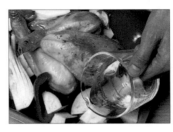

4 After 30 minutes, add the eggplant, red bell pepper, fennel, and garlic cloves to the pan. Drizzle the vegetables with the remaining oil, and season to taste with salt and pepper.

5 Add the remaining sprigs of thyme to the roasting pan, tucking the sprigs in among the vegetables. Return the chicken and vegetables to the oven, and cook for 30–50 minutes more, basting and turning the vegetables occasionally during cooking.

6 To find out if the chicken is cooked, push the tip of a small sharp knife between the thigh and breast—if the juices run clear, rather than pink, it is done. The vegetables should be tender and beginning to brown. Serve the chicken and vegetables from the pan.

Energy 798Kcal/3310kJ; Protein 43.3g; Carbohydrate 23.7g, of which sugars 6.1g; Fat 59.3g, of which saturates 13.5g; Cholesterol 208mg; Calcium 45mg; Fiber 4.2g; Sodium 183mg.

CHICKEN with FORTY CLOVES of GARLIC

This dish does not have to be mathematically exact, so do not worry if you have 35 or even 50 cloves of garlic—the important thing is that there should be lots. The smell that emanates from the oven as the chicken and garlic cook is indescribably delicious.

SERVES 4–5

5–6 whole heads of garlic
1 tablespoon butter
3 tablespoons olive oil
4–4½ pounds chicken
1¼ cups all-purpose flour, plus 1 teaspoon
5 tablespoons white port, Pineau
    de Charentes, or other white,
    fortified wine
2–3 fresh tarragon or
    rosemary sprigs
2 tablespoons crème fraîche (optional)
a few drops of lemon juice (optional)
salt and ground black pepper

1 Separate three of the heads of garlic into cloves, and peel them. Remove the first layer of papery skin from the remaining heads of garlic, and cut off the tops to expose the cloves, if you like, or leave them whole. Preheat the oven to 350°F.

2 Heat the butter and 1 tablespoon of the olive oil in a flameproof casserole that is just large enough to take the chicken and garlic. Add the chicken, and cook over medium heat, turning it frequently, for 10–15 minutes, until it is browned all over.

3 Sprinkle in 1 teaspoon flour, and cook for 1 minute. Add the port or wine. Tuck in the whole heads of garlic and the peeled cloves with the sprigs of tarragon or rosemary. Pour over the remaining oil, and season to taste with salt and pepper.

4 Mix the main batch of flour with sufficient water to make a firm dough. Roll it out into a long sausage, and press it around the rim of the casserole, then press on the lid, folding the dough up and over it to create a tight seal. Cook in the oven for 1½ hours.

5 To serve, lift off the lid to break the seal, and remove the chicken and whole garlic to a serving platter and keep warm. Remove and discard the herb sprigs, then place the casserole on the stovetop, and whisk the remaining ingredients to combine the garlic cloves with the juices. Add the crème fraîche, if using, and a little lemon juice to taste, if using. Process the sauce in a food processor or blender until smooth. Reheat the garlic sauce in a clean pan, if necessary, and serve it with the chicken.

Energy 616Kcal/2565kJ; Protein 37.7g; Carbohydrate 31.6g, of which sugars 2.9g; Fat 36.5g, of which saturates 10.4g; Cholesterol 173mg; Calcium 64mg; Fiber 2.6g; Sodium 151mg.

CHICKEN BAKED with SHALLOTS, GARLIC, and FENNEL

This is a very simple and delicious way to cook chicken. If you have time, leave the chicken to marinate for a few hours for the best flavor.

2 Preheat the oven to 375°F. Add the wedges of fennel to the chicken, then season with salt, and stir well to mix. Transfer the chicken to the oven, and cook for 50–60 minutes, stirring once or twice, until the chicken is thoroughly cooked. The chicken juices should run clear, not pink, when the thick thigh meat is pierced with a skewer or the point of a small sharp knife.

3 Transfer the chicken and vegetables to a serving dish, and keep them warm. Skim off some of the fat, and bring the cooking juices to a boil, then pour in the cream. Stir, scraping up all the juices. Whisk in the red currant jelly, followed by the mustard. Check the seasoning, adding a little sugar, if necessary.

4 Finely chop the remaining garlic clove with the feathery fennel tops, and mix them with the parsley. Pour the sauce over the chicken, and then sprinkle the chopped garlic and herb mixture over the top. Serve immediately with rice or baked potatoes.

COOK'S TIPS

• If possible, use the fresh, new season's garlic for this dish, as it is plump, moist, and full of flavor. Purple-skinned garlic is considered by many cooks to have the best flavor.

• The cut surfaces of fennel will quickly discolor, so do not prepare it too far in advance of using it. If you must prepare it beforehand, then put the wedges into a bowl of cold water acidulated with a little lemon juice.

SERVES 4

3½–4 pounds chicken, cut into
    8 pieces, or 8 chicken portions
9 ounces shallots, peeled
1 head of garlic, separated into cloves
4 tablespoons extra virgin olive oil
3 tablespoons tarragon vinegar
3 tablespoons white wine or
    vermouth (optional)
1 teaspoon fennel seeds, crushed
2 bulbs fennel, cut into wedges, feathery
    tops reserved
⅔ cup heavy cream
1 teaspoon red currant jelly
1 tablespoon tarragon mustard
a little sugar (optional)
2 tablespoons chopped fresh Italian parsley
salt and ground black pepper

1 Place the chicken pieces, shallots, and all but one of the garlic cloves in a large, shallow, flameproof dish. Add the olive oil, tarragon vinegar, white wine or vermouth, if using, and the crushed fennel seeds. Season to taste with plenty of ground black pepper, then set aside in a cool place, and leave to marinate for 2–3 hours.

Energy 743Kcal/3075kJ; Protein 43.1g; Carbohydrate 5.7g, of which sugars 5.6g; Fat 60.9g, of which saturates 22.2g; Cholesterol 266mg; Calcium 96mg; Fiber 3.9g; Sodium 176mg.

STOVED CHICKEN

"Stovies" were originally potatoes slowly cooked on the stove with onions and drippings or butter until falling to pieces. This version includes a delicious layer of bacon and chicken.

2 Heat the butter and oil in a large, heavy frying pan, add the chopped bacon and chicken pieces, and cook, turning occasionally, until brown on all sides. Using a slotted spoon, transfer the chicken and bacon to the earthenware dish. Reserve the fat in the pan.

3 Sprinkle the remaining chopped thyme over the chicken, season with salt and pepper, then cover with the remaining onion slices, followed by a neat, overlapping layer of the remaining potato slices. Season the top layer of potatoes with more salt and ground black pepper.

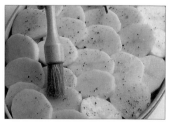

SERVES 4

2¼ pounds baking potatoes, cut into
  ¼-inch slices
2 tablespoons butter, plus extra
  for greasing
2 large onions, thinly sliced
1 tablespoon chopped fresh thyme
1 tablespoon vegetable oil
2 large bacon strips, chopped
4 large chicken portions, halved
2½ cups chicken stock
1 bay leaf
salt and ground black pepper

COOK'S TIP

Instead of chicken portions, choose eight chicken thighs or chicken drumsticks.

1 Preheat the oven to 300°F. Arrange a thick layer of half the potato slices in a large, lightly greased, earthenware baking dish, then cover with half the onions. Sprinkle with half of the chopped fresh thyme, and season with salt and pepper to taste.

4 Pour the chicken stock into the dish, add the bay leaf, and brush the potatoes with the reserved fat from the frying pan. Cover tightly with foil and bake for about 2 hours, or until the chicken is cooked and tender.

5 Preheat the broiler to medium-hot, then remove the foil from the earthenware dish, and place the dish under the broiler. Cook until the slices of potato are beginning to turn golden brown and crisp. Remove the bay leaf, and serve immediately.

Energy 500Kcal/2107kJ; Protein 50g; Carbohydrate 48.2g, of which sugars 8.9g; Fat 13.2g, of which saturates 5.4g; Cholesterol 144mg; Calcium 51mg; Fiber 3.9g; Sodium 405mg.

POT-ROAST CHICKEN with LEMON and GARLIC

This is a rustic dish that is easy to prepare. Lardons are thick strips of bacon fat; if you can't get them, use fatty bacon instead. Serve with thick bread to mop up the juices.

SERVES 4

2 tablespoons olive oil
2 tablespoons butter
1 cup smoked lardons, or coarsely
   chopped fatty bacon
8 garlic cloves, peeled
4 onions, cut into fourths
2 teaspoons all-purpose flour
2½ cups chicken stock
2 lemons, thickly sliced
3 tablespoons chopped fresh thyme
1 chicken, about 3–3½ pounds
2 × 14-ounce cans cannellini
   or navy beans, drained
   and rinsed
salt and ground black pepper

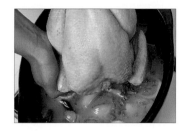

3 Bring the sauce to a boil, stirring constantly until thickened, then place the chicken on top. Season well. Transfer the casserole to the oven. Cook for 1 hour, basting the chicken once or twice during cooking to insure it stays moist.

4 Baste the chicken again. Stir the beans into the casserole, and return it to the oven for 30 minutes more, or until the chicken is cooked through and tender. Carve the chicken into thick slices, and serve with the beans.

1 Preheat the oven to 375°F. Heat the oil and butter in a flameproof casserole that is large enough to hold the chicken with a little room around the sides. Add the lardons or bacon, and cook until golden. Remove with a slotted spoon, and drain on paper towels.

2 Add the garlic and onions, and brown over high heat. Stir in the flour, then the stock. Return the lardons to the pan with the lemon, thyme, and seasoning.

Energy 887Kcal/3696kJ; Protein 62.5g; Carbohydrate 45.5g, of which sugars 12.9g; Fat 51.7g, of which saturates 16g; Cholesterol 256mg; Calcium 187mg; Fiber 13.9g; Sodium 1519mg.

POUSSINS and NEW POTATO POT-ROAST

Pot-roasts are traditionally associated with the colder months, but this delicious version is a simple summer dish that makes the most of new season potatoes.

SERVES 4

2 poussins, about 1¼ pounds each
2 tablespoons butter
1 tablespoon honey
1¼ pounds small new potatoes
1 red onion, halved
   lengthwise and cut
   into thin wedges
4–5 small fresh rosemary sprigs
2 bay leaves
1 lemon, cut into wedges
scant 2 cups hot chicken stock
salt and ground black pepper

1 Soak a clay chicken brick in cold water for 20 minutes, then drain. Cut the poussins in half, along the breast bones.

2 Melt the butter, combine it with the honey, and brush over the poussins. Season with salt and pepper.

3 Place the small new potatoes and onion wedges in the base of the chicken brick. Tuck the rosemary sprigs, bay leaves, and lemon wedges in among the vegetables. Pour over the hot chicken stock (see Cook's Tip).

4 Place the halved poussins on top of the vegetables. Cover the chicken brick, and place it in an unheated oven. Set the oven to 400°F, and cook for about 55–60 minutes, or until the poussin juices run clear and the vegetables are tender. Uncover the chicken brick for the last 10 minutes of cooking to add more color to the poussins, if necessary.

COOK'S TIPS
• Make sure the stock is hot, but not boiling when it is added to the chicken brick, otherwise the brick may crack.
• A poussin is a baby chicken—usually around 4–6 weeks old. Poussins can be cooked by broiling, roasting, or pot-roasting, but are especially tender and moist cooked in a chicken brick.

Energy 443Kcal/1852kJ; Protein 30.1g; Carbohydrate 24.2g, of which sugars 5.4g; Fat 25.8g, of which saturates 8.9g; Cholesterol 158mg; Calcium 23mg; Fiber 1.5g; Sodium 153mg.

CORN-FED CHICKEN with WINTER VEGETABLES

Chicken cooked in a clay pot remains beautifully moist and tender. Flavored with lemon, parsley, and tarragon, serve this as an alternative to a traditional Sunday roast.

SERVES 4

3 large carrots, cut into batons
1 celery heart, thickly sliced
2 red onions, cut into fourths
a few fresh thyme sprigs
3½ pounds corn-fed chicken
3 tablespoons butter, softened
1 tablespoon chopped fresh parsley
1 tablespoon chopped fresh tarragon
1 small lemon, halved
1¼ cups dry white wine or
   chicken stock
salt and ground black pepper

COOK'S TIP
Cook some potatoes in the oven at the same time to accompany the pot roast—baked potatoes or roast potatoes both go well with this main course. Or, if you like, serve the pot-roast with creamy mashed potatoes.

1 Soak a chicken brick or large clay pot in cold water for 20 minutes, then drain. Place the carrots, celery, red onions, and thyme in the pot.

2 Wash the chicken, and dry thoroughly. Combine the butter, parsley, and tarragon. Ease up the breast skin of the chicken, and spread the butter under it, taking care not to puncture the skin. Place the lemon halves inside the chicken.

3 Rub the chicken with seasoning, and nestle on top of the vegetables. Add the wine or chicken stock, and cover. Place the chicken brick or pot in an unheated oven. Set the oven temperature to 400°F, and cook for about 1¾ hours, or until the chicken is cooked.

4 Remove the lid from the brick or pot, and cook for 10 minutes more, or until the chicken is golden brown.

Energy 717Kcal/2975kJ; Protein 47.3g; Carbohydrate 13.8g, of which sugars 12.3g; Fat 47.4g, of which saturates 16.6g; Cholesterol 261mg; Calcium 89mg; Fiber 4.1g; Sodium 314mg.

CHICKEN GUMBO with OKRA, HAM, TOMATOES, and SHRIMP

This classic Creole dish is really a very hearty soup, but is usually served over rice as a delicious and filling main course, like a stew.

SERVES 4

2 tablespoons olive oil
1 onion, chopped
8 ounces skinless, boneless chicken
    breast portions, cut into
    small chunks
¼ cup all-purpose flour
1 teaspoon paprika
2 tablespoons tomato paste
2½ cups well-flavored chicken stock
14-ounce can chopped tomatoes
    with herbs
a few drops of Tabasco
6 ounces okra
1 red, orange, or yellow bell pepper,
    seeded and chopped
2 celery sticks, sliced
1⅓ cups diced lean cooked ham
8 ounces large shrimp, peeled, deveined
    and heads removed, but with
    tails intact
salt and ground black pepper
boiled rice, to serve

1 Soak a large clay pot or chicken brick in cold water for 20 minutes, then drain. Heat the oil in a large frying pan, add the chopped onion, and cook over a medium heat for about 5 minutes, stirring occasionally, until softened and lightly golden.

2 Add the chicken chunks to the pan, and sauté for 1–2 minutes, to seal. Stir in the flour, paprika, and tomato paste, and cook, stirring constantly, for 1–2 minutes.

3 Gradually add the stock, stirring constantly, then bring the sauce to the boil, stirring. Add the chopped tomatoes, then remove the pan from the heat. Add a few drops of Tabasco, and season with salt and pepper.

4 Cut the okra pods in half if they are large, then add them to the clay pot or chicken brick with the chopped red, orange, or yellow pepper and the sliced celery. Add the chicken and tomato mixture, and stir well to mix.

5 Cover the clay pot or chicken brick, and place it in an unheated oven. Set the oven to 400°F, and cook for 30 minutes.

6 Remove the clay pot or chicken brick from the oven, then add the diced ham and the shrimp, and stir well to combine. Cover the pot or brick, and return it to the oven for about 10 minutes, or until the ham is heated through and the shrimp are just cooked. To serve, spoon some freshly boiled rice into four warmed, individual serving plates or bowls, and ladle over the gumbo.

VARIATIONS

Replace the cooked ham with crabmeat or cooked and shelled mussels or, for a special occasion, replace the peeled shrimp with crayfish, and replace the ham with cooked and shelled oysters.

COOK'S TIPS

• Okra is a favorite ingredient in the southern states of the USA and in African and Caribbean cooking. When buying, look for firm, bright green pods that are less than 4 inches long. Larger pods may be slightly tough and fibrous. When cooked, okra produces a rather viscous substance that thickens the liquid in which it is cooked—an essential part of many traditional okra recipes.
• If you don't have a bottle of Tabasco sauce at hand, add about ½ teaspoon chili powder, or a finely chopped fresh or dried chile. Remove the seeds from the chile if you would prefer the gumbo to be only medium-hot.

CHICKEN and SHRIMP JAMBALAYA

This colorful mixture of rice, bell peppers, and tomatoes with chicken, ham, and shrimp is flavored with garlic and fresh herbs and a few dashes of fiery Tabasco sauce. It's an ideal dish for big family gatherings and celebrations.

SERVES 10

2 chickens, each about 3–3½ pounds
1-pound piece raw smoked ham
⅓ cup lard or bacon fat
½ cup all-purpose flour
3 onions, thinly sliced
2 green bell peppers, seeded and sliced
1½ pounds tomatoes, peeled
    and chopped
2–3 garlic cloves, crushed
2 teaspoons chopped fresh thyme or
    1 teaspoon dried thyme
24 jumbo shrimp, peeled with
    tails intact
2½ cups long grain rice
5 cups water
2–3 dashes Tabasco sauce
3 tablespoons chopped fresh Italian
    parsley, plus tiny fresh parsley sprigs
    to garnish
salt and ground black pepper

1 Cut each chicken into ten pieces, and season the pieces well with salt and pepper. Dice the ham, discarding the rind and fat.

2 Melt the lard or bacon fat in a large, heavy frying pan. Add the chicken pieces, in several batches, cook them over medium heat until they are golden brown all over, then lift them out with a slotted spoon, and set them aside.

3 Reduce the heat. Sprinkle the flour into the fat in the pan, and stir with a wooden spoon until the roux turns a golden brown color. Return the chicken pieces to the pan.

4 Add the diced ham, onions, green bell peppers, tomatoes, garlic, and thyme, and stir well to mix. Cook, stirring regularly, for about 10 minutes, then add the shrimp and mix lightly.

5 Stir the rice into the frying pan, and pour in the water. Season well with salt, black pepper, and Tabasco sauce. Bring to a boil, then cook, stirring occasionally, until the rice is tender and all the liquid has been fully absorbed. Add a little extra boiling water if the rice looks like it is drying out before it is cooked. Check the seasoning, and add salt, pepper, and more Tabasco if necessary.

6 Mix the chopped fresh Italian parsley into the finished dish, garnish with tiny sprigs of Italian parsley, and serve the jambalaya immediately with plenty of crusty bread.

Energy 740Kcal/3079kJ; Protein 50.6g; Carbohydrate 52.9g, of which sugars 7.7g; Fat 36.1g, of which saturates 11.1g; Cholesterol 240mg; Calcium 79mg; Fiber 2.2g; Sodium 593mg.

RISOTTO with CHICKEN

This is a classic risotto combination of creamy rice and tender cubes of chicken, flavored with aromatic saffron, prosciutto, white wine, and Parmesan cheese.

SERVES 6

2 tablespoons olive oil
8 ounces skinless, boneless chicken breast
    portions, cut into 1-inch cubes
1 onion, finely chopped
1 garlic clove, finely chopped
2¼ cups risotto rice
½ cup dry white wine
¼ teaspoon saffron threads
7½ cups simmering chicken stock
2 ounces prosciutto, cut into
    thin strips
2 tablespoons butter, diced
⅓ cup freshly grated Parmesan cheese,
    plus extra to serve
salt and ground black pepper
fresh Italian parsley sprigs,
    to garnish

1 Heat the olive oil in a large frying pan over medium-high heat. Add the cubes of chicken, and cook, stirring occasionally with a wooden spoon, until they start to turn white.

2 Reduce the heat to low, and add the chopped onion and garlic. Cook, stirring occasionally, until the onion is soft. Stir in the risotto rice, then sauté for 2 minutes, stirring constantly, until all the rice grains are coated in oil.

3 Add the dry white wine to the rice mixture, and cook, stirring constantly, until the wine has been absorbed. Add the saffron threads to the simmering stock, and stir well, then add ladlefuls of hot stock to the rice mixture, letting each ladleful be fully absorbed before adding the next.

4 When the rice is about three-quarters cooked, add the strips of prosciutto, and stir well. Continue cooking, stirring occasionally, until the rice is just tender and the risotto is creamy.

5 Add the butter and the Parmesan, and stir in well. Season with salt and pepper to taste. Serve the risotto hot, sprinkled with a little more Parmesan, and garnished with Italian parsley.

Energy 418Kcal/1744kJ; Protein 17.9g; Carbohydrate 60.9g, of which sugars 0.8g; Fat 9.5g, of which saturates 3.8g; Cholesterol 44mg; Calcium 72mg; Fiber 0.1g; Sodium 194mg.

CHICKEN PIRI-PIRI

*This is a classic Portuguese dish, based on a hot sauce made from Angolan chiles. It is
popular wherever there are Portuguese communities, and is often served in South Africa.*

SERVES 4

4 chicken breast portions
2–3 tablespoons olive oil
1 large onion, thinly sliced
2 carrots, cut into thin strips
1 large parsnip or 2 small parsnips,
    cut into thin strips
1 red bell pepper, seeded and sliced
1 yellow bell pepper, seeded
    and sliced
4 cups chicken or vegetable stock
3 tomatoes, peeled, seeded,
    and chopped
generous dash of piri-piri sauce
1 tablespoon tomato paste
½ cinnamon stick
1 fresh thyme sprig, plus extra
    fresh thyme to garnish
1 bay leaf
1½ cups white long grain rice
1 tablespoon lime or lemon juice
salt and ground black pepper

1 Preheat the oven to 350°F. Rub the
chicken skin with a little salt and ground
black pepper. Heat 2 tablespoons of the
olive oil in a large frying pan, add the
chicken portions, and cook over medium
heat, turning occasionally, until golden
brown on all sides. Transfer to a plate,
using a metal spatula.

2 Add some more oil to the pan if
necessary, add the sliced onion, and
cook for 2–3 minutes, until slightly
softened. Add the carrot and parsnip
strips and the bell pepper slices, and stir-
fry for a few minutes more. Cover the
pan, and cook for 4–5 minutes, until all
the vegetables are quite soft.

3 Pour in the chicken or vegetable stock,
then add the tomatoes, piri-piri sauce,
tomato paste, and cinnamon stick. Stir in
the thyme and bay leaf. Season to taste,
and bring to a boil. Using a ladle, spoon
off 1¼ cups of the liquid, and set aside
in a small pan.

4 Put the rice in the base of a large
earthenware dish. Using a slotted spoon,
scoop the vegetables out of the pan, and
spread them over the rice. Arrange the
chicken pieces on top. Pour over the
spicy chicken stock from the pan, cover
tightly, and cook in the oven for about
45 minutes, until both the rice and
chicken are completely tender.

5 Meanwhile, heat the reserved chicken
stock, adding a few more drops of piri-
piri sauce and the lime or lemon juice.

6 To serve, spoon the piri-piri chicken
and rice onto warmed serving plates.
Serve the remaining sauce separately or
poured over the chicken.

Energy 557Kcal/2337kJ; Protein 44.3g; Carbohydrate 75.4g, of which sugars 15.5g; Fat 8.8g, of which saturates 1.5g; Cholesterol 105mg; Calcium 73mg; Fiber 5.8g; Sodium 122mg.

CHICKEN BIRIANI

Easy to make and very tasty, this is the ideal one-pot dish for a family supper.

SERVES 4

10 green cardamom pods
1½ cups basmati rice, soaked and drained
½ teaspoon salt
2–3 cloves
2-inch cinnamon stick
3 tablespoons vegetable oil
3 onions, sliced
4 skinless, boneless chicken
     breast portions, each about
     6 ounces, cubed
¼ teaspoon ground cloves
1 teaspoon ground cumin
1 teaspoon ground coriander
½ teaspoon ground black pepper
3 garlic cloves, chopped
1 teaspoon finely chopped fresh
     ginger root
juice of 1 lemon
4 tomatoes, sliced
2 tablespoons chopped fresh cilantro
⅔ cup plain yogurt
4–5 saffron threads, soaked in
     2 teaspoons hot milk
⅔ cup water
toasted sliced almonds and fresh cilantro
     sprigs, to garnish
plain yogurt, to serve

1 Preheat the oven to 375°F. Remove the seeds from half the cardamom pods, and grind them finely, using a mortar and pestle. Set the seeds aside.

2 Bring a flameproof casserole of water to a boil, and add the soaked and drained basmati rice, then stir in the salt, the remaining whole cardamom pods, the whole cloves, and cinnamon stick. Boil the rice for 2 minutes, then drain, leaving the whole spices in the rice.

3 Heat the oil in the flameproof casserole, and cook the onions for about 8 minutes, until softened and browned. Add the cubed chicken and the ground spices, including the ground cardamom seeds. Mix well, then add the chopped garlic, ginger, and lemon juice. Stir-fry the mixture together for 5 minutes.

4 Arrange the sliced tomatoes on top. Sprinkle on the cilantro, spoon the yogurt on top, and cover with the rice.

5 Drizzle the saffron milk over the rice, and add the water. Cover, and bake for 1 hour. Garnish with almonds and cilantro, and serve with extra yogurt.

Energy 563Kcal/2359kJ; Protein 45.4g; Carbohydrate 70g, of which sugars 12.5g; Fat 11.3g, of which saturates 1.7g; Cholesterol 105mg; Calcium 152mg; Fiber 3.2g; Sodium 138mg

CHICKEN CASSEROLE with WINTER VEGETABLES

A casserole of wonderfully tender chicken, root vegetables, and lentils, finished with crème fraîche, mustard, and tarragon.

SERVES 4

12 ounces onions
12 ounces leeks
8 ounces carrots
1 pound rutabaga
2 tablespoons oil
4 chicken portions, about 2 pounds
    total weight
½ cup green lentils
2 cups chicken stock
1¼ cups apple juice
2 teaspoons cornstarch
3 tablespoons crème fraîche
2 teaspoons whole-grain mustard
2 tablespoons chopped fresh tarragon
salt and ground black pepper
fresh tarragon sprigs, to garnish

1 Preheat the oven to 375°F. Wash and peel the onions, leeks, carrots, and rutabaga, and then coarsely chop them.

COOK'S TIP
Chop the vegetables into similarly sized pieces so that they cook evenly.

2 Heat the oil in a large, flameproof casserole. Season the chicken portions with plenty of salt and pepper, and brown them in the hot oil until golden. Drain on paper towels.

3 Add the onions to the casserole, and cook for 5 minutes, stirring, until they begin to soften and color. Add the leeks, carrots, rutabaga, and lentils to the casserole, and stir over medium heat for 2 minutes.

4 Return the chicken to the pan, then add the stock, apple juice, and seasoning. Bring to a boil, and cover. Reduce the heat, and cook gently for 60 minutes, or until the chicken and lentils are tender.

5 In a small bowl, blend the cornstarch with about 2 tablespoons water to make a smooth paste, and add to the casserole with the crème fraîche, whole-grain mustard, and chopped tarragon. Adjust the seasoning, then simmer gently for about 2 minutes, stirring, until thickened slightly, before serving, garnished with tarragon sprigs.

Energy 477Kcal/2010kJ; Protein 46.8g; Carbohydrate 45.7g, of which sugars 24.9g; Fat 13.2g, of which saturates 4.5g; Cholesterol 118mg; Calcium 151mg; Fiber 8.1g; Sodium 141mg.

COQ au VIN

This French country casserole was traditionally made with an old boiling bird, marinated overnight in red wine, then simmered gently until tender. Modern recipes use tender roasting birds to save time and because boiling fowl are not readily available.

SERVES 6

3 tablespoons light olive oil
12 shallots
8 ounces rindless fatty bacon
   strips, chopped
3 garlic cloves, finely chopped
8 ounces small mushrooms, halved
6 boneless chicken thighs
3 boneless chicken breast
   portions, halved
1 bottle red wine
salt and ground black pepper
3 tablespoons chopped fresh parsley,
   to garnish

For the bouquet garni
3 sprigs each fresh parsley, thyme, and sage
1 bay leaf
4 peppercorns

For the beurre manié
2 tablespoons butter, softened
¼ cup all-purpose flour

1 Heat the oil in a large, flameproof casserole, and cook the shallots for about 5 minutes, or until golden. Increase the heat, then add the chopped bacon, garlic, and mushrooms and cook for 10 minutes more, stirring frequently.

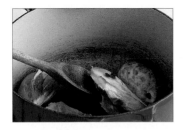

2 Use a slotted spoon to transfer the cooked ingredients to a plate, then brown the chicken portions in the oil remaining in the pan, turning them until they are golden brown all over. Return the cooked shallots, garlic, mushrooms, and bacon to the casserole, and pour in the red wine.

3 Tie the ingredients for the bouquet garni in a bundle in a small piece of cheesecloth, and add to the casserole. Bring to a boil, reduce the heat, and cover the casserole with a tightly fitting lid, then simmer for 30–40 minutes.

4 To make the beurre manié, cream the butter and flour together in a small bowl, using your fingers or a spoon to make a smooth paste.

5 Add small lumps of the beurre manié paste to the bubbling casserole, stirring well until each piece has melted into the liquid before adding the next. When all the paste has been added, bring the casserole back to a boil and simmer for 5 minutes.

6 Season the casserole to taste with salt and pepper, and serve garnished with chopped fresh parsley and accompanied by boiled potatoes.

Energy 538Kcal/2240kJ; Protein 43.5g; Carbohydrate 7g, of which sugars 2.8g; Fat 28.2g, of which saturates 8.9g; Cholesterol 170mg; Calcium 50mg; Fiber 1 1g; Sodium 610mg.

MEDITERRANEAN DUCK with HARISSA and SAFFRON

Harissa is a fiery chili sauce from north Africa. Mixed with cinnamon, saffron, and preserved lemon, it gives this colorful casserole an unforgettable flavor.

SERVES 4

1 tablespoon olive oil
4–4½ pounds duck, quartered
1 large onion, thinly sliced
1 garlic clove, crushed
½ teaspoon ground cumin
1⅔ cups duck or chicken stock
juice of ½ lemon
1–2 teaspoon harissa
1 cinnamon stick
1 teaspoon saffron threads
½ cup black olives
½ cup green olives
peel of 1 preserved lemon,
    rinsed, drained, and cut into
    fine strips
2–3 lemon slices
2 tablespoons chopped fresh
    cilantro, plus extra leaves
    to garnish
salt and ground black pepper

1 Heat the oil in a flameproof casserole. Add the duck quarters, and cook until browned all over. Remove the duck with a slotted spoon, and set aside. Add the onion and garlic to the oil remaining in the casserole, and cook for 5 minutes, until soft. Add the ground cumin, and cook, stirring, for 2 minutes.

COOK'S TIP
The term "duck" refers to birds over two months old. The rich flavor of duck is best appreciated when a duck reaches its full-grown size. Look for a duck with a supple, waxy skin with a dry appearance. It should have a long body with tender, meaty breasts.

2 Pour in the stock and lemon juice, then add the harissa, cinnamon, and saffron. Bring to a boil. Return the duck to the casserole, and add the olives, preserved lemon peel, and lemon slices. Season with salt and pepper.

3 Lower the heat, partially cover the casserole, and simmer gently for about 45 minutes, or until the duck is cooked through. Discard the cinnamon stick. Stir in the chopped cilantro, and garnish with the cilantro leaves.

Energy 262Kcal/1095kJ; Protein 26.6g; Carbohydrate 8.3g, of which sugars 5.9g; Fat 34g, of which saturates 13.5g; Cholesterol 135mg; Calcium 79mg; Fiber 2.8g; Sodium 709mg.

BRAISED SAUSAGES with ONIONS, CELERY ROOT, and APPLE

This richly flavored casserole is comfort food at its best—serve with mashed potatoes and a glass or two of full-bodied red wine on a cold winter night.

SERVES 4

3 tablespoons sunflower-seed oil
1 pound duck or venison sausages
2 onions, sliced
1 tablespoon all-purpose flour
1⅔ cups hard cider
12 ounces celery root, cut into
    large chunks
1 tablespoon Worcestershire sauce
1 tablespoon chopped fresh sage
2 small cooking apples, cored
    and sliced
salt and ground black pepper

1 Preheat the oven to 350°F. Heat the oil in a frying pan, add the sausages, and cook for about 5 minutes, until evenly browned. Transfer to an earthenware casserole dish.

2 Drain off any excess oil from the pan to leave 1 tablespoon. Add the onions, and cook until golden.

3 Stir in the flour, then gradually add the hard cider, and bring to a boil, stirring. Add the celery root, and cook for 2 minutes. Stir in the Worcestershire sauce and sage. Season well.

4 Pour the celery root mixture over the sausages, then cover, and cook in the oven for 30 minutes. Add the apples, and cook for 10–15 minutes, or until the apples are just tender.

VARIATION
You can use good quality pork and herb sausages instead, if you like.

Energy 538Kcal/2240kJ; Protein 43.5g; Carbohydrate 7g, of which sugars 2.8g; Fat 28.2g, of which saturates 8.9g; Cholesterol 170mg; Calcium 50mg; Fiber 1.1g, Sodium 610mg.

CASSOULET

Based on the traditional French dish, this recipe is full of delicious flavors and makes a welcoming and warming meal.

SERVES 6

3–4 boneless duck breast portions, about
    1 pound total weight
8 ounces thick-cut fatty pork
    or unsmoked fatty bacon strips
1 pound Toulouse or garlic sausages
3 tablespoons vegetable oil
1 pound onions, chopped
2 garlic cloves, crushed
2 × 15-ounce cans cannellini beans, rinsed
    and drained
8 ounces carrots, coarsely chopped
14-ounce can chopped tomatoes
1 tablespoon tomato paste
bouquet garni
2 tablespoons chopped fresh thyme or
    1 tablespoon dried
2 cups well-flavored chicken stock
2 cups fresh white or whole-wheat
    bread crumbs
salt and ground black pepper
fresh thyme sprigs,
    to garnish
warm crusty bread,
    to serve

1 Preheat the oven to 325°F. Cut the duck portions and pork or bacon strips into large pieces. Twist the sausages to shorten them, and then cut them into short lengths.

COOK'S TIP
Cannellini beans are large white beans with a nutty flavor. They are especially popular in Italy, particularly in Tuscany, where they are included in a variety of pasta and soup dishes. Cannellini beans are sometimes referred to as white kidney beans or fazola beans.

2 Heat the oil in a large, flameproof casserole. Cook the meat, in batches, until well browned. Remove from the pan with a slotted spoon, and drain on paper towels.

3 Add the onions and garlic to the casserole, and cook for 3–4 minutes, or until softened, stirring frequently.

4 Stir in the beans, carrots, tomatoes, tomato paste, bouquet garni, thyme, and seasoning. Return the meat to the casserole, and mix until well combined.

VARIATION
Canned lima beans or borlotti beans can be used in this recipe instead of the cannellini beans.

5 Add enough of the stock just to cover the meat and beans. (The cassoulet shouldn't be swimming in juices; if the mixture becomes too dry during the cooking time, add a little more stock or water.) Bring to a boil. Cover the casserole tightly, and cook in the oven for 1 hour.

6 Remove the cassoulet from the oven, and add a little more stock or water, if necessary. Remove the bouquet garni.

7 Sprinkle the bread crumbs in an even layer over the top of the cassoulet, and return to the oven, uncovered, for 40 minutes more, or until the meat is tender and the top crisp and lightly brown. Garnish with fresh thyme sprigs, and serve hot with plenty of warm crusty bread to mop up the juices.

Energy 739Kcal/3085kJ; Protein 40.2g; Carbohydrate 49.6g, of which sugars 11.6g; Fat 44.8g, of which saturates 14.2g; Cholesterol 142mg; Calcium 118mg; Fiber 9.4g; Sodium 1848mg.

PIGEONS in STOUT

Pigeons are usually sold in breast portions, as the edible meat is mainly on the breast. The flesh is dark and, like most small birds, dry, so casseroling them in stout is an ideal cooking method. When buying the pigeon breasts, ask your poulterer for the carcasses for stock, if possible. Serve with spiced rice and a watercress or arugula salad.

SERVES 6

6 ounces thick fatty bacon
2 medium onions, finely chopped
2 or 3 garlic cloves, crushed
seasoned flour, for coating
¼ cup butter
1 tablespoon olive oil
6 pigeon breasts
2 tablespooons Irish whiskey (optional)
2½ cups chicken stock
1¼ cups stout
6 ounces white mushrooms
beurre manié, if needed (see Cook's tip)
1–2 tablespoons rowan jelly
sea salt and ground black pepper

1 Preheat the oven to 300°F. Trim the fatty bacon, and cut it into strips. Cook gently in a large, flameproof casserole until the fat runs out, then add the two chopped onions and crushed garlic, and continue cooking until they are soft. Remove from the casserole, and set aside.

2 Coat the breast portions thickly with seasoned flour. Add the butter and oil to the pan, heat until the butter is foaming, then add the meat, and brown well on all sides. Pour in the Irish whiskey, if using. Carefully set it alight, and shake the pan until the flames go out—this improves the flavor.

3 Stir in the stock, stout, and the mushrooms, and bring slowly to the boil. Cover closely, and cook in the preheated oven for 1½–2 hours, or until the pigeons are tender.

4 Remove from the oven, and lift the pigeons onto a serving dish. Thicken the gravy, if necessary, by adding small pieces of beurre manié, stirring until the sauce thickens. Stir in rowan jelly to taste, and adjust the seasoning. Serve the pigeons with the gravy while hot.

COOK'S TIP
To make beurre manié, mix together 1 tablespoon of butter with 1 tablespoon flour. Add small pieces of the mixture to the boiling gravy or sauce, and stir until thickened.

Energy 436Kcal/1817kJ; Protein 38.7g; Carbohydrate 6.7g, of which sugars 5.3g; Fat 27.2g, of which saturates 6.2g; Cholesterol 33mg; Calcium 48mg; Fiber 1.7g; Sodium 639mg

MARINATED SQUAB in RED WINE

The time taken to marinate and cook this casserole is well rewarded by the fabulous rich flavor of the finished dish. Stir-fried green cabbage and celery root mash are delicious accompaniments to this casserole.

SERVES 4

4 squabs, about 8 ounces each
2 tablespoons olive oil
I onion, coarsely chopped
3¼ cups cremini
    mushrooms, sliced
I tablespoon all-purpose flour
1¼ cups game stock
2 tablespoons chopped fresh parsley
salt and ground black pepper
Italian parsley,
    to garnish

For the marinade
I tablespoon light olive oil
I onion, chopped
I carrot, peeled and chopped
I celery stalk, chopped
3 garlic cloves, sliced
6 allspice berries, bruised
2 bay leaves
8 black peppercorns, bruised
⅔ cup red wine vinegar
⅔ cup red wine
3 tablespoons red currant jelly

2 Preheat the oven to 300°F. Heat the oil in a large, flameproof casserole, and cook the onion and mushrooms for about 5 minutes, or until the onion has softened, but not browned.

3 Meanwhile, drain the squabs, and strain the marinade into a pitcher, then set both aside separately.

4 Sprinkle the flour over the squabs, and add them to the casserole, breast sides down. Pour in the marinade and stock, and add the chopped parsley and seasoning. Cover, and cook for 2½ hours.

5 Check the seasoning, then serve the squabs on warmed plates, and ladle the sauce over them. Garnish with parsley.

I Combine all the ingredients for the marinade in a large bowl. Add the squabs, and turn them in the marinade, then cover the bowl, and chill for about 12 hours, turning the squabs frequently.

VARIATIONS
If you are unable to buy squabs, this recipe works equally well with chicken or rabbit. Buy portions, and make deep slashes in the flesh so that the marinade soaks into, and flavors right to, the center of the pieces of meat.

Energy 428Kcal/1785kJ; Protein 32.0g; Carbohydrate 16.7g, of which sugars 12.4g; Fat 23.3g, of which saturates 1.3g; Cholesterol 0mg; Calcium 51mg; Fiber 2g; Sodium 135mg.

GUINEA FOWL with BEANS and CURLY KALE

Cooking lean poultry, such as guinea fowl, chicken, or turkey in a clay pot or chicken brick gives a delicious, moist result. Here, the guinea fowl is cooked on top of a colorful bed of herb-flavored beans and vegetables.

2 Remove the shallots, garlic, and celery with a slotted spoon, and place in the chicken brick. Stir in the tomatoes and beans. Tuck in the thyme and bay leaves.

3 Put the guinea fowl in the pan, and brown on all sides, then pour in the wine and stock, and bring to a boil. Lift the bird out of the pan, place it on top of the vegetables in the chicken brick, and then pour the liquid over the top. Cover, and place in an unheated oven, and set to 400°F. Cook for 1 hour.

4 Add the curly kale to the chicken brick, nestling it among the beans. Cover, and cook for 10–15 minutes, or until the guinea fowl is tender. Season the bean mixture, and serve.

COOK'S TIP

Guinea fowl and quail were both originally classified as game birds, but nowadays farmed varieties are sold, making them available in the stores all year round.

VARIATION

Use chard, collard greens, or Savoy cabbage in place of curly kale.

SERVES 4

3 pounds guinea fowl
3 tablespoons olive oil
4 shallots, chopped
1 garlic clove, crushed
3 celery stalks, sliced
14-ounce can chopped tomatoes
2 × 14-ounce cans mixed
   beans, drained
5 fresh thyme sprigs
2 bay leaves
⅔ cup dry white wine
1¼ cups well-flavored
   chicken stock
6 ounces curly kale
salt and ground black pepper

1 Soak a clay chicken brick in cold water for 20 minutes, then drain. Rub the guinea fowl with 1 tablespoon of the olive oil, and season. Place the remaining oil in a frying pan, add the shallots, garlic, and celery, and cook for 4–5 minutes.

Energy 617Kcal/2585kJ; Protein 53.1g; Carbohydrate 32.9g, of which sugars 8.7g; Fat 28.6g, of which saturates 1.5g; Cholesterol 0mg; Calcium 98mg; Fiber 11.6g; Sodium 1017mg.

BRAISED PHEASANT with WILD MUSHROOMS, CHESTNUTS, and BACON

Pheasant at the end of their season are not suitable for roasting, so consider this tasty casserole enriched with wild mushrooms and chestnuts. Allow two birds for four people.

SERVES 4

2 mature pheasants
¼ cup butter
5 tablespoons brandy
12 pearl onions, peeled
1 celery stalk, chopped
2 ounces unsmoked rindless bacon,
　cut into strips
3 tablespoons all-purpose flour
2¼ cups chicken stock, boiling
6 ounces peeled, cooked chestnuts
4 cups fresh ceps, trimmed and
　sliced, or ¼ cup dried porcini
　mushrooms, soaked in warm
　water for 20 minutes
1 tablespoon lemon juice
salt and ground black pepper
watercress sprigs,
　to garnish

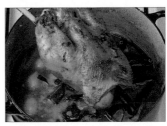

2 Wipe out the casserole, and melt the remaining butter. Add the onions, celery, and bacon, and brown lightly. Stir in the flour. Remove from the heat.

3 Stir in the stock, adding it gradually so that it is completely absorbed by the flour. Add the chestnuts, mushrooms, the pheasants, and their juices. Bring back to a gentle simmer, then cover, and cook in the oven for 1½ hours.

4 Transfer the cooked pheasants and vegetables to a warmed serving plate. Bring the sauce back to a boil, add the lemon juice, and season to taste. Pour the sauce into a pitcher or gravy boat, and garnish the birds with watercress.

COOK'S TIP
Cooking and peeling fresh chestnuts can be hard work, so look out for ready-peeled canned or vacuum-packed varieties.

1 Preheat the oven to 325°F. Season the pheasants inside and out with salt and pepper. Melt half of the butter in a large, flameproof casserole, and brown the pheasants over medium heat. Transfer the pheasants to a shallow dish, and pour off the cooking fat. Return the casserole to the heat, and brown the sediment. Add the brandy, stir well to loosen the sediment using a flat wooden spoon, then pour all the cooking juices over the pheasants.

COOK'S TIP
When buying pheasant, choose birds that look fresh. They should be plump and firm, with supple skin. Game birds have a strong odor, but they should never smell unpleasant or "off."

Energy 883Kcal/3699kJ; Protein 86.8g; Carbohydrate 32.3g, of which sugars 6.9g; Fat 41.6g, of which saturates 15.8g; Cholesterol 35mg; Calcium 205mg; Fiber 2.9g; Sodium 920mg.

GROUSE with ORCHARD FRUIT STUFFING

Tart apples, plums, and pears make a fabulous orchard fruit stuffing that complements the rich gamey flavor of grouse perfectly.

SERVES 2

juice of ½ lemon
2 young grouse
¼ cup butter
4 Swiss chard leaves
¼ cup Marsala
salt and ground black pepper

For the stuffing
2 shallots, finely chopped
1 tart stovecooking apple, peeled, cored,
 and chopped
1 pear, peeled, cored, and chopped
2 plums, halved, pitted
 and chopped
large pinch of apple pie spice

1 Sprinkle the lemon juice over the grouse, and season well. Melt half the butter in a flameproof casserole, add the grouse, and cook for 10 minutes, or until browned. Use tongs to remove the grouse from the casserole, and set aside.

2 Add the shallots to the fat remaining in the casserole, and cook until softened but not colored. Add the apple, pear, plums, and apple pie spice, and cook for about 5 minutes, or until the fruits are just beginning to soften. Remove the casserole from the heat, and spoon the hot fruit mixture into the body cavities of the birds.

3 Truss the birds neatly with string. Smear the remaining butter over the birds, and wrap them in the chard leaves, then replace them in the casserole.

4 Pour in the Marsala, and heat until simmering. Cover tightly, and simmer for 20 minutes, or until the birds are tender, taking care not to overcook them. Leave to rest in a warm place for about 10 minutes before serving.

COOK'S TIP
There isn't a lot of liquid in the casserole for cooking the birds. They are steamed rather than boiled, so it is very important that the casserole has a heavy base and a tight-fitting lid, otherwise the liquid may evaporate and the chard will burn on the base of the pan.

Energy 508Kcal/2121kJ; Protein 46.9g; Carbohydrate 19.5g, of which sugars 18.7g; Fat 24.3g, of which saturates 13.8g; Cholesterol 53mg; Calcium 185mg; Fiber 4.2g; Sodium 406mg.

SPICY VENISON CASSEROLE

Being low in fat but high in flavor, venison is an excellent choice for healthy, yet rich,
casseroles. Cranberries and orange bring a festive fruitiness to this spicy recipe.
Serve with small baked potatoes and green vegetables.

SERVES 4

1 tablespoon olive oil
1 onion, chopped
2 celery sticks, sliced
2 teaspoons ground allspice
1 tablespoon all-purpose flour
1½ pounds stewing venison, cubed
8 ounces fresh or frozen cranberries
grated rind and juice of 1 orange
3¾ cups beef or venison stock
salt and ground black pepper

1 Heat the oil in a flameproof casserole.
Add the onion and celery, and fry for
about 5 minutes, or until softened.

2 Meanwhile, mix the ground allspice
with the flour, and either spread the
mixture out on a large plate or place in
a large plastic bag. Toss a few pieces of
venison at a time (to prevent them
becoming soggy) in the flour mixture
until they are all lightly coated. Spread
the floured venison out on a large plate
until ready to cook.

3 When the onion and celery are just
softened, remove them from the
casserole using a slotted spoon, and set
aside. Add the venison pieces to the
casserole in batches, and cook until well
browned and sealed on all sides.

COOK'S TIP
Freshly made stock is always best, but if
you are short of time, look for cartons
of fresh stock in the chilled food
sections of large supermarkets.

4 Add the cranberries and the orange
rind and juice to the casserole along
with the stock, and stir well. Return the
vegetables and the browned venison to
the casserole, and heat until simmering.
Cover tightly, and reduce the heat.

5 Simmer for about 45 minutes, or
until the venison is tender, stirring
occasionally. Season the venison
casserole to taste with salt and pepper
before serving.

VARIATIONS
Farmed venison is increasingly easy to
find and is available from good butchers
and many large supermarkets. It makes a
rich and flavorful stew, but lean pork or
braising steak could be used in place of
the venison, if you prefer. You could
also replace the cranberries with pitted
and halved ready-to-eat prunes and, for
extra flavor, use either ale or stout
instead of about half the stock.

Energy 242Kcal/1025kJ; Protein 38.3g; Carbohydrate 10.4g, of which sugars 7.1g; Fat 6.6g, of which saturates 1.8g; Cholesterol 84mg; Calcium 27mg; Fiber 1.4g; Sodium 105mg.

VENISON SAUSAGES with RED WINE GRAVY

Strongly flavored, meaty sausages are delicious with a robust red wine gravy flavored with shiitake mushrooms. Serve with soft polenta, mashed potatoes or plenty of thickly sliced crusty bread to mop up the delicious gravy.

SERVES 4

1 tablespoon sunflower-seed oil (optional)
12 venison or wild boar sausages
2 leeks, sliced
2 plump garlic cloves, sliced
3 cups shiitake mushrooms, quartered
1 tablespoon all-purpose flour
2½ cups red wine
2 tablespoons chopped mixed fresh herbs,
    such as Italian parsley and marjoram
salt and ground black pepper

1 Pour the sunflower-seed oil, if using, into a large frying pan, add the venison or wild boar sausages, and cook over a medium heat for 15–20 minutes, turning frequently.

2 Add the leeks, garlic, and mushrooms, and mix well. Cook the vegetables for 10–15 minutes, or until the leeks are soft and beginning to brown.

3 Sprinkle in the flour, and gradually pour in the red wine, stirring with a wooden spoon and pushing the sausages around to mix the flour and the liquid smoothly with the leeks.

4 Bring slowly to the boil, reduce the heat, and simmer for 10–15 minutes, stirring occasionally, or until the gravy is smooth and glossy. Season the gravy with salt and pepper to taste, and then sprinkle the mixed herbs over the sausages. Serve immediately with polenta or mashed potatoes.

COOK'S TIP
Shiitake mushrooms have a slightly floury-looking medium to dark gray-brown cap. They have a firm and meaty texture that becomes silky when cooked. The stalks can be tough so discard if necessary.

Energy 246Kcal/1026kJ; Protein 7.8g; Carbohydrate 11.7g, of which sugars 2.9g; Fat 7.8g, of which saturates 3g; Cholesterol 15mg; Calcium 71mg; Fiber 3g; Sodium 447mg.

CASSEROLED VENISON with STOUT

Venison, both wild and (more usually) farmed, is now widely available. It is popular on restaurant menus and, increasingly, available for home cooks from butchers and the better supermarkets. Serve with boiled or baked potatoes and red cabbage.

SERVES 6

2 pounds stewing venison, such as shoulder
3 tablespoons seasoned flour
2 tablespoons olive oil
2 or 3 large onions, sliced
5 or 6 juniper berries, crushed
3 allspice berries
rind of ½ lemon or orange
2 tablespoons butter
1¼ cups chicken or beef stock
⅔ cup red wine vinegar or cider vinegar
1¼ cups stout or red wine
salt and ground black pepper

1 Preheat the oven to 350°F. Cut the meat into 2-inch cubes. Toss the meat in the seasoned flour. Shake off, and reserve the excess flour.

2 Heat the olive oil in a heavy frying pan, and fry the meat in it until well browned all over. Lift out the pieces with a slotted spoon, and put them into a casserole.

3 Add the onions to the casserole with the juniper berries and allspice, a little salt and black pepper and the lemon or orange rind.

4 Melt the butter in the pan in which the meat was browned, add the reserved flour, and stir and cook for 1 minute. Mix the stock, vinegar, and stout or red wine together, and gradually add to the pan, stirring until it boils and thickens.

5 Pour the sauce over the meat in the casserole, cover closely, and cook in the oven for 1 hour. Reduce the temperature to 300°F, and cook for a further 2 hours, or until the venison is tender. Check the casserole occasionally, and add a little extra stock or water if required. Serve piping hot.

COOK'S TIP
Venison is not difficult to cook but, like other game, it is lean, so marinating, basting, and braising all help to offset any tendency to dryness.

Energy 294Kcal/1233kJ; Protein 34.7g; Carbohydrate 9.3g, of which sugars 4.9g; Fat 10.6g, of which saturates 3.9g; Cholesterol 84mg; Calcium 37mg; Fiber 1.3g; Sodium 114mg

BRAISED RABBIT

Rabbit now features frequently on restaurant menus. It is delicious served with potatoes boiled in their skins and a lightly cooked green vegetable.

SERVES 4–6

1 rabbit, prepared and jointed by
   the butcher
2 tablespoons seasoned flour
2 tablespoons olive oil or vegetable oil
2 tablespoons butter
4 ounces fatty bacon
1 onion, roughly chopped
2 or 3 carrots, sliced
1 or 2 celery sticks, trimmed and sliced
1¼ cups chicken stock
1¼ cups hard cider or stout
a small bunch of parsley leaves, chopped
salt and ground black pepper

1 Soak the joints in cold salted water for at least two hours, then pat them dry with paper towels, and toss them in seasoned flour. Preheat the oven to 400°F.

2 Heat the oil and butter together in a heavy flameproof casserole. Shake off (and reserve) any excess flour from the rabbit joints, and brown them on all sides. Lift out and set aside.

3 Add the bacon to the casserole, and cook for a few minutes, then remove and set aside with the rabbit. Add the vegetables to the casserole, and cook gently until just coloring, then sprinkle over any remaining seasoned flour to absorb the fats in the casserole. Stir over a low heat for 1 minute, to cook the flour. Add the stock and cider or stout, stirring, to make a smooth sauce.

4 Return the rabbit and bacon to the casserole, and add half of the chopped parsley and a light seasoning of salt and pepper. Mix gently together, then cover with a lid, and put into the preheated oven. Cook for 15–20 minutes, then reduce the temperature to 300°F for about 1½ hours, or until the rabbit is tender. Add the remaining parsley and serve.

COOK'S TIP

Buy rabbit whole or jointed, from butchers and good supermarkets. To make Rabbit Pie, prepare as above, then allow to cool. Remove the meat from the bones, and then return the meat to the casserole, taste for seasoning, and turn into a suitable pie dish, ensuring that the meat is covered by the sauce. (Add a sliced hard-boiled egg and a few quartered white mushrooms, if you like.) Cover with shortcrust or rough-puff pastry, and cook in the oven heated to 400°F for about 30 minutes, or until the filling is hot and the pastry is golden brown and cooked through.

Energy 368Kcal/1535kJ; Protein 32.9g; Carbohydrate 10.5g, of which sugars 5.8g; Fat 19.7g, of which saturates 8g; Cholesterol 133mg; Calcium 88mg; Fiber 1.4g; Sodium 567mg

RABBIT with RED WINE and PRUNES

This is a favorite French dish and is often found on the menus of small country restaurants. It has a wonderfully rich flavor, and the prunes add a delicious sweetness to the sauce. Serve with crisp, golden sautéed potatoes.

SERVES 4

8 rabbit portions
2 tablespoons vegetable oil
2 onions, finely chopped
2 garlic cloves, finely chopped
4 tablespoons Armagnac or brandy
1¼ cups dry red wine
1 teaspoon soft light brown sugar
16 ready-to-eat prunes
⅔ cup heavy cream
salt and ground black pepper

VARIATIONS
• Chicken can also be cooked in this way. Use 4 chicken drumsticks and 4 thighs in place of the rabbit portions.
• The prunes can be replaced with ready-to-eat dried apricots—these go well with the rabbit and particularly well with chicken.

1 Season the rabbit portions liberally with salt and pepper. Heat the vegetable oil in a large, flameproof casserole, and fry the rabbit portions in batches until they are golden brown on all sides.

2 Remove the browned rabbit portions from the casserole, add the chopped onion and garlic, and cook, stirring occasionally, until the onion is softened.

3 Return the rabbit to the casserole, add the Armagnac or brandy, and ignite it. When the flames have died down, pour in the wine. Stir in the sugar and prunes, cover, and simmer for 30 minutes.

4 Remove the rabbit from the casserole, and keep warm. Add the cream to the sauce, and simmer for 3–5 minutes, then season to taste and serve immediately.

Energy 543Kcal/2259kJ; Protein 29.3g; Carbohydrate 19.4g, of which sugars 18.2g; Fat 79.9g, of which saturates 15.3g; Cholesterol 156mg; Calcium 99mg; Fiber 3g; Sodium 81mg.

SLOW COOKER MEAT

Slow cooking is suitable for all kinds of meat, but it works its magic best on less tender cuts, helping to improve and enhance their flavor and texture. Although beef and pork are great for robust dishes, such as Beef and Mushroom Pudding, they can also be used to make lighter modern meals, like Spicy Pork Casserole with Dried Fruit. Most lamb cuts are naturally tender and succulent, and the slow cooker ensures they stay that way—try Moroccan Lamb with Honey and Prunes for a delicious meal. Whatever meat you choose, and whether you are looking for a simple supper or an impressive dinner, you will find plenty of recipes here for delicious pot roasts, braised dishes, casseroles, and stews.

STEAK and KIDNEY PIE with MUSTARD GRAVY

Peppery mustard gravy flavored with bay leaves and parsley complements the tasty chunks of succulent beef and kidney in this classic pie. Cooking the puff pastry topping separately from the filling ensures it remains perfectly crisp—and is a perfect technique to use when making the pie using a slow cooker.

SERVES 4

1½ pounds stewing steak
8 ounces ox or lamb's kidney
3 tablespoons oil
1 tablespoons sweet butter
2 onions, chopped
2 tablespoons all-purpose flour
1¼ cups beef stock
1 tablespoon tomato paste
2 teaspoons English mustard
2 bay leaves
13 ounces puff pastry
beaten egg, to glaze
1 tablespoon chopped fresh parsley
salt and ground black pepper
creamed potatoes and green vegetables,
    to serve

2 Heat 2 tablespoons of the oil in a frying pan, and brown the beef on all sides. Remove from the pan with a slotted spoon, and place in the ceramic cooking pot. Switch the slow cooker on to high.

3 Add the kidney to the frying pan, and brown for 1–2 minutes before adding to the beef. Add the remaining oil and the butter to the pan, add the onions and cook for 5 minutes, until just beginning to color. Sprinkle with the flour, and stir in, then remove the pan from the heat.

4 Gradually stir the stock into the pan, followed by the tomato puree and mustard. Return to the heat, and bring to the boil, stirring constantly, until thickened. Pour the gravy over the meat, then add the bay leaves and season. Stir well, and cover with the lid. Reduce the cooker to low, and cook for 5–7 hours, or until the meat is very tender.

VARIATION
To make a richer version, use half the quantity of stock, and add ⅔ cup stout or red wine.

5 While the beef is cooking, roll out the pastry and, using a dinner plate as a guide, cut out a 10-inch round. Transfer the pastry round to a baking sheet lined with parchment paper.

6 Using a sharp knife, mark the pastry into quarters, cutting almost but not quite through it. Decorate with pastry trimmings, then flute the edge. Cover with plastic wrap, and place in the refrigerator until ready to cook.

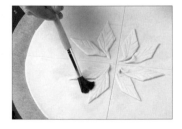

7 Toward the end of the beef's cooking time, preheat the oven to 400°F. Brush the pastry all over with beaten egg to glaze, then bake for about 25 minutes, or until well risen, golden-brown and crisp.

8 To serve, stir the chopped parsley into the steak and kidney stew, and spoon onto warmed serving plates. Cut the baked pie crust into four, using the markings as a guide, and top each portion of stew with a wedge of pastry. Serve immediately with rich, creamed potatoes and green vegetables.

1 Using a sharp knife, cut the stewing steak into 1-inch cubes. Remove all fat and skin from the kidney, and cut into cubes or thick slices.

Energy 637Kcal/2652kJ; Protein 18.7g; Carbohydrate 46.2g, of which sugars 5.2g; Fat 43.4g, of which saturates 13.1g; Cholesterol 259mg; Calcium 99mg; Fiber 2.7g; Sodium 578mg.

PROVENÇAL BEEF STEW

Known in France as daube de boeuf à la Provençal, *after the earthernware pot it was originally cooked in, this deliciously rich, fruity stew makes a perfect winter supper dish. Serve with mashed or boiled new potatoes and green vegetables.*

SERVES 4

3 tablespoons olive oil
4 ounces lean salt pork or
   thick-cut bacon, diced
3 pounds stewing steak cut into
   1½-inch pieces
1 large onion, chopped
2 carrots, sliced
2 ripe tomatoes, peeled, seeded
   and chopped
2 teaspoons tomato paste
2 garlic cloves, very finely chopped
1 cup fruity red wine
⅔ cup beef stock
1 bouquet garni
1 small onion, studded with 2 cloves
grated zest and juice of ½ unwaxed orange
1 tablespoon chopped fresh parsley
salt and ground black pepper

1 Heat 1 tablespoon of the oil in a large heavy frying pan, then add the salt pork or bacon, and cook over a medium heat for 4–5 minutes, stirring frequently, until browned and the fat is rendered.

2 Using a slotted spoon, transfer the pork or bacon to the ceramic cooking pot, and switch the slow cooker to high.

3 Working in batches, add the beef to the pan in a single layer (do not overcrowd the pan, or the meat will stew in its own juices and not brown). Cook for 6–8 minutes, until browned, turning to color all sides.

4 Transfer the beef to the ceramic cooking pot, and continue browning the rest of the meat in the same way, adding more oil when needed.

5 Pour the wine and stock over the beef in the ceramic cooking pot, then add the bouquet garni and the onion. Add the remaining oil and the onion to the frying pan, and cook gently for 5 minutes. Stir in the carrots, and cook for a further 5 minutes, until softened. Stir in the tomatoes, tomato paste, and garlic, then transfer to the ceramic cooking pot.

6 Cover with the lid, and switch the slow cooker to low. Cook for 5–7 hours, or until the beef and vegetables are very tender. Uncover, and skim off any fat. Season, discard the bouquet garni and clove-studded onion, and stir in the orange zest and juice and the parsley.

Energy 547Kcal/2286kJ; Protein 55.8g; Carbohydrate 8.7g, of which sugars 7.2g; Fat 27.8g, of which saturates 8.9g; Cholesterol 170mg; Calcium 43mg; Fiber 2g; Sodium 682mg.

BRAISED BEEF in a RICH PEANUT SAUCE

Like many dishes brought to the Philippines by the Spanish, this slow-cooking Estofado,
renamed Kari Kari by the Philippinos, retains much of its original charm. Peanuts are used
to thicken the juices, yielding a rich, sweet, glossy sauce.

SERVES 4

2 pounds braising chuck,
   shin, or blade steak
3 tablespoons vegetable oil
2 onions, chopped
2 cloves garlic, crushed
1 teaspoon paprika
pinch of ground turmeric
8 ounces celeriac or rutabaga, peeled
   and cut into ¾-inch dice
1¾ cups boiling beef stock
1 tablespoon fish or anchovy sauce
2 tablespoons tamarind sauce (optional)
2 teaspoons soft light brown sugar
1 bay leaf
1 sprig thyme
2 tablespoons smooth peanut butter
3 tablespoons converted white rice
1 teaspoon white wine vinegar
salt and ground black pepper

1 Using a sharp knife, cut the beef into 1-inch cubes. Heat 2 tablespoons of the oil in a pan, and fry the beef, turning until well browned all over.

2 Transfer the meat and any juices to the ceramic cooking pot, and switch the slow cooker to high.

3 Add the remaining 1 tablespoon oil to the frying pan, add the onions, and fry gently for 10 minutes until softened.

4 Add the garlic, paprika, and turmeric to the pan, and cook for 1 minute. Transfer the mixture to the ceramic pot, and add the celeriac or swede.

5 Pour in the stock, fish or anchovy sauce, and taramind sauce, if using, and add the sugar, bay leaf, and thyme. Cover with the lid, then reduce the heat to low, and cook for 4 hours, or until the beef and vegetables are just tender.

6 Turn the slow cooker up to high, then remove about 4 tablespoons of the cooking juices to a bowl, and blend with the peanut butter. Stir the mixture into the casserole, sprinkle with the rice, and stir again to combine.

7 Cover the pot, and cook for about 45 minutes, or until the rice is cooked and the sauce has thickened slightly. Stir in the wine vinegar, and season to taste.

COOK'S TIP
This stew makes a meal in itself so needs no accompaniments. However, a simple green salad served on the side makes a refreshing palate cleanser.

Energy 577Kcal/2408kJ; Protein 48.9g; Carbohydrate 14.1g, of which sugars 8.9g; Fat 36.8g, of which saturates 12.2g; Cholesterol 141mg; Calcium 70mg; Fiber 2.4g; Sodium 561mg

BEEF and MUSHROOM PUDDING

Based on a great British classic, this steamed savory pudding has a light herb pastry crust made with a mixture of suet and butter for both taste and color. A mouthwatering mixture of dried porcini and cremini mushrooms gives the filling an intense flavor.

SERVES 4

½ cup dried porcini mushrooms
2 cups near-boiling beef stock
1½ pounds braising steak
4 tablespoons all-purpose flour
3 tablespoons sunflower-seed oil
1 large onion, finely chopped
8 ounces cremini or flat mushrooms,
    thickly sliced
1 bay leaf
1 tablespoon Worcestershire sauce
⅓ cup port or red wine
salt and ground black pepper

For the pastry
2½ cups self-rising flour
½ teaspoon baking powder
½ teaspoon salt
1 tablespoon each chopped parsley
    and fresh thyme
1½ cups beef or vegetable suet (chilled,
    grated shortening)
¼ cup butter, frozen and grated
1 egg, lightly beaten
about ⅔ cup cold water

1 Put the dried mushrooms in a bowl, and pour over the stock. Leave to soak for about 20 minutes.

2 Meanwhile, trim the meat, and cut into ¾-inch pieces. Place the flour in a bowl, season, then add the meat and toss to coat. Heat the oil in a frying pan, and fry the meat in batches until browned on all sides. Transfer to the ceramic cooking pot.

3 Add the onion to the pan, and cook gently for 10 minutes, or until softened. Transfer to the ceramic cooking pot, then add the cremini mushrooms and the bay leaf.

4 In a bowl or pitcher, combine the Worcestershire sauce with the port or wine, then pour into the ceramic cooking pot. Drain the soaked porcini mushrooms, pouring the stock into the pot, then chop them and add to the pot.

5 Stir the ingredients together, then cover with the lid, and cook on high or auto for 1 hour. Reduce the heat to low, and cook for a further 5–6 hours, or until the meat and onions are tender. Remove the bay leaf, then leave the mixture to cool completely.

6 To make the pastry, butter a deep 7½-cup heatproof bowl. Sift the flour, baking powder, and salt into a mixing bowl, and stir in the herbs followed by the suet and butter. Make a well in the center, add the egg and enough cold water to mix, and gather into a soft dough.

7 Lightly knead the dough for a few seconds on a floured surface until smooth. Cut off a quarter of the dough, and wrap in plastic wrap. Shape the rest into a ball, and roll out into a round large enough to line the bowl. Lift up the pastry, and carefully place in the bowl, pressing it against the sides, and allowing the excess to fall over the sides. Roll out the reserved pastry to make a round large enough to use as a lid for the pudding.

8 Spoon in the cooled filling and enough of the gravy to come to within ½ inch of the rim. (Reserve the remaining gravy to serve with the pudding.) Brush the top edge of the pastry with water, and place the lid on top. Press the edges together to seal, and trim off any excess.

9 Cover the heatproof bowl with a pleated, double thickness layer of parchment paper, and secure under the rim using string. Cover with pleated foil to allow the pudding to rise.

10 Put an inverted saucer or metal pastry ring in the base of the cleaned ceramic cooking pot, and place the heatproof bowl on top. Pour in enough near-boiling water to come just over halfway up the sides of the bowl. Cover with the lid, and cook on high for 3 hours.

11 Carefully remove the pudding from the slow cooker, then take off the foil, string, and greaseproof paper. Loosen the edges of the pudding, and invert onto a warmed serving plate.

Energy 1061Kcal/4444kJ; Protein 70g; Carbohydrate 75.1g, of which sugars 4.8g; Fat 54.3g, of which saturates 24.5g; Cholesterol 265mg; Calcium 319mg; Fiber 4.4g; Sodium 941mg.

BRAISED BEEF with HORSERADISH

This dark rich beef with a spicy kick makes an ideal alternative to a meat roast.
The meat slowly tenderizes in the slow cooker, and all the flavors blend together
beautifully. It is also a great dish for entertaining, because it can be prepared in advance
and then simply left to simmer on its own until you are ready to serve.

SERVES 4

2 tablespoons all-purpose flour
4 × 6-ounce braising steaks
2 tablespoons sunflower-seed oil
12 small shallots, peeled and halved
1 garlic clove, crushed
¼ teaspoon ground ginger
1 teaspoon curry powder
2 teaspoons dark molasses sugar
2 cups near-boiling beef stock
1 tablespoon Worcestershire sauce
2 tablespoons creamed horseradish
8 ounces baby carrots, trimmed
1 bay leaf
salt and ground black pepper
2 tablespoons chopped fresh chives,
    to garnish
roast vegetables, to serve

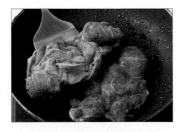

1 Place the flour in a large, flat dish, and season with salt and black pepper. Toss the steaks in the flour to coat.

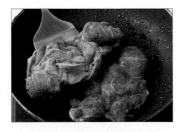

2 Heat the oil in a pan, and quickly brown the steaks on both sides. Transfer them to the ceramic cooking pot.

3 Add the halved shallots to the pan, and cook gently for 10 minutes, or until golden and beginning to soften. Stir in the garlic, ginger, and curry powder and cook for 1 minute more, then remove the pan from the heat.

4 Tip the shallot mixture into the ceramic cooking pot, spreading it over the meat, and sprinkle with the sugar.

5 Pour the beef stock over the shallots and meat, then add the Worcestershire sauce, horseradish, baby carrots, and bay leaf. Stir to combine, then season with salt and black pepper. Cover with the lid, and cook on high or auto for 1 hour.

6 Reduce the slow cooker to low, or leave on auto, and continue to cook the stew for a further 5–6 hours, or until the beef and vegetables are very tender.

7 Remove the bay leaf from the stew, and sprinkle with the chopped chives before serving with roast vegetables.

COOK'S TIPS

• Choose a medium curry powder for flavoring the stew. There is already plenty of bite from the horseradish, so you don't want to overpower the meat flavors entirely with a very strong, spicy curry powder.
• To give the stew a really robust flavor, replace ¾ cup of the stock with red wine.
• The sweet flavor of roasted parsnips and butternut squash goes particularly well with the spicy bite of horseradish. Cook plenty of roast potatoes too—they are the perfect accompaniment to braised beef, and are great for mopping up the delicious gravy.

Energy 478Kcal/2010kJ; Protein 62.5g; Carbohydrate 17.7g, of which sugars 9.6g; Fat 18.1g, of which saturates 7.4g; Cholesterol 176mg; Calcium 65mg; Fiber 2.5g; Sodium 423mg.

HUNGARIAN CHOLENT

A traditional Sabbath dish of the Ashkenazi Jews, cholent is a long-simmered dish of beans, grains, meat, and vegetables. The addition of whole boiled eggs is a classic feature. Don't forget to start soaking the beans the day before; they need at least 8 hours.

3 Meanwhile, heat the oil in a pan, add the onion, and cook gently for about 10 minutes, or until soft. Transfer the onions to the ceramic cooking pot.

4 Add the garlic, beans, barley, paprika, cayenne pepper, celery, tomatoes, carrots, turnip, potatoes, beef, and stock to the onions, and stir to combine.

5 Cover the pot with the lid, and cook on low for 5–6 hours, or until the meat and vegetables are tender. Add the rice, stir, and season with salt and pepper.

6 Rinse the eggs in tepid water, then lower them, one at a time, into the hot stock. Cover, and cook for a further 45 minutes, or until the rice is cooked. Serve hot, making sure each portion contains a whole egg.

SERVES 4

1⅓ cups dried navy beans
2 tablespoons olive oil
1 onion, chopped
4 garlic cloves, finely chopped
2 ounces pearl barley
1 tablespoon ground paprika
pinch of cayenne pepper
1 celery stick, chopped
14-ounce can chopped tomatoes
3 carrots, sliced
1 small turnip, diced
2 baking potatoes, peeled and cut into
  chunks
1½-pound mixture of beef brisket, stewing
  beef, and smoked beef, cut into cubes
4 cups boiling beef stock
2 tablespoons converted white rice
4 eggs, at room temperature
salt and ground black pepper

1 Place the beans in a large bowl. Pour over plenty of cold water to cover, and leave to soak for at least 8 hours, or overnight if you like.

2 Drain the beans well, then place them in a large pan, cover with fresh cold water, and bring to the boil. Boil them steadily for about 10 minutes, skimming off any froth that rises to the surface, then drain well, and set aside.

Energy 860Kcal/3607kJ; Protein 58.9g; Carbohydrate 74.2g, of which sugars 13.7g; Fat 38.8g, of which saturates 12.7g; Cholesterol 341mg; Calcium 164mg; Fiber 10.9g; Sodium 639mg.

SPICED BEEF

This is a classic Irish dish, although it is a modern version of the traditional recipe, as it omits the initial pickling stage and takes only three or four days to cure, in comparison with ten days for the older method. Serve on thinly sliced brown bread, with chutney.

SERVES 6

1 tablespoon coarsely ground
    black pepper
2 teaspoons ground ginger
1 tablespoon juniper berries, crushed
1 tablespoon coriander seeds, crushed
1 teaspoon ground cloves
1 tablespoon ground allspice
3 tablespoons soft dark brown sugar
2 bay leaves, crushed
1 small onion, finely chopped
4 pounds corned beef, silverside or tail end
1¼ cups Guinness
fruit chutney and brown bread, to serve

COOK'S TIP

• As a first course, serve the beef thinly sliced with homemade brown bread and a fruit chutney, such as apple and raisin.
• Spiced beef is excellent as finger food for parties, sliced thinly and served with sour cream lightly flavored with horseradish and black pepper.

1 First, spice the beef: blend the pepper, spices, and sugar thoroughly, then mix in the bay leaves and onion. Rub the mixture into the meat, then put it into a suitable lidded container, and refrigerate for 3–4 days, turning and rubbing with the mixture daily.

2 Put the meat into the ceramic cooking pot, and barely cover with cold water. Cover with the lid, and switch on to auto or high. Cook for 3 hours, then leave on auto or reduce to low, and cook for a further 3–4 hours, until the meat is very tender. For the last hour add the Guinness.

3 When the joint is cooked, leave it to cool in the cooking liquid. Wrap in foil, and keep in the refrigerator until required, then slice thinly to serve. It will keep for about 1 week.

Energy 309Kcal/1301kJ; Protein 53.6g; Carbohydrate 2g, of which sugars 2g; Fat 9.7g, of which saturates 3.6g; Cholesterol 137mg; Calcium 15mg; Fiber 0g; Sodium 140mg

HOT and SOUR PORK

This has all the flavor of a stir-fry without the hassle of last-minute cooking. Using lean pork tenderloin and reducing the temperature to low after an hour means that the meat remains wonderfully moist and tender, while the vegetables retain their crunchy texture.

SERVES 4

1 tablespoon dried Chinese mushrooms
⅔ cup boiling vegetable stock
12 ounces pork tenderloin
4 ounces baby corn kernels
1 green bell pepper
8 ounces pineapple chunks
   in natural juice
4 teaspoons cornstarch
1 tablespoon sunflower-seed oil
4 ounces water chestnuts
1-inch piece ginger root, grated
1 red chile, seeded and finely chopped
1 teaspoon Chinese five-spice powder
1 tablespoon sherry vinegar
1 tablespoon dark soy sauce
1 tablespoon hoisin sauce
plain boiled or fried rice,
   to serve

1 Put the mushrooms in a heatproof bowl, then pour over the hot stock, and leave to soak for 15–20 minutes.

2 Trim away any visible fat from the pork and cut into ½-inch slices. Slice the baby corn kernels lengthwise. Halve, seed, and slice the green pepper. Drain the pineapple chunks, reserving the juice. Drain the mushrooms, reserving the stock, and slice any large ones.

3 In a bowl, blend the cornstarch with a little of the reserved pineapple juice, then slowly stir in the remainder.

4 Heat the oil in a non-stick frying pan. Add the pork, and sear for 30 seconds on each side, or until lightly browned. Transfer to the ceramic cooking pot, and add the vegetables, pineapple chunks, and water chestnuts.

5 In a bowl, combine the ginger, chile, and five-spice powder with the vinegar, soy sauce, hoisin sauce and reserved stock. Pour in the pineapple juice mixture, then tip into the frying pan and bring to the boil, stirring constantly. As soon as the mixture thickens, pour over the pork and vegetables.

6 Cover with the lid, and switch the slow cooker to high. Cook for 1 hour, then reduce the temperature to low, and cook for 1–2 hours, or until the pork is cooked and the vegetables retain some crispness. Serve with rice.

Energy 358Kcal/1509kJ; Protein 19.9g; Carbohydrate 49.4g, of which sugars 36.3g; Fat 10.3g, of which saturates 2.8g; Cholesterol 60.4mg; Calcium 43mg; Fiber 2.7g; Sodium 405mg.

BOSTON BAKED BEANS

*The slow cooker was actually invented for making baked beans. Molasses gives the beans
a very rich flavor and dark color, but you can replace it with maple syrup if you prefer.*

SERVES 8

2½ cups dried navy beans
4 whole cloves
2 onions, peeled
1 bay leaf
6 tablespoons tomato ketchup
2 tablespoons molasses
2 tablespoons dark brown sugar
1 tablespoon Dijon-style mustard
2 cups unsalted vegetable stock
8-ounce piece of salt pork
salt and ground black pepper

1 Rinse the beans, then place in a large
bowl. Cover with cold water, and leave
to soak for at least 8 hours or overnight.

2 Drain and rinse the beans. Place them
in a large pan, cover with plenty of cold
water, and bring to the boil. Boil gently
for about 10 minutes, then drain, and tip
into the ceramic cooking pot.

3 Stick 2 cloves in each of the onions.
Add them to the pot with the bay leaf,
burying them in the beans.

4 In a bowl, blend together the ketchup,
molasses, sugar, mustard, and stock, and
pour over the beans. Add more stock,
or water, if necessary, so that the beans
are almost covered with liquid. Cover
with the lid, and switch the slow cooker
to low. Cook for 3 hours.

5 Toward the end of the cooking time,
place the salt pork in a pan of boiling
water, and cook for 3 minutes.

6 Using a sharp knife, score the pork
rind in deep ½-inch cuts. Add the salt
pork to the ceramic cooking pot,
pushing it down just below the surface
of the beans, skin side up. Cover the
pot with the lid, and cook for a further
5–6 hours, until the beans are tender.

7 Remove the pork from the beans, and
set aside until cool enough to handle,
Using a sharp knife, slice off the rind and
fat, and finely slice the meat.

8 Using a spoon, skim off any fat from
the top of the beans, then stir in the
pieces of meat. Season to taste with salt
and black pepper, and serve hot.

COOK'S TIPS
• Be sure to taste the beans before adding
any more salt. The salt pork will have
already added plenty, so you may only
need to season with black pepper.
• To make a vegetarian version of these
beans, simply leave out the salt pork.
They are just as good cooked without.

Energy 228Kcal/968kJ; Protein 13.4g; Carbohydrate 43.9g, of which sugars 19.4g; Fat 1g, of which saturates 0.1g; Cholesterol 0mg, Calcium 140mg, Fiber 9.5g; Sodium 334mg.

ITALIAN PORK SAUSAGE STEW

This hearty casserole, made with spicy sausages and navy beans, is flavored with fragrant fresh herbs and dry Italian wine. Serve with Italian bread for mopping up the delicious juices. Remember to leave time for the beans to soak before cooking.

SERVES 4

1¼ cups dried navy beans
2 sprigs fresh thyme
2 teaspoons olive oil
1 pound fresh Italian pork sausages
1 onion, finely chopped
2 sticks celery, finely diced
1¼ cups dry red or white wine,
    preferably Italian
1 sprig of fresh rosemary
1 bay leaf
1¼ cups boiling
    vegetable stock
7-ounce can chopped tomatoes
¼ head dark green cabbage such as
    cavolo nero or Savoy, finely shredded
salt and ground black pepper
chopped fresh thyme, to garnish
crusty Italian bread, to serve

1 Put the navy beans in a large bowl, and cover with cold water. Leave to soak for at least 8 hours, or overnight.

2 Drain the beans, and place in a pan with the thyme sprigs and at least twice their volume of cold water. Bring to the boil, and boil steadily for 10 minutes, then drain, and place in the ceramic cooking pot, discarding the thyme.

3 Meanwhile, heat the oil in a pan, and cook the sausages until browned all over. Transfer to the ceramic cooking pot, and tip away all but 1 tablespoon of the fat in the frying pan.

4 Add the onion and celery to the pan, and cook gently for 5 minutes, until softened but not colored. Add the wine, rosemary, and bay leaf, and bring to the boil. Pour over the sausages, add the stock, and season with salt and pepper. Cover with the lid, switch the slow cooker to high, and cook for 5–6 hours, until the beans are tender.

5 Stir the chopped tomatoes and the shredded cabbage into the stew. Cover, and cook for 30–45 minutes, or until the cabbage is tender but not overcooked. Divide between warmed plates, garnish with a little chopped fresh thyme, and serve with crusty Italian bread.

COOK'S TIP
The tomatoes are added toward the end of cooking, because their acidity would prevent the beans from becoming tender if added earlier.

Energy 620Kcal/2593kJ; Protein 28.4g; Carbohydrate 47.4g, of which sugars 9.9g; Fat 30.9g, of which saturates 10.8g; Cholesterol 67.5mg; Calcium 205mg; Fiber 7.6g; Sodium 1139mg.

PORK and POTATO HOT-POT

Long, slow cooking makes the pork chops meltingly tender and allows the potato slices to soak up all the delicious juices from the meat. Perfect for a family meal or casual supper with friends, simply serve with lightly cooked green vegetables.

SERVES 4

2 tablespoons butter
1 tablespoon oil
1 large onion, very thinly sliced
1 garlic clove, crushed
generous 3 cups white mushrooms, sliced
¼ teaspoon dried mixed herbs
2 pounds potatoes, thinly sliced
4 thick pork chops
3 cups vegetable or chicken stock
salt and ground black pepper

1 Use 1 tablespoon of the butter to grease the base and halfway up the sides of the ceramic cooking pot.

2 Heat the oil in a frying pan, add the sliced onion, and cook gently for about 5 minutes, until softened and translucent.

3 Add the garlic and mushrooms to the pan, and cook for a further 5 minutes, until softened. Remove the pan from the heat, and stir in the mixed herbs.

4 Spoon half the mushroom mixture into the base of the ceramic cooking pot, then arrange half the potato slices on top, and season with salt and ground black pepper.

5 Using a sharp knife, trim as much fat as possible from the pork chops, then place them on top of the potatoes in a single layer. Pour about half the stock over the top to cover the potatoes and prevent them from discoloring.

6 Repeat the layers of the mushroom mixture and potatoes, finishing with a layer of neatly overlapping potatoes. Pour over the remaining stock; it should just cover the potatoes, so use a little more or less if necessary. Dot the remaining butter on top of the potatoes, and cover with the lid.

7 Cook the stew on high for 4–5 hours, or until the potatoes and meat are tender when pierced with a thin skewer. If you like, place the hot-pot under a medium broiler for 5–10 minutes to brown before serving.

Energy 511Kcal/2132kJ; Protein 17.9g; Carbohydrate 41.5g, of which sugars 6.5g; Fat 31.5g, of which saturates 12.1g; Cholesterol 67mg; Calcium 40mg; Fiber 3.7g; Sodium 529mg.

POTATO and SAUSAGE CASSEROLE

There are many variations of this traditional Irish supper dish, known as Irish coddle, but the basic ingredients are the same wherever you go—potatoes, sausages, and bacon.

SERVES 4

1 tablespoon vegetable oil
8 large pork sausages
4 bacon slices, cut into 1-inch pieces
1 large onion, chopped
2 garlic cloves, crushed
4 large baking potatoes, peeled
   and thinly sliced
¼ teaspoon fresh sage
1¼ cups vegetable stock
salt and ground black pepper

COOK'S TIPS
• For an authentic Irish feel, serve this delicious, hearty casserole with braised green cabbage.
• Choose good quality sausages, because it will make all the difference to the final result. Many Irish artisan butchers export quality Irish sausages, so it is well worth keeping an eye out for them.

1 Heat the oil in a frying pan. Gently fry the sausages for about 5 minutes, turning frequently until they are golden but not cooked through. Remove from the frying pan, and set aside. Tip away all but about 2 teaspoons of fat from the pan.

2 Add the bacon to the pan, and fry for 2 minutes. Add the onion, and fry for about 8 minutes, stirring frequently until golden. Add the garlic, and fry for a further 1 minute, then turn off the heat.

3 Arrange half the potato slices in the base of the ceramic cooking pot. Spoon the bacon and onion mixture on top. Season well with salt and ground black pepper, and sprinkle with the fresh sage. Cover with the remaining potato slices.

4 Pour the stock over the potatoes, and top with the sausages. Cover with the lid, and cook on high for 3–4 hours, or until the potatoes are tender and the sausages cooked through. Serve hot.

Energy 717Kcal/2984kJ; Protein 20.5g; Carbohydrate 49.9g, of which sugars 6.1g; Fat 49.8g, of which saturates 18.1g; Cholesterol 78.1mg; Calcium 73mg; Fiber 4g; Sodium 1322mg.

PORK TENDERLOINS with PRUNE STUFFING

The sweet flavor and rich texture of dried fruit, such as prunes, goes particularly well with pork. If you want to ring the changes, dried apricots or figs can be used instead.

SERVES 4

1 tablespoon butter
1 shallot, very finely chopped
1 stick celery, very finely chopped
finely grated rind of ½ orange
½ cup (about 12) pitted, ready-to-eat
   prunes, chopped
½ cup fresh white bread crumbs
2 tablespoons chopped fresh parsley
pinch of grated nutmeg
2 x 8-ounce pork tenderloins, trimmed
6 slices Parma ham or prosciutto
1 tablespoon olive oil
⅔ cup dry white wine
salt and ground black pepper
mashed root vegetables and wilted
   bok choy, to serve

1 Melt the butter in a frying pan, add the shallot and celery, and fry gently until soft. Tip into a bowl, and stir in the orange rind, prunes, bread crumbs, parsley, and nutmeg. Season and leave to cool.

2 Slice down the length of each tenderloin, cutting three-quarters of the way through.

3 Open out each pork tenderloin, and lay it out on a board. Cover the meat with a piece of oiled plastic wrap, then gently bash with a rolling pin until the meat is about ¼ inch thick.

4 Arrange 3 slices of the ham on a board, and place one tenderloin on top. Repeat with the remaining ham and pork.

5 Divide the prune and bread-crumb stuffing between the tenderloins, then fold over to enclose the filling.

6 Wrap the ham around one stuffed tenderloin, and secure with one or two wooden toothpicks. Repeat with the remaining ham and tenderloins.

7 Heat the oil in the clean frying pan and quickly brown the wrapped pork fillets all over, taking care not to dislodge the cocktail sticks, before transferring them to the ceramic cooking pot.

8 Pour the white wine into the frying pan, and bring almost to the boil, then pour over the pork.

9 Cover the ceramic cooking pot with the slow cooker lid, and cook on high for 1 hour, then reduce the temperature to low, and cook for a further 2–3 hours, or until the pork is cooked completely through and tender.

10 Remove the toothpicks from the meat, and cut the pork into slices. Arrange on warmed plates, and spoon over some of the cooking juices. Serve with mashed root vegetables and wilted bok choy leaves.

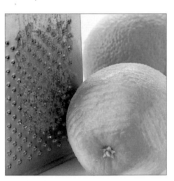

Energy 245Kcal/1077kJ; Protein 17.3g; Carbohydrate 14.6g, of which sugars 11.3g; Fat 10.0g, of which saturates 4g; Cholesterol 59mg; Calcium 34mg; Fiber 2g; Sodium 378mg.

SPICY PORK CASSEROLE with DRIED FRUIT

Inspired by the South American mole—*a paste of chili, shallots, and nuts—this casserole is thickened and flavored with a similar mixture, which really brings out the taste of the onions, meat, and sweet dried fruit. Part of the* mole *is added at the end of cooking to retain its fresh flavor. Serve the casserole with rice and a green salad.*

SERVES 6

1½ tablespoons all-purpose flour
2¼ pounds shoulder or leg of pork,
    cut into 1½-inch cubes
2 tablespoons olive oil
scant 2 cups fruity white wine
⅔ cup vegetable stock or water
1½ cups ready-to-eat prunes
1½ cups ready-to-eat dried apricots
grated rind and juice of 1 small orange
pinch of molasses sugar
2 tablespoons chopped fresh parsley
1 fresh green or red chile, seeded
    and finely chopped
salt and ground black pepper
plain boiled rice, to serve

For the *mole*
3 ancho chiles and 2 pasilla chiles
    (or other varieties of large,
    medium-hot dried red chiles)
2 tablespoons olive oil
2 large onions, finely chopped
3 garlic cloves, chopped
1 fresh green chile, seeded and
    chopped
2 teaspoons ground coriander
1 teaspoon mild Spanish paprika
    or pimenton
½ cup blanched almonds,
    toasted
1 tablespoon chopped fresh oregano
    or ½ teaspoon dried oregano

1 Make the *mole* paste first. Toast the dried chiles in a dry frying pan over a low heat for 1–2 minutes, stirring, until they are aromatic. Remove the chiles from the heat, place in a small bowl, and pour over warm water to cover. Leave to soak for about 30 minutes.

2 Drain the chiles, reserving the soaking water, then remove, and discard the woody stalks and seeds.

3 Heat the oil in a frying pan, and fry the onions over a low heat for about 10 minutes, until soft. Remove two-thirds of the onions from the pan, and set aside. Add the garlic, fresh green chile, and ground coriander to the pan, and cook for a further 5 minutes.

4 Transfer the onion mixture to a food processor, and add the drained chiles, paprika or pimenton, almonds, and oregano. Process the mixture, adding 3–4 tablespoons of the chile soaking liquid to make a workable paste.

5 Place the flour in a shallow dish, and season with salt and black pepper. Add the pork, and toss well to coat.

6 Wipe the frying pan clean with paper towels, and heat the olive oil. Fry the pork in two batches over a high heat for 5–6 minutes, stirring frequently, until it is sealed on all sides. Transfer the pork to the ceramic cooking pot with a slotted spoon, and switch the slow cooker to high.

7 Add the reserved fried onions to the pan. Pour in the wine and stock or water, and simmer for 1 minute. Stir in half the *mole* paste, bring back to the boil, and bubble for a few seconds before pouring over the pork. Stir to mix, then cover with the lid and cook for 2 hours.

8 Stir the fruit, orange juice, and sugar into the stew. Switch the slow cooker to low, and cook for a further 2–3 hours, or until the pork is very tender.

9 Stir in the remaining *mole* paste, and cook for 30 minutes. Serve sprinkled with orange rind, parsley, and fresh chile.

Energy 477Kcal/1999kJ; Protein 40.7g; Carbohydrate 25.6g, of which sugars 21g; Fat 19.1g, of which saturates 3.8g; Cholesterol 105mg; Calcium 86mg; Fiber 4.1g; Sodium 149mg.

CIDER-GLAZED GAMMON

This is a classic buffet centerpiece, which is ideal for Christmas or Thanksgiving. A fresh cranberry sauce provides the perfect foil to the richness of the meat and can be made in the slow cooker the day before if you want to serve the gammon hot, rather than cold. Soaking smoked gammon overnight helps to remove the excess salts.

SERVES 8

4½-pound middle gammon joint,
   soaked overnight, if smoked
2 small onions
about 30 whole cloves
3 bay leaves
10 black peppercorns
⅔ cup medium-dry hard cider
3 tablespoons soft light brown sugar

For the cranberry sauce

3 cups cranberries
scant I cup superfine sugar
grated rind and juice of 2 clementines
2 tablespoons port

I Drain the gammon joint, if soaked overnight, then place it in the ceramic cooking pot. Stud the onions with 6 of the cloves, and add to the cooking pot with the bay leaves and peppercorns.

2 Pour over enough cold water to just cover the gammon. Switch the slow cooker to high, cover with the lid, and cook for I hour. Skim off any scum from the surface, re-cover, and cook for a further 4–5 hours. Check once during cooking, and skim the surface, if necessary.

COOK'S TIP

The gammon should remain barely covered with water during cooking. There should be little evaporation from the slow cooker, but if necessary, top up with a small amount of boiling water.

3 Carefully lift the gammon joint out of the slow cooker using large forks or slotted spoons, and place it in a roasting pan or ovenproof dish. Leave to stand for about 15 minutes until cool enough to handle.

4 Meanwhile, make the glaze. Pour the cider into a small pan, add the soft brown sugar, and heat gently, stirring, until dissolved. Simmer for 5 minutes to make a sticky glaze, then remove from the heat, and leave to cool for a few minutes, so that it thickens slightly.

5 Preheat the oven to 425°F. Using a pair of scissors, snip the string off the gammon, then carefully slice off the rind, leaving a thin, even layer of fat over the meat.

6 Using a sharp knife, score the fat into a neat diamond pattern. Press a clove into the center of each diamond, then spoon over the glaze. Bake for about 25 minutes, or until the fat is brown, glistening, and crisp. Remove from the oven, and set aside until ready to serve.

7 Meanwhile, make the cranberry sauce. Wash the ceramic cooking pot, then add all the ingredients for the cranberry sauce to it. Switch the slow cooker to high, and cook uncovered for 20 minutes, stirring continuously, until the sugar has dissolved completely.

8 Cover the pot with the lid, and cook on high for 1½–2 hours, or until the cranberries are tender. Transfer the sauce to a pitcher or bowl, or keep warm in the slow cooker until ready to serve with the gammon. (The sauce can be served hot or cold.)

COOK'S TIPS

• If serving hot, cover the gammon with foil, and leave to rest for 15 minutes before carving.
• If you prefer, serve the ham with redcurrant sauce or jelly. You can also use honey in place of the soft brown sugar for the glaze, if you like.

Energy 404Kcal/1689kJ; Protein 44.1g; Carbohydrate 15.2g, of which sugars 14.8g; Fat 18.8g, of which saturates 6.3g; Cholesterol 57mg; Calcium 25mg; Fiber 1g; Sodium 220mg.

VEAL STEW with TOMATOES

This classic French dish is traditionally made with lean and mildly flavored veal.
Pork tenderloin makes an excellent, and economical, alternative.

SERVES 4

2 tablespoons all-purpose flour
1½ pounds boneless veal shoulder,
    trimmed and cut into cubes
2 tablespoons sunflower-seed oil
4 shallots, very finely chopped
1¼ cups boiling vegetable
    or chicken stock
⅔ cup dry white wine
1 tablespoon tomato paste
8 ounces tomatoes, peeled, seeded,
    and chopped
4 ounces mushrooms, quartered
grated zest and juice of 1 small
    unwaxed orange
bouquet garni
salt and ground black pepper
2 tablespoons chopped fresh parsley,
    to garnish

1 Put the flour in a small plastic bag, and season with salt and pepper. Drop the pieces of meat into the bag a few at a time, and shake to coat with the flour.

2 Heat 1 tablespoon of the oil in a pan, add the shallots, and cook gently for 5 minutes. Transfer to the ceramic cooking pot, and switch to high or auto.

3 Add the remaining 1 tablespoon oil to the pan, and fry the meat in batches until well browned on all sides, then transfer to the ceramic cooking pot.

4 Pour the stock and white wine into the pan. Add the tomato paste, and bring to the boil, stirring. Pour the sauce over the meat. Add the tomatoes, mushrooms, orange zest and juice, and bouquet garni to the pot, and stir briefly to mix the ingredients. Cover with the lid, and cook for about 1 hour.

5 Reduce the temperature to low, or leave on auto and cook for 3–4 hours, or until the meat and mushrooms are very tender. Remove the bouquet garni, check the seasoning, and add more salt and ground black pepper if necessary. Garnish with fresh parsley, and serve.

Energy 323Kcal/1358kJ; Protein 38.2g; Carbohydrate 13.8g, of which sugars 5.4g; Fat 10.6g, of which saturates 2.3g; Cholesterol 141mg; Calcium 47mg; Fiber 1.7g; Sodium 314mg.

GREEK MEATBALLS in RICH TOMATO SAUCE

*There are many versions of these sausage-shaped meatballs, known as yiouvarlakia
or soudzoukakia. These are made with lamb, but beef makes an excellent alternative.*

SERVES 4

1 cup fresh white bread crumbs
1 egg, lightly beaten
finely grated rind of ½ small orange
½ teaspoon dried oregano
1 pound ground lamb
1 small onion, peeled and grated
2 cloves garlic, crushed
1 tablespoon all-purpose flour
2 tablespoons olive oil
salt and ground black pepper
Italian parsley, to garnish

For the sauce
1 onion, very finely chopped
14-ounce can chopped tomatoes
⅔ cup hot lamb or beef stock
1 bay leaf

1 Put the bread crumbs, beaten egg,
orange rind, and oregano in a bowl, and
stir together. Add the lamb, onion, and
garlic, and season with salt and pepper.
Mix together until thoroughly combined.

2 Using dampened hands, so that the
mixture doesn't stick, press the meat
mixture into small sausage-shapes, about
2 inches long, and roll them in flour.
Place in the refrigerator for 30 minutes
to firm up slightly.

COOK'S TIP
Serve these meatballs with a refreshing
salad and plenty of fresh, country-style
crusty bread for mopping up the juices.
Alternatively, serve with pitta bread so
that guests can stuff the breads with
meatballs and fresh green salad.

3 Heat the oil in a large frying pan, and
add the meatballs, working in batches if
necessary. Cook for 5–8 minutes, turning
the meatballs, until evenly browned all
over. Transfer to a plate, and set aside,
leaving the fat and juices in the pan.

4 To make the sauce, add the onion to
the pan, and cook for 3–4 minutes, until
beginning to soften. Pour in the chopped
tomatoes, bring to the boil, and cook
gently for 1 minute.

5 Transfer the sauce to the ceramic
cooking pot, and stir in the stock.
Add the bay leaf, and season with salt
and ground black pepper.

6 Arrange the meatballs in a single layer in
the sauce. Cover with the lid, and cook on
high or auto for 1 hour. Reduce the
temperature to low, or leave on auto, and
cook for a further 4–5 hours. Serve
garnished with sprigs of fresh Italian parsley.

Energy 363Kcal/1515kJ; Protein 26.1g; Carbohydrate 15g, of which sugars 5.3g; Fat 22.5g, of which saturates 8.3g; Cholesterol 141mg; Calcium 68mg; Fiber 1.5g; Sodium 239mg.

LANCASHIRE HOT-POT

This dish is traditionally made without browning the lamb or vegetables, and relies on long,
slow cooking to develop the flavor. You can brown the top under the broiler, if you like.

SERVES 4

8 shoulder or loin lamb chops,
    about 2 pounds in total weight
2 pounds potatoes, thinly sliced
2 onions, peeled and sliced
2 carrots, peeled and sliced
1 stick celery, trimmed and sliced
1 leek, peeled and sliced
generous 3 cups white mushrooms, sliced
1 teaspoon dried mixed herbs
small sprig of rosemary
2 cups lamb or beef stock
1 tablespoon butter, melted
salt and ground black pepper

3 Pour the meat stock into the ceramic
cooking pot, then cover with the lid, and
switch the slow cooker to high or auto.
Cook for 1 hour, then reduce the
temperature to low, or leave on auto,
and cook for 6–8 hours or until tender.

4 Brush the top layer of potatoes with
melted butter. Place under a preheated
broiler, and cook for 5 minutes, or until
the potatoes are lightly browned. Serve
immediately.

1 Trim the lamb chops of excess fat.
Place a layer of sliced potatoes in the
base of the ceramic cooking pot, and
top with some sliced vegetables and a
sprinkling of dried herbs, salt, and black
pepper. Place four of the chops on top.

2 Repeat the layers of sliced potato,
vegetables, dried herbs, and meat,
tucking the rosemary sprig down the
side of the pot. Continue layering up the
remaining vegetables, finishing with a
neat layer of potatoes on the top.

Energy 850Kcal/3544kJ; Protein 44.7g; Carbohydrate 45.3g, of which sugars 10.1g; Fat 55.8g, of which saturates 26.5g; Cholesterol 186mg; Calcium 72mg; Fiber 4.3g; Sodium 274mg.

LAMB PIE with MUSTARD THATCH

*Here, a traditional shepherd's pie is given a contemporary twist with a tangy topping
of mashed potato flavored with peppery mustard. Serve with vegetables.*

SERVES 4

1 pound lean ground lamb
1 onion, very finely chopped
2 celery sticks, thinly sliced
2 carrots, finely diced
1 tablespoon cornstarch blended into
    ⅔ cup lamb stock
1 tablespoon Worcestershire sauce
2 tablespoons chopped fresh rosemary,
    or 2 teaspoons dried
1¾ pounds floury potatoes, diced
4 tablespoons milk
1 tablespoon whole-grain mustard
2 tablespoons butter
salt and ground black pepper

1 Heat a non-stick frying pan, then add
the lamb, breaking it up with a wooden
spoon, and cook until lightly browned all
over. Add the onion, celery, and carrots
to the pan and cook for 2–3 minutes,
stirring frequently.

2 Stir the stock and cornstarch mixture
into the pan. Bring to the boil, stirring
constantly, then remove from the heat.
Stir in the Worcestershire sauce and
rosemary, and season well with salt
and ground black pepper.

3 Transfer the mixture to the ceramic
cooking pot, and switch the slow cooker
to high. Cover, and cook for 3 hours.

4 Toward the end of the cooking time,
cook the potatoes in a large pan of
boiling salted water until tender. Drain
well, mash, and stir in the milk, mustard,
and butter. Season to taste.

5 Spoon the mashed potatoes on top
of the lamb, spreading the mixture out
evenly. Cook for a further 45 minutes.
Brown the topping under a preheated
broiler for a few minutes, if you like,
then serve immediately.

Energy 458Kcal/1920kJ; Protein 26.5g; Carbohydrate 42.2g, of which sugars 8.1g; Fat 21.5g, of which saturates 10.6g; Cholesterol 101mg; Calcium 84mg; Fiber 3.5g; Sodium 264mg.

MOUSSAKA

This classic Greek dish topped with a light egg and cheese sauce is delicious in summer or winter, served with a crisp leafy salad. Try to find small, sweet eggplants with firm, shiny skins because they have much the best flavor. For an authentic touch, look out for Kefolotiri cheese in delicatessens and specialist food stores—although if you can't find it, Cheddar cheese will give equally good results.

SERVES 6

2 pounds small or medium eggplants,
    thinly sliced
4 tablespoons olive oil
I onion, finely chopped
2 garlic cloves, crushed
I pound lean ground lamb
14-ounce can chopped tomatoes
I teaspoon dried oregano
pinch of ground cinnamon
salt and ground black pepper

For the topping
¼ cup butter
½ cup all-purpose flour
2½ cups milk
pinch of freshly grated nutmeg
¾ cup grated Kefolotiri or
    mature Cheddar cheese
I egg yolk
2 tablespoons fresh white bread crumbs

I Layer the eggplant slices in a strainer or colander, sprinkling each layer with salt. Place the strainer over a bowl, and leave to drain for 20 minutes. Rinse the eggplant slices thoroughly under cold running water, and pat dry with paper towels.

VARIATION
You can use zucchini in place of the eggplants, if you prefer. Simply slice the zucchini, brush with olive oil, and broil as before. There is no need to salt the zucchini slices.

2 Lightly brush the eggplant slices with about half the oil, then arrange the slices in a single layer on a baking sheet. Place the baking sheet under a medium broiler, and cook, turning once, until the eggplant slices are softened and golden brown on both sides.

3 Arrange half the eggplant slices in the bottom of the ceramic cooking pot, and switch the slow cooker to high. Set aside the remaining slices.

4 Heat the remaining olive oil in a heavy pan, add the onion, and fry gently for about 10 minutes, or until softened. Add the garlic and lamb, and cook, stirring and breaking up the meat with a wooden spoon, until the meat is evenly browned.

5 Stir the tomatoes, oregano, and cinnamon into the meat mixture, season generously with salt and ground black pepper, and slowly bring to the boil over a gentle heat.

6 Spoon the lamb mixture into the slow cooker, covering the aubergine slices. Arrange the remaining aubergine slices on top, cover, and cook for 2 hours.

7 Meanwhile, make the cheese topping. Melt the butter in a pan, stir in the flour, and cook for one minute. Gradually stir in the milk, bring to the boil over a low heat, stirring constantly, and cook until thick and creamy. Lower the heat, and simmer for I minute. Remove from the heat, season, then stir in the nutmeg and two-thirds of the cheese.

8 Leave the sauce to cool for 5 minutes, then beat in the egg yolk. Pour the sauce over the eggplant slices. Cover, and cook for a further 2 hours, or until the topping is lightly set.

9 Sprinkle the remaining cheese and the bread crumbs over the top, and cook under a broiler for 3–4 minutes, or until golden brown. Leave to stand for 5–10 minutes before serving.

Energy 444Kcal/1850kJ; Protein 24.1g; Carbohydrate 1.5g, of which sugars 11.2g; Fat 31g, of which saturates 14g; Cholesterol 93.5mg; Calcium 268mg; Fiber 4.1g; Sodium 266mg.

MOROCCAN LAMB with HONEY and PRUNES

This classic dish of the Moroccan Jews is eaten at Rosh Hashanah—the Jewish
New Year—when sweet foods are served in anticipation of a sweet new year to come.

SERVES 6

generous ½ cup pitted prunes
1½ cups hot tea
2¼ pounds stewing or braising lamb,
    such as shoulder
2 tablespoons olive oil
1 onion, chopped
½ teaspoon ground ginger
½ teaspoon curry powder
pinch of freshly grated nutmeg
2 teaspoons ground cinnamon
¼ teaspoon saffron threads
2 tablespoons hot water
5 tablespoons clear honey
scant 1 cup near-boiling lamb
    or beef stock
salt and ground black pepper
1 cup blanched almonds, toasted
2 tablespoons chopped fresh cilantro
    and 3 hard-boiled eggs,
    cut into wedges, to garnish

1 Put the prunes in a heatproof bowl, then pour over the tea, and leave to soak. Meanwhile, trim the lamb and cut into chunky pieces, no larger than 1 inch. Heat the oil in a frying pan, and sauté the lamb in batches for 5 minutes, stirring frequently, until well-browned. Remove with a slotted spoon, and transfer to the ceramic cooking pot.

2 Add the onion to the frying pan, and cook for 5 minutes, until starting to soften. Stir in the ginger, curry powder, nutmeg, cinnamon, salt, and a large pinch of black pepper, and cook for 1 minute. Add to the ceramic cooking pot with the meat and its juices.

3 Drain the prunes, adding the soaking liquid to the lamb. Cover the prunes.

4 Soak the saffron in the hot water for 1 minute, then add to the cooking pot with the honey and stock. Cover with the lid, and cook on high or auto for 1 hour. Reduce the temperature to low, and cook for a further 5–7 hours, or until the lamb is very tender.

5 Add the prunes to the cooking pot, and stir to mix. Cook for 30 minutes, or until warmed through. Serve sprinkled with the toasted almonds and chopped cilantro, and topped with the wedges of hard-boiled egg.

Energy 490Kcal/2051kJ; Protein 43.6g; Carbohydrate 23.8g, of which sugars 23.4g; Fat 25.2g, of which saturates 10.3g; Cholesterol 279mg; Calcium 41mg; Fiber 1.4g; Sodium 197mg.

LAMB in DILL SAUCE

In this recipe, the lamb is cooked with vegetables to make a clear well-flavored broth,
which is then thickened with an egg and cream mixture to make a smooth, delicate sauce.

SERVES 6

3 pounds lean boneless lamb
1 small onion, trimmed and quartered
1 carrot, peeled and thickly sliced
1 bay leaf
4 sprigs of fresh dill, plus 3 tablespoons
   chopped
1 thinly pared strip of lemon rind
3 cups near-boiling lamb
   or vegetable stock
8 ounces small shallots
1 tablespoon olive oil
1 tablespoon sweet butter
1 tablespoon all-purpose flour
4 ounces frozen baby peas, defrosted
1 egg yolk
⅓ cup light cream,
   at room temperature
salt and ground black pepper
new potatoes and carrots, to serve

1 Trim the lamb and cut into 1-inch
pieces. Place in the ceramic cooking pot
with the onion, carrot, bay leaf, sprigs of
dill, and lemon rind. Pour over the stock,
cover, and cook on high for 1 hour. Skim
off any scum, then re-cover, and cook for
a further 2 hours on high or 4 hours on
low, until the lamb is fairly tender.

2 Meanwhile, put the shallots in a
heatproof bowl, and pour over enough
boiling water to cover. Leave to cool,
then drain, and peel off the skins.

3 Remove the meat from the pot.
Strain the stock, discarding the vegetables
and herbs. Clean the pot. Return the
meat and half the stock (reserving the
rest), cover, and switch to high.

4 Heat the oil and butter in a pan, add
the shallots and cook gently, stirring, for
10–15 minutes, or until browned and
tender. Turn off the heat, then transfer
the shallots to the cooking pot, using a
slotted spoon.

5 Sprinkle the flour over the fat
remaining in the pan, then stir in the
reserved stock, a little at a time. Bring
to the boil, stirring all the time until
thickened, then stir into the lamb and
shallot mixture. Stir in the peas, and
season with salt and pepper. Cook on
high for 30 minutes until piping hot.

6 Blend the egg yolk and the cream
together, then stir in a few spoonfuls
of the hot stock. Add to the casserole
in a thin stream, stirring until slightly
thickened. Stir in the chopped dill, and
serve immediately, with steamed new
potatoes and carrots.

Energy 631Kcal/2629kJ; Protein 60.9g; Carbohydrate 7g, of which sugars 3.5g; Fat 40g, of which saturates 17.5g; Cholesterol 249mg; Calcium 123mg; Fiber 1.9g; Sodium 566mg.

TUSCAN POT-ROASTED SHOULDER of LAMB

This delicious boned and rolled shoulder of lamb, studded with rosemary sprigs and garlic, then cooked on a bed of vegetables, makes a perfect alternative to a traditional meat roast. Check that the lamb will fit comfortably in the slow cooker before you start.

SERVES 6

1 tablespoon olive oil
3 pounds lamb shoulder, trimmed,
   boned, and tied
3 large garlic cloves
12 small fresh rosemary sprigs
4 ounces lean rinded smoked bacon,
   chopped
1 onion, chopped
3 carrots, finely chopped
3 celery sticks, finely chopped
1 leek, finely chopped
⅔ cup red wine
1¼ cups lamb or vegetable stock
14 ounces can chopped tomatoes
3 sprigs of fresh thyme
2 bay leaves
14 ounces small cannellini beans,
   drained and rinsed
salt and ground black pepper
potatoes or warm crusty bread,
   to serve

1 Heat the oil in a large frying pan, and brown the lamb on all sides. Remove from the pan, and leave to stand until it is cool enough to handle.

2 Meanwhile, cut the garlic cloves into quarters. When the lamb is cool enough, make twelve deep incisions all over the meat. Push a piece of garlic and a small sprig of rosemary into each incision.

COOK'S TIP
Lamb can be quite a fatty meat, so ask your butcher to trim off as much excess fat as possible from the joint, before boning, rolling, and tying it.

3 Add the bacon, onion, carrot, celery, and leek to the pan, and cook for about 10 minutes until soft, then transfer to the ceramic cooking pot. Stir the red wine into the cooking pot.

4 Add the stock and chopped tomatoes to the pot, and season with salt and pepper. Add the thyme and bay leaves, submerging them in the liquid. Place the lamb on top, cover with the lid, and cook on high for 4 hours.

5 Lift the lamb out of the pot, and stir the beans into the vegetable mixture. Return the lamb, re-cover, and cook for a further 1–2 hours, or until the lamb is cooked and tender.

6 Remove the lamb from the ceramic cooking pot using slotted spoons, cover with foil to keep warm, and leave to rest for 10 minutes.

7 Remove the string from the lamb, and carve the meat into thick slices. Remove the thyme and bay leaves from the vegetable and bean mixture, and carefully skim off any fat from the surface. Spoon the vegetables onto warmed serving plates, and arrange the sliced lamb on top. Serve with potatoes or warm bread.

VARIATIONS
• Small cannellini beans have a delicate yet distinctive flavor that goes particularly well in this dish. However, you can use other mildly flavored beans instead, such as butter beans or cannellini beans.
• Try using 1 teaspoon fresh oregano in place of the thyme, if you prefer. This classic Italian herb tastes just as good.

Energy 710Kcal/2958kJ; Protein 60.2g; Carbohydrate 13.7g, of which sugars 4.8g; Fat 44.6g, of which saturates 19.4g; Cholesterol 229mg; Calcium 58mg; Fiber 4.7g; Sodium 864mg.

LAMB and CARROT CASSEROLE with BARLEY

Barley and carrots make natural partners for lamb and mutton. In this convenient casserole, the barley extends the meat and adds to the flavor and texture as well as thickening the sauce. This warming dish is comfort food at its very best.

SERVES 6

1½ pounds braising lamb
1 tablespoon vegetable oil
2 onions
1½ pounds carrots, thickly sliced
4–6 celery sticks, sliced
3 tablespoons pearl barley, rinsed
2½ cups near-boiling lamb or
    vegetable stock
1 teaspoon fresh thyme leaves or pinch of
    dried mixed herbs
salt and ground black pepper
spring cabbage and jacket potatoes,
    to serve

1 Trim all excess fat from the lamb, then cut the meat into 1¼-inch pieces. Heat the oil in a frying pan, add the lamb, and fry until browned. Remove from with a slotted spoon, and set aside.

2 Slice the onions, and add to the pan. Fry gently for 5 minutes until golden. Add the carrots and celery, and cook for a further 3–4 minutes, or until beginning to soften. Transfer the vegetables to the ceramic cooking pot, and switch the slow cooker to high.

3 Sprinkle the pearl barley over the vegetables in the cooking pot, then arrange the lamb pieces on top.

4 Lightly season with salt and ground black pepper, then scatter with the herbs. Pour the stock over the meat, so that all of the meat is covered.

5 Cover the slow cooker with the lid, and cook on auto or high for 2 hours. Lift the lid and, using a large spoon, skim off any scum that has risen to the surface of the casserole.

6 Re-cover the pot, and leave on auto, or switch to low, and cook for a further 4–6 hours, or until the meat, vegetables, and barley are tender. Serve with spring cabbage and jacket potatoes.

Energy 304Kcal/1263kJ; Protein 23.2g; Carbohydrate 13g, of which sugars 11.3g; Fat 18g, of which saturates 7.5g; Cholesterol 84mg; Calcium 53mg; Fiber 3.6g; Sodium 110mg

LAMB STEWED with TOMATOES and GARLIC

This simple rustic stew comes from the plateau of Puglia in Italy, where sheep graze beside the vineyards. Serve simply, with fresh crusty bread and a green leaf salad.

SERVES 4

2½ pounds braising lamb
2 tablespoons all-purpose flour,
   seasoned with ground black pepper
4 tablespoons olive oil
2 large cloves garlic, finely chopped
1 sprig fresh rosemary
⅔ cup dry white wine
⅔ cup lamb or beef stock
½ teaspoon salt
1 pound fresh tomatoes, peeled and
   chopped, or 14-ounce can
   chopped tomatoes
salt and ground black pepper

4 Season with salt and pepper, and stir in the tomatoes. Cover the cooking pot with the lid, and switch the slow cooker to high or auto. Cook for 1 hour.

5 Reduce the heat to low or leave on auto and cook for a further 6–8 hours, or until the lamb is tender. Taste, and adjust the seasoning before serving.

VARIATION
For Lamb with Butternut Squash, sauté 1½ pounds cubed lamb fillet in 1 tablespoon oil, then transfer to the ceramic cooking pot. Fry 1 chopped onion and 2 crushed garlic cloves until soft, and add to the lamb with 1 cubed butternut squash, 14-ounce can chopped tomatoes, ⅔ cup lamb stock, and 1 teaspoon dried marjoram. Cover, and cook on low for 5–6 hours.

1 Trim all fat and gristle from the lamb, and cut into 1-inch cubes. Toss in the flour to coat. Set aside the excess flour.

2 Heat the oil in a pan, and fry the lamb, in two batches for 5 minutes, stirring, until browned. Lift out the lamb, and transfer to the ceramic cooking pot.

3 Add the garlic, and cook for a few seconds before adding the rosemary, wine, and stock. Bring almost to the boil, stirring, to remove any meat sediment from the pan. Pour over the lamb.

Energy 636Kcal/2656kJ; Protein 62.4g; Carbohydrate 11.5g, of which sugars 3.9g; Fat 35.5g, of which saturates 12.2g; Cholesterol 222mg; Calcium 62mg; Fiber 1.4g; Sodium 508mg.

ONE-POT, CLAY-POT MEAT

Nothing quite matches the flavor of meat that has
simmered in the oven for hours with tasty root vegetables
and aromatic herbs, especially when a little beer or wine
has been poured into the pot, as in Pot-roast Beef with
Guinness, Pork cooked in Cider with Parsley Dumplings,
or Osso Bucco with Risotto Milanese. Equally delicious
are sustaining stews, such as Boeuf Bourguignon and
Braised Lamb with Apricots and Herb Dumplings.
For sophisticated entertaining, why not try Calf's Liver
with Slow-cooked Onions, Marsala, and Sage, or Noisettes
of Pork with Creamy Calvados and Apple Sauce?

CITRUS BEEF CURRY

*This superbly aromatic Thai-style curry is not too hot but full of
flavor. For a special meal, it goes perfectly with fried noodles.*

SERVES 4

1 pound round steak
2 tablespoons sunflower-seed oil
2 tablespoons medium curry paste
2 bay leaves
1⅔ cups coconut milk
1¼ cups beef stock
2 tablespoons lemon juice
3 tablespoons Thai fish sauce
1 tablespoon sugar
4 ounces pearl onions, peeled but
    left whole
8 ounces new potatoes, halved
1 cup unsalted roasted peanuts,
    coarsely chopped
4 ounces fine green beans, halved
1 red bell pepper, seeded and
    thinly sliced
unsalted roasted peanuts,
    to garnish (optional)

1 Trim any fat off the beef, and cut the
beef into 2-inch strips.

2 Heat the sunflower-seed oil in a large,
heavy pan, add the curry paste, and
cook over medium heat for 30 seconds,
stirring constantly.

3 Add the beef, and cook, stirring, for
2 minutes, until it is beginning to brown
and is thoroughly coated with the spices.

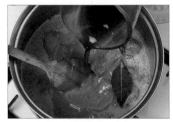

4 Stir in the bay leaves, coconut milk,
stock, lemon juice, fish sauce, and sugar,
and bring to a boil, stirring.

5 Add the onions and potatoes, then
bring back to a boil, reduce the heat,
and simmer, uncovered, for 5 minutes.

6 Stir in the peanuts, beans, and bell
pepper, and simmer for 10 minutes
more, or until the beef and potatoes are
tender. Serve in shallow bowls, with a
spoon and fork, to enjoy all the rich and
creamy juices. Sprinkle with extra
unsalted roasted peanuts, if you like.

Energy 476Kcal/1990kJ; Protein 33.8g; Carbohydrate 27.5g, of which sugars 16.3g; Fat 26.4g, of which saturates 6.6g; Cholesterol 69mg;
Calcium 77mg; Fiber 4.1g; Sodium 169mg.

IRISH STEW

Simple and delicious, this is the quintessential Irish main course. Traditionally, mutton chops are used, but as they are harder to find these days, you can use lamb instead.

SERVES 4

3 pounds boneless lamb chops, cut into
   large chunks
I tablespoon vegetable oil
3 onions
4 large carrots
3¾ cups water
4 large potatoes, cut into
   large chunks
I large fresh thyme sprig
I tablespoon sweet butter
I tablespoon chopped
   fresh parsley
salt and ground black pepper

I Trim any fat from the lamb. Heat the oil in a large, flameproof casserole, and brown the meat on all sides. Remove from the casserole.

2 Cut the onions into fourths, and thickly slice the carrots. Add them to the casserole, and cook for 5 minutes, stirring, or until the onions are browned. Return the meat to the casserole with the water. Bring to a boil, reduce the heat, cover, and simmer for I hour.

3 Add the potatoes and thyme to the casserole, and cook for I hour more.

4 Leave the stew to settle for a few minutes. Remove the fat from the liquid with a spoon, then stir in the butter and the parsley. Season well before serving.

Energy 898Kcal/3763kJ; Protein 70.4g; Carbohydrate 60g, of which sugars 19.1g; Fat 43.6g, of which saturates 19.5g; Cholesterol 255mg; Calcium 104mg; Fiber 7g; Sodium 359mg.

POT-ROAST BEEF with GUINNESS

This heart-warming, rich pot-roast is ideal for a winter supper. Brisket of beef has the best flavor, but this dish works equally well with a traditional rolled pot-roast.

SERVES 6

2 tablespoons vegetable oil
2 pounds rolled brisket of beef
10 ounces onions, coarsely chopped
2 celery stalks, thickly sliced
1 pound carrots, cut into large chunks
1½ pounds potatoes, peeled and cut
  into large chunks
2 tablespoons all-purpose flour
2 cups beef stock
1¼ cups Guinness
1 bay leaf
3 tablespoons chopped fresh thyme
1 teaspoon light brown sugar
2 tablespoons whole-grain mustard
1 tablespoon tomato paste
salt and ground black pepper

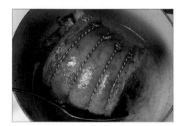

1 Preheat the oven to 350°F. Heat the oil in a large, flameproof casserole, and brown the meat, turning frequently, until golden all over.

3 Add the celery, carrot, and potato to the casserole, and cook over medium heat for 2–3 minutes, or until they are just beginning to color.

5 Add the bay leaf, thyme, sugar, mustard, tomato paste, and plenty of seasoning. Place the meat on top, cover tightly, and transfer to the oven.

2 Remove the meat from the casserole, and drain it on a double layer of paper towels. Add the chopped onions to the casserole, and cook for about 4 minutes, or until they are just beginning to soften and turn brown, stirring constantly.

4 Stir in the flour, and cook for 1 minute more, stirring constantly. Pour in the beef stock and the Guinness and stir until thoroughly combined. Bring the sauce to a boil, stirring constantly with a wooden spoon.

6 Cook for about 2½ hours, or until the vegetables and meat are tender. Adjust the seasoning, and add another pinch of sugar, if necessary. To serve, remove the meat, and carve into thick slices. Serve with the vegetables and plenty of gravy.

Energy 402Kcal/1691kJ; Protein 35.5g; Carbohydrate 33.8g, of which sugars 11.9g; Fat 13.6g, of which saturates 4.4g; Cholesterol 81mg; Calcium 58mg; Fiber 4g; Sodium 142mg.

CLAY-POT BEEF with RED BELL PEPPERS

Using a clay pot to cook lean meat keeps it moist and juicy. Here it is cooked with sweet bell peppers and onion in a rich red wine sauce.

SERVES 6

2½ pounds top round steak
    or pot-roast of beef, neatly tied
2 garlic cloves
2 tablespoons sunflower-seed oil
1 large onion, chopped
1¼ cups beef stock
1 tablespoon tomato paste
⅔ cup red wine
bouquet garni
4 sweet romano red bell
    peppers, halved lengthwise
    and seeded
1 tablespoon butter, softened
1 tablespoon all-purpose flour
salt and ground black pepper

1 Soak the clay pot in cold water for 20 minutes, then drain. Using a sharp knife, make about 20 small incisions in the beef. Cut the garlic cloves into thin slivers, and insert into the cuts.

2 Season the beef with salt and pepper. Heat the sunflower-seed oil in a large frying pan, add the beef, and cook, stirring frequently with a wooden spoon until browned on all sides. Remove the beef from the pan, and set aside.

3 Add the onion to the frying pan, and cook over low heat for 5–8 minutes, stirring occasionally, until light golden. Transfer the onion to the clay pot.

4 Place the beef on top of the onion in the clay pot, then combine the beef stock, tomato paste, and wine, and pour over the beef.

5 Add the bouquet garni to the pot, then cover the pot, and place it in an unheated oven. Set the oven to 400°F and cook for 1 hour. Uncover the pot, baste the meat, and add the bell pepper halves, arranging them around the meat. Cook, uncovered, basting occasionally, for about 45 minutes more, until the beef is tender and cooked through.

6 To serve, transfer the beef to a large warmed serving dish with the bell peppers and onion. Drain the juices from the pot into a pan, and heat gently.

7 Blend together the butter and flour to make a smooth paste, then gradually add small pieces of the paste to the sauce, whisking until well blended. Bring the sauce to a boil, and simmer gently for about 1 minute, whisking constantly, until the sauce is thickened slightly. Pour into a sauce boat, and serve with the beef and vegetables.

VARIATIONS
Romano bell peppers are an elongated variety available in large supermarkets. If you can't find them, use ordinary bell-shaped peppers instead—the dish will be just as good. If you like, use green, orange, or yellow peppers in place of red.

COOK'S TIPS
• The butter and flour paste used in step 7 to thicken the sauce is known as a beurre manié. The paste is always made from equal quantities of all-purpose flour and softened butter. It is used for thickening casseroles, sauces, and occasionally soups.
• A bouquet garni is a selection of aromatic herbs used to flavor soups, stocks, or casseroles. The most widely used herbs include thyme, parsley, rosemary, and bay leaves. Fresh herbs can be tied together with string, or dried herbs can be wrapped in a small cheesecloth square and secured with string. Ready-made bouquet garnis of dried herbs are sold in many supermarkets.

Energy 420Kcal/1760kJ; Protein 44.7g; Carbohydrate 15.5g, of which sugars 11.7g; Fat 18.6g, of which saturates 6.9g; Cholesterol 113mg; Calcium 42mg; Fiber 3g; Sodium 154mg.

BEEF CARBONADE

This rich, dark stew of beef cooked slowly with lots of onions, garlic, and beer is a classic casserole from the north of France and neighboring Belgium.

SERVES 6

3 tablespoons vegetable oil
3 onions, sliced
3 tablespoons all-purpose flour
½ teaspoon mustard powder
2¼ pounds stewing beef (shank or chuck), cut into large cubes
2–3 garlic cloves, finely chopped
1¼ cups dark beer or ale
⅔ cup water
1 teaspoon dark brown sugar
1 fresh thyme sprig
1 fresh bay leaf
1 celery stalk
salt and ground black pepper

For the topping
¼ cup butter
1 garlic clove, crushed
1 tablespoon Dijon mustard
3 tablespoons chopped fresh parsley
6–12 slices of French bread

1 Preheat the oven to 325°F. Heat 2 tablespoons of the oil in a large, heavy pan, and cook the onions over low heat, stirring occasionally, until softened. Remove from the pan, and set aside.

2 Meanwhile, combine the flour and mustard, and season. Toss the beef in the flour. Add the remaining oil to the pan, and heat over high heat. Brown the beef all over, then transfer it to a deep, earthenware baking dish.

3 Reduce the heat, and return the onions to the pan. Add the garlic, cook briefly, then add the beer or ale, water, and sugar. Tie the thyme and bay leaf together, and add to the pan with the celery. Bring to a boil, stirring, then season with salt and pepper.

4 Pour the sauce over the beef, and mix well. Cover tightly, then place in the oven, and cook for 2½ hours. Check the beef once or twice to make sure that it is not too dry, adding a little extra water, if necessary. Test for tenderness, allowing an extra 30–40 minutes' cooking time if necessary.

5 To make the topping, beat together the butter, crushed garlic, Dijon mustard, and 2 tablespoons of the chopped fresh parsley. Spread the flavored butter thickly over the bread. Increase the oven temperature to 375°F. Taste and season the stew, then arrange the prepared bread slices, buttered side uppermost, on top. Bake for 20 minutes, or until the bread topping is browned and crisp. Sprinkle the remaining chopped fresh parsley over the top to garnish, and serve immediately.

Energy 532Kcal/2234kJ; Protein 41.1g; Carbohydrate 40g, of which sugars 10.7g; Fat 21.8g, of which saturates 9.1g; Cholesterol 108mg; Calcium 102mg; Fiber 2.7g; Sodium 409mg.

BOEUF BOURGUIGNON

The classic French dish of beef cooked in Burgundy style, with red wine, small pieces of bacon, shallots, and mushrooms, is baked for several hours at a low temperature.

SERVES 6

6 ounces rindless fatty bacon
 strips, chopped
2 pounds lean braising steak, such as
 top round steak
2 tablespoons all-purpose flour
3 tablespoons sunflower-seed oil
2 tablespoons butter
12 shallots
2 garlic cloves, crushed
2⅓ cups mushrooms, sliced
scant 2 cups robust red wine
⅔ cup beef stock or consommé
1 bay leaf
2 sprigs each of fresh thyme, parsley,
 and marjoram
salt and ground black pepper

1 Preheat the oven to 325°F. Heat a large, flameproof casserole, then add the bacon, and cook over medium heat, stirring occasionally, until the pieces are crisp and golden brown.

2 Meanwhile, cut the beef into 1-inch cubes. Season the flour, and use to coat the meat. Use a slotted spoon to remove the bacon from the casserole, and set aside. Add and heat the oil, then brown the beef, in batches, and set aside with the bacon.

COOK'S TIP

Beef consommé, which can be used as an alternative to beef stock in this recipe, is a clear, light soup. It is sold in cans, or in cartons as a fresh soup. Fresh beef stock is also available in cartons.

3 Add the butter to the fat remaining in the casserole. Cook the shallots and garlic until they are just beginning to color, then add the mushrooms, and cook for 5 minutes more. Return the bacon and beef to the casserole, and stir in the wine and stock or consommé. Tie the herbs together into a bouquet garni, and add to the casserole.

4 Cover, and cook in the oven for 1½ hours, or until the meat is tender, stirring once or twice during the cooking time. Season to taste, and serve with creamy mashed root vegetables, such as celery root and potatoes.

COOK'S TIP

Boeuf Bourguignon freezes very well. Transfer the mixture to a dish so that it cools quickly, then pour it into a rigid plastic container. Push all the cubes of meat down into the sauce or they will dry out. Freeze for up to 2 months. Thaw overnight in the refrigerator, then transfer to a flameproof casserole, and add ⅔ cup water. Stir well, then bring to a boil, stirring occasionally, and simmer steadily for at least 10 minutes, or until the meat is piping hot.

Energy 459Kcal/1913kJ; Protein 39g; Carbohydrate 8.1g, of which sugars 3.1g; Fat 24.7g, of which saturates 8.9g; Cholesterol 122mg; Calcium 37mg; Fiber 1.2g; Sodium 497mg.

BEEF HOTCHPOT with HERB DUMPLINGS

Tender chunks of beef braised in beer, flavored with shallots and mushrooms, and finished with parsley- and thyme-flavored dumplings.

SERVES 4

⅓ cup dried porcini mushrooms
4 tablespoons warm water
3 tablespoons butter
2 tablespoons sunflower-seed oil
⅔ cup lardons or cubed pancetta
2 pounds lean braising steak, cut
    into chunks
3 tablespoons all-purpose flour
scant 2 cups beer
scant 2 cups beef stock
bouquet garni
8 shallots
2 cups white mushrooms
salt and ground black pepper
fresh thyme sprigs,
    to garnish

For the herb dumplings
1 cup self-rising flour
scant ½ cup shredded suet
½ teaspoon salt
½ teaspoon mustard powder
1 tablespoon chopped fresh parsley
1 tablespoon chopped fresh thyme

1 Soak a clay pot in cold water for 20 minutes, then drain. Place the porcini mushrooms in a bowl, add the warm water, and leave to soak. In a frying pan, melt half the butter with half the oil, add the lardons or pancetta, and quickly brown. Remove with a slotted spoon, and transfer to the clay pot.

2 Add the beef to the frying pan, and brown, in batches, then, using a slotted spoon, transfer to the clay pot. Sprinkle the flour into the fat remaining in the pan, and stir well.

3 Stir the beer and stock into the flour, and bring to a boil, stirring constantly until thickened and smooth. Strain the mushroom soaking liquid, and add to the frying pan along with the porcini. Season well. Pour the sauce over the meat in the clay pot, then add the bouquet garni. Cover the pot, and place in an unheated oven. Set the oven to 400°F. Cook for 30 minutes, then reduce the oven temperature to 325°F, and cook for 1 hour more.

4 Heat the remaining butter and oil in a frying pan, and cook the shallots until golden. Remove and set aside. Add the white mushrooms and sauté for 2–3 minutes. Stir the shallots and mushrooms into the pot, and cook for 30 minutes.

5 Combine the dumpling ingredients with sufficient cold water to bind to a soft, sticky dough. Divide into 12 small balls, and place on top of the hotchpot. Cover, and cook for 25 minutes.

Energy 527Kcal/2194kJ; Protein 10.3g; Carbohydrate 39.1g, of which sugars 6.4g; Fat 35.5g, of which saturates 14.9g; Cholesterol 50mg; Calcium 169mg; Fiber 3.1g; Sodium 789mg.

SLOW-BAKED BEEF with a POTATO CRUST

This recipe makes the most of braising beef by marinating it in red wine and topping it with a cheese-flavored grated potato crust that bakes to a golden, crunchy consistency.

SERVES 4

1½ pounds lean stewing beef, diced
1¼ cups red wine
3 juniper berries, crushed
pared strip of orange rind
2 tablespoons olive oil
2 onions, cut into chunks
2 carrots, cut into chunks
1 garlic clove, crushed
3 cups white mushrooms
⅔ cup beef stock
2 tablespoons cornstarch
salt and ground black pepper

For the crust

1 pound potatoes, grated
1 tablespoon olive oil
2 tablespoons creamed horseradish
½ cup grated sharp
    Cheddar cheese
salt and ground black pepper

1 Place the diced beef in a nonmetallic bowl. Add the wine, juniper berries, and orange rind, and season with pepper. Mix the ingredients together, then cover, and leave to marinate for at least 4 hours or overnight if possible.

COOK'S TIP

Use a large-holed, coarse grater on the food processor for the potatoes. They will hold their shape better while being blanched than if you use a finer blade.

2 Preheat the oven to 325°F. Drain the diced stewing beef, reserving the marinade in a bowl.

3 Heat the oil in a large, flameproof casserole, and cook the meat, in batches, for 5 minutes to brown and seal. Add the onions, carrots, and garlic, and cook for 5 minutes. Stir in the mushrooms, red wine marinade, and beef stock.

4 Mix the cornstarch with water to make a smooth paste, and stir into the beef mixture. Season, cover, and cook in the oven for 1½ hours.

5 Prepare the crust about 45 minutes before the end of the cooking time for the beef. Start by blanching the grated potatoes in boiling water for 5 minutes. Drain well, and then squeeze out all the extra liquid.

6 Stir in the olive oil, horseradish, grated cheese, and seasoning, then sprinkle the mixture evenly over the surface of the beef. Increase the oven temperature to 400°F, and cook for 30 minutes more, until the potato crust is crisp and light golden brown. Serve immediately.

Energy 641Kcal/2678kJ; Protein 45.9g; Carbohydrate 36.6g, of which sugars 10.8g; Fat 29.6g, of which saturates 10.6g; Cholesterol 111mg; Calcium 152mg; Fiber 4.2g; Sodium 306mg.

CALFS' LIVER with SLOW-COOKED ONIONS, MARSALA, and SAGE

Liver and onions are an international favorite, from British liver with onion gravy to the famous Venetian dish of Fegato alla Veneziana. Inspired by Italian cooking, this dish is good served with polenta, either soft or set and broiled.

3 Add the remaining oil to the pan, and fry the remaining sage leaves for about 30 seconds, then leave them to drain on paper towels.

4 Add the remaining butter and extra oil to the pan, and increase the heat to high. Season the flour, then dip the liver in it, and fry quickly for about 2 minutes on each side until browned, but still pink in the middle. Use a slotted spoon or metal spatula to transfer the liver to warm plates, and keep warm.

5 Immediately add the Marsala to the pan, and let it bubble fiercely until reduced to a few tablespoons of sticky glaze. Distribute the onions over the liver, and spoon over the Marsala juices. Sprinkle with the fried sage leaves and extra parsley, and serve immediately.

SERVES 4

3 tablespoons olive oil, plus extra for shallow frying
2 tablespoons butter
1¼ pounds mild onions, thinly sliced
small bunch of fresh sage leaves
2 tablespoons chopped fresh parsley, plus a little extra to garnish
½ teaspoon sugar
1 tablespoon balsamic vinegar
2 tablespoons all-purpose flour
1½ pounds calves' liver, thinly sliced
⅔ cup Marsala
salt and ground black pepper

1 Heat half the oil with half the butter in a large, wide, heavy pan, and cook the onions, covered, over very gentle heat for 30 minutes. Stir once or twice.

2 Chop five of the sage leaves, and add them to the pan with the chopped parsley, a pinch of salt, the sugar, and balsamic vinegar. Cook, uncovered and stirring frequently with a wooden spoon, until the onions are very tender and a golden brown color. Taste for seasoning, and add salt and pepper as necessary. Tip the onions into a heatproof dish, and keep warm.

VARIATION
Chicken liver and onion bruschetta
Cook the onions as above, replacing the sage with 1 teaspoon chopped fresh thyme. Fry 14 ounces chicken livers in 2 tablespoons butter and 1 tablespoon olive oil until browned but still pink in the center. Flame the chicken livers with 3 tablespoons cognac, and add 5 ounces seeded, skinned grapes (optional). Heat the grapes through, then toss them into the cooked onions. Heap the mixture onto thick slices of toasted country bread rubbed with oil and garlic or onto thick slices of broiled polenta. Serve sprinkled with chopped fresh parsley.

Energy 427Kcal/1777kJ; Protein 32.5g; Carbohydrate 14.9g, of which sugars 12.1g; Fat 22.1g, of which saturates 6.5g; Cholesterol 638mg; Calcium 44mg; Fiber 1.8g; Sodium 163mg.

BLACK BEAN CHILI CON CARNE

Fresh green and dried red chiles add plenty of fire to this classic Tex-Mex dish of tender beef cooked in a spicy tomato sauce.

SERVES 6

1¼ cups dried black beans
1¼ pounds braising steak
2 tablespoons vegetable oil
2 onions, chopped
1 garlic clove, crushed
1 fresh green chile, seeded and
　finely chopped
1 tablespoon paprika
2 teaspoons ground cumin
2 teaspoons ground coriander
14-ounce can chopped tomatoes
1¼ cups beef stock
1 dried red chile, crumbled
1 teaspoon hot pepper sauce
1 red bell pepper, seeded and chopped
salt
fresh cilantro, to garnish
boiled rice, to serve

1 Put the beans in a large pan. Add enough cold water to cover them, bring to a boil, and boil vigorously for about 10 minutes. Drain, tip into a clean bowl, cover with cold water, and leave to soak for about 8 hours or overnight.

2 Preheat the oven to 300°F. Cut the braising steak into small cubes. Heat the vegetable oil in a large, flameproof casserole. Add the chopped onion, crushed garlic, and chopped green chile, and cook them gently for 5 minutes, until soft. Use a slotted spoon to transfer the mixture to a plate.

3 Increase the heat to high, add the meat to the casserole, and brown on all sides, then stir in the paprika, ground cumin, and ground coriander.

4 Add the tomatoes, beef stock, dried chile, and hot pepper sauce. Drain the beans, and add them to the casserole, with enough water to cover. Bring to simmering point, cover, and cook in the oven for 2 hours. Stir occasionally, and add extra water, if necessary.

5 Season the casserole with salt, and add the chopped bell pepper. Replace the lid, return the casserole to the oven, and cook for 30 minutes more, or until the meat and beans are tender. Sprinkle over the fresh cilantro, and serve with rice.

COOK'S TIP
Red kidney beans are traditionally used in chili con carne, but in this recipe, black beans are used instead. They are the same shape and size as red kidney beans but have a shiny black skin. They are also known as Mexican or Spanish black beans.

VARIATION
Use ground beef in place of the cubed braising steak.

Energy 289Kcal/1216kJ; Protein 27.3g; Carbohydrate 24.7g, of which sugars 7.8g; Fat 9.7g, of which saturates 2.0g; Cholesterol 45mg; Calcium 61mg; Fiber 7.8g; Sodium 65mg.

NOISETTES of PORK with CREAMY CALVADOS and APPLE SAUCE

This dish gives the impression of being far more difficult to prepare than it really is, so it is ideal as part of a formal menu to impress guests. Buttered gnocchi or griddled polenta and red cabbage are suitable accompaniments.

SERVES 4

2 tablespoons all-purpose flour
4 noisettes of pork, about 6 ounces each,
   firmly tied
2 tablespoons butter
4 baby leeks, thinly sliced
1 teaspoon mustard seeds,
   coarsely crushed
2 tablespoons Calvados
⅔ cup dry white wine
2 eating apples, peeled, cored,
   and sliced
⅔ cup heavy cream
2 tablespoons chopped fresh Italian parsley
salt and ground black pepper

1 Place the flour in a bowl, and add plenty of seasoning. Turn the noisettes in the flour mixture to coat them lightly.

2 Melt the butter in a large, heavy frying pan, and cook the noisettes until golden on both sides. Remove from the pan, and set aside.

3 Add the leeks to the fat remaining in the pan, and cook for 5 minutes. Stir in the mustard seeds, and pour in the Calvados, then carefully ignite it to burn off the alcohol. When the flames have died down, pour in the wine, and replace the pork. Cook gently for 10 minutes, turning the pork frequently.

4 Add the sliced apples to the pan, and pour in the cream. Simmer for about 5 minutes, or until the apples are tender and the sauce is thick and creamy. Taste for seasoning, then stir in the chopped fresh parsley, and serve immediately.

Energy 553Kcal/2304kJ; Protein 40.6g; Carbohydrate 14.3g, of which sugars 6.1g; Fat 32.9g, of which saturates 18.3g; Cholesterol 175mg; Calcium 72mg; Fiber 2.8g; Sodium 173mg.

PANCETTA and FAVA BEAN RISOTTO

This delicious risotto makes a healthy and filling meal, when served with mixed salad greens. Use smoked bacon instead of pancetta, if you like.

SERVES 4

8 ounces frozen baby fava beans
1 tablespoon olive oil
1 onion, chopped
2 garlic cloves, finely chopped
6 ounces smoked pancetta, diced
1¾ cups risotto rice
5 cups chicken stock
2 tablespoons chopped fresh mixed herbs,
    such as parsley, thyme, and oregano
salt and ground black pepper
coarsely chopped fresh parsley, to garnish
shavings of Parmesan cheese, to serve
    (see Cook's Tip)

1 First, cook the fava beans in a large flameproof casserole of lightly salted, boiling water for about 3 minutes, until tender. Drain, and set aside.

2 Heat the olive oil in the casserole. Add the chopped onion, chopped garlic, and diced pancetta, and cook gently for about 5 minutes, stirring occasionally.

3 Add the rice to the casserole and cook for 1 minute, stirring. Add 1¼ cups of the stock, and simmer, stirring frequently until it has been absorbed.

4 Continue adding the stock, a ladleful at a time, stirring frequently until the rice is just tender and creamy, and almost all of the liquid has been absorbed. This will take 30–35 minutes. It may not be necessary to add all the stock.

5 Stir the beans, mixed herbs, and seasoning into the risotto. Heat gently, then serve garnished with the chopped fresh parsley and sprinkled with shavings of Parmesan cheese.

COOK'S TIP
To make thin Parmesan cheese shavings, take a rectangular block or long wedge of Parmesan, and firmly scrape a vegetable peeler down the side of the cheese to make shavings. The swivel-bladed type of peeler is best for this job.

Energy 511Kcal/2132kJ; Protein 18g; Carbohydrate 77.6g, of which sugars 1.6g; Fat 13.9g, of which saturates 4g; Cholesterol 28mg; Calcium 55mg; Fiber 3.9g; Sodium 556mg.

POT-ROAST LOIN of PORK with APPLE

*Roasted pork loin with crisp cracklings and a lightly spiced apple and raisin stuffing
makes a wonderful Sunday-lunch main course.*

SERVES 6–8

4 pounds boned loin of pork
1¼ cups hard cider
⅔ cup sour cream
1½ teaspoons salt

For the stuffing
2 tablespoons butter
1 small onion, chopped
1 cup fresh white bread crumbs
2 apples, cored, peeled, and chopped
scant ½ cup raisins
finely grated rind of 1 orange
pinch of ground cloves
salt and ground black pepper

1 Preheat the oven to 425°F. To make
the stuffing, melt the butter in a frying
pan, and cook the onion over low heat
for 10 minutes, until soft. Stir in all the
remaining stuffing ingredients.

2 Put the pork, rind side down, on a
board. Make a horizontal cut between
the meat and the outer layer of fat,
cutting to within 1 inch of the edges to
make a pocket.

3 Push the prepared stuffing into the
pocket. Roll up the pork lengthwise, and
tie firmly with string. Score the rind at
¾-inch intervals with a sharp knife.

4 Pour the hard cider and sour cream
into a large casserole. Stir to combine,
then add the pork, rind side down.
Transfer to the oven, and cook,
uncovered, for 30 minutes.

5 Turn the pork over, so that the rind
is on top. Baste with the juices, then
sprinkle the rind with salt. Cook for
1 hour more, basting after 30 minutes.
Reduce the oven temperature to 350°F.
Cook for 1½ hours, then remove the
casserole from the oven, and leave the
pork to stand for about 20 minutes
before carving.

COOK'S TIP
Do not baste during the final 1½ hours of
roasting, so the cracklings become crisp.

Energy 398Kcal/1667kJ; Protein 49.7g; Carbohydrate 13g, of which sugars 8.2g; Fat 15.5g, of which saturates 7.1g; Cholesterol 160mg; Calcium 50mg; Fiber 0.7g; Sodium 239mg.

BRAZILIAN PORK and RICE CASSEROLE

We tend to associate Brazil with beef recipes, but there are also some excellent pork recipes, including this hearty dish of marinated pork, vegetables, and rice.

SERVES 4–6

1¼ pounds lean pork, such as tenderloin,
    cut into strips
4 tablespoons vegetable oil
1 onion, chopped
1 garlic clove, crushed
1 green bell pepper, cut into pieces
about 1¼ cups chicken or
    vegetable stock
generous 1 cup long grain rice
⅔ cup light cream
1⅔ cups freshly grated
    Parmesan cheese
salt and ground black pepper

For the marinade
½ cup dry white wine
2 tablespoons lemon juice
1 onion, chopped
4 juniper berries, lightly crushed
3 cloves
1 fresh red chile, seeded and
    thinly sliced

1 Mix the marinade ingredients in a shallow dish, add the pork strips, and leave to marinate for 3–4 hours, stirring occasionally. Transfer the pork to a plate using a slotted spoon, and pat dry. Strain the marinade and set aside.

2 Heat the oil in a heavy pan, add the pork strips, and cook for a few minutes until evenly brown. Transfer to a plate using a slotted spoon.

3 Add the chopped onion and the garlic to the pan, and cook for 3–4 minutes. Stir in the pieces of bell pepper, and cook for 3–4 minutes more, then return the pork strips to the pan. Pour in the reserved marinade and the stock. Bring to a boil, and season with salt and pepper, then lower the heat, cover the pan, and simmer gently for 10 minutes, or until the meat is nearly tender.

VARIATION
Strips of chicken breast meat can be used in this recipe instead of the lean pork tenderloin.

4 Preheat the oven to 325°F. Cook the rice in plenty of lightly salted boiling water for 8 minutes, or until three-fourths cooked. Drain well. Spread half the rice over the base of a buttered, earthenware dish. Using a slotted spoon, make a neat layer of the meat and vegetables on top, then spread over the remaining rice.

5 Stir the cream and 2 tablespoons of the grated Parmesan into the liquid in which the pork was cooked. Tip into a pitcher, then carefully pour the cream mixture over the rice, and sprinkle with the remaining Parmesan. Cover with foil, and bake for 20 minutes, then remove the foil, and cook for 5 minutes more, until the top is lightly brown.

Energy 490Kcal/2040kJ; Protein 31.7g; Carbohydrate 33.3g, of which sugars 3g; Fat 73.9g, of which saturates 10.2g; Cholesterol 91mg; Calcium 342mg; Fiber 0.6g; Sodium 340mg.

PORK COOKED in HARD CIDER with PARSLEY DUMPLINGS

Pork and fruit are a perfect combination. If you don't want to make dumplings, serve creamy mashed potatoes with the stew.

SERVES 6

½ cup pitted prunes,
    coarsely chopped
½ cup ready-to-eat dried apricots,
    coarsely chopped
1¼ cups hard cider
2 tablespoons all-purpose flour
1½ pounds lean boneless pork, cut
    into cubes
2 tablespoons vegetable oil
12 ounces onions, coarsely chopped
2 garlic cloves, crushed
6 celery stalks, coarsely chopped
2 cups stock
12 juniper berries, lightly crushed
2 tablespoons chopped fresh thyme
15-ounce can black-eyed
    peas, drained
salt and ground black pepper

For the dumplings
1 cup self-rising flour
scant ½ cup vegetable suet
3 tablespoons chopped fresh parsley
6 tablespoons water

1 Preheat the oven to 350°F. Place the coarsely chopped prunes and dried apricots in a small bowl. Pour over the hard cider, and leave to soak for at least 20 minutes.

VARIATION
This recipe can also be made with lean lamb—leg steaks or diced shoulder would be ideal cuts to choose. Omit the juniper berries, try cannellini beans in place of the black-eyed peas, and use red onions rather than brown ones.

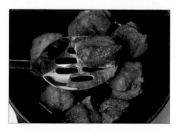

2 Season the flour, then toss the pork in the flour to coat. Reserve any leftover flour. Heat the oil in a large, flameproof casserole. Brown the meat, in batches, adding a little more oil if necessary. Remove the meat with a slotted spoon, and drain on paper towels.

3 Add the onions, garlic, and celery to the casserole, and cook for 5 minutes. Add any reserved flour, and cook for 1 minute more.

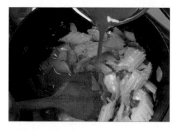

4 Blend in the stock until smooth. Add the hard cider and fruit, juniper berries, thyme, and plenty of seasoning. Bring to a boil, add the pork, cover tightly, and then cook in the oven for 50 minutes.

5 Just before the end of the cooking time, prepare the dumplings. Sift the flour into a large bowl, add a pinch of salt, then stir in the suet and chopped fresh parsley. Add the water gradually, and mix all the ingredients together to form a smooth, slightly sticky dough.

6 Remove the casserole from the oven, then stir in the black-eyed peas, and adjust the seasoning. Divide the dumpling mixture into six, form into rough rounds, and place on top of the stew. Return the casserole to the oven, then cover, and cook for 20–25 minutes more, or until the dumplings are cooked and the pork is tender.

COOK'S TIP
Black-eyed peas, or beans as they are called in Britain, are also sometimes referred to as cowpeas. They are a medium-size, cream-colored pea with a distinctive black spot or "eye" on the inner curve. They have a smooth, creamy texture and a subtle flavor. Black-eyed peas are a popular addition to soups and casseroles and are widely used in southern American cuisines.

Energy 468Kcal/1968kJ; Protein 32.6g; Carbohydrate 46.9g, of which sugars 21g; Fat 16.5g, of which saturates 5.9g; Cholesterol 71mg; Calcium 174mg; Fiber 8.2g; Sodium 437mg.

PORK TENDERLOIN with SPINACH and PUY LENTILS

Lean pork tenderloin, wrapped in spinach and cooked in a clay pot on a bed of tiny French green lentils, flavored with coconut.

SERVES 4

1¼–1½ pounds pork tenderloin
1 tablespoon sunflower-seed oil
1 tablespoon butter
8–12 large spinach leaves
1 onion, chopped
1 garlic clove, finely chopped
1-inch piece fresh ginger root,
    finely grated
1 fresh red chile, finely
    chopped (optional)
generous 1 cup Puy lentils
3 cups chicken or vegetable stock
scant 1 cup coconut cream
salt and ground black pepper

1 Soak a small clay pot in cold water for about 15 minutes, then drain. Cut the pork tenderloin widthwise into two equal pieces. Season the pork well with salt and ground black pepper.

2 Heat the sunflower-seed oil and butter in a large, heavy frying pan, add the pork tenderloin, and cook over high heat until browned on all sides. Remove the meat from the pan using a metal spatula, and set aside.

3 Meanwhile, add the spinach leaves to a large pan of boiling water, and cook for 1 minute, or until just wilted. Drain immediately in a colander, and refresh under cold running water. Drain well.

4 Lay the spinach leaves on the counter, overlapping them slightly to form a rectangle. Place the pork on top, and wrap the leaves around the pork to enclose it completely.

5 Add the onion to the oil in the frying pan, and cook for about 5 minutes, stirring occasionally, until softened. Add the chopped garlic, grated ginger, and finely chopped chile, if using, and cook for 1 minute more.

6 Add the lentils to the onion mixture in the frying pan, and then stir in the chicken or vegetable stock. Bring to a boil, then boil rapidly for 10 minutes. Remove the pan from the heat, and stir in the coconut cream until thoroughly blended. Transfer the onion and lentil mixture to the clay pot, and arrange the pork tenderloins on top.

7 Cover the clay pot, and place it in an unheated oven. Set the oven to 375°F, and cook for 45 minutes, or until the lentils and pork are cooked.

8 To serve, remove the spinach-wrapped pork tenderloins from the clay pot using a slotted spoon or tongs, and cut the pork into thick slices. Stir the lentils, and spoon them, with some of the cooking juices, onto warmed, individual plates, and top each portion with a few of the pork slices.

VARIATIONS
• Wrap the pork in slices of prosciutto, instead of the spinach leaves, and tie in place with string or secure with wooden toothpicks. Remove before slicing.
• Use 4 large chicken or duck breast portions in place of the pork tenderloin. Check the chicken or duck after about 30 minutes cooking time. Cut the breast portions into thick, diagonal slices to serve. The chicken would also be good wrapped with prosciutto.

Energy 399Kcal/1683kJ; Protein 42.3g; Carbohydrate 39.1g, of which sugars 5g; Fat 9.2g, of which saturates 4g; Cholesterol 87mg; Calcium 81mg; Fiber 3.5g; Sodium 206mg.

POTATO and SAUSAGE CASSEROLE

You will find numerous variations of this traditional supper dish throughout Ireland, but the basic ingredients are the same wherever you go—potatoes, sausages, and bacon.

2 Heat the oil in a frying pan, add the bacon, and cook for 2 minutes, stirring. Add the onions and cook for 5–6 minutes, until golden. Add the garlic and cook for 1 minute, then remove the mixture from the pan, and set aside.

3 Cook the sausages in the same pan for 5–6 minutes, until golden brown.

4 Arrange the potatoes in the base of the prepared dish. Spoon the bacon and onion mixture on top. Season to taste with salt and pepper, and sprinkle with the fresh sage. Pour in the stock, and top with the sausages. Cover and bake for about 1 hour, or until the potatoes and sausages are tender. Serve hot with crusty bread.

SERVES 4

1 tablespoon vegetable oil
4 bacon strips, cut into
    1-inch pieces
2 large onions, chopped
2 garlic cloves, crushed
8 large pork sausages
4 large baking potatoes, peeled and
    thinly sliced
1 tablespoon chopped fresh sage
1¼ cups vegetable stock
salt and ground black pepper
crusty bread, to serve

1 Preheat the oven to 350°F. Lightly grease a large, shallow earthenware baking dish, and set aside.

Energy 526Kcal/2201kJ; Protein 19.6g; Carbohydrate 53.4g, of which sugars 7.5g; Fat 27.4g, of which saturates 9.7g; Cholesterol 56mg; Calcium 71mg; Fiber 3.8g; Sodium 1214mg.

SAUSAGE POPOVER

This is one of those dishes that is classic comfort food—perfect for lifting the spirits on cold days. Use only the best sausages for this adult version, which includes chives.

SERVES 4–6

1½ cups all-purpose flour
2 tablespoons chopped fresh
    chives (optional)
2 eggs
1¼ cups milk
⅓ cup white vegetable fat
1 pound good quality pork sausages, such
    as Cumberland sausages
salt and ground black pepper

VARIATION

For a young children's supper, make small, individual sausage popovers: omit the chopped fresh chives from the batter and cook small cocktail sausages in muffin pans until golden. Add the batter and cook for 10–15 minutes, or until puffed and golden brown.

1 Preheat the oven to 425°F. Sift the flour into a bowl with a pinch of salt and pepper. Make a well in the center of the flour. Whisk the chives, if using, with the eggs and milk, then pour this into the well in the flour. Gradually whisk the flour into the liquid to make a smooth batter. Cover, and leave to stand for at least 30 minutes.

2 Put the vegetable fat into a small roasting pan, and place in the oven for 3–5 minutes, until very hot. Add the sausages, and cook for 15 minutes. Turn the sausages twice during cooking.

3 Pour the batter over the sausages, and cook for about 20 minutes, or until the batter is risen and golden. Serve immediately.

Energy 448Kcal/1071kJ; Protein 15.6g; Carbohydrate 33.1g, of which sugars 4.9g; Fat 29.2g, of which saturates 11.7g; Cholesterol 111mg; Calcium 188mg; Fiber 1.7g; Sodium 692mg.

ROAST LAMB with BEANS and GREEN PEPPERCORNS

Roasting the lamb slowly on a bed of beans results in a dish that combines meltingly tender meat with vegetables all in one pot.

SERVES 6

8–10 garlic cloves, peeled
4–4½ pounds leg of lamb
2 tablespoons olive oil
14 ounces spinach leaves
14-ounce can small cannellini or
    navy beans, drained
14-ounce can lima beans, drained
2 large, fresh rosemary sprigs, plus extra
    to garnish
1–2 tablespoons drained, bottled
    green peppercorns

1 Preheat the oven to 300°F. Set four garlic cloves aside, and slice the rest lengthwise into three or four pieces. Make shallow slits in the skin of the lamb, and insert a piece of garlic in each.

2 Heat the olive oil in a heavy, shallow flameproof casserole or a roasting pan that is large enough to hold the leg of lamb. Add the reserved garlic cloves and the fresh spinach leaves to the casserole or pan, and cook over medium heat, stirring occasionally, for 4–5 minutes, or until the spinach is wilted.

3 Add the beans, and tuck the rosemary sprigs and peppercorns among them. Place the lamb on top, then cover the casserole or roasting pan with foil or a lid. Roast the lamb for 3–4 hours, until it is cooked to your taste. Serve the lamb and beans hot, garnished with the remaining fresh rosemary sprigs.

Energy 705Kcal/2945kJ; Protein 74.3g; Carbohydrate 22.2g, of which sugars 4.2g; Fat 35.9g, of which saturates 15.4g; Cholesterol 246mg; Calcium 186mg; Fiber 8.7g; Sodium 775mg.

MIDDLE-EASTERN ROAST LAMB
and POTATOES

When the Eastern aroma of the garlic and saffron comes wafting out of the oven, this
deliciously garlicky lamb won't last very long.

SERVES 6–8

6 pounds leg of lamb
4 garlic cloves, halved
4 tablespoons olive oil
juice of 1 lemon
2–3 saffron threads, soaked in
   1 tablespoon boiling water
1 teaspoon mixed dried herbs, oregano,
   or marjoram
1 pound small baking potatoes,
   thickly sliced
2 large or 4 small onions,
   thickly sliced
salt and ground black pepper
fresh thyme, to garnish

1 Make eight evenly spaced incisions in the leg of lamb, press the halved garlic cloves into the slits, and place the lamb in a large nonmetallic dish.

2 Combine the olive oil, lemon juice, saffron mixture, and herbs. Rub over the lamb, and marinate for 2 hours.

3 Preheat the oven to 350°F. Layer the potato and onion slices in a large roasting pan. Lift the lamb out of the marinade, and place it on top of the sliced potato and onions, fat side up, and season well with plenty of salt and ground black pepper.

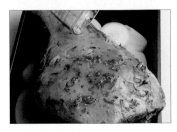

4 Pour the marinade over the lamb, then roast for 2 hours, basting occasionally. Remove from the oven, and cover with foil, then let rest for 10 minutes before carving. Garnish with thyme.

Energy 719Kcal/2997kJ; Protein 74.4g; Carbohydrate 13g, of which sugars 3.5g; Fat 41.2g, of which saturates 17.7g; Cholesterol 282mg; Calcium 33mg; Fiber 1.3g; Sodium 169mg.

LAMB SHANKS with BEANS and HERBS

A hearty winter meal, the lamb shanks are slowly cooked in a clay pot until tender on a bed of tasty beans and vegetables.

SERVES 4

1 cup dried cannellini beans, soaked
   overnight in cold water
⅔ cup water
3 tablespoons olive oil
4 large lamb shanks, about 8 ounces each
1 large onion, chopped
1 pound carrots, cut into thick chunks
2 celery stalks, cut into thick chunks
1 pound tomatoes, cut into fourths
1 cup vegetable stock
4 fresh rosemary sprigs
2 bay leaves
salt and ground black pepper

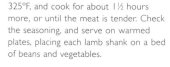

1 Soak a large clay pot in cold water for 20 minutes, then drain. Drain, and rinse the cannellini beans, place in a large pan of unsalted boiling water, and boil rapidly for 10 minutes, then drain.

2 Place the ⅔ cup water in the soaked clay pot, and then add the drained cannellini beans.

3 Heat 2 tablespoons of the olive oil in a large frying pan, add the lamb shanks, and cook over high heat, turning the lamb shanks occasionally, until brown on all sides. Remove the lamb shanks with a slotted spoon, and set aside.

4 Add the remaining oil to the pan, then add the onion, and sauté for 5 minutes, until soft and translucent.

5 Add the carrots and celery to the pan, and cook for 2–3 minutes. Stir in the tomatoes and vegetable stock, and mix thoroughly. Transfer the vegetable mixture to the clay pot, and season well with salt and pepper, then add the fresh rosemary and bay leaves, and stir again to combine.

6 Place the lamb shanks in a layer on top of the beans and vegetables. Cover the clay pot, and place it in an unheated oven. Set the oven to 425°F, and cook for about 30 minutes, or until the liquid is bubbling.

7 Reduce the oven temperature to 325°F, and cook for about 1½ hours more, or until the meat is tender. Check the seasoning, and serve on warmed plates, placing each lamb shank on a bed of beans and vegetables.

COOK'S TIP

Lamb shanks are small cuts from the lower end of the leg. One shank is an ideal-sized portion for one. Until recently you would have had to order them from the butcher, but they are now becoming increasingly available from larger supermarkets. To obtain a tender result, shanks should be cooked for a long time at a low heat.

VARIATIONS

• Dried lima beans or the smaller navy beans can be used in place of the cannellini beans.

• If you like, two 14-ounce cans cannellini beans can be used in this dish—simply place the drained beans in the soaked clay pot with the water, and continue from step 3.

• A variety of other root vegetables would work well in this recipe—try chopped rutabaga, sweet potatoes, butternut squash, parsnips, or celery root instead of the carrots. In spring, a mixture of baby turnips and baby carrots would also be good.

Energy 743Kcal/3121kJ; Protein 79.2g; Carbohydrate 39.7g, of which sugars 18.7g; Fat 30.9g, of which saturates 10.1g; Cholesterol 225mg; Calcium 127mg; Fiber 12.3g; Sodium 200mg.

LAMB with TOMATOES and BELL PEPPERS

Select lean tender lamb from the leg for this lightly spiced curry with juicy bell peppers and wedges of onion. Serve warm nan bread to mop up the tomato-rich juices.

3 Cut two of the onions into wedges (six from each onion), and add to the oil remaining in the pan. Cook the onions over medium heat for 10 minutes, or until they are beginning to color. Add the bell peppers, and cook for 5 minutes. Use a slotted spoon to remove the vegetables from the pan, and set aside.

4 Meanwhile, chop the remaining onion. Add it to the oil remaining in the pan with the garlic, chile, and ginger, and cook for 4–5 minutes, stirring frequently, until the onion has softened.

5 Stir in the curry paste and canned tomatoes with the reserved yogurt. Return the lamb to the pan, season, and stir well. Bring to a boil, then reduce the heat, and simmer for 30 minutes.

SERVES 6

3¼ pounds lean boneless lamb, cubed
1 cup plain yogurt
2 tablespoons sunflower-seed oil
3 onions
2 red bell peppers, seeded and cut
   into chunks
3 garlic cloves, finely chopped
1 fresh red chile, seeded and chopped
1-inch piece fresh ginger root, peeled and
   chopped
2 tablespoons mild curry paste
2 × 14-ounce cans chopped tomatoes
large pinch of saffron threads
1¾ pounds plum tomatoes, halved,
   seeded, and cut into chunks
salt and ground black pepper
chopped fresh cilantro,
   to garnish

1 Mix the lamb with the yogurt in a bowl. Cover, and chill for about 1 hour.

2 Heat the oil in a large pan. Drain the lamb, and reserve the yogurt, then cook the lamb, in batches, until it is golden on all sides—this will take about 15 minutes in total. Remove the lamb from the pan using a slotted spoon, and set aside.

6 Pound the saffron to a powder in a mortar, then stir in a little boiling water to dissolve the saffron. Add this liquid to the curry and stir well. Return the onion and bell pepper mixture to the pan, then stir in the fresh tomatoes. Bring the curry back to simmering point and cook for 15 minutes. Garnish with chopped fresh cilantro to serve.

Energy 559Kcal/2343kJ; Protein 54.4g; Carbohydrate 20.5g, of which sugars 18.8g; Fat 29.6g, of which saturates 13.5g; Cholesterol 191mg; Calcium 139mg; Fiber 4.6g; Sodium 278mg.

BRAISED SHOULDER of LAMB with PEARL BARLEY and BABY VEGETABLES

In this wonderful, slow-cooked stew, the pearl barley absorbs all the rich meat juices and stock to become full-flavored and nutty in texture when cooked.

SERVES 4

4 tablespoons olive oil
1 large onion, chopped
2 garlic cloves, chopped
2 celery stalks, sliced
a little all-purpose flour
1½ pounds boneless shoulder of lamb, cut
    into cubes
3¾–4 cups lamb stock
⅔ cup pearl barley
8 ounces baby carrots
8 ounces baby turnips
salt and ground black pepper
2 tablespoons chopped fresh marjoram,
    to garnish

1 Heat 3 tablespoons of the oil in a flameproof casserole. Cook the onion and garlic until softened, add the celery, then cook until the vegetables brown.

2 Season the flour, and toss the lamb in it. Use a slotted spoon to remove the vegetables from the casserole.

3 Add and heat the remaining oil with the juices in the casserole. Cook the lamb, in batches, until brown. When all the meat is browned, return it to the casserole with the onion mixture. Stir in 3¾ cups of the stock. Add the pearl barley. Cover, then bring to a boil, reduce the heat, and simmer for 1 hour, or until the pearl barley and lamb are completely tender.

4 Add the baby carrots and turnips to the casserole for the final 15 minutes of cooking. Stir the meat occasionally during cooking, and add the remaining stock, if necessary. Stir in seasoning to taste, and serve piping hot, garnished with marjoram. Warm, crusty bread would make a good accompaniment.

Energy 565Kcal/2364kJ; Protein 37.2g; Carbohydrate 37.2g, of which sugars 11g; Fat 30.9g, of which saturates 10.4g; Cholesterol 128mg; Calcium 85mg; Fiber 3.9g; Sodium 180mg.

BRAISED LAMB with APRICOTS and HERB DUMPLINGS

A rich and fruity lamb casserole, topped with light, herbed dumplings, which is delicious served with baked potatoes and broccoli.

SERVES 6

2 tablespoons sunflower-seed oil
1½ pounds lean lamb
    tenderloin, cut into
    1-inch cubes
12 ounces pearl onions, peeled
1 garlic clove, crushed
3 cups white mushrooms
¾ cup small ready-to-eat
    dried apricots
1 cup well-flavored lamb or
    beef stock
1 cup red wine
1 tablespoon tomato paste
salt and ground black pepper
fresh herb sprigs,
    to garnish

For the dumplings
1 cup self-rising flour
scant ½ cup shredded
    vegetable suet
1–2 tablespoons chopped fresh
    mixed herbs

1 Preheat the oven to 325°F. Heat the oil in a large, flameproof casserole, add the lamb, and cook over high heat until browned all over, stirring occasionally. Remove the meat from the casserole using a slotted spoon, then set aside, and keep warm.

2 Reduce the heat slightly, then add the pearl onions, crushed garlic, and whole mushrooms to the oil remaining in the casserole, and cook them gently for about 5 minutes, stirring occasionally with a wooden spoon.

3 Return the meat to the casserole, then add the dried apricots, stock, wine, and tomato paste. Season to taste with salt and pepper, and stir to mix.

4 Bring to a boil, stirring, then remove the casserole from the heat, and cover. Transfer the casserole to the oven, and cook for 1½–2 hours, until the lamb is cooked and tender, stirring once or twice during the cooking time and adding a little extra stock, if necessary.

5 Meanwhile, make the dumplings. Place the flour, suet, herbs, and seasoning in a bowl, and stir to mix. Add enough cold water to make a soft, elastic dough. Divide the dough into small, marble-size pieces and, using lightly floured hands, roll each piece into a small ball.

6 Remove the lid from the casserole, and place the dumplings on top of the braised lamb and vegetables.

7 Increase the oven temperature to 375°F. Return the casserole to the oven, and cook for 20–25 minutes more, until the herb dumplings are cooked. Serve immediately, garnished with the fresh herb sprigs.

VARIATIONS
Use lean beef or pork in place of the lamb, and substitute shallots for the pearl onions, if you like.

Energy 499Kcal/2091kJ; Protein 28.5g; Carbohydrate 36.7g, of which sugars 20.2g; Fat 24.4g, of which saturates 10.1g; Cholesterol 86mg; Calcium 132mg; Fiber 4.8g; Sodium 277mg.

ITALIAN LAMB MEATBALLS with CHILI TOMATO SAUCE

Serve these piquant Italian-style meatballs with pasta and leafy salad greens. Sprinkle with a little grated Parmesan cheese for that extra Italian touch.

SERVES 4

1 pound lean ground lamb
1 large onion, grated
1 garlic clove, crushed
1 cup fresh white bread crumbs
1 tablespoon chopped fresh parsley
1 medium egg, lightly beaten
2 tablespoons olive oil
salt and ground black pepper
4 tablespoons finely grated Parmesan
     cheese and arugula leaves, to serve

For the sauce
1 onion, finely chopped
14-ounce can chopped tomatoes
scant 1 cup bottled strained tomatoes
1 teaspoon granulated sugar
2 fresh green chiles, seeded and
     finely chopped
2 tablespoons chopped fresh oregano
salt and ground black pepper

1 Soak a small clay pot in cold water for 15 minutes, then drain. Place the ground lamb, onion, garlic, bread crumbs, parsley, and seasoning in a bowl and mix well. Add the beaten egg, and mix to bind the meatball mixture together.

2 Shape the mixture into 20 small, even-size balls. Heat the olive oil in a frying pan, add the meatballs, and cook over high heat, stirring occasionally, until they are browned all over.

VARIATIONS
Lean ground beef or bulk sausage can be used in place of the ground lamb in this dish.

3 Meanwhile, to make the sauce, combine the onion, chopped tomatoes, bottled strained tomatoes, sugar, chopped chiles, and oregano. Season well, and pour the sauce into the clay pot.

4 Place the meatballs in the sauce, then cover, and place in an unheated oven. Set the oven to 400°F, and cook for 1 hour, stirring after 30 minutes. Serve with Parmesan cheese and arugula.

Energy 443Kcal/1853kJ; Protein 33.1g; Carbohydrate 22.5g, of which sugars 11.1g; Fat 25.3g, of which saturates 10.3g; Cholesterol 148mg; Calcium 246mg; Fiber 3g; Sodium 389mg.

FRAGRANT LAMB CURRY
with CARDAMOM-SPICED RICE

Wonderfully aromatic, this Indian-style lamb biriani, with the meat and rice cooked together, is a delicious meal in itself.

SERVES 4

1 large onion, cut into fourths
2 garlic cloves
1 small fresh green chile, halved
    and seeded
2-inch piece fresh ginger root
1 tablespoon ghee
1 tablespoon vegetable oil
1½ pounds boneless shoulder or leg of
    lamb, cut into chunks
1 tablespoon ground coriander
2 teaspoons ground cumin
1 cinnamon stick, broken into 3 pieces
⅔ cup thick plain yogurt
⅔ cup water
⅓ cup ready-to-eat dried apricots,
    cut into chunks
salt and ground black pepper

For the rice

1¼ cups basmati rice
6 cardamom pods, split open
2 tablespoons butter, cut into small pieces
3 tablespoons toasted cashew nuts or
    sliced almonds

For the garnish

1 onion, sliced and fried until golden
a few fresh cilantro sprigs

1 Soak a large clay pot in cold water for 20 minutes, then drain. Place the onion, garlic, chile, and ginger in a food processor or blender, and process with 1 tablespoon water, to a smooth paste.

COOK'S TIP

Serve a cooling yogurt raita and a fresh fruit chutney or relish as an accompaniment.

2 Heat the ghee and vegetable oil in a heavy frying pan. Cook the lamb chunks, in batches, over high heat until golden brown. Remove from the pan using a slotted spoon, and set aside.

3 Add the onion paste to the remaining oil left in the pan, stir in the ground coriander and cumin, add the cinnamon stick pieces, and cook for 1–2 minutes, stirring constantly with a wooden spoon.

4 Return the meat to the pan, then gradually add the yogurt, a spoonful at a time, stirring well between each addition with a wooden spoon. Season the meat well with plenty of salt and pepper, and stir in the water.

5 Transfer the contents of the frying pan to the prepared clay pot, cover with the lid, and place the pot in an unheated oven. Set the oven to 350°F, and cook for 45 minutes.

6 Meanwhile, prepare the basmati rice. Place it in a bowl, cover with cold water, and leave to soak for 20 minutes. Drain the rice, and place it in a large pan of boiling salted water, bring back to a boil, and cook for 10 minutes. Drain, and stir in the split cardamom pods.

7 Remove the clay pot from the oven, and stir in the chopped ready-to-eat apricots. Pile the cooked rice on top of the lamb, and dot with the butter. Drizzle over 4 tablespoons water, then sprinkle the cashew nuts or sliced almonds on top. Cover the pot, reduce the oven temperature to 300°F, and cook the meat and rice for 30 minutes.

8 Remove the lid from the pot, and fluff up the rice with a fork. Spoon into warmed individual bowls, then sprinkle over the fried onion slices, and garnish with the sprigs of fresh cilantro.

Energy 769Kcal/3208kJ; Protein 43.6g; Carbohydrate 67.6g, of which sugars 14.5g; Fat 36.2g, of which saturates 15g; Cholesterol 142mg; Calcium 134mg; fl 2.6g; Sodium 252mg.

LAMB and CARROT CASSEROLE with BARLEY

Barley and carrots make natural partners for lamb and mutton. In this convenient casserole, the barley supplements the meat and adds to the flavor and texture, as well as thickening the sauce. The dish is comfort food at its best. Serve with boiled or baked potatoes and a green vegetable, such as spring cabbage.

SERVES 6

1 pound stewing lamb
1 tablespoon oil
2 onions, sliced
1½ pounds carrots, thickly sliced
4–6 celery sticks, sliced
3 tablespoons pearl barley, rinsed
stock or water
salt and ground black pepper
chopped fresh parsley, to garnish

1 Trim the lamb, and cut it into bitesize pieces. Heat the oil in a flameproof casserole, and brown the lamb.

2 Add the vegetables to the casserole, and fry them briefly with the meat. Add the barley and enough stock or water to cover, and season to taste.

3 Cover the casserole, and simmer gently or cook in a slow oven, 300°F for 1–1½ hours, until the meat is tender. Add extra stock or water during cooking if necessary. Serve garnished with the chopped fresh parsley.

COOK'S TIP
Tougher cuts of meat cook more evenly if they are cut into small, even-size cubes; 1 inch is ideal. They should be slightly larger than the vegetables being cooked in the stew because these will take a little longer to cook than the meat. Although excess fat should be removed, some marbling is useful for keeping the meat moist. Any excess fat can be skimmed off after cooking.

Energy 304Kcal/1263kJ; Protein 23.2g; Carbohydrate 13g, of which sugars 11.3g; Fat 18g, of which saturates 7.5g; Cholesterol 84mg; Calcium 53mg; Fiber 3.6g; Sodium 110mg

LAMB and PUMPKIN COUSCOUS

Pumpkin is a very popular Moroccan ingredient, and this is a traditional couscous recipe,
with echoes of the very early vegetable couscous dishes made by the Berbers.

SERVES 4–6

½ cup garbanzo beans, soaked overnight
 and drained
1½ pounds lean lamb
2 large onions, sliced
pinch of saffron threads
¼ teaspoon ground ginger
½ teaspoon ground turmeric
1 teaspoon ground black pepper
5 cups water
1 pound carrots
1½ pounds pumpkin
⅔ cup raisins
2¼ cups couscous
salt
fresh parsley sprigs, to garnish

1 Place the garbanzo beans in a large
pan of boiling water. Boil for 10 minutes,
then reduce the heat, and cook for
1–1½ hours, until tender. Place in cold
water, and remove the skins by rubbing
with your fingers. Drain.

2 Cut the lamb into bitesize pieces,
place in the pan with the sliced onions,
and add the saffron, ginger, turmeric,
pepper, and salt. Pour in the water, and
stir well, then slowly bring to a boil.
Cover the pan, and simmer for about
1 hour, until the meat is tender.

3 Peel or scrape the carrots, and cut
them into large chunks. Cut the pumpkin
into 1-inch cubes, discarding the skin,
seeds, and pith.

4 Stir the carrots, pumpkin, and raisins
into the meat mixture with the
garbanzos, cover the pan, and simmer
for 30–35 minutes more, stirring
occasionally, until the vegetables and
meat are completely tender.

5 Meanwhile, prepare the couscous
according to the instructions on the
package, and steam on top of the stew,
then fork lightly to fluff up. Spoon the
couscous onto a warmed serving plate,
add the stew, and stir the stew into the
couscous. Extra gravy can be served
separately. Sprinkle some tiny sprigs
of fresh parsley over the top, and
serve immediately.

Energy 725Kcal/3034kJ; Protein 34.8g; Carbohydrate 115.4g, of which sugars 69.5g; Fat 16.6g, of which saturates 6.0g; Cholesterol 86mg; Calcium 282mg; Fiber 21.5g; Sodium 297mg.

OSSO BUCCO with RISOTTO MILANESE

Two one-pot dishes in one recipe, both so utterly delicious that it seemed churlish to omit them from this collection. Osso Bucco is a traditional Milanese veal stew and is classically accompanied by this saffron-scented risotto.

SERVES 4

¼ cup butter
1 tablespoon olive oil
1 large onion, chopped
1 leek, finely chopped
3 tablespoons all-purpose flour
4 large portions of veal shanks, hind cut
2½ cups dry white wine
salt and ground black pepper

For the risotto
2 tablespoons butter
1 onion, finely chopped
1¾ cups risotto rice
4 cups chicken stock
½ teaspoon saffron threads
4 tablespoons white wine
⅔ cup freshly grated
    Parmesan cheese

For the gremolata
grated rind of 1 lemon
2 tablespoons chopped fresh parsley
1 garlic clove, finely chopped

1 Heat the butter and oil until sizzling in a large, heavy frying pan. Add the onion and leek, and cook gently for about 5 minutes. Season the flour and toss the veal in it, then add to the pan, and cook over high heat until it browns.

2 Gradually stir in the wine, and heat until simmering. Cover the pan, and simmer for 1½ hours, stirring occasionally. Use a slotted spoon to transfer the veal to a warmed serving dish, then boil the sauce over high heat until it is reduced and thickened to the required consistency.

3 Make the risotto about 30 minutes before the end of the cooking time for the stew. Melt the butter in a large pan, and cook the onion until softened.

4 Stir in the rice to coat all the grains in butter. Add a ladleful of boiling chicken stock, and mix well. Continue adding the boiling stock a ladleful at a time, letting each portion be completely absorbed before adding the next.

5 Pound the saffron threads in a mortar, then stir in the wine. Add the saffron-scented wine to the risotto, and cook for a final 5 minutes. Remove the pan from the heat, and stir in the Parmesan.

6 Combine the lemon rind, chopped parsley, and garlic for the gremolata. Spoon some risotto onto each plate, then add some veal. Sprinkle each with a little gremolata, and serve immediately.

Energy 899Kcal/3754kJ; Protein 46.3g; Carbohydrate 90.6g, of which sugars 7.1g; Fat 27.4g, of which saturates 14.2g; Cholesterol 178mg; Calcium 249mg; Fiber 2.4g; Sodium 427mg.

OSTRICH STEW with SWEET POTATOES and GARBANZO BEANS

Lean and firm, ostrich meat marries well with the soft-textured sweet potatoes and garbanzo beans in this quick and easy, rich-flavored stew.

SERVES 4

3 tablespoons olive oil
1 large onion, chopped
2 garlic cloves, finely chopped
1½ pounds ostrich fillet, cut into
    short strips
1 pound sweet potatoes, peeled
    and diced
2 × 14-ounce cans chopped tomatoes
14-ounce can garbanzo beans, drained
salt and ground black pepper
fresh oregano, to garnish

COOK'S TIP
Steamed couscous is a quick and easy accompaniment to this healthy stew, but it would also be good served with rice, or simply some warm, crusty bread.

1 Heat half the olive oil in a flameproof casserole. Add the chopped onion and garlic, and cook over medium heat, stirring occasionally, for about 5 minutes, or until softened but not colored. Remove from the casserole using a slotted spoon, and set aside. Add the remaining oil to the casserole, and heat.

2 Cook the meat, in batches, over high heat until browned. When the last batch is cooked, replace the meat and onions, and stir in the potatoes, tomatoes, and garbanzos. Bring to a boil, reduce the heat, and simmer for 25 minutes, or until the meat is tender. Season, and serve, garnished with the fresh oregano.

Energy 639Kcal/2682kJ; Protein 19g; Carbohydrate 51.2g, of which sugars 16.5g; Fat 27.9g, of which saturates 8.2g; Cholesterol 98mg; Calcium 108mg; Fiber 9.7g; Sodium 393mg.

SLOW COOKER VEGETARIAN AND SIDE DISHES

Just because you follow a vegetarian diet doesn't
mean you need to miss out on fabulous-tasting food.
This chapter makes use of all kinds of wonderful vegetables,
beans, and grains to make fabulous
slow-cooked main meals that will appeal just as much
to meat-eaters as they do to vegetarians. Try rich and creamy
Rosemary Risotto with Borlotti Beans, or aromatic Vegetable
Kashmiri for a hearty main meal. If you are looking for a
special side dish, why not try Potato, Onion, and Garlic
Gratin, or Spicy Tamarind Garbanzo Beans. Whatever you are
in the mood for, you are sure to find the perfect
meat-free recipe in this chapter.

MUSHROOM and FENNEL HOT-POT

Hearty and richly flavored, this tasty stew makes a marvelous vegetarian main dish, but it can also be served as an accompaniment to meat dishes. Dried mushrooms swell up a great deal after soaking, so a little goes a long way in terms of both flavor and quantity.

SERVES 4

½ cup dried shiitake mushrooms
1 small head of fennel
2 tablespoons olive oil
12 shallots, peeled
3 cups white mushrooms, trimmed
   and halved
1 cup dry hard cider
½ cup sun-dried tomatoes
½ cup sun-dried tomato paste
1 bay leaf
salt and ground black pepper
chopped fresh parsley,
   to garnish

1 Place the dried shiitake mushrooms in a heatproof bowl. Pour over just enough hot water to cover them, and leave to soak for about 15 minutes. Meanwhile, trim and slice the fennel.

2 Heat the oil in a heavy pan. Add the shallots and fennel, then sauté for about 10 minutes over a medium heat, until the vegetables are softened and just beginning to brown. Add the button mushrooms to the pan, and cook for a further 2–3 minutes, stirring occasionally.

3 Transfer the vegetable mixture to the ceramic cooking pot. Drain the shiitake mushrooms, adding 2 tablespoons of the soaking liquid to the cooking pot. Chop them, and add them to the pot.

4 Pour the cider into the pot, and stir in the sun-dried tomatoes and tomato paste. Add the bay leaf. Cover with the lid, and cook on high for 3–4 hours, or until the vegetables are tender.

5 Remove the bay leaf, and season to taste with salt and black pepper. Serve sprinkled with plenty of chopped parsley.

SWEET and SOUR MIXED-BEAN HOT-POT

This impressive-looking dish, topped with sliced potatoes, is incredibly easy, making the most of dried and canned ingredients from the kitchen pantry and combining them with a deliciously rich and tangy tomato sauce.

SERVES 6

3 tablespoons butter
4 shallots, peeled and finely chopped
⅓ cup all-purpose or whole-wheat flour
1¼ cups bottled strained tomatoes
½ cup unsweetened apple juice
4 tablespoons soft light brown sugar
4 tablespoons tomato ketchup
4 tablespoons dry sherry
4 tablespoons cider vinegar
4 tablespoons light soy sauce
14-ounce can lima beans
14-ounce can small cannellini beans
14-ounce can garbanzo beans
6 ounces green beans, cut into
    1-inch lengths
3 cups mushrooms, sliced
1 pound unpeeled potatoes
1 tablespoon olive oil
1 tablespoon chopped fresh thyme
1 tablespoon fresh marjoram
salt and ground black pepper
fresh herbs, to garnish

3 Rinse the beans, and drain well. Place them in the ceramic cooking pot with the green beans and mushrooms, and pour over the sauce. Stir well, then cover with the lid, and cook on high for 3 hours.

4 Meanwhile, thinly slice the potatoes, and parboil them for 4 minutes. Drain well, then toss them in the oil so that they are lightly coated all over.

5 Stir the fresh herbs into the bean mixture, and season with salt and pepper. Arrange the potato slices on top of the beans, overlapping them slightly so that they completely cover them. Cover the pot, and cook for a further 2 hours, or until the potatoes are tender.

6 Place the ceramic cooking pot under a medium broiler, and cook for 4–5 minutes to brown the potato topping. Serve garnished with herbs.

1 Melt the butter in a pan, add the shallots, and fry gently for 5–6 minutes, until softened. Add the flour, and cook for 1 minute, stirring all the time, then gradually stir in the tomatoes.

2 Add the apple juice, sugar, tomato ketchup, sherry, vinegar, and light soy sauce to the pan, and stir in. Bring the mixture to the boil, stirring constantly until it thickens.

VARIATIONS
• You can vary the proportions and types of beans used, depending on what you have in the pantry. Kidney beans and borlotti beans would work well and can be either interchanged with any of the beans used here, or combined with them.
• Try using snow peas or sugar snap peas in place of the green beans, if you prefer.

Energy 483Kcal/2042kJ; Protein 18.5g; Carbohydrate 73.3g, of which sugars 24.8g; Fat 13.8g, of which saturates 4.5g; Cholesterol 14mg; Calcium 134mg; Fiber 10.9g; Sodium 826mg.

ROOT VEGETABLE CASSEROLE with CARAWAY DUMPLINGS

Stirring soft cheese into the cooking juices gives this incredibly easy casserole a wonderfully creamy richness, while thickening and flavoring it at the same time. Light zucchini dumplings spiced with caraway complete the meal.

SERVES 3

1¼ cups dry hard cider
¾ cup boiling vegetable stock
2 leeks
2 carrots
2 small parsnips
8 ounces potatoes
1 sweet potato, weighing about 6 ounces
1 bay leaf
1½ teaspoons cornstarch
4 ounces full-fat soft cheese with garlic and herbs
salt and ground black pepper

For the dumplings
1 cup self-rising flour
1 teaspoon caraway seeds
½ cup shredded vegetable suet (chilled, grated shortening
1 zucchini, grated
about 5 tablespoons cold water

1 Reserve 1 tablespoon of the cider, and pour the rest into the ceramic cooking pot with the stock. Cover with the lid, and switch the slow cooker to high.

2 Meanwhile, prepare the vegetables. Trim the leeks, and cut into ¾-inch slices. Peel the carrots, parsnips, potatoes, and sweet potato, and cut into ¾-inch chunks.

3 Add the vegetables to the ceramic cooking pot with the bay leaf. Cover with the lid, and cook for 3 hours.

4 In a small bowl, blend the cornstarch with the reserved cider. Add the cheese, and mix together until combined, then gradually blend in a few spoonfuls of the cooking liquid. Pour over the vegetables, and stir until thoroughly mixed. Season with salt and black pepper. Cover, and cook for a further 1–2 hours, or until the vegetables are almost tender.

5 Toward the end of the cooking time, make the dumplings. Sift the flour into a bowl, and stir in the caraway seeds, suet, zucchini, salt, and black pepper. Stir in the water, adding a little more if necessary, to make a soft dough. With floured hands, shape the mixture into 12 dumplings, about the size of walnuts.

6 Carefully place the dumplings on top of the casserole, cover with the lid, and cook for a further hour, or until the vegetables and dumplings are cooked. Adjust the seasoning, and serve in warmed deep soup plates.

VARIATION
To make a non-vegetarian version of this dish, add some fried chopped bacon or pancetta to the pot with the vegetables.

Energy 616Kcal/2584kJ; Protein 11.9g; Carbohydrate 74.9g, of which sugars 17.1g; Fat 28.9g, of which saturates 15.9g; Cholesterol 35mg; Calcium 256mg; Fiber 9.5g; Sodium 369mg.

SPICY-HOT MIXED-BEAN CHILI
with CORNBREAD TOPPING

Inspired by traditional Texan cooking, this chili combines Tex-mex with classic Texan cornbread. The delicious topping offers the starch component of the dish, making this dish a filling one-pot meal with no need for accompaniments.

SERVES 4

generous ½ cup dried red
    kidney beans
generous ½ cup dried
    black-eyed peas
1 bay leaf
1 tablespoon vegetable oil
1 large onion, finely chopped
1 garlic clove, crushed
1 teaspoon ground cumin
1 teaspoon chili powder
1 teaspoon mild paprika
½ teaspoon dried marjoram
1 pound mixed vegetables such
    as potatoes, carrots, eggplants,
    parsnips, and celery
1 vegetable bouillon cube
14-ounce can chopped tomatoes
1 tablespoon tomato paste
salt and ground black pepper

For the cornbread topping
2¼ cups fine cornmeal
2 tablespoons whole-wheat flour
1½ teaspoons baking powder
1 egg, plus 1 egg yolk lightly beaten
1¼ cups milk

1 Put the dried beans in a large bowl, and pour over at least twice their volume of cold water. Leave to soak for at least 6 hours, or overnight.

2 Drain the beans, and rinse well, then place in a pan with 2½ cups of cold water and the bay leaf. Bring to the boil, and boil rapidly for 10 minutes. Turn off the heat, leave to cool for a few minutes, then tip into the ceramic cooking pot, and switch the slow cooker to high.

3 Heat the oil in a pan, add the onion and cook for 7–8 minutes. Add the garlic, cumin, chili powder, paprika, and marjoram, and cook for 1 minute. Tip into the ceramic cooking pot, and stir.

4 Prepare the vegetables, peeling or trimming them as necessary, then cut into ¾-inch chunks.

5 Add the vegetables to the mixture, making sure that those that may discolor, such as potatoes and parsnips, are submerged. It doesn't matter if the other vegetables are not completely covered. Cover with the lid, and cook for 3 hours, or until the beans are tender.

6 Add the bouillon cube and chopped tomatoes to the cooking pot, then stir in the tomato paste, and season with salt and ground black pepper. Replace the lid, and cook for a further 30 minutes, until the mixture is at boiling point.

7 To make the topping, combine the cornmeal, flour, baking powder, and a pinch of salt in a bowl. Make a well in the center, and add the egg, egg yolk, and milk. Mix, then spoon over the bean mixture. Cover, and cook for 1 hour, or until the topping is firm and cooked.

Energy 613Kcal/2595kJ; Protein 29.6g; Carbohydrate 97.4g, of which sugars 15.8g; Fat 14.5g, of which saturates 3.4g; Cholesterol 112mg; Calcium 257mg; Fiber 13.1g; Sodium 113mg.

SWEET PUMPKIN and PEANUT CURRY

Rich, sweet, spicy and fragrant, the flavors of this delicious Thai-style curry really come together with long, slow cooking. Serve with rice or noodles for a substantial supper dish.

3 Add the lime leaves, galangal, pumpkin and sweet potatoes to the cooking pot. Pour the stock and ⅔ cup of the coconut milk over the vegetables, and stir to combine. Cover with the lid and cook on high for 1½ hours.

4 Stir the mushrooms, soy sauce, and Thai fish sauce into the curry, then add the chopped peanuts, and pour in the remaining coconut milk. Cover, and cook on high for a further 3 hours, or until the vegetables are very tender.

5 Spoon the curry into warmed serving bowls, garnish with the pumpkin seeds and chiles, and serve immediately.

SERVES 4

2 tablespoons vegetable oil
4 garlic cloves, crushed
4 shallots, finely chopped
2 tablespoons yellow curry paste
1⅔ cups near-boiling vegetable stock
1¼ cups coconut milk
2 kaffir lime leaves, torn
1 tablespoon chopped fresh galangal
1 pound pumpkin, peeled, seeded, and diced
8 ounces sweet potatoes, diced
1½ cups cremini mushrooms, sliced
1 tablespoon soy sauce
2 tablespoons Thai fish sauce
scant 1 cup peanuts, roasted and chopped
⅓ cup pumpkin seeds, toasted, and fresh green chile flowers, to garnish

1 Heat the oil in a frying pan. Add the garlic and shallots, and cook over a medium heat, stirring occasionally, for 10 minutes, until softened and beginning to turn golden.

2 Add the yellow curry paste to the pan, and stir-fry over a medium heat for 30 seconds, until fragrant. Tip the mixture into the ceramic cooking pot.

COOK'S TIP
Fresh chile flowers make an impressive garnish for a special-occasion dinner, and will make the curry look authentically Thai. To make chile flowers, hold each chile by the stem and slit the chile in half lengthwise, keeping the stem end intact. Continue slitting the chile in the same way to make thin strips. Put the chiles in a bowl of iced water, and leave for several hours to curl up like flower petals.

Energy 337Kcal/1404kJ; Protein 10.3g; Carbohydrate 21.7g, of which sugars 10.8g; Fat 23.8g, of which saturates 4g; Cholesterol 0mg; Calcium 168mg; Fiber 5.1g; Sodium 554mg.

VEGETABLE KASHMIRI

Delicious vegetables cooked in a spicy and aromatic yogurt sauce make a lovely vegetarian main meal. You can use any combination of your favorite vegetables.

SERVES 4

2 teaspoons cumin seeds
8 black peppercorns
2 green cardamom pods, seeds only
2-inch cinnamon stick
½ teaspoon grated nutmeg
3 tablespoons vegetable oil
1 fresh green chile, seeded and chopped
1-inch piece of fresh ginger root, grated
1 teaspoon chili powder
½ teaspoon salt
2 large potatoes, cut into 1-inch chunks
8 ounces cauliflower florets
1⅔ cups boiling vegetable stock
⅔ cup strained plain yogurt
8 ounces okra, thickly sliced
toasted sliced almonds and
    sprigs of fresh cilantro,
    to garnish

4 In a bowl, stir a few spoonfuls of the hot stock into the yogurt, then pour over the vegetable mixture, and stir until thoroughly combined.

5 Add the okra to the pot, stir, cover, and cook for a further 1½–2 hours, or until all the vegetables are very tender.

6 Serve the curry straight from the ceramic cooking pot, or spoon into a warmed serving dish. Sprinkle with toasted almonds and fresh cilantro sprigs to garnish.

1 Put the cumin seeds, peppercorns, cardamom seeds, cinnamon stick, and nutmeg in a mortar or spice grinder, and grind to a fine powder.

2 Heat the oil in a frying pan, add the chile and ginger, and fry for 2 minutes, stirring all the time. Add the chili powder, salt, and ground spice mixture, and fry gently for 2–3 minutes, stirring constantly to prevent the spices from sticking to the pan.

3 Transfer the mixture to the ceramic cooking pot, and stir in the potatoes and cauliflower. Pour in the stock, cover with the lid, and cook on high for 2 hours.

Energy 294Kcal/1231kJ; Protein 9g; Carbohydrate 35.5g, of which sugars 7g; Fat 13.8g, of which saturates 4g; Cholesterol 6mg; Calcium 161mg; Fiber 5.1g; Sodium 427mg.

VEGETABLE and CASHEW NUT BIRYANI

Full of the flavors of India, this hearty supper dish is great for chilly winter evenings. The nuts add protein, and the combination of eggplant and parsnips is delicious.

SERVES 4

1 small eggplant, sliced
3 onions
2 garlic cloves
1-inch piece of fresh ginger root, peeled
about 4 tablespoons sunflower-seed oil
3 parsnips, chopped into ¾-inch pieces
1 teaspoon ground cumin
1 teaspoon ground coriander
½ teaspoon chili powder
3 cups boiling vegetable stock
1 red bell pepper, seeded and sliced
generous 1½ cups converted basmati or
    white rice
1½ cups unsalted cashew nuts
¼ cup golden raisins
salt and ground black pepper
2 hard-boiled eggs, quartered, and sprigs
    of fresh cilantro to garnish

1 Layer the eggplant slices in a strainer or colander, lightly sprinkle with salt, and leave to drain for 30 minutes. Rinse thoroughly under cold running water, pat dry, and cut into bitesize pieces.

2 Roughly chop one of the onions, and place in a food processor with the garlic and ginger. Add 3 tablespoons cold water, and process to a smooth paste.

3 Finely slice the remaining onions. Heat 2 tablespoons of the oil in a large frying pan, add the onions, and fry gently for 10–15 minutes, until they are soft and golden. Add the eggplant and parsnips, and cook for 3–4 minutes to soften. Transfer to the ceramic cooking pot.

4 Add 1 tablespoon oil to the pan, add the onion paste, and cook, stirring, for 3–4 minutes. Stir in the cumin, coriander, and chili powder and cook for 1 minute.

5 Gradually stir one-third of the stock into the pan, then transfer the mixture to the ceramic cooking pot, and switch the slow cooker to high. Add the remaining stock and the pepper, then season, and cover with the lid. Cook for 2–3 hours, or until the vegetables are almost tender.

6 Spoon the rice in a layer over the vegetables, then re-cover, and cook for 45 minutes–1 hour until the rice is tender and most of the stock has been absorbed. If the rice becomes too dry, add an extra 2 tablespoons stock.

7 Meanwhile, heat the remaining 1 tablespoon of oil in a clean frying pan, add the cashew nuts, and stir-fry for about 2 minutes. Add the golden raisins, and fry for a few seconds until they swell up. Remove the pan from the heat, and drain the nuts and raisins on paper towels.

8 Add half the cashew nuts and raisins to the vegetable rice, and gently fold in using a fork. Turn off the slow cooker, cover with the lid, and leave the biryani to stand for 5 minutes to finish cooking.

9 Spoon the vegetable biryani onto a warmed serving dish, and scatter with the remaining nuts and raisins. Garnish with quartered eggs and fresh cilantro, and serve immediately.

Energy 801Kcal/3360kJ; Protein 18.7g; Carbohydrate 103.4g, of which sugars 25.7g; Fat 37.6g, of which saturates 6.7g; Cholesterol 0mg; Calcium 129mg; Fiber 9.2g; Sodium 230mg.

PILAF with SAFFRON and PICKLED WALNUTS

Fragrant saffron gives this lovely rice dish a warm, spiced flavor and glorious color.
The pickled walnuts, which are available in large supermarkets and delicatessens, have a
strong, really distinctive flavor that goes well with the spices, pine nuts, and dried fruit.

SERVES 4

1 teaspoon saffron strands
½ cup pine nuts
3 tablespoons olive oil
1 large onion, finely chopped
3 garlic cloves, crushed
¼ teaspoon ground allspice
1½-inch piece fresh ginger root, grated
3 cups boiling vegetable stock
generous 1½ cups converted rice
½ cup pickled walnuts, drained and
    roughly chopped
¼ cup raisins
3 tablespoons roughly chopped fresh
    parsley or cilantro
salt and ground black pepper
parsley or cilantro leaves,
    to garnish
plain yogurt, to serve

1 Put the saffron strands in a heatproof bowl with 1 tablespoon boiling water, and leave to stand.

2 Meanwhile, heat a large frying pan and dry-fry the pine nuts until golden. Set them aside until needed.

COOK'S TIP

Saffron is the most expensive spice in the world because the stigmas of the saffron crocus have to be hand-picked. Ground turmeric makes a cheaper alternative and gives a similar golden-yellow color and warm flavor and aroma. Simply leave out step 1, and stir in ½ teaspoon ground turmeric with the allspice and the ginger.

3 Heat the oil in a pan, add the onion, and fry gently for 8 minutes. Stir in the garlic, allspice, and ginger, and cook for 2 minutes, stirring constantly. Transfer the mixture to the ceramic cooking pot.

4 Pour the boiling vegetable stock into the cooking pot, and stir to combine, then cover with the lid, and switch the slow cooker to high. Cook for 1 hour.

5 Sprinkle the rice into the cooking pot, then stir to mix thoroughly. Re-cover with the lid, and cook for 1 hour, or until the rice is almost tender and most of the stock has been absorbed. Add a little extra boiling stock or water to the pot if the mixture is already becoming dry.

6 Stir the saffron and soaking liquid into the rice, then add the pine nuts, pickled walnuts, raisins, and parsley or cilantro, and stir well to combine. Season to taste with salt and ground black pepper.

7 Re-cover the ceramic cooking pot with the lid, and cook for a further 15 minutes, until the rice is very tender and all the ingredients are completely warmed through. Garnish with fresh parsley or cilantro leaves, and provide a bowl of natural yogurt on the side for guests to serve themselves.

VARIATION

For a spicy mushroom pilaf, cook 3 sliced shallots in 1 tablespoon oil until soft. Stir in ½ teaspoon ground turmeric and 1 teaspoon each cumin and coriander. Transfer to the ceramic cooking pot. Add 3 cups hot vegetable stock. Cover with the lid, and cook on high for 30 minutes. Stir in a generous 1½ cups converted rice, and cook for 30 minutes. Fry 8 ounces mixed mushrooms in 1 ounce butter until soft, then stir into the ceramic cooking pot, and season to taste. Cook for a further 30 minutes, then serve.

Energy 585Kcal/2450kJ; Protein 10.2g; Carbohydrate 77.1g, of which sugars 11.1g; Fat 28.5g, of which saturates 3.1g; Cholesterol 0mg; Calcium 72mg; Fiber 2g; Sodium 222mg.

ROSEMARY RISOTTO with BORLOTTI BEANS

Using easy-cook Italian rice means that all the wine and stock can be added at the same time, rather than ladleful by ladleful, as with a traditional risotto. The gentle, constant heat of the slow cooker produces a delicious risotto that is still thick and creamy.

SERVES 3

14-ounce can borlotti beans
1 tablespoon butter
1 tablespoon olive oil
1 onion, finely chopped
2 garlic cloves, crushed
½ cup dry white wine
generous 1 cup converted Italian rice
3 cups boiling vegetable stock
4 tablespoons mascarpone cheese
1 teaspoon chopped fresh rosemary
¾ cup freshly grated Parmesan cheese,
   plus extra to serve (optional)
salt and ground black pepper

1 Drain the borlotti beans in a colander, rinse well under cold running water, and drain again. Place about two-thirds of the beans in a food processor or blender, and process to a coarse puree. Tip the remaining beans into a bowl, and set aside for later.

2 Heat the butter and oil in a pan, add the onion and garlic, and fry gently for 7–8 minutes until soft. Transfer the mixture to the ceramic cooking pot, and stir in the wine and bean puree. Cover with the lid, and cook on high for 1 hour.

3 Add the rice to the pot, then stir in the stock. Re-cover with the lid, and cook for about 45 minutes, stirring once halfway through cooking. The rice should be almost tender, and most of the stock should have been absorbed.

4 Stir the reserved beans, mascarpone, and rosemary into the risotto. Cover again with the lid, and cook for a further 15 minutes, until the rice is tender but still has a little bite.

5 Stir the Parmesan cheese into the risotto, and season to taste with salt and ground black pepper. Turn off the slow cooker, cover, and leave to stand for about 5 minutes, so that the risotto absorbs the flavors fully and the rice completes cooking.

6 Spoon the rice into warmed serving bowls, and serve immediately, sprinkled with extra Parmesan, if you like.

VARIATIONS
• Try using different herbs to vary the flavor. Fresh thyme or marjoram would make a good alternative to rosemary.
• To make a lower-fat version of this dish, use Quark cheese in place of the mascarpone. It offers the same creamy texture with much less fat.

Energy 651Kcal/2740kJ; Protein 25g; Carbohydrate 87g, of which sugars 4.6g; Fat 22.2g, of which saturates 10.5g; Cholesterol 41.9mg; Calcium 357mg; Fiber 7.1g; Sodium 1462mg.

COUSCOUS-STUFFED BELL PEPPERS

The peppers are softened in boiling water before filling to ensure really tender results.
Choose red, yellow, or orange peppers for this dish, but avoid green ones, because they
tend to discolor after a couple of hours of cooking and do not have such a sweet taste.

SERVES 4

4 bell peppers
½ cup instant couscous
⅓ cup boiling vegetable stock
1 tablespoon olive oil
2 teaspoons white wine vinegar
2 ounces dried apricots, finely chopped
3 ounces feta cheese, cut into tiny cubes
3 ripe tomatoes, skinned, seeded,
 and chopped
3 tablespoons toasted pine nuts
2 tablespoons chopped fresh parsley
salt and ground black pepper
Italian parsley, to garnish

1 Halve the peppers lengthwise, then remove the core and seeds. Place the peppers in a large heatproof bowl, and pour over boiling water to cover. Leave to stand for about 3 minutes, then drain thoroughly, and set aside.

2 Meanwhile, put the couscous in a small bowl, and pour over the stock. Leave to stand for about 5 minutes until all the water has been absorbed.

3 Using a fork, fluff up the couscous, then stir in the oil, vinegar, apricots, feta cheese, tomatoes, pine nuts, and parsley, and season to taste with salt and ground black pepper.

COOK'S TIP
Be sure to taste the stuffing before adding any more salt. Feta cheese can be very salty already, so you may not need to add any extra.

4 Fill the peppers with the couscous mixture, gently packing it down using the back of a spoon.

5 Place the peppers, filling side up, in the ceramic cooking pot, then pour ⅔ cup near-boiling water around them.

6 Cover with the lid, switch the slow cooker to high, and cook for 2–3 hours, or until the peppers are tender. Brown under a hot broiler for 2 minutes, and serve garnished with fresh parsley.

Energy 303Kcal/1266kJ; Protein 33.7g; Carbohydrate 33.6g, of which sugars 17g; Fat 15.8g, of which saturates 3.9g; Cholesterol 13mg; Calcium 105mg; Fiber 4.3g; Sodium 285mg.

PARSNIPS and GARBANZO BEANS in GARLIC, ONION, CHILI, and GINGER PASTE

The sweet flavor of parsnips goes very well with the spices in this Indian-style vegetable stew. It makes an ideal meal for vegetarians, because garbanzo beans are high in protein. Complete the meal with warm Indian breads, such as chapati or naan.

SERVES 4

5 garlic cloves, finely chopped
1 small onion, chopped
2-inch piece fresh ginger root, chopped
2 green chiles, seeded and finely chopped
5 tablespoons cold water
4 tablespoons peanut oil
1 teaspoon cumin seeds
2 teaspoons coriander seeds
1 teaspoon ground turmeric
½ teaspoon chili powder or mild paprika
½ cup cashew nuts, toasted and ground
8 ounces tomatoes, peeled and chopped
14-ounce can garbanzo beans, drained
  and rinsed
2 pounds parsnips, cut into
  ¾-inch chunks
1½ cups boiling vegetable stock
juice of 1 lime, to taste
salt and ground black pepper
chopped fresh cilantro leaves, toasted
  cashew nuts and plain yogurt, to serve

1 Reserve 2 teaspoons of the garlic, then place the remainder in a food processor or blender with the onion, ginger, and half the chile. Add the water, and process to make a smooth paste.

2 Heat the oil in a large frying pan, add the cumin seeds, and cook for about 30 seconds. Stir in the coriander seeds, turmeric, chili powder or paprika, and the ground cashew nuts. Add the ginger and chili paste, and cook, stirring frequently, until the paste bubbles and the water begins to evaporate.

COOK'S TIPS
• Buy spices in small quantities, and store them in a cool, dark place. Try to use them within a few months, because they quickly lose their flavor.
• Frying spices before adding to the cooking pot intensifies their taste.

3 Add the tomatoes to the pan, and cook for 1 minute. Transfer the mixture to the ceramic cooking pot, and switch the slow cooker to high.

4 Add the garbanzo beans and parsnips to the pot, and stir to coat in the spicy tomato mixture, then stir in the stock, and season with salt and pepper. Cover with the lid, and cook on high for 4 hours, or until the parsnips are tender.

5 Stir half the lime juice, the reserved garlic and green chile into the stew. Re-cover and cook for 30 minutes more, then taste and add more lime juice if needed. Spoon onto plates, and sprinkle with fresh cilantro leaves and toasted cashew nuts. Serve immediately with a generous spoonful of plain yogurt.

Energy 453Kcal/1899kJ; Protein 14.8g; Carbohydrate 50.1g, of which sugars 16.6g; Fat 23g, of which saturates 4.3g; Cholesterol 0mg; Calcium 148mg; Fiber 15.8g; Sodium 394mg.

ONIONS STUFFED with GOAT CHEESE and SUN-DRIED TOMATOES

Long, slow cooking is the best way to get maximum flavor from onions, so the slow cooker is the natural choice for these delicious stuffed onions. Serve with a rice or cracked wheat pilaf to make a great vegetarian main course.

SERVES 4

2 large onions
2 tablespoons olive oil (or use oil from the sun-dried tomatoes)
⅔ cup firm goat cheese, crumbled or cubed
1 cup fresh white bread crumbs
8 sun-dried tomatoes in olive oil, drained and chopped
1 garlic clove, finely chopped
½ teaspoon fresh thyme
2 tablespoons chopped fresh parsley
1 small egg, beaten
3 tablespoons pine nuts
⅔ cup near-boiling vegetable stock
salt and ground black pepper
chopped fresh parsley, to garnish

1 Bring a large pan of water to the boil. Add the whole onions in their skins, and boil for 10 minutes.

2 Drain the onions, and leave until cool enough to handle, then cut each onion in half horizontally, and peel. Using a teaspoon, remove the center of each onion, leaving a thick shell.

3 Very finely chop the flesh from one of the scooped-out onion halves, and place in a bowl. Stir in 1 teaspoon of the olive oil or oil from the sun-dried tomatoes, then add the goat cheese, breadcrumbs, sun-dried tomatoes, garlic, thyme, parsley, egg, and pine nuts. Season with salt and pepper, and mix well.

4 Divide the stuffing among the onions, and cover each one with a piece of oiled foil. Brush the base of the ceramic cooking pot with 1 tablespoon of the oil, then pour in the stock. Arrange the onions in the base of the cooking pot, cover with the lid, and cook on high for 4 hours, or until the onions are very tender but still hold their shape.

5 Carefully remove the onions from the slow cooker, and transfer them to a broiler pan. Remove the foil, and drizzle the tops with the remaining 1 teaspoon oil. Brown under a medium broiler for 3–4 minutes, taking care not to burn the nuts. Serve immediately, garnished with fresh chopped parsley.

VARIATIONS

• Try using feta cheese in place of the goat cheese, and add chopped fresh mint, currants, and pitted black olives in place of the other flavorings.
• Alternatively, use 6 ounces Roquefort or Gorgonzola in place of the goat cheese, and add about ¾ cup chopped walnuts and 1 cup very finely chopped celery in place of the sun-dried tomatoes and pine nuts.

Energy 330Kcal/1370kJ; Protein 13.8g; Carbohydrate 14.3g, of which sugars 11.3g; Fat 24.7g, of which saturates 8.4g; Cholesterol 83.7mg; Calcium 98mg; Fiber 1.9g; Sodium 349mg.

ORANGE CANDIED SWEET POTATOES

Candied sweet potatoes are the classic accompaniment to a traditional Thanksgiving dinner. For a really fresh, festive look, serve with extra orange segments.

SERVES 8

2 pounds sweet potatoes
⅔ cup orange juice
2 tablespoons maple syrup
1 teaspoon freshly grated ginger
½ teaspoon ground cinnamon
½ teaspoon ground cardamom
1 teaspoon salt
ground black pepper
orange segments, to serve (optional)

VARIATION
You can serve this rich vegetable dish as a puree if you prefer (but omit the orange segments). Transfer the cooked candied sweet potatoes to a food processor, adding a little of the sauce, and blend until smooth. You may need to add a little more of the sauce to make a soft, creamy, spoonable puree.

1 Peel the potatoes and cut them into ¾-inch cubes. Put them in a large heatproof bowl, and pour over just enough boiling water to cover. Leave to stand for 5 minutes.

2 Meanwhile, put the orange juice, maple syrup, spices, and salt in the ceramic cooking pot, and stir to mix. Switch the slow cooker to high.

3 Drain the sweet potato cubes, and add to the ceramic cooking pot. Gently stir to coat in the spicy orange mixture. Cover, and cook for 4–5 hours, until tender, stirring twice during cooking.

4 Stir the orange segments, if using, into the sweet potatoes, and season to taste with pepper. Serve immediately.

Energy 53Kcal/226kJ; Protein 2.9g; Carbohydrate 13.7g, of which sugars 11.8g; Fat 0g, of which saturates 0g; Cholesterol 0mg; Calcium 5mg; Fiber 0.2g; Sodium 158mg.

POTATO, ONION, and GARLIC GRATIN

This tasty side dish makes the perfect accompaniment to roasts, stews, and broiled meat or fish. Cooking the potatoes in stock with onions and garlic gives them a really rich flavor.

3 Pour just enough of the stock into the pot to cover the potatoes. Cover with the lid, and cook on low for 8–10 hours, or on high for 4–5 hours, until the potatoes are tender.

4 If you like, brown the potatoes under a hot broiler for 3–4 minutes. Serve sprinkled with a little salt and ground black pepper.

VARIATIONS
• To make this dish more substantial, sprinkle 1 cup of grated Gruyère cheese over the top of the cooked potatoes, and brown under a preheated broiler for 3–4 minutes until golden-brown and bubbling.
• Alternatively, crumble scant 1 cup soft goat cheese on the gratin 30 minutes before the end of cooking.
• To vary the flavor, try using chopped rosemary or sage in place of the thyme, or use crushed juniper berries instead.

SERVES 4

3 tablespoons butter
1 large onion, finely sliced into rings
2–4 garlic cloves, finely chopped
½ teaspoon dried thyme
2 pounds waxy potatoes, very finely sliced
scant 2 cups boiling vegetable stock
sea salt and ground black pepper

1 Grease the inside of the ceramic cooking pot with 1 tablespoon of the butter. Spoon a thin layer of onions onto the base of the cooking pot, then sprinkle over a little of the chopped garlic, thyme, salt, and pepper.

2 Carefully arrange an overlapping layer of potato slices on top of the onion mixture in the ceramic cooking pot. Continue to layer the ingredients in the pot until all the onions, garlic, herbs and potatoes are used up, finishing with a layer of sliced potatoes.

Energy 260Kcal/1092kJ; Protein 5.1g; Carbohydrate 41.9g, of which sugars 6.4g; Fat 9.1g, of which saturates 5.4g; Cholesterol 21mg; Calcium 31mg; Fiber 3.3g; Sodium 171mg.

BROWN RICE with LIME and LEMONGRASS

*It is unusual to find brown rice given the Thai treatment, but the nutty flavor of the grains
is enhanced by the fragrance of limes and lemongrass in this delicious dish.*

3 Heat the oil in a large pan. Add the onion, and cook over a low heat for 5 minutes. Stir in the ginger, coriander and cumin seeds, lemongrass, and lime rind and cook for 2–3 minutes. Tip the mixture into the ceramic cooking pot.

4 Pour the stock into the pot, briefly stir to combine, then cover with the lid, and switch the slow cooker to high. Cook for 1 hour.

5 Rinse the rice in cold water until the water runs clear, then drain, and add to the ceramic cooking pot. Cook for 45 minutes–1½ hours, or until the rice is tender and has absorbed the stock.

6 Stir the fresh cilantro into the rice, and season with salt and pepper. Fluff up the grains with a fork, and serve garnished with strips of scallion and toasted coconut, and lime wedges.

SERVES 4

2 limes
1 lemongrass stalk
1 tablespoon sunflower-seed oil
1 onion, chopped
1-inch piece fresh ginger root, peeled and
    very finely chopped
1½ teaspoons coriander seeds
1½ teaspoons cumin seeds
3 cups boiling vegetable stock
1½ cups converted brown rice
4 tablespoons chopped fresh cilantro
salt and ground black pepper
scallions, toasted coconut strips, and lime
    wedges, to garnish

1 Using a zester or fine grater, pare the rind from the limes, taking care not to remove any of the bitter white pith. Set the rind aside.

2 Cut off the lower portion of the lemongrass stalk, discarding the papery top end of the stalk. Finely chop the lemongrass and set aside.

Energy 308Kcal/1304kJ; Protein 5.6g; Carbohydrate 64g, of which sugars 5.1g; Fat 5.1g, of which saturates 0.9g; Cholesterol 0mg; Calcium 17mg; Fiber 2g; Sodium 129mg.

SPICY TAMARIND GARBANZOS

Garbanzo beans make a good base for many vegetarian dishes. Here, they are tossed
with sharp tamarind and spices to make a deliciously light vegetarian lunch or side dish.

SERVES 4

1¼ cups dried garbanzo beans
2 ounces tamarind pulp
3 tablespoons vegetable oil
½ teaspoons cumin seeds
1 onion, very finely chopped
2 garlic cloves, crushed
1-inch piece of fresh ginger root, peeled
    and grated
1 fresh green chile, finely chopped
1 teaspoon ground cumin
1 teaspoon ground coriander
¼ teaspoon ground turmeric
½ teaspoon salt
8 ounces tomatoes, skinned
    and finely chopped
½ teaspoon garam masala
chopped fresh chiles and chopped
    onion, to garnish

1 Put the garbanzo beans in a large bowl, and pour over cold water to cover. Leave to soak for at least 8 hours, or overnight.

2 Drain the beans, and put in a pan with at least double the volume of cold water. (Do not add salt to the water, because this will toughen the beans and spoil the final dish.)

3 Bring the water to the boil, and boil vigorously for at least 10 minutes. Skim off any scum, then drain the garbanzo beans, and tip into the ceramic cooking pot.

4 Pour 3 cups of near-boiling water over the beans, and switch the slow cooker to high. Cover with the lid, and cook for 4–5 hours, or until the beans are just tender.

5 Toward the end of the cooking time, put the tamarind in a bowl, and break up with a fork. Pour over ½ cup of boiling water, and leave to soak for about 15 minutes.

6 Tip the tamarind into a strainer, and discard the water. Rub the pulp through, discarding any stones and fiber.

7 Heat the oil in a large pan, add the cumin seeds, and fry for 2 minutes, until they splutter. Add the onion, garlic, and ginger, and fry for 5 minutes. Add the cumin, coriander, turmeric, chile, and salt, and fry for 3–4 minutes. Add the tomatoes, garam masala, and tamarind pulp, and bring to the boil.

8 Stir the tamarind mixture into the chickpeas, cover, and cook for a further 1 hour. Either serve straight from the ceramic cooking pot, or spoon into a warmed serving dish, and garnish with chopped chiles and onion.

COOK'S TIP
To save time, make double the quantity of tamarind pulp, and freeze in ice-cube trays. It will keep for up to 2 months.

Energy 777Kcal/1164kJ; Protein 12.8g; Carbohydrate 32.6g, of which sugars 5.3g; Fat 11.5g, of which saturates 1.3g; Cholesterol 0mg; Calcium 103mg; Fiber 7.1g; Sodium 274mg.

COCONUT, TOMATO, and LENTIL DHAL with TOASTED ALMONDS

Richly flavored and utterly moreish, this lentil dish makes a filling supper served with warm naan bread and plain yogurt. Split red lentils give the dish a vibrant color, but you could use larger yellow split peas instead, although they will take a little longer to cook.

SERVES 4

2 tablespoons vegetable oil
1 large onion, very finely chopped
3 garlic cloves, chopped
1 carrot, diced
2 teaspoons cumin seeds
2 teaspoons yellow mustard seeds
1-inch piece fresh ginger root, grated
2 teaspoons ground turmeric
1 teaspoon mild chili powder
1 teaspoon garam masala
1 cup split red lentils
1⅔ cups boiling vegetable stock
1⅔ cups coconut milk
5 tomatoes, peeled, seeded, and chopped
juice of 2 limes
4 tablespoons chopped fresh cilantro
salt and ground black pepper
¼ cup sliced almonds, toasted, to garnish

1 Heat the oil in a pan. Add the onion, and cook for 5 minutes, until softened, stirring occasionally.

2 Add the garlic, carrot, cumin, mustard seeds, and ginger to the pan. Cook for 3–4 minutes, stirring, until the seeds begin to pop, the aromas are released, and the carrot softens slightly.

COOK'S TIP
This dish reheats well, so it is worth making a double batch and freezing half. Thaw, then add a little water, and reheat.

3 Add the ground turmeric, chili powder, and garam masala to the pan and cook, stirring, for 1 minute, or until the flavors begin to mingle.

4 Tip the mixture into the ceramic cooking pot. Add the lentils, stock, coconut milk, and tomatoes, and season with salt and pepper. Stir well. and cover the pot with the lid.

5 Cook on high for 2 hours, or until the lentils are soft, stirring halfway through the cooking time to prevent the lentils sticking. Stir the lime juice and 3 tablespoons of fresh cilantro into the dhal.

6 Check the seasoning, and cook for a further 30 minutes. To serve, sprinkle with the remaining fresh cilantro and the toasted almonds.

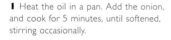

Energy 335Kcal/1421kJ; Protein 16.6g; Carbohydrate 46.3g, of which sugars 14.3g; Fat 10.6g, of which saturates 1.4g; Cholesterol 0mg; Calcium 99mg; Fiber 5.5g; Sodium 230mg.

SPICED INDIAN RICE with SPINACH, TOMATOES, and CASHEW NUTS

This all-in-one rice dish makes a delicious, nutritious vegetarian meal but can also be served as an accompaniment to a spicy meat curry. Ghee, the clarified butter used in much Indian cooking, is available in cans from large supermarkets and Asian stores.

SERVES 4

2 tablespoons sunflower-seed oil
1 tablespoon ghee or sweet butter
1 onion, finely chopped
2 garlic cloves, crushed
3 tomatoes, peeled, seeded, and chopped
1½ cups converted brown rice
1 teaspoon each ground coriander
    and ground cumin, or 2 teaspoons
    dhana jeera powder
2 carrots, coarsely grated
3 cups boiling vegetable stock
6 ounces baby spinach leaves, washed
½ cup unsalted cashew nuts, toasted
salt and ground black pepper

1 Heat the oil and ghee or butter in a heavy-based pan, add the onion, and fry gently for 6–7 minutes, until soft. Add the garlic and chopped tomatoes, and cook for a further 2 minutes.

2 Rinse the rice in a strainer under cold water, drain well, and tip into the pan. Add the coriander and cumin or dhana jeera powder, and stir for a few seconds. Turn off the heat, and transfer the mixture to the ceramic cooking pot.

3 Stir in the carrots, then pour in the stock, season with salt and pepper, and stir to mix. Switch the slow cooker on to high. Cover, and cook for 1 hour.

4 Lay the spinach on the surface of the rice, replace the lid, and cook for a further 30–40 minutes, or until the spinach has wilted and the rice is cooked and tender.

5 Stir the spinach into the rice, and check the seasoning, adding a little more salt and pepper if necessary. Sprinkle the cashew nuts over the rice, and serve.

COOK'S TIP
If baby spinach leaves are unavailable, use larger fresh spinach leaves instead. Remove any tough stalks, and chop the leaves roughly before adding to the rice.

Energy 473Kcal/1989kJ; Protein 10.1g; Carbohydrate 77.1g, of which sugars 9.2g; Fat 18g, of which saturates 4.5g; Cholesterol 8mg; Calcium 111mg; Fiber 4.8g; Sodium 349mg.

ONE-POT, CLAY-POT VEGETARIAN AND SIDE DISHES

The great thing about these vegetarian dishes is that
many of them are made with ingredients you will
almost certainly have in your kitchen, so they are the
recipes you'll make time and time again for all
the family. Pan Haggerty, for instance, owes its
excellent flavor to three simple ingredients: potatoes,
Cheddar cheese, and chives. Vegetable Korma is very
adaptable, and Fettuccine with Butter and Parmesan
is as easy as its name suggests.

RATATOUILLE

A highly versatile vegetable stew from Provence. Ratatouille is delicious hot or cold, on its own or with eggs, pasta, fish, or meat—particularly roast lamb.

SERVES 6

2 pounds ripe, well-
 flavored tomatoes
½ cup olive oil
2 onions, thinly sliced
2 red bell peppers, seeded and
 cut into chunks
1 yellow or orange bell pepper,
 seeded and cut into chunks
1 large eggplant, cut into chunks
2 zucchini, cut into thick slices
4 garlic cloves, crushed
2 bay leaves
1 tablespoon chopped
 fresh thyme
salt and ground black pepper

1 To peel the tomatoes, plunge them into a bowl of boiling water for about 30 seconds, remove them using a slotted spoon, and then refresh in cold water. Peel off the skins and coarsely chop the tomato flesh.

2 Heat a little of the oil in a large, heavy pan, and cook the onions for 5 minutes. Add the bell peppers, and cook for 2 minutes more. Drain. Add the eggplant and more oil, and cook gently for 5 minutes. Add the remaining oil and zucchini, and cook for 3 minutes. Drain.

3 Add the garlic and tomatoes to the pan with the bay leaves and thyme, and a little salt and pepper. Cook gently until the tomatoes have softened and are turning pulpy.

4 Return all the vegetables to the pan, and cook gently, stirring frequently, for about 15 minutes, until they are fairly pulpy but have retained a little texture. Season with more salt and pepper to taste, if required.

COOK'S TIPS
• There are no specific quantities for the vegetables when making ratatouille, so you can, to a large extent, vary the quantities and types of vegetables, depending on what you have in the refrigerator.
• If the tomatoes are a little tasteless, add 2–3 tablespoons tomato paste and a pinch of sugar to the mixture along with the tomatoes.
• Eggplants no longer need to be salted to draw out the bitter juices, however, this salting process does help prevent them from soaking up too much oil during cooking. So, if you have the time, it is worth sprinkling the eggplant chunks with salt and leaving them in a colander in the sink for about 30 minutes to drain. Rinse them well, and pat dry with paper towels before frying.

Energy 204Kcal/848kJ; Protein 4.3g; Carbohydrate 13.3g, of which sugars 12.5g; Fat 15.2g, of which saturates 2.3g; Cholesterol 0mg; Calcium 49mg; Fiber 4.5g; Sodium 64mg.

VEGETABLE KORMA

The blending of spices is an ancient art in India. Here the aim is to produce a subtle, aromatic curry rather than an assault on the senses.

SERVES 4

¼ cup butter
2 onions, sliced
2 garlic cloves, crushed
1-inch piece fresh ginger root, grated
1 teaspoon ground cumin
1 tablespoon ground coriander
6 cardamom pods
2-inch piece cinnamon stick
1 teaspoon ground turmeric
1 fresh red chile, seeded and
    finely chopped
1 potato, peeled and cut into
    1-inch cubes
1 small eggplant, chopped
1½ cups mushrooms, thickly sliced
¾ cup water
1 cup green beans, cut into 1-inch lengths
4 tablespoons plain yogurt
⅔ cup heavy cream
1 teaspoon garam masala
salt and ground black pepper
fresh cilantro sprigs, to garnish
boiled rice and poppadums,
    to serve

2 Add the potato cubes, eggplants, and mushrooms and the water. Cover the pan, bring to the boil, then lower the heat, and simmer for 15 minutes. Add the beans, and cook, uncovered, for 5 minutes. With a slotted spoon, remove the vegetables to a warmed serving dish and keep hot.

3 Allow the cooking liquid to bubble up until it has reduced a little. Season with salt and pepper, then stir in the yogurt, cream, and garam masala. Pour the sauce over the vegetables, and garnish with fresh cilantro. Serve with boiled rice and poppadums.

1 Melt the butter in a heavy pan. Add the onions, and cook for 5 minutes, until soft. Add the garlic and ginger, and cook for 2 minutes, then stir in the cumin, coriander, cardamom pods, cinnamon stick, turmeric, and finely chopped chile. Cook, stirring constantly, for 30 seconds.

VARIATION

All kinds of vegetables and pulses can be used for this korma; try broccoli, carrots, cauliflower, peas, canned or fresh beans, and canned chickpeas.

Energy 381Kcal/1577kJ; Protein 5.1g; Carbohydrate 20.9g, of which sugars 9.9g; Fat 31.4g, of which saturates 19.3g; Cholesterol 78mg; Calcium 95mg; Fiber 3.9g; Sodium 108mg.

TOFU and VEGETABLE THAI CURRY

Traditional Thai ingredients—chiles, galangal, lemongrass, and kaffir lime leaves—give this curry a wonderfully fragrant aroma.

SERVES 4

6 ounces tofu, drained
3 tablespoons dark soy sauce
1 tablespoon sesame oil
1 teaspoon chili sauce
1-inch piece fresh ginger root,
    finely grated
8 ounces cauliflower
8 ounces broccoli
2 tablespoons vegetable oil
1 onion, sliced
1⅔ cups coconut milk
⅔ cup water
1 red bell pepper, seeded
    and chopped
6 ounces green beans, halved
1½ cups shiitake or white
    mushrooms, halved
shredded scallions, to garnish
boiled jasmine rice or noodles,
    to serve

For the curry paste
2 fresh chiles, seeded
    and chopped
1 lemongrass stalk, chopped
1-inch piece fresh galangal, chopped
2 kaffir lime leaves
2 teaspoons ground coriander
a few fresh cilantro sprigs, including
    the stalks

1 Cut the drained tofu into 1-inch cubes, and place in an ovenproof dish. Combine the soy sauce, sesame oil, chili sauce, and ginger, and pour over the tofu. Toss gently to coat all the cubes evenly, then leave to marinate for at least 2 hours or overnight, turning and basting the bean curd occasionally.

2 To make the curry paste, place the chopped chiles, lemongrass, galangal, kaffir lime leaves, ground coriander, and fresh cilantro in a food processor, and process for a few seconds until well blended. Add 3 tablespoons water, and process to a thick paste.

3 Preheat the oven to 375°F. Using a large sharp knife, cut the cauliflower and broccoli into small flowerets, and cut any stalks into thin slices.

4 Heat the vegetable oil in a frying pan, add the sliced onion, and cook gently for about 8 minutes, or until soft and lightly browned. Stir in the prepared curry paste and the coconut milk. Add the water, and bring to a boil.

5 Stir in the red bell pepper, green beans, cauliflower, and broccoli. Transfer to a Chinese sand pot or earthenware casserole. Cover, and place in the oven.

6 Stir the tofu and marinade, then place the dish in the top of the oven, and cook for 30 minutes, then stir them into the curry with the mushrooms. Reduce the oven temperature to 350°F, and cook for about 15 minutes, or until the vegetables are tender. Garnish with scallions, and serve with boiled jasmine rice or noodles.

COOK'S TIP
Tofu is made from soybeans and is sold in blocks. It is a creamy white color and has a solid gel-like texture. Tofu has a bland flavor, and its absorbent nature means that it takes on the flavors of marinades or any other food that it is cooked with.

Energy 212Kcal/883kJ; Protein 10.7g; Carbohydrate 16.2g, of which sugars 13.8g; Fat 12g, of which saturates 1.8g; Cholesterol 0mg; Calcium 329mg; Fiber 5.2g; Sodium 126mg.

MIXED BEAN and EGGPLANT TAGINE with MINT YOGURT

In this traditional-style Moroccan dish, the mixed beans and eggplant provide both texture and flavor, which are enhanced by the herbs and chiles.

SERVES 4

generous ½ cup dried red kidney beans, soaked overnight in cold water and drained
generous ½ cup dried black-eyed peas or cannellini beans, soaked overnight in cold water and drained
2½ cups water
2 bay leaves
2 celery stalks, each cut into 4 batons
5 tablespoons olive oil
1 eggplant, about 12 ounces, cut into chunks
1 onion, thinly sliced
3 garlic cloves, crushed
1–2 fresh red chiles, seeded and finely chopped
2 tablespoons tomato paste
1 teaspoon paprika
2 large tomatoes, coarsely chopped
1¼ cups vegetable stock
1 tablespoon each chopped fresh mint, parsley, and cilantro
salt and ground black pepper
fresh herb sprigs, to garnish

For the mint yogurt
⅔ cup plain yogurt
2 tablespoons chopped fresh mint

1 Place the soaked and drained kidney beans in a large pan of unsalted boiling water. Bring back to a boil, and boil rapidly for 10 minutes, then drain. Place the soaked and drained black-eyed peas or cannellini beans in a separate large pan of unsalted boiling water, and boil rapidly for 10 minutes, then drain.

2 Place the 2½ cups of water in a soaked bean pot or a large tagine, add the bay leaves, celery, beans, and peas. Cover, and place in an unheated oven. Set the oven to 375°F, and cook for 1–1½ hours, or until the beans and peas are tender. Drain.

3 Heat 4 tablespoons of the oil in a large frying pan or cast-iron tagine base. Add the eggplant chunks, and cook, stirring, for 4–5 minutes, until evenly browned. Remove and set aside.

4 Add the remaining oil to the tagine base or frying pan, then add the onion, and cook, stirring, for 4–5 minutes, until softened. Add the garlic and chiles, and cook for 5 minutes more, stirring frequently, until the onion is golden.

VARIATIONS
• Use 2–3 teaspoons harissa paste or chili sauce instead of fresh chiles.
• A mixture of zucchini and red and yellow bell peppers can be used instead of the eggplant. Cut them into small chunks, and cook them in the oil as in step 3 above.

5 Reduce the oven temperature to 325°F. Add the tomato paste and paprika, and cook, stirring constantly, for 1–2 minutes. Add the tomatoes, browned eggplant, drained red kidney beans, black-eyed peas or cannellini beans, and stock. Season with salt and pepper.

6 Cover the iron tagine base with the earthenware lid or, if using a frying pan, transfer the contents to a clay tagine. Place in the oven, and cook for 1 hour.

7 Meanwhile, combine the yogurt, mint, and scallions, and place in a small serving dish. To serve, add the mint, parsley, and cilantro to the tagine, and lightly mix through the vegetables. Season to taste. Garnish with fresh herb sprigs, and serve with the mint yogurt.

COOK'S TIP
The cooking time for the beans and peas will vary depending on their age. Older legumes will take longer to cook until tender. The tagine will happily keep warm once it's ready, so if you are serving this to guests, it is a good idea to allow extra time for the legumes to become tender.

Energy 328Kcal/1377kJ; Protein 14.9g; Carbohydrate 35.2g, of which sugars 9.3g; Fat 15.3g, of which saturates 2.2g; Cholesterol 0mg; Calcium 96mg; Fiber 12.8g; Sodium 28mg.

MOROCCAN BRAISED GARBANZO BEANS

This sweet and spicy vegetarian dish is a real treat. Serve it hot as a main course with rice or couscous, or serve cold as a salad, drizzled with olive oil and lemon juice.

SERVES 4

1½ cups dried garbanzo beans, soaked
   overnight in cold water
2 tablespoons olive oil
2 onions, cut into wedges
2 teaspoons ground cumin
¼ teaspoon ground turmeric
¼ teaspoon cayenne pepper
1 tablespoon ground coriander
1 teaspoon ground cinnamon
1¼ cups vegetable stock
2 carrots, sliced
½ cup ready-to-eat dried
   apricots, halved
scant ½ cup raisins
¼ cup sliced almonds
2 tablespoons chopped fresh cilantro
2 tablespoons chopped fresh
   Italian parsley
salt and ground black pepper

3 Meanwhile, place the olive oil and onions in a frying pan, and cook for about 6 minutes, or until softened. Add the cumin, turmeric, cayenne, coriander, and cinnamon, and cook for 2–3 minutes. Stir in the stock, carrots, apricots, raisins, and almonds and bring to a boil.

4 Drain the garbanzo beans, add the spicy vegetable mixture, and stir. Cover, and return to the oven for 30 minutes.

5 Season with salt and pepper, lightly stir in half the fresh cilantro and parsley, and serve sprinkled with the remainder.

1 Soak a bean clay pot in cold water for 20 minutes, then drain. Place the garbanzo beans in a pan with plenty of cold water. Bring to a boil, and boil rapidly for 10 minutes, then place the garbanzo beans in the bean pot, cover with lukewarm water, and cover.

2 Place the bean pot in an unheated oven, and set the temperature to 400°F. Cook for 1 hour, then reduce the oven temperature to 325°F. Cook for 1 hour more, or until the garbanzo beans are cooked through and tender.

COOK'S TIP
The cooking time for the garbanzo beans will vary depending on their age—if old, they could take 30 minutes more.

Energy 403Kcal/1696kJ; Protein 17.1g; Carbohydrate 58.5g, of which sugars 27.1g; Fat 12.8g, of which saturates 1.4g; Cholesterol 0mg; Calcium 167mg; Fiber 10.9g; Sodium 45mg.

JAMAICAN BLACK BEAN POT

Molasses imparts a rich treacly flavor to the spicy sauce, which incorporates a stunning mix of black beans, vibrant red and yellow bell peppers, and orange butternut squash.

SERVES 4

1¼ cups dried black beans
1 bay leaf
2 tablespoons vegetable oil
1 large onion, chopped
1 garlic clove, chopped
1 teaspoon mustard powder
1 tablespoon molasses
2 tablespoons dark brown sugar
1 teaspoon dried thyme
½ teaspoon dried chili flakes
1 teaspoon vegetable bouillon powder
1 red bell pepper, seeded and diced
1 yellow bell pepper, seeded and diced
1½ pounds butternut squash or pumpkin,
    seeded and cut into
    ½-inch dice
salt and ground black pepper
fresh thyme sprigs, to garnish
cornbread or plain boiled rice, to serve

1 Soak the beans overnight in plenty of water, then drain, and rinse well. Place in a large pan, cover with fresh water, and add the bay leaf. Bring to a boil, then boil rapidly for 10 minutes. Reduce the heat, cover the pan, and simmer for about 30 minutes, until tender. Drain, reserving the cooking water. Preheat the oven to 350°F.

COOK'S TIPS
• To prepare squash or pumpkin, cut it in half using a large sharp knife, then cut off the skin. Remove the seeds using a spoon, and cut the flesh into chunks. Choose firm specimens that are blemish-free.
• If you don't have bouillon powder, then dissolve half a bouillon cube in the bean cooking water.

2 Heat the vegetable oil in a flameproof casserole, add the onion and garlic, and sauté for about 5 minutes, until softened, stirring occasionally. Stir in the mustard powder, molasses, sugar, dried thyme, chili flakes, and seasoning. Cook for about 1 minute, stirring, then stir in the black beans.

3 Add enough water to the reserved liquid to make 1⅔ cups, mix in the bouillon powder, and pour into the casserole. Bake for 25 minutes.

4 Add the bell peppers and squash or pumpkin, and mix well. Cover, then bake for 45 minutes. Garnish with thyme.

Energy 297Kcal/1252kJ; Protein 15.1g; Carbohydrate 45.9g, of which sugars 20.3g; Fat 7.1g, of which saturates 1g; Cholesterol 0mg; Calcium 129mg; Fiber 12.6g; Sodium 16mg.

OKRA and TOMATO TAGINE

A spicy vegetarian dish that is delicious served either with other vegetable dishes or as a side dish to accompany a meat tagine.

SERVES 4

12 ounces small okra
5–6 tomatoes
2 small onions
2 garlic cloves, crushed
1 fresh green chile, seeded
1 teaspoon paprika
a small handful of fresh
    cilantro leaves
2 tablespoons
    vegetable oil
juice of 1 lemon
½ cup water

1 Preheat the oven to 350°F. Trim the okra, then cut the pods into ½-inch lengths. Set aside.

2 Peel, seed, and coarsely chop the tomatoes. Set aside. Chop one of the onions, place in a food processor with 4 tablespoons water, the garlic, spices, and cilantro, and process to a paste.

3 Thinly slice the second onion. Heat the oil in a flameproof casserole or pan, and cook the onion for 5–6 minutes, until it turns golden brown. Transfer to a plate with a slotted spoon.

4 Reduce the heat, and pour the onion and cilantro paste over the onions. Cook for 1–2 minutes, stirring frequently, then add the okra, tomatoes, and lemon juice. Pour in the water, and stir well to mix. Cover tightly, and transfer to the oven. Bake for about 15 minutes, until the okra is tender.

5 Transfer the tagine to a serving dish, sprinkle with the fried onion rings, and serve immediately.

VARIATION
Canned, chopped tomatoes can be used instead of the fresh tomatoes in this recipe—simply add the contents of a 7-ounce can with the okra in step 4.

Energy 115Kcal/482kJ; Protein 4.2g; Carbohydrate 9.6g, of which sugars 8.5g; Fat 7g, of which saturates 1.2g; Cholesterol 0mg; Calcium 182mg; Fiber 6g; Sodium 26mg.

PAN HAGGERTY

Use a firm-fleshed potato that will hold its shape when cooked. For a change,
try adding chopped ham or salami between the layers.

SERVES 2

1 large onion
1 pound potatoes
2 tablespoons olive oil
2 tablespoons butter
2 garlic cloves, crushed
1 cup grated sharp
   Cheddar cheese
3 tablespoons chopped fresh chives, plus
   extra to garnish
salt and ground black pepper

1 Halve and thinly slice the onion. Peel and thinly slice the potatoes.

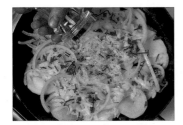

2 Heat the oil and butter in a large heavy or nonstick frying pan. Remove from the heat and cover the base with a layer of potatoes, followed by layers of onion slices, garlic, cheese, chives, and plenty of seasoning.

VARIATIONS
• Other hard cheeses, such as Red Leicester or Monterey Jack, work well in this recipe.
• For a slightly sweeter flavor and extra color, use 1 sliced red onion in place of the brown-skinned variety.

3 Continue layering, ending with grated cheese. Cover with a lid or foil, and cook the pan haggerty over gentle heat on the stovetop for about 30 minutes, or until the potatoes and onion are tender when tested with a knife.

4 Preheat the broiler to hot. Uncover the pan, cover the pan handle with foil to protect it, if necessary, and brown the top under the broiler. Serve the pan haggerty straight from the pan, sprinkled with extra chives to garnish.

Energy 542Kcal/2257kJ; Protein 19.6g; Carbohydrate 12.2g, of which sugars 7.2g; Fat 33.9g, of which saturates 15g; Cholesterol 60mg; Calcium 429mg; Fiber 3.3g; Sodium 413mg.

MEDITERRANEAN BAKED VEGETABLES

This colorful selection of vegetables is baked in a shallow clay pot, known as a tian *in Provence, where it is also the name given to the food baked in it.*

SERVES 4–6

5 tablespoons olive oil
2 onions, halved and sliced
1 garlic clove, crushed
1 tablespoon finely chopped
   fresh sage
4 large, well-flavored
   tomatoes, quartered
3 zucchini, thickly sliced
2 small yellow bell peppers, cut into
   fourths and seeded
2 small red bell peppers, cut into fourths
   and seeded
4 tablespoons fresh white or whole-wheat
   bread crumbs
4 tablespoons freshly grated
   Parmesan cheese
8–10 pitted black olives
salt and ground black pepper
sage leaves,
   to garnish

1 Heat 2 tablespoons of the olive oil in a frying pan, add the onions, and cook, stirring occasionally, until softened. Add the garlic, and continue cooking until the onions are really soft and golden. Stir in the sage, and season well.

2 Transfer the onions to a large oval *tian* or earthenware baking dish. Spread them evenly, then arrange the tomatoes, zucchini, and bell peppers on top.

3 Preheat the oven to 400°F. Drizzle the remaining oil over the mixed vegetables, and season to taste. Bake for 30 minutes.

4 Sprinkle the fresh bread crumbs and Parmesan cheese over the vegetables, and arrange the olives on top. Return to the oven for 10–15 minutes more, or until the vegetables are tender. Serve garnished with the sage leaves.

Energy 260Kcal/1083kJ; Protein 9.5g; Carbohydrate 24.9g, of which sugars 15.4g; Fat 14.2g, of which saturates 3.7g; Cholesterol 10mg; Calcium 192mg; Fiber 4.9g; Sodium 275mg.

PORTABELLO MUSHROOMS with HAZELNUTS

Large mushrooms, full of texture and flavor, are topped with crunchy hazelnut pieces,
fresh parsley, and garlic-flavored olive oil.

SERVES 4

2 garlic cloves
grated rind of 1 lemon
6 tablespoons olive oil
8 large portabello mushrooms
½ cup hazelnuts, coarsely chopped
2 tablespoons chopped fresh parsley
salt and ground black pepper

1 Crush the garlic cloves with a little salt using a mortar and pestle or on a cutting board. Place the crushed garlic in a small bowl, and stir in the grated lemon rind and the olive oil. If time allows, leave the mixture to stand to enable the flavors to steep.

2 Preheat the oven to 400°F. Arrange the mushrooms, stalk side up, in a single layer in a large, ovenproof earthenware dish. Drizzle about 4 tablespoons of the oil mixture over them, and bake for 10 minutes.

3 Remove the mushrooms from the oven, and baste them with the remaining oil mixture, then sprinkle the chopped hazelnuts evenly over the top. Bake for 10–15 minutes more, or until the mushrooms are tender. Season with salt and pepper, and sprinkle with chopped parsley. Serve immediately.

COOK'S TIP
Almost any unsalted nuts can be used in place of the hazelnuts in this recipe—try pine nuts, cashew nuts, almonds, or walnuts. Nuts can go rancid quickly, so, for the freshest flavor, either buy nuts in small quantities or buy them in shells and remove the shells just before use.

Energy 255Kcal/1052kJ; Protein 5.2g; Carbohydrate 1.7g, of which sugars 1g; Fat 25.4g, of which saturates 3.1g; Cholesterol 0mg; Calcium 43mg; Fiber 3.1g; Sodium 12mg.

ROASTED SQUASH with RICE STUFFING

Gem squash has a sweet, subtle taste that contrasts well with the olives and sun-dried tomatoes in this recipe. The rice adds substance without changing any of the flavor.

SERVES 4 AS A FIRST COURSE

4 whole gem squashes
8 ounces cooked white long grain rice
   (about ½ cup raw weight)
3 ounces sun-dried tomatoes in oil,
   drained and chopped
½ cup pitted black olives, chopped
4 tablespoons soft goat cheese
2 tablespoons olive oil
1 tablespoon chopped fresh basil leaves,
   plus basil sprigs, to serve
yogurt and mint dressing and salad
   greens, to serve

1 Preheat the oven to 350°F. Using a sharp knife, trim the base of each squash, slice off the top of each, and scoop out and discard the seeds.

2 Mix the rice, tomatoes, olives, cheese, half the oil ,and the basil in a bowl.

3 Oil a shallow baking dish with the remaining oil, just large enough to hold the squash side by side. Divide the rice mixture among the squash, and place them in the dish.

4 Cover with foil, and bake for about 45 minutes, until the squash are tender when pierced with a skewer. Garnish with basil sprigs, and serve with a yogurt and mint dressing and salad greens.

VARIATION
Try ricotta cheese or cream cheese with garlic and herbs in place of the soft goat cheese in this recipe.

Energy 208Kcal/870kJ; Protein 6.3g; Carbohydrate 23.1g, of which sugars 4.6g; Fat 10.6g, of which saturates 3.9g; Cholesterol 14mg; Calcium 97mg; Fiber 2.5g; Sodium 93mg.

CHEESE-TOPPED ROAST BABY VEGETABLES

A simple way of serving baby vegetables that really brings out their flavor.

SERVES 4

2¼ pounds mixed baby vegetables, such as
  eggplant, onions or shallots, zucchini,
  corn cobs, and mushrooms
1 red bell pepper, seeded and cut into
  large pieces
1–2 garlic cloves, finely chopped
1–2 tablespoons olive oil
2 tablespoons chopped fresh
  mixed herbs
8 ounces cherry tomatoes
1 cup coarsely grated
  mozzarella cheese
salt and ground black pepper
black olives, to serve (optional)

1 Preheat the oven to 425°F. Cut the
vegetables in half lengthwise.

2 Place the halved baby vegetables and
bell pepper pieces in an ovenproof dish
with the garlic and plenty of salt and
ground black pepper. Drizzle the oil over,
and toss the vegetables to coat them.
Bake the vegetables for 20 minutes, or
until they are tinged brown at the edges,
stirring once during the cooking time.

3 Remove the dish from the oven, and
stir in the chopped fresh mixed herbs.
Sprinkle the cherry tomatoes over the
surface, and top with the coarsely grated
mozzarella cheese. Return the dish to
the oven, and bake for 5–10 minutes
more, until the cheese has melted and is
bubbling. Serve immediately with black
olives, if you like.

COOK'S TIP

This dish can also be made with a mixture
of regular-sized vegetables. Simply chop
them into bitesize pieces, and continue
from Step 2.

VARIATION

Use 2–3 fresh rosemary sprigs in place of
the chopped fresh mixed herbs.

Energy 212Kcal/883kJ; Protein 9.2g; Carbohydrate 24.3g, of which sugars 18.4g; Fat 9.4g, of which saturates 4.5g; Cholesterol 17mg; Calcium 174mg; Fiber 4.8g; Sodium 128mg.

POTATOES and PARSNIPS BAKED with GARLIC and CREAM

As the potatoes and parsnips cook, they gradually absorb the garlic-flavored cream, while the cheese browns to a crisp finish.

SERVES 4–6

3 large potatoes, total weight about
   1½ pounds
12 ounces small or
   medium parsnips
scant 1 cup light cream
7 tablespoons milk
2 garlic cloves, crushed
butter, for greasing
about 1 teaspoon freshly grated nutmeg
¾ cup coarsely grated
   Gruyère cheese
salt and ground black pepper

1 Peel the potatoes and parsnips, and cut them into thin slices using a sharp knife. Place them in a large pan of salted boiling water, and cook for 5 minutes. Drain, and leave to cool slightly.

2 Meanwhile, pour the light cream and milk into a heavy pan, add the crushed garlic, and bring to a boil over medium heat. Remove the pan from the heat, and leave to stand at room temperature for about 10 minutes to let the flavor of the garlic steep into the cream and milk mixture.

3 Lightly grease a 10-inch rectangular earthenware baking dish. Preheat the oven to 350°F.

4 Arrange the potatoes and parsnips in layers in the greased earthenware dish, sprinkling each layer with a little freshly grated nutmeg and plenty of salt and ground black pepper.

5 Pour the garlic-flavored cream and milk mixture into the dish, and then press the sliced potatoes and parsnips down into the liquid. The liquid should come to just underneath the top layer of vegetables. Cover the dish with a piece of lightly buttered foil or parchment paper, and bake for 45 minutes.

6 Remove the dish from the oven, and remove the foil or parchment from the dish. Sprinkle the grated Gruyère cheese over the vegetables in an even layer.

7 Return the dish to the oven, and bake, uncovered, for 20–30 minutes more, or until the potatoes and parsnips are tender (see Cook's Tip) and the topping is golden brown.

COOK'S TIPS
• If you have one, use a mandolin or a food processor fitted with a slicing blade to slice the potatoes and parsnips evenly and thinly for this gratin.
• At the end of the cooking time, to test if the vegetables are tender, insert a sharp knife through the middle of the potatoes and parsnips. The knife should slide in easily, and the vegetables should feel soft.

VARIATIONS
• Use sweet potatoes in place of some or all of the ordinary potatoes—choose orange-fleshed ones for a pretty color contrast with the parsnips. Other root vegetables, such as Jerusalem artichokes and carrots, would also work well.
• Other hard cheeses would be equally good in this recipe—try Cheddar or Red Leicester, or go for the even more strongly flavored Parmesan or Romano.

Energy 241Kcal/1009kJ; Protein 7.8g; Carbohydrate 27g, of which sugars 6.4g; Fat 11.7g, of which saturates 7.2g; Cholesterol 31mg; Calcium 174mg; Fiber 3.8g; Sodium 126mg.

NEW POTATOES and VEGETABLES BAKED TURKISH-STYLE

Here's a meal in a pot that's suitable for feeding large numbers of people. It's lightly spiced and has plenty of garlic—who could refuse?

SERVES 4

4 tablespoons olive oil
1 large onion, chopped
2 eggplants, cut into
    small cubes
4 zucchini, cut into small chunks
1 green bell pepper, seeded
    and chopped
1 red or yellow bell pepper,
    seeded and chopped
1 cup fresh or frozen peas
4 ounces green beans
1 pounds new or salad
    potatoes, cubed
½ teaspoon ground cinnamon
½ teaspoon ground cumin
1 teaspoon paprika
4–5 tomatoes, peeled
14-ounce can chopped tomatoes
2 tablespoons chopped fresh parsley
3–4 garlic cloves, crushed
1½ cups vegetable stock
salt and ground black pepper
black olives and fresh parsley,
    to garnish

1 Preheat the oven to 375°F. Heat 3 tablespoons of the oil in a large, heavy frying pan, add the onion, and cook over medium heat until golden.

2 Add the eggplant and sauté for about 3 minutes, then add the zucchini, bell peppers, peas, beans and potato cubes, together with the cinnamon, cumin, paprika, and seasoning. Continue to cook for 3 minutes more, stirring the mixture constantly. Transfer the vegetables to an ovenproof dish.

3 Halve the fresh tomatoes, remove the seeds using a teaspoon, and then chop the tomato flesh. Mix the tomato flesh with the canned tomatoes, chopped parsley, crushed garlic, and the remaining olive oil in a bowl.

4 Pour the vegetable stock over the eggplant and bell pepper mixture, and then spoon the tomato mixture evenly over the top. Cover the dish with foil, and bake for 30–45 minutes. Serve hot, garnished with olives and parsley.

Energy 332Kcal/1387kJ; Protein 11.4g; Carbohydrate 42.5g, of which sugars 21.6g; Fat 14g, of which saturates 2.4g; Cholesterol 0mg; Calcium 110mg; Fiber 10.1g; Sodium 41mg.

MEDITERRANEAN VEGETABLES BAKED in GOLDEN BATTER

Crunchy golden batter surrounds these vegetables, making them delicious and filling.
Serve with salad as a light lunch, or with broiled sausages for a more substantial meal.

SERVES 6

1 small eggplant, trimmed, halved, and
    thickly sliced
1 egg
1 cup all-purpose flour
1¼ cups milk
2 tablespoons fresh thyme leaves, or
    2 teaspoon dried
1 red onion
2 large zucchini
1 red bell pepper
1 yellow bell pepper
4–5 tablespoons sunflower-seed oil
2 tablespoons freshly grated
    Parmesan cheese
salt and ground black pepper
fresh herbs, to garnish

1 Place the eggplant in a colander or strainer, sprinkle generously with salt, and leave for 10 minutes. Drain, rinse well, and pat dry on paper towels.

2 Meanwhile, beat the egg in a bowl, then gradually beat in the flour and a little milk to make a smooth thick paste. Gradually blend in the rest of the milk, add the thyme leaves and seasoning to taste, and stir until smooth. Leave the batter in a cool place until required. Preheat the oven to 425°F.

COOK'S TIP
As with Yorkshire pudding, it is essential to get the fat in the dish really hot before adding the batter, which should sizzle slightly as it goes in. If the fat is not hot enough, the batter will not rise well. Use a dish that is not too deep.

3 Cut the onion into fourths, slice the zucchini, and seed the bell peppers, then cut them into fourths. Put the oil in a shallow roasting pan, and heat in the oven. Add the vegetables, toss them in the oil to coat thoroughly, and return the pan to the oven for 20 minutes.

4 Give the batter another whisk, then pour it over the vegetables, and return the pan to the oven for 30 minutes. When the batter is puffed up and golden, reduce the heat to 375°F for about 10 minutes, or until the edges are crisp. Sprinkle with Parmesan and herbs.

Energy 231Kcal/966kJ; Protein 8.9g; Carbohydrate 24.1g, of which sugars 8.9g; Fat 11.7g, of which saturates 2.9g; Cholesterol 40mg; Calcium 181mg; Fiber 3.3g; Sodium 93mg.

TRUFFADE

Baked until meltingly soft, this warming cheese and potato supper is the perfect slow-baked dish to come home to. In France, where it originated, it would be made with a Tomme or Cantal cheese—look for them in good cheese stores.

SERVES 4–6

a little sunflower-seed oil or melted butter
1 large onion, thinly sliced
1½ pounds baking potatoes, very
    thinly sliced
1¼ cups grated hard cheese, such as
    Tomme, Cantal, or sharp Cheddar
freshly grated nutmeg
salt and ground black pepper
mixed salad greens,
    to serve

VARIATION

In France, they make a non-vegetarian version of this dish, which is cooked with finely diced fatty bacon (lardons), and the cheese is chopped, not grated. The ingredients are mixed and cooked slowly in a little lard in a heavy frying pan on top of the stove.

1 Preheat the oven to 350°F. Lightly grease the base of a shallow baking dish or roasting pan with the sunflower-seed oil or melted butter.

2 Arrange a layer of sliced onion over the base of the dish, then add a layer of sliced potatoes, and about half of the grated cheese. Finish with the remaining onions and a layer of sliced potatoes.

3 Brush the top layer of potatoes with oil or melted butter, and season with nutmeg, salt, and pepper.

4 Sprinkle the remaining grated cheese over the top and bake for about 1 hour, or until the vegetables are tender and the top is golden brown. Leave the dish to stand for about 5 minutes, then serve, cut in wedges, with a salad.

POTATOES BAKED with TOMATOES

This simple, hearty dish from the south of Italy is best made in the summer, when fresh, ripe tomatoes are in season and bursting with flavor.

SERVES 6

6 tablespoons olive oil
2 large red or yellow onions, thinly sliced
2¼ pounds baking potatoes, thinly sliced
1 pound well-flavored tomatoes, sliced,
    with their juice
1 cup freshly grated Parmesan or
    Cheddar cheese
a few fresh basil leaves
¼ cup water
salt and ground black pepper

1 Preheat the oven to 350°F. Brush a large baking dish generously with 2 tablespoons of the oil.

2 Arrange a layer of some of the thinly sliced onions in the base of the prepared dish, followed by a layer of the potatoes and tomatoes.

3 Drizzle a little of the olive oil over the potatoes and tomatoes, and sprinkle with some of the grated cheese. Season generously with plenty of salt and ground black pepper.

4 Continue to layer the vegetables in the dish until they are used up, ending with an overlapping layer of potatoes and tomatoes.

5 Reserve a sprig of fresh basil for the garnish, tear the remaining leaves into small pieces, and add them here and there among the vegetables. Sprinkle the top with the remaining grated cheese, and drizzle with the rest of the oil. Pour the water evenly over the vegetables and cheese, then bake for about 1 hour, or until the vegetables are tender.

6 Check toward the end of the cooking time and, if the top begins to brown too much, place a sheet of foil, parchment paper, or a flat baking tray on top of the dish. Garnish with the remaining basil, once it is cooked, and serve hot.

VARIATION

If you can't get hold of really flavorsome tomatoes, a 14-ounce can of chopped plum tomatoes can be used instead.

Truffade: Energy 117Kcal/494kJ; Protein 3.2g; Carbohydrate 20.8g, of which sugars 3.4g; Fat 2.9g, of which saturates 1.7g; Cholesterol 7mg; Calcium 40mg; Fiber 1.6g; Sodium 48mg.
Potatoes Baked with Tomatoes: Energy 339Kcal/1418kJ; Protein 11.7g; Carbohydrate 34.4g, of which sugars 8.2g; Fat 18.1g, of which saturates 5.8g; Cholesterol 19mg; Calcium 262mg; Fiber 3.4g; Sodium 236mg.

BAKED SCALLOPED POTATOES with FETA CHEESE and OLIVES

Thinly sliced potatoes are cooked with Greek feta cheese and black and green olives and olive oil. This dish is a good one to serve with toasted pita bread.

SERVES 4

4–6 large, unpeeled potatoes, total weight
   about 2 pounds
⅔ cup extra virgin olive oil
leaves from a fresh rosemary sprig
2½ cups coarsely crumbled
   feta cheese
1 cup pitted mixed black and
   green olives
1¼ cups hot vegetable stock
salt and ground black pepper
toasted pita bread,
   to serve

1 Preheat the oven to 400°F. Bring a large pan of lightly salted water to a boil, and cook the potatoes for 15 minutes, until only just tender.

2 Drain the potatoes, and set them aside until they are cool enough to handle. Carefully remove the peel from the potatoes using a small sharp knife, and then cut them into thin slices.

3 Brush the base and sides of a 6¼-cup rectangular, ovenproof dish with some of the olive oil.

COOK'S TIP
Cooking the potatoes with their skins on not only helps to preserve their vitamin content, but will also ensure that the potatoes cook more evenly. If you prefer, peel them before they are cooked.

4 Arrange half the potatoes in the dish in an even layer. Top with half of the rosemary, cheese, and olives, and season with salt and pepper. Arrange the rest of the potatoes in an even layer on top.

5 Add the remaining rosemary leaves, crumbled cheese, and olives, and drizzle with the remaining olive oil. Pour the hot vegetable stock over the top, and season the top layer with salt and plenty of ground black pepper.

6 Bake for 35 minutes, covering the dish loosely with foil after about 20 minutes to prevent the potatoes from getting too brown. Serve hot, straight from the dish with the toasted pita bread.

VARIATION
Thinly sliced sun-dried tomatoes would make a delicious addition.

Energy 584Kcal/2429kJ; Protein 14.8g; Carbohydrate 37.3g, of which sugars 4g; Fat 42.7g, of which saturates 13.7g; Cholesterol 48mg; Calcium 279mg; Fiber 3.1g; Sodium 1662mg.

TOMATO, FETA CHEESE, and OLIVE TARTS

These upside-down tartlets are filled with vegetables and chunks of salty cheese. They
make the perfect first course, or may be served with salad greens for a lunchtime snack.

SERVES 4

1 ounce sun-dried
   eggplant slices
1¼ cups boiling water
3 tablespoons sunflower-seed oil
1 onion, thinly sliced
2 cups white mushrooms, sliced
1 garlic clove, crushed
12–16 cherry tomatoes, halved
8 black or green olives, pitted
   and chopped
1 cup crumbled feta cheese
12 ounces ready-made
   puff pastry
salt and ground black pepper

1 Preheat the oven to 400°F. Place the eggplant slices in a shallow dish. Pour over the boiling water, and leave to soak for 10 minutes. Rinse in cold water, drain, and dry on paper towels. Cut the eggplant slices in half or fourths, depending on their size.

2 Heat 2 tablespoons of the sunflower-seed oil in a frying pan, and cook the onion over medium heat for 4–5 minutes. Add the mushrooms, and cook for 3–4 minutes, or until the onions are light golden. Remove and set aside.

3 Heat the remaining oil in the pan, add the eggplant slices and garlic, and cook for 1–2 minutes. Lightly oil four individual cazuelas. Mix the halved tomatoes with the onions, mushrooms, eggplant, olives, and feta cheese, and divide among the cazuelas. Season well.

4 Roll out the pastry thinly into an oblong, then cut out four rounds, each slightly larger than the diameter of the cazuelas. Place the pastry on top of the vegetable and cheese mixture, tucking the overlap down inside the dish.

5 Bake for 20 minutes, or until the pastry is risen and golden. Cool slightly, then invert onto individual warmed serving plates to serve.

COOK'S TIP
Choose cherry tomatoes on the vine for the very best flavor.

Energy 506Kcal/2105kJ; Protein 11.1g; Carbohydrate 35.9g, of which sugars 4.1g; Fat 37.7g, of which saturates 5.2g; Cholesterol 20mg; Calcium 175mg; Fiber 1.6g; Sodium 989mg.

FRITTATA with LEEK, RED PEPPER, and SPINACH

Apart from the fact that Italian frittata does not usually contain potato and is generally slightly softer in texture, it is not hugely different from Spanish tortilla. This combination of sweet leek, red bell pepper, and spinach is delicious with the egg.

3 Add the spinach, and cover the pan. Allow the spinach to wilt in the steam for 3–4 minutes, then stir to mix it into the vegetables, adding the pine nuts.

4 Beat the eggs with salt, pepper, the remaining cumin, basil, and parsley. Add to the frying pan, and cook over gentle heat until the base of the omelet sets and turns golden brown. Pull the edges of the omelet away from the sides of the pan as it cooks, and tilt the pan so that the uncooked egg runs underneath.

SERVES 3–4

2 tablespoons olive oil
1 large red bell pepper, seeded and diced
½–1 teaspoon ground cumin
3 leeks (about 1 pound), thinly sliced
5 ounces baby spinach leaves
3 tablespoons pine nuts, toasted
5 extra large eggs
1 tablespoon chopped fresh basil
1 tablespoon chopped fresh Italian parsley
salt and ground black pepper
watercress, to garnish and ⅔ cup freshly
  grated Parmesan cheese, to serve

1 Heat a heavy, nonstick frying pan, and add the olive oil. Add the diced red bell pepper, and cook over medium heat, stirring occasionally, for 6–8 minutes, until the bell pepper is soft and beginning to brown. Add ½ teaspoon of the ground cumin, mix well, and cook for 1–2 minutes more.

2 Stir in the thinly sliced leeks, then partly cover the pan, and cook gently for about 5 minutes, or until the leeks have softened and collapsed. Season the cooked vegetables with plenty of salt and ground black pepper.

5 Preheat the broiler. Flash the frittata under the hot broiler to set the egg on top, but do not let it become too brown. Cut the frittata into wedges, and serve warm, garnished with watercress and sprinkled with Parmesan.

VARIATION

A delicious way to serve frittata is to pack it into a slightly hollowed-out loaf, and then drizzle it with olive oil. Wrap tightly in plastic wrap, and stand for 1–2 hours before cutting into slices.

Energy 267Kcal/1107kJ; Protein 12.7g; Carbohydrate 7.1g, of which sugars 6.2g; Fat 21.2g, of which saturates 3.4g; Cholesterol 238mg; Calcium 131mg; Fiber 4.2g; Sodium 144mg.

LENTIL FRITTATA

Throughout the Mediterranean, a variety of thick, vegetable omelets are cooked. This tasty supper dish combines green lentils, red onions, broccoli, and cherry tomatoes.

SERVES 4–6

scant ½ cup green lentils
8 ounces small broccoli flowerets
2 red onions, halved and thickly sliced
2 tablespoons olive oil
8 eggs
3 tablespoons milk or water
3 tablespoons chopped mixed herbs, such
    as oregano, parsley, tarragon, and
    chives, plus extra sprigs to garnish
6 ounces cherry tomatoes, halved
salt and ground black pepper

1 Place the lentils in a pan, cover with cold water, and bring to a boil. Reduce the heat, and simmer for 25 minutes, until tender. Add the broccoli, return to a boil, and cook for 1 minute.

VARIATIONS
Add about ⅔ cup freshly grated Parmesan cheese or 1 cup diced mozzarella cheese to the egg mixture.

2 Meanwhile place the onion slices and olive oil in a shallow, earthenware dish or cazuela about 9–10 inches in diameter, and place in an unheated oven. Set the oven to 400°F, and cook for 25 minutes.

3 In a bowl, whisk together the eggs, milk or water, a pinch of salt, and plenty of black pepper. Stir in the herbs. Drain the lentils and broccoli, and stir into the onions. Add the cherry tomatoes. Stir gently to combine.

4 Pour the egg mixture evenly over the vegetables. Reduce the oven to 375°F. Return the dish to the oven, and cook for 10 minutes, then push the mixture into the center of the dish, using a spatula, letting the raw mixture in the center flow to the edges.

5 Return the dish to the oven and cook the frittata for 15 minutes more, or until it is just set. Garnish with sprigs of fresh herbs, and serve the frittata warm, cut into thick wedges.

Energy 200Kcal/836kJ; Protein 13.6g; Carbohydrate 11.3g, of which sugars 3.6g; Fat 11.7g, of which saturates 2.7g; Cholesterol 254mg; Calcium 76mg; Fiber 2.4g; Sodium 105mg.

BULGUR WHEAT, ASPARAGUS, and FAVA BEAN PILAF

Nutty-textured bulgur wheat is usually simply soaked in boiling water until it is softened, but it can be cooked like rice to make a pilaf. Here it is combined with fava beans, herbs, and lemon and orange rinds, which add a fresh, springtime flavor.

SERVES 4

1½ cups bulgur wheat
3–3¾ cups warm vegetable stock
8 ounces asparagus spears
2 cups frozen fava
    beans, thawed
8 scallions, chopped
1 tablespoon grated lemon rind
1 tablespoon grated orange rind
3 tablespoons butter, cut into
    small pieces
4 tablespoons chopped fresh Italian parsley
2 tablespoons chopped fresh dill, plus
    extra sprigs to garnish
salt and ground black pepper

1 If using a clay pot, soak in cold water for 20 minutes, then drain. Place the bulgur wheat in the clay pot or in a shallow, ovenproof earthenware dish, and pour over ½ cups of the stock. Season with salt and pepper.

VARIATIONS

• Try using fresh green beans and either fresh or frozen peas in place of the asparagus and fava beans and, instead of using dill, stir in plenty of chopped fresh mint along with the parsley.
• If you'd like to add a little extra color to the pilaf, then stir in some finely shredded red bell pepper, or some peeled and seeded wedges of tomato.
• To make a richer pilaf, stir in some finely grated Parmesan cheese along with the butter in step 6.

2 Cut the asparagus spears into 1-inch lengths, discarding any hard, woody ends from the stems. (Peel white asparagus spears, if necessary.) Add the asparagus pieces to the clay pot or dish, and gently stir these into the bulgur wheat.

3 Cover the clay pot or dish tightly, and place in an unheated oven. Set the oven to 400°F, and then cook the bulgur wheat and asparagus for 20 minutes.

4 Meanwhile pop the fava beans out of their shells, and then stir the beans into the bulgur pilaf after it has cooked for about 20 minutes, adding a little more stock at the same time. Re-cover the clay pot or dish, and return the dish to the oven for about 10 minutes.

COOK'S TIP

If your clay pot or earthenware dish doesn't have its own lid, then cover the pot or dish with foil, crimping it around the edge to seal. Or, if the top of the dish is completely flat, then you can simply place a flat, heavy baking sheet on top.

5 Stir in the scallions, grated lemon rind, and grated orange rind. Add a little more stock, if necessary. Cover, and return to the oven for 5 minutes.

6 Dot the pieces of butter over the top of the pilaf, and leave to stand, covered, for 5 minutes.

7 Add the chopped parsley and dill to the pilaf, and stir well with a fork, to fluff up the bulgur wheat and distribute the herbs evenly. Check the seasoning, and add salt and plenty of black pepper. Serve the pilaf hot, garnished with sprigs of fresh dill.

Energy 285Kcal/1188kJ; Protein 10.5g; Carbohydrate 40.8g, of which sugars 2.7g; Fat 9.8g, of which saturates 5.4g; Cholesterol 21mg; Calcium 93mg; Fiber 5.5g; Sodium 71mg.

BASMATI RICE and NUT PILAF

Vegetarians will love this simple pilaf. Add wild or cultivated mushrooms, if you like.

SERVES 4

1–2 tablespoons sunflower-seed oil
1 onion, chopped
1 garlic clove, crushed
1 large carrot, coarsely grated
generous 1 cup basmati
   rice, soaked
1 teaspoon cumin seeds
2 teaspoons ground coriander
2 teaspoons black mustard
   seeds (optional)
4 green cardamom pods
scant 2 cups vegetable
   stock or water
1 bay leaf
½ cup shelled walnuts and/or unsalted
   cashew nuts
salt and ground black pepper
fresh parsley or cilantro sprigs, to garnish

1 Heat the oil in a large frying pan. Add the onion, garlic, and carrot, and cook for 3–4 minutes, stirring occasionally.

2 Drain the rice, and add it to the pan with the cumin seeds, ground coriander, black mustard seeds, if using, and the green cardamom pods. Cook for about 1 minute, stirring to coat the grains in oil.

3 Pour in the vegetable stock or water, add the bay leaf, and season well with salt and pepper. Bring to a boil, then lower the heat, cover, and simmer very gently for 10–12 minutes.

4 Remove the pan from the heat without lifting the lid. Leave to stand in a warm place for about 5 minutes, then check the rice. If it is cooked, there will be small steam holes on the surface of the rice. Remove the bay leaf and the cardamom pods.

5 Stir the walnuts and/or cashew nuts into the rice mixture. Taste to check the seasoning, and add more salt and pepper if necessary. Spoon into warmed individual bowls or onto a large platter, garnish with the sprigs of fresh parsley or cilantro, and serve immediately.

COOK'S TIPS
• Use whichever nuts you prefer in this pilaf—even unsalted peanuts taste good—although almonds, brazil nuts, cashew nuts, or pistachio nuts add a slightly more exotic flavor.
• If you don't have basmati rice, then use any other long grain rice. Thai jasmine rice has a particularly good flavor.

Energy 370Kcal/1538kJ; Protein 7.3g; Carbohydrate 48.7g, of which sugars 3.2g; Fat 16g, of which saturates 1.4g; Cholesterol 0mg; Calcium 38mg; Fiber 1.5g; Sodium 8mg.

VEGETABLE COUSCOUS with SAFFRON and HARISSA

This spicy, North African dish makes an excellent main meal, or serve as part of a vegetarian buffet.

SERVES 4

3 tablespoons olive oil
1 onion, chopped
2 garlic cloves, crushed
1 teaspoon ground cumin
1 teaspoon paprika
14-ounce can chopped tomatoes
1¼ cups vegetable stock
1 cinnamon stick
generous pinch of saffron threads
4 baby eggplants, cut into fourths
8 baby zucchini, trimmed
8 baby carrots
1⅓ cups couscous
15-ounce can garbanzo beans, drained
¾ cup pitted prunes
3 tablespoons chopped fresh parsley
3 tablespoons chopped fresh cilantro
2–3 teaspoons harissa
salt

1 Heat the olive oil in a large pan. Add the onion and garlic, and cook gently for 5 minutes, until soft. Add the cumin and paprika, and cook, stirring, for 1 minute.

2 Add the tomatoes, stock, cinnamon stick, saffron, eggplant, zucchini, and carrots, and season with salt. Bring to a boil, cover, lower the heat, and cook gently for 20 minutes, until the vegetables are just tender.

3 Line a steamer or colander with a double thickness of cheesecloth. Soak the couscous according to the instructions on the package.

COOK'S TIPS
• Couscous is made from durum wheat and has a similar appearance to semolina. It has a very mild flavor and takes on the flavor of any ingredients it is mixed with. Most couscous is sold precooked and needs only to be rehydrated in boiling water or according to the package instructions.
• Harissa is a spicy paste made from red chiles, cilantro, caraway, garlic, salt, and olive oil. Its bright red/orange color is an indicator of its fiery flavor. It is sold in cans, jars, and tubes.

4 Add the garbanzos and prunes to the vegetables, stir, and cook for 5 minutes.

5 Spread the couscous in the steamer. Place it on top of the vegetables, cover, and cook for 5 minutes, until the couscous is hot.

6 Stir the herbs into the vegetables. Heap the couscous onto a serving dish. Using a slotted spoon, remove the vegetables from the pan, and add to the couscous. Spoon over a little sauce, and toss gently. Stir the harissa into the remaining sauce, and serve separately.

Energy 463Kcal/1942kJ; Protein 16.2g; Carbohydrate 73.4g, of which sugars 26.9g; Fat 13.5g, of which saturates 1.9g; Cholesterol 0mg; Calcium 152mg; Fiber 12.7g; Sodium 267mg.

VEGETABLE PAELLA

A colorful assortment of vegetables is cooked slowly with rice to make this tasty—slightly spicy—vegetarian meal.

SERVES 4

1 large eggplant
3 tablespoons extra virgin olive or
    sunflower-seed oil
2 onions, cut into fourths
    and sliced
2 garlic cloves, crushed
1½ cups short grain Spanish or
    risotto rice
5–6¼ cups vegetable stock
1 red bell pepper, halved, seeded,
    and sliced
1 yellow bell pepper, halved, seeded,
    and sliced
7 ounces fine green beans, halved
scant 2 cups cremini mushrooms,
    cut into fourths, or
    cremini or white
    mushrooms, halved
1 dried chile, crushed
1 cup frozen peas
salt and ground black pepper
fresh cilantro leaves,
    to garnish

1 Soak a clay pot or Chinese sand pot in cold water for 20 minutes, then drain. Cut the eggplant in half lengthwise, then cut it crosswise into thin slices.

COOK'S TIP

Although nowadays eggplants don't need to be salted to remove the bitter flavor they used to have, salting them does insure that they absorb less oil when they are cooked. So, if you have the time, layer the slices in a colander and sprinkle each layer with salt. Leave the slices to drain for about 30 minutes, then rinse thoroughly, and pat dry before cooking.

2 Heat 2 tablespoons of the olive oil in a large frying pan, add the eggplant slices, and quickly sauté until slightly golden. Transfer to the clay pot.

3 Add the remaining oil, then add the onion, and cook, stirring occasionally, for a few minutes until golden.

4 Add the garlic and rice, and cook for 1–2 minutes, stirring, until the rice becomes transparent. Pour in 3¾ cups of the stock into the clay pot, then add the rice mixture.

5 Add the peppers, halved green beans, mushrooms, and crushed chile, and season to taste. Stir to mix, then cover the pot, and place in an unheated oven.

6 Set the oven to 400°F, and cook for 1 hour, or until the rice is almost tender. After 40 minutes, remove the pot from the oven, and add a little more stock to moisten the paella. Stir well, re-cover, and return to the oven.

7 Add the peas and a little more stock to the paella, and cook for 10 minutes more. Adjust the seasoning, and sprinkle over the cilantro. Lightly stir through, and then serve.

VARIATIONS

• Almost any coarsely chopped or sliced vegetables can be used in this dish. Broccoli, carrots, cauliflower, zucchini, and okra are all suitable—or try using frozen corn in place of all or some of the peas.
• For a tomato-flavored paella, use a 14-ounce can chopped tomatoes in place of 1½ cups of the stock.

Energy 458Kcal/1911kJ; Protein 11.8g; Carbohydrate 80g, of which sugars 14.3g; Fat 10.3g, of which saturates 1.5g; Cholesterol 0mg; Calcium 80mg; Fiber 7.1g; Sodium 10mg.

CLAY-POT RISOTTO with SPINACH and SAFFRON

Rice cooks to perfection in the moist environment of a clay pot. This risotto can be made without the constant checking required when cooked on top of the stove.

SERVES 4

a few saffron threads
2 tablespoons boiling water
1 tablespoon olive oil
¼ cup butter
1 onion, finely chopped
1¾ cups risotto rice
3¾ cups warm vegetable stock
⅔ cup dry white wine
8 ounces baby spinach leaves
1¼ cups hot vegetable stock
scant ½ cup shelled
    walnuts, chopped
3 ounces Parmesan cheese, very
    finely shaved
salt and ground black pepper

1 Soak a large clay pot in cold water for 20 minutes, then drain. Meanwhile, place the saffron in a bowl, cover with the boiling water, and leave to steep.

2 Heat the oil and half the butter in a large, heavy pan. Add the finely chopped onion and cook gently for 5 minutes, or until soft, stirring occasionally. Add the rice and stir over the heat for about 3 minutes, until the grains are thoroughly coated in oil and butter.

COOK'S TIP
Risotto rice is short grain rice that is widely used in Italy to make a variety of different types of risotto. Arborio rice is the most widely available type, but you may also find carnaroli and Vialone Nano. When cooked, risotto rice has a creamy consistency, but the grains retain a slight "bite" to their texture.

3 Pour the warm stock into the clay pot, add the saffron water, wine, and the rice mixture, and stir together. Cover, and place in an unheated oven. Set the oven to 375°F, and cook for 50 minutes, stirring after 30 minutes.

4 Stir in the spinach, add the stock, then cover, and cook for 10 minutes, or until the rice is tender. Stir in the walnuts, the remaining butter, and half the Parmesan cheese. Season, and serve sprinkled with the remaining Parmesan cheese.

Energy 630Kcal/2618kJ; Protein 17.2g; Carbohydrate 72.6g, of which sugars 2.3g; Fat 26.9g, of which saturates 11.4g; Cholesterol 45mg; Calcium 356mg; Fiber 1.8g; Sodium 362mg.

TAGLIATELLE BAKED with MUSHROOMS, GORGONZOLA, and WALNUTS

This rich, creamy dish is perfect served as a lunch or supper dish with mixed salad greens.

2 Meanwhile, add the tagliatelle to a large pan of lightly salted, boiling water, and cook according to the package instructions, or until just tender.

3 Remove the mushrooms and leeks and set aside. Crumble the Gorgonzola cheese into the pan, and stir over gentle heat, until melted. Stir in the creams and the dry vermouth or white wine, and season to taste.

SERVES 4

2 tablespoons butter
1 tablespoon vegetable oil
4 cups cremini mushrooms, halved
2 leeks, thinly sliced
14 ounces mixed spinach and
    plain tagliatelle
6 ounces Gorgonzola cheese
⅔ cup heavy cream
scant 1 cup thick light cream
6 tablespoons dry vermouth
    or white wine
½ cup walnuts, finely chopped
1 cup freshly grated Parmesan cheese
salt and ground black pepper

1 Preheat the oven to 400°F. Melt the butter with the vegetable oil in a large sauté pan or deep, heavy frying pan, add the cremini mushrooms and the thinly sliced leeks, and stir-fry the vegetables over medium heat for 4–5 minutes.

4 Drain the pasta, and divide it among four individual cazuelas or other shallow ovenproof earthenware dishes. Top with the mushrooms and leeks, spreading them over the pasta. Pour over the sauce, sprinkle the chopped walnuts and Parmesan cheese on top, and bake for about 15 minutes, or until the cheese is golden brown and bubbling.

VARIATION
Any type of pasta shapes can be used in this bake in place of the tagliatelle. However, other long ribbon pasta, such as linguine and bucatini, and hollow tube pasta that scoop up the sauce, such as macaroni, penne, or rigatoni, will work particularly well.

Energy 1050Kcal/4384kJ; Protein 35.3g; Carbohydrate 79.9g, of which sugars 8.2g; Fat 65.3g, of which saturates 34g; Cholesterol 137mg; Calcium 559mg; Fiber 6.5g; Sodium 808mg.

SPAGHETTI with ARUGULA PESTO

This is the pesto for real arugula lovers. It is sharp and peppery, and delicious for a summer pasta meal with a glass of chilled dry white wine.

SERVES 4

4 garlic cloves
6 tablespoons pine nuts
2 large handfuls of arugula, total weight
    about 5 ounces, stalks removed
⅔ cup freshly grated
    Parmesan cheese
⅔ cup freshly grated
    Romano cheese
6 tablespoons extra virgin olive oil
14 ounces fresh or dried spaghetti
salt and ground black pepper
freshly grated Parmesan and Romano
    cheese, to serve

1 Put the garlic and pine nuts in a food processor or blender, and process until finely chopped. Add the arugula, grated Parmesan and Romano, and olive oil.

2 Add salt and pepper to taste, and process for 5 seconds. Stop, and scrape down the side of the bowl, then process for 5–10 seconds more, until a smooth paste is formed.

3 Cook the spaghetti in a large pan of salted, boiling water until just tender, or according to the package instructions.

4 Spoon the pesto into a large mixing bowl. Just before the pasta is ready, add one or two ladlefuls of the cooking water to the pesto, and stir well to mix.

5 Drain the pasta, tip it into the bowl of pesto, and toss well to mix. Serve immediately, with the grated cheeses handed separately.

VARIATION
To temper the flavor of the arugula and make the pesto milder, add ½ cup ricotta or mascarpone cheese to the pesto in step 4, and mix thoroughly before adding the water.

Energy 621Kcal/2610kJ; Protein 26.1g; Carbohydrate 75.6g, of which sugars 4.8g; Fat 25.9g, of which saturates 6.4g; Cholesterol 25mg; Calcium 392mg; Fiber 4.2g; Sodium 362mg.

PASTA SHELLS with TOMATOES and RICOTTA

Nothing could be simpler than hot pasta tossed with fresh ripe tomatoes, ricotta cheese, and sweet basil. Serve it on hot summer days—it is surprisingly refreshing.

SERVES 4–6

3 cups dried conchiglie
generous ½ cup ricotta cheese
6 ripe plum tomatoes, diced
2 garlic cloves, crushed
a handful of fresh basil leaves, shredded,
    plus extra basil leaves to garnish
4 tablespoons extra virgin olive oil
salt and ground black pepper

1 Cook the pasta in salted boiling water according to the package instructions.

VARIATIONS
• Use diced mozzarella instead of ricotta.
• An avocado is the ideal ingredient for adding extra color and flavor to this pasta dish. Halve, pit, and peel, then dice the flesh. Toss it with the hot pasta at the last minute.

2 Meanwhile, put the ricotta cheese in a large mixing bowl, and mash with a fork until soft and creamy.

3 Add the diced tomatoes (see Cook's Tip), crushed garlic, and shredded basil to the softened ricotta cheese, with salt and pepper to taste, and mix well. Add the olive oil, and whisk thoroughly. Taste for seasoning.

4 Drain the cooked pasta, tip it into the ricotta and tomato mixture, and toss well. Garnish with basil leaves, and serve immediately, sprinkled with black pepper.

COOK'S TIP
If you like, peel the tomatoes before you dice them, by plunging them into boiling water for 30 seconds, and then refresh in cold water before peeling.

Energy 318Kcal/1342kJ; Protein 9.6g; Carbohydrate 46.5g, of which sugars 5.7g; Fat 11.8g, of which saturates 3.2g; Cholesterol 9mg; Calcium 21mg; Fiber 2.5g; Sodium 9mg.

BUCKWHEAT NOODLES with CABBAGE, POTATOES, and CHEESE

This is a very unusual pasta dish from Valtellina in the Italian Alps. The pale brown buckwheat noodles called pizzoccheri *are unique to this area.*

SERVES 6

14 ounces Savoy cabbage, cut into
   ½-inch strips
2 potatoes, total weight about 7 ounces,
   cut into 5¼-inch slices
14 ounces dried pizzoccheri
   (buckwheat noodles)
6 tablespoons butter
1 large bunch fresh sage
   leaves, shredded
2 garlic cloves
7 ounces Fontina cheese, rind removed
   and thinly sliced
2–3 tablespoons freshly grated Parmesan
   cheese, plus extra to serve
salt and ground black pepper

COOK'S TIPS
• Look for packages of dried pizzoccheri
pasta in Italian delicatessens.
• Fontina is an Italian mountain cheese
with a sweet, nutty taste. If you cannot
get it, look for Taleggio, Gruyère, or
Emmenthal—they are all similar cheeses.

1 Bring a very large pan of salted water to a boil. Add the cabbage strips and potato slices, and boil for 5 minutes.

2 Add the pasta to the pan, stir well, and let the water return to a boil over high heat. Lower the heat, and simmer for about 15 minutes, or according to the instructions on the package, until the pasta is just tender.

3 Drain the pasta and vegetables, and set aside. Melt the butter in the pan. Add the sage and whole garlic cloves, and cook over low to medium heat until the garlic is golden and sizzling. Lift the garlic out of the pan, and discard it. Set the sage and garlic butter aside.

4 Pour one-fourth of the pasta and vegetable mixture into a warmed large bowl, and arrange about one-third of the Fontina slices on top. Repeat these layers until all the ingredients have been used, then sprinkle with the grated Parmesan. Pour the sage and garlic butter over the top, and serve immediately, with extra grated Parmesan handed separately.

VARIATION
You could use chard or spinach instead of the cabbage. Spinach will need much less cooking, so add it to the pan about 5 minutes before the end of the cooking time in step 2.

FETTUCCINE with BUTTER and PARMESAN

Very few ingredients are needed to make this incredibly simple dish. It comes from northern Italy, where butter and cheeses are the most popular ingredients for serving with pasta. This dish is especially popular with children.

SERVES 4

14 ounces fresh or
   dried fettuccine
¼ cup sweet butter, cubed
1⅓ cups freshly grated
   Parmesan cheese
salt and ground black pepper

VARIATIONS
• Other long pasta would be just as good
in this recipe; try spaghetti, linguine, or
tagliatelle. Spinach- or tomato-flavored
versions would also work well.
• Try freshly grated Romano cheese
instead of the Parmesan.

1 Cook the pasta in a large pan of salted boiling water until just tender, or according to the instructions on the package. Drain thoroughly, then tip the pasta into a large warmed bowl.

2 Add the cubes of butter and the grated Parmesan, one-third at a time, tossing the pasta after each addition until it is evenly coated. Season to taste, and serve immediately.

Buckwheat Noodles: Energy 469Kcal/1958kJ; Protein 17.9g; Carbohydrate 70.7g, of which sugars 4.4g; Fat 13.9g, of which saturates 8.3g; Cholesterol 37mg; Calcium 351mg; Fiber 3.5g; Sodium 308mg.
Fettucine with Butter and Parmesan: Energy 565Kcal/2379kJ; Protein 23.4g; Carbohydrate 74.2g, of which sugars 3.4g; Fat 21.5g, of which saturates 12.6g; Cholesterol 55mg; Calcium 372mg; Fiber 2.9g; Sodium 392mg.

PASTA TWISTS with PESTO

Bottled pesto is a useful stand-by, but if you have a food processor or blender, it is very easy to make a delicious homemade version.

SERVES 4

2 cups fresh basil leaves, plus
    extra fresh basil leaves,
    to garnish
2–4 garlic cloves
4 tablespoons pine nuts
½ cup extra virgin olive oil
1⅓ cups freshly grated
    Parmesan cheese, plus
    extra to serve
⅓ cup freshly grated
    Romano cheese
3½ cups dried fusilli
salt and ground black pepper

1 Put the basil, garlic, and pine nuts in a food processor. Add 4 tablespoons of the oil. Process until chopped, then stop the machine, and scrape the bowl.

2 Turn the machine on again, and gradually add the remaining olive oil in a thin, steady stream through the feeder tube. You may need to stop the machine and scrape down the sides of the bowl once or twice to make sure that everything is evenly mixed.

3 Scrape the mixture into a large bowl, and beat in the cheeses with a wooden spoon. Taste, and add salt and ground black pepper if necessary.

4 Cook the pasta in a large pan of salted boiling water for 10 minutes, or according to the instructions on the package, until just tender. Drain the pasta well, then add it to the bowl of pesto, and toss well. Serve immediately, garnished with the extra fresh basil leaves. Hand around the extra shaved Parmesan separately.

COOK'S TIP
Fresh pesto can be made up to 2–3 days in advance. To store it, transfer the pesto to a small bowl, and pour a thin film of olive oil over the surface. Cover the bowl tightly with plastic wrap and keep it in the refrigerator.

Energy 799Kcal/3343kJ; Protein 28.3g; Carbohydrate 75g, of which sugars 4.2g; Fat 44.9g, of which saturates 11.1g; Cholesterol 35mg; Calcium 472mg; Fiber 3.8g; Sodium 389mg.

PASTA with CHEESE and CREAM

The Italian name for this dish—Mezzanotte—means middle of the night, which is when this rich and filling dish is eaten—after a night on the tiles. When you arrive home hungry from a party, it's just the thing to sober you up!

SERVES 4

3½ cups dried rigatoni
3 egg yolks
7 tablespoons grated Parmesan cheese
scant 1 cup ricotta cheese
4 tablespoons heavy cream
nutmeg
3 tablespoons butter
salt and ground black pepper

1 Cook the pasta according to the instructions on the package.

2 Meanwhile, combine the egg yolks, grated Parmesan, and ricotta in a bowl. Add the cream and mix with a fork.

3 Grate in nutmeg to taste, then season with plenty of black pepper and a little salt. Drain the pasta thoroughly when cooked. Return the clean pan to the heat. Melt the butter, add the drained pasta, and toss over medium heat.

4 Turn off the heat under the pan, and add the ricotta mixture. Stir well with a large spoon for 10–15 seconds, or until all the pasta is coated in sauce. Serve immediately in warmed individual bowls with plenty of ground black pepper.

Energy 670Kcal/2816kJ; Protein 29.2g; Carbohydrate 75.7g, of which sugars 4.9g; Fat 30g, of which saturates 16.5g; Cholesterol 220mg; Calcium 359mg; Fiber 2.9g; Sodium 357mg.

ARTICHOKE SALAD

Artichokes are grown widely in country gardens—as much for their architectural qualities in the garden as for the table. This salad makes a versatile first course, and is equally good served hot or cold.

SERVES 4

4 artichokes
juice of I lemon
3¾ cups homemade vegetable stock and
   water mixed
2 garlic cloves, chopped
I small bunch parsley
6 whole peppercorns
I tablespoon olive oil, plus extra
   for drizzling

I To prepare the artichokes: trim the stalks of the artichokes close to the base, cut the very tips off the leaves, and then divide them into quarters. Remove the inedible hairy choke (the central part), carefully scraping the hairs away from the heart at the base of the artichoke.

2 Squeeze a little of the lemon juice over the cut surfaces of the artichokes to prevent discoloration.

3 Put the artichokes into a pan, and cover with the stock and water, garlic, parsley, peppercorns, and olive oil. Cover with a lid, and cook gently for I hour, or until the artichokes are tender. They are ready when the leaves will come away easily when pulled.

4 Remove the artichokes with a slotted spoon, and keep them warm if serving hot. Boil the cooking liquor hard without the lid, to reduce by half, and then strain.

5 To serve, arrange the artichokes in small serving dishes, and pour over the reduced juices. Drizzle over a little extra olive oil and lemon juice. Provide finger bowls and a large bowl for the leaves. To eat, pull a leaf away from the artichoke, and scrape the fleshy part at the base with your teeth. Discard the remainder of the leaves, and then eat the heart at the base.

VARIATION
The fleshy bases of the leaves and the artichoke heart or "fond" can be nibbled warm or cold with a dip such as hollandaise sauce or a vinaigrette. Serve with finger bowls and a large dish for the debris.

Energy 59Kcal/245kJ; Protein 0.7g; Carbohydrate 7.8g, of which sugars 7.3g; Fat 3.1g, of which saturates 0.5g; Cholesterol 0mg; Calcium 25mg; Fiber 2.4g; Sodium 61mg

BEETS with LEMON DRESSING

Beets are often grown in large kitchen gardens attached to country houses in England, where they feature on menus in the summer. They are widely enjoyed and often used fresh rather than in the pickled form more familiar in other northern European countries.

SERVES 4

1 pound evenly-sized raw beets
grated rind and juice of ½ lemon
⅔ cup extra virgin olive oil (or a mixture
    of olive and sunflower-seed oil, blended
    to taste)
sea salt and ground black pepper
chopped fresh chives, to garnish (optional)

COOK'S TIP
To avoid the beets "bleeding" during cooking, twist off the tops rather than cutting them with a knife.

1 Twist off the tops from the beets (see Cook's tip), and cook in a large pan of salted boiling water for about 30 minutes, or until the beets are tender. Pinch the skin between two fingers: when cooked, the skin will come away easily. Drain the beets, and allow them to cool.

2 Peel when cool, and slice into wedges into a bowl. Add the lemon rind and juice, and the oil; season to taste. Mix gently in the dressing and serve.

VARIATION
Serve as a side dish or a first course, adding a few chopped chives, if you like.

Energy 265Kcal/1097kJ; Protein 1.9g; Carbohydrate 8.6g, of which sugars 7.9g; Fat 25.1g, of which saturates 3.6g; Cholesterol 0mg; Calcium 23mg; Fiber 2.2g; Sodium 74mg

CAULIFLOWER with TOMATOES and CUMIN

This makes an excellent side dish to serve with broiled meat or fish.

SERVES 4

2 tablespoons sunflower-seed or olive oil
1 onion, chopped
1 garlic clove, crushed
1 small cauliflower, broken into florets
1 teaspoon cumin seeds
good pinch of ground ginger
4 tomatoes, peeled, seeded,
    and quartered
¾ cup water
1–2 tablespoons lemon juice (optional)
salt and ground black pepper
2 tablespoons chopped fresh
    cilantro (optional)

VARIATIONS

• Use a 7-ounce can of chopped tomatoes instead of the fresh tomatoes.
• Broccoli florets can be used in place of the cauliflower, if you like.

1 Heat the oil in a flameproof casserole, add the onion and garlic, and stir-fry for 2–3 minutes, until the onion is softened. Add the cauliflower and stir-fry for 2–3 minutes more, until the cauliflower is flecked with brown. Add the cumin seeds and ginger, and stir-fry briskly for 1 minute, then add the peeled, seeded, and quartered tomatoes, the water, and some salt and pepper to taste.

2 Bring to a boil, then reduce the heat, cover with a plate or with foil, and simmer for 6–7 minutes, or until the cauliflower is just tender.

3 Stir in a little lemon juice to sharpen the flavor, if you like, and adjust the seasoning if necessary. Sprinkle over the chopped fresh cilantro, if using, and serve immediately.

ROAST VEGETABLES with FRESH HERBS and CHILI SAUCE

Oven roasting brings out all the flavors of these classic Mediterranean vegetables. Serve them hot with broiled or roast meat or fish.

SERVES 4

2–3 zucchini
1 large onion
1 red bell pepper
16 cherry tomatoes
2 garlic cloves, chopped
pinch of cumin seeds
1 teaspoon fresh thyme or 4–5 torn
    fresh basil leaves
4 tablespoons olive oil
juice of ½ lemon
1–2 teaspoons harissa
fresh thyme sprigs, to garnish

COOK'S TIP

Harissa is a spicy paste made from a base of beets and carrots and flavored with chiles, coriander seeds, caraway, garlic, salt, and olive oil. It is a popular ingredient in northern African cooking and is sold in small pots—look for its distinctive orangey red color.

1 Preheat the oven to 425°F. Trim the zucchini, and then cut them into long thin strips. Cut the onion into thin wedges, and cut the red bell pepper into fairly large chunks, discarding the seeds and core.

VARIATION

Other vegetables would work well in this dish. Add wedges of red and yellow bell peppers in place of one of the zucchini, or add chunks of eggplant.

2 Place the vegetables in a large roasting pan, add the tomatoes, chopped garlic, cumin seeds, and thyme or basil. Sprinkle with the olive oil, and toss to coat. Cook in the oven for 25–30 minutes, until the vegetables are very soft and slightly charred at the edges.

3 Blend the lemon juice with the harissa, and stir into the roasted vegetables just before serving, garnished with the fresh thyme sprigs.

Cauliflower with Tomatoes and Cumin: Energy 106Kcal/441kJ; Protein 4.5g; Carbohydrate 7.3g, of which sugars 6.5g; Fat 6.7g, of which saturates 1g; Cholesterol 0mg; Calcium 32mg; Fiber 3g; Sodium 19mg.
Roast Vegetables with Fresh Herbs: Energy 154Kcal/635kJ; Protein 3.7g; Carbohydrate 8.2g, of which sugars 7.6g; Fat 12g, of which saturates 1.8g; Cholesterol 0mg; Calcium 48mg; Fiber 2.8g; Sodium 8mg.

ROASTED TOMATOES and GARLIC

*These are so simple to prepare, yet taste absolutely wonderful. Use a large, shallow
earthenware dish that will let the tomatoes sear and char in a very hot oven.*

SERVES 4

8 well-flavored tomatoes (see Cook's
    Tip), halved
12 garlic cloves, unpeeled
4 tablespoons extra virgin olive oil
3–4 bay leaves
salt and ground black pepper
3 tablespoons fresh oregano leaves,
    to garnish

COOK'S TIP
If possible, use ripe plum tomatoes for
this recipe, as they not only keep their
shape and their delicious flavor, but also
do not fall apart when roasted at such a
high temperature. Leave the stalks on the
tomatoes, if you like.

1 Preheat the oven to 450°F. Select a
large, shallow ovenproof dish that will
hold all the tomato halves snugly in a
single layer. Arrange the tomato halves
in the dish, and then tuck the whole,
unpeeled garlic cloves evenly in among
the tomatoes.

2 Brush the tomatoes with the oil, add
the bay leaves, and sprinkle black pepper
over the top. Bake for about 45 minutes,
or until the tomatoes have softened and
are sizzling in the dish. Season with salt
and more black pepper, if needed.
Garnish with oregano leaves, and serve.

Energy 138Kcal/571kJ; Protein 2g; Carbohydrate 6.6g, of which sugars 5.6g; Fat 11.7g, of which saturates 1.8g; Cholesterol 0mg; Calcium 36mg; Fiber 2.5g; Sodium 19mg.

SLOW-COOKED SPICED ONIONS

Onions marinated and baked in a spicy sauce are delicious with broiled or roasted meats.
Choose a good, extra virgin olive oil for a rich, peppery flavor.

SERVES 4

1½ pounds Bermuda or red onions
6 tablespoons olive or sunflower-seed oil
   or a mixture of both
pinch of saffron threads
½ teaspoon ground ginger
1 teaspoon ground black pepper
1 teaspoon ground cinnamon
1 tablespoon sugar

3 Fold a large piece of foil into three, and place over the top of the casserole or ovenproof dish, securing it with a lid.

4 Cook in the oven for 45 minutes, or until the onions are very soft and tender, then increase the oven temperature to 400°F. Remove the lid and foil, and cook for 5–10 minutes more, or until the onions are lightly glazed. Serve immediately.

COOK'S TIP
When slicing onions, chop off the neck and just a little of the base to help the onion stay together. Score a line down the side of the onion, and peel off the outer skin and first layer of flesh.

1 Slice the onions very thinly, and place them in a shallow dish. Blend together the olive and/or sunflower-seed oil, saffron, ground ginger, black pepper, cinnamon, and sugar, and pour over the onions. Stir gently to mix, then set the onions aside for about 2 hours.

2 Preheat the oven to 325°F, and pour the onions and the marinade into a casserole or ovenproof dish.

COOK'S TIP
Onions grown in warmer climates are milder than those from cooler regions. Consequently, Bermuda onions have a mild, sweet flavor. Their skins are a rich golden color, and they are one of the largest varieties available.

Energy 224Kcal/926kJ; Protein 2.1g; Carbohydrate 17.3g, of which sugars 13.4g; Fat 16.9g, of which saturates 2.4g; Cholesterol 0mg; Calcium 60mg; Fiber 2.4g, Sodium 6mg.

OVEN-ROASTED RED ONIONS

The wonderful taste of these sweet red onions is enhanced still further with the powerful flavors of fresh rosemary and juniper berries, and the added tangy sweetness from the balsamic vinegar.

SERVES 4

4 large or 8 small red onions
3 tablespoons olive oil
6 juniper berries, crushed
8 small rosemary sprigs
2 tablespoons balsamic vinegar
salt and ground black pepper

VARIATION
Add a similar quantity of long, thin potato wedges to the onion. Use a larger dish so that the vegetables are still in one layer.

COOK'S TIP
To help hold back the tears during preparation, chill the onions first for about 30 minutes, and then remove the root end last. The root contains the largest concentration of the sulfuric compounds that make the eyes water.

1 Soak a clay onion baker in cold water for 15 minutes, then drain. If the base of the baker is glazed, only the lid will need to be soaked.

2 Trim the roots from the onions and remove the skins, if you like. Cut the onions from the tip to the root, cutting the large onions into fourths, and the small onions in half.

3 Rub the onions with olive oil, salt and pepper, and the juniper berries. Place the onions in the baker, inserting the rosemary in among them. Pour the remaining olive oil and vinegar over.

4 Cover and place in an unheated oven. Set the oven to 400°F, and cook for 40 minutes. Remove the lid, and cook for 10 minutes more.

Energy 128Kcal/530kJ; Protein 1.8g; Carbohydrate 11.9g, of which sugars 8.4g; Fat 8.6g, of which saturates 1.2g; Cholesterol 0mg; Calcium 38mg; Fiber 2.1g; Sodium 5mg.

ROASTED SWEET POTATOES, ONIONS, and BEETS in COCONUT and GINGER PASTE

Sweet potatoes and beets take on a wonderful sweetness when roasted, and are delicious with savory onions and aromatic coconut, ginger, and garlic paste.

SERVES 4

2 tablespoons peanut or mild olive oil
1 pound sweet potatoes, peeled and cut
   into thick strips or chunks
4 beets, cooked, peeled and cut
   into wedges
1 pound small onions, halved
1 teaspoon coriander seeds,
   lightly crushed
3–4 small whole fresh red chiles
salt and ground black pepper
chopped fresh cilantro, to garnish

For the paste
2 large garlic cloves, chopped
1–2 fresh green chiles, seeded
   and chopped
1 tablespoon chopped fresh ginger root
3 tablespoons chopped fresh cilantro
5 tablespoons coconut milk
2 tablespoons peanut or mild olive oil
grated rind of ½ lime
½ teaspoon light brown sugar

1 To make the paste, process the garlic, chiles, ginger, cilantro, and coconut milk in a food processor or blender.

2 Tip the spicy paste into a small bowl, and beat in the peanut or olive oil, grated lime rind, and brown sugar. Preheat the oven to 400°F.

3 Heat the oil in a large roasting pan in the oven for 5 minutes. Add the sweet potatoes, beets, onions, and coriander seeds, tossing them in the hot oil. Roast the vegetables for 10 minutes.

4 Stir in the spicy paste and the whole red chiles. Season the vegetables well with salt and pepper, and shake the roasting pan to toss the vegetables, and coat them thoroughly with the paste.

5 Return the vegetables to the oven, and cook for 25–35 minutes more, or until both the sweet potatoes and onions are fully cooked and tender. During cooking, stir the mixture two or three times with a wooden spoon to prevent the coconut and ginger paste from sticking to the roasting pan. Serve the vegetables immediately, sprinkled with a little chopped fresh cilantro.

COOK'S TIP
Try to buy orange-fleshed sweet potatoes for this dish—they not only look more attractive than white-fleshed ones, but they are also more nutritious.

Energy 272Kcal/1143kJ; Protein 4.4g; Carbohydrate 39.8g, of which sugars 19.2g; Fat 11.8g, of which saturates 1.7g; Cholesterol 0mg; Calcium 98mg; Fiber 6.3g; Sodium 122mg.

ZUCCHINI in TOMATO SAUCE

This rich-flavored Mediterranean dish can be served hot or cold, either as a side dish or as part of a tapas meal. Cut the zucchini into fairly thick slices, so that they retain their texture and stay slightly crunchy.

SERVES 4

1 tablespoon olive oil
1 onion, chopped
1 garlic clove, chopped
4 zucchini, thickly sliced
14-ounce can chopped tomatoes, drained
2 tomatoes, peeled, seeded,
   and chopped
1 teaspoon vegetable bouillon powder
1 tablespoon tomato paste
salt and ground black pepper

VARIATION

Add 1 or 2 sliced and seeded red, green, or yellow bell peppers with the zucchini in step 1.

1 Heat the olive oil in a heavy pan, add the chopped onion and garlic, and sauté for about 5 minutes, or until the onion is softened, stirring occasionally. Add the thickly sliced zucchini, and cook for 5 minutes more.

2 Add the canned and fresh tomatoes, bouillon powder, and tomato paste. Stir well, then simmer for 10–15 minutes, until the sauce is thickened and the zucchini are just tender. Season to taste and serve.

BAKED FENNEL with a CRUMB CRUST

The delicate aniseed flavor of baked fennel makes it a very good accompaniment to all kinds of dishes, from pasta and risotto to roast chicken.

SERVES 4

3 fennel bulbs, cut lengthwise
   into fourths
2 tablespoons olive oil
1 garlic clove, chopped
1 cup day-old whole-
   wheat bread crumbs
2 tablespoons chopped fresh Italian parsley
salt and ground black pepper
a few fronds of fennel leaves, to
   garnish (optional)

COOK'S TIPS

• When buying fennel, look for compact, unblemished white-green bulbs. The leaves should look fresh and green. Tougher specimens will have bulbs that spread at the top.

• Fennel has a distinctive licorice flavor, which particularly complements fish dishes. All parts of the plant are edible including the bulb, the celery-like stalks, and the feathery leaves.

1 Cook the fennel in a pan of boiling salted water for 10 minutes. Preheat the oven to 375°F.

2 Drain the fennel, and place in a large earthenware baking dish, then brush with half of the olive oil.

VARIATION

To make a cheese-topped version, add 4 tablespoons finely grated strong-flavored cheese, such as sharp Cheddar, Dry Jack, or Parmesan, to the bread-crumb mixture in step 3.

3 In a small bowl, combine the chopped garlic, whole-wheat bread crumbs, and chopped fresh Italian parsley, then stir in the rest of the olive oil. Sprinkle the mixture evenly over the fennel, then season well with salt and pepper.

4 Bake the fennel for about 30 minutes, or until it is tender and the bread-crumb topping is crisp and golden brown. Serve the baked fennel hot, garnished with a few fronds of fennel leaves, if you like.

Courgettes in Tomato Sauce: Energy 92Kcal/382kJ; Protein 4.8g; Carbohydrate 9.4g, of which sugars 8.9g; Fat 4g, of which saturates 0.8g; Cholesterol 0mg; Calcium 64mg; Fiber 3.5g; Sodium 16mg.
Baked Fennel with a Crumb Crust: Energy 114Kcal/477kJ; Protein 3g; Carbohydrate 12.6g, of which sugars 3.1g; Fat 6.1g, of which saturates 0.8g; Cholesterol 0mg; Calcium 67mg; Fiber 4.3g; Sodium 114mg.

BRAISED LETTUCE and PEAS with MINT

Based on the traditional French way of braising peas with lettuce in butter, this dish is delicious with simply cooked fish, or roast or broiled duck.

2 Toss the vegetables in the butter, then sprinkle in the sugar, ½ teaspoon salt and plenty of black pepper. Cover, then cook very gently for 5 minutes, stirring once.

3 Add the peas and mint sprigs to the pan. Toss the peas in the buttery juices, then pour in the stock or water.

4 Cover the pan, and cook over gentle heat for 5 minutes more, until the peas are almost tender, then remove the lid from the pan. Increase the heat to high and cook, stirring occasionally, until the cooking liquid has reduced to a few tablespoons.

5 Stir in the remaining butter, and adjust the seasoning. Transfer to a warmed serving dish, and garnish with the extra mint. Serve immediately.

VARIATIONS

• Braise about 9 ounces baby carrots with the lettuce.

• Use 1 lettuce, shredding it coarsely, and omit the fresh mint. Toward the end of cooking, stir in about 5 ounces arugula—preferably the slightly stronger-flavored, wild variety—and cook briefly until it has just wilted.

• Cook 4 ounces chopped smoked bacon or pancetta with 1 small chopped red or white onion in the butter. Use 1 bunch of scallions, and omit the mint. Stir in some chopped fresh Italian parsley before serving. This version is also very good with small, white summer turnips, braised with the lettuce.

SERVES 4

¼ cup butter
4 Bibb lettuces,
  halved lengthwise
2 bunches scallions
1 teaspoon sugar
14 ounces shelled peas (about
  2¼ pounds in pods)
a few fresh mint sprigs, plus extra fresh
  mint to garnish
½ cup light vegetable or chicken stock
  or water
salt and ground black pepper

1 Melt half the butter in a wide, heavy pan over low heat. Add the lettuce halves and scallions.

Energy 164Kcal/680kJ; Protein 9.2g; Carbohydrate 9.8g, of which sugars 3.4g; Fat 10.1g, of which saturates 3.2g; Cholesterol 27mg; Calcium 69mg; Fiber 3.7g; Sodium 64mg.

BRAISED LEEKS with CARROTS

Sweet carrots and leeks go well together and are good finished with a little chopped mint,
chervil, or parsley. This is a good accompaniment to roast beef, lamb, or chicken.

SERVES 4

5 tablespoons butter
1½ pounds carrots, thickly sliced
a little sugar
2 fresh bay leaves
5 tablespoons water
1½ pounds leeks, cut into 2-inch lengths
1½ cups white wine
2 tablespoons chopped fresh mint, chervil,
    or parsley
salt and ground black pepper

1 Melt 2 tablespoons of the butter in
a wide, heavy pan, and cook the carrots
without letting them brown, for about
5 minutes. Add the bay leaves, seasoning,
sugar, and the water. Bring to a boil,
cover, and cook for 10 minutes, or until
the carrots are just tender.

2 Uncover the pan, and boil until the
juices have evaporated, leaving the
carrots moist and glazed. Remove the
carrots from the pan, and set aside.

3 Melt 2 tablespoons of the remaining
butter in the pan. Add the leeks, and
cook over low heat for 4–5 minutes,
without letting them brown.

4 Add seasoning, a good pinch of sugar,
the wine, and half the chopped herbs.
Heat until simmering, then cover, and
cook gently for 5–8 minutes, until the
leeks are tender, but not collapsed.

5 Uncover the leeks, and turn them in
the buttery juices. Increase the heat,
and then boil the liquid rapidly until it is
reduced to a few tablespoons.

6 Add the carrots to the leeks, and
reheat them gently, stirring occasionally,
then add the remaining butter. Adjust
the seasoning, if necessary. Transfer to a
warmed serving dish, and serve sprinkled
with the remaining chopped herbs.

VARIATION
Braised leeks in tarragon cream
Cook 2 pounds leeks, cut into 2-inch
lengths, in 3 tablespoons butter as
step 3. Season with salt and pepper, add
a pinch of sugar, 3 tablespoons tarragon
vinegar, 6 fresh tarragon sprigs or
1 teaspoon dried tarragon, and
4 tablespoons white wine. Cover, and
cook as step 4. Add ⅔ cup heavy cream,
and let bubble and thicken. Adjust the
seasoning, and serve sprinkled with plenty
of finely chopped fresh tarragon leaves.
A spoonful of tarragon-flavored mustard
is good stirred into these creamy leeks.
Serve with fish or chicken dishes.

Energy 240Kcal/994kJ; Protein 4.1g; Carbohydrate 18.7g, of which sugars 16.7g; Fat 14.8g, of which saturates 8.8g; Cholesterol 35mg; Calcium 103mg; Fiber 8.1g; Sodium 148mg.

BRAISED RED CABBAGE with BEETS

The moist, gentle cooking of the clay pot finishes this vegetable dish to perfection.
Serve with casseroles and roast meats—it is especially delicious with roast pork.

SERVES 6–8

1½ pounds red cabbage
1 Bermuda onion, thinly sliced
2 tablespoons olive oil
2 tablespoons light molasses sugar
2 tart eating apples, peeled, cored,
    and sliced
1¼ cups vegetable stock
4 tablespoons red wine vinegar
13 ounces raw beets, peeled
    and coarsely grated
salt and ground black pepper

COOK'S TIP
When buying cabbage, choose one that
is firm and heavy for its size. The leaves
should look healthy—avoid any with
curling leaves or blemishes. These
guidelines apply to any type of cabbage—
red, green, or white.

1 Soak a large clay pot or bean pot in
cold water for 20 minutes, then drain.
Finely shred the red cabbage, and place
in the clay pot.

2 Place the onion and olive oil in a
heavy frying pan, and sauté until soft and
transparent. Stir in the sugar, and cook
the onion gently until it is caramelized
and golden. Take care not to overcook.

3 Stir in the apple slices, stock, and wine
vinegar, then transfer to the clay pot.
Season with salt and pepper.

4 Cover and place in an unheated oven.
Set the oven temperature to 375°F,
and cook for 1 hour. Stir in the beets,
re-cover the pot, and cook for about
20–30 minutes more, or until the
cabbage and beets are tender.

Energy 99Kcal/415kJ; Protein 2.5g; Carbohydrate 16.2g, of which sugars 15g; Fat 3.1g, of which saturates 0.4g; Cholesterol 0mg; Calcium 63mg; Fiber 3.5g; Sodium 39mg.

SPINACH BRAISED with SWEET POTATOES

Sweet potatoes make an interesting alternative to the ordinary variety. Here the garlic and ginger subtly complement the flavors of the potatoes and spinach.

SERVES 4

2 tablespoons sunflower-seed oil
1 onion, chopped
1 garlic clove, finely chopped
1-inch piece fresh ginger root,
    peeled and grated
½ teaspoon cayenne pepper
1½ pounds sweet potatoes
⅔ cup vegetable or
    chicken stock
8 ounces spinach
3 tablespoons pine nuts, toasted
salt and ground black pepper

1 Soak a clay potato pot in cold water for 20 minutes, then drain. Heat the oil in a large frying pan, add the onion, garlic, ginger, and cayenne pepper, and cook gently, stirring occasionally, for about 8 minutes, or until the onion is softened.

2 Peel the sweet potatoes, and cut them into 1-inch chunks. Add the chunks to the frying pan, and stir to coat them in the oil and spices.

COOK'S TIP
To toast pine nuts, heat a heavy frying pan, and add the nuts, cook them for 3–4 minutes, or until they turn a golden brown color, stirring occasionally. Watch the nuts carefully—they will scorch and burn quickly if toasted for too long.

VARIATIONS
• Add a drained, 14-ounce can garbanzo beans to the potato mixture after 30 minutes cooking, and stir well.
• Use baby new potatoes in place of the sweet potatoes.

3 Transfer the potato mixture to the clay pot, and add the stock. Cover the pot, and place in an unheated oven. Set the oven to 425°F, and cook for about 50–60 minutes, or until the potatoes are just tender, stirring gently halfway through cooking.

4 Wash the spinach, and shred coarsely. Stir into the potatoes with the toasted pine nuts, re-cover the clay pot, and cook for 5 minutes more in the oven. Remove from the oven, and let stand for 5 minutes. Adjust the seasoning, and serve immediately.

Energy 293Kcal/1231kJ; Protein 5.4g; Carbohydrate 38.5g, of which sugars 11.8g; Fat 14.2g, of which saturates 1.4g; Cholesterol 0mg; Calcium 141mg; Fiber 5.7g; Sodium 147mg.

ROOT VEGETABLE GRATIN with INDIAN SPICES

Subtly spiced with curry powder, turmeric, coriander, and mild chili powder, this rich gratin is substantial enough to serve on its own for lunch or supper. It also makes a good accompaniment to a vegetable or bean curry.

2 Preheat the oven to 350°F. Melt half the butter in a heavy pan, add the curry powder, ground turmeric, and coriander, and half the chili powder. Cook, stirring constantly, for 2 minutes, then leave to cool slightly. Drain the vegetables, then pat them dry with paper towels. Place in a bowl, add the spice mixture and the shallots, and mix well.

3 Arrange the vegetables in a shallow baking dish, seasoning well with salt and pepper between the layers. Combine the cream and milk, pour the mixture over the vegetables, then sprinkle the remaining chili powder on top.

4 Cover the dish with baking parchment and bake for 45 minutes. Remove the baking parchment, dot the vegetables with the remaining butter, and bake for 50 minutes more, or until the top is golden brown. Serve the gratin garnished with chopped parsley.

SERVES 4

2 large potatoes, about 1 pound total weight
2 sweet potatoes, about 10 ounces total weight
6 ounces celery root
1 tablespoon sweet butter
1 teaspoon curry powder
1 teaspoon ground turmeric
½ teaspoon ground coriander
1 teaspoon mild chili powder
3 shallots, chopped
⅔ cup light cream
⅔ cup milk
salt and ground black pepper
chopped fresh Italian parsley, to garnish

1 Cut the potatoes, sweet potatoes, and celery root into thin, even slices using a sharp knife or the slicing attachment on a food processor. Immediately place the vegetables in a bowl of cold water to prevent them from discoloring.

COOK'S TIP
The cream adds a delicious richness to this gratin. However, you can use low-fat milk, if you prefer a lighter meal.

Energy 268Kcal/1129kJ; Protein 5.8g; Carbohydrate 37.7g, of which sugars 9.8g; Fat 11.6g, of which saturates 7.1g; Cholesterol 31mg; Calcium 127mg; Fiber 3.6g; Sodium 117mg.

LEEKS in CREAM SAUCE

This versatile vegetable makes a great winter standby, and leeks find their way into many dishes, including casseroles and soups. Simple buttered leeks are underrated as a side dish, and this recipe makes a tasty accompaniment for plain broiled food, such as chops or chicken, or it can be served as a light lunch or supper on its own.

SERVES 4–6

4 large or 8 medium leeks
1¼ cups milk
8 fatty strips of bacon, trimmed and
    sliced (optional)
1 egg, lightly beaten
⅔ cup light cream
1 tablespoon mild mustard
¾ cup grated cheese (optional)
salt and ground black pepper

1 Slice the leeks into fairly large chunks. Put them into a pan with the milk. Season, and bring to the boil. Reduce the heat, and simmer for 15–20 minutes, or until tender. Drain well, and turn the leeks into a buttered shallow baking dish, reserving the cooking liquor.

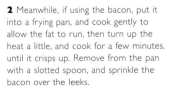

2 Meanwhile, if using the bacon, put it into a frying pan, and cook gently to allow the fat to run, then turn up the heat a little, and cook for a few minutes, until it crisps up. Remove from the pan with a slotted spoon, and sprinkle the bacon over the leeks.

3 Rinse the pan used for the leeks. Blend the beaten egg, light cream, and mustard together, and mix it with the reserved cooking liquor. Return to the pan, and heat gently without boiling, allowing the sauce to thicken a little. Taste, and adjust the seasoning with salt and freshly ground black pepper. Pour the sauce over the leeks and bacon.

4 Sprinkle with grated cheese, if using, and brown for a few minutes under a hot broiler. (Alternatively, the leeks may served immediately without browning.) Serve with plain broiled meat or poultry, if you like.

VARIATION
The bacon may be broiled and served separately, if you prefer.

Energy 238Kcal/993kJ; Protein 18.6g; Carbohydrate 9g, of which sugars 7.9g; Fat 14.4g, of which saturates 7.3g; Cholesterol 90mg; Calcium 172mg; Fiber 3.5g; Sodium 830mg

GRIDDLE POTATOES

This attractive dish has traditionally been cooked with leftover cooked potatoes that have been boiled in their skins. It makes a tasty accompaniment to broiled meat or fish, or would be served as a light meal with glasses of milk or buttermilk.

SERVES 4–6

2 onions, peeled and chopped
1–1½ pounds whole cooked potatoes,
    boiled in their skins
a mixture of butter and oil, for
    shallow frying
salt and ground black pepper

1 Put the onions in a large pan, and scald them briefly in boiling water. Refresh under cold water, and drain well. Peel and slice the potatoes.

2 Put a mixture of butter and oil into a large, heavy frying pan, and heat well.

3 When the fat is hot, fry the onion until tender. Add the potato slices, and brown them together, turning the potato slices to brown as evenly as possible on both sides. Transfer to a warmed serving dish, and season with salt and pepper. Serve very hot.

Energy 163Kcal/681kJ; Protein 3.4g; Carbohydrate 26.4g, of which sugars 5g; Fat 5.5g, of which saturates 3.3g; Cholesterol 13mg; Calcium 26mg; Fiber 2.6g; Sodium 49mg

ROASTED POTATOES with GARLIC and RED ONIONS

These mouthwatering potatoes are a fine accompaniment to just about anything.
The key is to use small firm potatoes; the smaller they are cut, the quicker they will cook.

SERVES 4

1½ pounds small firm potatoes
2 tablespoons butter
2 tablespoons olive oil
2 large or 4 small red onions, cut
    into wedges
8 garlic cloves, unpeeled
2 tablespoons chopped fresh rosemary or
    2 teaspoons dried
salt and ground black pepper

COOK'S TIP

Choose waxy or new potatoes that will hold their shape for this dish. You can peel them, or simply scrub them well, and leave the skins on.

1 Preheat the oven to 450°F. Peel, and cut the potatoes into fourths, rinse them, and pat dry on paper towels.

2 Put the butter and oil in a roasting pan, and heat in the oven. When the butter has melted and is foaming, add the potatoes, onion wedges, and garlic cloves to the roasting pan.

3 Sprinkle over the rosemary, toss well, then spread out the vegetables.

4 Place the pan in the oven, and roast for about 25 minutes, until the potatoes are golden and tender when tested with a fork. Shake the pan from time to time to redistribute the vegetables. When cooked, season with salt and pepper.

Energy 254Kcal/1063kJ; Protein 4.5g; Carbohydrate 35.4g, of which sugars 8.1g; Fat 11.5g, of which saturates 4.2g; Cholesterol 13mg; Calcium 59mg; Fiber 3.7g; Sodium 63mg.

POTATO GRATIN

Potatoes, layered with mustard butter and baked until golden, are perfect to serve with a green salad, or as an accompaniment to a vegetable or nut roast.

SERVES 4

4 large potatoes, about 2 pounds
   total weight
2 tablespoons butter
1 tablespoon olive oil
2 large garlic cloves, crushed
2 tablespoons Dijon mustard
1 tablespoon lemon juice
1 tablespoon fresh thyme leaves, plus
   extra to garnish
¼ cup vegetable stock
salt and ground black pepper

1 Thinly slice the potatoes, using a knife, mandolin, or a slicing attachment on a food processor. Place the potato slices in a bowl of cold water to prevent them from discoloring.

2 Preheat the oven to 400°F. Heat the butter and oil in a deep, flameproof frying pan. Add the garlic, and cook gently for 2–3 minutes until light golden, stirring constantly. Stir in the mustard, lemon juice, and thyme. Remove from the heat, and pour the mixture into a pitcher.

3 Drain the potatoes, and pat dry with paper towels. Place a layer of potatoes in the pan, season, and pour over one-third of the butter mixture. Arrange another layer of potatoes on top, pour over half of the remaining butter mixture, and season. Arrange a final layer of potatoes on top, pour over the remainder of the butter mixture and the stock. Season, and sprinkle with the reserved thyme.

4 Cover the potatoes with parchment paper, and bake for 1 hour, then remove the paper, return to the oven, and cook for 15 minutes, or until golden.

VARIATION
Any root vegetables can be used: try sweet potatoes, parsnips, or turnips.

Energy 238Kcal/1002kJ; Protein 3.9g; Carbohydrate 36.3g, of which sugars 3g; Fat 9.6g, of which saturates 4.5g; Cholesterol 16mg; Calcium 15mg; Fiber 2.3g; Sodium 70mg.

NEW POTATOES with THYME and LEMON

These potatoes are the perfect accompaniment to meat or poultry. You can even use old potatoes, cut into chunks, ideal for serving as an alternative with a traditional roast.

SERVES 4

1½ pounds small new potatoes
4 garlic cloves, sliced
8 fresh thyme sprigs
4 strips finely pared lemon rind
5 tablespoons olive oil
coarsely ground black pepper
coarse sea salt

COOK'S TIPS

• Thyme is an aromatic, woody herb that goes particularly well with lemon. It has a strong aroma and pungent flavor and grows wild in most warm climates. Thyme is often associated with dishes from the Mediterranean.

• You could easily make this dish with older potatoes—simply peel them, if you like, then cut them into even chunks or wedges before adding them to the pot.

1 Soak a clay potato pot in cold water for 20 minutes, then drain. Scrub the new potatoes, and rinse thoroughly in cold water. Place the potatoes in the pot.

2 Add the sliced garlic cloves, thyme sprigs, and pared lemon rind to the pot, tucking them in among the potatoes. Sprinkle over plenty of coarsely ground black pepper and coarse sea salt.

3 Drizzle over the olive oil. Cover with the lid, and place in an unheated oven. Set the oven to 400°F, and cook for 1 hour, or until just tender.

4 If you like, remove the lid, and bake for 15–20 minutes more, until slightly golden. If you like to keep the skins soft, remove the potatoes from the oven, and leave to stand for 10 minutes.

Energy 242Kcal/1011kJ; Protein 2.9g; Carbohydrate 27.2g, of which sugars 2.2g; Fat 14.3g, of which saturates 2.1g; Cholesterol 0mg; Calcium 10mg; Fiber 1.7g; Sodium 19mg.

POTATOES BAKED with FENNEL, ONIONS, GARLIC, and SAFFRON

Potatoes, fennel, and onions flavored with garlic, saffron, and spices make a sophisticated and attractive accompaniment to fish or chicken or egg-based, main-course dishes.

SERVES 4–6

1¼ pounds small waxy potatoes, cut into
    chunks or wedges
good pinch of saffron threads
    (12–15 threads)
1 head of garlic, separated into
    individual cloves
12 small red or yellow onions, peeled
    but left whole
3 fennel bulbs, cut into wedges, feathery
    tops reserved for garnish (optional)
4–6 fresh bay leaves
6–9 fresh thyme sprigs
¾ cup fish, chicken or vegetable stock
2 tablespoons sherry or
    balsamic vinegar
½ teaspoon sugar
1 teaspoon fennel seeds,
    lightly crushed
½ teaspoon paprika
3 tablespoons olive oil
salt and ground black pepper

1 Boil the potato chunks or wedges in a pan of lightly salted, boiling water for 8–10 minutes. Drain well. Preheat the oven to 375°F. Soak the saffron threads in 2 tablespoons warm water for 10 minutes.

2 Peel and finely chop two of the garlic cloves and set aside. Place the potato chunks or wedges, whole red or yellow onions, remaining unpeeled garlic cloves, fennel wedges, fresh bay leaves, and fresh thyme sprigs in a large roasting pan or dish. Mix together the stock and the saffron and its soaking liquid in a pitcher or measuring cup.

3 Add the vinegar and sugar to the stock mixture, then pour the liquid over the vegetables. Stir in the fennel seeds, paprika, chopped garlic, and oil, and season with salt and pepper.

4 Cook the vegetables in the oven for 1–1¼ hours, stirring occasionally, until they are just tender. Chop the reserved fennel tops, if using, and sprinkle them over the vegetables to garnish. Season the vegetables with more salt and pepper and serve immediately.

COOK'S TIP

Sherry vinegar has a rich, mellow flavor and it makes a good addition to a variety of sauces and dressings. It can be used simply to add extra piquancy to a dish. Try sprinkling a little over oven-roasted vegetables or add a teaspoon or two to soups, sauces, or stews.

Energy 162Kcal/676kJ; Protein 4.4g; Carbohydrate 23.6g, of which sugars 7.1g; Fat 6.2g, of which saturates 0.9g; Cholesterol 0mg; Calcium 49mg; Fiber 4.9g; Sodium 23mg.

LENTIL DHAL with ROASTED GARLIC and WHOLE SPICES

This spicy lentil dhal makes a sustaining and comforting meal when served with rice or Indian breads and any dry-spiced dish, particularly a cauliflower or potato dish. It's something of a cheat to have in a one-pot cookbook, since there's a spicy garnish that needs to be cooked—in a small frying pan—at the end.

SERVES 4–6

3 tablespoons butter or ghee
1 onion, chopped
2 fresh green chiles, seeded and chopped
1 tablespoon chopped fresh ginger root
1 cup yellow or red lentils
3¾ cups water
3 tablespoons roasted garlic puree
1 teaspoon ground cumin
1 teaspoon ground coriander
7 ounces tomatoes, peeled and diced
a little lemon juice
salt and ground black pepper
2–3 tablespoons fresh cilantro sprigs,
    to garnish

For the spicy garnish
2 tablespoons peanut oil
4–5 shallots, sliced
2 garlic cloves, thinly sliced
1 tablespoon butter or ghee
1 teaspoon cumin seeds
1 teaspoon mustard seeds
3–4 small dried red chiles
8–10 fresh curry leaves

1 First begin the spicy garnish. Heat the oil in a large, heavy pan. Add the shallots, and cook them over medium heat, stirring occasionally, until they are crisp and browned. Add the garlic and cook, stirring frequently, for a moment or two until the garlic colors slightly. Use a slotted spoon to remove the mixture from the pan, and set aside.

COOK'S TIP
Ghee is type of clarified butter that has had all the milk solids removed by heating—it was originally made to extend the life of butter in India. It is the main cooking fat used in Indian cooking. Because the milk solids have been removed, ghee has a high smoking point and can therefore be cooked at higher temperatures than ordinary butter. Look for it in Indian and Asian stores.

2 Melt the butter or ghee in the pan, and cook the onion, chiles, and ginger for 10 minutes, until golden.

3 Stir in the lentils and water, then bring to a boil, reduce the heat, and part-cover the pan. Simmer, stirring occasionally, for 50–60 minutes, until similar to a very thick soup.

4 Stir in the roasted garlic puree, cumin, and ground coriander, then season to taste with salt and pepper. Cook over low heat for 10–15 minutes more, uncovered, stirring frequently.

5 Stir in the tomatoes, and then adjust the seasoning, adding a little lemon juice to taste if necessary.

6 To make the spicy garnish: melt the butter or ghee in a frying pan. Add the cumin and mustard seeds, and cook until the mustard seeds pop. Stir in the chiles, curry leaves, and the shallot mixture, then immediately swirl the mixture into the cooked dhal. Garnish with cilantro, spicy fried shallots, and garlic, and serve.

Energy 233Kcal/978kJ; Protein 9.5g; Carbohydrate 23.8g, of which sugars 3.1g; Fat 11.8g, of which saturates 5.3g; Cholesterol 20mg; Calcium 28mg; Fiber 2.5g; Sodium 73mg.

RICE with DILL and FAVA BEANS

This is a favorite rice dish in Iran. The combination of fava beans, plenty of fresh dill, and warm spices works very well, and the saffron rice adds a splash of bright color.

SERVES 4

1½ cups basmati rice,
    soaked in cold water and drained
3 cups water
3 tablespoons butter
1½ cups frozen baby fava beans,
    thawed and peeled
6 tablespoons finely chopped fresh dill,
    plus fresh dill sprigs to garnish
1 teaspoon ground cinnamon
1 teaspoon ground cumin
2–3 saffron threads, soaked in
    1 tablespoon boiling water
salt

1 Tip the rice into a large pan with the water. Add a little salt. Bring to a boil, then simmer very gently for 5 minutes. Drain, rinse in warm water, and drain again.

2 Melt the butter in the rinsed-out pan. Pour two-thirds of the melted butter into a bowl, and set aside. Spoon enough rice into the pan to cover the base. Add a fourth of the beans and a little dill.

3 Spread over another layer of rice, then a layer of beans and dill. Repeat the layers until all the beans and dill have been used, ending with a layer of rice. Cook over gentle heat for 8 minutes, until nearly tender.

4 Pour the reserved melted butter evenly over the rice, then sprinkle the ground cinnamon and cumin over the top. Cover the pan with a clean dish towel or cloth and a tight-fitting lid, lifting the corners of the towel or cloth back over the lid. Cook over low heat for 25–30 minutes.

5 Spoon about 3 tablespoons of the cooked rice into the bowl of saffron water and then mix the rice and liquid together. Spoon the remaining rice mixture onto a large serving plate and spoon the saffron rice on one side to garnish. Serve immediately, decorated with fresh sprigs of dill.

Energy 364Kcal/1521kJ; Protein 9.3g; Carbohydrate 60.7g, of which sugars 1.2g; Fat 9.1g, of which saturates 5.3g; Cholesterol 21mg; Calcium 84mg; Fiber 4g; Sodium 72mg.

BASMATI RICE with VEGETABLES

Serve this tasty dish with roast chicken, broiled lamb chops, or pan-fried fish. Add the vegetables near the end of cooking so that they remain crisp.

SERVES 4

1¾ cups basmati rice
3 tablespoons vegetable oil
1 onion, chopped
2 garlic cloves, crushed
3 cups water or vegetable stock
⅔ cup fresh or drained canned
  corn kernels
1 red or green bell pepper, seeded
  and chopped
1 large carrot, grated
fresh chervil sprigs,
  to garnish

1 Rinse the rice in a strainer under cold water, then leave to drain thoroughly for about 15 minutes.

2 Heat the oil in a large pan, and cook the onion for a few minutes over medium heat, until it starts to soften.

3 Add the rice to the pan, and cook for about 10 minutes, stirring constantly to prevent the rice from sticking to the base of the pan. Stir in the garlic.

4 Pour in the water or stock, and stir well. Bring to a boil, then lower the heat. Cover, and simmer for 10 minutes.

5 Sprinkle the corn over the rice, spread the bell pepper on top, and sprinkle over the grated carrot. Cover tightly, and steam over low heat until the rice is tender, then mix with a fork. Pile onto a serving plate. and garnish with chervil.

Energy 449Kcal/1877kJ; Protein 8.1g; Carbohydrate 83g, of which sugars 7.7g; Fat 9.3g, of which saturates 1.1g; Cholesterol 0mg; Calcium 30mg; Fiber 1.8g; Sodium 85mg.

SAFFRON RICE with ONION and CARDAMOM

This delightfully fragrant, buttery pilaf is wonderful with both Indian and Middle-eastern dishes, especially ones featuring fish, shellfish, chicken, or lamb.

2 Toast the saffron threads in a dry, heavy frying pan over low heat for about 2 minutes, then place in a small bowl, and add 2 tablespoons warm water. Leave to soak for 10–15 minutes.

3 Melt the butter in the pan, then cook the onion with the cardamom pods very gently for 8–10 minutes, until soft and buttery yellow.

4 Add the drained rice to the pan, and stir to coat the grains in the butter. Add the salt and bay leaves, then stir in the stock or water and saffron with its liquid. Bring the rice to a boil, stir, then reduce the heat to very low, and cover tightly. Cook the rice for 10–12 minutes, until it has absorbed all the liquid.

5 Lay a clean, folded dish towel over the pan under the lid, and press on the lid to wedge it firmly in place. Leave the rice to stand for 10–15 minutes to continue cooking in its own heat.

6 Fluff up the grains of cooked rice with a fork. Tip it into a warmed serving dish, and serve immediately as an accompaniment to a spicy main course.

SERVES 4

1¾ cups basmati rice
good pinch of saffron threads (about 15 threads)
2 tablespoons butter
1 onion, finely chopped
6 green cardamom pods, lightly crushed
1 teaspoon salt
2–3 fresh bay leaves
2½ cups well-flavored chicken or vegetable stock or water

1 Put the rice into a strainer, and rinse well under cold running water. Tip it into a bowl, add cold water to cover, and set aside to soak for 30–40 minutes. Drain in the strainer.

COOK'S TIP
After boiling, when all the liquid has been absorbed, basmati rice is set aside to finish cooking in its own heat and become tender. Wedging a folded dish towel under the pan lid ensures the heat is not lost and the steam is absorbed.

Energy 366Kcal/1528kJ; Protein 6.7g; Carbohydrate 71.1g, of which sugars 0.9g; Fat 5.6g, of which saturates 3.3g; Cholesterol 13mg; Calcium 22mg; Fiber 0.2g; Sodium 38mg.

GARLIC CHIVE RICE with MUSHROOMS

*Rice is readily steeped with the pungent aroma and taste of garlic chives, creating a dish
with an excellent flavor. Serve with vegetarian dishes, fish, or chicken.*

SERVES 4

4 tablespoons peanut oil
9 ounces mixed mushrooms,
   thickly sliced
1 ounce garlic chives, chopped
1¾ cups long grain rice
1 small onion, finely chopped
2 fresh green chiles, seeded and
   finely chopped
½ cup fresh cilantro
2½ cups vegetable or mushroom stock
1 teaspoon salt
½ cup toasted cashew nuts
ground black pepper

5 Add the rice to the onions, and cook
over low heat, stirring frequently, for
4–5 minutes, until the onion is softened.
Pour in the stock mixture, then stir in
the salt and plenty of black pepper.

6 Bring to a boil, stir, and reduce the
heat to very low. Cover tightly, and cook
for 15–20 minutes, until the rice has
absorbed all the liquid. Lay a clean,
folded dish towel over the pan under
the lid, and press on the lid to wedge it
firmly in place. Leave to stand in a warm
place for 10 minutes, letting the towel
absorb the steam while the rice
becomes completely tender.

7 Add the cooked mushroom and chive
mixture to the rice, and mix well. Stir in
the chopped fresh cilantro leaves, then
adjust the seasoning. Serve immediately,
sprinkled with the toasted cashew nuts.

1 Heat half the oil in a large frying pan,
and cook the thickly sliced mushrooms
for 5–6 minutes, stirring occasionally,
until they are tender and browned.

2 Add half of the garlic chives to the
frying pan, and cook for 1–2 minutes.
Remove them with a slotted spoon, and
set aside. Wash and drain the rice.

3 Add the remaining oil to the pan, add
the chopped onion and chiles,
and cook over gentle heat, stirring
occasionally, for 10–12 minutes, until
the onions have softened.

4 Set half the remaining garlic chives
aside. Cut the stalks off the cilantro, and
set the leaves aside. Puree the remaining
chives and the cilantro stalks with the
stock in a food processor or blender.

COOK'S TIP
You'll find garlic chives in Asian and Thai
food stores.

Energy 504Kcal/2100kJ; Protein 10.4g; Carbohydrate 73.8g, of which sugars 1.0g, Fat 10.2g, of which saturates 2.6g; Cholesterol 0mg; Calcium 41mg; Fiber 1.6g; Sodium 533mg.

SLOW COOKER DESSERTS AND CAKES

From baked custards and poached fruit to steamed puddings and luscious cakes, this tempting chapter is perfect for anyone with a sweet tooth. Try old-fashioned favorites such as Poached Pears in Red Wine, Baked Stuffed Apples and Tapioca Pudding, or indulge yourself with a really wicked treat such as Chocolate Chip and Banana Pudding. When you are looking for a little something to enjoy mid-afternoon with a cup of tea or coffee, try any one of the fabulous cakes—Frosted Carrot and Parsnip Cake, Chocolate Cheesecake Brownies or Moist Golden Ginger Cake. One mouthful of any of these delights and you will be in heaven.

COCONUT CUSTARD

This classic Thai dessert, made with rich, creamy coconut milk, is often served with a selection of fresh fruit. Mangoes and tamarillos go particularly well.

2 Strain the mixture into a pitcher, then pour into four individual heatproof glasses, ramekins, or one single ovenproof dish. Cover the containers with plastic wrap.

3 Place the dishes in the slow cooker, and, if necessary, pour a little more boiling water around them to reach just over halfway up their sides.

4 Cover the ceramic cooking pot with the lid, then cook for 3 hours, or until the custards are lightly set. Test with a fine skewer or toothpick; it should come out clean.

5 Carefully lift the dishes out of the slow cooker, and leave to cool. Once cool, chill in the refrigerator until ready to serve. Decorate the custards with a light dusting of confectioners' sugar, and serve with sliced fruit.

SERVES 4

4 eggs
generous ⅓ cup soft light brown sugar
1 cup coconut milk
1 teaspoon vanilla, rose or jasmine extract
confectioners' sugar, to decorate
sliced fresh fruit, to serve

COOK'S TIP
Line the bases of individual ramekins with rounds of parchment paper, then lightly oil the sides. After cooking and chilling, run a knife around the insides of the custards and turn out onto individual dessert plates.

1 Pour about 1 inch of hot water into the base of the ceramic cooking pot, and switch the slow cooker onto low. Whisk the eggs and sugar in a bowl until smooth. Gradually add the coconut milk and flavored extract, and whisk well.

Energy 175Kcal/738kJ; Protein 7.5g; Carbohydrate 22.7g, of which sugars 22.7g; Fat 6.7g, of which saturates 2g; Cholesterol 227mg; Calcium 57mg; Fiber 0g; Sodium 151mg.

TAPIOCA PUDDING

Another Thai-style dessert, this version of the classic tapioca pudding is made from large
pearl tapioca and coconut milk and is served warm. It is very good served with lychees.

SERVES 4

⅔ cup large pearl tapioca
2 cups very hot water
generous ½ cup superfine sugar
pinch of salt
I cup coconut milk
9 ounces prepared tropical fruits
shredded lime rind and shaved fresh
    coconut, to decorate (optional)

COOK'S TIP

This dish includes a lot of sugar—as it
would in Thailand—but you may prefer to
reduce the sugar according to taste.

I Put the tapioca in a bowl and pour
over enough warm water to cover
generously. Leave the tapioca to soak for
I hour, until the grains swell, then drain
well, and set aside.

2 Pour the measured water into the
ceramic cooking pot, and switch the
slow cooker to high. Add the sugar and
salt, and stir until dissolved. Cover with
the lid, and heat for about 30 minutes,
until the water reaches boiling point.

3 Add the tapioca and coconut milk and
stir well. Cover pot and cook for a further
I–I½ hours, or until the tapioca grains
become transparent.

4 Spoon into one large dish or four
individual bowls, and serve warm with
tropical fruits, decorated with the lime
rind and coconut shavings, if using.

Energy 273Kcal/1164kJ; Protein 2.7g; Carbohydrate 66.7g, of which sugars 41.9g; Fat 1.3g, of which saturates 0.4g; Cholesterol 0mg; Calcium 43mg; Fiber 1.7g; Sodium 73mg.

POACHED PEARS in RED WINE

The pears take on a red blush from the wine and make a very pretty dessert. It works best in a small slow cooker, which ensures that the pears stay submerged during cooking.

SERVES 4

1 bottle fruity red wine
¾ cup superfine sugar
3 tablespoons clear honey
1 cinnamon stick
1 vanilla bean, split lengthwise
large strip of lemon or orange rind
2 whole cloves
2 black peppercorns
4 firm ripe pears
juice of ½ lemon
mint leaves, to garnish
whipped cream or sour cream, to serve

1 Pour the red wine into the ceramic cooking pot. Add the sugar, honey, cinnamon stick, vanilla bean, lemon or orange rind, cloves, and peppercorns. Cover with the lid, and cook on high for 30 minutes, stirring occasionally.

2 Meanwhile, peel the pears using a vegetable peeler, leaving the stem intact. Take a very thin slice off the base of each pear so it will stand square and upright. As each pear is peeled, toss it in the lemon juice to prevent the flesh browning when exposed to the air.

3 Place the pears in the spiced wine mixture. Cover with the lid, and cook for 2–4 hours, turning the pears occasionally, until they are just tender; be careful not to overcook them.

COOK'S TIP
The cooking time will depend on the size and ripeness of the pears. Small, ripe pears will cook quickly; large, hard pears will take longer.

4 Transfer the pears to a bowl, using a slotted spoon. Continue to cook the wine mixture uncovered for a further hour, until reduced and thickened a little, then turn off the slow cooker, and leave to cool. Alternatively, to save time, pour the cooking liquor into a pan, and boil briskly for 10–15 minutes.

5 Strain the cooled liquid over the pears, and chill for at least 3 hours. Place the pears in four individual serving dishes, and spoon a little of the wine syrup over each one. Garnish with fresh mint, and serve with whipped or sour cream.

Energy 87Kcal/367kJ; Protein 0.5g; Carbohydrate 16.6g, of which sugars 16.6g; Fat 0.2g, of which saturates 0g; Cholesterol 0mg; Calcium 19mg; Fiber 3.3g; Sodium 7mg.

WINTER FRUIT POACHED in MULLED WINE

Poaching fresh apples and pears with dried apricots and figs in a spicy wine syrup makes
a delicious winter dessert. Serve on its own or with a generous spoonful of thick cream.

SERVES 4

1¼ cups fruity red wine
1¼ cups fresh apple or orange juice
thinly pared strip of orange or
    lemon peel
3 tablespoons clear honey
1 small cinnamon stick
4 whole cloves
4 cardamom pods, split
2 pears, such as Anjou or Bosc
8 ready-to-eat figs
12 ready-to-eat dried unsulphured apricots
2 eating apples, peeled, cored and thickly
    sliced

1 Pour the wine and apple or orange
juice into the ceramic cooking pot.
Add the citrus peel, honey, cinnamon
stick, cloves, and cardamom pods. Cover
with the lid, and cook on high for 1 hour.

2 Peel, core, and halve the pears,
keeping the stalk intact if possible.
Place in the slow cooker with the figs
and apricots. Cook for 1 hour. Gently
turn the pears, then add the sliced
apples, and cook for a further 1½–2
hours, or until all the fruit is tender.

3 Using a slotted spoon, carefully
remove the fruit from the cooking pot,
and place in a serving dish. Set aside
while you finish making the syrup.

4 Strain the syrup into a pan, discarding
the spices, then bring to the boil. Boil
vigorously for about 10 minutes, until
reduced by about one-third. Pour over
the fruit, and serve hot or cold.

COOK'S TIP
Choose tart, well-tasting apples such as
Winesap, Rome Beauty, and Cortland.
They stand up particularly well against the
sweet dried fruits and spicy, robust red
wine syrup.

Energy 347Kcal/1476kJ; Protein 5g; Carbohydrate 78.1g, of which sugars 78.1g; Fat 1.9g, of which saturates 0g; Cholesterol 0mg; Calcium 284mg; Fiber 11.4g; Sodium 72mg.

BAKED STUFFED APPLES

Using Italian amaretti to stuff the apples gives a lovely almondy flavor, while dried cranberries and candied fruit add sweetness and color. Make sure that you choose a variety of apple that will remain firm during the long cooking time.

3 Add the nuts and dried cranberries or sour cherries and candied fruit to the bowl, and mix well, then set aside the filling while you prepare the apples.

4 Wash and dry the apples. Remove the cores, using an apple corer, then carefully enlarge each core cavity to twice its size, using the corer to shave out more flesh. Using a sharp knife, score each apple around its equator.

5 Divide the filling among the apples, packing it into the hole, then piling it on top. Stand the apples in the cooking pot, and cover with the lid. Reduce the temperature to low, and cook for 4 hours, or until tender. Transfer the apples to warmed serving plates, and spoon the sauce over the top. Serve with cream, crème fraîche, or vanilla ice cream.

SERVES 4

6 tablespoons butter, softened
3 tablespoons orange or apple juice
scant ½ cup light brown sugar
grated rind and juice of ½ orange
¼ teaspoon ground cinnamon
2 tablespoons crushed amaretti
¼ cup pecan nuts, chopped
¼ cup dried cranberries
   or sour cherries
¼ cup luxury mixed candied fruit, chopped
4 large stovecooking apples, such as
   York Imperial
cream, crème fraîche, or vanilla
   ice cream, to serve

1 Grease the ceramic cooking pot with 1 tablespoon of the butter, then pour in the fruit juice, and switch to high.

2 Put the remaining butter, the sugar, orange rind and juice, cinnamon, and amaretti crumbs in a bowl and mix well.

COOK'S TIP
The cooking time will depend on the type and size of apples used.

Energy 347Kcal/1457kJ; Protein 1.6g; Carbohydrate 42.4g, of which sugars 41.3g; Fat 20.3g, of which saturates 10.3g; Cholesterol 40mg; Calcium 27mg; Fiber 3g; Sodium 131mg.

PAPAYA COOKED with GINGER

Spicy ginger enhances the delicate flavor of papaya perfectly. This recipe is excellent for busy people because it takes no more than 10 minutes to prepare and can then just be left to cook gently. Be careful not to overcook papaya or the flesh will become watery.

SERVES 4

⅔ cup hot water

3 tablespoons raisins

shredded finely pared rind and juice
    of 1 lime

2 ripe papayas

2 pieces crystallized ginger in syrup,
    drained, plus 1 tablespoon syrup from
    the jar

8 amaretti or other dessert cookies,
    coarsely crushed

¼ cup pistachio nuts, chopped

1 tablespoon light brown sugar

4 tablespoons crème fraîche, plus extra
    to serve

VARIATION

Try using chopped almonds and strained plain yogurt in place of the pistachio nuts and crème fraîche.

1 Pour the water into the base of the ceramic cooking pot, and switch the slow cooker to high. Put the raisins in a small bowl, and pour over the lime juice. Stir to combine, then leave to soak for at least 5 minutes, while preparing the remaining ingredients.

2 Cut the papayas in half, and scoop out and discard their seeds using a teaspoon.

3 Finely chop the crystallized ginger, and combine with the cookies, raisins, and lime juice, lime rind, two-thirds of the nuts, sugar, and crème fraîche.

4 Fill the papayas with the mixture, and place in the cooking pot. Cover, and cook for 1–1½ hours. Drizzle with the ginger syrup, sprinkle with the remaining nuts, and serve with crème fraîche.

Energy 302Kcal/1272kJ; Protein 4.1g; Carbohydrate 45.6g, of which sugars 36.6g; Fat 12.8g, of which saturates 5.7g; Cholesterol 17mg; Calcium 70mg; Fiber 5.7g; Sodium 136mg.

VERMONT BAKED MAPLE CUSTARD

Maple syrup has a really distinctive flavor and gives these little baked custards a wonderfully rich taste. Try to find pure maple syrup—it will make all the difference.

SERVES 6

3 eggs
½ cup maple syrup
1 cup warm milk
⅔ cup warm light cream
1 teaspoon vanilla extract
whole nutmeg, to grate

COOK'S TIP

Warming the milk and cream until tepid will help the custard cook and set more quickly. You can do this in a pan on the stovetop, or more simply, pour the milk and cream into a heatproof bowl or pitcher, and place in the slow cooker filled with near-boiling water to a depth of about 2 inches. Switch the slow cooker to high, and leave for 30 minutes. Remove the milk, then turn the slow cooker to low, and use the hot water in the ceramic cooking pot to cook the custards.

1 Beat the eggs in a large bowl, then whisk in the maple syrup, followed by the warm milk, cream, and the vanilla extract. Grate in a little nutmeg.

2 Strain the custard mixture into six individual ramekins—first checking that the dishes will all fit inside the ceramic cooking pot in a single layer. Carefully cover each ramekin with a piece of kitchen foil, then place them in the ceramic cooking pot.

3 Pour very hot water around the dishes, to come three-quarters of the way up their sides. Cover with the lid, and cook on low for 2½–3 hours, or until set. To test, insert a skewer in the middle; it should come out clean.

4 Transfer the custards to a wire rack. Leave for 5 minutes, and serve warm, or leave to cool completely, then chill. Remove from the refrigerator about 30 minutes before serving.

Energy 174Kcal/735kJ; Protein 8.6g; Carbohydrate 24.5g, of which sugars 18.7g; Fat 5.3g, of which saturates 1.6g; Cholesterol 116mg; Calcium 97mg; Fiber 9.1g; Sodium 120mg.

PETITS POTS de CRÈME au MOCHA

The name of these classic French baked custards comes from the baking cups, called pots de crème. *The addition of coffee gives the dessert an even richer, more indulgent flavor.*

SERVES 4

1 teaspoon instant coffee powder
1 tablespoon soft light brown sugar
1¼ cups milk
⅔ cup heavy cream
4 ounces semisweet chocolate
1 tablespoon coffee liqueur (optional)
4 egg yolks
whipped cream and candied cake
  decorations, to decorate (optional)

1 Put the instant coffee and sugar in a pan, and stir in the milk and cream. Bring to the boil over a medium heat, stirring constantly, until the coffee and sugar have dissolved completely.

2 Remove the pan from the heat, and add the chocolate. Stir until the chocolate has melted, then stir in the coffee liqueur, if using.

3 In a bowl, whisk the egg yolks, then slowly whisk in the chocolate mixture until well blended. Strain the custard mixture into a large pitcher, and divide equally among *pots de crème* or ramekins —first checking that they will all fit inside the ceramic cooking pot.

4 Cover each *pot de crème* or ramekin with a piece of foil, then transfer to the ceramic cooking pot. Pour enough hot water around the dishes to come just over halfway up their sides. Cover the slow cooker with the lid, and cook on high for 2½–3 hours, or until they are just set and a knife inserted into the middle comes out clean.

5 Carefully remove the pots from the cooker, and leave to cool. Cover, and chill until ready to serve, then decorate with whipped cream and candied cake decorations, if you like.

Energy 443Kcal/1840kJ; Protein 8.3g; Carbohydrate 23.7g, of which sugars 23.7g; Fat 35.7g, of which saturates 20.2g; Cholesterol 264mg; Calcium 196mg; Fiber 0.2g; Sodium 74mg.

HOT BANANAS with RUM and RAISINS

These sticky, sweet baked bananas are utterly moreish and make a great dessert all year round. The rich sauce becomes almost toffee-like during cooking, and is irresistible.

3 Add the bananas to the melted butter and sugar mixture, cover with the lid, and cook for about 30 minutes, or until the fruit is almost tender, turning over the bananas halfway through cooking time.

4 Sprinkle the nutmeg and cinnamon over the bananas, then pour in the rum and raisins. Stir very gently to mix, then re-cover, and cook for 10 minutes.

5 Carefully lift the bananas out of the ceramic cooking pot, and arrange on a serving dish or individual plates. Spoon over the sauce, then sprinkle with almonds, if using. Serve hot with whipped cream or vanilla ice cream.

COOK'S TIP
Choose almost-ripe bananas with even-colored skins. Overripe bananas will not hold their shape during cooking, and will give mushy results.

SERVES 4

2 tablespoons seedless raisins
3 tablespoons dark rum
3 tablespoons sweet butter
¼ cup soft light brown sugar
4 slightly under-ripe bananas, peeled and
    halved lengthwise
¼ teaspoon grated nutmeg
¼ teaspoon ground cinnamon
¼ cup sliced almonds, toasted (optional)
whipped cream or vanilla ice cream,
    to serve

1 Put the raisins in a bowl and spoon over 2 tablespoons of the rum. Set aside, and leave to soak.

2 Cut the butter into small cubes, and place in the ceramic cooking pot with the sugar and remaining 1 tablespoon rum. Switch the slow cooker to high, and leave uncovered for 15 minutes, until the butter and sugar have melted.

VARIATION
If you don't like the taste of rum, try using an orange liqueur, such as Cointreau, instead. It makes a very good alternative and is a little less overpowering.

Energy 323Kcal/1355kJ; Protein 3g; Carbohydrate 47.1g, of which sugars 44.7g; Fat 12.1g, of which saturates 5.6g; Cholesterol 21mg; Calcium 33mg; Fiber 1.9g; Sodium 72mg.

CHOCOLATE CHIP and BANANA PUDDING

*Rich, dense and sticky, this steamed pudding served with a glossy chocolate sauce is
a great winter dessert. For an extra treat, serve with a scoop of vanilla ice cream.*

SERVES 4

1¾ cups self-rising flour
6 tablespoons sweet butter
2 ripe bananas
6 tablespoons superfine sugar
1¼ cups milk
1 egg, lightly beaten
⅔ cup chocolate chips or
   chopped unsweetened chocolate

For the chocolate sauce
½ cup superfine sugar
¼ cup water
1¼ cups semisweet chocolate chips or
   chopped unsweetened chocolate
2 tablespoons sweet butter
2 tablespoons brandy or orange juice

1 Grease and line the base of a 4-cup
heatproof bowl with parchment paper.
Put an inverted saucer in the bottom of
the ceramic cooking pot, and pour in
about 1 inch of hot water. Turn the slow
cooker to high.

2 Sift the flour into a large mixing bowl,
and rub in the butter until the mixture
resembles coarse bread crumbs. In a
separate bowl, mash the bananas, then
stir into the flour and butter mixture.
Add the sugar, and mix well.

3 In a clean bowl, whisk together the
milk and egg, then beat into the banana
mixture. Stir in the chocolate chips or
chopped chocolate, and spoon into the
prepared heatproof bowl. Cover with
a double thickness of buttered foil, and
place in the ceramic cooking pot. Pour
enough boiling water around the bowl
to come just over halfway up the sides.

4 Cover the slow cooker, and cook on
high for 3–4 hours, or until the pudding
is well risen and a skewer inserted in the
middle comes out clean. Turn off the
slow cooker, and leave the pudding in
the water while you make the sauce.

5 Put the sugar and water in a heavy
pan, and heat gently, stirring occasionally
with a wooden spoon, until all the sugar
has dissolved. Remove from the heat,
add the chocolate, and stir until melted,
then add the butter in the same way.
Stir in the brandy or orange juice.

6 Remove the pudding from the slow
cooker, and run a knife around the inside
of the bowl to loosen it. Turn it out
onto a warmed serving dish, and serve
hot, with the sauce poured over.

Energy 926Kcal/3890kJ; Protein 11.1g; Carbohydrate 131.9g, of which sugars 93.2g; Fat 41.1g, of which saturates 24.6g; Cholesterol 118mg; Calcium 266mg; Fiber 3.3g; Sodium 378mg.

STICKY COFFEE and PEAR PUDDING

This dark and moist fruity pudding is complemented with a tangy citrus-flavored cream.
It is delicious served hot, but is equally good cold; serve at room temperature rather than
chilled to enjoy its rich flavor and wonderful texture at their best.

SERVES 6

½ cup butter, softened, plus extra
    for greasing
2 tablespoons ground coffee
1 tablespoon near-boiling water
½ cup toasted skinned hazelnuts
4 small ripe pears
juice of ½ orange
generous ½ cup golden superfine sugar,
    plus 1 tablespoon for baking
2 eggs, beaten
½ cup self-rising flour
3 tablespoons maple syrup
fine strips of orange rind, to decorate

For the orange cream
1¼ cups whipping cream
1 tablespoon confectioners' sugar, sifted
finely grated rind of ½ orange

1 Pour about 1 inch of hot water into the ceramic cooking pot. Place an upturned saucer or metal pastry ring in the base, then turn onto high. Grease and line the base of a deep 17-inch fixed-base cake pan or soufflé dish.

COOK'S TIPS
• If you can't find ready-toasted skinned hazelnuts, prepare your own. Toast the nuts under a hot broiler for about 3 minutes, turning frequently until well browned. Leave to cool, and rub off the skins before grinding.
• Many supermarkets and specialist food stores sell flavored coffees. Try using a hazelnut-flavored coffee for this dessert.

2 Put the ground coffee in a small bowl, and pour the water over. Leave to infuse for 4 minutes, then pour through a fine strainer. Place the hazelnuts in a coffee grinder, and grind until fine.

3 Peel, halve, and core the pears. Thinly slice across the pear halves part of the way through, then brush them all over with the orange juice.

4 Beat the butter and the larger quantity of superfine sugar together in a bowl until very light and fluffy. Gradually beat in the eggs. Sift the flour, then fold into the mixture in the bowl. Add the hazelnuts and coffee. Spoon the mixture into the pan or soufflé dish, and level the surface.

5 Pat the pears dry on paper towels, and arrange in a circle in the sponge mixture, flat side down. Brush them with some of the maple syrup, then sprinkle with the 1 tablespoon superfine sugar.

6 Cover the top of the pan or soufflé dish with kitchen foil, and place in the ceramic cooking pot. Pour enough boiling water around the pan or dish to come slightly more than halfway up the sides. Cover with a lid, and cook for 3–3½ hours, until firm and well risen.

7 Meanwhile, make the orange cream. Whip the cream, confectioners' sugar, and orange rind until soft peaks form. Spoon into a serving dish and chill until needed.

8 Leave the sponge to cool in the pan for about 10 minutes, then turn over onto a serving plate. Lightly brush with the remaining maple syrup, then decorate with orange rind, and serve with the orange cream.

Energy 852Kcal/3571kJ; Protein 12.5g; Carbohydrate 107g, of which sugars 45g; Fat 44.5g, of which saturates 23.8g; Cholesterol 169mg; Calcium 362mg; Fiber 5.3g; Sodium 493mg.

STEAMED CHOCOLATE and FRUIT PUDDINGS

Drenched in a rich chocolate syrup, this wickedly indulgent steamed pudding makes a great alternative to a traditional Christmas pudding—although it is a fabulous treat at any time of year, the addition of cranberries gives it an unmistakably festive flavor.

SERVES 4

vegetable oil, for greasing
1 apple
¼ cup cranberries, thawed
    if frozen
¾ cup soft dark brown sugar
½ cup soft margarine
2 eggs, lightly beaten
½ cup self-rising flour, sifted
3 tablespoons unsweetened cocoa powder

For the syrup
4 ounces semisweet chocolate, chopped
2 tablespoons clear honey
1 tablespoon sweet butter
½ teaspoon vanilla extract

1 Pour 1 inch of hot water into the cooking pot, and switch the slow cooker to high. Grease four ovenproof bowls with oil, then line with parchment paper.

2 Peel and core the apple, then dice the flesh. Place in a mixing bowl, then add the cranberries and 1 tablespoon of the sugar. Mix well, then divide the fruit mixture among the prepared bowls , gently patting it down into the base of each one.

3 Place the remaining sugar in a clean mixing bowl, and add the margarine, eggs, flour, and cocoa. Beat together with a wooden spoon until combined and smooth and creamy.

4 Spoon the mixture into the heatproof bowls, and cover each with a double thickness of greased foil. Place the puddings in the ceramic cooking pot, and pour in enough very hot water to come about two-thirds up the sides.

5 Cover with a lid, and cook on high for 1½–2 hours, or until the puddings are well-risen and firm to the touch. Carefully remove from the slow cooker, and leave to stand for 10 minutes.

6 Meanwhile, make the chocolate syrup. Put the chocolate, honey, butter, and vanilla extract in a heatproof bowl and place in the hot water in the slow cooker. Leave for 10 minutes, until the butter has melted, then stir until smooth.

7 Run a knife around the edge of the puddings to loosen, then turn over onto warmed individual plates. Serve immediately with the chocolate syrup.

Energy 739Kcal/3094kJ; Protein 9.1g; Carbohydrate 88.3g, of which sugars 77.2g; Fat 41.3g, of which saturates 14.4g; Cholesterol 124mg; Calcium 103mg; Fiber 3.1g; Sodium 438mg.

HOT DATE PUDDINGS with TOFFEE SAUCE

Fresh dates make this pudding less rich than the classic dried date version, but it still makes an utterly indulgent dessert. Ideally, peel the dates, because their skins can be tough. Squeeze them between your thumb and forefinger, and the skins will slip off.

3 Put the dates in a heatproof bowl, pour over the boiling water, and mash well with a potato masher to make a fairly smooth paste.

4 Sift the flour and baking soda over the creamed butter and sugar mixture, and fold in. Add the date paste, and gently fold in.

SERVES 6

¼ cup butter, softened
½ cup light brown sugar
2 eggs, beaten
generous 1 cup fresh dates,
    peeled, pitted,
    and chopped
5 tablespoons boiling water
1 cup self-rising flour
½ teaspoon baking soda

For the sauce
¼ cup butter,
    at room temperature
½ cup light brown sugar
4 tablespoons heavy cream
2 tablespoons brandy

1 Grease six individual pudding molds or pans—first making sure that they will all fit in the slow cooker. Pour enough very hot water into the ceramic cooking pot to reach a depth of ¾ inch. Switch the slow cooker to high.

2 Put the butter and sugar in a mixing bowl, and beat until pale and fluffy. Gradually beat in the eggs.

5 Spoon the mixture into the greased molds or pans. Cover each with a piece of foil. Place in the ceramic cooking pot, and pour enough boiling water around the puddings to come just over halfway up the sides. Cover with the lid, and cook on high for 1½–2 hours, or until well risen and firm. Remove the puddings from the slow cooker.

6 Meanwhile, make the sauce. Put the butter, sugar, cream, and brandy in a pan and heat very gently, stirring occasionally, until the mixture is smooth. Increase the heat, and boil for 1 minute.

7 Turn the warm puddings out onto individual dessert plates. Spoon sauce over each one, and serve immediately.

Energy 462Kcal/1932kJ; Protein 5.1g; Carbohydrate 50.3g, of which sugars 35.9g; Fat 26.9g, of which saturates 16g; Cholesterol 138mg; Calcium 109mg; Fiber 1.1g; Sodium 244mg.

FRESH FRUIT BREAD and BUTTER PUDDING

Fresh currants add a tart touch to this scrumptious hot pudding. For the best results, use a wide, shallow dish rather than a narrow, deep one, but make sure it fits comfortably in the slow cooker. Serve drenched with a generous splash of fresh cream.

SERVES 4

3 tablespoons butter, softened,
   plus extra for greasing
6 medium-thick slices of day-old bread,
   crusts removed
1 cup prepared redcurrants
   and raspberries
3 eggs, beaten
1/4 cup golden superfine sugar
1 1/4 cups creamy milk
1 teaspoon vanilla extract
freshly grated nutmeg
2 tablespoons raw sugar
light cream, to serve

1 Generously butter a 4-cup round or oval baking dish—first checking that it fits in your slow cooker.

2 Pour about 1 inch of very hot water into the ceramic cooking pot. Place an upturned saucer or metal pastry ring in the base, and switch the cooker to high.

3 Spread the slices of bread generously with the butter, then use a long serrated knife to cut them in half diagonally.

VARIATIONS
• Try using slices of Italian panettone in place of the white bread. It gives a particularly rich, indulgent result.
• Use fresh blueberries or blackcurrants in place of the fruit used here.
• When fresh berries and currants are unavailable, use chopped ready-to-eat dried apricots instead.

4 Arrange the buttered bread triangles in the dish in neat layers, overlapping the slices, with the buttered side facing up.

5 Scatter the fresh currants and berries over the bread and between the slices, ensuring that there is an even quantity of fruit throughout the pudding.

6 Place the eggs and superfine sugar in a large mixing bowl, and briefly beat together. Gradually whisk in the milk, vanilla extract and a large pinch of freshly grated nutmeg until well mixed.

COOK'S TIP
Always buy whole nutmegs. Once grated, the spice loses its flavor quickly.

7 Place the baking dish in the ceramic cooking pot, then slowly pour the egg and milk mixture over the bread, pushing the bread slices down to submerge them, and making sure they are thoroughly soaked. Sprinkle the raw sugar and a little nutmeg over the top, then cover the dish with foil.

8 Pour near-boiling water around the dish, so that the water level comes just over halfway up the sides of the dish. Cover with the lid, and cook on high for 3–4 hours, or until a skewer inserted into the center comes out clean.

9 Carefully remove the dish from the slow cooker and, if you like, briefly brown the top of the pudding under a hot broiler. Cool slightly, then serve with the light cream.

Energy 405Kcal/1700kJ; Protein 12.6g; Carbohydrate 53.7g, of which sugars 30.7g; Fat 16.9g, of which saturates 8.6g; Cholesterol 202mg; Calcium 234mg; Fiber 2.1g; Sodium 405mg.

RICH CHOCOLATE CAKE

This rich, dense steamed chocolate cake filled with a decadently creamy buttercream
makes a perfect teatime treat. Serve with a big cup of strong coffee.

SERVES 8

4 ounces semisweet chocolate, chopped
   into small pieces
3 tablespoons milk
10 tablespoons butter, at room
   temperature
scant 1 cup soft light brown sugar
3 eggs, lightly beaten
1¾ cups self-rising flour
1 tablespoon unsweetened
   cocoa powder
confectioners' sugar and unsweetened
   cocoa powder,
   for dusting

For the chocolate buttercream
6 tablespoons butter,
   at room temperature
1 cup iconfectioners' sugar
1 tablespoon unsweetened cocoa powder
½ teaspoon vanilla extract

1 Grease and line a deep 7-inch fixed-base cake pan or soufflé dish with parchment paper. Pour about 2 inches very hot water into the ceramic cooking pot, then turn the slow cooker to high.

2 Put the chocolate and milk into a heatproof bowl, and place in the cooking pot. Leave for about 10 minutes, until the chocolate softens, then stir until smooth. Remove, and leave to cool for a few minutes.

3 Meanwhile, place the butter and sugar in a mixing bowl, and beat together until light and fluffy. Beat in the eggs, a little at a time, then stir in the chocolate mixture until well mixed.

4 Sift the flour and cocoa over the chocolate mixture, and fold in until evenly mixed. Spoon into the prepared pan or dish, and cover the top with a piece of foil. Put a saucer in the bottom of the ceramic cooking pot, then rest the pan on top. If necessary, pour in more boiling water to come just over halfway up the sides of the pan.

5 Cover the slow cooker with the lid, and cook for 3–3½ hours, or until firm to the touch and a fine skewer inserted into the middle comes out clean. Carefully lift the pan out of the cooking pot, and leave to stand on a wire rack for 10 minutes. Turn out, and leave to cool. Remove the lining paper.

6 To make the buttercream, put the butter in a large bowl, and beat until very soft. Sift over the confectioners' sugar and cocoa powder, then stir together. Add the vanilla extract and beat until the buttercream is light and fluffy.

7 Very carefully, cut the cake in half horizontally, and spread a thick, even layer of the buttercream on one of the cut halves. Sandwich the cakes back together, then dust with a mixture of confectioners' sugar and cocoa and serve.

Energy 564Kcal/2363kJ; Protein 6.6g; Carbohydrate 70g, of which sugars 51g; Fat 30.5g, of which saturates 18.2g; Cholesterol 146mg; Calcium 129mg; Fiber 1.5g; Sodium 321mg.

CHOCOLATE CHIP WALNUT CAKE

The tangy flavor of orange works well in this chocolate and nut loaf. It can be finished simply with a generous dusting of confectioners' sugar, or as here with a zesty orange topping.

SERVES 8

1 cup all-purpose flour
¼ cup cornstarch
1 teaspoon baking powder
½ cup butter, at room temperature
½ cup golden superfine sugar
2 eggs, lightly beaten
½ cup semisweet, milk or white
   chocolate chips
½ cup chopped walnuts
finely grated rind of ½ orange

For the topping
1 cup confectioners' sugar, sifted,
   plus 1 teaspoon for dusting
4 teaspoons–2 tablespoons freshly
   squeezed orange juice
walnut halves, to decorate

4 Gently fold about half of the sifted flour mixture into the creamed butter and sugar mixture, then add the rest with the chocolate chips, walnuts, and orange rind. Fold in until just blended, taking care not to overmix.

5 Spoon the mixture into the prepared loaf pan, and loosely cover with a piece of foil, allowing some space at the top for the cake to rise as it cooks.

6 Put the loaf pan on the pastry ring or saucer inside the ceramic cooking pot. Pour enough boiling water around the loaf pan to come two-thirds of the way up the sides.

7 Cover the slow cooker with a lid, and cook for 2½–3 hours, or until a fine skewer pushed into the center of the cake comes out clean. Carefully remove the cake from the slow cooker, and stand it on a wire rack for 10 minutes, then turn out and leave to cool on the rack.

8 To decorate the cake, place the 1 cup confectioners' sugar in a mixing bowl. Stir in 4 teaspoons of the orange juice, adding a little more if needed, to make the consistency of thick cream. Drizzle the mixture over the cake, then decorate with walnut halves dusted with the 1 teaspoon confectioners' sugar. Leave the topping to set before serving.

1 Grease and line a 1 pound loaf pan, with a capacity of 3¾ cups, with parchment paper. Place a metal pastry ring or upturned saucer in the base of the ceramic cooking pot, and pour in about 1 inch very hot water. Switch the slow cooker to high.

2 Sift the flour, cornstarch, and baking powder together twice, so that the dry ingredients are well mixed and aerated, then set aside.

3 Place the butter in a large mixing bowl, and beat until creamy. Add the golden superfine sugar, and continue beating until light and fluffy. Add the eggs a little at a time, beating well after each addition.

Energy 395Kcal/1655kJ; Protein 4.7g; Carbohydrate 51g, of which sugars 36.9g; Fat 20.5g, of which saturates 9.9g; Cholesterol 87mg; Calcium 19mg; Fiber 0.9g; Sodium 171mg.

FROSTED CARROT and PARSNIP CAKE

A delicious twist on the classic plain carrot cake, this version is wonderfully light and crumbly. The grated vegetables help to keep it moist, and account for its excellent keeping qualities. Cooked meringue spread over the top makes a change from the usual cream cheese topping, and makes a stunning contrast to the wholesome, crumbly cake.

SERVES 8

oil, for greasing
1 orange or lemon
2 teaspoons superfine sugar
¾ cup butter or margarine
¾ cup soft light brown sugar
3 eggs, lightly beaten
6 ounces carrots and parsnips, grated
⅓ cup golden raisins
1 cup self-rising flour
½ cup self-rising whole-wheat flour
1 teaspoon baking powder

For the topping
¼ cup superfine sugar
1 egg white
pinch of salt

1 Put an upturned saucer or metal pastry cutter in the base of the ceramic cooking pot, and pour in about 1 inch hot water. Turn the slow cooker to high. Lightly grease a deep 7-inch round fixed-based cake pan or soufflé dish with oil, and line the base with parchment paper.

2 Finely grate the orange or lemon rind, taking care not to take off any of the white pith. Selecting the longest shreds, put about half the rind in a bowl, and mix with the superfine sugar. Arrange the sugar-coated rind on a sheet of waxed paper, and leave in a warm place to dry.

3 Put the butter or margarine and brown sugar in a large mixing bowl, and beat together until pale and fluffy. Add the eggs a little at a time, beating well after each addition. Stir in the unsugared orange or lemon rind, grated carrots and parsnips, and golden raisins.

4 Sift the flours and baking powder together, adding any bran left in the sieve, then gradually fold into the carrot and parsnip mixture.

5 Transfer the mixture to the prepared pan, and level the surface. Cover loosely with greased foil, then place in the ceramic cooking pot, on top of the saucer or pastry cutter. Pour sufficient boiling water around the pan to come just over halfway up the sides.

6 Cover the slow cooker with the lid, and cook for 3–5 hours, or until a skewer inserted in the center of the cake comes out clean. Carefully lift the pan out of the slow cooker, and leave to stand for 5 minutes. Turn the cake out onto a wire rack, and leave until cool.

7 To make the topping, place the superfine sugar in a bowl over the near-simmering water in the slow cooker. Squeeze the juice from the orange or lemon, and add 2 tablespoons of the juice to the sugar. Stir over the heat until the sugar dissolves. Remove from the heat, add the egg white and salt, and whisk for 1 minute with an electric beater.

8 Return the bowl to the heat, and whisk for about 6 minutes until the mixture becomes stiff and glossy, holding a good shape. Remove from the heat, and allow to cool for about 5 minutes, whisking frequently.

9 Swirl the meringue topping over the cake, and leave for 1 hour to firm up. To serve, sprinkle with the sugared orange or lemon rind.

VARIATION
If you do not like parsnips, you can make this cake with just carrots, or replace the parsnips with the same weight of grated zucchini. Add a pinch of cinnamon and nutmeg to the mixture.

Energy 410Kcal/1718kJ; Protein 5.9g; Carbohydrate 53g, of which sugars 38.2g; Fat 20.8g, of which saturates 12.2g; Cholesterol 132mg; Calcium 98mg; Fiber 1.9g; Sodium 290mg.

CHOCOLATE CHEESECAKE BROWNIES

A very dense chocolate brownie mixture is swirled with creamy cheese to give a marbled effect. Cut into small squares for little mouthfuls of absolute heaven.

MAKES 9

2 ounces bittersweet chocolate (minimum
   70 per cent cocoa solids),
   chopped
¼ cup sweet butter
5 tablespoons light brown sugar
I egg, beaten
¼ cup all-purpose flour

For the cheesecake mixture
½ cup full-fat cream cheese
2 tablespoons superfine sugar
I teaspoon vanilla extract
½ beaten egg

I Line the base and sides of a 6-inch square fixed-base cake pan with parchment paper. Pour about 2 inches of very hot water into the ceramic cooking pot, and switch to high.

2 Put the chocolate and butter in a heatproof bowl, and place in the slow cooker. Leave to stand for 10 minutes.

3 Meanwhile, make the cheesecake mixture. Put the cream cheese, sugar, and vanilla extract in a clean mixing bowl, and beat together. Gradually beat in the egg until the mixture is very smooth and creamy. Set aside.

4 Stir the chocolate and butter mixture until completely melted and smooth, then remove the bowl from the slow cooker. Add the brown sugar, and stir to combine. Place an upturned saucer or metal pastry ring in the base of the ceramic cooking pot.

5 Add the beaten egg to the melted chocolate mixture a little at a time, and beat well until thoroughly mixed, then sift over the flour, and gently fold in.

6 Spoon the chocolate mixture into the base of the pan. Drop small spoonfuls of the cheesecake mixture on top. Using a skewer, swirl the mixtures together.

7 Cover the pan with foil, and place in the slow cooker. Pour in more boiling water around the pan to come just over halfway up the sides. Cook for 2 hours, or until just set in the cent. Remove the pan from the slow cooker, and place on a wire rack to cool. Cut into squares.

Energy 174Kcal/727kJ; Protein 2.9g; Carbohydrate 16.2g, of which sugars 14g; Fat 11.3g, of which saturates 6.8g; Cholesterol 65mg; Calcium 25mg; Fiber 0.2g; Sodium 86mg.

LIGHT FRUIT CAKE

This incredibly easy all-in-one fruit cake has a crumbly texture. The combination
of whole-wheat flour and long slow cooking ensures that it stays beautifully moist.

SERVES 12

2 eggs
generous ½ cup butter,
    at room temperature
1 cup light brown sugar
1¼ cups self-rising flour
1¼ cups whole-wheat
    self-rising flour
pinch of salt
1 teaspoon apple pie spice
2½ cups luxury mixed
    dried fruit

3 Spoon the mixture into the prepared cake pan, and level the surface. Cover the pan with a piece of buttered foil.

4 Put the pan in the slow cooker, and pour in enough boiling water to come just over halfway up the sides of the pan. Cover with the lid, and cook for 4–5 hours, or until a skewer inserted into the middle of the cake comes out clean.

5 Remove the cake from the slow cooker, and place on a wire rack. Leave the cake to cool in the pan for about 15 minutes, then turn out and leave to cool completely. To store, wrap the cake in waxed paper and then foil, and keep in a cool place.

1 Line the base and sides of a deep 7-inch round or 6-inch square fixed-base cake pan with parchment paper. Place an upturned saucer or metal pastry ring in the base of the ceramic cooking pot, then pour in about 1 inch of very hot water. Switch the slow cooker to high.

2 Crack the eggs into a large mixing bowl. Add the butter and sugar, then sift over the flours, salt, and spice, adding any bran left in the sieve. Stir together with a wooden spoon until mixed, then add the dried fruit, and beat for 2 minutes until the mixture is smooth and glossy.

COOK'S TIP
Choose a good quality brand of luxury dried fruits. It should contain a good mix of currants, golden raisins, mixed peel and candied cherries, as well as other dried fruits.

Energy 351Kcal/1482kJ; Protein 4.9g; Carbohydrate 63g, of which sugars 46g; Fat 10.6g, of which saturates 6g; Cholesterol 60.8mg; Calcium 78.6mg; Fiber 2.3g; Sodium 148mg.

MARBLED SPICE CAKE

This cake can be baked in a fluted ring-shaped cake mold called a kugelhupf *or* gugelhupf, *which originates from Germany and Austria, or in a plain ring-shaped cake pan. The marbled effect looks particularly good when the cake is baked in a ring like this.*

SERVES 8

6 tablespoons butter, at room
   temperature, plus extra for greasing
generous I cup all-purpose flour,
   plus extra for dusting
½ cup soft light brown sugar
2 eggs
few drops of vanilla extract
I½ teaspoons baking powder
3 tablespoons milk
2 tablespoons malt extract or molasses
I teaspoon apple pie spice
½ teaspoon ground ginger
¾ cup confectioners' sugar, sifted, to
   decorate

I Grease and flour a 5-cup *kugelhupf* mold or ring-shaped cake pan. Put an inverted saucer or large metal pastry cutter in the base of the slow cooke,r and pour in about 2 inches hot water. Switch the slow cooker to high.

2 Put the butter and sugar in a bowl, and beat together until light and fluffy.

3 In a separate bowl, beat together the eggs and vanilla extract, then gradually beat into the butter and sugar mixture, adding a little at a time and beating well after each addition.

COOK'S TIP

To make a marbled chocolate and vanilla cake, stir I tablespoon chocolate essence into the cake mixture, in place of the malt extract or molasses and spices.

4 Sift together the flour and baking powder to combine, then fold the flour into the butter and sugar mixture, adding a little of the milk between each addition until evenly combined.

5 Spoon about one-third of the mixture into a small bowl, and stir in the malt extract or molasses, mixed spice, and ginger until just combined.

6 Drop a large spoonful of the light mixture into the cake pan, followed by a spoonful of the dark mixture. Continue alternating spoonfuls of the light and dark mixtures until all the mixture has been used. Run a knife or skewer through the mixtures to give a marbled effect.

7 Cover the pan with foil, and place in the ceramic cooking pot. Pour a little more boiling water around the pan to come just over halfway up the sides. Cover the slow cooker with the lid, and cook for 3–4 hours. To test if it is done, insert a skewer into the middle of the cake; it should come out clean.

8 Carefully lift the cake out of the slow cooker, and leave in the pan for about 10 minutes before turning out onto a wire rack to cool.

9 To decorate, place the confectioners' sugar in a bowl, and add just enough warm water to make a smooth frosting with the consistency of light cream. Quickly drizzle the mixture over the cake, then leave to set before serving the cake in thick slices.

Energy 215Kcal/902kJ; Protein 2.8g; Carbohydrate 33g, of which sugars 20.3g; Fat 8.8g, of which saturates 5.2g; Cholesterol 49mg; Calcium 84mg; Fiber 0.5g; Sodium 172mg.

BLUEBERRY MUFFIN PUDDING

You can't cook traditional muffins in a slow cooker, but this delicious alternative will satisfy your cravings. It's especially good served barely warm with custard or crème fraîche. Take the eggs and buttermilk out of the refrigerator at least an hour before you start mixing.

SERVES 4

6 tablespoons butter, plus extra
    for greasing
6 tablespoons soft light brown sugar
7 tablespoons buttermilk, at room
    temperature
2 eggs, lightly beaten, at room temperature
2 cups self-rising flour
pinch of salt
1 teaspoon ground cinnamon
¼ cup fresh blueberries
2 teaspoons raw sugar,
    for sprinkling
custard or crème fraîche, to serve

1 Place an upturned saucer or metal pastry ring in the base of the slow cooker. Pour in about 2 inches of very hot water, then switch the slow cooker to high. Lightly grease a 6¼-cup heatproof dish with butter, first making sure that it will fit the inside of your slow cooker.

2 Put the butter and sugar in a heatproof pitcher, and place in the ceramic cooking pot. Leave uncovered for 20 minutes, stirring, until melted.

3 Remove the pitcher from the slow cooker, and leave to cool until tepid, then stir in the buttermilk followed by the beaten egg, until well mixed.

COOK'S TIP
Because less liquid evaporates from the pudding in a slow cooker, the mixture is thicker than a conventional muffin batter.

4 Sift the flour, salt, and cinnamon into a mixing bowl. Stir in the blueberries, then make a hollow in the middle. Pour in the buttermilk mixture, and quickly stir until just combined. Do not overmix.

5 Spoon the mixture into the prepared dish, then sprinkle the top with the raw sugar. Cover with a piece of buttered foil, and place in the ceramic cooking pot. Pour in a little more boiling water around the dish, if necessary, to come halfway up the sides.

6 Cover the slow cooker with the lid, and cook for 3–4 hours, until a skewer inserted in the middle comes out clean. Remove from the slow cooker, and let the pudding cool slightly before serving with custard or crème fraîche.

Energy 499Kcal/2101kJ; Protein 10.1g; Carbohydrate 76.2g, of which sugars 34.4g; Fat 19.2g, of which saturates 10.7g; Cholesterol 153mg; Calcium 262mg; Fiber 2.2g; Sodium 367mg.

PUMPKIN and BANANA CAKE

Rather like a cross between a carrot cake and banana bread, this luscious cake is an excellent way of using some of the scooped-out pumpkin flesh after making Halloween lanterns. A cream cheese topping provides a delicious contrast with the dense moist cake.

SERVES 12

2 cups self-raising self-rising flour
1½ teaspoons baking powder
½ teaspoon ground cinnamon
½ teaspoon ground ginger
pinch of salt
10 tablespoons soft light brown sugar
¾ cup pecans or walnuts, chopped
4 ounces pumpkin flesh, coarsely grated
2 small bananas, peeled and mashed
2 eggs, lightly beaten
⅔ cup sunflower-seed oil

For the topping
¼ cup butter, at room temperature
⅔ cup soft cheese
¼ teaspoon vanilla extract
1 cup confectioners' sugar
pecan halves, to decorate

1 Line the base and sides of a deep 8-inch round fixed-base cake pan or soufflé dish with parchment paper. Place an upturned saucer or metal pastry ring in the base of the ceramic cooking pot, then pour in about 1 inch of very hot water. Switch the slow cooker to high.

2 Sift the flour, baking powder, cinnamon, ginger, and salt into a large mixing bowl to combine. Stir in the sugar, chopped pecans and, and grated pumpkin until thoroughly mixed. Make a slight hollow in the middle of the dry ingredients.

3 In a separate bowl, combine the bananas, eggs, and sunflower-seed oil, then stir into the dry ingredients. Turn into the prepared pan, and level the surface.

4 Cover the pan with a piece of buttered foil, and place in the slow cooker. Pour in sufficient boiling water to come just over halfway up the sides of the pan.

5 Cover the pot with the lid, and cook on high for 4–4½ hours, or until the cake is firm and a skewer inserted into the middle comes out clean.

6 Carefully remove the cake from the slow cooker, and stand the pan on a wire rack to cool for 15 minutes. Turn out, and leave to cool completely, then peel off the lining paper.

7 To make the topping, put the butter, soft cheese, and vanilla extract in a bowl, and beat until blended and smooth. Sift in the confectioners' sugar, and beat again until smooth and creamy. Thickly spread the topping over the top of the cake, and decorate with pecan halves. Chill in the refrigerator for at least 1 hour before serving, to allow the topping to harden.

Energy 374Kcal/1567kJ; Protein 5.1g; Carbohydrate 43.7g, of which sugars 28.7g; Fat 21.3g, of which saturates 6.5g; Cholesterol 58mg, Calcium 101.7mg; Fiber 1g; Sodium 203mg.

MOIST GOLDEN GINGER CAKE

This is the ultimate ginger cake: instead of the traditional molasses, a mixture of light corn syrup and malt extract gives a really sticky, moist texture. Because of the long, slow cooking, the cake matures sufficiently to eat right away. However, the flavor improves and the texture becomes stickier if it is wrapped and kept for a day or two.

SERVES 10

generous ¾ cup light brown sugar
½ cup butter
⅔ cup light corn syrup
1 ounce malt extract
1½ cups self-rising flour
½ cup all-purpose flour
2 teaspoons ground ginger
pinch of salt
1 egg, lightly beaten
½ cup milk, at room temperature
½ teaspoon baking soda

2 Place the sugar, butter, light corn syrup, and malt extract in a heatproof bowl that will fit inside the slow cooker. Place in the ceramic cooking pot and leave for 15 minutes, or until melted.

3 Remove the bowl from the slow cooker, and stir until smooth. Place an upturned saucer or metal pastry ring in the base of the ceramic cooking pot.

1 Line the base of a deep 7-inch round fixed-base cake pan or soufflé dish with parchment. paper. Pour 2 inches of very hot water into the ceramic cooking pot. Switch to high.

4 Sift the flours, ginger, and salt into a separate mixing bowl. Pour the melted butter and sugar mixture into the flour, and beat until smooth. Stir in the beaten egg until well mixed.

VARIATION

To turn this moist cake into a tempting treat for kids, try decorating it with plain lemon frosting and scattering with multi-colored sugar sprinkles. To make the frosting, put ¾ cup confectioners' sugar in a bowl, and stir in just enough lemon juice to make a smooth frosting with the consistency of light cream. Drizzle over the cake, and scatter with sprinkles.

5 Pour the milk in a pitcher, and stir in the baking soda. Pour the mixture into the ginger cake mixture, and stir until combined.

6 Pour the cake mixture into the prepared cake pan or soufflé dish, cover with foil, and place in the cooking pot.

7 Pour a little more boiling water around the pan or dish to come just over halfway up the sides. Cover with the lid, and cook for 5–6 hours, or until firm and a fine skewer inserted into the middle of the cake comes out clean.

8 Remove the cake from the slow cooker, and place the pan or dish on a wire cooling rack. Leave to cool for 15 minutes, then turn out and leave to cool completely before serving in slices.

COOK'S TIP

Because this cake improves with keeping, it is the perfect choice when you are expecting guests, because you can make it several days in advance.

Energy 289Kcal/1216kJ; Protein 3.4g; Carbohydrate 48g, of which sugars 31.1g; Fat 10.6g, of which saturates 6.4g; Cholesterol 48mg; Calcium 98mg; Fiber 0.7g; Sodium 211mg.

ONE-POT, CLAY-POT DESSERTS AND CAKES

The clever cook who saves time and effort by mastering one-pot and clay-pot cooking deserves a sweet reward, and what better way to celebrate success than with Baked Maple and Pecan Croissant Pudding or Honey-baked Figs—cooked in a clay pot, of course—served with Hazelnut Ice Cream. Black Cherry Clafoutis is another treat or, for pots of pleasure, try sweet and tangy Citrus and Caramel Custards, which are baked in individual cazuelas, or elegant and impressive Plum Charlottes with Foamy Kirsch Sauce.

PLUM CHARLOTTES with FOAMY KIRSCH SAUCE

These individual desserts, cooked in mini earthenware dishes, conceal a fresh plum filling and are served on a pool of light, frothy Kirsch-flavored sauce.

SERVES 4

½ cup butter, melted
4 tablespoons raw sugar
1 pound ripe plums, pitted and
    thickly sliced
2 tablespoons sugar
2 tablespoons water
¼ teaspoon ground cinnamon
¼ cup ground almonds
8–10 large slices of
    white bread

For the Kirsch sauce
3 egg yolks
3 tablespoons sugar
2 tablespoons Kirsch

1 Preheat the oven to 375°F. Line the base of four individual 4-inch diameter deep, earthenware ramekin dishes with parchment paper. Brush evenly and thoroughly with a little of the melted butter, then sprinkle each dish with a little of the raw sugar, rotating the dish in your hands to coat the base and sides of each dish evenly.

VARIATIONS

• Slices of peeled pear or apple can be used in this recipe instead of the pitted, sliced plums.
• If using apples or pears, replace the Kirsch in the foamy sauce with Calvados or another apple brandy.
• If you are short of time, drained canned fruit, such as pineapple, apricots, pears, or plums can be used—simply stir in the ground almonds as in step 2, and add to the prepared ramekins.

2 Place the plum slices in a pan with the sugar, water, and ground cinnamon, and cook gently for 5 minutes, or until the plums have softened slightly. Leave them to cool, then stir in the ground almonds.

3 Cut the crusts off the bread, and then use a plain cookie cutter to cut out four rounds to fit the bases of the ramekins. Dip the bread rounds into the melted butter, and fit them into the dishes. Cut four more rounds to fit the tops of the dishes, and set aside.

4 Cut the remaining bread into strips, dip into the melted butter, and use to line the sides of the ramekins completely.

5 Divide the plum mixture among the lined dishes. Place the bread rounds on top, and brush with the remaining butter. Place the ramekins on a baking sheet, and bake for 25 minutes.

6 Just before the charlottes are ready, place the egg yolks and superfine sugar for the sauce in a bowl. Whisk together until pale. Place the bowl over a pan of simmering water, and whisk in the Kirsch. Continue whisking until the mixture is very light and frothy.

7 Remove the charlottes from the oven, and turn out onto warm serving plates. Pour a little sauce over and around the charlottes, and serve immediately.

COOK'S TIP

For an extra indulgent dessert, serve the plum charlottes with lightly whipped heavy cream flavored with extra Kirsch and sweetened to taste with a little sifted confectioners' sugar.

Energy 600Kcal/2513kJ; Protein 9.1g; Carbohydrate 69.6g, of which sugars 44.2g; Fat 32.5g, of which saturates 16.5g; Cholesterol 218mg; Calcium 128mg; Fiber 3.1g; Sodium 467mg.

BAKED MAPLE and PECAN CROISSANT PUDDING

This variation of the classic English bread and butter pudding uses croissants, which give a light, fluffy texture. Pecans, brandy-laced golden raisins, and maple-syrup-flavored custard complete this mouthwatering dessert.

SERVES 4

generous ½ cup golden raisins
3 tablespoons brandy
¼ cup butter, plus extra
    for greasing
4 large croissants
⅓ cup pecan nuts,
    coarsely chopped
3 eggs, lightly beaten
1¼ cups milk
⅔ cup light cream
½ cup maple syrup
2 tablespoons raw sugar
maple syrup and half-and-half cream, to
    serve (optional)

1 Place the golden raisins and brandy in a small pan, and heat gently, until warm. Leave to stand for 1 hour. Soak a small clay pot in cold water for 15 minutes, then drain, leave for 2–3 minutes, and lightly grease the base and sides.

2 Cut the croissants (see Cook's Tip) into thick slices, then spread with butter on one side.

3 Arrange the croissant slices, butter side uppermost and slightly overlapping, in the soaked clay pot. Sprinkle the brandy-soaked golden raisins and the coarsely chopped pecan nuts over the buttered croissant slices.

4 In a large bowl, beat the eggs and milk together, then gradually beat in the light cream and maple syrup.

5 Pour the egg custard through a strainer, over the croissants, fruit, and nuts in the dish. Leave to stand for 30 minutes, so that some of the egg custard liquid is absorbed by the croissants.

6 Sprinkle the raw sugar evenly over the top, then cover the dish, and place in an unheated oven. Set the oven to 350°F, and bake for 40 minutes. Remove the lid, and continue to cook for about 20 minutes, or until the custard is set, and the top is golden.

7 Leave the dessert to cool for about 15 minutes before serving warm with extra maple syrup and a little half-and-half cream, if you like.

COOK'S TIPS
• This dessert is perfect for using up leftover croissants. Slightly stale, one-day-old croissants are easier to slice and butter; they also soak up the custard more easily. Thickly sliced one-day-old bread or large slices of brioche could be used instead.
• Pecan nuts are an elongated nut in a glossy red oval-shaped shell, but are usually sold shelled. They are native to the United States and have a sweet, mild flavor. Pecans are most commonly used in pecan pie, but are also popular in ice creams and cakes. Walnuts can be substituted for pecans in most recipes, and they would be perfect in this one if you don't have any pecan nuts.

Energy 731Kcal/3056kJ; Protein 15g; Carbohydrate 72.3g, of which sugars 49.4g; Fat 45.6g, of which saturates 19.5g; Cholesterol 226mg; Calcium 217mg; Fiber 1.8g; Sodium 507mg.

COCONUT RICE PUDDING

A delicious adaptation of the classic creamy rice pudding, this dessert is flavored with coconut milk and finished with a coconut crust.

SERVES 4

scant ½ cup short
   grain rice
3 tablespoons sugar
½ teaspoon vanilla extract
1¼ cups milk
1⅔ cups coconut milk
7 tablespoons light cream
2 tablespoons dry unsweetened
   shredded coconut or slivers of
   fresh coconut

VARIATION

If you like, this dessert can be made
with extra milk instead of the light cream.
Use whole milk, to be sure of achieving a
rich, creamy flavor.

1 Soak a small clay pot in cold water for
15 minutes, then drain. Add the rice,
sugar, vanilla extract, milk, coconut milk,
and cream.

2 Cover the clay pot, and place in a
cold oven. Set the oven to 350°F, and
cook for 1 hour.

3 Remove the lid from the clay pot, stir
the pudding gently, then re-cover and
cook for 30–45 minutes more, or until
the rice is tender.

4 Remove the lid, stir the pudding, then
sprinkle with dry or fresh coconut, and
bake uncovered for 10–15 minutes.

Energy 259Kcal/1087kJ; Protein 5.8g; Carbohydrate 34g, of which sugars 19.9g; Fat 11.6g, of which saturates 8.2g; Cholesterol 19mg; Calcium 153mg; Fiber 1g; Sodium 153mg.

CITRUS and CARAMEL CUSTARDS

*These Spanish-style custards, made rich with cream and egg yolks, are delicately scented
with tangy citrus flavors and aromatic cinnamon.*

SERVES 4

scant 2 cups milk
⅔ cup light cream
1 cinnamon stick, broken
    in half
thinly pared rind of ½ lemon
thinly pared rind of ½ orange
4 egg yolks
1 teaspoon cornstarch
3 tablespoons sugar
grated rind of ½ lemon
grated rind of ½ orange
a little confectioners' sugar,
    for sprinkling

1 Place the milk and cream in a pan.
Add the cinnamon stick and the strips of
pared citrus rind. Bring to a boil, then
simmer for 10 minutes.

2 Preheat the oven to 325°F. Whisk the
egg yolks, cornstarch, and sugar together.
Remove the rinds and cinnamon from
the hot milk and cream, and discard.
Whisk the hot milk and cream into the
egg yolk mixture.

3 Stir the grated citrus rind into the
custard mixture. Pour into four individual
cazuelas, each about 5 inches in
diameter. Place in a roasting pan, and
pour warm water into the pan to reach
three-fourths of the way up the sides.
Bake for 25–30 minutes, or until the
custards are just set. Remove the dishes
from the water. Leave to cool, then chill.

4 Preheat the broiler to high. Sprinkle
the custards with confectioners' sugar
and place under the broiler until the
tops turn golden brown and caramelize.

COOK'S TIPS
• Prepare the grated rind first, then cut a
few strips of rind from the ungrated side
of the citrus fruits, using a swivel-bladed
vegetable peeler.
• You can use a special cook's gas-gun or
salamander to caramelize the tops instead
of broiling them.

Energy 225Kcal/939kJ; Protein 8g; Carbohydrate 16.6g, of which sugars 16.6g; Fat 14.6g, of which saturates 7.3g; Cholesterol 229mg; Calcium 197mg; Fiber 0g; Sodium 69mg.

HONEY-BAKED FIGS with HAZELNUT ICE CREAM

This is a delectable dessert—fresh figs are baked in a lightly spiced lemon and honey syrup and served with a gorgeous, homemade roasted hazelnut ice cream.

SERVES 4

1 lemongrass stalk,
   finely chopped
1 cinnamon stick, coarsely broken
4 tablespoons honey
scant 1 cup water
8 large figs

For the hazelnut ice cream
scant 2 cups heavy cream
¼ cup sugar
3 egg yolks
¼ teaspoon vanilla extract
¾ cup hazelnuts

1 To make the ice cream, place the cream in a pan, and heat gently until almost boiling. Place the sugar and egg yolks in a bowl, and beat until creamy.

2 Pour a little of the cream onto the egg yolk mixture, and stir. Pour into the pan, and mix with the rest of the cream. Cook over low heat, stirring constantly, until the mixture thickens slightly and lightly coats the back of the spoon—do not let it boil. Pour into a bowl, then stir in the vanilla, and leave to cool.

3 Preheat the oven to 350°F. Spread out the hazelnuts on a baking sheet, and roast for 10–12 minutes, or until they are golden. Leave the nuts to cool, then place them in a food processor or blender, and process until they are coarsely ground.

4 Transfer the ice cream mixture to a metal or plastic freezer container, and freeze for 2 hours, or until the mixture feels firm around the edge. Remove the container from the freezer, and whisk the ice cream to break down the ice crystals. Stir in the ground hazelnuts, and freeze the mixture again until half-frozen. Whisk again, then freeze until firm.

COOK'S TIPS
• If you like, rather than whisking the semifrozen ice cream, tip it into a food processor, and process until smooth.
• There are several different types of figs available, and they can all be used in this recipe. Choose from green-skinned figs that have an amber-colored flesh, dark purple-skinned fruit with a deep red flesh, or green/yellow-skinned figs with a pinky-colored flesh.

5 Place the lemongrass, cinnamon stick, honey, and water in a small pan and heat gently until boiling. Simmer the mixture for 5 minutes, then leave the syrup to stand for 15 minutes.

6 Meanwhile, soak a small clay pot in cold water for 15 minutes. Cut the figs into fourths, leaving them intact at the bases. Place the figs in the clay pot, and pour over the honey-flavored syrup.

7 Cover the clay pot, and place in an unheated oven. Set the oven to 400°F, and bake the figs for about 15 minutes, or until tender.

8 Take the ice cream from the freezer about 10 minutes before serving, to soften slightly. Transfer the figs to serving plates. Strain a little of the cooking liquid over the figs, and then serve them with a scoop or two of hazelnut ice cream.

VARIATION
This recipe also works well with halved, pitted nectarines or peaches—simply cook as from step 6, and serve with the homemade ice cream.

Energy 909Kcal/3770kJ; Protein 8.2g; Carbohydrate 48.7g, of which sugars 48.4g; Fat 77.1g, of which saturates 39.6g; Cholesterol 305mg; Calcium 206mg; Fiber 4.2g; Sodium 60mg.

SPICED PEARS with a NUT TOPPING

*An all-time favorite, this dessert has a crunchy pecan nut and oat topping,
which complements the spicy pears hidden beneath.*

SERVES 4–6

2 pounds pears
2 tablespoons lemon juice
3 tablespoons sugar
1 teaspoon apple pie spice
½ teaspoon grated nutmeg
vanilla ice cream,
    to serve

For the nut topping
⅔ cup all-purpose flour
6 tablespoons butter
¼ cup light molasses sugar
½ cup pecan nuts or
    walnuts, chopped
scant ½ cup rolled oats

COOK'S TIP
Look for golden-skinned Forelle pears,
which are especially good for cooking, or
try Anjou, Bosc, or Seckel pears.

1 Soak a small clay pot in cold water for
15 minutes, then drain. Peel the pears
if you like, then halve them, and remove
the cores. Cut each pear into six
wedges, and toss in the lemon juice.

2 Place the pears in the clay pot, add
the sugar, apple pie spice, and nutmeg,
and mix together. Place in an unheated
oven, set the oven to 400°F, and cook
for 25 minutes.

3 Meanwhile, prepare the nut topping.
Sift the flour into a bowl, and rub in the
butter with your fingertips, then stir in
the sugar, nuts, and rolled oats.

4 Uncover the clay pot, and stir gently
to rearrange the fruit. Spoon the nut
mixture over the pears, then return the
clay pot to the oven for 25–30 minutes,
or until the topping is golden. Serve
warm, with vanilla ice cream.

Energy 365Kcal/1523kJ; Protein 3.5g; Carbohydrate 42.9g, of which sugars 33.2g; Fat 21g, of which saturates 7.4g; Cholesterol 27mg; Calcium 57mg; Fiber 4.3g; Sodium 82mg.

NECTARINES BAKED with ALMONDS and PISTACHIO NUTS

Fresh nectarines stuffed with a ground almond and chopped pistachio nut filling, baked in a clay pot until meltingly tender, then served with a passion fruit sauce.

SERVES 4

½ cup ground almonds
1 tablespoon sugar
1 egg yolk
⅓ cup shelled pistachio
   nuts, chopped
4 nectarines
scant 1 cup orange juice
2 ripe passion fruits
3 tablespoons Cointreau or other
   orange liqueur

1 Soak a small clay pot, if using, in cold water for 15 minutes. Mix the ground almonds, sugar, and egg yolk to a paste, then stir in the pistachio nuts.

2 Cut the nectarines in half, and carefully remove the pits with the tip of a knife. Pile the ground almond and pistachio filling into the nectarine halves, and then place them in a single layer in the base of the clay pot or in a cazuela.

3 Pour the orange juice around the nectarines, then cover the pot or dish, and place it in an unheated oven. Set the oven to 400°F, and cook the nectarines for 15 minutes.

4 Remove the lid from the pot or dish, and bake for 5–10 minutes more, or until the nectarines are soft. Transfer the nectarines to individual, warmed serving plates, and keep warm.

5 Cut the passion fruits in half, scoop out the seeds, and stir into the cooking juices in the clay pot or dish with the liqueur. Spoon the sauce around the nectarines, and serve.

Energy 277Kcal/1159kJ; Protein 7.5g; Carbohydrate 27.8g, of which sugars 27.2g; Fat 14.1g, of which saturates 1.5g; Cholesterol 0mg; Calcium 63mg; Fiber 3.8g, Sodium 78mg.

BREAD and BUTTER PUDDING with WHISKEY SAUCE

This is comfort food at its very best. The whiskey sauce is heavenly, but if you are not keen on the alcohol, the pudding can also be served with chilled cream or vanilla ice cream—the contrast between the hot and cold is delicious.

SERVES 6

8 slices of white bread, buttered
⅔–¾ cup golden raisins, or mixed
    dried fruit
½ teaspoon grated nutmeg
¾ cup superfine sugar
2 extra large eggs
1¼ cups light cream
scant 2 cups milk
1 teaspoon of vanilla extract
light brown sugar,
    for sprinkling (optional)

For the whiskey sauce
10 tablespoons butter
generous ½ cup superfine sugar
1 egg
3 tablespoons Irish whiskey

1 Preheat the oven to 350°F . Remove the crusts from the bread, and put four slices, buttered side down, in the base of an ovenproof dish. Sprinkle with the fruit, some of the nutmeg and 1 tablespoon sugar.

2 Place the remaining four slices of bread on top, buttered side down, and sprinkle again with nutmeg and 1 tablespoon sugar.

3 Beat the eggs lightly, add the cream, milk, vanilla extract, and the remaining sugar, and mix well to make a custard. Pour this mixture over the bread, and sprinkle light brown sugar over the top, if you like to have a crispy crust. Bake in the preheated oven for 1 hour, or until all the liquid has been absorbed and the pudding is risen and brown.

4 Meanwhile, make the whiskey sauce: melt the butter in a heavy pan, add the superfine sugar, and dissolve over gentle heat. Remove from the heat, and add the egg, whisking vigorously, and then add the whiskey. Serve the pudding on hot serving plates, with the whiskey sauce poured over the top.

Energy 757Kcal/3168kJ; Protein 11.7g; Carbohydrate 82g, of which sugars 65.2g; Fat 40.8g, of which saturates 24.3g; Cholesterol 207mg; Calcium 232mg; Fiber 0.9g; Sodium 472mg

FRESH CURRANT BREAD and BUTTER PUDDING

Fresh mixed red- and black currants add a tart touch to this scrumptious hot dessert in which layers of custard-soaked bread are cooked to a crisp golden crust.

SERVES 6

8 medium-thick slices day-old white bread,
    crusts removed
¼ cup butter, softened
1 cup red currants
1 cup black currants
4 eggs, beaten
6 tablespoons sugar
2 cups creamy milk
1 teaspoon vanilla extract
freshly grated nutmeg
2 tablespoons raw sugar
light cream, to serve

1 Preheat the oven to 325°F. Butter a 5-cup ovenproof earthenware dish, and set aside.

VARIATION
A mixture of blueberries and raspberries would work just as well as the currants.

2 Spread the slices of bread generously with the butter, then cut them in half diagonally. Layer the slices in the dish, buttered side up, sprinkling the currants between the layers.

3 Beat the eggs and sugar lightly together in a large mixing bowl, then gradually whisk in the creamy milk and vanilla extract along with a large pinch of freshly grated nutmeg.

4 Pour the milk mixture over the bread, pushing the slices down into the liquid. Sprinkle the raw sugar and a little more nutmeg over the top. Place the dish in a roasting pan, and fill with hot water to come halfway up the sides of the dish. Bake for 40 minutes, then increase the oven temperature to 350°F, and bake for about 20 minutes more, or until the top is golden brown. Serve warm, with light cream.

Energy 328Kcal/1377kJ; Protein 10.3g; Carbohydrate 42.2g, of which sugars 25.4g; Fat 14.3g, of which saturates 7.4g; Cholesterol 156mg; Calcium 186mg; Fiber 1.9g; Sodium 321mg.

APRICOT PANETTONE PUDDING

Panettone and pecan nuts make a rich addition to this "no-butter" version of a traditional bread and butter pudding.

SERVES 6

sunflower-seed oil,
   for greasing
12 ounces panettone, sliced
   into triangles
¼ cup pecan nuts
⅓ cup ready-to-eat dried
   apricots, chopped
generous 2 cups whole milk
1 teaspoon vanilla extract
1 extra large egg, beaten
2 tablespoons maple syrup
nutmeg
raw sugar,
   for sprinkling

1 Lightly grease a 4-cup ovenproof earthenware dish. Arrange half of the panettone triangles in the dish, sprinkle over half the pecan nuts and all of the chopped, dried apricots, then add another layer of panettone on top.

COOK'S TIP

Panettone is a light fruit cake originally from northern Italy, but now popular all over the world. It is traditionally eaten at festivals, such as Christmas or Easter. Panettone is baked in cylindrical molds, giving it a distinctive shape. You can now find panettone in different flavors—the coffee-flavored type is particularly good.

2 Heat the milk and vanilla extract in a small pan until the milk just simmers. Put the egg and maple syrup in a large bowl, grate in about ½ teaspoon nutmeg, then whisk in the hot milk.

3 Preheat the oven to 400°F. Pour the egg mixture over the panettone, lightly pressing down the slices of cake so that they are submerged. Leave the dessert to stand for about 10 minutes, to let the panettone slices soak up a little of the liquid.

4 Sprinkle over the reserved pecan nuts and sprinkle a little raw sugar and freshly grated nutmeg over the top. Bake for 40–45 minutes, until the dessert is risen and golden brown. Serve hot.

Energy 294Kcal/1237kJ; Protein 9.4g; Carbohydrate 43.2g, of which sugars 21.8g; Fat 10.4g, of which saturates 3.7g; Cholesterol 44mg; Calcium 180mg; Fiber 2.3g; Sodium 248mg.

PEAR, ALMOND, and GROUND RICE PIE

Ground rice gives a distinctive, slightly grainy texture to desserts that goes particularly
well with fall fruit. Pears and almonds are a divine combination.

2 Place the butter and sugar in a mixing bowl, and beat together using a wooden spoon or electric mixer until light and fluffy, then beat in the eggs, one at a time, and the almond extract. Fold in the flour and the ground rice.

3 Carefully spoon the creamed mixture over the pears in the tart pan or pie dish, and then level the surface with a metal spatula.

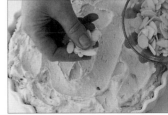

4 Sprinkle the sliced almonds evenly over the top of the creamed mixture, then bake the flan for about 30 minutes, or until the topping springs back when touched lightly and is a golden brown color. Serve warm or cold with custard or crème fraîche.

SERVES 6

4 ripe pears
2 tablespoons light brown sugar
½ cup sweet butter,
    at room temperature
generous ½ cup sugar
2 eggs
a few drops of
    almond extract
⅔ cup self-rising flour
⅓ cup ground rice
¼ cup sliced almonds
pouring custard or crème fraîche,
    to serve

I Preheat the oven to 350°F. Grease a shallow 10-inch tart pan or pie dish, then peel the pears, cut them into fourths, and arrange them in the dish. Sprinkle with the brown sugar.

Energy 396Kcal/1656kJ; Protein 5.2g; Carbohydrate 50.9g, of which sugars 34.8g; Fat 20.2g, of which saturates 10.7g; Cholesterol 104mg; Calcium 92mg; Fiber 2.9g; Sodium 190mg.

SPICED BLACKBERRY and APPLE CRUMBLE

Any fruit can be used in this popular dessert, but you can't beat the favorites of blackberry and apple. Hazelnuts and cardamom seeds give the topping extra flavor.

SERVES 4–6

butter, for greasing
I pound tart stovecooking apples
I cup blackberries
grated rind and juice of I orange
¼ cup light brown sugar
custard, to serve

For the topping
I½ cups all-purpose flour
6 tablespoons butter
⅓ cup sugar
¼ cup chopped hazelnuts
½ teaspoon crushed cardamom seeds

VARIATIONS
This dessert can be made with all kinds of fruit. Try plums, apricots, peaches, or pears, alone or in combination with apples. Rhubarb is especially good when partnered with bananas.

I Preheat the oven to 400°F. Grease a 5-cup baking dish with plenty of butter. Peel and core the apples, then slice them into the prepared baking dish. Level the surface with the back of a spoon, then sprinkle the blackberries over the top. Sprinkle the orange rind and light brown sugar evenly over the top of the fruit, then pour over the orange juice. Set the fruit mixture aside while you make the topping.

2 Sift the flour into a large bowl, and rub in the butter with your fingertips until the mixture resembles coarse bread crumbs. Stir in the sugar, hazelnuts, and cardamom seeds, then sprinkle the topping over the fruit.

3 Press the topping around the edges of the dish to seal in the juices. Bake for 30–35 minutes, or until the topping is golden. Serve hot, with custard.

Energy 336Kcal/1413kJ; Protein 4g; Carbohydrate 53.2g, of which sugars 30.8g; Fat 13.4g, of which saturates 6.8g; Cholesterol 27mg; Calcium 72mg; Fiber 3g; Sodium 81mg.

TARTE TATIN

This upside-down apple tart is remarkably easy to make—especially if you use ready-rolled pastry. The apples are cooked in butter and sugar to make a caramel topping.

SERVES 6–8

3 eating apples
juice of ½ lemon
¼ cup butter, softened
⅓ cup sugar
9 ounces ready-rolled puff pastry
cream, to serve

COOK'S TIPS

• Tarte Tatin is a popular traditional French dessert. It is basically an upside-down apple pie cooked in a pan. The tart is inverted before serving to reveal a rich caramel topping.

• To turn out the tarte Tatin, place the serving plate upside down on top of it, then, protecting your hands and arms with pot holders, hold both pan and plate firmly together and deftly turn them over. Lift off the pan.

1 Preheat the oven to 425°F. Cut the apples in fourths, and then remove the cores. Toss the apple quarters in the lemon juice.

2 Spread the butter over the base of an 8-inch heavy, ovenproof omelet pan. Sprinkle the sugar over the base of the pan, and arrange the apple wedges on top, rounded side down.

3 Cook over medium heat for about 15 minutes, or until the sugar and butter have melted and the apples are golden. Cut the pastry into a 10-inch round, and place on top of the apples; tuck in the edges with a knife. Place the pan in the oven, and bake for 15–20 minutes, or until the pastry is golden. Carefully invert the tart onto a serving plate, then cool slightly before serving with cream.

Energy 208Kcal/872kJ; Protein 1.9g; Carbohydrate 23.5g, of which sugars 12.4g; Fat 12.8g, of which saturates 3.3g; Cholesterol 13mg; Calcium 25mg; Fiber 0.1g; Sodium 136mg.

BLACK CHERRY CLAFOUTIS

Clafoutis is a batter pudding that originated in the Limousin area of central France. It is often made with cream in place of milk and traditionally uses slightly tart black cherries.

SERVES 6

butter, for greasing
2 cups fresh black
    cherries, pitted
¼ cup plain flour
½ cup confectioners' sugar, plus extra
    for dusting
4 eggs, beaten
1 cup whole milk
2 tablespoons cherry liqueur, such as
    Kirsch or maraschino
vanilla ice cream,
    to serve

1 Preheat the oven to 350°F. Grease a 5-cup baking dish with butter, and add the cherries.

2 Sift the flour and confectioners' sugar into a large bowl, then gradually whisk in the beaten eggs until the mixture is smooth. Whisk in the milk until well blended, then stir in the liqueur.

3 Pour the batter into the baking dish, and then stir gently to insure that the cherries are evenly distributed. Transfer to the oven, and bake for about 40 minutes, or until just set and light golden brown. Insert a small knife into the center of the dessert to test if it is cooked in the middle; the blade should come out clean.

4 Let the dessert cool for at least 15 minutes, then dust liberally with confectioners' sugar just before serving, either warm or at room temperature. Vanilla ice cream goes well with it.

VARIATIONS
Try other fruit or nut liqueurs in this dessert. Almond-flavored liqueur is delicious teamed with cherries, while hazelnut, raspberry, or orange liqueurs will also work well. Other fruits that can be used in this dessert include blackberries, blueberries, plums, peaches, nectarines, and apricots.

Energy 167Kcal/704kJ; Protein 6.7g; Carbohydrate 23.8g, of which sugars 20.6g; Fat 4.5g, of which saturates 1.5g; Cholesterol 129mg; Calcium 89mg; Fiber 0.8g; Sodium 66mg.

LEMON SURPRISE PUDDING

This is a much-loved dessert that many of us remember from childhood. The surprise is the unexpected sauce concealed beneath the delectable sponge cake.

SERVES 4

¼ cup butter, plus extra
    for greasing
grated rind and juice of 2 lemons
½ cup sugar
2 eggs, separated
½ cup self-rising flour
1¼ cups milk

1 Preheat the oven to 375°F. Use a little butter to grease the base and sides of a 5-cup baking dish.

COOK'S TIP
Lemons are often waxed before packing. If a recipe uses the rind of the lemons, either buy unwaxed lemons or scrub the rind thoroughly to remove the wax.

2 Beat the lemon rind, butter, and sugar in a bowl until pale and fluffy. Add the egg yolks and flour, and beat together well. Gradually whisk in the lemon juice and milk (don't be alarmed—the mixture will curdle horribly.) In a grease-free bowl, whisk the egg whites until they form stiff peaks.

3 Fold the egg whites lightly into the lemon mixture, using a metal spoon, then pour into the prepared baking dish.

4 Place the dish in a roasting pan, and pour in hot water to come halfway up the side of the dish. Bake for 45 minutes until golden. Serve immediately.

Energy 319Kcal/1341kJ; Protein 7g; Carbohydrate 43.1g, of which sugars 33.8g; Fat 14.5g, of which saturates 8.1g; Cholesterol 126mg; Calcium 166mg; Fiber 0.4g; Sodium 190mg.

STRAWBERRY OAT CRUNCH

This simple dessert looks good and tastes delicious. The strawberries form a tasty filling between the crisp oat layers.

SERVES 4

1¼ cups rolled oats
½ cup whole-wheat flour
6 tablespoons butter
2 tablespoons pear and
    apple concentrate
1¼ pounds strawberries
2 teaspoon arrowroot
plain yogurt, custard, or cream,
    to serve

VARIATIONS

• Use dried apricots (chop half and cook the rest to a puree with a little apple juice) instead of the strawberries.
• Add a few chopped almonds or walnuts to the oat mixture.

COOK'S TIP

You'll find pear and apple concentrate in good health-food stores.

1 Preheat the oven to 350°F. Mix the oats and flour in a bowl. Melt the butter with the apple and pear concentrate in a pan, and stir into the bowl.

2 Process half the strawberries in a food processor, and chop the rest. Mix the arrowroot with a little of the strawberry puree in a small pan, then add the rest of the puree. Heat gently until thickened, then stir in the chopped strawberries.

3 Spread half the oat mixture over the base of a shallow 7-inch round ovenproof earthenware dish to form a layer at least ½ inch thick. Top the oat mixture with the chopped and pureed strawberry mixture, then add the remaining oat mixture, patting it down gently to form an even layer. Bake the oat crunch for about 30 minutes, until golden brown. Serve warm or cold, with yogurt, custard, or cream.

Energy 339Kcal/1425kJ; Protein 7g; Carbohydrate 49.8g, of which sugars 13g; Fat 13.8g, of which saturates 6.5g; Cholesterol 27mg; Calcium 61mg; Fiber 4.3g; Sodium 98mg.

MOIST APPLE CAKE

This delicious cake is perhaps best in autumn, when homegrown apples are in season. It has a lovely crunchy top and can be served cold, as a cake, or warm with chilled cream or custard as a dessert.

MAKES I CAKE

2 cups self-rising flour
good pinch of salt
pinch of ground cloves
½ cup butter,
   at room temperature
3 or 4 stovecooking apples
generous ½ cup superfine sugar
2 eggs, beaten
a little milk to mix
granulated sugar,
   to sprinkle over

I Preheat the oven to 375°F, and butter an 8-inch cake pan.

2 Sieve the flour, salt, and ground cloves into a bowl. Cut in the butter, and rub in until the mixture is like fine bread crumbs. Peel and core the apples. Slice them thinly, and add to the rubbed in mixture with the sugar.

3 Mix in the eggs and enough milk to make a fairly stiff dough, then turn the mixture into the prepared pan, and sprinkle with granulated sugar.

4 Bake in the preheated oven for 30–40 minutes, or until springy to the touch. Cool on a wire rack. When cold store in an airtight container until ready to serve.

Per cake Energy 2315Kcal/9717kJ; Protein 37g; Carbohydrate 312.5g, of which sugars 145.3g; Fat 110.9g, of which saturates 61.1g; Cholesterol 702mg; Calcium 948mg; Fiber 10.7g; Sodium 1.68g

APPLE PIE

This is one of the most popular desserts on every informal menu and, when well made, there is nothing to beat it. Bake in a traditional metal pie plate so that the pastry base will be perfectly cooked. Serve with chilled whipped cream, or vanilla ice cream.

SERVES 6

2 cups all-purpose flour
generous ½ cup butter, or mixed butter
    and white vegetable shortening
2 tablespoons superfine sugar
3 tablespoons very cold milk or water

For the filling
1½ pounds stovecooking apples
½ cup golden raisins (optional)
a little grated lemon rind (optional)
6 tablespoons superfine sugar
a pat of butter or 1 tablespoon of water
a little milk, to glaze
confectioners' sugar and whipped cream,
    to serve

1 Sieve the flour into a large mixing bowl, add the butter and cut it into small pieces. Rub the butter into the flour with the fingertips, or using a pastry cutter, lifting the mixture as much as possible to aerate.

2 Mix the superfine sugar with the chilled milk or water, add to the bowl and mix with a knife or fork until the mixture clings together. Turn onto a floured worktop, and knead lightly once or twice until smooth.

3 Wrap in parchment paper or foil, and leave in the refrigerator to relax for 20 minutes before using. Meanwhile, preheat the oven to 400°F.

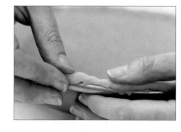

4 Roll out one-third of the pastry, and use to line a 9-inch pie plate. Use any trimmings to make a second layer of pastry around the top edge of the pie plate.

5 To make the filling, peel, core, and slice the apples, and arrange half of them on the pastry base, then sprinkle over the golden raisins and lemon rind, if using. Top with the superfine sugar, the remaining apples, and butter or water.

6 Roll out the remainder of the pastry to make a circle about 1 inch larger than the pie plate. Dampen the pastry edging on the rim, and lay the top over the apples, draping it gently over any lumps to avoid straining the pastry. Press the rim well to seal. Knock up the edge with a knife, and pinch the edges neatly with the fingers to make a fluted edge.

7 Brush the pastry lightly with milk, and bake the pie in the preheated oven for about 30 minutes, or until the pastry is nicely browned and crisp and the fruit is cooked.

8 To serve, dust the pastry with confectioners' sugar, and serve hot, warm or cold, but not straight from the refrigerator.

VARIATION
The same filling may be used to make a deep pie in a 10-inch deep oval pie dish, although only about three-quarters of the quantity of pastry will be needed for the topping.

Energy 393Kcal/1650kJ; Protein 4.1g; Carbohydrate 56.3g, of which sugars 27.7g; Fat 18.4g, of which saturates 11.4g; Cholesterol 46mg; Calcium 68mg; Fiber 2.5g; Sodium 136mg

SLOW COOKER PRESERVES AND DRINKS

Although the slow cooker isn't suitable for fast-boiling jams, jellies, and marmalades to setting point, it is perfect for making rich chutneys and relishes. The long, slow cooking develops their flavor to such an extent that long-maturation is unnecessary, and many can be eaten immediately. It is particularly good for making textured preserves because the fruit and vegetables retain their shape well. Fruit curds, such as the traditional fresh lemon curd, are easier than those made conventionally, because there is no need for constant stirring. You will also find a number of delicious drinks here including Mexican Hot Chocolate and Hot Spiced Wine.

MANGO CHUTNEY

No Indian meal would be complete without this classic chutney. Its gloriously sweet, tangy flavor complements the warm taste of spices perfectly. It is also great served with chargrilled chicken or duck breasts, and will liven up cheese sandwiches a treat.

3 Stir the sugar, chile, ginger, garlic, bruised cardamoms, bay leaf, and salt into the mango mixture until the sugar has dissolved completely.

4 Cover, and cook for 2 hours, then uncover, and let the mixture cook for a further 1 hour, or until the chutney is reduced to a thick consistency and no excess liquid remains. Stir the chutney every 15 minutes during the last hour.

5 Remove and discard the bay leaf and the chile. Spoon the chutney into hot sterilized jars, and seal. Store for 1 week before eating, and use within 1 year.

COOK'S TIP
To make a more fiery chutney, seed and slice two green chiles, and stir into the chutney mixture with the other spices.

MAKES 1 POUND

3 firm mangoes
½ cup cider vinegar
scant 1 cup light brown sugar
1 small red finger chile or jalapeño chile, split
1-inch piece of fresh ginger root, peeled and finely chopped
1 garlic clove, finely chopped
5 cardamom pods, bruised
1 bay leaf
½ teaspoon salt

1 Peel the mangoes, and cut out the pit, then cut the flesh into small chunks or thin wedges.

2 Put the chopped mango in the ceramic cooking pot. Add the cider vinegar, stir briefly to combine, and cover the slow cooker with the lid. Switch to high, and cook for about 2 hours, stirring the chutney halfway through the cooking time.

Per 450g/1lb: Energy 1045Kcal/4465kJ; Protein 4.1g; Carbohydrate 272.5g, of which sugars 271.1g; Fat 0.9g, of which saturates 0.5g; Cholesterol 0mg; Calcium 908mg; Fiber 11.7g; Sodium 1002mg.

BUTTERNUT, APRICOT, and ALMOND CHUTNEY

*Coriander seeds and turmeric add a slightly spicy touch to this rich golden chutney. It is
delicious spooned onto little savory canapés or with melting cubes of mozzarella cheese;
it is also good in sandwiches, helping to spice up bland or run-of-the-mill fillings.*

MAKES ABOUT 4 POUNDS

1 small butternut squash, weighing
   about 1¾ pounds
2 cups golden granulated sugar
1¼ cups cider vinegar
2 onions, finely chopped
1 cup ready-to-eat dried apricots,
   chopped
finely grated rind and juice of 1 orange
½ teaspoon turmeric
1 tablespoon coriander seeds
1 tablespoon salt
1 cup sliced almonds

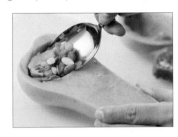

1 Halve the butternut squash, and scoop
out the seeds. Peel off the skin, then cut
the flesh into ½-inch cubes.

2 Put the sugar and vinegar in the
ceramic cooking pot, and switch to high.
Heat for 30 minutes, then stir until the
sugar has dissolved.

3 Add the butternut squash, onions,
apricots, orange rind and juice, turmeric,
coriander seeds, and salt to the slow
cooker, and stir well.

4 Cover with the lid, and cook for
5–6 hours, stirring occasionally. After
about 5 hours the chutney should be
a fairly thick consistency with relatively
little liquid. If it is still quite runny at this
stage, cook uncovered for the final hour.
Stir in the flaked almonds.

5 Spoon the chutney into warmed
sterilized jars, cover, and seal. Store in
a cool, dark place, and allow to mature
for at least 1 month before eating.
Use within 2 years. Once opened, store
the chutney in the refrigerator, and use
within 2 months.

Per 1.8kg/4lb: Energy 2770Kcal/11723kJ; Protein 41.7g; Carbohydrate 532.6g, of which sugars 524.1g; Fat 67.3g, of which saturates 5.9g; Cholesterol 0mg; Calcium 807mg; Fiber 31.6g; Sodium 5967mg.

SWEET and HOT DRIED-FRUIT CHUTNEY

This rich, thick and slightly sticky preserve of spiced dried fruit is a wonderful way to enliven cold roast turkey left over from Christmas or Thanksgiving dinner.

MAKES ABOUT 3 POUNDS, 6 OUNCES

1½ cups ready-to-eat dried apricots
1½ cups dried dates, pitted
1⅓ cups dried figs
⅓ cup candied citrus peel
1 cup raisins
½ cup dried cranberries
⅓ cup cranberry juice
1¼ cups cider vinegar
1 cup superfine sugar
finely grated rind of 1 lemon
1 teaspoon apple pie spice
1 teaspoon ground coriander
1 teaspoon cayenne pepper
1 teaspoon salt

1 Roughly chop the apricots, dates, figs, and citrus peel, then put all the dried fruit in the ceramic cooking pot. Pour over the cranberry juice, stir, then cover with the lid, and switch the slow cooker on to low. Cook for 1 hour, or until the fruit has absorbed most of the juice.

2 Add the cider vinegar and sugar to the fruit mixture. Turn the slow cooker up to the high setting, and stir until the sugar has dissolved.

3 Re-cover, and cook for 2 more hours, or until the fruit is very soft and the chutney fairly thick (it will thicken further as it cools). Stir in the lemon rind, mixed spice, coriander, cayenne pepper, and salt. Cook uncovered for 30 minutes, until little excess liquid remains.

4 Spoon the chutney into warmed sterilized jars, cover, and seal. Store in a cool, dark place. Open within 10 months of making. Once opened, store in the refrigerator, and use within 2 months.

VARIATIONS

Pitted dried prunes can be substituted for the dates, and dried sour cherries for the dried cranberries. Apple juice can be used instead of the cranberry juice.

Per 1.5kg/3lb 6oz: Energy 2873Kcal/12248kJ; Protein 32g; Carbohydrate 714.3g, of which sugars 703.5g; Fat 6.8g, of which saturates 0.2g; Cholesterol 0mg; Calcium 1075mg; Fiber 52.1g; Sodium 2358mg.

BEET, DATE, and ORANGE PRESERVE

With its vibrant red color and rich earthy flavor, this distinctive chutney is good with
salads as well as full-flavored cheeses such as mature Cheddar, Stilton, or Gorgonzola.

MAKES ABOUT 3 POUNDS

1¼ cups malt vinegar
1 cup granulated sugar
12 ounces raw beets
12 ounces apples
8 ounces red onions, very finely chopped
1 garlic clove, crushed
finely grated rind of 2 oranges
1 teaspoon ground allspice
1 teaspoon salt
1 cup chopped dried dates

1 Put the vinegar and sugar in the ceramic cooking pot. Cover with the lid, and switch the slow cooker to high. Leave until steaming hot.

2 Meanwhile, scrub or thinly peel the beets, then cut into ½-inch pieces. Peel, quarter, and core the apples, and cut into ½-inch pieces.

3 Stir the vinegar mixture with a wooden spoon until the sugar has dissolved. Add the beets, apples, onions, garlic, orange rind, ground allspice, and salt. Stir everything together, then re-cover and cook for 4–5 hours, stirring occasionally until very tender.

4 Stir in the dates, and cook for a further hour until the mixture is really thick. Stir once or twice during this time to prevent the chutney catching on the base of the ceramic cooking pot.

5 Spoon the chutney into warmed sterilized jars, cover, and seal. Store in a cool, dark place, and open within 5 months of making. Refrigerate after opening, and use within 1 month.

COOK'S TIP
For really speedy preparation and a deliciously fine-textured chutney, put the peeled beets through the coarse grating blade of a food processor. Alternatively, you can simply grate the beets by hand.

Per 1.4kg/3lb: Energy 1632Kcal/6949kJ; Protein 16.8g; Carbohydrate 413.7g, of which sugars 406g; Fat 1.5g, of which saturates 0.2g; Cholesterol 0mg; Calcium 278mg; Fiber 23.1g; Sodium 2241mg.

CARROT and ALMOND RELISH

This Middle Eastern classic, usually made with long fine strands of carrot, is available from many supermarkets. This version, using coarsely grated carrots, is just as good.

3 Switch the slow cooker to high, and cook for about 2 hours, or until the carrots and ginger are almost tender, stirring only if the mixture looks dry around the edges.

4 Stir in the lemon rind, and cook for a further 1 hour, until the mixture is thick. Stir once toward the end of the cooking time to prevent the mixture from sticking to the base of the pot.

5 Put the almonds in a frying pan, and toast over a low heat until just beginning to color. Gently stir into the relish, taking care not to break the almonds.

6 Spoon the relish into warmed sterilized jars, cover, and seal. Store in a cool, dark place, and leave to mature for 1 week. The relish will keep unopened for up to 1 year. However, once the jars have been opened, store them in the refrigerator, and use within 2 weeks.

MAKES ABOUT 1½ POUNDS

1 tablespoon coriander seeds
1¼ pounds carrots, grated
2 ounces fresh ginger root, finely shredded
1 cup superfine sugar
½ cup white wine vinegar
2 tablespoons clear honey
1½ teaspoons salt
finely grated rind of 1 lemon
½ cup sliced almonds

1 Crush the coriander seeds, using a mortar and pestle. Put them in the ceramic cooking pot with the carrots, ginger, and sugar, and mix well.

2 Put the vinegar, honey, and salt in a pitcher, and stir until the salt has dissolved completely. Pour the mixture over the carrots. Mix well, cover, and leave for 1 hour.

Per 675g/1½lb: Energy 1407Kcal/5947kJ; Protein 13.7g; Carbohydrate 289.6g, of which sugars 285.8g; Fat 29.4g, of which saturates 2.7g; Cholesterol 0mg; Calcium 268mg; Fiber 15.7g; Sodium 2898mg.

PAPAYA and LEMON RELISH

This chunky relish is best made with a firm, unripe papaya. The slow, gentle cooking
allows all the flavors to mellow. Serve with roast meats, or with cheese and crackers.

MAKES I POUND

I large unripe papaya
I onion, very thinly sliced
generous ¾ cup red wine vinegar
juice of 2 lemons
¾ cup golden superfine sugar
I cinnamon stick
I bay leaf
½ teaspoon hot paprika
½ teaspoon salt
I cup golden raisins

I Peel the papaya, and cut it lengthwise
in half. Remove the seeds, then cut the
flesh into small chunks.

2 Place the papaya in the ceramic
cooking pot, add the onion slices, and stir
in the vinegar. Switch the slow cooker to
high, cover, and cook for 2 hours.

3 Add the lemon juice, sugar, cinnamon
stick, bay leaf, paprika, salt, and golden
raisins, and stir thoroughly until the sugar
has completely dissolved.

4 Cook the chutney, uncovered, for a
further I hour to allow the mixture to
reduce slightly; the relish should be fairly
thick and syrupy.

5 Ladle the chutney into hot sterilized
jars. Seal, and store for I week before
using. Open within I year of making.
Once opened, store in the refrigerator,
and use within 2 weeks.

Per 150g/1lb: Energy 1294Kcal/5511kJ; Protein 8.1g; Carbohydrate 332.7g, of which sugars 332.7g, Fat 1.4g, of which saturates 0g; Cholesterol 0mg; Calcium 272mg; Fiber 16.1g; Sodium 111mg.

CHRISTMAS MINCEMEAT

In many mincemeat recipes, the raw ingredients are simply mixed together. Here, gentle cooking develops and intensifies the flavor, so that the mincemeat may be used right away without being left to mature. At the same time, heating it to simmering point helps prevent fermentation, and this allows a much longer shelf-life.

MAKES ABOUT 4 POUNDS

1 pound stovecooking apples
¾ cup candied citrus peel
½ cup candied cherries
½ cup ready-to-eat dried apricots
1 cup blanched almonds
⅔ cup brandy
1 cup currants
1⅓ cups golden raisins
3¼ cups seedless raisins
1 cup soft dark brown sugar
1⅔ cups suet (chilled, grated shortening)
    or vegetarian suet
2 teaspoons ground ginger
1 teaspoon ground allspice
1 teaspoon ground cinnamon
½ teaspoon grated nutmeg
grated rind and juice of 1 lemon
grated rind and juice of 1 orange

1 Peel, core, and chop the stovecooking apples, then roughly chop the citrus peel, candied cherries, apricots, and blanched almonds.

2 Reserve half the brandy, and put the rest into the ceramic cooking pot with all the other ingredients. Stir well until thoroughly mixed.

3 Cover the ceramic cooking pot with the lid, and switch the slow cooker to high. Cook for 1 hour.

4 Stir the mixture well, then re-cover the pot, and reduce the temperature to low. Cook for a further 2 hours, stirring halfway through cooking to prevent the mixture from overheating and sticking to the sides of the pot.

5 Remove the lid, and leave the mixture to cool completely, stirring occasionally.

6 Stir the reserved brandy into the mincemeat, and spoon the mixture into sterilized jars. Cover, and store in a cool, dry place for up to six months. Once opened, store in the refrigerator, and use within two weeks.

Per 1.75g/4lb: Energy 7149Kcal/30087kJ; Protein 55.6g; Carbohydrate 1114g, of which sugars 1088.3g; Fat 267.7g, of which saturates 106.3g; Cholesterol 0mg; Calcium 1228mg; Fiber 47.3g; Sodium 774mg.

CONFIT of SLOW-COOKED ONIONS

This jam of slow-cooked, caramelized onions in sweet-sour balsamic vinegar will keep for several days in a sealed jar in the refrigerator. You can use red, white, or yellow onions, but yellow onions will give the sweetest result. Shallots will also make an excellent confit.

2 Cover the pot with the lid, then place a folded dish towel on top. Cook the onions for 5 hours, stirring the mixture several times during the cooking time to ensure the onions soften evenly.

3 Season well with salt and ground black pepper, then add the thyme, bay leaf, sugar, balsamic vinegar, and red wine. Gently stir with a wooden spoon until the sugar has completely dissolved, then stir in the prunes.

4 Re-cover, and cook for 1½–2 hours, or until the mixture is thick and sticky. Adjust the seasoning, adding more sugar and/or vinegar to taste. When cool, store the confit in the refrigerator. Serve either cold or warm.

SERVES 6

2 tablespoons extra virgin olive oil
1 tablespoon butter
1¼ pounds onions, thinly sliced
3–5 fresh thyme sprigs
1 bay leaf
2 tablespoons light brown sugar, plus a
little extra
2 tablespoons balsamic vinegar,
plus a little extra
½ cup red wine
¼ cup ready-to-eat prunes, chopped
salt and ground black pepper

1 Put the oil and butter in the ceramic cooking pot, and heat on high for about 15 minutes, until the butter has melted. Add the onions, and stir to coat.

Energy 133Kcal/556kJ, Protein 1.2g, Carbohydrate 16.5g, of which sugars 14.6g, Fat 5.9g, of which saturates 1.8g, Cholesterol 5mg, Calcium 26mg, Fiber 1.6g, Sodium 20mg.

FRESH LEMON CURD

This classic tangy, creamy curd is still one of the most popular of all the curds. Delicious spread thickly over freshly baked white bread or served with pancakes, it also makes a wonderfully rich, zesty sauce spooned over fresh fruit tarts.

3 Put the eggs and yolks in a bowl, and beat together with a fork. Strain the eggs into the lemon mixture, and whisk well until combined. Cover the bowl with foil, then return it to the slow cooker.

4 Cook the lemon curd on low for 1–2 hours, stirring every 15 minutes, until thick enough to lightly coat the back of a wooden spoon.

5 Pour the curd into small warmed sterilized jars. Cover, and seal. Store in a cool, dark place, ideally in the refrigerator, and use within 3 months. Once opened, store in the refrigerator.

MAKES ABOUT 1 POUND

finely grated rind and juice of 3 lemons
  (preferably unwaxed or organic)
1 cup superfine sugar
½ cup sweet butter, diced
2 extra large eggs
2 extra large egg yolks

COOK'S TIP
To make sharp, tangy lime curd, replace the lemons with the grated zest and juice of 4 large ripe, juicy limes. Lime curd has a lovely pale greenish hue.

1 Pour about 2 inches very hot water into the ceramic cooking pot. Switch the slow cooker to high. Put the lemon rind and juice, sugar, and butter in the largest heatproof bowl that will fit inside the slow cooker.

2 Put the bowl into the slow cooker, then pour enough near-boiling water around it to come just over halfway up the sides. Leave for about 15 minutes, stirring occasionally, until the sugar has dissolved and the butter melted. Remove, and allow to cool for a few minutes. Turn the slow cooker to low.

Per 450g/1lb: Energy 1968Kcal/8224kJ; Protein 22.4g; Carbohydrate 215.3g, of which sugars 215.3g; Fat 118.9g, of which saturates 66.9g; Cholesterol 1102mg; Calcium 277mg; Fiber 0g; Sodium 895mg.

BLUSHING PEARS

As this pickle matures, the fruits absorb the color of the vinegar, giving them a glorious
pink hue. Their deliciously spicy, sweet-and-sour flavor is especially good with cold turkey
at Christmas, or with game pie, well-flavored cheese, or paté.

MAKES ABOUT 3 POUNDS

I small lemon
2¼ cups golden granulated sugar
2 cups raspberry vinegar
3-inch cinnamon stick
6 whole cloves
6 allspice berries
⅔ cup water
2 pounds firm pears

I Using a sharp knife, thinly pare a few
strips of rind from the lemon. Squeeze
out the juice, and add to the ceramic
cooking pot with the strips of rind.

2 Add the sugar, vinegar, spices, and
water, and switch the slow cooker to
high. Cover, and leave to heat for about
30 minutes, then stir until the sugar has
completely dissolved. Re-cover with the
lid, and heat for a further 30 minutes.

3 Meanwhile, prepare the pears.
Peel and halve the pears, then scoop out
the cores using a melon baller or small
teaspoon. If the pears are very large, cut
them into quarters rather than halves.

4 Add the pears to the slow cooker,
cover, and cook for 1½–2 hours, turning
them occasionally to coat them in the
syrup. Check the pears frequently; they
should be tender and translucent but
still retain their shape.

5 Using a slotted spoon, remove the
pears from the slow cooker, and pack
into hot sterilized jars, adding the spices
and strips of lemon rind.

6 Remove any scum from the surface of
the syrup, then ladle it over the pears.
Cover, and seal. Store for a few days
before eating, and use within 2 weeks.

Per 1.3kg/3lb: Energy 2133Kcal/9086kJ; Protein 5g; Carbohydrate 560.3g, of which sugars 560.3g; Fat 0.9g, of which saturates 0g; Cholesterol 0mg; Calcium 230mg; Fiber 19.8g; Sodium 50mg.

HOT SPICED WINE

On a cold winter evening, there is nothing more welcoming than a glass of warm spicy wine. The slow cooker is particularly useful when you are making the wine for guests: you can prepare the spiced wine up to four hours before your guests arrive, and the slow cooker will keep it at the ideal serving temperature until you are ready to serve.

SERVES 8

¼ cup soft light brown sugar
⅔ cup near-boiling water
2 small oranges, preferably unwaxed
6 whole cloves
1 stick cinnamon
½ whole nutmeg
1½ bottles red wine, such as Bordeaux
⅔ cup brandy

1 Put the sugar in the ceramic cooking pot, and pour in the near-boiling water. Stir until the sugar has dissolved, then switch the slow cooker to high.

COOK'S TIP
Use heatproof glasses with a handle, so that guests can hold the hot wine easily.

2 Rinse the oranges, then press the cloves into one, and add it to the slow cooker with the cinnamon, nutmeg, and wine. Halve the remaining orange, then slice, and set aside. Cover the slow cooker with the lid, and cook on high or auto for 1 hour, then reduce to low or leave on auto, and heat for 3 hours.

3 Stir the brandy into the spiced wine, and add the orange slices. Heat for a further 1 hour.

4 Remove the whole orange and the cinnamon stick. The wine is now ready to serve and can be kept hot for up to 4 hours. Serve in heatproof glasses.

CRANBERRY and APPLE PUNCH

When you are throwing a party, it is good to have a non-alcoholic punch available. Here, the slow cooker extracts maximum flavor from fresh ginger and lime peel.

SERVES 6

1 lime
2-inch piece of fresh ginger root, peeled
   and thinly sliced
¼ cup superfine sugar
scant 1 cup near-boiling water
2 cups cranberry juice
2 cups clear apple juice
ice and chilled sparkling mineral water
   or soda water, to serve (optional)

1 Pare the rind off the lime, and place in the ceramic cooking pot with the ginger and sugar. Pour over the water, and stir until the sugar dissolves. Cover with the lid, and heat on high or auto for 1 hour, then reduce the temperature to low or leave on auto, and heat for a further 2 hours. Switch off the slow cooker, and leave the syrup to cool completely.

2 When cold, pour the syrup through a fine strainer into a large serving pitcher or punch bowl, and discard the lime rind and ginger.

3 Squeeze the juice from the lime, and pour through a strainer into the syrup. Stir in the cranberry and apple juices. Cover, and chill in the refrigerator for at least 3 hours, or until ready to serve.

4 To serve, pour or ladle the punch over plenty of ice in tall glasses, and top up with sparkling mineral water or soda water, if using.

COOK'S TIP
You can now buy all kinds of different apple juices made from specific varieties of apple. They have distinctive flavors, and it is well worth searching them out.

Hot Spiced Wine: Energy 162Kcal/675kJ; Protein 0.2g; Carbohydrate 6.8g, of which sugars 6.8g; Fat 0g, of which saturates 0g; Cholesterol 0mg; Calcium 12mg; Fiber 0g; Sodium 10mg.
Cranberry and Apple Punch: Energy 111Kcal/475kJ; Protein 0.1g; Carbohydrate 27.9g, of which sugars 16.5g; Fat 0.1g, of which saturates 0g; Cholesterol 0mg; Calcium 8mg; Fiber 0g; Sodium 2mg.

MEXICAN HOT CHOCOLATE

Blending or whisking the hot chocolate before serving gives it a wonderfully frothy texture. The slow cooker is particularly good for heating the milk in this recipe, because the gentle heating process allows the cinnamon and cloves to infuse and flavor the hot chocolate with a deliciously warm and spicy flavor.

SERVES 4

4 cups milk
1 cinnamon stick
2 whole cloves
4 ounces bittersweet chocolate, chopped
    into small pieces
2–3 drops of almond extract
whipped cream and cocoa powder or
    grated chocolate, to serve (optional)

COOK'S TIP
Traditional Mexican hot chocolate is always warmly spiced. It is a popular breakfast drink, often served with delicious deep-fried *churros*, which are Mexican sugared doughnuts.

1 Pour the milk into the ceramic cooking pot. Add the cinnamon stick and cloves, cover with the lid, and switch the slow cooker to high. Leave to heat the milk and infuse the spices for 1 hour, or until the milk is almost boiling.

2 Add the chocolate pieces and almond extract to the milk, and stir until melted. Turn off the slow cooker.

3 Strain the mixture into a blender (it may be necessary to do this in two batches), and whizz on high speed for about 30 seconds, until frothy. Alternatively, whisk the mixture in the ceramic cooking pot with a hand-held electric whisk or a wire whisk.

4 Pour or ladle the hot chocolate into warmed heatproof glasses. If you like, top each with a little whipped cream and a dusting of cocoa powder or grated chocolate. Serve immediately.

NORMANDY COFFEE

The Normandy region of northern France is known for its abundant apple orchards, and its name is often given to dishes made with apple juice or apple sauce. This recipe combines the sweet-tart flavor of apples and spices to make a delicious, tangy coffee.

SERVES 4

2 cups apple juice
2 tablespoons soft brown sugar, to taste
2 oranges, thickly sliced
2 small cinnamon sticks
2 whole cloves
pinch of ground allspice
2 cups hot, freshly brewed strong black
    coffee
halved cinnamon sticks, to serve (optional)

COOK'S TIPS
• For a good flavor, use strong coffee: espresso or filter-/plunger-brewed at scant ½ cup coffee per 4 cups water.
• To make an alcoholic drink, replace a quarter of the apple juice with the French apple brandy, Calvados. Stir in the brandy after straining the spice-infused apple juice and removing the spices.

1 Pour the apple juice into the ceramic cooking pot, and switch the slow cooker on to high.

2 Add the sugar, oranges, cinnamon sticks, cloves, and allspice to the pot, and stir. Cover, and heat for 20 minutes.

3 Stir the mixture until the sugar has dissolved completely, then cover with the lid, and heat for 1 hour.

4 When the juice is hot and infused with the spices, switch the slow cooker to low to keep warm for up to 2 hours.

5 Strain the juice into a bowl, discarding the orange slices and spices.

6 Pour the hot coffee into the juice, and stir. Quickly pour into warmed mugs or espresso-style cups, adding a halved cinnamon stick to each, if you like.

Mexican Hot Chocolate: Energy 262Kcal/1102kJ; Protein 9.9g; Carbohydrate 30g, of which sugars 29.7g; Fat 12.3g, of which saturates 7.6g; Cholesterol 17mg; Calcium 309mg; Fiber 0.7g; Sodium 109mg.
Normandy Coffee: Energy 85Kcal/363kJ; Protein 0.2g; Carbohydrate 22.2g, of which sugars 22.2g; Fat 0.1g, of which saturates 0g; Cholesterol 0mg; Calcium 11mg; Fiber 0g; Sodium 3mg.

USEFUL ADDRESSES

MANUFACTURERS

Contact the following slow cooker manufacturers for retail advice, online orders and customer services, including parts and repairs.

UNITED KINGDOM

Lakeland Ltd
Customer Services Department
Alexandra Buildings
Windermere
Cumbria LA23 1BQ
Tel: (01539 4) 88100
www.lakeland.co.uk

Morphy Richards
Customer Services Department
Talbot Road
Mexborough
South Yorkshire
S64 8AJ
Tel: (01709) 582 402
www.morphyrichards.com

Prima
Contact shop.prima-international.com for online orders, retail advice and customer service centres in your area.

Russell Hobbs
Customer Services Department
Pifco Ltd
Failsworth
Manchester
M35 0HS
Tel: (0161) 681 8588
www.russell-hobbs.com

TEFAL
Contact www.tefal.co.uk for online orders, retail advice and customer service centres in your area.

UNITED STATES

Farberware Inc
Customer Services Department
Tel: (800) 253-9054
www.farberware.com

Hamilton Beach
Customer Services Department
55353 Lyon Industrial Drive
New Hudson
MI 48165
Tel: (1-800) 851-8900
www.hamiltonbeach.com

Kirby & Allen
Customer Services Department
1330 Livingstone Avenue
North Brunswick
NJ 08902
Tel: (732) 246-1460
Email: customerservice@kirby-allen.com
www.kirby-allen.com

Proctor Silex HB/PS
Customer Services Department
234 Springs Road
Washington, NC 27889
Tel: (US) (1-800) 851-8900
      (Can) (1-800) 267-2826
      (Mexico) (01-800) 71-16-100
www.proctor-silex.com

Rowecraft
Customer Services Department
24 Critchett Road
Raymond, NH 03077
www.rowecraft.com

Russell Hobbs
Customer Services Department
Myers Electric
416 Whalley Avenue
New Haven
CT 06511-3097
Tel: (toll free) 1-888-HOBBS-20
www.russell-hobbs.com

West Bend
Customer Services Department
PO Box 2780
West Bend
WI 53095
Tel: (262) 334-6949
www.west-bend.com

Windmere/Applica
Tel: (1-800) 557 9463
Contact applicaconsumeraffairs@fox-international.com for retail advice and customer service centers in your area.
www.windmere.com

AUSTRALIA

Morphy Richards
Contact www.morphyrichards.com for customer service centres in your area.

Russell Hobbs
Contact www.russell-hobbs.com for online orders, retail advice and customer service centres in your area.

TEFAL
Contact www.tefal.com for customer service centres in your area.

NEW ZEALAND

Morphy Richards
Contact www.morphyrichards.com for customer service centres in your area.

Russell Hobbs
Contact www.russell-hobbs.com for online orders, retail advice and customer service centres in your area.

TEFAL
Customer Services Department
PO Box 64-302
Botany Town Centre
East Tamaki
1730 Auckland
Tel: (0800) 700 711
www.tefal.com

INDEX